The ‘Pacifist Principle’ in the Italian and Japanese Constitutions in the Wake of the War in Ukraine

Giovanni Cavaggion
Editor

The 'Pacifist Principle' in the Italian and Japanese Constitutions in the Wake of the War in Ukraine

Springer

Editor
Giovanni Cavaggion
University of Milan
Milan, Italy

ISBN 978-3-032-23107-9 ISBN 978-3-032-23108-6 (eBook)
https://doi.org/10.1007/978-3-032-23108-6

This book was published with the support of the University of Milan, Call My First SEED Grant 2023 – DM 737/2021 (Italian Ministry for University and Research – MUR), project "The 'pacifist principle' in the Italian and Japanese Constitutions in the wake of the war in Ukraine" (PEACE-ITA-JPN – PI Prof. Giovanni Cavaggion).

This Springer imprint is published by the registered company Springer Nature Switzerland AG
The registered company address is: Gewerbestrasse 11, 6330 Cham, Switzerland

Acknowledgements

The editor would like to express his deepest gratitude to Prof. Arianna Angeli, Prof. Giulia Bistagnino, Prof. Filippo Dornetti, and Prof. Fabio Guidali, irreplaceable members of the PEACE-ITA-JPN research group. Without their indispensable contribution, on both a professional and personal level, this book would not have been possible. It has been truly a pleasure to work with such passionate and knowledgeable scholars, and friends.

Special thanks are due to Prof. Akihiko Kimijima, who hosted the research group at Ritsumeikan University in Kyoto in December 2024 to jointly discuss the Italian and Japanese pacifist clauses in a stimulating and vibrant series of workshops. His advice and guidance were crucial in shaping the studies that led to the final conference and to this book.

Last but not least, thanks to all contributing authors who shared their knowledge and expertise with the research group, greatly enriching the scientific value of this book and of all the connected project activities.

Contents

Contributors

Arianna Angeli University of Milan, Milan, Italy

Elisa Bertolini Bocconi University, Milan, Italy

Giulia Bistagnino University of Milan, Milan, Italy

Andrea Carati University of Milan, Milan, Italy

Giovanni Cavaggion University of Milan, Milan, Italy

Massimo Cavino University of Eastern Piedmont, Novara, Italy

Andrea De Petris Università degli Studi Internazionali (UNINT), Rome, Italy

Filippo Dornetti University of Milan, Milan, Italy

Oliviero Frattolillo Roma Tre University, Rome, Italy

Fabio Guidali University of Milan, Milan, Italy

Akihiko Kimijima Ritsumeikan University, Kyoto, Japan

Marco Labbate University of Urbino, Urbino, Italy

Mario G. Losano Accademia delle Scienze, Turin, Italy

Massimiliano Malvicini University of Eastern Piedmont, Novara, Italy

Amoreno Martellini University of Urbino, Urbino, Italy

Craig Martin Washburn University School of Law, Topeka, KS, USA

Alessandro Pascolini University of Padua, Padua, Italy

Piotr Podemski University of Warsaw, Warsaw, Poland

Andrea Salvatore Sapienza Università di Roma, Rome, Italy

Marco Zappa Ca' Foscari University of Venice, Venice, Italy

Introduction

Giovanni Cavaggion

The "pacifist principle" is a fundamental principle of both the Italian and Japanese Constitutions. This book explores the evolution of the debate on the scope and meaning of the Italian and Japanese constitutional "pacifist clauses" that was generated by the war in Ukraine, by adopting an interdisciplinary perspective spanning across different social sciences and, more precisely, Japanese history, Italian history, Italian public and constitutional law, Japanese public and constitutional law, political philosophy, political science, and comparative law.

Article 11 of the Constitution of Italy of 1948 provides that "Italy repudiates war as an instrument of aggression against the freedom of other peoples and as a means for the settlement of international disputes; Italy agrees, on conditions of equality with other States, to the limitations of sovereignty that may be necessary to a world order ensuring peace and justice among the Nations; Italy promotes and encourages international organisations furthering such ends". Article 9 of the Constitution of Japan of 1947 provides that "Aspiring sincerely to an international peace based on justice and order, the Japanese people forever renounce war as a sovereign right of the nation and the threat or use of force as means of settling international disputes. In order to accomplish the aim of the preceding paragraph, land, sea, and air forces, as well as other war potential, will never be maintained. The right of belligerency of the State will not be recognized".

The actual scope of these constitutional provisions and their role in shaping the respective peoples, legal systems, foreign policies, and national identities has historically been the object of a heated legal and political debate in both Italy and Japan.

From a practical point of view, it has not been particularly controversial that the "pacifist clauses" allow (and even oblige) Italy and Japan to turn to "war" as a

G. Cavaggion (✉)
University of Milan, Milan, Italy
e-mail: giovanni.cavaggion@unimi.it

G. Cavaggion (ed.), *The 'Pacifist Principle' in the Italian and Japanese Constitutions in the Wake of the War in Ukraine*,
https://doi.org/10.1007/978-3-032-23108-6_1

means of self-defence of last resort, when this is necessary to ensure the survival of the liberal democratic constitutional system when faced with an existential threat (such as a "war" of invasion/annexation waged by a foreign power). Scholars, however, disagree on whether (and to what extent) these provisions allow Italy and Japan to provide aid to a third country engaged in a war of their own.

Until 2022 the issue has emerged in the state of the art mainly in relation to peacekeeping and/or military operations (often endorsed by the UN), which were significantly limited and restrained both legally and in a spatial and temporal perspective.

The Russian invasion of Ukraine, however, presented the Italian and Japanese constitutional systems (and societies) with an entirely new dilemma, as the State requesting their aid (Ukraine) is facing a fully fledged war of invasion and annexation: a "total war", that is, the very same kind of "war" rejected by the "pacifist clauses", and the very same kind of "war" against which, according to the said clauses, self-defence is not only allowed, but necessary.

This book wishes to explore this dilemma and, consequently, the evolution of the debate on the scope and meaning of the constitutional "pacifist principles" (or "pacifist clauses") in Italy and Japan that was generated by the start of the war in Ukraine. The book presents the outcomes of the research project (funded by the University of Milan and by the Italian Ministry for University and Research in the framework of the Call "My First SEED Grant 2023" – DM 737/2021) "The 'pacifist principle' in the Italian and Japanese Constitutions in the wake of the war in Ukraine" (PEACE-ITA-JPN), and builds upon the findings presented and discussed at the project's final conference (held at the University of Milan on the 15th and 16th of May 2025).

In order to provide readers with a comprehensive analysis of the subject matter, the book adopts an interdisciplinary approach, spanning across different social sciences and, more precisely, Japanese history, Italian history, Italian public and constitutional law, Japanese public and constitutional law, political philosophy, political science, and comparative law.

The historical perspective is vital for reconstructing and understanding the debate, the political and social context, and the national and international cultural climate in which the constitutional "pacifist clauses" originated in the post-World War II period in both Italy and Japan, as well as for understanding their evolution and transformation throughout the second half of the twentieth century.

The constitutional perspective is essential for clarifying the legal meaning of the pacifist clauses in the Italian and Japanese legal systems, their prescriptive force, the sense in which they have historically been interpreted, and thus the way in which they have influenced (and continue to influence) the decisions of democratic institutions in the face of different forms of "war" and of the use of force in the context of international crises.

The comparative perspective contextualizes the Italian and Japanese pacifist clauses within a broader framework, expanding the point of observation to include other European legal systems and societies that have chosen to regulate, at the constitutional level, the approach of public powers and of their peoples to war and peace.

Lastly, the philosophical and political theory perspective outlines the perimeter of the theoretical framework within which the study of the Japanese and Italian cases unfolds, identifying and defining the conceptual and interpretive tools necessary to understand the evolution of the constitutional pacifist clauses and the growing tension to which they are exposed in the current historical phase of global disorder.

Consequently, the book is divided into four sections, devoted, respectively, to Italy, Japan, the comparative and transnational perspective, and the philosophical and political theory perspective.

The section devoted to Italy is opened by Massimo Cavino and Massimiliano Malvicini, who analyse the genesis, the intended meaning, and the scope of Article 11 of the Italian Constitution, which enshrines the so-called pacifist clause, as well as the other constitutional provisions that regulate war. They explore the historical context that brought to the constitutionalization of the repudiation of war and examine the boundaries of this constitutional provision, in the context of the international obligations and alliances of the Italian Republic (in particular, its membership of NATO and of the European Union). The chapter highlights that Article 11 cannot be considered a "pacifist" clause in a radical (literal) sense, and proceeds to examine the compatibility of the constitutional repudiation of war with Italy's engagement in various types of military operations and missions throughout the history of the Republic.

Amoreno Martellini reconstructs the history of Italian pacifism from its reorganization after the end of World War II (at the time in which Article 11 of the Constitution was drafted) to its crisis and transformation in the 1970s and 1980s. He highlights how the different expressions of the "pacifist culture" struggled to find a true unity of intent and failed to mobilize significant sectors of the Italian civil society. A special focus is dedicated to the turning point of the first "march for peace" from Perugia to Assisi that brought new languages and new forms of participation to the universe of pacifist protest, hence managing, at last, to intercept the anxieties of newer generations. At the same time, the deployment of the Italian military in the so-called "peace missions" or in the aftermath of natural disasters promoted a rethinking of the role of armies in contemporary societies. The chapter highlights the inversion of the terms of discourse on war and peace produced by these phenomena, as pacifism entered the new era inaugurated by the end of the Cold War.

Marco Labbate explores the historical context in which pacifism developed in Italy in the second half of the twentieth century and the evolution of radical pacifism in post-war Italy, by focusing, in particular, on its principles and their role in mobilizations for the recognition of conscientious objection between 1945 and 1972, when civilian service was institutionalized as an alternative to military service. He examines the difference between the cultural framework at the foundation of Article 11 and the one that underlies conscientious objection, focusing on three core ideas: the moral refusal of violence, which emphasizes the consistency of peaceful means and ends; antinuclearism, which rejects the doctrine of just war in the atomic era and advocates for universal objection; and antimilitarism, which frames military service as a tool of capitalist power within a broader class struggle. The chapter also highlights the marginal role of Article 11 in pacifist mobilizations and how the pacifist clause was rarely leveraged as a constitutional or political argument in the opposition to military service.

Alessandro Pascolini writes about the activism of Italian scientists for nuclear disarmament (or at least for the control of nuclear weapons) in the second half of the twentieth century, with particular regard to the Russell-Einstein Manifesto (1955) and the genesis of the Pugwash conferences (from 1957). The chapter devotes a special focus to the physicist Edoardo Amaldi, who was immediately involved in the Pugwash conferences and urged students and colleagues to engage in national and international arms control actions. The chapter also outlines the role of other Italian scientists that, in addition to their involvement in Pugwash, created an institution for the training of international arms control experts, ISODARCO, active since 1966, and USPID, since 1982, to study the problems raised by weapons of mass destruction and develop operational proposals for their containment.

Lastly, in the final chapter of this section, I examine the doctrinal and political debate concerning the compatibility of the different forms of support that Italy provided to Ukraine, following the Russian invasion in 2022, with the "pacifist clause" enshrined in Article 11 of the Italian Constitution. I argue that the war in Ukraine revealed a sharp contrast, never truly resolved since the entry into force of the 1948 Constitution, between "radical pacifist" interpretations of Article 11, according to which Italy should have remained perfectly neutral in the conflict, and "internationalist" interpretations of the same clause, according to which the right to use war as an instrument of self-defence, in cases in which this is allowed by international law, shall allow Italy to provide help to other States that are facing an unjust war of aggression. The chapter underlines the importance of developing an independent constitutional definition of the concepts of "war" and "peace" and argues that such a definition can only point towards the conclusion that Italy's support for Ukraine is compatible with the national pacifist clause.

The section devoted to Japan is opened by Akihiko Kimijima, who explores the genesis, intended meaning, and scope of Article 9 of the Japanese Constitution and of the perpetual renunciation of war and the right to maintain a military. A special focus is dedicated to the "six faces" of the Japanese pacifist clause that prescribe a commitment to peace in six different perspectives. In this sense, Article 9 can be looked at from Washington DC (Japanese-American relations and American calls for a rearmament of Japan), the Japanese Empire (renunciation of nationalist and imperialist stances by the Japanese State, also as a means to keep the emperor in power), the Japanese people (commitment to peace to the Japanese people, by the Japanese government and the emperor), Okinawa (tension between the Japanese pacifist clause and the militarization of Okinawa in the wake of the Cold War), East Asia (commitment to peace by the Japanese people to other Eastern Asian peoples and especially to those that suffered from Japanese imperialist and colonialist policies), and the world (reliance of the Japanese people on the international community of States as the only instrument to protect peace and build peaceful relations among the world's peoples).

Filippo Dornetti then reconstructs the origins of Article 9, while highlighting the American and Western influence in its drafting. He investigates secondary sources and archival material to capture the intellectual milieu that surrounded the formulation of the Japanese constitutional pacifist principle and the growing commitment of the Japanese society to the value of peace. A special focus is devoted to the intellectual connection between E. Herbert Norman and Colonel Charles L. Kades, as Norman, a distinguished historian and diplomat, served as a GHQ-SCAP official in the months leading up to the drafting of the Constitution by the SCAP, in which Kades played a crucial role. The chapter highlights the particular interpretation of the "feudal remnants" in post-war Japan which was shared by both Norman and Kades, as evidence of their broader ideological alignment and of the wider circulation of ideas that shaped the drafting of Article 9.

Oliviero Frattolillo goes on to examine the historical evolution of the Japanese defence build-up in the post-World War II period, adopting a transnational perspective. He highlights how Japanese defence policies, especially during the Cold War, found their legal basis in the Japan-United States Security Treaty (signed in 1951 and revised in 1960) rather than in the Constitution and in Article 9 (and the pacifist clause that it enshrines). A particular attention is devoted to outlining the mounting tension, in the political and social debate, between growing national and international security concerns and the commitment (from a legal and cultural perspective) to upholding the pacifist principle in its originally intended scope and meaning.

This tension is further explored, in a constitutional perspective, by Elisa Bertolini, who highlights the contradiction between the "pacifist clause" of Article 9 and the policies adopted by Japanese governments through the years, since 1948, with particular regard to the renunciation of the right to maintain a military, which was effectively bypassed by several subsequent policies. The chapter argues that Japanese governments consistently tried to find ways to rearm the country while carefully avoiding formal amendments to the text of the constitutional pacifist clause, also due to its lasting (and rising) popularity among the electorate. This divergence between the constitutional text and the actual policies adopted by constitutional bodies could, however, in the long run, end up depriving the pacifist clause of its normative (prescriptive) nature.

The same issue is explored, from an historical point of view, by Marco Zappa, who discusses, in a critical perspective, the evolution of the Japanese security strategy, by using primary and secondary sources and focusing, in particular, to the policies developed from the 1990s to the present day. He observes that after the end of the Cold War the calls for an amendment of Article 9 of the Constitution, aimed at realigning its text to the reality of Japan's role in the world order, became prominent in the Japanese political debate. As a matter of fact, such an amendment could be even seen as an inevitability, as the defence policies adopted by the Liberal Democratic Party gradually moved towards a substantial (re-)militarization of the country, which is, in theory, in open contradiction with the constitutional pacifist clause. In this perspective, the chapter also analyses the more recent developments of Japanese security policies and the doubts surrounding their compatibility with the pacifist Constitution.

In the last chapter of the section, Craig Martin describes the "tragic demise" of Japan's constitutional war constraints, as in the last decade the Japanese government intensified its efforts to radically "reinterpret" Article 9 through an executive branch fiat, aimed at allowing uses of force that had long been understood to be prohibited by the Constitution. With the Russian invasion of Ukraine in February 2022, the government seized the opportunity to issue a new national security strategy that fundamentally reoriented Japanese military capability, posture, and doctrine, in ways that completed, at last, the reinterpretation of Article 9, effectively overturning the remaining prohibition on the maintenance of armed forces and other war potential. These moves were widely considered illegitimate and ultimately unconstitutional yet were not overturned by the judiciary. The chapter explains why and how these "reinterpretations" represent an arguably illegitimate process of eviscerating constitutional constraints on executive power, which is undermining the rule of law in Japan and abandoning the pacifist principles that have constituted a defining element of Japan's post-war constitutional identity. It also suggests that this process of constitutional transformation has implications that extend far beyond Japan's borders and implicates fundamental questions about the relationship between domestic constitutional law and international legal constraints on the use of force.

The section dedicated to the comparative and transnational perspective is opened by Mario G. Losano, who analyses the genesis, the content, and the application of the pacifist clauses enshrined in the Constitutions of Italy, Japan, and Germany. Through a multidisciplinary approach that entails geopolitical, historical, and legal perspectives in the interpretation of the pacifist principle in these countries, the chapter highlights similarities and differences between the three constitutional systems. A special focus is dedicated to the struggle that the constitutional pacifist clauses encounter in adapting to the new forms of "war" (or, rather, "non-wars") that characterize the current historical phase. The chapter untangles the difficulties in adapting constitutional provisions devised in the context of the aftermath of World War II to the liquid reality of our time, in which the very definition of what a "war" is could be the object of debate and disagreements.

Fabio Guidali then focuses on a transnational and European historical perspective, by studying the role and activities of the European Society of Culture, founded in 1950 by law philosopher Umberto Campagnolo, which brought together many of the leading European intellectuals of the post-World War II era. The society advocated for the autonomy of culture from politics, the essentiality of dialogue, and the political commitment of literati, artists, and scientists. The chapter shows that the European Society of Culture was able to create safe spaces of shared reflection for intellectuals from both Western and Eastern Europe during the harshest years of the Cold War, with a view on building bridges between societies and promoting the value of peace in the complex context of the second half of the twentieth century. A special focus is devoted to the magazine *Comprendre* and in particular on the issues of the early 1950s dedicated to the atomic bomb, the Iron Curtain, and the sense of dialogue, which shaped a particular and concrete angle of the search for pacifism, promoted by intellectuals confident in their ability of steering peoples and societies towards a peaceful future.

Piotr Podemski goes on to explore the issue of war and peace in the Polish constitutional system inaugurated with the Constitution of 2 April 1997. The relevant constitutional provisions are analysed in the broader context of Polish constitutional traditions, ranging from the so-called nobles' democracy of the sixteenth to eighteenth centuries, through the partition era of foreign domination (1795–1918), to the Constitutions of the twentieth-century Polish statehood (both sovereign and non-sovereign). The analysis examines the legal provisions governing the decision to declare a state of war or peace while also exploring the legal consequences of such decisions, including the states of emergency, the restrictions of civil liberties and human rights, and the principles governing the deployment of Polish armed forces beyond the national territory. A special focus is devoted to the practical application of the relevant provisions of the 1997 Constitution in matters relating to war and peace, particularly in the context of Poland's accession to NATO in 1999, the participation of Polish armed forces in military interventions led by the United States in Afghanistan (2002–2021) and Iraq (2003–2011), as well as in light of the ongoing Russian aggression against Ukraine (post-2014), in the wake of which the role of Poland has been one of the most prominent in the comparative perspective.

Andrea De Petris then provides an in-depth study of the "pacifist clause" enshrined in Article 26 of the German Basic Law (the third, alongside Italy and Japan, of the "pacifist Constitutions" of the defeated powers of World War II), as well as the other constitutional provisions that regulate war and other kinds of military operations in which Germany might take part. He dedicates a particular attention to the judgements of the Federal Constitutional Court in which the interpretative basis of the constitutional pacifist principle was further defined and perfected. Lastly, the chapter analyses the unprecedented increase in military spending approved by the Bundestag in March 2025: a measure that could have a significant impact on the constitutional conception of the pacifist principle in the German legal system and on Germany's emerging role as a leader of the effort towards a rearmament of Europe.

In the last chapter of the section, Arianna Angeli investigates the "pacifist clauses" (including the clauses regulating Euro-Atlantic integration and the clauses of neutrality) enshrined in the Constitutions of the countries of the former Soviet space, by focusing specifically on the cases of Ukraine, Georgia, and Moldova. She demonstrates that in the wake of the increasing "assertiveness" of the Russian Federation in the international context, these three countries were forced to significantly reimagine the constitutional provisions that constrain State institutions when it comes to foreign policy decisions that are vital for the preservation of peace. In particular, the chapter analyses the ways in which these constitutional foreign policy clauses have been reinterpreted or amended in the context of the large-scale aggression of the Russian Federation against Ukraine.

The section devoted to the philosophical and political perspective is opened by Giulia Bistagnino, who explores the ethics of war, traditionally framed within a tripartite structure: pacifism, which rejects war altogether; just war theory, which seeks to justify war under specific conditions; and political realism, which treats war as an inevitable and necessary instrument of politics. However, contemporary debates have brought to the emergence of more nuanced positions and "grey areas", such as those theorized by "contingent pacifism", which argue that while war is not necessarily unjust in principle, real-world conditions rarely, if ever, meet the moral requirements for justifiable warfare. The chapter analyses the different forms of contingent pacifism, which may: emphasize epistemic uncertainty, collective responsibility, and the moral risks of participation in war; employ probabilistic reasoning to assess the likelihood of just war criteria being met; or argue that structural and cultural forces make genuinely just wars exceedingly rare. By engaging with these perspectives, the chapter assesses (and challenges) the definition of the Italian and Japanese constitutional provisions on the rejection of war as "pacifist clauses", a definition that becomes all the more relevant due to the empirical and theoretical challenges presented by the Russian invasion of Ukraine.

In the following chapter, Andrea Salvatore provides a map of the various philosophical theories on the problem of war, pivoting from the best known (and most controversial) among them: the so-called "just war theory", which asserts the possibility of distinguishing between permissible (whether permitted or commanded) and impermissible wars on the grounds of a normative criterion (whether moral or legal), based on a concept of justice as fairness. Legitimate wars, in this view, are justified if and in so far as they meet certain criteria of justice and are therefore regarded as "just". Starting from this definition, all alternative positions can be, indeed, derived *ex contrario*. The chapter demonstrates that understanding the "just war theory" and its nuances is, indeed, crucial to understand the terms of the fracture between the "radical pacifist" and "internationalist" interpretations of the pacifist clauses enshrined in the Italian and Japanese Constitutions in the wake of the war in Ukraine.

Lastly, Andrea Carati explores the different theories of peace proposed by the liberal school of International Relations, among which the theory of "democratic peace" emerged as the most robust and compelling. He reviews the literature that, since the 1990s, has provided empirical corroboration of the existence of a "zone of peace" created by democracies, based on the proposition that democracies rarely engage in war with each other, which has been validated by historical evidence and quantitative studies. He highlights that, despite this substantial empirical evidence, the democratic peace theory has been increasingly questioned in many ways, from both methodological and political-normative perspectives. The chapter argues that, in light of the challenges that democracy is facing in the current world order, coupled with the resurgence of great power competition and warfare (as demonstrated by the Russian invasion of Ukraine), the democratic peace theory is now showing all its weaknesses.

The authors of this volume wish to submit their reflections (developed in the wake of the war in Ukraine) to the scholarly and political debate, in the hope that they may contribute to the studies on peace (and war) in a global context in which, as highlighted by the new conflicts in Palestine, Kashmir, and Iran, the cultural and constitutional ideal of a global order founded on peaceful relations among States and peoples, that inspired the drafting of the "pacifist" Constitutions of Italy and Japan in the aftermath of the Second World War, appears to be increasingly receding.

Italy

The "Pacifist Principle" and the "Use of Force" in the Italian Constitution

Massimo Cavino and Massimiliano Malvicini

1 The Pacifist Principle in Article 11 of the Constitution: The Constitutional Debate[1]

Any analysis of the provisions imposed on the Italian Republic with regard to international relations must commence from Article 11 of the Constitution and, in particular, its genesis.[2]

Thus, even before referring to the debates in the Italian Constituent Assembly (operating between June 1946 and December 1947), it is worthwhile to focus on the documents of the Commission for Studies pertaining to the Reorganisation of the State (also known as the "Forti Commission", operating between September 1945 and June 1946) at the behest of the Minister for the Constituent Assembly Pietro Nenni with preliminary responsibilities in relation to the work of the Assembly.[3]

As can be read in the minutes of the meetings held by the first sub-committee of the Commission, there were essentially three issues discussed:

(a) The appropriateness of a declaration on the international policy of the Italian Republic.

[1] Please note that any translation from the official report and document (e.g. Parliamentary report, public statement, press releases, etc.) is done by the authors for informational and scientific purposes only.

[2] For a detailed analysis see Cassese (1980), pp. 505–549.

[3] See D'Alessio (1979).

M. Cavino · M. Malvicini (✉)
University of Eastern Piedmont, Novara, Italy
e-mail: massimo.cavino@uniupo.it; massimiliano.malvicini@uniupo.it

G. Cavaggion (ed.), *The 'Pacifist Principle' in the Italian and Japanese Constitutions in the Wake of the War in Ukraine*,
https://doi.org/10.1007/978-3-032-23108-6_2

(b) The determination of the body empowered in general to represent it in international relations, with the related and delicate problems of the competence to declare war and to stipulate international treaties.
(c) The mechanisms for adapting domestic law to international law, both in relation to treaties and in relation to the rules of general international law.[4]

Notwithstanding the last two issues (which only tangentially concern the subject of our reflections), with regard to the advisability of constitutionalising a specific direction of Italy's international policy, the discussion began with the report presented by two commissioners and scholars of international law, Professors Roberto Ago and Gaetano Morelli. They stressed the opportunity to include in the text of the Constitution a declaration highlighting the "peace policy of observance of international law" and adherence to all forms and types of international and "supranational" organisations, accompanied by a renunciation of war as an instrument of national policy.

However, this proposal was rejected. Conversely, an orientation emerged from the discussion favouring the constitutionalisation of a mere reference, somewhat generic and of ambiguous nature (according to some experts, due to purely political intent; according to others, as a binding legal statement), to the peace purposes pursued by the Italian Republic.

Despite their "vagueness", the conclusions of the "Forti Commission" represented one of the references for the work of the Constituent Assembly, whose work was inevitably influenced not only by the changed international framework (with the creation of the United Nations) but also by the events surrounding the finalisation of the Peace Treaty with the Allied Powers.[5]

The first discussions on the subject date back to December 1946. They took place within the so-called Committee of the Seventy-Five, a special body set to design and propose a draft Constitution and, in particular, within the first sub-committee, which was responsible for drafting the articles on the rights and duties of citizens and the relationship between the Italian State and other legal systems.

At that point, the first formulation of the principle of renouncing war as "an instrument of conquest or offence to the freedom of other peoples" was proposed by Giuseppe Dossetti. In the perspective of this Christian Democrat exponent, this affirmation, flanked by the provision that "The State allows, under conditions of reciprocity, the limitations of sovereignty necessary for the organisation and defence of peace", corresponded to a general "widespread and concordant awareness of this post-war period" to such an extent as to be found, with almost identical wording,

[4] Ministero per la Costituente—Commissione di studi attinenti alla riorganizzazione dello Stato, Relazione all'Assemblea Costituente, Volume I, Problemi costituzionali—Organizzazione dello Stato, Roma, Failli, 1947, p. 67, http://legislature.camera.it/_dati/costituente/documenti/ministero-costituente/p8_Vol1.pdf.

[5] Leanza (2006), p. 310 ss.

even in the coeval French Constitution of 27 October 1946 (which, in turn, had illustrious roots in certain provisions of the French Constitutional Charter of 1791).[6]

On the whole, Dossetti's proposal met with the favour of almost all the commissioners and, apart from a few interventions aimed at pointing out the critical issues concerning the last part of Article 5 of the Project, the one concerning the legitimacy of the Italian State's self-limitation of sovereignty, it was approved in the sitting of 3 December.[7] However, this passage did not prevent the text of the future Article 11 of the Constitution from undergoing some changes in the course of subsequent stages.

An initial intervention was carried out within the Drafting Committee (the so-called Committee of the Eighteen) formed by the Bureau of the "Committee of the Seventy-Five" and led not only to the specification of the necessary conditions for the cession of Italian sovereignty (under conditions of reciprocity and equality) but also to the provision that this self-limitation of the state *imperium* would be functional to the establishment and functioning of "an international organisation that would ensure peace" as well as "justice for the peoples". Likewise, the amendment proposed by Emilio Lussu, aimed at inserting a reference to the possibility of ceding sovereignty in favour of a European and international organisation, was not approved in the sitting of 24 January.

Other alterations took place during the Assembly debate, before the text drafted by the "Committee of the Eighteen". The first of these was the shift from *rejection* to *repudiation of* war, which was finalised on the basis of a precise orientation of the constituents, who took a middle position between condemnation, which they considered to be of ethical rather than political and legal value, and renunciation.[8]

The second was represented by the specification that such repudiation would be directed not only against war as a tool of conquest and aggression by the Italian Republic towards other nations but also as a means of resolving international disputes; thereby, the constitutional text incorporated the expression adopted in Article 1 of the Briand-Kellogg Pact, signed in Paris on 27 August 1928.[9]

---

[6] Also recalled by Elia (2003), pp. 7–15.

French Constitution, 3 September1791 - Title VI:

"La Nation française renonce à entreprendre aucune guerre dans la vue de faire des conquêtes, et n'emploiera jamais ses forces contre la liberté d'aucun peuple".

Articles 14 and 15 of the Preamble of French Constitution, 27 October 1946:

"14. La République française, fidèle à ses traditions, se conforme aux règles du droit public international. Elle n'entreprendra aucune guerre dans des vues de conquête et n'emploiera jamais ses forces contre la liberté d'aucun peuple.

15. Sous réserve de réciprocité, la France consent aux limitations de souveraineté nécessaires à l'organisation et à la défense de la paix".

[7] Assemblea Costituente, Committee for the Constitution - Commissione per la Costituzione, First Sub-committee - Prima sottocommissione, Official report, 3 December 1946, pp. 452–453.

[8] Assemblea costituente, Official report - Resoconto stenografico, 24 March 1947 (afternoon), p. 2429 ss.

[9] Art. 1 "The High Contracting Parties solemnly declare in the names of their respective peoples that they condemn recourse to war for the solution of international controversies", available at: https://avalon.law.yale.edu/20th_century/kbpact.asp.

Finally, these changes were accompanied by the replacement of the expression approved in the sub-committee on limitations of sovereignty, to be carried out on an equal footing with other states; the change of the reference to peace and justice for peoples to the protection of these values "among the nations", which the constituents considered more formally correct; and lastly, the specification that—to further these objectives—the Republic would promote international organisations aimed at these ends.[10]

In general, from the reading of the Constituent Assembly's proceedings, a clear impression emerges that, with regard to the pacifist principle, there was a shared intent to condemn war and to promote a broad (and somewhat vague) openness of the Italian legal system to forms of international collaboration. Aside from the few dissenting positions, such as those expressed by Russo Perez (Fronte dell'uomo qualunque)[11] and Nitti (Unione democratica nazionale),[12] the convergence in this area can also be explained by the desire to exclude from political contention the issue of the specific geopolitical stance of the nascent Republic in relation to the post-war geopolitical scenario. This was achieved by affirming—through a drafting technique characterised by a high degree of abstraction—the importance of both the pacifist and internationalist principles.[13]

2 The Interpretation of Article 11 with Regard to the International Law on the Justification of the Use of Force

In general terms, in light of the constitutional debate, it can be stated that the repudiation of war enshrined in the first part of Article 11 of the Italian Constitution has a scope limited to the hypothesis of the use of force as a means of settling international disputes and as an offence against the freedom of other peoples. In other words, the constitutional system does not exclude the legitimacy of war to defend one's own freedom and that of other peoples and, in general, when it is necessary to implement obligations arising from participation in international organisations aimed at achieving an order that ensures peace and justice among nations.[14]

At the same time, it is well known that the Constitution does not define war—perhaps with the intention of deferring to international law[15] or more likely because defining an ostensibly obvious concept proves quite difficult: war consists in the

[10] Assemblea costituente, Official report, 24 March 1947 (afternoon), pp. 2433–2434.

[11] Assemblea costituente, Official report, 14 March 1947 (afternoon), p. 2090.

[12] Assemblea costituente, Official report, 18 March 1947 (afternoon), p. 2253.

[13] As underlined by Faraguna (2018), pp. 75–81, which takes up Sunstein's notion of "incompletely theorized agreements" (Harvard Law Review, 1995, n. 8, p. 1733 ss.).

[14] For a detailed analysis see Sicardi (1999), p. 99 e ss.; Cabras (2006), p. 297 e ss.

[15] De Vergottini (2022), p. 78.

deliberate use of force by one State against another, aimed at compelling it to adopt a specific position. The use of alternative terms to "war" (such as armed conflict, serious international crisis, etc.) has been prompted, on the one hand, by a sort of "pacifist exorcism", as if by renouncing the signifier one could banish the meaning; and, on the other hand, by the political desire not to take too firm a stance on the value of "renunciation", around which attention has focused in the interpretation of Article 11 of the Constitution. Yet, beyond these terminological variations, it remains firmly established that Italy may enter into war.

This is not, as often argued, the outcome of an evolutionary interpretation of Article 11,[16] which would have seen the second part progressively prevailing over the first[17] to the detriment of the intention of the constituents,[18] since the constituents themselves, despite the strong lexical choice of the term "repudiation",[19] rejected the option—albeit considered—of neutralisation.[20]

Moreover, and right from the start, the interpretation of Article 11 did not stand in the way of adherence to the Atlantic alliance,[21] which was certainly incompatible with a neutralising reading, even though it was also supported by voices within the parliamentary majority that deliberated on it.[22]

The basis of the legitimacy of the use of force does not reside, moreover, in Article 11 alone but also in Articles 10 and 117 paragraph 1 of the Constitution, that is, in the general reference to international law, and on that level a first element of complexity emerges, according to the nature and degree of elaboration of its norms.

Established and generally recognised customary norms and covenant norms do not pose a problem: wars fought in response to aggression against one's own State, based on the generally recognised principle of individual self-defence; wars fought in reaction to aggression committed against another State, based on the principle of collective self-defence (which, from being legitimate, becomes obligatory in the case of treaties obliging intervention to aid allies)[23]; and wars fought within the framework of the explicit activation of the device on the use of force within the United Nations system[24] are certainly compatible with our constitutional order.

---

[16] Solutions that were clear and unequivocal were not put forward by constitutional scholars of the early Republican era. See the different position by Balladore Pallieri (1949), p. 337; Crosa (1951), p. 106; Lavagna (1953); Biscaretti di Ruffia (1954), p. 320, Bon Valsassina (1955), p. 4 e *passim*; Amorth (1948), p. 46 e ss.

[17] See Sicardi (1999), cit., p. 108.

[18] De Vergottini (2022), cit., p. 75. In the same perspective De Vergottini (2022), p. 5 e ss.

[19] Cassese (1975), p. 565 e ss.; Cartabia and Chieffi (2006), p. 267 e s.; Benvenuti (2010), p. 33 e ss., (2020), p. 3 e ss.; (2013), p. 261 e ss.

[20] De Vergottini (2004), p. 40; Cabras (2006), p. 313 e ss.; Guazzarotti (2018), p. 80.

[21] N. Lupo, *L'art.11 della Costituzione e l'appartenenza dell'Italia all'Alleanza atlantica*, in *il Filangieri*, Quaderno 2022, cit., p. 19 e ss., in particolare p. 28 ss.

[22] Brunelli (2020), p. 584 e ss.

[23] I.e. the Gulf War (1990), the Afghanistan war (2001) and the Ukrainian war (2022-).

[24] I.e. the Libyan war (2011).

More controversial is the hypothesis of war waged as a reaction to serious violations of human rights,[25] and that of pre-emptive defence is entirely illegitimate. With respect to these, reliance has been placed on international custom; however, these practices appear to lack the constituent elements of *longa repetitio* (for both cases) and *opinio iuris* (particularly for the latter).

3 Participation in War and Declaration of a State of War: Distinction Between Declaration of a State of War and Declaration of War

As we have seen, the discipline of Article 11 of the Constitution cannot be read from a neutralising perspective, and therefore Italy can certainly be part of a belligerent relationship. In light of this premise, it is necessary to consider whether Italian participation in a war necessarily entails the activation of the constitutional measures resulting from the application of Article 78 of the Constitution, under which "The Chambers shall declare a state of war and confer on the Government the necessary powers".

The prevailing constitutionalist doctrine tends to answer this question positively by emphasising "how the need for the resolution referred to in the article in question arises whenever there is a situation qualifying as war under international law, even if the parties to the conflict do not define it as such".[26] Article 78 of the Italian Constitution is essentially considered as the provision regulating the concrete exercise of the *ius ad bellum*; however, it follows that, noting Italy's frequent participation in wars in the absence of its application, it has come to be affirmed that it is substantially unimplemented.

This interpretation is not tenable. It places undue emphasis on the first part of the provision while overlooking the second, which is in fact crucial to a correct reading. The key term is the adjective *necessary*. Pursuant to Article 78 of the Constitution, the declaration of a state of war cannot be separated from the conferral upon the government of the *necessary* powers—powers which the Executive does not ordinarily possess but which *necessity* requires it to be granted.

The pertinent question, therefore, is whether participation in a war *necessarily* entails the need to confer upon the government powers additional to those it ordinarily holds; the answer must be negative.

This question also requires that the debate within the Constituent Assembly be situated in its proper historical context: while it is true that the framers[27] tended to

[25] De Vergottini (1999), p. 124 e s.

[26] With a different position Mortati (1962), p. 598; A. Giardina, *Articolo. 78*, in *Commentario della Costituzione a cura di G. Branca*, cit., 1979, p. 104, Vedaschi, *Articolo 78*, in *La Costituzione italiana*, cit., vol. II, p.135.

[27] Patroni Griffi (2006), p. 1532.

conflate the concepts of *declaration of war* and *deliberation on the state of war*, thus treating Article 78 as addressing the *ius ad bellum*, it must nonetheless be stressed that their understanding of war was rooted in the notion of an event which, by its very nature, demanded recourse to exceptional measures. This conception stands in contrast to the broader range of situations in which Italy has subsequently found itself involved in international conflicts—circumstances that have been redefined as contingencies manageable within the framework of ordinary legal mechanisms.

Thus, the content of the parliamentary decision required by Article 78 of the Constitution is to be traced back "rather than to the choice on the *an of* participation in the war (the so-called choice on the war), *to the option on the need to provoke*, following involvement in the conflict, *those modifications and alterations of the internal order provided for at the time of the onset of wartime* (the so-called choice on the state of war)".[28] Modifications and alterations that go beyond the granting of the necessary powers to the government, such as: the extension of the term of the Chambers pursuant to Article 60, paragraph 2, of the Constitution; the attribution of broader jurisdiction to military courts pursuant to Article 103, paragraph 3, of the Constitution; and the exception to the right to appeal to the Supreme Court of Cassation against judgements and measures on personal freedom pursuant to Article 111, paragraph 7, of the Constitution.

When Italy's participation in a war does not require (as has been the case thus far) recourse to such modifications and alterations to the normal functioning of the constitutional order, a declaration of a state of war will therefore not be necessary.

From the consideration that Italy's participation in a war does not necessarily entail the deliberation of a state of war, there follows the clear distinction between the *declaration of war* and the declaration of the president of the Republic referred to in paragraph 9 of Article 87 of the Constitution (in the sense attributed to it by international law of a prior and unequivocal warning of the start of hostilities, pursuant to Article 1 of the Third Hague Convention of 1907): the declaration of a state of war, as deliberated by the Chambers, fulfils its function in terms of the constitutional guarantee ensured by the intervention of the head of state in exceptional circumstances that justify parliamentary deliberation.

4 Wars and Missions

Within the framework of the United Nations and, more generally, international law, the difference between international military missions and wars lies in the fact that the former are carried out with the consent of the State on whose territory the operations take place or without the necessary involvement of other States. This distinction has never been accepted by the Italian legislature, which has expunged the word "war" from its lexicon, thereby lumping all international military operations into a

[28] Opinion of Carnevale (2019), p. 49 e s.

confused *genus*. Nonetheless, it retains its validity and makes it possible to classify the cases of the use of force by Italy in the Republican period and to note that they include, in addition to a very high number of missions, six wars, all fought without the need to declare a state of war pursuant to Article 78 of the Constitution[29]: the Gulf War of 1991, the Kosovo War of 1999, the Afghanistan War of 2001, the Iraq War of 2003, the Libyan War of 2011, and the Ukraine War of 2022.

The ideological difficulty in acknowledging that Italy may engage in war has been reflected in the regulation of the use of force, with particular reference to the application of the Military Penal Code in times of peace and of war.

In this regard, the legislative developments concerning Article 9 of the Military Criminal Code of War (*Codice Penale Militare di Guerra*, or *c.p.m.g.*) are of particular interest, which provided for its applicability "to expeditionary forces abroad for military operations". The provision was subject to a series of derogations, leading to its substantial disuse.[30] With the initiation of the mission in Lebanon on 21 August 1982, characterised by the deployment of a significant contingent of 519 military personnel,[31] the non-applicability of the *c.p.m.g.* was discussed. However, this was not determined by a legislative act but rather through the approval of an order of the day by both Chambers of Parliament, thus leaving the matter unresolved.

During the Gulf War, and precisely to emphasise the intention to deny that it constituted a war, it was decided to apply the Military Criminal Code of Peace (*Codice Penale Militare di Pace*, or *c.p.m.p.*). Only with Law No. 6 of 3 January 2002, which converted Decree-Law No. 421 of 1 December 2001, adopted in relation to the war in Afghanistan, was Article 9 of the *c.p.m.g.* modified, declaring its applicability—even in peacetime—to "expeditionary forces abroad for armed military operations, from the moment they cross the national borders or embark on a ship or aircraft, or, for the crews of these, from the moment they are informed of the destination of the mission".

What could have been a stable legal framework was, however, rapidly overridden by Law No. 15 of 27 February 2002, which, converting Decree-Law No. 451 of 2001, established that the *c.p.m.g.* would apply to troops deployed in Afghanistan

---

[29] Two types of international military missions are usually distinguished: those carried out by sending military personnel abroad to participate in defence arrangements prepared with allies, which do not involve the use of force (essentially NATO operations), and those carried out by sending military personnel abroad to contribute to resolving various types of crises involving the use of force (essentially UN missions). A list of active and completed missions is available on https://www.difesa.it/OperazioniMilitari/op_intern_corso/Pagine/Operazioni_int.aspx.

However, international military missions may also include operations that do not require the involvement of another State, such as escort or patrol operations. For example, one may recall the 1987 naval mission for protection and clearance of mines in the Persian Gulf (see Massai 1988, pp. 209 e ss) or the provisions of Article 5 of Law No. 130/2011, which permit the deployment of military personnel on merchant ships to defend against potential acts of piracy.

[30] See Cevolin, *L'impiego di forze armate all'estero: profili procedurali*, in *Pubblicazioni Centro Studi per la Pace*, www.studiperlapace.it, 2000, p. 6 e ss.; Rivello (2004), p. 81 e ss.

[31] See Decree-Law No. 686/1982, converted by Law No. 820/1982, and later integrated by Law No. 11/1984.

but not to other international military operations. Law No. 42 of 18 March 2003 confirmed this same dual-track approach.

The most recent legislative intervention is contained in Article 19 of Law No. 145 of 2016, which establishes the general applicability of the *c.p.m.p.* for all international military operations while allowing the legislator to assess the appropriateness of applying, by derogation, the *c.p.m.g.*.

The legislator therefore fails to establish an unambiguous criterion for the applicability of military penal codes, thereby leaving ample room for discretion. A coherent discipline would require the application of the military criminal code to international military missions not involving the use of force and the application of the military criminal code to international military missions involving the use of force and, of course, to wars.

However, this, as we have said, is prevented by ideological reasons that lead the legislator to shy away from the application of wartime rules during peacetime and to claim to be in peacetime even when Italy is, in fact, at war.

5 The Gulf War (1990)

On 2 August 1990, Iraq invaded Kuwait and, following a swift military campaign, declared its annexation on 8 August.[32] The invasion was justified by the Iraqi authorities on the basis of territorial claims dating back to Kuwait's attainment of independence in 1961, as well as by contingent reasons linked to oil policy: the government in Baghdad accused Kuwait and the United Arab Emirates of exceeding their OPEC production quotas, thereby causing serious harm to the Iraqi economy. The international response was immediate. The United Nations Security Council adopted its first resolution, Resolution 660, on the very same day, 2 August. This resolution formed the basis for subsequent UN actions and immediately defined the scope of future measures: the invasion of Kuwait was characterised as a breach of international peace and security and was accordingly condemned. Acting pursuant to Articles 39 and 40 of the Charter of the United Nations, the Security Council demanded the immediate and unconditional withdrawal of Iraqi forces and the commencement of negotiations between the parties to resolve their disputes. This resolution was followed, over the ensuing months, by further resolutions, none of which authorised the use of force.[33]

It was in this context that Italian action took place.[34]

[32] For a detailed account of the main events see Villani (1991), p. 15 ss.

[33] No. 661, 6 August 1990; No. 662 del 9 August; No. 664, 18 August; No. 665, 25 August; No. 666, 13 September; No. 667, 16 September; No. 669, 24 September, No. 670 del 25 September; No. 674 del 29 October; No. 678, 28 November. https://main.un.org/securitycouncil/en/content/resolutions-adopted-security-council-1990.

[34] The first regulatory interventions were the Decree-Law No. 216/1990 and the Decree-Law No. 220/1990.

On 14 August 1990, the Council of Ministers adopted a resolution in which Italy's commitment to restoring international law and security was reaffirmed, and it was decided to send a naval group to the eastern Mediterranean to compensate for the removal of the US units that had moved to the Gulf; the same naval group, following the decisions taken at the Western European Union ministerial meeting of 21 August in Paris, would also move to Gulf waters. On 22 August 1990, Foreign Minister De Michelis and Foreign Minister Rognoni presented to the Senate the government communications on the crisis and the decisions taken.[35] They emphasised, on the one hand, the unity of the international community's response as expressed by the positions taken by the League of Arab Countries, the European Economic Community (EEC), the Western European Union (WEU), and, above all, the United Nations (UN); on the other hand, the need for a major military commitment to ensure that the economic sanctions established internationally could be effective, so as to avoid war. On the basis of these communications, the Senate approved the motion (a similar motion was approved the following day by the Chamber of Deputies) with which it committed the government to continue its action in the field of international coordination to implement the directives of the UN Security Council.

The diplomatic route and recourse to economic sanctions had no effect. Thus, on 29 November 1990, noting the inadequacy of the measures taken up to that point, the Security Council, acting under Chapter VII of the UN Charter, adopted Resolution No. 678,[36] with which it authorised "to use all necessary means to enforce and apply Resolution 660 and all subsequent relevant resolutions and to re-establish peace and international security in the region" if the Iraqi troops did not withdraw by 15 January 1991. An ultimatum was therefore issued, and after the deadline had expired to no avail, the armed forces of a coalition of several States went to war against Iraq on the night of 16–17 January 1991.

Then, on 17 January 1991, the Italian Government decided to take part in the conflict supported by the resolutions of the Senate and the Chamber of Deputies[37] committing it to join the military action against Iraq in order to fully implement Directive No. 678 in compliance with the duties of cooperation imposed by membership of the UN.[38] The government's position had been expressed in the communications made to the Senate by Prime Minister Giulio Andreotti in the morning session of 16 January 1991. It recalled all the unsuccessful attempts at a peaceful settlement of the crisis and emphasised that "the Charter of the United Nations,

[35] Senate of the Republic, Official report, 22 August 1990, No. 430.

[36] The resolution was adopted with 12 votes in favour (Canada, Colombia, Côte d'Ivoire, Ethiopia, Finland, France, Malaysia, the United Kingdom, Romania, the United States, USSR, Zaire), 1 abstention (China), and 2 votes against (Cuba and Yemen).

[37] Chamber of deputies, Official reports, 16 and 17 January 1991, No.574; Senate of the Republic, Official reports, 16 and 17 January 1991, No. 476, No. 477 and No. 478. On this matter see Bettinelli (1991), p. 375 s.

[38] For a detailed reconstruction of the public debate upon these events, see Ciglioni (2022), p. 228 ss.

which sets as one of its purposes those of safeguarding future generations from the scourge of war and of creating the conditions in which justice and respect for obligations under treaties and other sources of international law may otherwise be maintained, provides for [and I highlight this part of the quote] *effective collective measures* to prevent and remove threats to peace and to suppress acts of aggression or other breaches of the peace". Recalling Resolution No. 678, the Prime Minister clarified: "We are not, therefore, in the hypothesis of war as a means of settling international disputes, which Italy repudiates with Article 11 of the Constitution. Our legal system conforms, under Article 10 of the Constitution, to the norms of generally recognised international law. The decision to take part, if not averted in extremis by the Iraqi Government, in the military action in the Gulf that the Italian Cabinet is submitting to Parliament for approval, is inspired by the provision in the second part of Article 11 by virtue of which Italy favours international organisations whose action tends to ensure peace and justice among nations".

It is evident in the Prime Minister's words the effort not to characterise military intervention as war.[39] Italian participation in the conflict is brought back by the government and by the political forces that support it in Parliament, to the category of *international police* operation. The argumentative effort is understandable: for the first time, Articles 11, first part, and 78 of the Constitution are evoked, not in the framework of an ideal debate but to respond to the urgency of a concrete event: "It is necessary to clarify these concepts in order to establish the nature and limits of the Government's constitutional powers in the current affair. Participation with other states in the actions in the Gulf is in accordance with the letter and spirit of Article 11 and therefore does not entail recourse to Article 78 of the Constitution itself, which provides for the deliberation of a state of war by the Houses of Parliament. We are not asking for a state of war to be declared. Instead, we are asking for Parliament's support for the action to be carried out with the cooperation of the naval and air units of our Armed Forces present in the Gulf, in the Gulf 2 and 'Locusta 90' missions respectively, for the implementation of the measures provided for in paragraphs 2, 3 and 4 of Security Council Resolution 678, for the defence of peace and the restoration of international security".

The justifications advanced by the government for Italy's participation in the conflict are therefore twofold but mutually contradictory. Firstly, the Prime Minister emphasised that the Iraqi invasion of Kuwait could not be considered an international dispute within the meaning of the first part of Article 11 of the Constitution.[40] This assertion would thus imply that recourse to the use of force could be regarded as a war—legitimate precisely because it was not aimed at resolving a dispute or at infringing upon the freedom of other peoples but rather at defending it (in accordance with generally recognised norms of international law). However, by subsequently invoking the second part of Article 11 and the actions of the United Nations,

[39] The same effort is evident in the decisions made by lawmakers. See Decree-Law No. 247/1990 and the Decree-law No. 17/1991.

[40] Position contested by Allegretti (1991), p. 387 e ss.

it is explicitly maintained that the military intervention in the Gulf cannot be considered a war, thereby denying the necessity of activating the mechanism provided for under Article 78 of the Constitution.

This contradiction depends on that conceptual overlap, on which we have already had occasion to dwell, between the concepts of declaration of war and declaration of a state of war. At the moment in which Italy adopted the positions taken by Security Council Resolution No. 678, it decided to adhere to the ultimatum contained therein and therefore made a formal declaration of war. However, participation in the war did not determine alterations in the normal functioning of the institutions such as to justify the declaration of a state of war with all its constitutional consequences.

The Gulf War was thus the first war of the Republican era, the first of a series that Italy would be able to fight without having to declare a state of war under Article 78 of the Constitution. What justified its legitimacy was the application of the generally recognised norm of international law authorising collective self-defence, with the fact that such self-defence was carried out through the UN framework assuming a merely ancillary character. Precisely because it was the first such instance, it raised questions which the government, and more broadly the republican institutions, struggled to formulate clearly and to resolve. Chief among these was the question of whether it was possible to participate in a war without declaring a state of war; and when faced with what appeared to be a dilemma, the preference was to deny the very nature of the decision taken.

The analysis of the events of 1990/1991 confirms our considerations on the ownership of the decision on the "*an*" and "*quomodo*" of participation in the war. The decision to "participate in the use of force"—this was the expression used by the Prime Minister—was taken by the government as part of an articulated diplomatic action and strategic design; it was up to Parliament to make it fully operational.[41]

6 The Kosovo War (1999)

The Kosovo War was part of the tragic events of the break-up of former Yugoslavia. The background was the bitter clash between the army of the Yugoslav Federation and the Kosovo independence movement *Ushtria Çlirimtare e Kosovës* (UÇK) in the Spring of 1998, which led the United Nation Security Council to pass Resolution No. 1160 of 31 March 1998.[42] The Security Council declared that it was acting under Chapter VII of the Charter, thus implicitly qualifying the Kosovo crisis as a situation threatening peace and condemning the excesses of Belgrade's troops and the terrorist acts committed by UÇK. Among other things, the resolution established a ban on all States selling arms to the Yugoslav Federation, including Kosovo.

---

[41] As the Prime Minister reported to the Senate of the Republic on 17 January 1991.

[42] https://digitallibrary.un.org/record/252117.

However, the fighting continued so that the Security Council passed Resolution No. 1199 of 23 September 1998,[43] in which it explicitly described the situation as a serious threat to peace. Additionally, the Security Council expressed concern over the serious humanitarian situation that was looming due to the high number of displaced persons (quantified at 230,000) and the increasingly bitter level of fighting; it called for an end to the violence and the withdrawal of Yugoslav troops so as to allow international observers and humanitarian aid. Most importantly, the Security Council decided that if the concrete measures imposed on the parties were not adopted, further actions and measures to maintain or restore peace in the region would be seriously considered and enacted.

The Yugoslav Federation refused to come to an agreement, which led to the reaction of North Atlantic Treaty Organisation (NATO). On 12 October 1998, the NATO issued an ultimatum to the Belgrade government, giving it 96 h to accept the conditions imposed, and adopted *an activation order* ordering the start of military operations. This forceful action led to an agreement between the warring parties and the NATO, signed on 15 October 1998. It provided for the withdrawal of Yugoslav troops by the following 27 October and the establishment of the *Kosovo Verification Mission* (KVM), a contingent of *Organization for Security and Co-operation in Europe* (*OSCE*) observers with verification tasks. However, the agreement did not last long as both sides failed to respect the ceasefire, with violence so severe against the Albanian population that it amounted to ethnic cleansing.

Ultimately, what led to the war was the failure of the Rambouillet Accords. At the Rambouillet conference between 6 February and 18 March 1999, the negotiations were geared towards achieving two objectives: the recognition of broad political autonomy for Kosovo, albeit within the Yugoslav federation, and a massive NATO troop presence in the region to guarantee the peaceful development of the situation. On 18 March 1999, the Yugoslav and Russian delegates refused to sign the agreement—the military content of which they disputed—which was thus only signed by NATO and Kosovo. The crisis was difficult to resolve: the *OSCE* international observers were sent back on 22 March, and on 23 March, NATO Secretary General Javier Solana declared that he had ordered an attack on the Federation of Yugoslavia, which was launched the following day.

The NATO attack was carried out with a massive bombing campaign on Yugoslav soil that did not spare the capital. Italy took a direct part by providing bases on its territory for the launching of bombers. In the late afternoon of 24 March 1999, the Vice-President of the Council of Ministers, Sergio Mattarella, reported to Parliament on the start of the military operations, emphasising how they were the consequence of the irresponsible Yugoslav attitude and found their justification not only in the consistent adherence to NATO policies but above all "in the clear impression that [...] the Belgrade Government wanted to carry out an ethnic cleansing of the region with an action of expulsion, when not of physically provoked victims, of the Kosovar minority". Sergio Mattarella insisted on the humanitarian basis of the attack: "We

[43] https://digitallibrary.un.org/record/260416.

are facing a blatant and very serious violation of human rights, ascertained and declared by the UN's Security Council". But in recalling the Security Council resolutions, he could not fail to recognise that none of them had expressly provided for recourse to the use of force, and for this reason he hypothesised the existence of an international custom legitimising the use of force for humanitarian reasons. The government's position was reiterated 2 days later in the communications to Parliament by the Prime Minister, Massimo D'Alema,[44] and approved by motions of both Houses.[45] He too recalled the responsibilities of the Belgrade government in rejecting the Rambouillet Agreements. He stressed that the lack of an express authorisation to use force by the United Nations had to be traced back to the paralysis of the UN Security Council, blocked by Russia's veto. Furthermore, he justified the armed intervention on humanitarian grounds. Among the speeches that animated the debate following the Prime Minister's communications to the Senate, the one by Leopoldo Elia deserves particular attention. Recalling the same precedent invoked by Sergio Mattarella, he prefigured the formation of an international custom: "Allow me to add that the intervention in Bosnia cannot be considered an unrepeatable exception but must be identified as the first application of a principle that had already been implemented outside Europe with the multinational force in Iraqi Kurdistan: the principle is that which legitimises humanitarian interference for the protection of human rights and peacekeeping, recalled in the preamble and first article of the North Atlantic Treaty. Moreover, not all international law, let alone nascent European public law, is contained in treaties. Their progress is also based on repeated behaviour, the basis of customary law, and above all of a *communis opinio* that unites all the countries involved in the intervention in Serbia today, even if it is opportune that we move very soon for the sake of certainty to written law".

The justifications provided by the government and accepted by Parliament for Italian participation in the Kosovo War are not acceptable. The assertion that the lack of UN authorisation should have been considered as irrelevant, because it was determined by the structure of the Security Council's decision-making procedure, can be seen as a radical criticism of the *UN system* itself but in itself does not allow the decision on the war to be rooted in the second part of Article 11 of the Constitution. As for the possibility of basing armed action on an international custom aimed at the protection of human rights, it should be emphasised that the very subjects that supported it had to admit that the Kosovo War would be the occasion of its first application[46]: thus configuring it as an instantaneous custom, the admissibility of which must be doubted.[47]

[44] Senate of the Republic, Official report, 26 March 1999.

[45] Chamber of deputies: Motions No. 6–00078 (Mussi and others), No. 6–00079 (Sbarbati and others), No. 6–00080 (Marinacci and others); Senate of the Republic: Motions No. 1–00378 (Salvi) and No. 1–00379 (Meluzzi).

[46] See Pinelli (2000), pp. 196 s.

[47] As stated also in Cavino and Malvicini (2023), p. 96 ss.

The inevitable conclusion that follows from the above discussion is the unconstitutionality of Italy's participation in the 1999 Kosovo War.[48]

7 The War in Afghanistan (2001)

The war against Afghanistan in October 2001 constituted the first response to the terrorist attack on the United States on 11 September 2001. It triggered a series of reactions in international politics with important repercussions with respect to the definition of the *ius ad bellum*. Among these developments was the elaboration by the United States of a doctrine of pre-emptive self-defence, which would later be invoked to justify the intervention in Iraq.

Equally important was the emergence of a position, broadly shared by the international community, which explicitly classified terrorist attacks as acts of war when they were fostered, if not directly planned and executed, by sovereign States. This view initially provoked intense debate, as it seemed to attribute the status of belligerents not to States themselves but to terrorist organisations, thereby introducing a new paradigm of warfare characterised by the indefiniteness of the enemy. Nevertheless, the sequence of events following 11 September—culminating in the invasion of Afghanistan—effectively re-situated the "war on terrorism" within the traditional framework of inter-state belligerency. A detailed consideration of the key stages of this process is thus necessary.

It is thus necessary to take as a starting point the NATO Council declaration of 12 September 2001, according to which, if it had been made clear that the attack of the previous day had originated outside the United States, the collective defence obligation set forth in Article 5 of the Treaty would have had to be applied.[49] Now, if one considers the nature and structure of the military apparatus of the Atlantic

[48] This was, after all, the reading provided, almost unanimously, by the Italian Constitutional Doctrine. For a reconstruction of the debate, see the essays collected in Dogliani and Sicardi (1999).

[49] "On September 12th, the North Atlantic Council met again in response to the appalling attacks perpetrated yesterday against the United States. The Council agreed that if it is determined that this attack was directed from abroad against the United States, it shall be regarded as an action covered by Article 5 of the Washington Treaty, which states that an armed attack against one or more of the Allies in Europe or North America shall be considered an attack against them all. The commitment to collective self-defence embodied in the Washington Treaty was first entered into in circumstances very different from those that exist now, but it remains no less valid and no less essential today, in a world subject to the scourge of international terrorism. When the Heads of State and Government of NATO met in Washington in 1999, they paid tribute to the success of the Alliance in ensuring the freedom of its members during the Cold War and in making possible a Europe that was whole and free. But they also recognised the existence of a wide variety of risks to security, some of them quite unlike those that had called NATO into existence. More specifically, they condemned terrorism as a serious threat to peace and stability and reaffirmed their determination to combat it in accordance with their commitments to one another, their international commitments and national legislation. Article 5 of the Washington Treaty stipulates that in the event of attacks falling within its purview, each Ally will assist the Party that has been attacked by taking such

Alliance, it is exceedingly difficult to give the concept of *attack directed* from abroad a meaning other than *directed by another State*.

Furthermore, the resolutions adopted by the UN Security Council must be considered. Resolution 1368 of 12 September 2001 reaffirmed the right to individual and collective defence in accordance with the Charter; it stated that the attacks of the previous day, like any terrorist act, constituted a threat to international peace and security, and it emphasised, in paragraph 3, that those responsible for aiding, abetting, and harbouring the perpetrators, organisers, and sponsors of the attacks would bear the consequences. And even more explicit was Resolution No. 1373 of 28 September 2001 that recalling the principle—established by the General Assembly with Declaration No. 2625 XXV of 1970 and reaffirmed by the Security Council itself with Resolution No. 1189 of 1998—by virtue of which every State has the duty to refrain from organising and encouraging acts of terrorism on the territory of other States, established, declaring that it was acting under Chapter VII of the Charter, that States should oppose any kind of support for the benefit of terrorists.

It can therefore be affirmed that the international community expressed itself decisively in supporting the view that terrorist attacks should be regarded as acts of war, for which States that had concretely facilitated or encouraged their commission would bear responsibility. Thus, once the support provided by the Afghan government to the terrorist organisation al-Qaeda—which had effectively claimed responsibility for the attacks—had been established, an armed response against it could be considered legitimate, both on the part of the United States and, more broadly, by all States, by virtue of the principle of collective self-defence, without the need for any further specific authorisations.

The United States, leading an alliance of eight countries,[50] went to war against Afghanistan on 7 October 2001 by launching Operation *Enduring Freedom*. Two days later, the Italian Prime Minister, Silvio Berlusconi, and the Italian Minister of Defence, Antonio Martino, reported to the Italian Parliament on the international situation, upholding the legitimacy of the American military operations and expressing the government's full support for them, which was translated into support actions of an essentially logistical nature. The communications were followed by acts of address of substantial adhesion to the positions of the Cabinet.[51] The following 7 November, Minister Martino reported to Parliament on Italy's participation in the war with the commitment of its own contingent. The government's communications were approved by resolutions of both Houses.[52]

---

action as it deems necessary. Accordingly, the United States' NATO Allies stand ready to provide the assistance that may be required as a consequence of these acts of barbarism".

[50] In addition to the United States, the United Kingdom, Italy, France, Germany, Canada, Australia, Poland.

[51] Chamber of deputies: Resolutions No. 6–00004 (Vito and others) and No. 6–00006 (Rutelli and others); Senate of the Republic: Motions No. 6–00008 (Schifani and others) and No. 6–00009 (Angius and others).

[52] Chamber of deputies: Resolutions No. 6–00009 (Vito and others) and No. 6–00010 (Rutelli and others); Senate of the Republic: Resolutions No. 6–00011 (Schifani and others) and No. 6–00012

In light of the preceding considerations, the constitutional legitimacy of Italy's participation in the Afghanistan War must be regarded as beyond doubt.[53]

At the regulatory level, particular attention must be paid to Decree-Law No. 421 of 1 December 2001, concerning *Urgent Provisions for the Participation of Military Personnel in the Multinational Operation Enduring Freedom*. Notably, Article 8 of this Decree-Law provided that the Italian expeditionary force would be subject to the Military War Criminal Code (*Codice Penale Militare di Guerra*), with reference to the observations previously made.

8 The Iraq War (2003)

The war against Iraq in 2003 must also be traced back to the events directly linked to the attacks of 11 September 2001. Iraq, accused of producing and possessing weapons of mass destruction, was in fact included among those that the Bush doctrine qualified as *Rogue States*.

The event that led to the 2003 invasion had its premises in the first Gulf War of 1991, at the end of which the UN Security Council had approved Resolution No. 687 of 3 April 1991,[54] which imposed on defeated Iraq the conditions of peace, consisting of the definition of borders with Kuwait, the repatriation of prisoners of war, the determination of the extent of reparations, and the launching of a demilitarisation policy.

With respect to demilitarisation, section C of the resolution stipulated that Iraq should unconditionally accept the obligation to adhere to the international conventions on the prohibition of chemical and bacteriological weapons; to destroy and not to produce for the future stockpiles of weapons or components for chemical and bacteriological weapons it possesses; to destroy and not to produce missiles with a range greater than 150 km; and not to acquire nuclear weapons. The fulfilment of these obligations was to be monitored by inspections conducted by the United Nations Special Commission (UNSCOM) under the coordination of the International Atomic Energy Agency (IAEA). After initial cooperation, the Iraqi government began to obstruct UNSCOM's action, going as far as to expel the inspectors in 1998. This led to a series of armed interventions, to some extent authorised by the UN,[55] which ended with the Anglo-American campaign of massive, targeted bombing called Operation *Desert Fox* between 16 and 19 December 1998. The following year, the space for a diplomatic solution reopened, which led the Security Council to adopt Resolution No. 1284 of 17 December 1999 by which a new monitoring commission, the *United Nations Monitoring, Verification, and Inspection*

(Angius and others).

[53] *Contra* De Fiores (2002), p. 89 e ss.

[54] https://digitallibrary.un.org/record/110709.

[55] Johnstone (2015), p. 239.

Commission (UNMOVIC), was set up. However, it failed to be granted authorisation by the Iraqi government to settle in the country for almost 2 years. This led the Security Council to approve Resolution 1441 of 8 November 2002, which set a 30-day deadline for the Iraqi government to submit a detailed report on the status of its disarmament. On 13 November, Iraq unconditionally accepted the terms of the resolution and delivered the requested report on the following 7 December; the Security Council expressed itself on 27 January 2003 in critical terms towards the positions taken up to that point by the Iraqi government but without detecting any illicit conduct and ordering the examination of a further report for the following 7 March.

In response to this development, a rift emerged within the Security Council. On one side, the American government, in line with the Bush doctrine, presented a report on 5 February, delivered by Secretary of State Colin Powell, aimed at demonstrating that Iraq had produced and held arsenals of weapons of mass destruction. On the other side, France, Germany, and Russia issued a joint statement on 10 February, asserting the necessity of continuing inspections. The turning point came on 24 February when the United States, the United Kingdom, and Spain presented a draft resolution to the Security Council aimed at authorising the use of force against Iraq. On 17 March, the proposal was withdrawn in the face of opposition, particularly from the French government, which had announced its intention to veto. However, the proponents decided to proceed unilaterally, outside the UN system. Thus, on 18 March, US President George W. Bush issued an ultimatum to Iraqi President Saddam Hussein, demanding that he leave the country within 48 h. The war began on 20 March and ended on 1 May of the same year.

The Italian position with respect to the conflict was expressed on 19 March 2003 by means of a communiqué issued by the General Secretariat of the Presidency of the Republic, which reported on the meeting of the Supreme Defence Council held on the same day. After an in-depth debate, the Council acknowledged the decisions that the government would subsequently present to Parliament for scrutiny. The communiqué underlined how these positions were consistent with the political line followed up to that time by the government, of support for the Anglo-American positions, and emphasised that "During the meeting, it was unanimously acknowledged that, given the fundamentally parliamentary character established by our Constitution, the determination of political direction—including the use of the Armed Forces and their structures—falls within the competence of the Government and Parliament, linked to one another by the relationship of confidence, including with regard to constitutional aspects". In terms of constitutional dynamics, the communiqué presents a framework that is entirely consistent with the structure which, as we have seen, characterises decisions on war within our legal system: the decision on the *an* by the government, the decision on the *quomodo* by Parliament, and the function of guaranteeing the development of the political direction exercised by the President of the Republic within the Supreme Defence Council. As regards the substance of the government's determinations, the communiqué listed six points:

1. Exclusion of the participation of Italian military personnel in wartime actions.

2. Exclusion of the supply and provision of armaments and military means of any kind.
3. Exclusion of the use of military facilities as bases for direct attacks on Iraqi targets.
4. Qualification of the Italian position—in accordance with the above stipulations—as non-belligerent.
5. Maintenance of the use of the bases for transit, refuelling, and vehicle maintenance needs, as well as authorisation to fly over national airspace.
6. Strengthening of the protection apparatus of the bases themselves.

The government therefore decided for *non-belligerency*, affirming that this position was a direct consequence of non-participation in the fighting and the exclusion of the supply of weapons and the use of bases on Italian territory for direct attacks and that it did not prevent the provision of significant logistical support to the Anglo-American alliance.[56] As we have seen, the declaration of non-belligerency represents a mode of participation in the war that is manifested in the active support for one of the parties to the conflict. It follows that non-belligerency can also be legitimately declared only with respect to a war that does not conflict with the limits to the use of force established by our Constitution.

And it is in the light of this consideration that the speech by the Prime Minister, Silvio Berlusconi, in the Chamber of Deputies on the same day, 19 March 2003, must be read.[57] In his speech he mentions: "perplexities about the legitimacy of the use of force to disarm Iraq, following the withdrawal of a draft of this further resolution before the Security Council. These are perplexities that would prevent, according to the exponents of the opposition, not only active participation (a situation that for Italy has always been excluded and is also to be excluded for the future), but even logistical support for military action through the authorisation to fly over national territory and the use of military bases, which for decades have been located in Italy in application of the Atlantic Pact". But Berlusconi believed that they could be overcome in consideration of the fact that the Anglo-American military action could be framed as part of the measures to forcibly implement the UN resolutions following the end of the first Gulf War, which, in the absence of a subsequent vote against by the Security Council, would have retained their validity. The assertion is contradictory in itself, given that the President of the Council himself had begun by pointing out that the American military initiative had started after the renunciation of submitting a new resolution to the Security Council "after a permanent member country of the Security Council, our friend and ally France, had legitimately—however, in my opinion, wrongly—announced that it would veto it".

It seems that, on the one hand, this position argued that the Iraqi disarmament resolutions are still in force because they are not contradicted by a subsequent vote against them; on the other hand, it is argued that the American intervention is brought about precisely by the French announcement of a vote against a forced

[56] On this topic see also Ronzitti (2021), p. 358.

[57] http://documenti.camera.it/_dati/leg14/lavori/stenografici/sed283/pdfs001.pdf.

execution of the same resolutions. The internal contradictions in the Prime Minister's speech led to two conclusions.

The first concerns the effort made to justify the use of force by framing it within the United Nations system: in no way is the hypothesis of a pre-emptive legitimate defence evoked, which, as we have seen, is instead the starting point for American decisions. And this makes it clear that even the Italian government did not consider this hypothesis as a valid justification for war.

The second concerns the constitutional legitimacy of Italy's participation in the war: since the American attack was conducted outside the UN security system and could not be considered legitimate defence, the government's decision to renounce neutrality for non-belligerence can only be considered illegitimate.

9 The War in Libya (2011)

Italy's participation in the war in Libya falls within the broader context of the events which, also as a result of the spread of the so-called Arab Spring across the North African geopolitical quadrant,[58] led, between February and October 2011, to the fall of Colonel Muammar Gaddafi's regime.

The beginning of the end of the Libyan regime is generally identified with the clashes between protesters in Benghazi and pro-government militias that took place between 15 and 17 February; within a few days, the worsening of the crisis led to the institutionalisation of a vast insurrectionary movement, coordinated by the Transitional National Council (TNC), which, over the next 7 months, thanks to the support of the international community, put an end to the *Jamahiriya* experience.[59]

Faced with the ongoing crisis, also at the instigation of the Arab League, it was mainly France, Great Britain, and the United States that worked to promote an intervention in Libya.[60] This was done through diplomatic action with the European Union and the United Nations. On 21 February, the Union's Foreign Affairs Council called for an immediate end to the use of force against demonstrators and for restraint on all sides but without providing for specific sanctions. Meanwhile, 1 week after the protests had begun, France called for a special session of the United Nations Security Council to adopt appropriate measures against the Libyan government. In response, on 26 February 2011, the Security Council, acting under Chapter VII of the United Nations Charter, adopted Resolution 1970, ordering the referral of Colonel Gaddafi to the International Criminal Court in The Hague—the body competent to investigate war crimes, crimes against humanity, and genocide. This step was necessary because Libya was not a party to the Rome Statute. The resolution also imposed an arms embargo and introduced targeted sanctions against key

[58] See Mercuri and Torelli (2012).

[59] For a detailed analysis see Cresti and Cricco (2012), spec. p. 203 ss.

[60] See v. Bartolini (2012), pp. 1012–1055.

figures of the regime, including travel bans on Gaddafi loyalists and relatives, as well as the freezing of their assets.

Between 28 February and 11 March, the European Council took further steps, tightening some UN-imposed sanctions, for example, by extending the embargo on the supply of any equipment that could be used against protesters and rebels and establishing a *no-fly zone* over Libyan airspace.

Faced with the worsening crisis in Libya, the Security Council passed Resolution No. 1973/2011 on 17 March.[61] Referring to the argument of humanitarian protection (i.e. the *Responsibility to Protect*—R2P principle),[62] and again relying on the standards contained in Chapter VII of the Charter, through Res. 1973/2011, the Security Council on the one hand authorised the Member States to take all necessary measures to safeguard the Libyan population from the threat of attack, possibly by resorting to regional agreements or organisations (but excluding the deployment of a foreign occupation force in any part of Libyan territory); on the other hand, it provided for the institutionalisation of the *no-fly zone* over Libya (already envisaged by the EU), authorising the Member States to act, individually and/or collectively, to ensure compliance and a tightening of the measures envisaged by Res. 1970.

In order to ensure compliance with Resolution 1973/2011, France, Great Britain, and the United States set up an international *coalition* (*coalition of the willing*) in which Belgium, Canada, Denmark, Norway, the Netherlands, Spain, Qatar, and the United Arab Emirates also took part alongside our country.

It began its activities on 19 March with Operation *Odyssey Dawn*, bombing some strategic installations on Libyan territory and attacking troops loyal to the regime. Subsequently, starting on 31 March (and until 31 October 2011), again in implementation of Resolution 1973/2011, military operations were placed under the aegis of NATO, which launched Operation *Unified Protector*, converging in it (also by virtue of Italian diplomatic efforts) the ongoing activities.

With respect to this scenario, also by virtue of the peculiar Italian-Libyan relations, the Italian government initially adopted a conciliatory position, trying to promote, especially through the action of Prime Minister Silvio Berlusconi, the path of dialogue with Gaddafi.

Nonetheless, as emerges from the urgent briefing given to the Chamber of Deputies and the Senate on 23 February by Foreign Minister Franco Frattini, when this prospect gradually disappeared,[63] the government moved closer to the positions expressed by the European Council and the UN Security Council, which had been

[61] The resolution was adopted with ten votes in favor (France, the United Kingdom, the United States, Bosnia and Herzegovina, Colombia, Gabon, Lebanon, Nigeria, Portugal, and South Africa) and five abstentions (Russia, China, Brazil, India, and Germany).

[62] See Scuccimarra (2016), p. 126 ss.; Morris (2013), p. 1270 ss.

[63] Chamber of deputies, Official report, 23 February 2011, No. 438, p. 20 ss.; Senate of the Republic, Official report, 23 February 2011 (afternoon), No. 508, p. 2 ss.

repeatedly supported by the President of the Republic, Giorgio Napolitano, as evidenced by the position taken by the Supreme Defence Council on 11 March.[64]

Particularly significant in this perspective were the summits held between the evening of 17 March and the morning of 18 March, which were also attended, among others, by the President of the Republic, to define Italy's position not only with respect to the contents of Resolution 1973/2011 (which was being finalised in New York at the time) but also with respect to the military commitment required, in view of the Paris summit scheduled for 19 March. Our country's adherence to the orientation expressed by the Security Council was formalised, *first and foremost*, through the decision of the Council of Ministers on 18 March to "authorise, like the other countries available, every appropriate initiative to guarantee humanitarian support to the civilian populations of Libya, ensuring an active role by Italy for the protection of civilians and areas under threat of attack, including the concession in use of existing military bases on national territory": a determination made, as can be read in the press release, by the Prime Minister, "shared with the President of the Republic" and "adopted with the consent of the Council".[65]

The government's position was communicated the same day to the joint Foreign Affairs and Defence Committees of the House and Senate by Ministers Frattini and La Russa.[66] On that occasion, the Minister of Defence dwelt on the need to take into consideration the hypothesis that, precisely because of the specific coverage provided by Res. 1973/2011, Italy's involvement could have gone beyond the mere granting of the use of Italian airbases (i.e. Amendola, Gioia Del Colle, Sigonella, Aviano, Trapani, Decimomannu, and Pantelleria), i.e. in the direction of a greater employment of our Armed Forces.

That being said, Italy's participation in the war in Libya (qualified, at an institutional level, as a humanitarian intervention)[67] was authorised by Parliament through the approval of two resolutions on 18 March,[68] which were followed by two other acts of address approved on 23 and 24 March (recalling the model of the Ruffino resolutions approved in 2001).[69]

---

[64] See the statement of the President of the Republic, Giorgio Napolitano: Rome, 11 March 2011https://archivio.quirinale.it/aspr/comunicati/PRESSRELEASE-001-008127/presidente/giorgio-napolitano/dichiarazione-del-presidente-napolitano-sulle-conclusioni-del-consiglio-europeo#n.

[65] Council of Ministers Press Release No. 131, 18 March 2011.

[66] See the Official report, 18 March 2011, No. by the III and IV Standing Committee (both houses, reunited), *Comunicazioni del governo sulle recenti determinazioni del consiglio di sicurezza dell'Onu in merito alla crisi in Libia.*

[67] As underlined by O. Croci e M. Valigi, *L'Italia e l'intervento internazionale in Libia*, cit., pp. 210–212.

[68] Chamber of deputies - III and IV Standing committee, 18 March 2011: Resolution No. 7–00520 (Nirenstein and others); Senate of the Republic—III and IV Standing committee 18 march 2011), Resolution Amato and others.

[69] Senate of the Republic: Resolution, No. 6–00071 (Gasparri and others), March 23, 2011, sitting, No. 525; Chamber of deputies: Resolutions, No. 6–00071 (Cicchitto and others); and No. 6–00072 (Franceschini and others), 24 March 2011, sitting, No. 452.

Even considering that the actions carried out internationally by the "coalition of the willing" were regarded by the Italian government as an urgent and temporary solution pending the full involvement of NATO, Italy's participation in the Libyan conflict, until mid-April, was limited to providing the use of bases on its territory and conducting maritime and aerial patrol missions, as well as operations aimed at blinding or suppressing Libyan radar air defences.[70] This cautious approach was consistent with the Italian government's broader reluctance to assume a direct role in ongoing operations, as confirmed, among other things, by statements made by Foreign Minister Franco Frattini during a hearing before the joint Defence and Foreign Affairs Committees on 19 April.[71]

A significant change in this respect was represented by the government's decision, under pressure from the United States and other international coalition countries, to take part in operations through direct action, i.e. bombing against military targets on Libyan territory, including in urban areas, especially in order to strengthen the position of the Transitional National Council (25 April).[72]

The President of the Republic was also in favour of the government's decision. On 26 April, at a meeting with representatives of the Combatant and Partisan Associations and the Associations of Arms, he described the government's decision as "the natural development of the choice made by Italy in mid-March, in accordance with the line established by the Supreme Defence Council (...) and therefore supported by broad consensus in Parliament".[73]

The evolution of the government's policy on Operation *Unified Protector* was the subject of parliamentary debate in the following weeks. In particular, in briefing the Senate and House Joint Committees on Foreign Affairs and Defence on the events in Libya, on 27 April, Ministers Frattini and La Russa confirmed the justification provided, among others, by the Head of State the previous day, dwelling, in particular, on the humanitarian basis of Resolution 1973/2011[74] (as well as on the commitments undertaken in NATO), as the basis for the legitimate use of our armed forces to neutralise the firepower of the pro-government military apparatus (used by Gaddafi against his fellow citizens), reiterating the illegitimacy of any solution involving the use of a ground force on Libyan territory, as well as indiscriminate bombing. The same reasons were at the basis of the debate in the House and Senate

[70] See Coticchia (2014), pp. 234–235.

[71] See the Official report, 19 April 2011, by the III and IV Standing Committee (both Houses, reunited), p. 6.

[72] See the President of the Council of Minister press release http://www.governo.it/Presidente/Comunicati/dettaglio.asp?d=63368. On this topic see Colombo and Varvelli (2012), p. 88.

[73] Speech by President of the Republic Giorgio Napolitano at the meeting with representatives of the Combatant and Partisan Associations and Associations of Arms, Rome, April 26, 2011, https://presidenti.quirinale.it/elementi/54814.

[74] See the Official report, 27 April 2011, by the III and IV Standing Committee (both Houses, reunited).

Assemblies, which confirmed their support for the government's approach by approving correlated acts of address on 3 and 4 May.[75]

In general, Italy's participation in the Libyan War allows us to make some general observations.Firstly, as the parliamentary debates and the public stances of government representatives testify, once the possibility of re-establishing a dialogue with the Ràis had disappeared, our country aligned itself—albeit on more moderate positions than other States—with the common "humanitarian" orientation expressed in the "European" and "United Nations" contexts. In contrast to what happened in Kosovo, the military actions undertaken by our country in the spring of 2011 fully conformed to the principles expressed in Resolution 1973/2011,[76] which more widely represented the parameter of legitimacy for NATO's actions until October 2011 (although greater doubts later emerged regarding the military operations carried out against pro-government troops, aimed not primarily at protecting the population but at enabling opposition forces to win the civil war in its final stages).[77]

Secondly, the events of 2011 confirm certain underlying dynamics that, as we have seen, characterised (and, in part, continue to characterise) the decision on whether and how to participate in the war. Thus, it is not surprising to see the leadership role assumed, on that occasion, by the government—in particular by the Prime Minister and the Ministers of Foreign Affairs and Defence—nor the exercise of influence by the Head of State,[78] who, while expressing his position (and that of the Supreme Defence Council) on several occasions, acted in accordance with the Constitution, exercising his power of influence by recalling the commitments undertaken by our country at the international level.

As for Parliament, although it is undeniable that it was involved only ex post facto with respect to the government's determinations, it is equally evident that, although it had the possibility, it did not consider sanctioning them nor did it express an alternative course of action to that of the government, except by committing the government "to set a certain time limit, to be communicated to Parliament, within which to conclude the targeted actions against specific military targets selected on Libyan territory", specifying that they "must in any case be implemented in full compliance with Article 11 of the Constitution and exclusively as an instrument of defence against hostile, real, concrete and current acts directed against our aircraft or against the civilian population, and under conditions of absolute safety for the civilian population itself and for our operators".[79] This dynamic also characterised

---

[75] Chamber of deputies: Motions No. 1–00633 (Franceschini and others); No. 1–00634 (Galletti, Della Vedova, Vernetti, Lo Monte and La Malfa); No. 1–00635 (Di Pietro and others); No. 1–00636 (Reguzzoni, Cicchitto and Sardelli); No. 1–00637 Mecacci and others; 3 May 2011, No. 470.

[76] With a different opinion M. Benvenuti, *L'Italia, la Costituzione e la (seconda) guerra di Libia*, in "Costituzionalismo.it", 9 April 2011.

[77] See N. Ronzitti, *Quale legittimità per le operazioni Nato e italiane in Libia?*, in *IAI- Istituto Affari Internazionali*, 11–12 settembre 2011, reperibile presso: https://www.iai.it/sites/default/files/iai1112.pdf.

[78] See Bellandi (2011), pp. 664–668; Furlan (2013), pp. 348–354.

[79] Chamber of deputies: Motion No. 1–00636 (Reguzzoni, Cicchitto and Sardelli), 3 May 2011.

the parliamentary debate concerning the conversion of Decree-Law no. 107 of 12 July 2011, which concerned, among other things, the protection of the civilian population, the financing of operations already carried out in implementation of Security Council Resolutions 1970/2011 and 1973/2011, and the authorisation of expenditure for those planned for the following month.[80]

10 Conclusion

In general terms, considering the constitutional debate, it can be stated that the repudiation of war, as enshrined in the first part of Article 11 of the Italian Constitution, is limited to the hypothesis of the use of force as a means of settling international disputes and as an offence against the freedom of other peoples.

In other words, the Italian constitutional system does not exclude the legitimacy of war to defend one's own freedom and that of other peoples and, in general, when it is necessary to implement obligations arising from participation in international organisations aimed at achieving an order that ensures peace and justice among nations.

The basis of the legitimacy of the use of force does not reside, moreover, in Article 11 alone but also in Articles 10 and 117 paragraph 1 of the Italian Constitution, that is, in the general reference to international law.

In this perspective, established and generally recognised customary norms and covenant norms do not pose a problem: wars fought in reaction to aggression against one's own State, based on the generally recognised principle of individual self-defence; wars fought in reaction to aggression committed against another State, based on the principle of collective self-defence (which, from being legitimate, becomes mandatory in the case of treaties obliging intervention to aid allies); and wars fought within the framework of the explicit activation of the device on the use of force within the United Nations system are certainly compatible with our constitutional order.

Within this framework, Article 78 of the Italian Constitution regulates the concrete exercise of the ius ad bellum, albeit it has never been applied, besides Italy's frequent participation in wars: all fought without the need to declare a state of war, in some cases complying with the constitutional principles (the Gulf War of 1991,

[80] Through Art. 7 of Decree-Law No. 107/2011 the provisions on criminal matters relating to the missions provided by the decree-law under consideration had been referred to Art. 5 of Decree-Law No. 209/2008, and, consequently, the military personnel engaged in international missions had been subjected to the discipline of the Peace Military Criminal Code and that carried by Art. 9, paragraphs 3 and 4 (subparagraphs a, b, c, and d), paragraphs 5 and 6, of Decree-Law No. 451/2001.

the war in Afghanistan, the war in Libya in 2011, and the war in Ukraine that began in 2022)[81] while in others not (the Kosovo War in 1999 and the Iraq War in 2003).

References

Amorth A (1948) La Costituzione italiana. Giuffrè, Milano, p 46 e ss

Balladore Pallieri G (1949) Diritto costituzionale secondo la nuova Costituzione. Giuffré, Milano, p 337

Bartolini G (2012) *L'operazione* Unified Protector *e la condotta delle ostilità in Libia*. Rivista di Diritto internazionale 4:1012–1055

Bellandi R (2011) Il Consiglio supremo di difesa e la crisi libica: quando il capo dello Stato si fa partecipe dell'indirizzo politico. Quaderni costituzionali (3):664–668

Benvenuti M (2010) Il principio del ripudio della guerra nell'ordinamento costituzionale italiano. Jovene, Napoli, p 33 e ss

Benvenuti M (2013) La prima proposizione dell'articolo 11 della Costituzione italiana tra (in) attualità e (in)attuazione. Un principio decostituzionalizzato o da ricostituzionalizzare? La Comunità Internazionale (2):261 e ss

Benvenuti M (2020) Ripudio della guerra e Costituzione italiana. In: Studi in onore di Vincenzo Atripaldi, vol I. Jovene, Napoli, p 3 e ss

Bettinelli E (1991) Guerre e operazioni di polizia internazionale. Il Foro italiano V:375 s

Biscaretti di Ruffia P (1954) Diritto costituzionale. Jovene, Napoli, p 320

Bon Valsassina P (1955) Il ripudio della guerra nella Costituzione italiana. CEDAM, Padova, p 4

Brunelli G (2020) Scelta atlantica e centralità del Parlamento nella politica costituzionale degasperiana. Quaderni costituzionali (3):584 e ss

Cabras D (2006) Il "ripudio della guerra" e l'evoluzione del diritto internazionale. Quaderni costituzionali (2):297

Carnevale P (2019) Guerra, Costituzione e legge. Qualche riflessione sul trattamento costituzionale della guerra anche alla luce della recente legge sulle missioni internazionali. In: Carnevale P, Greppi E, Roudier K (eds) Il diritto della guerra e della pace. Editoriale Scientifica, Napoli, p 49 e s

Cartabia M, Chieffi L (2006) Art. 11. In: Bifulco R, Celotto A, Olivetti M (eds) Commentario alla Costituzione, vol I. UTET, Torino, p 267 e s

Cassese A (1975) *Articolo 11*, in *Commentario della Costituzione a cura di G. Branca*. Zanichelli-Il Foro, Bologna-Roma, p 565 e ss

Cassese A (1980) Politica estera e relazioni internazionali nel disegno emerso alla Assemblea Costituente. In: De Siervo U (ed) Scelte della Costituente e cultura giuridica—tomo II: Protagonisti e momenti del dibattito costituzionale. Il Mulino, Bologna, pp 505–549

Cavino M, Malvicini M (2023) Le guerre dell'Italia repubblicana. il Mulino, Bologna, p 96 ss

Ciglioni L (2022) L'Italia e la guerra del Golfo. Carocci, Roma, p 228 ss

Colombo A, Varvelli A (2012) L'Italia e la crisi libica. In: Colombo A, Greco E (eds) La politica estera dell'Italia. Edizione 2012. Il Mulino, Bologna, p 88

Coticchia F (2014) Qualcosa è cambiato? L'evoluzione della politica di difesa italiana dall'Iraq alla Libia (1991-2011). Pisa University Press, Pisa

Cresti F, Cricco M (2012) Storia della Libia contemporanea: dal dominio ottomano alla morte di Gheddafi. Carocci, Roma, p 203 ss

Crosa E (1951) Diritto costituzionale. Torino, UTET, p 106

[81] For a more in-depth analysis see M. Cavino, M. Malvicini, *Le guerre dell'Italia repubblicana*, cit., p. 217.

D'Alessio G (ed) (1979) *Alle origini della Costituzione italiana. I lavori preparatori della "Commissione per studi attinenti alla riorganizzazione dello stato"* (1945–1946). Il Mulino, Bologna
De Fiores C (2002) L'intervento militare in Afghanistan. Profili di diritto costituzionale interno e internazionale. Politica del diritto (1):89 e ss
De Vergottini G (1999) La Costituzione e l'intervento NATO nella ex-Jugoslavia. Quaderni costituzionali (1):124 e s
De Vergottini G (2004) Guerra e costituzione. Nuovi conflitti e sfide alla democrazia. Il Mulino, Bologna, p 40
De Vergottini G (2022) La Costituzione e il ritorno della guerra. Osservatorio AIC (3):78
Dogliani M, Sicardi S (eds) (1999) Diritti umani e uso della forza. Profili di diritto costituzionale interno e internazionale. Giappichelli, Torino
Elia L (2003) In: Colombo A (ed) L'articolo 11 della Costituzione: pace, guerra, ordine internazionale. Atti di un seminario tenuto il 16 gennaio 2003—La Margherita Area Studi, Roma, pp 7–15
Faraguna P (2018) Costituzione senza confini? Principi e fonti costituzionali tra sistema sovranazionale e diritto internazionale. In: Cortese F, Caruso C, Rossi S (eds) Immaginare la Repubblica. Mito e attualità dell'Assemblea Costituente. FrancoAngeli, Milano, pp 75–81
Furlan F (2013) Presidente della Repubblica e politiche di sicurezza internazionale tra diarchia e garanzia. Giuffrè, Milano, pp 348–354
Guazzarotti A (2018) Articolo 11. In: Clementi F, Cuocolo L, Rosa F, Vigevani GE (eds) La Costituzione italiana. Commento articolo per articolo, vol I. Il Mulino, Bologna, p 80
Johnstone I (2015) When the security council is divided: imprecise authorizations, implied mandates, and the "unreasonable veto". In: Weller M (ed) The Oxford handbook of the use of force in international law. Oxford University Press, Oxford, p 239
Lavagna C (1953) Basi per uno studio delle figure giuridiche soggettive contenute nella Costituzione italiana. CEDAM, Padova
Leanza U (2006) Il principio internazionalista nella Costituente. In: Labriola S (ed) Valori e principi del regime repubblicano, vol I. Laterza, Roma-Bari, p 310 ss
Massai A (1988) La missione italiana nel Golfo Persico. Quaderni Costituzionali 1:209 e ss
Mercuri M, Torelli SM (eds) (2012) La primavera araba. *Origini ed effetti delle rivolte che stanno cambiando il Medio Oriente*. Vita e Pensiero, Milano
Morris J (2013) Lybia and Syria: R2P and the spectre of the swinging pendulum. Int Aff (5):1270 ss
Mortati C (1962) Istituzioni di diritto pubblico. CEDAM, Padova, p 598
Patroni Griffi A (2006) Art.78. In: Bifulco R, Celotto A, Olivetti M (eds) Commentario alla Costituzione, a cura vol. II. UTET, Torino, p 1532
Pinelli C (2000) *Argomenti e posizioni nel dibattito dei costituzionalisti sulla guerra del* Kosovo. In: Ronzitti N (ed) NATO, conflitto in Kosovo e Costituzione italiana. Giuffrè, Milano, p 196 s
Rivello R (2004) Le operazioni militari all'estero e le fonti de diritto internazionale penale. In: Porro G (ed) Studi di diritto internazionale umanitario. Giappichelli, Torino, p 81 e ss
Ronzitti N (2021) Diritto internazionale dei conflitti armati. Giappichelli, Torino, p 358
Scuccimarra L (2016) Proteggere l'umanità. *Sovranità e diritti umani nell'epoca globale*. Il Mulino, Bologna, p 126 ss
Sicardi S (1999) I mille volti della guerra, la Costituzione e il diritto internazionale. In: Dogliani M, Sicardi S (eds) Diritti umani e uso della forza. Profili di diritto costituzionale interno e internazionale. Giappichelli, Torino, p 99
Villani U (1991) Lezioni su l'ONU e la crisi del Golfo. Cacucci, Bari, p 15 ss

From "Vapid Pacifism" to "Aggressive Pacifism". Themes, Languages, and Organisational Forms of Pacifist Culture from the Post-War Period to the End of the Short Century

Amoreno Martellini

A premise: for reasons that it would now take too long to explain, I have never considered it correct, as far as Italy is concerned, to speak of a pacifist movement. The objectives, methods, envisaged scenarios, and even the ideals of reference are too different to have even the vaguest idea of a unitary movement, and very often the different expressions of pacifist culture are too conflicting to think they could march together towards any objective, whatever it was. It could be argued that all expressions of pacifism had as their common denominator the fact that they were aimed at the search for peace: but we know by now from experience—and, alas, also from tragically contemporary experiences—that proclaiming the will to peace is not sufficient in itself to define pacifist behaviour.

1 The Post-War Period

The pacifist idea in its many forms and declinations has gone through seasons of profound and continuous transformations in the history of republican Italy.[1]

[1] I limit myself to providing only the essential bibliographical references. In general, for a more complete and detailed exposition on the history of Italian pacifism in Republican Italy, I refer to my *Fiori nei cannoni* (2006) and Goglia et al. (2006). On more specific topics for women's pacifist associationism: Scarantino (2006) and Gabrielli (2005). For the history of conscientious objection: Labbate (2020) and Vecchio (1993). For the relationship between pacifism and the two mass cultures: Menozzi (2008) and Guiso (2006).

A. Martellini (✉)
University of Urbino, Urbino, Italy
e-mail: amoreno.martellini@uniurb.it

G. Cavaggion (ed.), *The 'Pacifist Principle' in the Italian and Japanese Constitutions in the Wake of the War in Ukraine*,
https://doi.org/10.1007/978-3-032-23108-6_3

It was reborn after the collapse of fascism and the end of the war as a tree with a very lush foliage, consisting of so many associations, so numerous that it is difficult to count them. But in spite of such a thick foliage, there were essentially three roots:

- The non-violent one (which contrasted with the fascist regime's pedagogy of violence).
- Anti-militarist in the anarchist and socialist tradition (which contrasted with fascism's exaltation of militarism and war).
- Federalist or unionist (which contrasted with the glorification of nationalism on which fascisms had based their world view).

In the immediate post-war period, when the material conditions made both the sustenance and the logistical organisation of the associative bodies particularly difficult, there were several dozen, certainly more than 30, movements taking their steps in the territory of pacifist culture, distributed fairly equally across each of the 3 roots. Each of them had its own structure, its own little newspaper, and its own associative offices: some were important bodies, Italian sections of international associations that would mark the history of pacifism in the years to come; others were tiny fragments, expressions of small, sometimes very small, local movements, they had no base behind them and consisting of their founders and their small circle of acquaintances: most of them would disappear without a trace. Faced with such a deployment of pacifist troops, even some of the protagonists of that world, of that associative fabric, were somewhat perplexed. In 1946, for example, Giovanni Pioli, defined as the "doyen" of Italian pacifism, wrote to one of the main inspirers of the non-violent movement.

In the Italian [pacifist] associations, I confess, I have little faith; [...] they seem like academies to me: with every war they have vanished "like dust in the wind", except to resurrect courageously when Janus' rule ends. I am very doubtful that the many members of the numerous "pro-peace" associations, put to the test, would, better than in the past, honour their pacifist sentiments. So what? What qualms will this vapid pacifism represent for the rulers? This is no reason not to spread the pacifist idea: agreed; but neither should we base great hopes on it.[2]

And even a few years later, Don Primo Mazzolari, who had dedicated an important part of his priestly mission to pacifist commitment,[3] was ironic about what he called "the merchants of peace":

You find them everywhere, the merchants of peace, blasting out their songs in the public squares, with loudspeaker reinforcements, trumpets, bass drums: "Take my peace, the only good one, the only authentic one, the pure unbreakable, stainless, water- and blood-resistant one, written in stone...The others, all the others, are counterfeits, surrogates, war hoaxes....Be wary of imitations".[4]

---

[2]Historical Archives of the Municipality of Jesi, Fondo Edmondo Marcucci, b. 70, vol.2, letter from Giovanni Pioli to Edmondo Marcucci, 18 August 1946.

[3]On this see Trionfini (2009).

[4]"Adesso", a. II, 1 July 1950, no.13.

Pioli's words and those of Mazzolari, in addition to testifying to the widespread diffusion of the pacifist idea—entirely understandable at the end of the most destructive war in the history of mankind—placed the emphasis on one of the atavistic and never resolved vices of Italian pacifism: its fragmentary nature and the inability of the individual associations to find a plan of convergence, a unifying perspective. The effort to reduce the scattered fragments *ad unum* was attempted several times in those early post-war years, once under the banner of the War Resisters International, other times by Aldo Capitini and the subjects that revolved around the Perugian movement: but the "peace hub" (this is the expression used by the Umbrian philosopher) remained for all those years a chimera, undermined from within by the strenuous defence of the peculiarities and quarrelsomeness of the small associations. Even from within the federalist universe there were those who proposed themselves as aggregators: "I would see the need to unite all efforts around the European Federalist Movement", proposed one of the most illustrious exponents of Italian federalism, the historian Gino Luzzatto, in a letter to one of Capitini's collaborators. Except then having to admit that the movement was in deep crisis due to the bloc policy inaugurated after the war by the victorious powers. Moreover, between the different souls of federalism (Europeanism, globalism, unionism, Citizens of the World) there was not always an identity of views, and on more than one occasion contrasts led to open rivalry. Finally, some of these souls had a rather critical opinion of the non-violent solution: while appreciating the choice of conscientious objectors from a moral standpoint, they nevertheless considered it a somewhat naive utopia to pursue the dream of world peace through individual choices, believing instead realistic or at least possible a scenario in which the overcoming of wars would be achieved through the union of all states or rather through the creation of a supranational body that would absorb all national sovereignty.

In addition to its fragmentary nature, Italian pacifism had to suffer another heavy limitation: its elitist dimension. Excluding the Partigiani della pace—which, however, responded to party logic, relied on the Partito comunista italiano (PCI) propaganda machine and its funding channels and therefore could not be compared to the movements we are referring to[5]—all other associations seemed the expression of an elitist, exclusive world, incapable of dialogue with the popular masses, largely involved, instead, in political conflict. Thus, still in the mid-1950s, a number of collaborators of the Perugian philosopher Aldo Capitini, the undisputed leader of the non-violent movement in Italy and one of the most tireless organisers of pacifist initiatives in the country, were beginning to denounce a certain weariness and a profound lack of confidence in the ability of pacifist language to make a breach in mass culture. "I see that we have not succeeded, that most are not interested in our problems and prefer indifference or the open and gregarious flocking to follow tradition [...]Our monologue is of no use [...]It is always us few",[6] complained some of

[5] Cerrai (2011).

[6] Historical Archives of the Municipality of Jesi, Fondo Edmondo Marcucci, b. 1, vol.2, draft from Edmondo Marcucci to Aldo Capitini, 16 December 1955.

them, by now rather demoralised. And Capitini himself, in the years around the time of the economic miracle, appeared not to have much faith in the possibility of involving in the pacifist battles a society increasingly distracted by the myths of well-being: "I ask continually", he confessed to one of his friends and collaborators, "and I receive very little, because everyone puts other needs ahead: clothes, travel, holidays, cars, etc.".[7]

However, in the first post-war 15 years, some of the main bodies of this restricted and aristocratic "little old world" took shape and came to life, bodies that would mark the path of the culture of peace in Italy and, in particular, its non-violent root for the following decades. It was this component of absolute pacifism, despite being the most elitist because it required the most extreme choices, that first captured the interest of the media of the time and gained space in the pages of newspapers and magazines, even the most popular ones, without, however, breaking the isolation in which the pacifist world had slipped.

The first case, which had wide media coverage, occurred in the late 1940s and concerned the first conscientious objector to military service, Pietro Pinna. Others here will have the task of analysing his choice and delving into its content and context; for the subject of this contribution, it will suffice to recall that the Pinna case introduced into the cultural debate of a country so marked by the weight of tradition, the disruptive theme of disobedience, used as an instrument of opposition to war. And he did so at a time when the subject was very pertinent indeed, due to all the issues surrounding the need to reform the army and to transform it from an instrument of a wartime dictatorship into a functional body for a peacetime democracy. The debate on this issue had been very lively within the Constituent Assembly and had continued when it had closed its doors. At the end of 1948, when the Constitution was still brand new, a newspaper with a large circulation such as *Il Messaggero* hosted the intervention of a long-standing general, who had been through both world wars, who, faced with the dreaded idea of reforming the army, felt compelled to reassure citizens (whom he evidently felt were concerned by this threat) that, even in the changes that would inevitably take place, "the two disciplinary cornerstones—obedience and subordination—would not be shaken". Finally, producing a more detailed definition of the term "obedience", the general used these words:

Obedience, therefore, consists of the "voluntary, conscious renunciation of a part of one's personality before a superior.[...]The majority finds in obedience a kind of repose of the spirit, freed from the torment of doubt and the burden of responsibility".[8]

It was precisely this idea of the renunciation of individual responsibility that the conscientious objectors rejected; and not only them, if truth be told: in parallel with the declarations of disobedience to the military authorities, in fact, in the early 1950s an action of civil disobedience also began on the part of a singular and disruptive character such as Danilo Dolci. He, too, was a follower of non-violent theories

[7] Ibid, b. 10, letter from Aldo Capitini to Edmondo Marcucci, 29 July 1962.

[8] "Il Messaggero", December 1948.Quoted in E. D'Onofrio, *La disciplina di noi soldati*, in "Vie Nuove", III, 19 December 1948, 50.

and techniques, but with him the theme of civil disobedience left the field of opposition to war and was brought into the arena (about to emerge in post-war Italy) of civil rights. His work, which began in 1952 in western Sicily, where death by starvation was still a daily occurrence, had to challenge not only the Mafia power, the sole manager of the economy in that area, but often also the action of the state, which, when it was not characterised by its absence, intervened with actions to oppose not the Mafia power but those who tried to oppose it: the presence of the State was marked by denunciations, arrests, expulsions with travel orders, sentences issued by the courts, and repressive action implemented by the forces of law and order on the basis of old laws of the fascist code in blatant contrast with the dictates and spirit of the new Constitution. It was as a result of one of these repressive actions, which had led to the interruption of a welfare initiative in favour of the poor people of Trappeto, that Dolci put down on paper his firm will to disobey the authorities. In March 1954, *L'Incontro*, the pacifist newspaper in Turin, published a series of articles by Dolci that retraced the events of his intervention in Sicily in the previous 2 years; one of them stated, among other aspects:

We will continue all our activities as before: i.e. assistance to the neediest population (including health care, medicines, etc.); continuation of the irrigation work that will give work to a thousand men (until water arrives in the countryside here there is hunger); documentation and information work so that people in Italy know what kind of life exists in this area [...]. As for the children: no policeman, no prefect of this world will be obeyed when his orders are against God's law.[9]

This stubborn disobedience, exercised with the weapons of non-violence, manifested itself again and again in the following years, in sometimes clamorous episodes, such as the "upside-down strike" or the numerous protest fasts or the initiatives put in place after the Belice earthquake, earning Dolci the nickname of "Italian Gandhi".[10] His action gained the support of many Marxist and Catholic intellectuals, and his figure became a polemical target of the conservative press and even more so of the reactionary press. But in fact, thanks to his disruptive actions, the theme of non-violence was able to leave the elitist circles of absolute pacifists and present itself to Italian society.

2 The Peace March

However, outside of Dolci's Sicilian initiatives and the courageous action of a small handful of conscientious objectors, the organisation of a pacifist movement continued to languish throughout the 1950s, and all peace initiatives remained confined within a circle of total isolation that failed to open up to the outside world and involve public opinion. It was precisely in order to break free of this *impasse* that in

---

[9] *The story of "Borgo di Dio"*, in "L'Incontro", VI, March 1954.

[10] See in this regard D. Dolci, *Processo all'articolo 4*, Sellerio, Palermo 1911.

the central years of the economic miracle Aldo Capitini began to devise the peace march: a participatory form different from the usual ones, a pacifist demonstration that would be able to welcome wider sectors of civil society, students, workers, and peasants: "it is made for them, this march", Capitini declared to the journalists present, "because the peasants know how to walk, while they are uncomfortable at conferences".[11]

The peace march that for the first time on 24 September 1961 walked the winding uphill roads from Perugia to the Rocca di Assisi was, first and foremost, a new form of expression, a modern language, borrowed from the Anglo-Saxon tradition but not yet practised in Italy.[12] The result was extraordinary: popular support was even unexpected, and for the first time the participants in a pacifist demonstration, organised outside and above the parties, were no longer counted in tens or even hundreds but thousands. But the surprise for Capitini himself was not so much the participation of peasants and, in general, of a large audience of workers but above all of many young people, who had come to Perugia from various parts of Italy and not necessarily with a precise political affiliation behind them. The march brought to the universe of pacifist protest a new form of participation that managed to intercept some of the anxieties of the youth universe, which was already in turmoil during those years. The encounter between these new languages of political participation (in the highest and noblest sense of the term) and the instances of renewal that came from the protest cultures certainly gave impetus to the pacifist cause, giving it a much wider audience than in the past; but at the same time it produced a profound renewal in the leadership and in the cultural (and political) references of the pacifist movement.

This openness to society is undoubtedly the most striking effect produced by the march; however, other benefits, less visible to the outside world, flowed from that experience. Firstly, the march produced that reunification of the scattered fragments of the pacifist world within a single "container": the Peace Council. This new body (which sought to translate into practice the long-standing theories on the "peace council") was supposed to bring together all pacifist associations of whatever inspiration, both those with a spiritual matrix, non-violence and "absolute pacifism", and those with an avowedly political or anti-militarist inspiration. In 1962, under the presidency of Capitini himself, the Consulta began its troubled existence and was immediately shaken by a series of criticisms and contrasts that directly affected the figure and role of the president himself. The first criticism was directed at Capitini from within the pacifist world, from his own companions on the road: some of the figures who had shared the idea and the non-violent action with him reproached him for having opened the doors of this pure and exclusive world of pacifism to people who gravitated in the orbit of the PCI, therefore indirectly to the USSR, who

[11] "L'Espresso", 1 October 1961.

[12] An account of the march and a collection of documents and materials were published by Einaudi shortly after the march, edited by Capitini himself: Capitini (1962). Recently these documents were republished under a different title for Edizioni dell'asino: Capitini (2016).

consequently had nothing to do with non-violent practice. Thus expressed, for example, Ines Zilli Gay of the Christian Youth Union:

That communists, who have preached violence and hatred, while aspiring to a classless society, and who are undoubtedly a ferment for a more just society, come to associate with Gandhians, seems to me one of the many Italian inconsistencies. All in peace, yes, under totalitarian regimes... And woe to those who move.[13]

Similar criticisms were also made by others gravitating in the small nebula of Italian non-violence and conscientious objection. But another criticism, perhaps even more violent, against Capitini came from outside, from some of the new companions coming from the galaxy of politics and drawn to the pacifist cause thanks to the peace march and the birth of the Consulta. In particular, a violent attack was directed at him by the radical leader Marco Pannella, who used expressions of a verbal violence that was rarely known within that world, devoid of any respect for the historic leader of Italian non-violence, to certify that the newborn body that was supposed to unify the efforts of the various fragments of Italian pacifism had already completed its task and would serve from then on rather to exalt their differences:

Dear Capitini, on several occasions, from all sides, there have been alarmed criticisms of your way of conducting the work of building and growing the Italian Consulta for Peace. Today, faced with episodes that once again demonstrate the daily truffle dust into which you have allowed, at least in the Consulta, those principles of democracy and "bottom-up management" that you have certainly contributed to spreading and developing in theory; in the face of ambiguous, reticent attitudes, from time to time exaggerated or frightened, corporal or "prima donna"; but above all taking note of the absolute sterility and political blindness that leads to see the representativeness and effectiveness of the National Council shrinking every day, today, I have only one reproach to make: That of having, with my friends, guiltily resented that 'human respect' which we all know is undue, and which, in democratic organisations, often means avoidance of responsibility. In Florence, however, we will discuss all this. Because in Florence, of course, we will be there rejecting this umpteenth and hypocritical attempt of yours to evade a precise and democratic debate.[...] We will then see who has legs to walk on and help others on their way, and who, with the worn-out crutch of vanity, egocentricity and wishful thinking, can instead only hope, at best, for the practical role of fellow-traveller, "useless-idiot", and unwitting epigone of the most vile frontalism.[14]

In fact, that the entry of so many new energies into the pacifist world had upset the cards on the table and introduced new communication codes was already visible to those who had observed those few black and white photos and the very rare colour ones published by some newspapers in the aftermath of the Perugia-Assisi march. The first contrast that leaps to the eye concerns what today we would call the *dress code*: the many young people wearing shirts open at the chest and with

[13] Historical Archives of the Municipality of Jesi, Fondo Edmondo Marcucci, b. 71, vol. 5, letter from Ines Zilli Gay to Edmondo Marcucci, 5 October 1961.

[14] State Archives of Perugia, Capitini Fund, b. 101.

rolled-up sleeves or coloured half-sleeved T-shirts and girls with flared skirts, bare arms, and shoulder bags offered the measure of the distance that separated their generation from Capitini's, closed in his grey suit with a narrow-brimmed hat of the same colour. A difference in attire to which corresponded a difference in attitude: festive, boisterous, and cheerful that of the former and compassionate and measured that of the latter. Beyond the outward attitudes, the two different communication codes can also be seen in other details, such as in the slogans and phrases written on the placards and banners that paraded with the marchers: some phrases referred to a generic, sometimes naïve pacifism ("no more atomic bombs", "peace and love", "let's bury the bomb not the men"); others referred to contemporary political scenarios and contained condemnations of ongoing wars, such as the one in Algeria, or of the imperialist system. Some placards portrayed the face of Gandhi, others that of Patrik Lumumba, who was assassinated a few months previously in the Congolese civil war and immediately ascended to the role of champion of the European left.

All in all, even if we pass from images to sounds, we can clearly see a clear change of register: the most popular pacifist hymn at that time was born in the world of the pro-Soviet political hymnody of the Partisans of Peace, the association that was a sort of *spin-off* of the PCI; it was entitled, somewhat unimaginatively, *Hymn of the Partisans of Peace* and was composed by the official cantor of the communist epic of those years, Raffaele Mario Offidani, better known by the pseudonym of Spartacus Picenus: the hymn exuded stale rhetoric and spread an idea of peace linked to the progressive achievements of the Soviet Union: "To bar the way we swear to the most horrendous and voracious war. We will fight for peace, united we will conquer death. The barbarous infernal war, no, it will not return![...] Let every mother come to us, to fight for her children against those who seek to damn them to death. Cursed be he who wishes the terrible fate for our cities unleashed on Hiroshima" (just to understand the gist).

Not even remotely comparable in tone, language, and musical structure to the song by Fausto Amodei (already the author of militant songs such as *Per i morti di Reggio Emilia*): he can be seen in some photos walking up to the Rocca di Assisi with his guitar slung over his shoulder surrounded by young people. On that occasion, assisted by an exceptional lyricist that was Franco Fortini, Amodei improvised what would be remembered (and recorded on vinyl) as the *Song of the Peace March:*

And if Berlin calls tell her to hang herself / Not to die for the rich! We don't like her any more / And if NATO calls, tell her to come back / Even the stones know it, you don't believe it any more [...] / And if the homeland asks you to offer your life / Answer that life is for you for now.

It was an expressive code that showed total absence of rhetoric, direct language, assertion of the right to self-determination outside the logic of blocs.

3 Pacifism and Revolution

In the following years and throughout the cycle of protests that culminated in 1968, pacifist marches multiplied in every part of Italy, becoming the most widespread form of pacifist protest; new forms of participation were also practised to express the usual contents of the rejection of war and violence: from the *provos-style* demonstrations in Milan to the protest against the 4 November celebrations and against the military parade on 2 June. The theme of peace had by then firmly entered as a central element in youth culture. However, it was precisely in the field of language and communication codes in general that the definitive generational change within the pacifist world took place: it was 1965 when, during one of the first marches against the American invasion of Vietnam, Capitini complained in a private letter to a friend and collaborator of his, about the use of excessively violent expressions by the young demonstrators:

If, on the one hand - Capitini wrote - we should be happy about the spontaneous multiplication [of pacifist marches], which also has a certain weight at such a serious time, on the other hand, the fact that some marches have gone too far seems to me to have so compromised this instrument that it is difficult to protest against the prefectural decisions to prohibit them. This is something that I deeply regret, [...] but I must recognise that we have not always been able to restrain ourselves in such marches, both in the use of terms, such as *Johnson the executioner*, and in the line-up, which no longer corresponds to a certain distance from today's political and especially military line-ups.[15]

Perhaps Capitini himself would have been even more impressed if he had known that a couple of years later, expressions of the same tenor as those that had seemed unacceptable to him on the lips of young demonstrators who were mostly politically aligned would also have been pronounced by one of the priests who had been most exposed in the battle for conscientious objection, Father Luigi Rosadoni. And the Prefect of Florence was also impressed, who used these words in a note sent to the Ministry of the Interior after a demonstration for Vietnam:

Instead, speaking in a language not used by even the most ideologically extreme speakers, he harshly condemned Johnson and his government's power groups for their colonialist and aggression policy towards the entire world, agreeing with the most advanced proposals of the Communists and Psiuppines regarding propaganda activities to be conducted nationally and locally.[16]

This decisive change of register in language, not necessarily more violent but certainly more defined and rooted from an ideological point of view, also overwhelmed pacifist culture down to its most absolute expressions, represented by that scanty band of conscientious objectors who continued to face military tribunals and

[15] State Archives of Perugia, Capitini Fund, b. 101, letter from Aldo Capitini to Giovanni Favilli, 8 June 1965.

[16] Central State Archive, Ministero dell'Interno, Gabinetto, 1967–1970, b. 52.Note by the Prefect of Florence, 11 April 1967.

military recluses: if the first objectors, those who had raised the issue in the previous decades, referred in their declarations to the primacy of individual conscience over state law, to the spiritual and Tolstoyan vision of non-violence, or, in the case of the first Catholic objector (1963), to the commandment "thou shalt not kill", the new generation of objectors introduced ideological elements into their declarations that made them think more of the anti-militarist spirit than the non-violent spirit.

"I refuse to become a soldier", wrote an anarchist objector in 1965, "because the army means the exploitation of labour, an apparatus destined to swallow incredible quantities of working hours and materials [...].The fact of living and fighting in Italy places before me, as a concrete objective of refusal, an army at the service of the Italian bourgeois ruling class".[17]

He was echoed in the same year by a Catholic objector:

I reject military service because I think that the Fatherland to whose defence citizens are called is a myth. I am convinced that today this myth is coldly used to cover up what in reality they are trying to keep standing at all costs: that is, an institute of power. I am convinced that with the motivation of the Fatherland they actually want to induce me to kill or be killed to defend the existence of the state to which I am subject and which is evidently only one of the possible organisations and probably not even the best.[18]

A few more years and a young member of the Evangelical Church justified his decision to refuse the uniform with these sentences:

As a believer and member of the Universal Church, I feel committed to being the salt of the earth within this capitalist society, where only a limited group of people hold economic-political power and exploit the masses. This society is held up by various structures, one of which and among the worst is the army, of which I do not wish to be a part.[19]

On the other hand, the contestative culture that flourished in the 1960s and culminated in the 1968 movement, which absorbed and made the theme of peace its own, elevating it to the status of a mainstay of youth culture, contained within it a series of contradictions that were also expressed in language (or perhaps started from language). These contradictions, which stemmed from the coexistence of nuclei of varying political and cultural inspiration, affected the very concept of revolution and its nature: for some components of the movement it was a non-violent revolution, a profound cultural transformation that would affect attitudes, outlooks, and social relations; other components, instead, dreamed of an armed revolt or guerrilla warfare (which for some was inspired by that taking place in various Third World situations while others had to find a new and original form, more suited to the industrial and metropolitan realities of the First World). This ideal divergence inevitably ended up also affecting the pacifist idea, producing a sort of schizophrenia that

---

[17] "L'Incontro", October 1965.

[18] Ibid, c.o..

[19] Quoted in Canestrini and Paladini (1973), p. 133. The statement belongs to the evangelical Gianfranco Truddaiu.

was already clearly expressed in the slogans shouted by thousands of young men and women during the demonstrations: slogans of a clearly non-violent matrix, such as "make love, don't make war" or "put flowers in your cannons", were answered, often even during the same demonstration, sometimes shouted by the same individuals, and other phrases of a different nature: "war no, guerrilla war yes", "Vietnam wins because it shoots", and "power comes from the barrel of a gun".

The same contradictory vision of peace and non-violence can be seen by drawing on the endless reservoir of song lyrics: this is obviously not the place for an in-depth analysis of this issue; it will suffice to recall how not all anti-war songs had a non-violent content, and not all of them referred to "a world of love". Some of them contained the same contradictory canon as the slogans: in the stanzas of a song written after the colonels' seizure of power in Greece, a young soldier was mentioned:

You were twenty years old in April / Your palms still full of love/Under a rag of a flag/They gave you a number and a rifle/Your head you bowed like a hero/In the air a smell of sewer / And you cried for shame/Of losing your humanity.

It would seem to be a vision in perfect non-violent style, a vision corroborated by the very title of the song (*Soldier dressed in olive*), except that it opens up in the refrain to a completely different vision of the struggle:

Take up the rifle unleash the fanfare / Aim at the colonel between the eyes and shoot / Burn all the uniforms at the stake / If anyone is in it they will pay for their days.

4 "You Good People What Peace You Seek": The Equivocation of Non-violence

Above all, some songs born in the world of political militancy tended to make the idea of peace coincide with a devious idea of acquiescence and acceptance of reality and of renouncing the struggle. This is the case of one of the most famous songs in the militant repertoire, *Contessa*, which in the refrain conveys this idea of peace to the young protesters: "you good people what peace you seek / peace to do what you want / but if this is the price we want war".

Which brings us back to one of the most controversial themes of this period: the idea that pacifism and non-violence are bourgeois privileges, which serve the ruling classes to ward off the threat of subversion of order. I deliberately use strongly ideologised language so that the contrast with what I am about to state stands out better, namely, that this vision of peace and non-violence, conveyed by the language of the most radicalised fringes of protest, seems to fit perfectly with the conduct, words, and intentions of our ruling class at certain dangerous turning points in republican history. In particular, to stay with those years, we should carefully observe what happened precisely in 1968, in the aftermath of Martin Luther King's death on 4 April of that year.

The fact that up to that moment the concept of non-violence in Italy had not enjoyed the favour of the ruling classes had been amply demonstrated, as we have seen, by the open hostility of the Catholic church—and therefore of the governing Catholic party—towards Capitini's initiatives (the curia in Perugia had even circulated a leaflet admonishing the faithful not to attend them), by the public institutions' opposition to Dolci's action in Sicily, and finally by the equidistant criticism, albeit for very different reasons, of Catholic and Marxist culture against conscientious objectors. Instead, following Martin Luther King's death, there was an unprecedented institutional involvement and participation in the mourning that started from the President of the Republic and the Prime Minister and went all the way down to the last mayor of the most remote town on the peninsula: telegrams of condolences, public funeral orations, commemorations in institutional venues, the naming of streets, and squares and schools giving a plastic image of how all the institutions of the state had rallied around the figure of the black reverend, glorifying his work and magnifying the virtues of non-violence. What had happened for this conversion to take place? And, above all, was it a true rethink on the subject? In reality, there is more than one doubt on this point, especially if we consider that this change of direction came only a few weeks after what had been the most violent episode of youth protest up to that point, the clashes in Valle Giulia a month earlier (1 March): an episode that had raised fears that the protest, until then contained and controlled without difficulty by the police, would turn into something more destabilising, rolling down the much more dangerous slope of violence. This exaltation of non-violent principles by public institutions that had never before shown any belief in them seems decidedly instrumental and functional to the time the country was going through: it was meant to propose to young people a model of behaviour considered by those who proposed it to be neutral, harmless, and not capable of destabilising social equilibrium. All in the pious illusion that the thousands of young men and women who drove the protest in the country had attentive ears to listen to what the ruling classes had to say to them and followed the models of behaviour they proposed.

This being an instrumental communication strategy, a clumsy attempt to downplay the protest became clear before the decade was out: on 20 December 1969 the *Corriere della Sera*, at the time the daily newspaper of order, an expression of the conservative and well-thinking Milanese bourgeoisie, dedicated its entire double-page spread to celebrating the virtues of non-violence and to exalting the personalities who had made it a reason for living, from Gandhi to Russel, and from King to Spoke and even La Pira, the most divisive political personality in the recent history of the governing party.[20] After having denigrated conscientious objectors for years, after having mocked the non-violent experiences of the youth communes during the hottest phase of the protest, and even after having heavily criticised La Pira himself for his pacifist choices considered almost heretical,[21] now the narrative changed

[20] "Il Corriere della Sera", 20 December 1969.

[21] On the figure and role of La Pira see Scivoletto (2003).

completely. Once again, it is a little hard to believe that this sudden change of course was dictated only by a sincere conversion to the reasons of absolute pacifism. And in fact, even in this case the editorial choice must be contextualised: only a week earlier, on 12 December, the bomb that exploded in Piazza Fontana in Milan, in the Banca dell'Agricoltura, had sown death and destruction and, at the same time, had launched the season of terrorism and massacre in the country.

Of course, we now know that the matrix of that bomb was to be sought in the folds of circles traceable to the subversive and neo-fascist right, but in those first few days after the massacre, faced with a country shocked by the event, the script of the "strategy of tension" provided that a number of institutional subjects should place the responsibility for the massacre on the left-wing extremist circles and anarchist circles. Thus, once again, faced with an explosive situation, with the dreaded danger that youthful discontent would find bad teachers capable of transforming that discontent into violence, a communication strategy was decided upon, centred on the value of non-violence, as an instrument of struggle that inspired good feelings in the youth and did not risk calling into question the existing social order.

Needless to say, this instrumental use of non-violence was not at all appreciated by the man who had practised that choice all his life. On the day after the public celebration of mourning for the death of Martin Luther King, in the pages of *Non-violent Action*, the magazine founded and directed by Capitini, a number of clear and definitive words appeared on this point, words that condemned without appeal "the tears of the new Pharisees" and distanced themselves from this lukewarm and cowardly idea of non-violence:

It is the thorn of all non-violent people and perhaps their greatest challenge, having to counter an image of non-violence as an absence of contestation and renunciation of struggle, as an opiate invitation to goodwill that does not change anything in the unjust de facto relationships, or at most entrusts renewal to the orderly course of time and to the sighing yearning of good consciences. Martin Luther King, who in one of his most impassioned writings in defence of non-violent action had pointed to the "good guys" [...] as the most significant obstacle, greater than that of his declared adversaries, on the path to liberation, found himself after his death—in extreme derision—with these very "good guys" in the front row singing his eulogy in chorus, reiterating to the world what they had always had in their hearts, him "apostle of non-violence". An apostle of that non-violence which was always denied, mocked, and opposed, as soon as it tended to take concrete form; an apostle vilified in life until the last of his days, beaten, imprisoned, and finally killed.[22]

[22] "Azione nonviolenta", April–May 1968, No.4–5.

5 Between Reform and Terror: Pacifism and Non-violence in the 1970s

Aldo Capitini died a few months later, in October 1968; the year before, Don Lorenzo Milani had died, and the year after (1969), Giovanni Pioli, the "doyen of pacifist spiritualism"; Gino Luzzatto, one of the most brilliant minds of federalism, had already died a few years earlier, in 1964, and Edmondo Marcucci, the historical collaborator and friend of Capitini and the terminal point of a network of relations between pacifists that embraced the whole world, had died in 1963.The generation that had driven the post-war pacifist season and formed the different souls of pacifism before the advent of the fascist dictatorship had by then almost completely left the scene. Italian pacifism presented itself to the decade that was about to open with radically renewed people, tools, and language.

On the other hand, once the cycle of the "long Sixty-Eight" was over, the domestic political scenario had profoundly changed (we will not even dwell on the international one for the sake of brevity) and was still changing rapidly. The previously mentioned Piazza Fontana massacre represented only the beginning of a season in which political violence would be the undisputed protagonist. In such a scenario, discourses on peace and non-violence risked being lost in a background noise that seemed to confuse Italian society. Yet the early part of the decade already saw some important novelties: firstly, in 1972, approval of the law recognising the right to conscientious objection to military service. Again, others will deal with this here, so I will not dwell on it, but it is evident how this was a step of great importance for the history of pacifism in general, not only of non-violence. On the other hand, throughout the decade, in addition to continuing the pacifist and anti-militarist marches and the protest demonstrations against the 4 November celebrations and against the 2 June military parade—forms of protest all borrowed from the 1960s—there was a progressive rapprochement of the various associations, movements, and peace organisations to anti-nuclear and environmental issues, which became the new frontiers of pacifist culture. This link was particularly strengthened in the second half of the decade, when a number of notable exponents of this culture decided to clarify the position of the non-violent in the context of environmental and nuclear issues. One of them, certainly not the most clueless, given his cultural background as a theoretical physicist, was Antonino Drago, who at the time was very much listened to in the non-violent world. Drago believed that "energy needs" and "defence needs", which required immediate responses, could be brought together in the proposal of a single, alternative development model that would involve the population in the development of alternative energy sources and a non-violent defence model:

> The fight against nuclear power goes against the entire institutional framework, both political and technical: now only a few small groups or grassroots movements are opposing what would be a qualitative leap in the power system. The struggle is hard and will certainly be long, because enormous interests are at stake (in Italy: 20,000 billion!), consolidated institutions (all scientific institutions) and political drives organised by decades of collective and bureaucratic work (all major parties)

[...]. So on two major social problems, that of the defence of the population and that of its energy support, today we are called upon to concretely express the alternative to this society. Traditional society tends to impose its solutions, which are in historical continuity and indeed strengthen its old bureaucratic and power apparatus. The new society is moving forward on the same problems by presenting alternative solutions that are concrete, already realised at the level of small groups and fully realisable for the whole of society, provided that people become aware of and want to set up social organisation from a different perspective.[...] In this historical moment, our political characterisation comes not only from choosing without ambiguity and regrets alternative energy sources (because we are among the few who choose without equivocation a decentralised society organised at community level) but also and above all from joining this political theme to that of non-violent popular defence, which is our specific political theme. It is this duality of themes that now characterises non-violence engaged in social struggles.[23]

In April 1977, the Non-violent Movement organised the conference *Nuclear Energy, Alternative Energy, New Model of Development* in Verona on these very issues during which the themes presented by Drago were developed from different points of view: scientific, economic, and ethical. But the underlying fact remained the profound bond that united the fight against war and the fight against nuclear energy, as if they were two sides of the same coin. The organisers wrote:

After years of opposition to the army as a macroscopic expression of organised and institutionalised violence, it is a logical consequence for us in the Non-violent Movement to join the fight against this new form of violence that the powers-that-be are imposing [the construction of nuclear power plants], passing it off as an "anchor of salvation" for the economic future of our country [...]. It is above all out of a desire for the "new society" that we oppose the construction of nuclear power plants; nuclear energy serves no other purpose than to continue the aberrant model of development that the Italian political class has imposed on us since the post-war period.[24]

Of course, attention to these emerging themes could not make the pacifist world close its eyes to the dramatic political situation the country was experiencing after falling into the nightmare of terrorism in the aftermath of the Piazza Fontana massacre; however, the most in-depth reflections on the role of non-violence and the culture of peace in a country dominated by political violence, rather than progressively developing and accompanying the growth of a social awareness of the phenomenon, seemed to be confined to the most dramatic moments of the decade, the massacres of 1974 and the Moro murder.

In 1974, in the aftermath of the *Italicus* massacre, the Torinese pacifist lawyer Bruno Segre, defender of almost all the first conscientious objectors, in the columns of the newspaper *L'Incontro*, which he inspired and directed, stigmatised the design

---

[23] A. Drago, *An alternative programme. Anti-nuclear struggle, alternative energy sources and non-violent popular defence*, in "Azione nonviolenta", a. XIV, March–April 1977.

[24] *Against nuclear energy for a new development model*, in ibid.

hidden behind the "strategy of terror": nothing that had not already been read or heard from other political subjects or in other social circles. But in this case, particular emphasis was placed on the danger posed by a secret service apparatus in the hands of the military structures, which was undoubtedly not very attentive to the subversive thrusts that came from or at least were heard from within the armed forces.[25] Indeed, the issue of the relationship between democracy and the armed forces was another major topic on which the pacifist world debated and mulled over during the 1970s, but to follow the course of that debate would take us far from the trajectory of this essay. Let us therefore return to the subject.

It was only in 1978, in the tragic days following the Moro murder, that the pacifist press published a comprehensive reflection on the relationship between terrorism and non-violence or rather on the role that non-violence can play in a society devastated by terrorism: *Non-violent Action* published on that occasion a long article signed by one of the founders of the League of Conscientious Objectors (LOC), the body representing the objectors, conceived after the passing of the 1972 law. The article, entitled *Terrorism and non-violence*, belonged to that large group of intermediate positions that were then summed up by the expression "neither with the state, nor with the Red Brigades", and, from this point of view, it read the Moro case as a ruthless tug of war between two violent systems, characterised by a "total lack of humanity", a characteristic that in fact prevented the opening of any negotiations. But—and this is perhaps the part that most concerns the issues dealt with in this essay—the need to justify to public opinion the inevitability of the "line of firmness" had ended, according to the author, by emphasising the role of violence even in the words and language used by the media, hiding the possible alternatives to that already written ending. One of these alternatives would have been, precisely, non-violence. Thus, the link between non-violence and information became a decisive theme:

This is why fighting for honest and correct information means fighting against terrorism, for participation, democracy, self-management, and non-violence; while excluding non-violence from information, or worse, qualifying it as "fascism", as the PCI recently did, violently repressing those who defend constitutional freedoms, means creating the ideal conditions for the spread of terrorism and armed violence, leaving the entire field of opposition to the real violence of the R.B..[26]

Instead, immediately after Moro's kidnapping, once again, and it was the third time, faced with the national emergency and the danger of a violent drift, even the ruling class returned to appeal to the beneficial virtues of non-violence, as had already happened after the clashes at Valle Giulia and after the Piazza Fontana massacre. I do not know if it is true that three clues are evidence; however, it seems to me that we can no longer speak of randomness but rather of a communicative scheme evidently considered effective by those who practised it. This time it was

---

[25] Sicor (pseud. di Bruno Segre), *La strategia del terrore*, in "L'Incontro", a. XXVI, n. 7–8, July–August 1974.

[26] M. Soccio, *Terrorism and Non-violence*, in "Azione nonviolenta", a. XV, May–June 1978.

Giulio Andreotti's turn to resort to it. Precisely on 16 March 1978, a few hours after the Via Fani massacre, Andreotti, who in his past years as Minister of Defence and also as Prime Minister, had certainly not distinguished himself for his commitment to the campaign for conscientious objection, far from it, and who several years earlier had consummated a definitive rift with La Pira on these issues of pacifism and non-violence, pushing the mayor of Florence to the fringes of the party, now in his capacity as Prime Minister, in the most dramatic hour of republican history he felt he had to address an "appeal to the conscience of non-violence" to the Italians so that "the tranquillity of life in Italian cities would be guaranteed".[27]

Again, the term *non-violence* was appropriated by the institutions and used instrumentally as a synonym for tranquillity and absence of conflict.

6 Inverse Canon

The 1980s represented the closing of the circle. As we have seen, the basic framework of Italian pacifism had profoundly changed in the preceding decades: the themes, languages, organisational forms, and the protagonists of the pacifist proposal themselves had changed. Each of the three roots from which the path of pacifism had begun—the non-violent, the federalist, and the anti-militarist—had undergone changes, hybridisations, and difficulties of various kinds. But all in all, the basic references had remained the same and were clear to all, to pacifists and to their detractors alike: whatever the means by which it was pursued (the creation of supranational bodies, the individual choice to renounce violence, collective action against military structures), the end was opposition to war and, from this point of view, the territories of those who opposed war, even at very high individual prices, and those who had chosen war as their profession were separated by a clear, almost Manichean division.

But in the first half of the 1980s, even these certainties began to waver. In fact, during that five-year period—in which political cultures were rapidly changing and, with them, the forms of media communication and the language of politics—two events overlapped that contributed to changing the perspective from which to observe these dynamics: on the one hand, the pacifist protests against the installation of Cruise missiles at the NATO base in Comiso, and on the other, the commitment of some contingents of the Italian army in Lebanon, as part of a multinational force.

The mission in Lebanon between 1982 and 1984, as we know, had become necessary to try to contain the violence and carnage that was destabilising an already historically delicate area. But beyond the more than valid reasons that justified it, it contributed substantially to changing Italian society's perception of the armed forces. Unprecedented media coverage, in fact, for the first time began to circulate

[27] "La Stampa", 17 March 1978.

so widely the expression "peacekeeping mission" (which was not new at all) that it became almost familiar in public discourse. It was a different image from the one we were used to associating with the army: the military did not *produce* violence but rather counteracted it; they did not destroy but helped populations after destruction. In short they no longer made wars but helped peace processes. The result was a wealth of popularity for the armed forces, a cross-class and cross-political popularity that they had never enjoyed before and whose most representative image was the emphatic and almost exasperated welcome that the contingents returning from Lebanon received in a "red city" such as Livorno.

During the same period, the protests against the installation of missiles at the Comiso base constituted the event of widest popular participation in a peace initiative. Hundreds of thousands (the largest demonstration was reported to be attended by 300,000) of men and women of all ages, but mostly by young people, paraded through the streets of many Italian cities; many also went to Sicily in front of the base's fences to practise passive resistance techniques, one of the most common tools of non-violent practice. But just as the anti-missile movement was proving to be the most powerful aggregator for the pacifist cause since the post-war period, dark shadows and disturbing suspicions were falling on it, polluting and compromising its image: on 3 September 1984, in his semi-annual report on internal security, Prime Minister Bettino Craxi revealed to the press the alarms received from the intelligence services, who were certain that those hypertrophic marches praising peace were actually hiding dangerous terrorists and professional violent men. The Prime Minister said that he had reason to believe that "pacifism and ecologism [were] polluted by provocative elements, exposed to become an easy vehicle for a strategy that was perhaps bloodless, but equally dangerous, because it was still directed to subversive ends" ("La Stampa", 5 September 1984).

A week later, given the hornet's nest stirred up by these statements in every political family, from the Greens to the Communists to the Catholic associations, Craxi argued his claims in more detail:

Seventy alleged terrorists or flankers are also active in anti-nuclear, anti-militarist and pacifist organisations. Recent terrorist documents confirm an "interest" in pacifism to exploit its aggressive potential. Craxi cites a recent volume written by terrorists in which the theme of the inclusion of the armed party in the great mass movements is addressed and claims that Autonomia is also interested in pacifism and ecologism.[28]

By this time, the stone had been thrown, and the images of those imposing marches bouncing off television screens and onto the pages of magazines and newspapers hinted at the idea of an "aggressive" pacifism and aroused mistrust, suspicion, and the ill-concealed concern in public opinion that those pacifists were keeping the shoots of violence warm, ready to burst forth again in a society still sensitive to the disasters caused by terrorism and political violence.

[28] "Repubblica", 11 September 1984.

The new narrative was now complete and had produced a total reversal of the terms of the discourse and an inversion of the semantic fields: the previously so clearly distinct and opposed territories of violence and non-violence now blurred and swapped places.

End-of-the-millennium pacifism was ready to enter the nebulous and confusing era that opened with the end of the Cold War.

References

Canestrini, Paladini (1973) L'ingiustizia militare.Natura e significato dei processi davanti ai giudici in divisa. Feltrinelli, Milan, p 133

Capitini A (ed) (1962) In marcia per la pace. Documenti e testimonianze sulla marcia Perugia-Assisi. Einaudi, Turin

Capitini A (ed) (2016) Persone che marciano per la pace. Perugia-Assisi 24 September 1961. Edizioni dell'asino, Rome

Cerrai S (2011) I partigiani della pace in Italia: tra utopia e sogno egemonico. Libreria Universitaria, Limena

Martellini (2006) Fiori nei cannoni (2006) Non-violence and antimilitarism in twentieth-century Italy. Donzelli, Rome

Gabrielli P (2005) La pace e la mimosa.L'Unione donne italiane e la costruzione della memoria (1944–1955). Donzelli, Rome

Goglia L, Moro R, Nuti L (eds) (2006) Guerra e pace nell'Italia del Novecento. Foreign policy, political culture and currents of public opinion. Il Mulino, Bologna

Guiso A (2006) La colomba e la spada: lotta per la pace e antiamericanismo nella politica del partito comunista italiano, 1949–1954. Rubettino, Soveria Mannelli

Labbate M (2020) Un'altra patria L'obiezione di coscienza nell'Italia repubblicana. Pacini, Pisa

Menozzi D (2008) *Chiesa, pace e guerra nel Novecento: verso una delegittimazione religiosa dei* conflitti. Il Mulino, Bologna

Scarantino A (2006) Women for Peace. *Maria Bajocco Remiddi e l'Associazione internazionale madri unite per la pace nell'Italia della guerra fredda.* Franco Angeli, Milan

Scivoletto A (2003) Giorgio La Pira. La politica come arte della pace. Studium, Rome

Trionfini P (ed) (2009) Tu non uccidere: Mazzolari e il pacifismo del Novecento. Morcelliana, Brescia

Vecchio G (1993) Pacifisti e obiettori nell'Italia di De Gasperi. Studium, Rome

The Pacifist Principles of Conscientious Objection

Marco Labbate

Contrary to common opinion, the "pacifist principle" enshrined in Article 11 of the Constitution is not a fundamental reference for objectors and movements that support its recognition. That "repudiation" of war is in fact inscribed in an area of legitimisation of war itself, however limited to the defence of the homeland. The non-violent movements that advocate conscientious objection go further: these include the total renunciation of war as an ethical instance, starting with its preparation, the impracticability of defensive warfare in the atomic age, or a frontal opposition to the institution of the army, seen as an instrument of power of the ruling class. However, before I delve into thc pacifist principles that animate conscientious objection, which have changed over the years, I intend to dwell on the notions on which Article 11 of the Constitution is based, as is evident from the acts of the Constituent Assembly. That debate, which took place between December 1946 and March 1947, helps us to understand the nature of a legal pacifism that affirms the repudiation of war as an instrument of offence or means of resolving international disputes, turning to the possibilities opened up by a new international law and the birth of the United Nations Organisation.

M. Labbate (✉)
University of Urbino, Urbino, Italy
e-mail: marco.labbate@uniurb.it

G. Cavaggion (ed.), *The 'Pacifist Principle' in the Italian and Japanese Constitutions in the Wake of the War in Ukraine*,
https://doi.org/10.1007/978-3-032-23108-6_4

1 The Constituent Assembly

The first formulation of the pacifist principle in the Constituent Assembly[1] was discussed on 3 December 1946 in the first subcommittee. It was part of a programme of 11 articles, presented by Giuseppe Dossetti[2] under the title *Proposals on the State as a legal system and its relations with other systems and on freedom of conscience and worship*. Point 4 read:

> The state renounces war as an instrument of conquest or offence against the freedom of other peoples. The state permits, under conditions of reciprocity, the limitations of sovereignty necessary for the organisation and defence of peace.[3]

This was nothing new in the international sphere. The direct inspiration was Articles 14 (inspired, in turn, by Title VI of the 1791 Constitution) and 15:

> [La Republique française] n'entreprendra aucune guerre dans des vues de conquête et n'emploiera jamais ses forces contre la liberté d'aucun peuple. Sous réserve de réciprocité, la France consent aux limitations de souveraineté nécessaires à l'organisation et à la défense de la paix.[4]

The proposed article was unanimously approved with a few changes after a brief debate. The only momentary divergence is not on the principle, which is widely shared, but on the advisability of introducing a limitation of state sovereignty into the Constitution. This is expressed by the demolabourist Mario Cevolotto, also meeting with the agreement of Christian Democrat Carmelo Carestia who considers the entire article superfluous. These doubts are answered by two interventions. Camillo Corsanego, a jurist, who is also a Christian Democrat, recalls the "ruins that have occurred in recent times", generated precisely by the "arrogance with which each state has sought to uphold its sovereignty in an absolute manner, without limitation". "A long period of peace between peoples" requires a binding of nations to an international order. Even more direct is Togliatti, confirming the relationship of harmony established with Dossetti during the work. On the one hand he addresses the newly established United Nations Organisation: that principle, laid down in the Constitution, serves to clarify Italy's position "in the face of that great movement of the entire world which, in an attempt to outlaw war, tends to create an international organisation in which forms of sovereignty different from those in force are beginning to emerge". But his gaze also turned to the past, to the war that Italy had helped to unleash by attacking other nations. Dossetti would finally reassure the doubters by recalling how the "conditions of reciprocity" were a prerequisite for any

[1] With respect to the debate in the Constituent Assembly: Carlassare (2013); Cassese (1975), pp. 565–588; Bonanate (2018).

[2] On the constituent profile of Giuseppe Dossetti: Melloni (1994), pp. 13–59; Dossetti (1995); Giorgi (2023); Pombeni and Dossetti (2013). Specifically with respect to his contribution on Article 11: Elia (2003), pp. 7–15.

[3] Antonietti et al. (1998), pp. 866–870.

[4] Conac et al. (2001) and Gudemet (2008).

limitation of sovereignty. The article was released by the subcommittee with a few changes: the two sentences are joined in a single sentence, the term "Republic" replaces "State", and the words "organisation" and "defence" are inverted, at Dossetti's suggestion, which took up the sentiment expressed by Tupini: the formula "defence and organisation of peace" would have accentuated the focus more on "the negative fact of avoiding wars" rather than on "the positive fact of international collaboration for the common good".[5] A new draft addressing the issues that emerged in more detail was prepared by the Commission for the Constitution:

> Italy renounces war as an instrument of conquest and offence against the freedom of other peoples and allows, on condition of reciprocity and equality, the limitations of sovereignty necessary for an international organisation that ensures peace and justice for peoples.

The term "Italy" is definitively preferred to "State" or "Republic", more functional in emphasising the break with the country's "wretched fascist parenthesis", based on the offence to the freedom of other peoples, and in inserting the new nation into a framework of international values against "any threat of reborn nationalism", as President Meuccio Ruini states in the report accompanying the draft Constitution.[6] Furthermore, the reference to the United Nations project becomes more explicit, and "peace" is now linked to "justice".

The discussion in plenary partly disengages from the need to mark the distance from the past in order to give the principle a more general character. I will ignore the debate on whether to include a more explicit reference to the European Federation and focus on the pacifist principle. On the one hand, there is an awareness of the importance of an article declaring "the reign of war", as the socialist Mancini emphatically states.[7] Ugo Damiani, the only representative of the Unionist Movement, finds in it "an enormous and fundamental importance that truly characterises the new historical epoch that has begun.[...] We renounce war: we no longer want to hear about it," he states, prefiguring the elimination of "this madness, this crime".[8] Critics who see in the wording an overly passive attitude also share this sentiment. Crispo calls for a more categorical commitment, taking the French Constitution as an example: the term "renunciation" in fact recalls "the idea of a right or a faculty.[...] And it seems inconceivable to me that the democratic state can be said to have the right to wage a war of conquest". That is why he proposes a clearer formula: "nor will it ever use violence against the freedom of any people".[9] "We", says an old socialist like Claudio Treves, "would like something more in this Article 4; we would like a more decisive statement. We would like Italy to set an example with this article of that future international law". The "abstract formulation condemning wars of conquest" must therefore be overcome in favour of "a more positive principle" that excludes war from the instruments "of international conflict

[5] Proceedings of the Constituent Assembly, First Subcommittee, 3 December 1947, pp. 451–454.

[6] Ibid, Report accompanying the Draft Constitution of the Italian Republic, 6 February 1947, p. 5.

[7] Plenary, 17 March 1947, p. 2018.

[8] Ibid, 8 March 1947, p. 1923.

[9] Ibid, 13 March 1947, pp. 2035–2036.

resolution", a principle closer to "the essence of our new democracy": the 20 years in which "the so-called armed prophets dominated, prophets who were nothing but prophets of lies" must be replaced by "the armour of the civil conscience of the world".[10] Along the same lines, Leo Valiani recalls in the debate the broader formula of the Briand-Kellogg Pact, where recourse to war was rejected "for the resolution of international differences" and "as an instrument of national policy".[11] The simple "renunciation of war as an instrument of conquest and offence to the freedom of other peoples" could be ambiguous: there have been "numerous" military interventions justified on the grounds of the freedom of peoples, such as those the United States was conducting in Greece and Turkey or fascist Italy in Ethiopia. Valiani's proposal, much applauded on the left, also considered the looming Cold War world: he argued for the inclusion of opposition to "all imperialism and all adherence to imperialist blocs".[12]

The voices critical of the pacifist principle come mainly from the Front of Everyman. General Bentivegna, while declaring himself "to be one of the most fervent apostles of the abolition of all wars" disputes "projects of this kind" in the context of the "iniquitous Peace Treaty" because they could "perpetuate the status quo".[13] Russo Perez, who later transited to the MSI, defines it as "ridiculous that we, an unarmed nation, with an army reduced only to the limits of a police force [...] should make such statements".[14] A similar opinion came from an authoritative voice, such as that of Francesco Saverio Nitti, who hoped the article would disappear because, abroad, it would have aroused hilarity if a weak and defenceless country had renounced the war of conquest.[15]

The Commission elaborates a new formula to balance the positions expressed, taking more account of the approach used in the Briand-Kellogg Pact:

> Italy repudiates war as an instrument of offence against the liberty of other peoples and for the settlement of international disputes and allows, on equal terms with other States, the limitations of sovereignty necessary for an international order that ensures peace and justice among peoples.

The compromise actually only partly incorporated the contents of the most significant amendment, that of the socialist Mario Zagari, signed by several MEPs, to which Valiani also adhered, withdrawing his own. The proposal was intended to strengthen "the new spirit" with respect to the "position of passivity" that still seemed to emerge: to the limitations of sovereignty it added a more assertive commitment to "promote" the creation and development of international organisations.[16]

---

[10] Ibid, 17 March 1947, pp. 2205–2207.

[11] Formigoni (2000), p. 312; Hathaway and Shapiro (2017).

[12] Ibid, pp. 2215–2217.

[13] Ibid, 13 March, pp. 2044–2045.

[14] Ibid, 14 March, pp. 2090–2091.

[15] Ibid, 18 March, p. 2253.

[16] The text of the amendment read: "Italy repudiates war as an instrument of national policy and as a means of settling international disputes. It promotes the creation and development of interna-

President Ruini would eventually persuade the proposers to withdraw the amendment, explaining the effort made to find an agreed wording: the preference for the verb "repudiate" followed the need that had emerged to widen the mesh of the pacifist principle. The expression "renunciation of the war of conquest" had in fact been prompted by "a cry of revolt and condemnation of the way in which war had been understood in the gloomy period from which we have emerged" but, as Nitti had put it, it appeared "exaggerated and grotesque" to speak in that way "in our conditions". Conversely, the verb "repudiate", if it might have appeared "by some accounts not fully happy", had "an energetic accent" that implied the "renunciation" and the "condemnation" of war. Compared to the resumption of the present formula of the Briand-Kellogg pact, supported by Valiani and present in Zagari's amendment (the one that asserted "the renunciation of war as an instrument of national policy"), the negation of war as a means of "resolving international controversies" was preferred, which was considered a clearer expression in a Constitution addressed to the people.[17]

The final draft of the article approved by the editorial board would, however, have revised the last part, adding a sentence inspired by Zagari's amendment:

Italy repudiates war as an instrument of offence against the liberty of other peoples and as a means of settling international disputes; it consents, on equal terms with other States, to the limitations of sovereignty necessary for an order that ensures peace and justice among nations; it promotes and encourages international organisations for this purpose.

In the economy of our discourse, the very broad consensus encountered by this article must be crossed with the cross-party consensus accompanying the approval of Article 52. The discussion on military obligation takes place in the context of prescribing the duty to defend the homeland, the only one in the entire Constitution to be emphasised with the adjective "sacred". It takes place in a particular phase of Republican history, in the midst of the consultations following the crisis of the third De Gasperi government. Ten days later De Gasperi would launch the new government, excluding Communists and Socialists. However, that fracture of Resistance unity did not entail a division over the defence model to be adopted. The final formulation of Article 52 certainly retains traces of the contradictory thrusts coming from securitarian instances, a strong desire for peace, a karst distrust of the army, the need to reaccredit it in the eyes of the country, and the condemnation of the recent past: while the beginning sanctifies the duty to defend the homeland, the last paragraph, inspired by Aldo Moro, who makes an explicit profession of anti-militarism,[18] prescribes, for this institution alone, the duty to be informed by the democratic spirit. In some speeches, across the parties, that prescription is crushed into an overturned automatism: compulsory conscription constitutes an instrument

tional organisations and permits, on an equal footing with other states, the relevant limitations of sovereignty".

[17] Ibid, pp. 2429–2435.

[18] Ap, Constituent Assembly, First Subcommittee, 15 November 1946, pp. 396 ff.

of democracy that shapes the army.[19] In practice, it would have remained a dead letter: the military institution, pardoned by the purge, spared from restructuring, would have enjoyed a structural separateness from political power.[20] However, the dissonances between the political areas appear marginal compared to the consensus that coalesces around the definition of the structure of a broadly framed army based on compulsory conscription, considered a guarantee for the opposing fears of an authoritarian involution that animate the camps. The duty to defend the homeland to be pursued also through an army built on the basis of compulsory conscription thus constitutes an explicit limit to the repudiation of war. And within this broad consensus was the rejection of all the pacifist amendments tabled by the deputies of the newly formed Socialist Party of Italian Workers, to which Zagari also belonged: that with first signatory Arrigo Cairo that envisaged non-compulsory military service, that of Umberto Calosso tying military expenditure to a lower figure than education, and that of Giovanni Ernesto Caporali who sought to introduce into the Constitution the recognition of conscientious objection, an act of prescience that would consider future objectors not as "irregulars" or "deserters" but as "advanced patrols of the new humanity". In his speech, a radical condemnation of war and a futuristic interpretation of "defence of the homeland", extended to the areas of assistance and solidarity, took shape:

Let conscientious objectors at least, the tenacious and die-hard opponents of violence [...] be granted the opportunity to cooperate in the defence of the soil of the fatherland in the areas of assistance and solidarity that share the risks and pain, but without the sad burden of carrying fratricidal weapons. War is fought by denying it and dishonouring it.[21]

The rapporteur Umberto Merlin dismissed the matter with a laconic quip, noting the absence in Italy of "a sect of conscientious objectors", while the inclusion in the Constitution of the "scruple of conscience", which the laws already "take into account for priests", could have had "very dangerous" consequences.[22] However, the presence of a component that, for technical reasons, is in favour of voluntary military service leaves, unintentionally, a space open for the future recognition of conscientious objection within the constitutional framework: if the duty to defend the homeland appears universal, the obligation of military service is subject to limits set by ordinary law.

[19] Speeches by Francesco Colitto (Uq) and Umberto Nobile (PCI), p. 4184 and p. 4109.

[20] Labanca (2009), pp. 75–82.

[21] Ibid, 20 May 1947, p. 4105.

[22] Ibid, sitting 22 May 1947, p. 4182.

2 The Non-violent Principle

Caporali's proposal for a recognition of conscientious objection in the Constitution had the support of two small groups behind it: one gathered around the former modernist priest Giovanni Pioli, and a more active one formed around the philosopher Aldo Capitini. The latter had started a Religion Movement in 1946, following the First Conference on the Modern Religious Problem in Italy. As well as contesting the hierarchical structure of traditional religions, it also addressed certain political issues. Conscientious objection is presented by the philosopher as a necessary position in the context of the foreshadowing of an armed clash between East and West in order to "argue, refusing arms, that the encounter must take place on the higher plane of a universal religious renewal, which is the synthesis of the two worlds and the enrichment for what they have of limited and insufficient value".[23] At the conclusion of the conference, the participants sent a letter to the constituents, with several requests, including the "full right not to join combatant formations with conscientious objectors". The following year, Capitini began to develop the idea of setting up, starting from the experience at hand, a "peace centre" that would break away from the Religious Movement to play a role of aggregation and confrontation on pacifism. From the *Convention of the representatives of Italian pacifist activities*, assembled on 11 October 1947, an Italian Association of War Resisters would be born which, inspired by the War Resisters International, would have to manifest the rejection of the means and instruments necessary to modern war, as well as of the blocs that were being constituted, and start groups of resistance throughout Italy.[24] Capitini went so far as to prefigure a Ministry for War Resistance that took into consideration the question of defence in the event of aggression but proposed training all citizens, from childhood onwards, in non-violent non-collaboration in a possible invasion:

> How many ways can one obstruct the invader without killing anyone! But one must learn, one must have certain means ready (e.g. scissors to cut telephone wires, nails to puncture tyres). Isn't an active non-collaboration of multitudes a third way beyond war and surrender?[...] Italy must set an example to itself, to Europe and to others in the world, insensitive to the possession of weapons, of different ways of affirming civilisation.[25]

Already from these brief notes, we can sense the gap between the pacifist principle that the Constituent Assembly fixed in the Constitution and that which animates the first pacifist groups in which a commitment to the recognition of the objection matures. In reality, this instance constitutes a minority position even among pacifist realities that is independent from the parties: the movements that turn to European or world federalism, to the development of the UN, and to the opportunities of international law do not exclude the possibility of war as an *extreme ratio* and look with

---

[23] Biblioteca Planettiana (BP), Fondo Marcucci (FM), sc.1, vol.1. b.1, From Aldo Capitini's report in Circular no. 1 First conference on the modern religious problem in Italy.

[24] Martellini (2006), pp. 65–70.

[25] A. Capitini, *Resistenza alla guerra* in "Il Mattino del Popolo", 13 March 1948.

detachment at "the more incisive work and more direct and exemplary responsibility that is less juridical and more conscience-focused".[26] The latter initiative realised by this first, circumscribed aggregation put into play by Capitini was the *Third meeting for the opposition to war and for conscientious objection*, to which the philosopher entrusted the task of giving the movement for peace an "extreme resoluteness".[27] In that meeting, the first in Italy dedicated to conscientious objection, the participants also provided a definition of it: "to commit oneself, as a minimum, to refusing to participate in war and its preparation, whatever one's religious and political convictions, associations and movements to which one belongs".[28] This is a broad conceptualisation, which goes beyond the mere refusal of military service: it involves men, women, young people, and the elderly and testifies to the primarily ethical character that the philosopher wishes to give to the expression "conscientious objection". Regardless of the modest results obtained by a movement with considerable organisational limitations and traversed by paralysing divisions, what is of interest here is above all the basis of a pacifist proposal that proposes a coincidence between means and ends. Subsumed with this choice is a political vision that imagines the future overcoming of the state form. The lexicon well represents a group with an intellectual matrix, whose commitment to peace is characterised by a strong spiritualistic tension and a cosmopolitan vision but is detached, for reasons of age or gender, from the possibility of concretely refusing military obligation. For it to be able to give its reflections greater impact, it needs the presence of young people to give the idea of conscientious objection a body.

This gap disappears when a young man from Ferrara, Pietro Pinna,[29] who had already met Capitini at one of the meetings of the Religious Movement, refuses military service at the Car di Monferrato. He was not the first conscientious objector. There had been some during the First World War, under fascism and also in the immediate post-war period. For the most part they had been Jehovah's Witnesses, and this would remain the most conspicuous group until conscientious objection was recognised in 1972: out of 706 objectors registered by the Ministry of Defence since 1945, 622 belonged to this congregation.[30] However, none of them had given public prominence to their actions. Conversely, the formula conscientious objection was so unfamiliar—"exotic" would have defined it as one of the first activists, the poet Guido Ceronetti[31]—that they had not even used the title of objectors for themselves. Also thanks to the support they received from Aldo Capitini, Giovanni Pioli, and the small group of pacifists from the experience of the Association of War

---

[26] A. Capitini, *Opposizione alla guerra*, "Il nuovo Corriere", 8 July 1948.

[27] Labbate (2020), pp. 28–29.

[28] Planettiana Library, Marcucci Fund, b. 11, f. 2.2a, typescript minutes.

[29] The story of Pietro Pinna has been reconstructed in numerous publications. In particular, I would like to point out: Capitini (1959), pp. 42 ff; Marcucci (2004), pp. 120–131; Martellini (2006), pp. 84–90; Vecchio (1993), pp. 146–150, Labbate (2022), pp. 21–51.

[30] Parliamentary Proceedings (PA), Senate, 30 November 1972. Intervention by Tanassi.

[31] State Archives of Perugia, Aldo Capitini Fund, b. 75, Letter from Ceronetti to Capitini, 19 January 1950.

Resisters that had been exhausted, Pinna's objection landed in newspapers and periodicals and received attention even abroad. Reading the words Pinna addresses to Capitini in his letters and, above all, in his memoir in which he justifies his reasons, we can see the influence of the philosopher's works, in the use of certain paradigms: non-violence, non-misunderstanding, and non-collaboration with evil.

> The war, "writes Pinna in his memoir", despite the self-sacrifice and heroism inspired by love of country, is essentially reduced to a total betrayal of the moral idea, completely destroying all sense of humanity, unforgivably disregarding the supreme value of human life. After nameless abominations and disasters, we then reap the fruits in the pride and insolence of the victors, in the hatred and lust for revenge on the part of the vanquished. I am told that the duty of every citizen is first and foremost to serve the fatherland. But I do not even remotely dream of refusing this. I only ask that the fatherland perform a service in which its sons are not forced to betray the principles of their conscience as men, and then they (and I with them, first) will be happy and honoured to serve it and give to it.[32]

The rejection of military service as inherent to the existence of war and the request to be able to participate in a defence of the homeland without weapons are recurrent aspects in the statements of the first objectors. Although expressed with a lexicon less informed by a religious dimension, the sentiment of Elevoine Santi is similar, who presented his conscientious objection, a few days after Pinna had been reformed for a non-existent heart condition. In his letter to the Minister of Defence and the President of the Republic explaining the reasons for his decision, he writes:

> By using the train, by switching on the electric light or if I save myself from death with penicillin, I find that others have worked and are working for me and I must help the whole of humanity. With war, humanity is destroyed; armies, even in peace, are the ones who prepare this destruction. Therefore, I refuse to serve in the army, as long as the army is an instrument of war. It is not cowardice that drives me to this step: I ask to do a harder and more dangerous service for a longer period as long as my service is of use to a part of the citizens of this world without harming anyone else.[33]

And the desire not to find himself in the position of shooting another human being leads the objector Mario Barbani to step out of line during the review of the chief of staff, General Marras, and lay the rifle at his feet. Behind the motivations of the Capitinian movement and the first objectors, the disgust for the war that has just been experienced and the terror that it might be renewed translates into a categorical rejection of its preparation. Whether reasoned or more instinctive, the objection proposal originates from a simple principle: the only way to banish war from history is to stop preparing for it, even for mere defensive purposes. This is a moral dimension that transcends the repudiation of Article 11.

It is significant how defence lawyers who are called upon to invent a line of defence against a crime that is not even contemplated in the codes—objectors are tried for disobedience—use other constitutional references. On the occasion of Pinna's trial, Agostino Buda and especially Bruno Segre, who would for a long time be the main defender of the objectors, constructed the line of defence, relying on the

---

[32] Ibid, Memoir by Pietro Pinna circulated at the trial.

[33] *Elevoine Santi, L'obbiettore di coscienza n. 2*, "L'Incontro", 1950, No.1.

assumptions of the Peace Treaty, the recently approved Universal Declaration of Human Rights, and, above all, on Article 2 of the Constitution which "recognises and guarantees the inviolable rights of man, both as an individual and in social groups".[34] Article 11 remains outside the military courts.

3 The Anti-atomic Principle

As the tensions of the Cold War escalated, the openings for debate that had been registered even in a circumscribed part of the Catholic world around the Pinna casc closed down, overwhelmed by the psychosis of a Soviet invasion. After the first cases, for about a decade, conscientious objection remained on the margins of public debate in Italy. Only in 1961 did it return to receive some attention: to end up in the press and drive parliamentary debates; however, it was not an objector in the flesh but one of fiction. The censorship committee had in fact banned the screening of Autant-Lara's film *Tu ne tueras point*, which recounted an event that actually took place in France. A young German seminarian, the author of a cold-blooded execution of a partisan during wartime and a conscientious objector, had been tried on the same day by the same military tribunal: the former was acquitted for obeying an order, the latter condemned. The censorship provoked numerous discussions and protests: the most clamorous was that of the Christian Democrat Mayor of Florence, Giorgio La Pira, who decided to defy the ban and screen the film as an important document in "calling government men and peoples to the great problems of peace, human nature and the State".[35] In the City Council, La Pira defended the choice, citing the intention to make people reflect "on the great themes of peace and war" and on the relationship between the "individual freedom" of the human person and the limits of State action "when it touches man's conscience and intelligence".[36] For La Pira, the film was one of the "poor and spiritual" means to be used in the apocalyptic ridge of the present era and "historical space within which" "peace forever" and "war forever" were still equally possible.[37] La Pira had already reflected on numerous occasions on war in the atomic age: the shadow of the hydrogen bomb explosion in October 1961 in the Soviet Union, the most devastating ever, stretched across his disobedience.[38] As he supposedly confided to the director, at least according to the latter's testimony, by projecting *Tu ne tueras point* he was protecting his morning "caffelatte" or that feriality that a nuclear war would have made

[34] Ciò che dice il difensore dell' "obbiettore di coscienza" "Corriere del Po", 5 September 1949.

[35] Fabbrini (1966), p. 23.

[36] "The Country", 2 December 1961.

[37] Bocchini Camaiani (1995), p. 253.

[38] To frame La Pira's reflection on peace: Possenti (2009); Giovannoni (2008), pp. 205–229; De Giuseppe (2001); Toschi (2007).

impossible.[39] This was not a new connection. If the question of peace had precipitated into the atomic age since its emergence in the post-war period,[40] even the discourse on conscientious objection could not avoid being confronted with the prospect of a nuclear war: it was a connection present as much in the reflection of pacifists close to Capitini and Pioli as in the Catholic world.[41] In *La* Via in 1950, MP Igino Giordani, the first to present a bill on objection together with social democrat Umberto Calosso, had linked conscientious objection and the hydrogen bomb: Pinna's action represented the "clue to a redemption of the Christian conscience against atomic madness", as it restored it to the logical rationality of evangelical morality that "puts forward [...] that commandment which enjoins:- Thou shalt not kill".[42] And the link between the nuclear age, the Christian unacceptability of war and the objection had pervaded Don Primo Mazzolari's reflection on peace, raised by the tense horizon of the Korean War. It had begun on the pages of *Adesso* in September 1950, around the questions raised by some young Brescian readers: if on the one hand Mazzolari had imagined the war of defence as an *extrema ratio*, in the face of violence that endangers his brother or the common good, and on the other hand he had opened up a space of doubt, which would gradually widen until he arrived, 5 years later, at the book *Tu non uccidere*: Here he had hypothesised the birth of an integral Christianity that would renounce armed defence in the context of the immense slaughter that tomorrow's war represented. These are, however, considerations that are muted by the tensions of the Cold War. What changes in the 1960s is therefore not the centrality of reflection on the nuclear weapon but the international context that softens the exaggerated tones of the previous decade. Reflection on the transformation in the atomic age of the ethical assumptions of defensive warfare, previously frozen by the escalation of tensions, is broadened on both the Catholic and secular sides. It is the fallout of a debate that runs through Western Europe, enlivened by the Campaign for Nuclear Disarmament. Inevitably, the discourse on conscientious objection is also involved.

A few days after La Pira's act of disobedience in Turin, the Cultural Union directed by Franco Antonicelli organised a debate with some relevant figures from Turin's intellectual scene: Gianni Rondolino, Bianca Guidetti Serra, and Norberto Bobbio. The ban on showing the film was compensated for by some theatre actors, who read the most significant dialogues. All that remains of that meeting is the transcript of Bobbio's speech, later published in the collection *Il terzo assente*. What stands out in his reflection is the clarity with which he elaborates a pacifist principle, adapting it to the epochal juncture of the atomic age. Bobbio identifies four ideologies that, seeing war as a "constitutive, essential element of our history", have proposed a justification for it: the one founded on the distinction between just and unjust wars; the one that considers war a lesser evil in the context of worse evils,

39 C. Autant-Lara, *Niente guerra*, "Il Ponte" no. 2 February 1962, pp.159 ff.

40 Vecchio (1993); Guiso (2006); De Giuseppe (2008), pp. 249–269.

41 Menozzi (2008).

42 I. Giordani, *Bomba a idrogeno e obiezione di coscienza*, in "La Via", 11 March 1950.

such as the loss of freedom, national honour, or faith; the one that understands war as a necessary evil for historical development; and the one that looks at war as a simple fact, a superior majesty to be accepted. The objector, considering war "an absolute evil", rejects each of these theories. However, the turning point in human history represented by the atomic age gives the rejection of war "a more current, broader, more universal significance". The "frightening race" towards atomic armaments, by projecting humanity into the prospect of a total war "that can lead to the annihilation of life on earth, that is, of human history itself", does away with all previous justifications and opens up the idea of a general conscientious objection:

> When the concept of a weapon includes a bomb that, as we read in the newspapers, alone has the explosive power of half of all the bombs dropped in the last war, I wonder if carrying weapons has not become a matter of conscience not only for the objector who protests in the name of his religious faith, but for each of us, in the name of humanity. Conscientious objection literally means that situation in which our conscience forbids us by its imperative to do injustice. If we question our conscience, we can no longer refuse to recognise that today [...] we are, at least potentially, all objectors.[43]

Looking at the nuclear age thus opens up a space in which the objector's choice from individual adherence to non-violence becomes an inescapable and universal question. The reflection on the change brought about by the atomic weapon involves the institution that had been most dedicated to the elaboration of a just war doctrine. The fear of a nuclear conflict reaches its peak with the Cuba crisis. The *radio message for the understanding and concord of peoples* addressed in those dramatic days by John XXIII to the rulers of the earth and to men of good will, with that repeated anaphora "peace, peace!", prepares the context of *Pacem in Terris*, which constitutes a turning point with respect to the traditional magisterium. In fact, already in the immediate post-war period prominent figures in the Church, such as Cardinal Alfredo Ottaviani or Bishop Evasio Colli, had questioned the viability of the doctrine of just war under atomic conditions.[44] The question had then been removed by the paranoia of an expansion of communism. The Latin version of the encyclical *Pacem in Terris*, much sharper than the more sugar-coated Italian translation, instead entailed an unequivocal break with the traditional idea of just war: "Aetate hac nostra quae vi atomica gloriatur, alienum est a ratione bellum iam aptum esse ad violata iura sarcienda".[45]

Although neither *Pacem in Terris* nor the magisterium of Pope Roncalli contains an explicit reference to conscientious objection, the ferments of the Johannine pontificate are decisive in triggering Catholic objection. In Catholic objectors, the moral

---

[43] N. Bobbio, in *Resistenza*, n. 12, 1961, republished in Bobbio (1989), pp. 139–142. Bobbio would later reconsider this thought, contemplating armed intervention when faced with a violation of international law. This does not change its value at that historical juncture.

[44] See the references to the chapter *Bellum omnino interdicendum* in Alfredo Ottaviani's *Institutiones iuris pubblici ecclesiastici* in Menozzi (2008), pp. 145–147; 170–173, and the pastoral letter for Lent 1949 by the bishop of Parma Evasio Colli (1956).

[45] There are numerous studies on *Pacem in Terris*: Santomassimo (2003), pp. 7–16; Martini (2005), pp. 607–652; Giovagnoli (2003), p. 141; Melloni (2010).

appeal to the non-violence of the Gospel message is combined with the catastrophic danger of an atomic conflict. The first objector, Giuseppe Gozzini, in addition to the profound motivations of faith, recalls, a few months before *Pacem in Terris* itself, "the historical political absurdity" whereby "the world can be destroyed by a choice that escapes human judgement and will".[46] At the same time, two priests ended up on trial for criminal apologia for their interventions in favour of the objectors. In an interview with the "Giornale del Mattino", the Scolopian Ernesto Balducci defended Gozzini, whose choice had been contested by the diocesan assistant of the female youth of Catholic Action in Florence, Father Luigi Stefani: if he had no doubts about supporting the "duty" of Catholics to desert in the face of total war, Balducci believed that even in times of peace, in the face of the risk of an apocalyptic conflict, objectors still deserved "silent admiration" for their testimony.[47] Two years later, in February 1965, Don Lorenzo Milani responded to the military chaplains who had defined conscientious objection as alien to the commandment of love and an expression of cowardice. The letter circulated in the press and published in *Rinascita* is particularly significant with respect to our focus because it is the first relevant document in which the discourse on conscientious objection crosses Article 11.[48]

The letter, rather than the objection, reflects above all on obedience to unjust commands. Don Milani connects the "repudiation of war as an instrument of offence against the liberty of other peoples" in Article 11 and the duty of defence of the homeland in Article 52, to reach the conclusion that most of the wars declared by Italy have been wars of aggression:

> Let us measure by this yardstick the wars to which the Italian people have been called in a century of history. If we see that the history of our army is interwoven with offences against the homelands of others, you will have to clarify whether in those cases the soldiers had to obey or object to what their conscience dictated. And then you will have to explain to us who defended the homeland and the honour of the homeland more: those who objected or those who, by obeying, made our homeland odious to the entire civilised world? Enough of high-sounding, generalised speeches. Get down to the practical. Tell us exactly what you taught the soldiers. Obedience at any cost? What if the order was the bombing of civilians, retaliation against a defenceless village, the summary execution of partisans, the use of atomic, bacteriological, chemical weapons, torture, the execution of hostages, summary trials for mere suspicions, decimations [...] a war of blatant aggression, the order of a rebel officer against the sovereign people, the repression of popular demonstrations?

Ill with leukaemia, he is unable to attend the trial but forwards a famous apologia to the judges. He once again returns to the role of Article 11, described as one of the "moral and social achievements" that underpinned his students' historical research:

> We therefore took our history books (humble secondary school texts) [...] and went back over a hundred years of Italian history in search of a "just war". In other words, a war that complied with Article 11 of the Constitution. It is not our fault if we did not find it.

---

[46] Archivio Centro Studi Sereno Regis (ACSSR), Fondo Mir Roma (FMR), b. 271, Declaration by Giuseppe Gozzini.

[47] *La Chiesa e la patria*, in "Giornale del mattino", 13 January 1963.For an in-depth study of the case: Bocchini Camaiani (2002), pp. 171–184.

[48] L. Milani, *I preti e la guerra*, in "Rinascita", 10 (1965).

In addition to the past, the gaze unravelling from Article 11 is directed at the present. Once again, the impossibility of a defensive war in the atomic age returns.

> In future warfare, the inadequacy of the terms of our theology and your legislation is even more evident. And I note that the only possible "defence" in a war of atomic missiles will be to shoot about 20 minutes before the "aggressor". But in the Italian language, shooting first is called aggression and not defence.[49]

The Catholic world's focus on conscientious objection is captured by the compromises between the souls of Catholicism in the conciliar constitution *Gaudium et spes*.[50] I leave out the evangelical dimension, to focus on the interpretation given to the defence war. On the one hand, compared to *Pacem in Terris*, *Gaudium et spes* follows a more traditional path: while tightening the casuistry even further, it recognises governments "once all possibilities for peaceful accommodation have been exhausted" "the right of legitimate defence" and considers "those who in the service of their country exercise their profession in the ranks of the army" as "servants of the security and freedom of their peoples". The same chapter, which condemns the arms race as "one of the most serious plagues of humanity", entrusts limiting measures to the international context: pending the emergence of "a public and universal authority endowed with effective power to guarantee all peoples security, observance of justice and respect for their rights", it is up to treaties between nations to proceed to an "arms reduction", which cannot take place "unilaterally" but "with equal rhythm on both sides". Despite the considerable lexical differences, the outline is similar to Article 11. On the other hand, *Pacem in Terris* is recalled in the consideration that "the subject of war" be approached "with a completely new mentality" in the context of means that, being able to "produce immense destruction", far exceed the limits of legitimate defence. However, atomic war is only evoked but never mentioned explicitly except in a footnote. Among the new acquisitions *of Gaudium et spes* is the cautious stance on conscientious objection through the wish for the enactment of laws that "humanely provide for the case of those who, for reasons of conscience, reject the use of arms, while nevertheless accepting some other form of service to the human community". This is a passage to be placed alongside the praise of those who "renounce violence in the vindication of their rights and resort to those means of defence that are, moreover, within the reach of even the weakest". Indeed, much of Catholic pacifism would have been disappointed by the tenuousness of the assertions. But these were lines that, however sketchy, gave an initial legitimacy to the objector and constituted a breach that subsequent reflection by the Church would deepen, not without tension.[51] The objections by Catholics, often supported by the intervention of priests and even bishops, became a stable element in the following years: in 1965, before the Council closed,

[49] The letter to the military chaplains is published with the title *I preti e la guerra* in "Rinascita", n. 10, 1965; the letter to the judges is filed by Don Milani's lawyer on the occasion of the opening hearing of the trial on 30 October 1965. For both see Milani (2017), pp. 929–961.

[50] Turbanti (2005), pp. 563–606.

[51] Formigoni (2008), pp. 231–248.

there was the objection by Giorgio Viola, in 1966 by Fabrizio Fabbrini, and in 1968 by Enzo Bellettato.

Therefore, the new attention that developed in the 1960s around the recognition of conscientious objection on the one hand drew on the broader reflection on nuclear war and on the other was favoured by the entry of Catholic institutions into the debate on the illegitimacy of modern war. The failure to reach a legislative determination generates, around the inaction of Parliament, a more active non-violent mobilisation that changes its forms, occupying public space. The non-violent proposal had already experienced a sudden visibility when Capitini, prompted by the construction of the wall in Berlin by the announcement of the resumption of nuclear experiments by Khrushchev and Kennedy, had organised the March for Peace and the Brotherhood of Peoples from Perugia to Assisi, inspired by those carried out by Bertrand Russell from Aldermaston to London: the danger brought by the atomic weapon was paraded in the placards together with the marchers. Following that experience, the philosopher founded the Consulta per la pace and the Movimento Nonviolento: in particular, the latter, to whose organisation Pietro Pinna was called, gave conscientious objection an unprecedented presence in the streets. These were not particularly participatory initiatives but the sit-downs with placards or public fasts by a handful of activists, often concluded by the intervention of the police who dragged the demonstrators away from the pavement, that added visibility in physical spaces to the intellectual debate. The square dimension would grow significantly after 1968, when conscientious objection became one of the forms of contestation against the state, perceived as authoritarian.

4 The Anti-militarist Principle

Even more than the points mentioned, it is other aspects of don Milani's letters that make them, for the young people of 1968, reference texts: the contestation of the myth of the Fatherland, the anti-authoritarian reflection on obedience, the consideration of young people as "responsible for everything",[52] and above all, the link between conscientious objection and the class question. Don Milani writes in one of the best known passages of *his Letter to the judges*:

> If, however, you have the right to divide the world into Italians and foreigners, then I will tell you that, in your sense, I have no homeland and claim the right to divide the world into the dispossessed and oppressed on the one hand, and the privileged and oppressors on the other. The former are my homeland, the latter my strangers.[...] Of course you will admit that the word Fatherland has been misused many times. Often it is merely an excuse to believe oneself exempt from thinking, from studying history, from choosing, when necessary, between the Fatherland and values much higher than it.[53]

---

[52] L. Milani, *Letter to the Judges*, cit.

[53] Id., *Letter to the Judges*, cit.

The application of a class dimension to the refusal of military service was not something new. It had informed early twentieth-century anti-militarism, had remained alive in anarchist groups, and had been reworked by the objectors of the early 1950s who came from this context such as Pietro Ferrua and Angelo Nurra.[54] But from the second part of the 1960s onwards, and even more markedly after Sixty-Eight, this nexus produces a koiné: it is the reference figure in the statements of Catholic, radical, libertarian, and non-violent objectors. It remains a foreign lexicon only in the motivations of Jehovah's Witnesses.

The conviction that conscientious objection had to be transformed from a "marginal act of the elite" to a "truly mass" phenomenon and "from a solitary manifestation of love for mankind" which suffered "the limits of religious and philosophical isolation" to a political and therefore collective act is a recurring element in the self-representation of the non-violent anti-militarist movement.[55] Even if the mass dimension remains a mirage, the existence of this perspective transforms the objector's perception of himself: no longer a solitary witness but part of a local or national anti-militarist group in which he militates and matures his choice and part of a collective of objectors scattered throughout the country. The common inspiration can be felt in the statements of objection which, in addition to marking the distance from the past, draw on a common lexicon that frames conscientious objection within a revolutionary, anti-militarist, and anti-authoritarian space.[56] The "community" of objectors is a portion of the broader contestation led by students and workers. This common approach led to the first group objections: four youth collectives were formed, which replaced personal statements with shared political manifestos, in which the individuality of the choice was thus removed.

From an analysis of the corpus of the various self-defences written by the objectors after Sixty-Eight, concluded by the two joint declarations written by the collectives in 1971 and 1972, we can grasp certain recurring paradigms, which provide conscientious objection with a new pacifist principle. The contestation of the army is connected to that of the other fulcrums of the bourgeois power system: the factory and the school. The army "does not serve for the defence of the fatherland" but "serves for repression".[57] To the image of the old anti-militarism that saw in the soldier the pupil of a "school of assassination" is added the robotic image of the automaton, which transfers the figure of the mass worker, employed on the assembly line, into the military system. The conscript completes the work of dehumanising the worker carried out by big industry and the indoctrination action of the school, making him "the cog in a gigantic mechanism",[58] accustomed to passivity and acriticality by the climate of repression within the army that compresses free-

[54] Ferrua (1997).

[55] ACSSR, MR, vol. 300, *Objection file* compiled by the International Antimilitarist Movement, February 1973.

[56] For an overview: Ventrone (2012), Martellini (2012), Tolomelli (2015) and Bravo (2008).

[57] Ibid, File 86, Collective Declaration I 1972.

[58] ACSSR, Fondo Mir e Mn Piemonte (FMP), vol.77, Statement by Giovanni Pistoi, 3 August 1969.

dom of expression. The action on the individual perpetrated by military service would reverberate in everyday life, producing a submissive and indifferent worker, ready to reiterate his "yes" to the ruling class. The army also performs a function of preserving political and economic power: the defence of borders is in fact only a façade, being delegated to American power. The investment in armaments and special corps is instead directed to internal policing tasks for the political control of the population: it performs anti-guerrilla functions to repress popular movements, as an "unemployment pocket" to relieve the social pressure of unemployed youth, and as a "scab" instrument to depress strikes.[59] At the same time it constitutes a "waste of time and energy" because it diverts resources away from social investments.[60] Thus, if in the past the manner in which the army practised its defence tasks was contested, now it was the institution itself that was being disavowed.

In contesting the bourgeois system, conscientious objectors thus conceive of themselves as part of the subordinate class participating in the struggle against the capitalist system. The same substitute civil service, to be performed in marginalised contexts of society, represents the prefiguration of a libertarian and socialist society, an alternative to that produced by a state that demands respect for Article 52 but forgets the other "fundamentals for the life of a community".[61] This approach also changes the organisation of mobilisation, which remains internal to the non-violent choice: it is articulated between the anti-militarist marches organised by the Non-violent Movement and the Radical Party, the spectacularisation of public initiatives, the dramatisation of the arrest of objectors through demonstrations that end with the handing over to the police, the self-detachment of young people who had received the precept card and were awaiting capture in civilian services set up autonomously at available institutions, the public denunciation of the conditions of detention in military prisons, and the dissemination of the trial procedures held by military courts, often indifferent to the constitutional dictate.

And it was precisely the new visibility of objection, to which the Radical Party[62] made a decisive contribution, that determined the law: in the autumn of 1972, a 38-day fast by Marco Pannella and Alberto Gardin that achieved international resonance prompted the chambers to recognise conscientious objection. Certainly the parliamentary majority needed to place it in a very different value framework from the anti-militarist one. The model of the "true" objector, an apostle of the denial of the use of violence in all circumstances, is opposed to the false objector, i.e. the "camouflaged violent people" of an "anti-militarist spirit" who make military service a "matter of speculation, including political speculation". This is how Defence Minister Mario Tanassi had branded them the previous year, when the measure had been approved in the Senate but the government had fallen before it passed the

---

[59] Ibid, File 86, Collective Declaration I 1972.

[60] Ibid, vol. 78, Letter from Mario Pizzola to the commander of the military district of L'Aquila, 8 February 1971.

[61] Memoriale dal prigione di Peschiera, in Gruppo antimilitarista padovano, *Processo all'obiettore*, Lanterna, Genoa, 1971, pp. 54 ff.

[62] Labbate (2020), pp. 192–197; Bonfreschi (2019), pp. 49–64.

House.[63] The romantic stereotype of the objector—evoked, for example, by rapporteur Vito Rosa—who makes the "simple prayer" mistakenly attributed to St. Francis his "vademecum", also has the function of reassuring those who fear that the measure belittles "the high task of our armed forces for the defence of the homeland and for the protection of peace and freedom of the Italian people".[64]

5 Conclusions

The law recognising conscientious objection was passed in the Senate plenary on 30 November 1972 and in the Chamber's Defence Commission on 14 December. The measure seemed to aim more to limit civil service than to organise it: the objector would have a longer term of 8 months, was assessed by a commission that investigated his sincerity, remained subject to military justice and to the Ministry of Defence, had to submit an application within a very tight timeframe, and if he refused civil service or military service after a contrary judgement by the commission was sentenced to 2–4 years in military prison (which was then reduced by a few months with extenuating circumstances). Despite the obvious restrictions, the law enshrined conscientious objection within the constitutional framework centred on Article 52. In this process, Article 11 remains on the margins. In the Senate it is succinctly recalled by Franco Antonicelli, a left-wing independent: the parliamentarian would have liked to establish a "direct relationship" between the two articles, recalling in the "reason of conscience" underlying the objector's request "an ideological affirmation of high value" already included in the Constitution, such as, precisely, "the repudiation of war" and the "use of weapons".[65] Instead, a generic formula is preferred, addressed only to the interiority of the individual: the objection stemmed from objection "in all circumstances to the personal use of weapons for unavoidable reasons of conscience". Of an opposite tenor is the tautological reference to Article 11 by Enrico Endrich to MSI. As this excludes Italy from being involved in a conflict as an aggressor country, the citizen who abstains from military service "implicitly refuses to defend his country in the event of war". Hence the deduction that "the conscientious objector is willing to make common cause with the enemy, which can only be an aggressor".[66]

Beyond the legislators' intentions, the recognition of civil service within the constitutional framework constituted a more significant novelty than it at first appeared: in fact, it sanctioned that broadening of the concept of defence of the homeland prescribed by Article 52, which had been the actual objective of movements and objectors, committed to giving it another layer of meaning. As the President of the

[63] AP, Senate, sitting 27 July 1971, p. 26513.

[64] Ibid, 29 November 1971, p. 3053.

[65] Ibid, 30 November 1972, p. 3088.

[66] Ibid, p. 3096.

Constitutional Court Branca had written in March 1971 in a letter to Luigi Anderlini, secretary of the League for the Recognition of Conscientious Objection, "many do not want to understand that one can defend the homeland [...] by performing, for it, civil services just as useful as military service".[67] However much the spirit of Law 772 gave military service a primacy in the concept of defending the homeland, the breach opened reinforced an interpretative line that the mobilisation for conscientious objection had always supported, that is, the legitimacy of a concept of defence that did not include the use of weapons. Throughout the 1970s and 1980s, the antimilitarist discourse coexisted with forms of contestation that addressed the interpretation of Article 52: the equalisation in value and therefore in time of civil and military service, the tax objection to military expenditure, and the elaboration of a model of non-violent popular defence. The questioning of the status quo by some objectors who self-reduced their civic service, going to trial, would generate a number of important pronouncements by the Constitutional Court that went in the direction requested by the non-violent movements: in 1985 the Court ruled that the law on conscientious objection did not constitute an exception to the duty of defence, which can also be fulfilled "through the exercising of adequate behaviour of non-armed social commitment".[68] In April of the following year, he declared Article 11 of Law no.772 unconstitutional, insofar as it removed the objector from his natural judge, who is the civilian judge: civilian service does not constitute a "mode" in which military service is performed, but a "limit" to its fulfilment and therefore represents "a profoundly different alternative" that renders the objector "extraneous" to the military forces.[69] Finally, in 1989, in line with the path taken, he arrives at the temporal equalisation of the two services. The new concept of defence of the homeland embraced by the Court, while focusing on Article 52, would also however have an impact on the interpretation of Article 11.[70]

At the same time, with the fall of the Berlin Wall, the military interventions that Italy joined during the 1990s generated the cementing of Article 11 of the Constitutional Court and pacifist mobilisation. Previously, at least in the reconnaissance conducted, Article 11 is not a stranger in the pacifist debate but remains rather lateral. It becomes evident during mobilisation against the Euro-missiles but more in terms of the legal debate, concerning the compatibility between the constitutional dictate and the installation of bases for long-range "first strike" and therefore offensive missiles.[71] Article 11 was also invoked by a number of women of the Nonviolent Movement in a public appeal to the President of the Republic Sandro Pertini,

---

[67] ACSSR, FMP, b. 74, letter from Branca to Anderlini, Rome, 8 March 1971.

[68] Constitutional Court Judgement No. 164, 24 May 1985.

[69] Constitutional Court Judgement No. 113 of 23 April 1986.

[70] Judgement of the Constitutional Court No. 470 of 19 July 1989.

[71] Francesco Bilancia, Claudio De Fiores, Paola Marsocci, Laura Ronchetti, Marco Ruotolo, *Guerra e Costituzione*, in "Costituzionalismo.it", 2003, issue 1. Cited in particular are Barbera (1984), pp. 439–476; Grassi (1986), pp. 79 ff; Ronzitti (1984), pp. 74 ff; Allegretti (1986), pp. 99–112. See also D. Gallo, Missili a Comiso contro la Costituzione, "Pace e Guerra", n. 23, 25 maggio 1983. p. 37.

when faced with the proposal to open the army to women volunteers. But the focus is actually Article 52: they ask to be employed "in the effective and immediate organisation of an alternative defence"[72] that positively implements that part of Article 11 that excludes war from the resolution of international disputes. In 1984, the journal "Pace e Costituzione" was established at the initiative of a group of jurists and physicians; it was subsequently renamed "Diritto alla pace". A central concern of the publication was to underscore the interdependence between the commitment to peace and the defense of the Constitution, with Article 11 emerging as one of the key pillars of this perspective.[73] And again, the "repudiation of war" is cited during the campaign of fiscal objection to military expenditure, after the 1989 Supreme Court ruling that acquitted three objectors: we can imagine a possible favourable ruling even by the Constitutional Court, which in reality did not occur, which would have had to assess the appeal of the Verbania First Instance Tax Commission regarding "the constitutional illegitimacy of tax regulations, where they oblige the taxpayer to pay that part of taxes which 'undoubtedly' [...] will be used to build and store homicidal and threatening weapons".[74]

It was the Gulf War when Article 11 became a cornerstone of pacifist mobilisation. Already Italy's participation in the naval mission in August 1990, decided before the agreement of the chambers, is seen as a breach of the Constitution.[75] It is an issue that becomes even more central when in January 1991, the parliament approves the resolution providing for Italy's participation in the military intervention. The Committee of Jurists "against war and for the protection of human rights" identifies an overstepping of the limits of the Constitution, which are insurmountable even for the government and parliamentary majorities.[76] The demonstrations were filled with placards attesting in various ways to the "repudiation of war".[77] The jurist Augusto Barbera, a PDS deputy, would respond to these positions by drawing on the "constraint resulting from participation in international organisations" in paragraph 3 of Article 11. In particular, against Ingrao, who in *l'Unità* had defined that constraint as "unfounded and unconstitutional" due to the privilege of the right of veto still present in the Security Council,[78] Barbera opposed the risk of delegitimising the United Nations Organisation, against the will of the constituents who had already demonstrated the right of veto.[79]

---

[72] Appello delle donne a Pertini "Azione Nonviolenta", No. 10, 1980.

[73] *Diritto internazionale e Costituzione della Repubblica Italiana di fronte all'installazione di basi nucleari straniere in Italia,* "Pace e Costituzione", n. 2, 15 luglio 1984, p. 3; *Nella Costituzione la garanzia di un ruolo di pace dell'Italia,* "Diritto alla Pace", n. 1-2 marzo-aprile 1986, p. 1.

[74] *Interpellata la Corte costituzionale*, "Azione Nonviolenta", No. 1, 1990. The order of the Constitutional Court rejecting the appeal addresses the appeal of the Brescia Tax Commission of first instance (Order No.65/1993 in https://www.cortecostituzionale.it/).

[75] *Editorial*, "Azione Nonviolenta", No. 8–9, 1990.

[76] *Appello. Contro la guerra le ragioni del diritto*, in "Il Manifesto", 29 January 1991.

[77] "Azione Nonviolenta", No. 3, 1991.

[78] Alberto Leiss, *La condizione umana è oggi in quel deserto*, "l'Unità", 20 January 1991.

[79] A. Barbera, *La Costituzione italiana e le guerre 'legali' dell'Onu*, "l'Unità", 5 February 1991.

The centrality of Article 11 in the pacifist discourse would have been further strengthened on the occasion of Italy's participation in subsequent conflicts, starting with NATO's armed operation in Kosovo, which lacked the legitimacy of the UN Security Council. On that occasion, there was a succession of complaints due to breach of Article 11 and Articles 78 and 87, as there was a lack of parliamentary coverage of both the granting of Italian bases to provide logistical support for military action and the participation of aircraft in raids.[80]

A case in point is the war in former Yugoslavia. Faced with the violence deployed by the Serbian army against Croats and Bosnians, non-violent groups were called upon to strike a balance between the prospect of unconstitutionality from which they viewed any armed intervention and the risk of slipping into inaction. Article 11 is thus invoked to legitimise the sending of conscientious objectors across national borders "to perform acts of peace and solidarity" with the population and to fully implement the European Convention on Human Rights and the 1966 International Covenant on Civil and Political Rights.[81] Several objectors allegedly moved their commitment there without being authorised by the Ministry of Defence, facing prosecution and sanctions.

In reality, that disobedience would later be legitimised in Law 230 of 1998 which, in addition to recognising conscientious objection as a subjective right, includes it within the pacifist principle of Article 11. The new law, in fact, by allowing civilian service abroad, regularised the hitherto "illegal" experience of the "white helmets" in ex-Yugoslavia and established a committee for the implementation of armed and non-violent civil defence,[82] opening the way to the constitution of civilian peace corps in armed conflicts (later implementation in the context of voluntary civil service).[83] This is an acquisition that would inform subsequent laws, e.g. Law 145 of 2016 on Italy's participation in international missions. While on the one hand it confirms that the idea of defence of the homeland, the constitutional cornerstone of the existence of the civil service, is not limited to what happens strictly within the borders, on the other hand, the civilian peace corps becomes one of the possible forms of intervention "to ensure peace between nations", alongside the Armed Forces and Police Forces, and thus an instrument for implementing the third paragraph of Article 11 of the Constitution.[84]

References

Allegretti U (1986) Una ricerca su Costituzione e nuove armi. Democrazia e diritto 2:99–111

Antonietti N, De Siervo U, Malgieri F (eds) (1998) I cattolici democratici e la Costituzione, vol 3. il Mulino, Bologna

---

[80] On this issue see: Vari (1999), pp. 119–133; Carnevale (2004), pp. 79–136.

[81] *Obiettori con i caschi bianchi al servizio della pace*, "Azione Nonviolenta", No. 3, 1995.

[82] Tullio (2000).

[83] See Article 1 paragraph 253 of Law 147/2013, at https://www.normattiva.it/.

[84] Law 145/2016, at https://www.normattiva.it/.

Barbera A (1984) Gli accordi internazionali: tra Governo, Parlamento e corpo elettorale. Quad cost 3:439–476
Bobbio N (1989) Il terzo assente. Edizioni Sonda, Milan-Turin
Bocchini Camaiani B (1995) Il dibattito sull'obiezione di coscienza: il "laboratorio fiorentino 1961–1966", in Rochat G (ed), La spada e la croce: i cappellani italiani nelle due guerre mondiali. Proceedings of the conference on the reformation and religious movements in Italy (Torre Pellice, 28–30 august 1994). Società di Studi Valdesi, Torre Pellice, pp 251–286
Bocchini Camaiani B (2002) Ernesto Balducci. *La chiesa e la modernità*. Laterza, Rome-Bari
Bonanate L (2018) Costituzione italiana: art. 11. Carocci, Rome
Bonfreschi L (2019) L'obiezione di coscienza come battaglia antimilitarista. Il Partito radicale dagli anni Sessanta al 1972. Ricerche di storia politica (1):49–64
Bravo A (2008) A colpi di cuore. Storie del Sessantotto. Laterza, Rome-Bari
Capitini A (1959) L'obbiezione di coscienza in Italia. Lacaita, Manduria
Carlassare L (2013) L'art.11 Cost. nella visione dei costituenti. Costituzionalismo.it 1
Carnevale P (2004) Il ruolo del Parlamento e l'assetto dei rapporti fra Camere e Governo nella gestione dei conflitti armati. Riflessioni alla luce della prassi seguita in occasione delle crisi internazionali del Golfo Persico, Kosovo e Afghanistan. In: Carnevale P (ed) Guerra e Costituzione. Giappichelli, Turin, pp 79–136
Cassese A (1975) Commento all'articolo 11 della Costituzione. In: Branca G (ed) Commentario della Costituzione. Principi fondamentali. Zanichelli-Foro italiano, Bologna-Rome, pp 565–588
Colli E Lettere pastorali 1932–1956 (ed. Triani P.). SEI, Turin
Conac G, Prétot X, Teboul G (eds) (2001) Le Preambule De La Constitution De 1946.Histoire, Analyse Et Commentaires. Dalloz
De Giuseppe M (2001) Giorgio La Pira. Un sindaco e le vie della pace. Centro Ambrosiano, Milan
De Giuseppe M (2008) Movimenti pacifisti e aperture terzomondiste. Aldo Capitini e l'ipotesi del terzo campo. In Canavero D, Formigoni G, Vecchio G (eds) Le sfide della pace. Istituzioni e movimenti intellettuali e politici tra Otto e Novecento. LED, Milan, pp 249–269
Dossetti G (1995) I valori della Costituzione. Edizioni San Lorenzo, Reggio Emilia
Elia L (2003) Intervento. In: Colombo A (ed) L'articolo 11 della Costituzione: pace, guerra, ordine internazionale. Atti di un seminario tenuto il 16 gennaio 2003. La Margherita Area Studi, Rome, pp 7–15
Fabbrini F (1966) Tu non ucciderai. Cultura Editrice, Florence
Ferrua P (1997) L'obiezione di coscienza anarchica in Italia.I pionieri. Editziones de su Arkiviubibrioteka T. Serra, Guasila
Formigoni G (2000) Storia della politica internazionale nell'età contemporanea (1815–1992). il Mulino, Bologna
Formigoni G (2008) La DC e il dibattito sulla pace nel mondo cattolico preconciliare. In: Canavero A, Formigoni G, Vecchio G (eds) Le sfide della pace. Istituzioni e movimenti intellettuali e politici tra Otto e Novecento. LED, Milan, pp 231–248
Giorgi L (2023) Giuseppe Dossetti. La politica come missione. Carocci, Rome
Giovagnoli A (ed) (2003) Pacem in terris tra azione diplomatica e guerra globale. Guerini e associati, Milan
Giovannoni PD (2008) La Pira e Firenze, "Città sul monte". In: Canavero A, Formigoni G, Vecchio G (eds) Le sfide della pace. Istituzioni e movimenti intellettuali e politici tra Otto e Novecento. LED, Milan, pp 205–229
Grassi S (1986) Le garanzie giuridiche in tema di pace. Democrazia e diritto
Gudemet Y (ed) (2008) Le Préambule de la Constitution de 1946. Panthéon-Assas, Paris
Guiso A (2006) La colomba e la spada: "lotta per la pace" e antiamericanismo nella politica del partito comunista italiano (1949–1954). Rubbettino, Soveria Mannelli
Hathaway O, Shapiro S (2017) The internationalists: how a radical plan to outlaw war remade the world. Simon & Schuster, New York
Labanca N (2009) La politica militare della Repubblica. Cornici e quadri In: Labanca N (ed) Gli italiani in guerra. Le armi della Repubblica dalla Liberazione a oggi. Utet, Turin, pp 66–156

Labbate M (2020) Un'altra patria. L'obiezione di coscienza nell'Italia repubblicana. Pacini, Pisa
Labbate M (2022) Non un uomo né un soldo. Obiezione di coscienza e servizio civile a Torino. Ega
Marcucci E (2004) Sotto il segno della pace. Biblioteca Planettiana, Jesi
Martellini A (2006) Fiori nei cannoni: nonviolenza e antimilitarismo nell'Italia del Novecento. Donzelli, Roma
Martellini A (2012) All'ombra delle altrui rivoluzioni. Parole e icone del Sessantotto. B. Mondadori, Milan
Martini L (2005) L'enciclica Pacem in terris. In: Franzinelli M, Bottoni R (eds) Chiesa e guerra. *Dalla benedizione delle armi alla Pacem in terris*. il Mulino, Bologna, pp 607–652
Melloni A (1994) *L'utopia come utopia*. In: Dossetti G (ed) La ricerca costituente, 1945–1992. il Mulino, Bologna, pp 1-81
Melloni A (2010) Pacem in terris. Storia dell'ultima enciclica di Papa Giovanni. Laterza, Rome-Bari
Menozzi D (2008) Chiesa, pace e guerra nel Novecento: verso una delegittimazione religiosa dei conflitti. il Mulino, Bologna
Milani L (2017) In: Ruozzi F, Canfora A, Oldano V, Tanzarella S (eds) Tutte le opere, vol II. A. Mondadori, Milan, pp 929–961
Pombeni P, Dossetti G (2013) *L'avventura politica di un riformatore cristiano*. il Mulino, Bologna
Possenti V (2009) Dentro il secolo breve.Paolo VI, Maritain, La Pira, Giovanni Paolo II. Rubbettino, Soveria Mannelli
Ronzitti N (1984) Politica di difesa, Costituzione e norme internazionali. Politica Internazionale (75)
Santomassimo G (2003) Alienum Est a ratione. La Pacem in Terris 40 anni dopo. Passato e presente 60:7–16
Tolomelli M (2015) L'Italia Dei movimenti. Politica e società nella Prima repubblica. Carocci, Rome
Toschi M (2007) Giorgio La Pira e il volto della pace. Opera Madonnina del Grappa, Florence
Tullio F (ed) (2000) La difesa civile e il progetto caschi bianchi: peacekeepers civilians disarmed. FrancoAngeli, Milan
Turbanti G (2005) Il tema della guerra al Concilio Vaticano II. In: Franzinelli M, Bottoni R (eds) Chiesa e guerra. Dalla benedizione delle armi alla Pacem in terris. il Mulino, Bologna, pp 563–606
Vari F (1999) La 'vecchia Costituzione' e la 'nuova' guerra: breve analisi della 'crisi del Kosovo'. In: Dogliani M, Sicardi S (eds) Diritti umani e uso della forza. Giappichelli, Turin, pp 119–133
Vecchio G (1993) Pacifisti e obiettori nell'Italia di De Gasperi (1948–1953). Studium, Rome
Ventrone A (2012) Vogliamo tutto. Perché due generazioni hanno creduto nella rivoluzione 1960–1988. Laterza, Rome-Bari

Italian Scientists for Nuclear Arms Control in the Cold War: A Concise Testimony

Alessandro Pascolini

1 Introduction

In the variegated multiplicity of groups and movements against nuclear weapons operating in Italy during the Cold War, this contribution focuses on a specific, limited group of scientists (mainly physicists) active both in Italy and internationally and on two structures they generated: the International School on Disarmament and Research on Conflicts (ISODARCO, born 1966) and Unione degli Scienziati per il Disarmo (USPID, Union of Scientists for Disarmament, created 1982). They also played an important role in the Pugwash Conferences on Science and World Affairs, which involve scientists and scholars on a global level. Both ISODARCO and USPID continue to the present time, but in this chapter only their activities up to the beginning of this century are considered. Most of the material presented here is based on personal recollections and unpublished documents, complement to scholarly research (Clavarino 2021, 2025, Foradori and Giacomello 2018).

Coming from different research fields and locations, and from often contrasting political cultures, these scientists shared the common goal of a special commitment to the knowledge and promotion of arms control, particularly for nuclear weapons. They thus created an informal, unstructured epistemic community on a national level (Foradori et al. 2017), which merged in the worldwide epistemic community of Pugwash.

These scientists consider themselves part of the broader pacifist movement, yet they assert a distinctive role in the anti-nuclear mobilization—one that stems from their expertise in the complexities of the issue within the international context. For them nuclear disarmament must be understood as a long, demanding, pragmatic,

A. Pascolini (✉)
University of Padua, Padua, Italy
e-mail: alessandro.pascolini@unipd.it

G. Cavaggion (ed.), *The 'Pacifist Principle' in the Italian and Japanese Constitutions in the Wake of the War in Ukraine*,
https://doi.org/10.1007/978-3-032-23108-6_5

and gradual process. It is therefore necessary to proceed through a combination of negotiations, legal constraints, unilateral measures, and concrete, verifiable initiatives. This approach to arms control differs from the maximalist demands of mass movements, which call for total disarmament while rejecting compromises and intermediate steps.

What these Italian scientists had in common was their continuous focus on global strategic issues and their reference to Edoardo Amaldi (1908–1989), as a guiding figure in their initiatives. Amaldi was one of the most prominent Italian scientists of the last century (Angela and Rubbia 1992). In the 1930s he belonged to the Enrico Fermi group in Rome, and after the ravages of World War II and the forced emigration of many scientists, he led the renaissance of Italian physics and was one of the main promoters of scientific collaboration among the European countries, as one of the founding fathers of the Conseil Européen pour la Recherche Nucleaire (CERN, created in 1954 in Geneva), and—at the beginning of the space race—a supporter of the first European Space Research Centre (ESRO, founded in 1964). Moreover, he was a staunch advocate of international detente and nuclear arms control throughout the Cold War (Clavarino 2017).

The underlying spirit guiding these Italian scientists, passed on to them mainly through Amaldi, was that which permeated the world community of nuclear physicists following the production of the nuclear weapon and the atomic bombing of Japan in August 1945.

2 The World Community of Nuclear Physicists and the Bomb

The atomic bombing of Hiroshima spread a feeling in the scientific community with a dual polarity: on the one hand a deep sense of guilt and on the other the need to take a responsible and critical role in the development of research and applications of nuclear physics and in strategic arms control.

J. Robert Oppenheimer explicitly spoke of "sin" in a lecture at the Massachusetts Institute of Technology, on 25 November 1947: "In some sort of crude sense which no vulgarity, no humor, no overstatement can quite extinguish, the physicists have known sin; and this is a knowledge which they cannot lose" (Schweber 2000).

The sense of co-responsibility spread throughout the world community of physicists: research on nuclear fission had been carried out in many countries, and the production of the bomb had required knowledge in vast fields of contemporary physics; therefore, many felt partly involved and therefore responsible. Understanding the qualitative difference of the nuclear weapon from other instruments of death and the resulting ethical and strategic implications became a subject of concerned attention by some of the Manhattan Project scientists themselves.

The results of these debates on ethical and political aspects were presented in the "Franck Report" (11 June 1945), largely inspired by Leo Szilard and written by

Eugene Rabinowitch. The report makes explicit the second polarity of scientist sentiment: the need for a new role for scientists in shaping future global atomic policy (Smith 1965; Price 1995): "The scientists on this Project do not presume to speak authoritatively on problems of national and international policy. However, we found ourselves, by the force of events of the last five years in the position of a small group of citizens cognizant of a grave danger for the safety of this country as well as for the future of all the other nations, of which the rest of mankind is unaware".

The Franck Report, which suggested for ethical reasons a bloodless demonstrative use of the nuclear weapon under construction, was to be taken as the founding "manifesto" by the scientists who immediately after Hiroshima felt obliged to use their knowledge and acquired social weight to promote international agreements to prevent the nuclear arms race and to inform and educate the public about nuclear energy: several associations created in various universities and laboratories merged into the Federation of American Scientists (FAS, January 1946).

In December 1945, Rabinowitch founded the *Bulletin of the Atomic Scientists*, which quickly became a communication tool for the international scientific community and an authoritative independent source of information and analysis of military issues.

The FAS soon realized the need to recreate the transnational scientific community characteristic of the 1920s and 1930s on the new issues. In 1946, it sent out information material on atomic energy to over 3000 non-American scientists, including Italian nuclear physicists, who, *in primis* Amaldi, during the war decided to stop research on fission in order to avoid the risk of being forced to take part into the German atomic project.

In the early 1950s, American and British scientists fought against the development of the thermonuclear weapon (H-bomb), a thousand times more powerful than the Hiroshima bomb; they were supported by the General Advisory Committee of the Atomic Energy Commission, chaired by Oppenheimer, in particular, as Fermi pointed out, "since there are no limits to the destructive power of this bomb, its very existence and the knowledge of its construction constitute a danger to all mankind".

The American test of the H-bomb (Castle Bravo on the Bikini Atoll, 1 March 1954) made a huge impression around the world, particularly because of the extensive radioactive contamination of the atmosphere.

3 The *Russell-Einstein Manifesto*

The event produced particular apprehension and indignation in the great philosopher, mathematician, and pacifist Bertrand Russell (Nobel Prize laureate in Literature in 1950). He decided to express his fears of a thermonuclear war in a broadcast on BBC radio, on 23 December 1954, under the title *Man's Peril* (Russell 1969, p. 17).

The broadcast made a deep impression, and Russell decided to persuade a number of eminent scientists from all over the world to join him in a statement warning governments and the general public and, in particular, calling on the scientific community to convene a conference on steps to avert this danger. Russell sent a draft of the statement to Einstein to seek his advice, and Einstein, just before dying, signed what became known as the *Russell-Einstein Manifesto*.

In ringing phrases, the *Manifesto* called on governments and the general public to take heed of the dangerous situation that had arisen from the progress of science in a world engaged in titanic struggles:

In the tragic situation which confronts humanity, we feel that scientists should assemble in conference to appraise the perils that have arisen as a result of the development of weapons of mass destruction, and to discuss a resolution in the spirit of the appended draft. We are speaking on this occasion, not as members of this or that nation, continent or creed, but as human beings, members of the species Man, whose continued existence is in doubt... We appeal, as human beings, to human beings: Remember your humanity, and forget the rest. If you can do so, the way lies open to a new Paradise; if you cannot, there lies before you the risk of universal death. (Bone 2003, ch. 16).

With the help of Joseph (Józef) Rotblat, a physicist who had left the Manhattan Project when it became clear that Germany was no longer capable of developing an atomic weapon, Russell began to procure other signatures to the statement. Although he was seeking Nobel laureates, more important to him was that the signatories should be politically balanced and come from the left and the right of the political spectrum. On 9 July 1955 Russell presented to a press conference the *Manifesto*, signed by nine prestigious scientists (including seven Nobel laureates).

4 The Pugwash Conferences on Science and World Affairs

Russell, with the collaboration of Rotblat and Cecil Powell (Nobel laureate in Physics in 1950), both signatories of the *Manifesto*, and the financial support of the American industrialist Cyrus Eaton, was able to convene the conference of scientists urged in the *Manifesto*, with the aim of a broad international participation and differing political opinions. The meeting was held in Pugwash (Canada) on July 1957 (Rotblat 1962).

The conditions of participation, which remained the rule for all subsequent activities, were invitations on an individual basis, each participant representing only himself, meetings were private, and participants would decide at the end whether to issue a public statement.

The majority of the 30 participants were physicists, along with chemists, biologists, and a jurist, coming from Australia, Austria, Canada, China, France, Japan, Poland, the United Kingdom, the United States, and the USSR. The first Pugwash conference demonstrated that scientists have a common goal that transcends national borders without violating fundamental loyalties. Due to their training and knowledge, scientists are capable of making a significant contribution to solving the complex problems that have arisen as a result of scientific progress.

With a view to new conferences, a Continuing Committee was set up, chaired by Russell and consisting of Powell, Rabinowitch, Rotblat, and Dmitri Skobeltsyn, director of the Lebedev Institute of Physics in Moscow.

Among the possible goals to be pursued (influencing governments, forming a channel of communication between scientists, and educating the public), strategic priority was assigned to convening small specialist meetings to discuss problems of immediate importance and aimed at influencing governments. In the years that followed, annual conferences were established, each gathering approximately 100 scientists. These events were structured into general plenary sessions and specialized parallel working groups. Their primary objective was to identify points of consensus and provide clarity on pressing contemporary scientific and geopolitical issues.

To address more technical subjects and urgent global challenges, specialized symposia and small-scale working groups were organized. The earliest symposia focused on the control of civilian nuclear energy and ballistic missile defence systems; first working groups dealt with biological weapons (1964–1966), European security (1964–1968), and chemical weapons (1974–1992). Often the groups functioned as an influential model of informal diplomacy (*Track Two Diplomacy*).

The deliberate choice to operate discreetly, avoiding mass media exposure and the dynamics of a mass movement, has shielded the Pugwash Conferences from generic and superficial pacifist or propagandistic positions. This approach has ensured the free flow and development of ideas in the realm of international relations—particularly in the field of arms control—and has enabled the formulation of precise recommendations, some of which have been acknowledged and adopted by world governments. The ensemble of conferences, symposia, working groups, and Council meetings has fostered a dense network of interpersonal and transnational relationships (Evangelista 1999), giving rise to a truly global epistemic community of scholars and scientists.

Throughout the prolonged and tense confrontation between the East and West, the Pugwash Conferences provided a continuous communication channel and an independent forum for the development of measures aimed at reducing the risk of war and halting the arms race, laying the groundwork for the eventual end of the Cold War (Kraft et al. 2018).

In 1995 the Norwegian Nobel Committee awarded its peace prize to the Pugwash Conferences and to its president and founder Joseph Rotblat "for their efforts to diminish the part played by nuclear arms in international politics and, in the longer run, to eliminate such arms".

5 Italian Participation in the Pugwash Conferences

Amaldi was invited to attend the conference in Pugwash but was unable to attend. However, he was convinced of the importance of this initiative and actively supported it from the very beginning; his first participation was in the Kitzbühel conference (1958), and he took part in another 11 conferences, the last one in Venice 1983.

Amaldi served in the Pugwash Continuing Committee from 1962 until 1972, when another Italian physicist, Francesco Calogero (born 1935), replaced him as a member of the committee. A former student of Amaldi in the 1950s, Calogero himself was already involved in arms control issues since the early 1960s, when he experienced the very tense atmosphere of the Cuban Missile Crisis. He soon became very active in this field, working in Rome with Amaldi in several initiatives in the field of arms control, including actions to promote the Italian ratification of NPT (Nuti 2015, p. 245).

Calogero was a leading personality of the community of Italian scientists here considered, with high responsibilities in ISODARCO, USPID, and Pugwash; throughout the Cold War he was the Italian scientist who wrote most intensively on arms control and security, publishing hundreds of articles on these topics. He was a pillar of Pugwash, serving as Secretary-General from 1989 to 1997; as such he had the honour to receive in the name of Pugwash the Nobel Peace Prize in 1995.

The role of Pugwash Secretary-General will be entrusted from 2002 to 2024 to another Italian physicist, Paolo Cotta-Ramusino (born in 1948). Over 100 other Italian scientists took part in Pugwash meetings in the period 1960–2006, several of them in numerous events. In particular, these scientists have contributed significantly to the goals of Pugwash, both by actively participating in the various initiatives and by organizing important events, in particular, two general conferences held in Venice in 1965 and 1983 (a third general conference took place in Bari in 2007).

The cosmologist Bruno Bertotti (1930–2018) and the chemist Giovanni Giacometti (1929–2018) were in charge of the actual making of the 14th Pugwash Conference (Venice, 11–16 April 1965). The Conference was sponsored by the Accademia Nazionale dei Lincei, and the Fondazione Cini offered their premises for the meeting; it was attended by 78 scientists and scholars from 20 countries.

The agenda was concerned with two main themes, *International Cooperation in Science* and *Problems of Disarmament*; the situation in Vietnam was considered as well. In Venice, the structure of the Stockholm International Peace Research Institute (SIPRI) was also discussed and finalized.

The 33rd Pugwash Conference, initially scheduled for 1983, was to be held in Warsaw. However, beginning in December 1981, Poland was placed under martial law, implemented to suppress political dissent, particularly the Solidarność movement. Under these conditions, the regular conduct of the conference became virtually unfeasible. Martin Kaplan, then Secretary-General of the Pugwash Conferences, consequently turned to the Italian national group with a request to consider relocating the event to Italy. The Director of ISODARCO, physicist Carlo Schaerf (born in 1935), together with the Secretary of the Pugwash Italian national group, physicist Alessandro Pascolini (born in 1944), obtained the Venetian administration to finance the conference and to assist with its logistical arrangements. The two physicists took care of the works of the Conference.

The Venice Conference on *Avoiding Nuclear and Other Wars and Reversing the Arms Race* was attended by 152 scientists and scholars from 34 countries and 7 international organizations, including Nobel laureates Dorothy Hodgkin (chemistry, 1964), Alfonso Garcia Robles (peace, 1982), and Abdus Salam (physics, 1979). A warm message of greetings was received from Italian President Sandro Pertini and presented by Amaldi in his opening speech held in Palazzo Ducale.

Most of the work focused on urgent issues such as disarmament, strategic armaments, European security, security problems in the Mediterranean and the Middle East, economic issues related to the arms race, arms transfers, and Third World security. Most of the invited and some of the proffered papers were collected in a book, edited by Rotblat and Pascolini (1984).

The Venice Conference played a significant role in broadening the community of scientists actively engaged with these issues in Italy while also facilitating international contacts for the members of the scientific committee of the newly established USPID association.

From 1965 to 2006, several members of this community also promoted 20 Pugwash symposia or workshops in Italy, on critical issues.

Among the various contributions of Italian scientists to the objectives of Pugwash, a recognized point of excellence is the original experience of ISODARCO, which has developed an advanced training programme on global issues of disarmament and arms control.

6 ISODARCO: The International School on Disarmament and Research on Conflicts

6.1 Origins and Early Development

The concept of establishing postgraduate-level training courses on disarmament was first proposed by Carlo Schaerf to Amaldi in 1962 (Schaerf 2017). At the time, Schaerf—a nuclear physicist affiliated with Stanford University—was actively involved in the Stanford Faculty Forum on Arms Control, which hosted presentations by experts from academia, the military, and government, followed by open discussions. His engagement with the forum deepened his interest in the broader implications of nuclear weapons and international security.

Amaldi and Schaerf recognized that, while international security and military strategy are largely political domains, a comprehensive understanding of these issues—especially in the nuclear age—requires grounding in technical and scientific disciplines. One major obstacle to fostering meaningful engagement between scientists and international relations experts lies in their distinct conceptual frameworks and professional languages, reflecting fundamentally different worldviews, rather than mere differences in terminology. Traditional educational trajectories in these fields remain largely siloed, and opportunities for interdisciplinary dialogue are limited. The courses envisioned by Schaerf and Amaldi sought to bridge this divide by offering structured, high-level, interdisciplinary training on the scientific and technical dimensions of global security, the arms race, and nuclear weapons deployment. The format was inspired by the summer schools organized by the

Italian Physical Society for young researchers: residential courses of a couple of weeks with advanced lectures delivered by leading scholars, facilitating both formal instruction and informal scholarly exchange.

Their initiative anticipated the international community's later recognition of the role of education in disarmament and non-proliferation. This recognition was formally articulated during the United Nations General Assembly's first special session on disarmament in 1978. The issue was revisited with renewed emphasis in Resolution 55/33/E of 20 November 2000, which requested that the UN Secretary-General prepare a comprehensive study. This study was subsequently submitted to the General Assembly's First Committee on 9 October 2002.

Drawing on personal networks and connections with the Pugwash Conferences, Schaerf and Amaldi convened the first course from 13 to 25 June 1966 in Frascati, near Rome. The event featured 9 lecturers and 3 representatives from international institutions and attracted 30 participants from 11 countries. The course was supported by the Geneva office of the Carnegie Endowment for International Peace, the Italian Prime Minister's Office, and the Ministry of Foreign Affairs, with the Ministry of Education providing the venue.

Amaldi opened the course by articulating its objectives and its intended function as an educational complement to the work of the Pugwash Conferences. The discussions in Frascati addressed a wide range of topics, including the effects of nuclear weapons, nuclear strategy, the relationship between armaments and global security, and the technical, economic, and political dimensions of disarmament.

To the best of current knowledge, this was the world's first advanced course devoted to the scientific study of the technological, economic, and political challenges associated with nuclear weapons and their potential elimination. It demonstrated the feasibility of engaging participants from both Western democracies and Socialist states in open, constructive dialogue on strategically sensitive issues.

A second course was held in 1968 at the Collegio Ghislieri in Pavia, with particular emphasis on international law, the role of the United Nations, and mechanisms for verifying disarmament agreements. Among the lecturers were Vasily Emelyanov, Jules Moch, Louis Sohn, and a young Francesco Calogero. Emelyanov, a former chair of the USSR Atomic Energy Commission, presented findings from a United Nations study on the consequences of nuclear war, to which he had contributed. Moch was a veteran of the French government under Léon Blum and a key figure in post-war French politics, while Sohn was among the foremost authorities on international law.

The third course, held in 1970 at Duino Castle near Trieste, assembled 60 scholars from 15 countries. Lecturers included Anatol Rapoport, Frank Barnaby (then Director of SIPRI), William Gutteridge, William Epstein (Director of the UN Disarmament Division), and emerging scholars such as Mary Kaldor (born in 1946) and Julian Perry Robinson (1941–2020). This session broadened the curriculum to include topics such as chemical and biological weapons and their control, the security concerns of developing nations, and the application of game theory and simulation models to international politics.

6.2 The Institutionalization of ISODARCO

The initial three ISODARCO courses were conducted without a formal organizational structure. In anticipation of the fourth course—and with the goal of garnering support from national and international institutions—a nonprofit association named ISODARCO was officially established in Rome on 18 January 1972. The founding members were five Italian physicists: Amaldi, Schaerf, Calogero, Pascolini, and Armando Reale (1933–2022). Of the original founders, Schaerf, Calogero, and Pascolini are still active.

Article 3 of the association's by-laws articulates its mission as follows:

The Association aims to foster interest in the scientific aspects of disarmament and peace by all possible means. In particular, it organizes, participates in, or collaborates with meetings, seminars, conferences, and professional and cultural training courses; it collects documentation and promotes and conducts research on these topics. The Association is non-partisan and non-profit.

Amaldi served as ISODARCO's inaugural president, and, upon Amaldi's death in 1989, Schaerf assumed the presidency. Technical amendments were later introduced to ensure compliance with evolving Italian legislation regarding nonprofit organizations. ISODARCO's membership has always consisted of a small cadre of Italian scientists—never exceeding nine and currently comprising eight.

Over the years, funding was provided mainly by American foundations, with occasional support by local institutions and universities—always on the condition that no sponsor may influence the content or conduct of the sessions.

ISODARCO has consistently maintained its identity as an educational institution, deliberately abstaining from issuing public statements or advocating for specific political positions. It has maintained a long-standing affiliation with the Pugwash Conferences, forming the nucleus of its Italian national group. Several members were instrumental in founding the *Unione degli Scienziati per il Disarmo* (Union of Scientists for Disarmament, USPID) in 1983. The early courses validated ISODARCO's foundational premise: the complex and interdisciplinary nature of issues surrounding war, peace, armaments, and disarmament necessitates engagement from experts across a wide range of academic and professional domains—not only scholars and researchers but also practitioners actively involved in strategic and arms control negotiations.

Over time, ISODARCO established a stable organizational framework. Course directors, appointed by the governing body, typically invite 10–15 lecturers, each of whom delivers 1 or 2 presentations and participates fully in all sessions and discussions. Participants are selected through a competitive application process based on academic and professional qualifications. They receive full board in exchange for a modest registration fee, which only partially offsets operational expenses.

Lecturers do not receive honoraria; however, they and one accompanying guest are provided with accommodation and meals. Travel costs are generally covered by the lecturers' home institutions, thereby providing indirect support for ISODARCO's financial sustainability. Despite limited funding and the absence of material incentives, the courses have consistently attracted prominent scholars due to their high academic standards and intellectually stimulating atmosphere. The programmes offer a rare platform for rigorous interdisciplinary dialogue within a collegial and diverse international community, enriched by a variety of national, ideological, disciplinary, and professional perspectives.

A distinctive feature of the ISODARCO courses—and one of their greatest strengths—is the emphasis on extended discussion following each presentation. Each session includes a 45-min lecture followed by 45 min of open dialogue, with priority given to younger participants. To encourage candid and constructive conversation, discussions are conducted under the Chatham House Rule: participants are requested not to attribute statements to specific individuals outside the course. This format empowers junior attendees to pose direct questions and allows all participants to express personal views—even those that may diverge from the official positions of their respective governments or institutions.

Another hallmark of the courses is the ample opportunity for informal interaction between lecturers and participants outside the formal sessions. Each course is limited to four sessions per day to allow time for unstructured engagement. Living together for approximately 10 days in a shared venue cultivates a vibrant intellectual community and provides numerous opportunities for private conversations, collaborative research, and professional networking.

A major factor in ISODARCO's continued success has been the steady participation of exceptional young individuals—typically in their twenties, including doctoral students and early-career professionals in fields such as research, diplomacy, law enforcement, military service, and public administration. Drawn from a wide range of countries and disciplines, these participants contribute significantly to the dynamic and globally engaged character of the institution.

6.3 New Themes and New Perspectives

The fourth ISODARCO course, held in Padua in 1972, focused on emerging technologies, their political and strategic implications, and their impact on the prospects for disarmament. Among the distinguished lecturers were historian David Carlton; Hans Morgenthau, a foundational figure in twentieth-century international relations theory; Thomas Schelling, who would later receive the Nobel Prize in Economics; and leading arms control experts Jack Ruina and George Rathjens, both of whom had contributed to the development of the first US thermonuclear devices. Other prominent figures included academician Oleg Reutov, a specialist in chemical weapons; Herbert Scoville of the US Arms Control and Disarmament Agency; and Herbert York, the inaugural director of the Livermore Laboratory. David Carlton would later play a pivotal role in ISODARCO, serving as editor of the conference proceedings and directing several courses.

Following four sessions centred on the arms race and prospects for arms control, the subsequent course—held in Urbino in 1974—shifted focus to international terrorism. At that time, terrorism in Europe and the United States was primarily driven by groups engaged in protracted nationalist campaigns of violence, such as the Provisional Irish Republican Army, the Basque separatist group ETA, the German Red Army Faction, and the Italian Red Brigades. The Urbino course attracted 60 lecturers and participants from 20 countries, representing a diverse array of professional backgrounds. A follow-up course on international terrorism was convened in 1978 in Ariccia (Rome).

The theme of terrorism and counterterrorism re-emerged on ISODARCO's agenda in the wake of the September 11, 2001, attacks in the United States, with courses held in 2006, 2007, and 2008. These sessions gave particular attention to the political and military responses to terrorism and their implications for human rights. Notably, ISODARCO facilitated the discussion of emotionally charged topics within a scholarly environment and among a highly diverse international audience.

Technological advancements in both nuclear and conventional weaponry—including space-based systems—and their implications for arms control were the subject of numerous ISODARCO courses. Notable venues included Nemi (Rome, 1976), Venice (1980, 1984, and 1988), Verona (1982), San Miniato (1986), and L'Aquila (1990). These courses welcomed a range of new generation of experts into ISODARCO's academic community, including Lawrence Freedman, Georgy Arbatov (then Director of the authoritative Institute for US and Canadian Studies in Moscow), General Mikhail Milstein, Catherine Kelleher (member of the US National Security Council), Jack Steinberger (Nobel Laureate in Physics, 1998), Richard L. Garwin (author of the first hydrogen bomb design), Frank von Hippel (then chairman of the FAS), and Rotblat.

A significant milestone in ISODARCO's history occurred in 1988 with the inaugural ISODARCO Beijing Seminar on Arms Control. This seminar was made possible through collaboration with the Institute of Applied Physics and Computational Mathematics and the China Institute of Contemporary International Relations. The initiative was born from discussions at the 1986 San Miniato course, where Hu Side—then Director of the China Academy of Engineering Physics—proposed hosting a similar event in China. The goal was to enable Chinese scholars from various disciplines and institutions to openly engage with international counterparts on issues of peace and global security.

The first Beijing Seminar brought together eight Western experts and 45 Chinese scholars. Participants represented a wide range of disciplines, including social sciences, political science, physics, diplomacy, the military, and the nuclear industry. Notably, the seminar marked the first occasion on which representatives of these Chinese institutions openly discussed strategic and disarmament issues among themselves.

This collaboration expanded over time, with regular participation by Chinese scholars and young researchers in ISODARCO's Italian courses and reciprocal contributions to biennial seminars held in China. In his study of the evolution of Chinese strategic thought, Evan Medeiros (2007) underscores the importance of the Beijing Seminars, identifying three key impacts: (1) the rapid expansion of these seminars facilitated increased interaction between Chinese and Western experts on arms control; (2) the breadth of topics addressed promoted a comprehensive understanding; and (3) the engagement of younger specialists exposed them to international perspectives.

In 1988, ISODARCO also launched winter sessions, made possible by support from local institutions. These courses were structured to include four daily sessions, allowing participants time for recreational activities such as skiing, ice skating, or hiking during daylight hours.

For several years, substantial international funding—most notably from the John D. and Catherine T. MacArthur Foundation and the Ford Foundation—enabled the organization of both summer and winter courses annually, along with biennial seminars in China and occasional special seminars.

The end of the Cold War ushered in new challenges and dimensions for arms control, including concerns over the international transfer of military technologies and their potential to spur proliferation; these issues were explored in courses held in Folgaria (1993), L'Aquila (1993), Pontignano (Siena, 1996), and Rovereto (2000).

The political transformations in Russia and Eastern Europe created a shifting international context—introducing new crises and conflicts but also generating fresh perspectives on European and global security. Between 1993 and 2005, many ISODARCO courses addressed these evolving dynamics with input from a new generation of scholars and practitioners.

Concurrently, military interest in cyberspace emerged, along with the development of autonomous and semi-autonomous weapon systems for hybrid operations. These emerging security challenges were the focus of courses held in Rovereto (1999), Trento (2002), and Andalo (Trento, 2012 and 2013).

6.4 Closing Observations

Over its first 50 years, ISODARCO has organized 52 courses, two seminars in Taipei, one in Amman, and one in Venice, along with 14 seminars in China in collaboration with Chinese counterparts. These events have engaged approximately 3000 participants from 80 different countries and some 150 distinguished lecturers, who, given their vast professional experience, could equally be classified as scientists, scholars, or policymakers.

Scholarly contributions presented during these events have resulted in the publication of 29 books by internationally recognized publishers, including Macmillan, John Wiley, St. Martin's Press, Dartmouth-Ashgate, Croom Helm, Palgrave, Routledge, Stanford University Press, and Bloomsbury.[1]

Through its sustained commitment to education on disarmament and non-proliferation, ISODARCO has made a significant and original

[1] A complete list of ISODARCO's publications can be found on the Association's website www.isodarco.it.

contribution—alongside Pugwash and other international organizations—to the formation and consolidation of the international epistemic community focused on arms control.

As noted by Foradori and Giacomello (2018), several distinctive characteristics define ISODARCO's approach to disarmament education in terms of its values, objectives, and methodologies. First, ISODARCO's courses are notable for their comprehensiveness and depth in addressing key issues. Second, they place significant emphasis on the scientific and technical dimensions of nuclear matters, which are essential for a nuanced understanding of nuclear strategies. Third, ISODARCO successfully bridges the gap between theory and practice by fostering interactions between scholars and practitioners, providing participants with a balanced perspective. Fourth, its pedagogical model is grounded in the belief that informed dialogue must be non-ideological and open to multiple viewpoints. Fifth, there is a strong commitment to intergenerational learning, with particular attention to mentoring younger participants. Finally, ISODARCO's extensive research and dissemination activities are integral to its educational mission.

In recognition of its contributions, US President Barack Obama commemorated ISODARCO's 50th anniversary with the following message:

The task of building a safer future requires people from around the world to engage in peaceful collaboration. For half a century, ISODARCO has brought women and men of different backgrounds and beliefs together to study and discuss pressing security concerns. By identifying problems, engaging in debate, and working in a spirit of common purpose to address issues ranging from the threat of nuclear weapons to conflict in cyberspace and the need for greater international cooperation, you are helping reduce the possibility of catastrophe and contributing to better understanding among peoples and states.

Similarly, in 2017, Sergio Mattarella, President of the Italian Republic, awarded ISODARCO the Gold Medal for Public Service, in recognition of its outstanding contributions to international discourse and the promotion of Italy's cultural legacy worldwide.

7 The Unione degli Scienziati per il Disarmo (USPID)

While Pugwash meetings were reserved to specialists and primarily aimed at influencing governments, and ISODARCO remained strictly dedicated to higher education, Italian scientists in the early 1980s founded USPID, the Unione degli Scienziati per il Disarmo (Union of Scientists for Disarmament) with a much broader spectrum of objectives in the field of the promotion of disarmament, including stimulating a specific awareness among the members of the scientific community and providing updated information to the Italian grassroots peace and disarmament movements, to the Italian government and parliament, and to the press and other media.

At the end of the 1970s, the onset of the Euromissile Crisis (the installation in Europe of Soviet SS-20 and NATO Pershing II and Tomahawk cruise missiles) and heightened tensions between the superpowers gave rise to mass mobilisation around the world (Moro 2017, pp. 208–210). In Italian scientific circles it became a sort of trigger for their social activation. In the autumn of 1981, at the Perugia congress of the Italian Physical Society, a group of physicists discussed how they might apply their expertise to the study of disarmament to search for potential solutions and offer guidance to both political institutions and civil society.

In November 1981 the Italian physicists took a public collective stand with an appeal to the President of the Republic, Sandro Pertini, urging him to carefully evaluate the current international situation, in particular, "the resumption of the nuclear arms race in Europe". Amaldi, Calogero, and Schaerf were among the six prominent physicists who personally delivered to Pertini the *Appello dei fisici italiani*, signed by 800 scientists.

In the cultural climate of the Appello, the USPID was formed in the autumn 1982 and gave itself a formal statute in April 1983, stating the main "scope of promoting and coordinating those scientific activities which contribute towards stopping the arms race, reducing the risk of war and bringing about a universal, controlled disarmament" (Bernardini et al. 2017, pp. 143–152).

In its statute, USPID claims to be "totally independent from any political party or organization" and to have been established "in response to the actual movement towards nuclear rearmament and the growing risk of nuclear war". The promoters explicitly intended to "fill the gap in the actual national situation", considering Italy as "one of the few Western countries in which research into the questions of peace and disarmament are almost entirely non-existent".

USPID aims at stimulating an awareness among the members of the scientific community of their particular responsibilities with respect to the risks and dangers of nuclear war, also producing original research on a number of topics: new technological developments in nuclear, chemical, bacteriological, and conventional arms; the impact of the new technologies on the arms race and the consequent social responsibilities of scientists; the true risk of nuclear war; the current state of nuclear arsenals; the evolution of the directions and strategic doctrines of the major powers; the conversion of the arms industry; and analyses of proposals for disarmament and the current state of negotiations.

This necessitated the establishment of a cultural space in which markedly diverse positions—from the most radical pacifist to the more moderate—could coexist within a framework of critical dialogue and mutual respect. It was implicitly understood that individuals affiliating with USPID would retain the freedom to pursue their own political objectives, albeit in separate contexts, thereby preventing the association from being subject to instrumentalization.

USPID's original board included physicists Carlo Bernardini (1930–2018), Bertotti, Calogero, Cotta Ramusino (born in 1948), Michelangelo De Maria (1942–2023), Roberto Fieschi (born in 1928), Francesco Lenci (born in 1942), and Schaerf. Although he never had a formal role in USPID, Amaldi gave his support to the association, granting it his remarkable national and international prestige.

The physicists were the "catalyst element" of the group, but the Union soon included other kind of scientists and experts; already at its foundation, USPID counted more than 600 members, distributed among some 25 local sections created at major universities, spread over the whole Italy, and in some research centres.

The major decisional body of USPID is the General Assembly of all associates, which expresses a National Secretary legally representing the Association, with full powers for the normal and extraordinary administration. The subsequent National Secretaries were de Maria (1983), Lenci (1984–1990), Giuseppe Nardulli (1990–1994), Cotta Ramusino (1995–1997), Nicola Cufaro (1998–2009), Diego Latella (2010–2019), and Francesco Forti (2020–present).

The coordination among the activities of the various sections was pivotal, and it turned out to be successful due to the work of the Committee for National Coordination, constituted by the secretaries of the local sections, and of the Scientific Committee, entrusted with the guidance of the Association.

7.1 Educational Activities

Many local sections of USPID have devoted significant efforts to education on armaments and disarmament, targeting various levels, particularly high school and university students.

In the mid-1980s, Franco Duprè organized a seminal lecture series on weaponry at the Department of Physics of the University of Rome "La Sapienza". The inaugural lecture, *The Birth and Evolution of Nuclear Weapons*, was delivered by Edoardo Amaldi. Subsequent lectures featured prominent figures such as Dimitri Batani, Carlo Bernardini, Bertotti, Cotta Ramusino, Ennio De Giorgi, Paolo Farinella (1953–2000), Lenci, Nardulli, Bruno Rossi, Schaerf, and Giorgio Tecce. These presentations addressed a wide range of topics related to science and disarmament, including the Strategic Defense Initiative, nuclear testing, arms control agreements, verification challenges, and conventional defence strategies.

Following the success of this initiative in Rome, similar seminars were organized at other universities—such as those in Milan, Florence, and Bologna. Research institutes of the Italian National Research Council, notably CNUCE and the Institute of Biophysics in Pisa, also hosted such programmes. Despite their success, these efforts remained largely informal.

Recognizing the growing importance of institutional frameworks for promoting a culture of peace, in 1989 Nardulli (1948–2008) was instrumental in establishing the Interdepartmental Research Center on Peace at the University of Bari. Beginning with the 1995–1996 academic year, he also led multiple editions of the Postgraduate Programme in Peace and Disarmament Policies and Technologies, which over time educated several hundred students.

USPID's commitment to peace education significantly influenced the development of academic programmes in the field. Its legacy includes the creation of interdepartmental peace studies programmes and university courses on peace and conflict at the universities of Pisa, Bari, Bologna, Milan, and Padua, among others.

In 1990 and 1992, in collaboration with the Interdepartmental Research Centre "University for Peace" at the University of Bologna and the Defense and Arms Control Studies Program at MIT, USPID organized two editions of the International Summer School on Global Security, Arms Control, and Disarmament, specifically designed for researchers and educators, who were preparing to teach courses or seminars on related subjects.

7.2 *Informing Politicians*

Since its establishment, USPID has consistently pursued the objective of informing governmental institutions and the Italian Parliament with rigorous analyses and critical perspectives on issues of strategic importance. As Lenci aptly remarked, "We, as Scientists for Disarmament, aspired to achieve something unprecedented in Italy: to become a credible and authoritative interlocutor for national institutions".

Avoiding sensationalism, USPID has consistently produced a series of carefully formulated documents, which emerged from internal discussions and consensus building within its Scientific Council, to be submitted to parliamentary committees and other institutional bodies. These contributions have addressed pivotal topics, including ballistic missile defence systems; the risks associated with horizontal nuclear proliferation; geopolitical developments following the 2003 US invasion of Iraq; the continued and unresolved deployment of US tactical nuclear weapons in Europe; and the multifaceted challenges related to Iran's nuclear programme.

The Scientific Council was received by the then President of the Chamber of Deputies, the Honourable Nilde Iotti, and by the then President of the Senate, Senator Francesco Cossiga. On those occasions, USPID presented a comprehensive document entitled *Initiative of American Strategic Defence and Research in Italy*. In November 1985, the Scientific Council delivered a detailed report on the same issue to the Foreign Affairs Committee of the Chamber of Deputies. Later, in September 1991, the Council produced a policy document entitled *Arms Control in the Middle East*, which was submitted to the Defense Committees of both branches of the Italian Parliament.

Scientists were under no illusion that their initiatives would be capable of producing a substantive effect on Italian military policy—which continued to adhere rigidly to NATO's strategic directives—yet they regarded it as an ethical and professional obligation to provide political authorities with rigorously accurate information and carefully considered perspectives on the prospects and imperatives of disarmament.

7.3 International Activities

Riding the wave of success of the first USPID international conference held in Bologna in the spring of 1984—organized by Fieschi under the patronage of then-mayor Renzo Imbeni—the USPID Scientific Council unanimously decided to pursue the organization of a recurring international conference on disarmament and arms control. The aim was to establish a forum for in-depth analysis of the rationale behind strategic choices, openly comparing various positions and strategies, and bringing together experts from all strategic blocs.

In October 1985, the First International Conference of Castiglioncello—a town in the province of Livorno—was held under the sponsorship of the Presidents of the Chamber of Deputies and the Senate. The initiative also received generous support from the town's mayor, Giuseppe Danesin. The conference, focused on nuclear weapons and Europe, was marked by significant international attendance and extensive coverage in the Italian media. It also contributed to establishing USPID as a respected interlocutor within the international community of scholars focused on disarmament and arms control. The conference proceedings—edited by Cotta Ramusino and Lenci—were published by the prestigious journal *Scientia*, as a special issue.

Since then, the Castiglioncello meetings have taken place every 2 years, consistently attracting notable figures from the international political, academic, and scientific arenas. Most foreign participants were from Pugwash and the faculty of ISODARCO, while from Italy important figures showed up over the years in Castiglioncello, including Luigi Anderlini (then President of Archivio Disarmo), Gilberto Bernardini, Daniel Bovet (Nobel Prize in Medicine, 1957), General Carlo Jean (then military advisor to the Italian President of the Republic), parliamentarian Giorgio La Malfa, General Fabio Mini, Federica Mogherini (later High Representative of the European Union for Foreign Affairs), and Giorgio Napolitano (former President of the Republic). On the occasion of the Castiglioncello conferences in 1987 and 1989, composer Luciano Berio offered two magnificent concerts, also featuring the singer Milva.

In 1986 and in 1987 the Academy of Sciences of the Soviet Union organized two conferences in Moscow, to which some members of USPID collaborated and several attended. The first one was dedicated to the Soviet moratorium on nuclear tests and the prospect for a comprehensive nuclear test ban treaty, while the second (with a broader attendance not only of scientists but also of representatives of the international cultural milieu) addressed the more general topic of reductions of nuclear weapons and international peace.

Speaking at the 1986 Forum—in agreement with Amaldi and other scientists—Calogero officially asked the Soviet government for the release of Andrei Sakharov (Nobel Peace Prize laureate in 1975) from confinement. Sakharov was indeed released and, during the 1987 forum, proposed "decoupling" the issue of so-called Euromissiles from that of strategic nuclear forces. This "decoupling" facilitated the signing of the Intermediate-Range Nuclear Forces Treaty (INF Treaty) in 1987, which led to the mutually verified and controlled dismantlement of all Soviet SS-20 and NATO Pershing II and Tomahawk Cruise missiles.

7.4 Communication

In the pre-Internet era, USPID faced considerable challenges in managing communication across its various operational levels—local, national, and international—amid constraints in human and financial resources. The goals of its dissemination activities included promoting and reporting on both local and national initiatives; providing timely updates to peace movements and the media; sharing insights from strategic analyses of global issues; circulating the outcomes of topical research; and distributing specialized materials otherwise difficult to obtain at the local level.

USPID's activities contributed to numerous scholarly publications on arms control, military strategy, environmental issues, and conflict studies. Notable among these are essay collections such as *Nuclear Weapons in Europe* (*Scientia*, 1986) and *Tecnologie avanzate: riarmo o disarmo?* (issued by Dedalo publishing house, 1988), along with the proceedings from the Castiglioncello Conferences, published annually since 1985. Furthermore, starting in 1984, USPID collaborated with the institute Archivio Disarmo to produce Italian translations of the *SIPRI Yearbook on Armaments, Disarmament and International Security*.

USPID-affiliated scholars also contributed to internationally recognized platforms such as *The Bulletin of the Atomic Scientists*. In addition, more accessible articles appeared in the *Science and Armaments* column of *Sapere* magazine (edited from 1983 by Carlo Bernardini), which also regularly published dossiers and assays on topics related to arms control.

From January 1984 to December 1992, USPID published the quarterly *Bollettino USPID*, which typically appeared two to three times per year. Edited by Lenci and astrophysicist Farinella, the *Bollettino*, although rudimentary in format—approximately 200 photocopied pages assembled informally—proved to be a valuable tool. It provided a comprehensive overview of USPID's positions, initiatives, and relevant developments, becoming a critical resource not only for the peace movement but also for specialized journalists and academics.

Reflecting on its editorial approach, Lenci stated: "In the *Bollettino*, I gathered informational material, documents, and contributions to ongoing debates, aiming to present as comprehensive a picture as possible of the various positions and initiatives". Each issue featured announcements, curated documents, and information derived from scientific journals, conference presentations, and reports from international networks—offering a diverse repository of thought-provoking materials for USPID members.

Production was carried out voluntarily by USPID members, supported by conscientious objectors fulfilling their civil service in lieu of mandatory military duty, pursuant to an agreement with the Italian Ministry of Defence.

Unsurprisingly, the advent of the Web rendered the *Bollettino USPID* obsolete. Its publication ceased in 1992, coinciding with the emergence of Mosaic, the first widely used Web browser, in 1993. Since then, the Association has transitioned its communication to its official website.

The final 2 years of the *Bollettino*, under Farinella's editorship, addressed critical topics such as NATO's transformation, military conscription and conscientious objection, and hazardous space activities. Notably, it also supported a campaign on behalf of Mordechai Vanunu, the Israeli nuclear technician who in 1986 revealed Israel's clandestine nuclear weapons programme to the British press. Subsequently abducted in Italy by Mossad and subjected to a closed-door trial in Israel, Vanunu was sentenced to 18 years in prison, including 11 in solitary confinement. Farinella's passionate advocacy on Vanunu's behalf stemmed solely from a principled defence of human rights and solidarity with Vanunu's courageous whistleblowing.

7.5 *After the End of the Cold War*

The conclusion of the Cold War, with the substantial reshaping of the political geography, marked a significant shift in global priorities, leading to a decline in public and academic interest in issues related to disarmament, particularly nuclear disarmament.

Simultaneously, emerging conflicts in Yugoslavia, Africa, and the Middle East demanded urgent attention from peace movements, particularly concerning the humanitarian consequences of conventional weapons, including anti-personnel mines. Concurrently, grassroots movements increasingly prioritized environmental concerns, focusing on issues such as acid rain, the greenhouse effect, ozone layer depletion, the hazardous disposal of waste, and the irresponsible exploitation of energy resources.

These new challenges required expertise distinct from the technical competencies traditionally offered by the hard sciences, thereby diminishing the relevance of one of USPID's core areas of action. Consequently, scientific engagement with USPID waned; by 1992, the organization had contracted to only 12 active local sections, and by 2025, only 5 remained (Bari, Bologna, Genoa, Pisa, and Trento).

During this period, USPID faced a profound crisis of identity and purpose, prompting an internal debate regarding its future orientation in the post-Cold War context. In the March 1990 issue of the *Bollettino*, Farinella initiated a discussion entitled *USPID: What Future?*, advocating for a transformation of the association into a body less narrowly focused on technical expertise and more attuned to broader social and political issues, as well as more responsive to the concerns of pacifist and environmentalist movements. Contributions from Bertotti and Latella, who presented differing perspectives, enriched the debate within the same issue.

Ultimately, the discussion concluded with a reaffirmation of USPID's identity as an association of scientists. Despite notable progress in the field of disarmament, numerous complex and unresolved issues remained. Consequently, one of the greatest challenges was maintaining both expert and public engagement with the persistent, though increasingly intangible, nuclear threat.

References

Angela P, Rubbia C (1992) Edoardo Amaldi. Scienziato e cittadino d'Europa. Leonardo Periodici, Milano

Bernardini C et al (2017) L'USPID. In: Greco P (ed) Fisica per la pace. Tra scienza e impegno civile. Carocci, Rome

Bone AG (ed) (2003) The collected papers of Bertrand Russell. Volume 28: Man's peril, 1954–55. Routledge, London

Clavarino L (2017) "Many countries will have the bomb: there will be hell". Edoardo Amaldi and the Italian physicists committed to disarmament, arms control and détente. In: Bini E, Londero I (eds) Nuclear Italy. An international history of Italian nuclear policies during the cold war. EUT edizioni, Trieste, pp 245–257

Clavarino L (2021) Italian physicists and the bomb: Edoardo Amaldi's network for arms control and peace during the cold war. J Contemp Hist 56(3):665–692

Clavarino L (2025) Italian epistemic communities in the arms control field. The case of USPID. In: Karamouzi E, Brunet L-A (eds) Beyond the Euromissiles: global histories of anti-nuclear activism. Bergahn, Oxford, pp 74–97

Evangelista M (1999) Unarmed forces. Cornell University Press, Ithaca

Foradori P et al (2017) Isodarco as an epistemic community. In Foradori P et al.(eds), Arms control and disarmament: 50 years of experience in nuclear education. Palgrave, London

Foradori P, Giacomello G (2018) Fighting nuclear proliferation through education. The remarkable story of ISODARCO. Modern Italy 23(3):331–344

Kraft A et al (2018) The Pugwash conferences and the global cold war: scientists, transnational networks, and the complexity of nuclear histories. J Cold War Studies Special Issue 20(1):1–240

Medeiros ES (2007) Reluctant restraint: the evolution of China's nonproliferation policies and practices in 1980–2004. Stanford University Press, Stanford

Moro R (2017) Anti-nuclear movements in 1980s Italy (1979–1984). In: Bini E, Londero I (eds) Nuclear Italy, nuclear Italy. An international history of Italian nuclear policies during the cold war. EUT edizioni, Trieste, pp 199–211

Nuti L (2015) The nuclear debate in Italian politics in the late 1970s and the early 1980s. In: Nuti L et al (eds) The Euromissile crisis and the end of the cold war. Stanford University Press, Stanford

Price M (1995) Roots of dissent: the Chicago met lab and the origins of the Franck report. Isis 86(2):222–244

Rotblat J (1962) History of the Pugwash conferences. Taylor and Francis, London

Rotblat J, Pascolini A (1984) The arms race at a time of decision. Macmillan, London

Russell B (1969) The autobiography of Bertrand Russell 1944–1969. 3 vols. George Allen and Unwin, London

Schaerf C (2017) ISODARCO, Scuola internazionale sul disarmo e la ricerca sui conflitti. In: Greco P (ed) Fisica per la pace. Tra scienza e impegno civile. Carocci, Rome, pp 175–191

Schweber SS (2000) In the shadow of the bomb: Oppenheimer, Bethe, and the moral responsibility of the scientist. Princeton University Press, Princeton

Smith AK (1965) A peril and a Hope: the scientists' movement in America: 1945–47. Chicago University Press, Chicago

The Tension of the Italian Constitutional Pacifist Principle in the Wake of the War in Ukraine

Giovanni Cavaggion

1 Introduction: Article 11 of the Italian Constitution Between the "Internationalist" and "Pacifist" Interpretations

Article 11 of the Italian Constitution enshrines the so-called "pacifist clause", according to which "Italy repudiates war as an instrument of aggression against the freedom of other peoples and as a means for the settlement of international disputes". The second part of the same article enshrines the so-called "internationalist clause", according to which "Italy agrees, on conditions of equality with other States, to the limitations of sovereignty that may be necessary to a world order ensuring peace and justice among the Nations; Italy promotes and encourages international organizations furthering such ends". The two parts of article 11 shall be understood as two deeply intertwined clauses, as confirmed by the fact that they are part of a single sentence, separated by just a semicolon (and not by a full stop). Consequently, the constitutional repudiation of war should always be interpreted in the light of Italy's commitment to developing constructive international relations through the establishment of specific supranational organizations vested with the power of preserving and promoting peace.[1]

Scholars have historically argued, over the years, about the actual meaning and scope of article 11, especially with regard to the constitutional pacifist clause. While

[1] On the origins and evolution of article 11 of the Italian Constitution see: Cartabia and Chieffi (2006), Cassese (1975) and Cavino and Malvicini (2023).

G. Cavaggion (✉)
University of Milan, Milan, Italy
e-mail: giovanni.cavaggion@unimi.it

G. Cavaggion (ed.), *The 'Pacifist Principle' in the Italian and Japanese Constitutions in the Wake of the War in Ukraine*,
https://doi.org/10.1007/978-3-032-23108-6_6

the majority of scholars believe that article 11 does not impose a radical renunciation of every form of the use of force in international relations,[2] others have claimed that it prescribes that any form of "war" or "violence" that does not involve directly (and exclusively) the defence of the homeland (the defence of the Italian territory) should be considered unconstitutional.[3]

Despite this long-standing doctrinal debate, it is hard to dispute that from a textual (the way in which the constitutional text was framed), theoretical (the way in which the pacifist clause has been interpreted by the majority of scholars), and practical (the way in which the pacifist clause has been interpreted by constitutional bodies such as Parliament, the Government, the President of the Republic, and other institutional actors such as political parties) perspective, as Massimo Cavino and Massimiliano Malvicini convincingly argued in their chapter,[4] article 11 has not been regarded, traditionally, as a truly "pacifist" principle, at least in the sense in which the concept of "pacifism" is commonly understood in common parlance (the complete refusal of every kind of violence).

This is evident, as a matter of fact, if one compares the text of article 11 with that of article 9 of the Japanese Constitution. While the latter provides for a clear renunciation of every form of the use of force, including for defensive aims[5] (and notwithstanding the divergence between this constitutional provision and its implementation by political and institutional actors[6]) the former contains an express repudiation of (only) "offensive wars" (war as an instrument of aggression against the freedom of other peoples), leaving the field open to interpretations when it comes to the constitutionality of other kinds of (defensive) use of force in international relations. Indeed, from a philosophical perspective, one could argue that while article 9 of the Japanese Constitution represents a case of positivization (translation into legally binding rules) of the "pacifist theory" of war, under which war is never justified or justifiable and always immoral (and, consequently, illegal), article 11 of the Italian Constitution represents a case of positivization of the "just war" theory, under which war could (and should) be justified, and regarded as moral (and, consequently, legal), in some specific cases and under some given conditions.[7]

In light of this framework, one could understandably wonder why we refer to article 11 of the Italian Constitution as a "pacifist" clause: after all, would it not be

---

[2] See, *ex multis*, Cartabia and Chieffi (2006), Cavino and Malvicini (2023), Benvenuti (2010), Rigano (2002), de Vergottini (1999), Baldassarre (2002), Cavino (1999), Rescigno (1999), Ferrari (1970), Cassese (1986), Motzo (1999), Arangio Ruiz (1975), Lattanzi (1997), and Pedrazzi (2001).

[3] See, *ex multis*, Allegretti (1991), Bettinelli (1992), Gianformaggio (1999), Ferrajoli (2002), Cecchetti (1993).

[4] See Cavino and Malvicini (2025).

[5] On article 9 of the Japanese Constitution and its interpretation see Kimijima (2010).

[6] On the divergence between the text of article 9 and the actual policies adopted by Japanese governments through the years, see Martin (2025), Bertolini (2025), Frattolillo (2025) Zappa (2025), and Beer (1998).

[7] See Bistagnino (2025).

contradictory to define as "pacifist" a clause that permits recourse to violence, or even war, albeit in a limited capacity?

The reason for this apparent contradiction lies, as I will try to argue, in the prescriptive and performative value of the "-ist" suffix applied to the value of "peace", which is a common feature, in the Italian legal system, when it comes to the definition of fundamental constitutional principles.[8] Fundamental principles outline an objective that the State (and all its articulations) must strive to reach, and this is the reason why, in the Italian constitutional system, we have a personalist, a pluralist, and a solidarist principle (article 2 of the Constitution), an egalitarianist principle (article 3 of the Constitution), a labourist principle (article 4 of the Constitution), an autonomist principle (article 5 of the Constitution), a secularist principle (articles 7 and 8 of the Constitution), an environmentalist principle (article 9 of the Constitution), and so on.

Therefore, when we refer to the first part of article 11 as to the "pacifist principle" or "pacifist clause", what we truly mean is that the Constitution requires that Italy strives to build a world in which international relations do not envision the use of violence (an international order built upon the fundamental value of "peace") and that it shall actively pursue this goal through the activities of its constitutional bodies.[9] This does not automatically mean, however, that there cannot be some specific instances in which, in order to achieve this ultimate objective, it becomes necessary to resort to non-peaceful means, especially when this is allowed by international law. In fact, the second clause of article 11 (the "internationalist clause") expressly contextualizes Italy's commitment to peace in the vaster framework of the rules that govern the relations between sovereign States and, more specifically, within the framework of the United Nations and their Charter.

It is clear, then, that Italy's role in the international landscape is shaped by the undying tension between these two "souls" of article 11: on the one end the commitment to peace and the repudiation of war as an instrument to threaten the freedom of other peoples and on the other hand the deference of national sovereignty to international law and supranational organizations when it comes to decisions on the resolution of international disputes. The precarious balance between these two souls of article 11 have historically outlined the (narrow) path in which the use of force (or even resorting to "war") has been regarded as legal according to the Italian Constitution.[10] A balance that, however, has been shaken to its core by the Russian invasion of Ukraine in 2022.

---

[8] See Luther (2002).

[9] See, *ex multis*, Bon Valsassina (1955) and Cassese (1975).

[10] For a comprehensive analysis of the cases in which Italy was involved in "wars" since the entry into force of the Constitution of 1948 see Cavino and Malvicini (2023).

2 The Unique Features of the War in Ukraine and the Measures Undertaken by Italy to Support the Ukrainian War of Defence

The Russian invasion of Ukraine has instantly revamped the latent doctrinal debate on the interpretation and scope of the Italian constitutional pacifist principle and the innate tension between the two souls of article 11. As a matter of fact, the unique features of this new conflict have greatly exacerbated this tension, to the point that, by looking at the doctrinal and political arguments of the last three years, it seems now almost impossible to reconcile the positions of those that would prioritize the pacifist soul of article 11 with the positions of those that would prioritize its internationalist soul instead.

The "uniqueness" of the war in Ukraine lays, I would argue, in at least four different factors.

Firstly, in the case of the war in Ukraine, the organizations ideally vested with the power of determining whether a "war" (or, rather, an instance of the use of force in international relations) is legal according to the rules of general international law (and, in particular, the United Nations) were unable to take any conclusive action (unlike in previous occasions, such as, e.g. the crises in Bosnia, in Kuwait, in Somalia, in Afghanistan, or in Libya).[11] The UN Security Council was (and still is) incapable of adopting a resolution condemning the Russian invasion and affirming the legality of the Ukrainian war of defence, due to the veto power recognized to Russia (and, for that matter, to China). This does not mean, of course, that the Russian invasion is not illegal under the fundamental principles of international law, but the lack of a specific binding act that clarifies the legal framework (by applying the general law to the specific case at hand) provides for a degree of uncertainty that can be leveraged in order to argue that there is no legal basis, according to international law, for third States to assist Ukraine in its defensive effort.

Secondly, the war in Ukraine is a war in which Italy did not choose to limit its involvement in the same way it did in previous cases in which the international legal context was similarly unclear due to the lack of a formal resolution by the UN Security Council (as, e.g. for the war in Iraq of 2003 or, to a lesser extent, the war in Libya of 2011). As a matter of fact, in previous similar cases (with the noticeable exception of the war in Kosovo in 1998), the Italian Government has often argued that, in the absence of a UN resolution authorizing the use of force, in order to comply with the pacifist clause enshrined in article 11 of the Constitution, Italy would have to limit its role, for example, by supplying only "non-lethal" equipment, carrying out only logistic and reconnaissance actions, or participating only in the "peacekeeping" and policing operations necessary once the actual "war" has ended.

Thirdly, the war in Ukraine is fought in the heart of the European continent and therefore incredibly close to the borders of the so-called "Western world" (or

[11] And notwithstanding the resolutions condemning the aggression adopted by the General Assembly of the United Nations, which, due to the organization's architecture, are deprived of a real effectiveness.

liberal-democratic world). While it is true that this is not the first war in Europe after the end of War World II, it is equally true that previous wars in the second half of the twentieth century were (or, at least, were perceived as) mainly wars of secession or civil wars (such as, for example, the wars in the Balkans).

Lastly, and more importantly, the war in Ukraine is a "total war": a war between two sovereign States (not between national groups or factions, not a civil war, not a war of secession, not a war on terror, not a regime change, not a peacekeeping mission, etc.), in which the aggressor attacks the aggressed in order to invade, conquer, and annex its territory and its people,[12] and hence does not limit the scope of the aggression to military objectives but openly targets civilian resources and infrastructures.[13] As a matter of fact, it could be maintained that the war in Ukraine is precisely the kind of "war" that was known by the Framers of the Italian Constitution (that had directly experienced the "total wars" of World War I and World War II) and therefore that this is exactly the kind of "war" that the members of the Constituent Assembly had in mind, and wanted to "repudiate", in 1948, when they were drafting article 11 and the pacifist clause. This is, as I will argue, paramount in understanding the constitutional perimeter that article 11 designs for Italy's involvement in the conflict.

In the face of a war with such unprecedented characteristics, in the February of 2022 the Italian Government's initial reaction was to issue an emergency decree having the force of law under article 77 of the Constitution (law decree no. 14/2022). The decree authorized the transfer to the Ukrainian Government (free of charge) of "non-lethal" military equipment and other materials "of protection".

A subsequent emergency decree (law decree no. 16/2022), issued by the Government just three days later, authorized the transfer to the Ukrainian Government (free of charge) of military instruments, materials, and other equipment, hence removing the "non-lethal" and "of protection" requirements, effectively greenlighting the transfer of offensive and lethal weaponry. The list of the specific weapons, materials, and equipment to be transferred was delegated to one or more classified governmental decrees, issued by the Ministry of Defence.[14]

The emergency decrees include *ad hoc* clauses that specifically derogate to the provisions of the Military Code and of the law on the exportation of weapons (law no. 185/1990) in order to expedite the transfers from a procedural perspective. At any rate, the relevant national legislative framework already allowed the supply of weapons to a third State in conformity with article 51 of the UN Charter, in cases in which said State is exercising its right to self-defence against an unjust aggression.[15]

[12] See Bilancia (2024) and Benvenuti (2022) pp. 21 ff.

[13] On the concept of "total war", see Chickering and Förster (2003). On the war in Ukraine of 2022 as a "total war", see Karlin (2024).

[14] For an in-depth analysis of the measures adopted by the Italian Government (and other constitutional bodies) and their criticalities, see Benvenuti (2022) pp. 33 ff.

[15] For the analysis of the relevant international and national legislative framework with regard to the transfer of weapons to a third State, see Pietrobon (2023).

In the following months, additional law decrees repeatedly extended the deadline for the transfers, in light of the continuation of the war.

All of the aforementioned decrees have been adopted within the larger collective policy framework of the European Union, with particular regard to the European Peace Facility established with Council Decision (CFSP) 2021/509 of 22 March 2021, and, more importantly, of NATO (under the leadership of the United States and President Biden that strongly advocated in favour of supporting Ukraine).[16]

Given this legislative state of the art, it can be safely stated that Italy has become a party of the Ukrainian conflict, at least since the adoption of law decree no. 16/2022.[17] While some scholars notoriously tried to develop a number of intermediate statuses in between "neutrality" and "belligerency" (such as, for example, "non-belligerency" or "qualified neutrality"),[18] according to the generally recognized provisions of international law, supplying weapons and other forms of assistance to one (and only one) of the parties of a conflict amounts to an involvement (although indirect) in the conflict itself.[19]

3 The Debate on the Scope and Interpretation of the Constitutional Pacifist Clause in the Wake of the War in Ukraine

In the wake of the Russian invasion, a non-negligible part of scholars has claimed that the decision of the Italian Government to support Ukraine's defensive effort by supplying lethal (offensive) weapons is actually incompatible with the pacifist clause enshrined in article 11, and therefore the emergency decrees (and other acts) adopted to this end should be considered unconstitutional. This position has been supported by resorting to a number of different arguments that share, nonetheless, a common hermeneutical bedrock.

According to a first group of scholars, the unconstitutionality of the Italian assistance to Ukraine derives precisely from the systemic interpretation of the two parts of article 11 (the pacifist and internationalist principles). According to this position, the two clauses, if considered as an ensemble, demand that the resolution to the conflict is pursued exclusively through those international organizations that are vested with the task of ensuring peace among nations (the organizations in which Italy participates, on conditions of equality with other States, by accepting the limitations of sovereignty necessary to a world order ensuring peace and justice). This would mean, in turn, that article 11 demands that the solution for the Ukrainian

[16] For an analysis of said framework see Bilancia (2024).

[17] See Cavino and Malvicini (2023).

[18] See, e.g. de Vergottini (2024).

[19] With specific regard to the war in Ukraine, see Volpi (2022), pp. XII ff., Cavino (2023), and Latino (2024) pp. 706 ff.

crisis is pursued through the system of the United Nations, while symmetrically prohibiting that said solution is pursued through NATO, as NATO is (allegedly) not an organization aimed at ensuring peace.[20]

Other scholars have argued that the Italian involvement in the war is illegal due to the absence, in the Italian constitutional system, of a provision that allows the Government to supply weapons and other forms of assistance to Ukraine. According to this interpretation, article 11, as well as the other constitutional clauses that regulate war (articles 52, 87, 78, and 60), concern exclusively wars aimed at the defence of the Italian Republic and do not provide a clear legal basis to assist a third State involved in a war that does not directly affect Italy's territory. Consequently, a legal basis for the assistance to Ukraine shall be sought outside of the perimeter of the national legal system and, more precisely, in the provisions of international (general and conventional) law. However, these provisions would be, on their own account, incompatible with the pacifist clause enshrined in article 11 and as such should be disregarded.[21]

Other scholars argued that, even notwithstanding the (alleged) contrast between the national Constitution and the rules of international law that would allow Italy to aid a third State involved in a war, the assistance to Ukraine would still be unconstitutional due to the lack of a resolution by the UN Security Council authorizing the use of force in Ukraine's defence and/or the lack of an international treaty (bilateral or multilateral) of collective defence under which Italy would be required to protect Ukraine in the event of an aggression (Ukraine is not a member of NATO or the European Union[22]). According to this interpretation, article 11 demands that Italy always remains neutral, except for cases in which the constitutional pacifist clause is "overwritten" by a specific obligation undertaken through the ratification of an international treaty. However, as this is not the case for the Ukrainian crisis, the decision on whether to provide support should be taken exclusively on the basis of article 11, which prohibits, as a general rule, Italy's involvement in the wars of third countries.[23]

Lastly, some scholars have embraced a radical interpretation of article 11, under which any stance that is not one of complete neutrality between the two belligerent parties (and therefore any form of military assistance to Ukraine) should be regarded as unconstitutional *per se*. This radical hermeneutical position, which would frame the Italian approach to peace and war in a way that strongly resembles the originally intended meaning of article 9 of the Japanese Constitution,[24] is justified by its proponents on the basis of (i) a systemic interpretation of article 11 in combination with article 52 of the Constitution, which imposes the "sacred duty" to "defend the

---

[20] This thesis was supported, e.g. by Azzariti (2022a), Caterina et al. (2022), Bucci (2022) pp. 182 ff., and Villone (2022a).

[21] This thesis was supported, e.g. by Azzariti (2022b), Algostino (2022) pp. 77 ff., Apostoli (2022) pp. 151 ff., and Ciervo (2022).

[22] On the possible accession of Ukraine to the European Union, see Scuto (2025).

[23] This thesis was supported, e.g. by Azzariti (2022b), De Fiores (2022) pp. 41 ff., Algostino (2022) pp. 77 ff., and Volpi (2022).

[24] On the intended meaning of article 9 of the Japanese Constitution, see Kimijima (2025).

homeland" upon all Italian citizens, and (ii) an originalist interpretation of article 11, in the light of the declarations of some of the Italian Framers in the proceedings of the Constituent Assembly. According to this interpretation, the only form of "war" that is not categorically prohibited by article 11 is the war for the defence of the territory of the Italian Republic (the "homeland") when it is the object of a direct threat (a foreign invasion or aggression). Any other form of belligerency or interference in a foreign war (a war that does not directly involve the Italian land), including providing weapons to a third State under attack, should be regarded as illegal.[25] Under this perspective, supplying weapons to Ukraine, thus enhancing its defensive capabilities and delaying Russia's victory, while becoming involved in the conflict, ultimately ends up prolonging the duration of the war and escalating its magnitude and its disruptive effects on the involved societies and populations, effectively undermining the objective of "peace" in international relations prescribed by article 11.

On the opposite side of the doctrinal spectrum, a different group of scholars argued in favour of the compatibility of the support that Italy provides to Ukraine with the pacifist clause of article 11, in particular, by leveraging its interpretation in combination with article 10 of the Constitution, which enshrines the clause of automatic adaptation of the national legal system to the fundamental principles of general international law ("The Italian legal system conforms to the generally recognised principles of international law").

These positions move from the premise that article 11 expressly repudiates only wars "of aggression", while article 52 imposes only wars "of defence of the homeland". They argue that in between these two extremes—one kind of "war" that is unequivocally prohibited and unconstitutional and one kind of "war" that is unequivocally required and constitutional—there exists an "empty space", deliberately designed by the Framers to give the Constitution the flexibility needed to provide Italy with a certain margin of political discretion in responding to international crises.[26] This "constitutional empty space" shall be navigated, in compliance with article 10, by using the rules of international law (general and conventional) as a compass, in order to distinguish between the cases in which a "war" (or other forms of use of violence in international relations) is prohibited (illegal) and cases in which the decision on whether to engage in activities of belligerency can be legally taken through the mechanisms of representative democracy. Therefore, according to these theories, article 11, and the Italian Constitution's approach to war and peace, should be completed (and complemented) by deferring to international law.[27]

It must be stressed that, in the case at hand, the legality of the Ukrainian war of resistance to the Russian invasion seems undisputable, with respect to both general and conventional international law. The Russian invasion of 2022 is evidently an

[25] This thesis was supported, e.g. by Azzariti (2022c), Algostino (2022), Caterina, Giannelli, and Siciliano (2022), Ainis (2022), De Fiores (2022), and Apostoli (2022).

[26] See Benvenuti (2022) p. 31.

[27] See Rossi (2022) and Latino (2024).

attack against the territorial integrity and the independence of a sovereign State, which is unequivocally prohibited by the general principles of international law and by article 51 of the United Nations Charter. As a matter of fact, article 51 is widely regarded as a conventional provision that codifies a norm belonging to the so-called *ius cogens* (the peremptory norms of international law)[28] and recognizes the inherent right of individual or collective self-defence if an armed attack occurs against a member State of the United Nations, until the Security Council has taken the measures necessary to maintain international peace and security, under the condition that the actions taken by the State in the exercise of this right are immediately reported to the Council itself.

Therefore, given that (i) supporting a State that is subject to an unjust aggression is undoubtedly permitted by the generally recognized norms of international law and that (ii) the Italian legal system conforms to the generally recognized principles of international law, (iii) providing weapons to Ukraine in order to resist Russia's invasion should be regarded as legal and compatible with article 11, if interpreted in the light of the clause of automatic adaptation to international law enshrined in article 10.[29]

It is precisely the manifest legality of the Ukrainian war of self-defence (and the manifest illegality of the Russian war of aggression), then, that ultimately brought the tension between the two souls of article 11 (and between the aforementioned opposing scholarly and political arguments) to its breaking point.

As a matter of fact, if the legality of the Ukrainian resistance according to international law is non-debatable, the only way to retain a radical pacifist stance and maintain that supporting Ukraine is prohibited by the constitutional pacifist clause is to argue that there is a divergence (an antinomy) between international law and article 11 of the Italian Constitution. Following this line of reasoning, article 11 and the pacifist clause should be regarded as a "counter-limit" to the general rule of the primacy of international law on national law,[30] and they would serve as a "brake" to the clause of automatic adaptation to the principles of general international law, thus preventing international law from deploying its effects in the Italian legal system in all instances in which it would allow Italy to take part into a war that is not a war of self-defence *stricto sensu* (a war for the defence of the homeland). This means, in other words, that resorting to the international clause enshrined in article 10 to complement (or, rather, to "correct") the scope of article 11 should be considered unconstitutional.

---

[28] See the decision of the ICJ in the Nicaragua Case. Nicaragua v. United States of America, Merits, ICJ, Judgment of 27 June 1986.

[29] This thesis was supported, e.g. by Benvenuti (2022), Cavino and Malvicini (2023), de Vergottini (2024), Flick (2022), Rossi (2022), Ventura and Pupo (2022) pp. 13 ff., Celotto (2022), De Minico (2023), Villone (2022b), Latino (2024), and Bilancia (2024).

[30] The primacy of international (and European) law on national law is prescribed, in the Italian legal system, by articles 10, 11, and 117 paragraph 1 of the Constitution, as interpreted by the Constitutional Court.

This is, ultimately, the hermeneutical position on which all of the "pacifist" arguments ended up converging as the war in Ukraine (and the scholarly debate) raged on, and the nature (and illegality) of the Russian aggression as a "total war" (a war for the conquest of the enemy's land and for the subjugation of its people) became more and more evident.[31]

4 Constitutional Law, and Not (Only) International Law, as the Legal Basis for the Italian Support to Ukraine

The unique features of the war in Ukraine (and especially the seemingly undisputable legality of the Ukrainian defensive effort) have generated a deep polarization of the debate, by pushing scholars and political and institutional actors on two opposite positions, effectively turning the internal (and innate) tension between the two souls of article 11 into a fully fledged antinomy,[32] centred on two antipodes: on the one hand a "radical pacifist" (or "egoistic") interpretation and on the other hand an "internationalist" (or "pragmatic") interpretation.

Those who argue against the legality of providing weapons (and other forms of assistance) to Ukraine ultimately ended up proposing an "egoistic" interpretation of the pacifist clause enshrined in article 11 of the Italian Constitution, in the sense that Italy would be permitted to resort to force only for its own sake and for its own defence, and consequently the only type of "war" not repudiated by the Constitution would be that undertaken for the defence of the homeland.[33] This would mean that Italy is prohibited from participating in the war of defence of another State and that when a foreign State is facing an unjust war of aggression (the very same "war" that is "repudiated" by the pacifist clause), Italy should remain inert (completely neutral), regardless of the reasons and actions of the belligerent parties (including the status of aggressor and aggressed). International law provisions that would make Italy abandon this stance of total neutrality should be considered incompatible with the national Constitution and, therefore, disregarded.

Conversely, those that argue in favour of the constitutional compatibility of Italy's support to Ukraine embrace an "internationalist" interpretation of article 11, under which the constitutional pacifist clause should be read in the light of the rules of general and conventional international law, with the consequence that Italy would be allowed to become involved in a conflict in order to support a foreign State that is legally defending itself from an unjust attack. In this perspective, international law would serve as the "judge" of the legality (or illegality) of any given war, and the constitutionality of Italy's intervention would be entirely dependent on its

[31] See, e.g. Algostino (2022), Apostoli (2022), De Fiores (2022), Ciervo (2022), and Caterina, Giannelli and Siciliano (2022).

[32] See Benvenuti (2022) pp. 20 ff.

[33] See, e.g. Caterina et al. (2022), Algostino (2022), Azzariti (2022c), De Fiores (2022), Ainis (2022), and Apostoli (2022).

compatibility with international provisions regulating warfare and/or the deliberations of international organizations such as the UN.

In light of this complex legislative and doctrinal context, I would argue that the "radical pacifist" arguments are correct in their premise: that it is not necessarily appropriate to refer (or, rather, defer) exclusively to international law when assessing the compatibility (or incompatibility) of Italy's involvement in "wars" (or other kinds of military operations) with article 11 of the Constitution (the constitutional pacifist clause). It seems to me that such an extensive deferral would ultimately deprive constitutional law of its normative nature, by making it entirely dependent on international law for the regulation of war and peace. An international law that, one might add, started to display its painstakingly evident shortcomings and its inability to effectively regulate States' behaviours in the global disorder of our time[34] precisely in the wake of the Russian invasion of Ukraine, in a downward spiral that continued with the war in Gaza in 2023, the conflict in Kashmir in 2025, and the wars in Iran in 2025 and 2026.

It is precisely in this era of profound disorder in international law and international relations, then, that one cannot help but wonder whether the legal basis for Italy's support to Ukraine (and for similar forms of support to foreign countries that are victim of an unjust aggression) might perhaps originate directly from the Constitution, rather than indirectly from international law, as the "classical" internationalist interpretations of article 11 would suggest.[35]

The conflict in Ukraine, due to its unique features, allows constitutional scholars to explore this possibility, as the heavy polarization of the doctrinal and political debate that it has generated revealed the (possible) underlying antinomies between constitutional and international law. In fact, to solve these antinomies, it becomes necessary to define the concept of "war" or, more specifically, the concept of "war" that is implied by article 11, as advocates of the "radical pacifist" interpretation argue that the "war" that is repudiated by the Constitution of 1948 is "every war that is not a war of defence of the homeland", while advocates of the "internationalist" interpretation argue that in order to define the "war" that is repudiated by the Constitution (and, symmetrically, the ones that are not), we should look at the rules of international law.

I would contend that, while it is indeed possible to infer an ontologically independent definition of "illegal war" directly from the Constitution, without relying on external legal systems (such as general or conventional international law), if one looks at article 11 in a systemic perspective, the resulting definition sharply diverges from that proposed by the radical pacifist interpretations and, specifically, does not coincide with that of "every war that is not a war for the defence of Italy's territory".

In order to outline a constitutional definition of "illegal war", it is necessary to move from the premise that, as already mentioned, there is at least one kind of "war" that is unmistakenly and unequivocally repudiated by article 11: the "war" as

---

[34] See Graziano (2024).

[35] See Cartabia and Chieffi (2006), Rescigno (1999), Baldassarre (2002), and Cavino (1999).

the Framers of 1948 had experienced it, the "total war", the war of invasion, of conquest, and of annexation of the enemy's territory and of its people. Indeed, the fact that at least this specific kind of "war" is undoubtedly repudiated by article 11 is the only common ground between the radical pacifist and internationalist interpretations of the Italian pacifist clause.

It cannot be denied, then, that the war in Ukraine possesses all of the features of the "war" repudiated by article 11, as it is undeniable that Russia aims at annexing at least part of (if not all) the Ukrainian territory (as proved by the territorial demands that have been advanced by the Russian Government in the peace negotiations that have been promoted with difficulty by the United States starting in 2025) and that Russia is waging a "total war" (a war that involves civilian objectives, infrastructures and the population of the enemy as a whole, and that aims at subjugating the enemy's Government and people by imposing Russia's control over them).

Article 11 would therefore certainly prohibit Italy from waging such a war and would authorize it to defend itself against such a war, but what does it prescribe, instead, when the same kind of war is waged by a foreign State, not against Italy but against a third country?

In this perspective, it must be noted that article 11 states that Italy "repudiates" war, and not that it "renounces" it, as it is the case, for example, for article 9 of the Japanese Constitution.[36] While it is true that a "repudiation" certainly implies a "renunciation", it is equally true that such a "renunciation" does not exhaust the content of article 11, as a "repudiation" also demands a "condemnation". As a matter of fact, many of the Framers of the Constitution of 1948 conceived article 11 as a form of "patriation" of the Kellogg-Briand Pact of 1928 (the Pact of Paris) that famously provided that "The High Contracting Parties solemnly declare in the names of their respective peoples that they *condemn* recourse to war for the solution of international controversies and *renounce* it as an instrument of national policy in their relations with one another".[37] Moreover, it is hard to overlook the fact that the Italian Constituent Assembly (even though some of its members argued in favour of a radical pacifist stance) expressly rejected, with a large majority, the so-called "Cairo amendment", which proposed to include a clause of "perpetual neutrality" (renunciation of every war that is not a war of defence of the homeland) in the text of the Constitution,[38] thus indicating that they thought that an involvement in foreign wars (a "non-neutral" stance) could be, at least in some cases, regarded as legal.

So the Italian Republic "renounces" and "condemns" (it "repudiates") war, but why is that? I am not convinced that the only reason is that war is prohibited by international law. The reason why Italy repudiates war is, I would argue, that war is

---

[36] See Kimijima (2010) and Kimijima (2025).

[37] See, e.g. the statements by Meuccio Ruini, in the proceedings of the Italian Constituent Assembly of 24 March 1947.

[38] See the proceedings of the Italian Constituent Assembly of 22 May 1947.

antithetical to the entire system of values on which the Constitution of 1948 was founded. It is the negation of the very cornerstone of the Italian "constitutional covenant": the "democratic method"[39] that was used to frame the Constitution, which is dialogical, non-violent, pluralistic, and compromising, and that makes it possible to find a peaceful (non-violent) synthesis between conflicting political, social, economic, and cultural visions of the world.[40]

If that is the case, the pacifist clause enshrined in article 11 must unfold its normative effects in two different dimensions. In a negative-internal dimension, the pacifist clause serves as a limit to the State's power to wage war or use violence in international relations. Italy repudiates "total war", "war of conquest", and "war of aggression", as it is the negation of the Italian fundamental constitutional values, and therefore it renounces using it as an instrument to offend the freedom of other peoples and as a means for the settlement of international disputes. In a positive-external dimension, the pacifist clause creates an obligation that constrains Italy's conduct in international relations: the obligation to (actively) condemn the resort, by other States, to the same kind of "war" that Italy renounces and, therefore, to a violent and anti-democratic course of action that is radically incompatible with the method for the resolution of conflicts that the Italian fundamental values prescribe. Differently put, the constitutional pacifist clause informs Italy's international behaviour not only when it comes to the actions that it might (and might not) take but also when it comes to the actions that it must regard as unacceptable from other States.

Moreover, if the pacifist clause is to be interpreted within the wider framework of the other fundamental constitutional values, the "egoistic" interpretations of article 11 (according to which Italy can and should resort to the use of force exclusively to protect itself and its territory but cannot use it to defend a third State that is subject to an unjust war of aggression) also fail to take into account the solidarist principle enshrined in article 2 of the Italian Constitution. In fact, if the pacifist principle and the solidarist principle are considered in a systemic perspective, together with the internationalist principle, it must follow that the fundamental value of solidarity also applies in the external dimension (to international relations), and that the Constitution prescribes (at least) a certain degree of solidarity between Italy and its people on the one hand and the other States and peoples of the world on the other.[41]

If this is the case then: (i) Italy clearly repudiates (renounces and condemns) "war" ("total war", "war of conquest", "war of aggression") as an instrument to offend the freedom of other peoples and as a means for the settlement of international disputes; (ii) in the presence of such a war that threatens to annihilate the constitutional system and the set of intertwined values on which it was built, citizens are bound to the "sacred" duty of defending the homeland enshrined in article 52 of the Constitution; and (iii) it stands to reason that the Constitution allows (or

---

[39] See Grosso (2010), pp. 251 ff.

[40] See Carlassare (2013) and Cassese (1975).

[41] See Bilancia (2024).

even demands) at least some forms of solidarity towards a foreign people that is facing the same "existential" threat that is described by articles 11 and 52 of the Italian Constitution and hence is exercising its "sacred" right (and duty) of self-defence against a "repudiated" war of aggression (as it is surely the case for the Ukrainian people).

In this perspective, then, the constitutional "empty space" that exists between the "war that is certainly prohibited" (repudiated) and the "war that is certainly mandatory" (the defence of the homeland) could be effectively filled not by resorting to international law but by referring directly to the fundamental principles of the Constitution.

If we embrace this constitutional interpretation of the meaning of "war" and of its "repudiation", it becomes possible, perhaps, to resolve the tension between the "pacifist" and "internationalist" souls of article 11 that emerged in the wake of the war in Ukraine.

Italy's participation in international organizations (and, more in general, its stance in the international community of States) should be always oriented towards pursuing the objective prescribed by article 11, which is that of a world order based on peace and in which international disputes are never resolved through war.[42] However, this does not mean that the definition of the "war" that is "repudiated" by article 11 shall be entirely deferred to the international legal system. If international organizations or international law authorize an unjust war, that war is, nonetheless, still repudiated by article 11.[43] Conversely, if international organizations or international law do not (clearly) recognize the legality of one State's defence against an unjust war (as it is the case for the UN and the war in Ukraine), that war is, nonetheless, still repudiated by article 11.

In other words, in the event of a divergency between international law and constitutional law in assessing the legality of a "war" (international endorsement of an unconstitutional war or international failure to endorse a constitutional war), constitutional law should necessarily prevail. This is also confirmed, after all, by the Italian Constitutional Court, which have stated that, as a general rule, the fundamental principles of the Constitution (to which article 11 clearly belongs) must always prevail on international law (including even the general principles of the international *ius cogens*).[44]

Therefore, as the war that Russia is waging against Ukraine is undeniably the exact type of war that is repudiated by article 11, the fact that the UN Security

---

[42] This is also recognized by the advocates for a radical pacifist interpretation of article 11. See, e.g. Allegretti (1991), Algostino (2022), Azzariti (2022a), Ciervo (2022), and De Fiores (2022).

[43] As a matter of fact, this perspective is also shared by the radical pacifist interpretations of article 11, as the same scholars that argue against the legality of Italy's support to Ukraine have argued, in previous cases (such as the military interventions in the Balkans, in Afghanistan, or in Libya), that even when the use of force is sanctioned by international organizations such as the United Nations, the pacifist clause would allow Italy to free itself from its international obligations, if they would require it to take part in acts of "war" or missions prohibited by the Constitution. See Allegretti (1991) and Caterina et al. (2022).

[44] See the decision no. 238/2014 of the Italian Constitutional Court. On the decision see, *ex multis*, Groppi (2015), Luciani (2015), and Bin (2016).

Council failed to condemn it (and to recognize the legality of Ukraine's defence), or the fact that Ukraine and Italy are (currently) not parties of a same treaty of collective defence, is ultimately irrelevant in assessing the constitutionality of the Italian Government's decision to transfer weapons (and other forms of assistance) to the Government in Kiev, provided that said decision is compliant with the constitutional fundamental principles that inform the concept of "illegal war" and prescribe its "condemnation" in international relations.

5 Towards a Constitutionally Oriented Definition of "Peace"

If one accepts that it is possible to infer an ontologically autonomous definition of the concept of (legal and illegal) "war" directly from the Italian Constitution, one must then wonder whether the same holds true for the concept of "peace".

The "egoistic" or "isolationist" interpretations of article 11, which were brought to their extreme consequences in the wake of the Russian invasion of Ukraine, theorize a sort of relativism of values in international relations that would demand that Italy always maintains a stance of complete and radical neutrality, even in a scenario in which an illiberal and antidemocratic State that rejects the Italian fundamental constitutional values (the values of the European and Western common constitutional tradition) invades, with the intention to conquer and annex, a State that embarked on a path towards embracing those very same liberal and democratic values.[45] The reason that justifies this complete and extreme neutrality (*rectius*, relativism) is, in this view, that supporting one of the belligerent parties would prolong the duration of the war and escalate its scope, while remaining neutral would provide for the fastest possible end of the hostilities, thus preventing possible escalations of the conflict and restoring a situation of "peace" (the situation required by article 11).

However, I would contend that, as demonstrated by the war in Ukraine, this interpretation oversimplifies the concept of "peace", by assuming that on the one hand "peace" means merely the "absence of war" and on the other hand that "peace" can only be achieved (or restored) through "pacifism" (by peaceful means and a complete and radical rejection of violence). Nevertheless, political philosophy teaches us that "peace" does not always amount to the "absence of war", and that there are a number of different "shades of grey" that must be taken into account in order to effectively adjust the constitutional and political theoretical framework to the complex reality of our time.[46]

Indeed, it is true that if everybody but the aggressor and the aggressed had remained neutral, the conflict in Ukraine would have ended a long time ago, hence terminating the "war" and restoring (formally) a situation of "peace". But is this

[45] See Ventura and Pupo (2022) p. 18.

[46] See Bistagnino (2025), Salvatore (2025), and Losano (2025).

really the notion of "peace" that is implied and prescribed by article 11? Can a foreign domination imposed and maintained through violence and the subjugation of the defeated people to the antidemocratic and illiberal regime enforced by the invader be really defined "peace"? Can allowing the aggressor to obtain the exact result that it intended to achieve by resorting to a "war" of the kind that the Constitution repudiates and thus illegally annexing the invaded territory (increasing, at the same time, the probability that in the future the same aggressor or other aggressors resort to the same instrument) be truly considered peace?

It seems to me that, as for the concept of "war", the concept of "peace" that article 11 prescribes should also be a constitutionally oriented one, compatible with the fundamental values on which the Italian Constitution was founded. A constitutionally oriented definition of "peace" cannot be reduced, then, to the fastest possible end of hostilities and should be balanced, instead, with the necessity of *effectively repudiating* (condemning) the resort to the kind of "war" that is prohibited by the national pacifist clause in the context of international relations.

This would mean, in turn, that Italy's behaviour in the international scenario can never be entirely relativist from a value perspective and, on the contrary, that it must be always informed by the values underlying the fundamental principles of the Constitution and by the democratic method that was used to shape them (to transform them into legal rules). While it is certainly true that (as confirmed by the Constitutional Court[47]) the Republic does not hold any values that it wishes to *impose* upon other peoples, this does not mean that the Republic does not have any values that it wishes to actively *defend* or *promote*.[48]

Ultimately, I believe that the pacifist clause enshrined in article 11 does not prescribe complete neutrality and value relativism in the international scenario but rather demands that, (at least) in the face of a "total war" (the "war" repudiated by article 11), Italy takes a side, according to the axiological system that inspired the Constitution of 1948.[49]

In this perspective, the promotion of a world order based on peace and justice among nations (the promotion of the value of "peace") can sometimes depend on the opposition to those "wars" that are of the kind repudiated by article 11, as these wars undermine the actual possibility of reaching, in the long term, the objective prescribed by the Constitution: peace in international relations. Differently put, sometimes peace can be best achieved and protected (also) through non-peaceful instruments. This is by no means a contradiction; on the contrary, it is often the rule when it comes to fundamental principles. Just as "true" peace can be sometimes achieved through non-peaceful actions, "true" equality can be sometimes achieved through discrimination (e.g. positive discriminations or affirmative actions), and the "true" protection of fundamental rights can be sometimes achieved through the imposition of duties (e.g. the duty to pay taxes to fund social and economic rights).

---

[47] See the decision no. 189/1987 of the Italian Constitutional Court.

[48] On the promotion and protection of values in international relations, see Iovane (2000).

[49] See Conti (2022).

If this is the case, then, actively pursuing and protecting "peace" (in a constitutionally oriented meaning) can, sometimes, be dependent on actions and initiatives that are aimed not only at promptly putting an end to the state of "war", but also at achieving "true" peace (a peace that does not allow the aggressor to benefit from resorting to war and does not condemn the aggressed to suffer unrepairable damages with regard to its freedom and sovereignty) and at preventing war from being used again in the future as an instrument of aggression against the freedom of other peoples and as a means for the settlement of international disputes.[50]

6 Conclusions

The debate surrounding the war in Ukraine showed that the "egoistic" interpretation of the Italian pacifist clause, according to which Italy repudiates war and therefore must always remain completely neutral between aggressors and aggressed, ends up producing an heterogenesis of ends, effectively enabling aggressor States (that reject the constitutional and European fundamental value of peace and use war as an instrument of conquest) to benefit from their illegal actions and to advance a vision of power relations in the international community of States that is antithetic to that prescribed by the Italian Constitution.

In this way, the ultimate objective, outlined by article 11, of a world order based on peace, moves further away, both in a practical perspective (resorting to war to impose one's views in international relations is tolerated) and in a theoretical perspective (the "peace" that is obtained through the prompt termination of hostilities is "peace" just in name).

If this is the case, then, I would argue that, if one takes into account the entire system of fundamental principles and values upon which the Italian constitutional order is founded, it is precisely an "egoistic" interpretation of article 11 that must be "repudiated" by the democratic, solidaristic, internationalist, pluralistic, and liberal matrix of the Constitution of 1948.

The pacifist clause of article 11 demands that Italy is proactive in building a world order ruled by peaceful relations and in which resorting to war is no longer an option. Until such a world order comes into being, however, article 11 prohibits Italy from retreating into a sort of "irenic isolationism", especially when the very conditions for the advent of a peaceful world order are being actively undermined, as in the case of Russia's invasion of Ukraine.

Obviously, this proactivity does not amount to an obligation to automatically become an active party of every armed conflict, but it stands to reason that the Constitution, at least, *authorizes* (does not prohibit) forms of support to the States and peoples that are defending themselves against an unjust aggression that has all the characteristics of the "war" repudiated by article 11. The means through which

[50] See Pietrobon (2023) and Pistorio (2022).

Italy can take action (according to the rules and procedures of every representative democracy) to repudiate these wars are multifaceted, which means that the forms of support that can be provided to the aggressed States (such as Ukraine) are also multifaceted and can include, of course, diplomatic means, as well as the offer of assistance, military equipment, or weapons.

It is certainly legitimate to question whether participation in collective defence treaties, such as those establishing NATO, truly contributes (especially in the current context of global disorder) to the pursuit of the objective of peace enshrined in article 11.[51] What is not debatable is, however, that Russia's invasion of Ukraine stands in clear opposition to the Italian constitutional pacifist clause and that, as a result, article 11 provides a valid legal basis for supporting Ukraine in its defensive effort.

References

Ainis M (2022) L'invio di armi all'Ucraina è contrario alla Costituzione. Il Fatto Quotidiano 6 April 2022

Algostino A (2022) Pacifismo e movimenti fra militarizzazione della democrazia e Costituzione. Costituzionalismo.it 4:67–90

Allegretti U (1991) Guerra del Golfo e Costituzione. Il Foro italiano 5:382–413

Apostoli A (2022) L'Italia è una Repubblica democratica fondata anche sul principio pacifista. Costituzionalismo.it 4:141–156

Arangio Ruiz G (1975) Difesa legittima (Diritto internazionale). In: Novissimo Digesto Italiano, vol V. Utet, Turin

Azzariti G (2022a) La mediazione non passa attraverso la Nato. Il Manifesto 5 March 2022

Azzariti G (2022b) Amato sbaglia, secondo Costituzione non possiamo inviare armi all'Ucraina. Il Riformista 9 April 2022

Azzariti G (2022c) La pace attraverso il diritto. Una conferenza internazionale per la sicurezza tra le nazioni. Costituzionalismo.it 4:3–14

Baldassarre A (2002) Globalizzazione contro democrazia. Laterza, Rome-Bari

Beer LW (1998) Peace in theory and practice under Article 9 of Japan's Constitution. Marquette Law Rev 81:815–830

Benvenuti M (2010) Il principio del ripudio della guerra nell'ordinamento costituzionale italiano. Jovene, Naples

Benvenuti M (2022) Le conseguenze costituzionali della guerra russo-ucraina. Prime considerazioni. Osservatorio costituzionale 3:20–46

Bertolini E (2025) Japanese rearmament and the constitution: a misalignment. In: Cavaggion G (ed) The 'Pacifist Principle' in the Italian and Japanese constitutions in the wake of the war in Ukraine. Springer Nature Switzerland, Cham

Bettinelli E (1992) Art. 52. In: Branca G (ed) Commentario alla Costituzione. Zanichelli, Bologna

Bilancia P (2024) Riflessioni sulle prospettive future per una difesa comune europea. In: Scritti in memoria di Beniamino Caravita di Toritto. Editoriale Scientifica, Naples, pp 1217–1232

Bin R (2016) L'adattamento dell'ordinamento italiano al diritto internazionale non scritto dopo la sent. 238/2014. Forum di Quaderni costituzionali: 1–10

[51] See, e.g. De Fiores (2020), Azzariti (2022a), Massa Pinto (2022), and Bucci (2022).

Bistagnino G (2025) Contingent or principled? On the philosophical distinctiveness of pacifism. In: Cavaggion G (ed) The 'Pacifist Principle' in the Italian and Japanese constitutions in the wake of the war in Ukraine. Springer Nature Switzerland, Cham
Bon Valsassina M (1955) Il ripudio della guerra nella Costituzione italiana. CEDAM, Padua
Bucci G (2022) Ragione del diritto e follia del potere di guerra. Costituzionalismo.it 4:175–194
Carlassare L (2013) L'art. 11 Cost. nella visione dei Costituenti. Costituzionalismo.it 1:1–17
Cartabia M, Chieffi L (2006) Art. 11. In: Bifulco R, Celotto A, Olivetti M (eds) Commentario alla Costituzione. Utet, Turin
Cassese A (1975) Art. 10-11. In: Branca G (ed) Commentario alla Costituzione. Zanichelli, Bologna
Cassese A (1986) Violenza e diritto nell'era nucleare. Laterza, Rome-Bari
Caterina E, Giannelli M, Siciliano D (2022) Il ripudio della guerra preso sul serio. Quattro tesi sull'incostituzionalità dell'invio di armi all'Ucraina. SIDIBlog 26 April 2022
Cavino M (1999) Lo scopo umanitario come causa di giustificazione dell'uso della forza. In: Dogliani M, Sicardi S (eds) Diritti umani e uso della forza. Profili di diritto costituzionale interno e internazionale. Giappichelli, Turin, pp 31–41
Cavino M (2023) Cessione di armi all'Ucraina: non belligeranza?. Eublog.eu 8 March 2023
Cavino M, Malvicini M (2023) Le guerre dell'Italia repubblicana. Il Mulino, Bologna
Cavino M, Malvicini M (2025) The 'pacifist principle' and the 'use of force' in the Italian Constitution. In: Cavaggion G (ed) The 'Pacifist Principle' in the Italian and Japanese constitutions in the wake of the war in Ukraine. Springer Nature Switzerland, Cham
Cecchetti M (1993) Il "ripudio della guerra" contenuto nella Carta Costituzionale, alla luce del diritto e delle prassi internazionali. La comunità internazionale 2:278–310
Celotto A (2022) L'Italia, l'art. 11 della Costituzione e la guerra. La lettura di Celotto. Formiche 6 March 2022
Chickering R, Förster S (2003) The shadows of total war. Cambridge University Press, Cambridge
Ciervo A (2022) Critica delle armi. L'articolo 11 della costituzione, la legge n. 185/1990 e l'invasione dell'Ucraina da parte della Federazione russa. Costituzionalismo.it 4:195–229
Conti GL (2022) Aristotele, l'atimia e la guerra in Ucraina. Rivista AIC: 1–2
De Fiores C (2020) Il principio pacifista, la ratifica dei Trattati internazionali e la questione della NATO. Democrazia e diritto 2:51–67
De Fiores C (2022) Il principio costituzionale pacifista, gli obblighi internazionali e l'invio di armi a paesi in guerra. Costituzionalismo.it 4:29–66
De Minico G (2023) I principi della guerra ammissibile secondo la nostra Costituzione. Il Sole 24 Ore 13 July 2023
de Vergottini G (1999) La Costituzione e l'intervento Nato nella ex Jugoslavia. Quaderni costituzionali 1:122–125
de Vergottini G (2024) Ripudio della guerra e neutralità alla luce dell'articolo 11 Cost. Federalismi.it 13 March 2024: 1–12
Ferrajoli L (2002) Neanche l'ONU può. La rivista del Manifesto 34
Ferrari G (1970) Guerra (stato di) (Diritto costituzionale). In: Enciclopedia del diritto, vol. XIX. Giuffrè, Milano
Flick GM (2022) Un reato arruolarsi da volontari in Ucraina. Legittime le armi a Kiev. La Repubblica 4 March 2022
Frattolillo O (2025) Whither pacifism in cold war Japan? An interpretive path (1947–1990). In: Cavaggion G (ed) The 'Pacifist Principle' in the Italian and Japanese constitutions in the wake of the war in Ukraine. Springer Nature Switzerland, Cham
Gianformaggio L (1999) Diritti umani e guerra. In: Dogliani M, Sicardi S (eds) Diritti umani e uso della forza. Profili di diritto costituzionale interno e internazionale. Giappichelli, Turin, pp 23–28
Graziano M (2024) Disordine mondiale. Perché viviamo in un'epoca di crescente caos. Mondadori, Milan
Groppi T (2015) La Corte costituzionale e la storia profetica. Considerazioni a margine della sentenza n. 238/2014 della Corte costituzionale italiana. Consulta online 1:1–9
Grosso E (2010) I doveri costituzionali. In: Lo statuto costituzionale del non cittadino. Jovene, Naples, pp 229–280

Iovane M (2000) La tutela dei valori fondamentali nel diritto internazionale. Editoriale Scientifica, Naples
Karlin M (2024) Rhe Return of Total War. Understanding – and Preparing for – a New Era of Comprehensive Conflict. Foreign Affairs November/December 2024
Kimijima A (2010) Article 9. In: Young NJ (ed) The Oxford international Encyclopedia of peace, vol 1. Oxford University Press, Oxford
Kimijima A (2025) Six faces of Article 9: Japan's constitutional pacifism and the world order. In: Cavaggion G (ed) The 'Pacifist Principle' in the Italian and Japanese constitutions in the wake of the war in Ukraine. Springer Nature Switzerland, Cham
Latino A (2024) L'invio di armi all'Ucraina fra Costituzione e diritto internazionale. DPCE online special issue 1:693–710
Lattanzi F (1997) Assistenza umanitaria e interventi di umanità. Giappichelli, Turin
Losano MG (2025) The constitutions of Japan, Italy and Germany reject war: and the current non-wars? In: Cavaggion G (ed) The 'Pacifist Principle' in the Italian and Japanese constitutions in the wake of the war in Ukraine. Springer Nature Switzerland, Cham
Luciani M (2015) I controlimiti e l'eterogenesi dei fini. Questione giustizia 1:84–93
Luther J (2002) Come interpretare i principi fondamentali della Costituzione. In: Luther J, Malfatti E, Rossi E (eds) I principi fondamentali della Costituzione italiana. Lezioni. Edizioni Plus, Pisa, pp 11–30
Martin C (2025) The tragic demise of Japan's constitutional war constraints. In: Cavaggion G (ed) The 'Pacifist Principle' in the Italian and Japanese constitutions in the wake of the war in Ukraine. Springer Nature Switzerland, Cham
Massa Pinto (2022) La solidarietà conflittuale come dovere di comprendere le ragioni dell'Altro, anche nella guerra Nato-Russia in Ucraina. Costituzionalismo.it 4:257–272
Motzo G (1999) Costituzione e guerra giusta alla periferia dell'impero. Quaderni costituzionali 2:373–375
Pedrazzi M (2001) L'uso della forza nel diritto internazionale: quali prospettive? Democrazia e diritto 2:119–128
Pietrobon A (2023) La fornitura di armi all'Ucraina: quali regole e quali cautele? Eurojus 3:134–150
Pistorio G (2022) La cessione di armamenti alle Forze armate ucraine, tra interpretazioni costituzionalmente e internazionalmente conformi e (ir)regolarità costituzionali. Rivista AIC: 1–5
Rescigno GU (1999) Riflessioni di un giurista sulla guerra e sulla pace. Quaderni costituzionali 2:376–377
Rigano F (2002) La guerra: profili di diritto costituzionale. In: La guerra profili di diritto internazionale e di diritto interno. Editoriale Scientifica, Napoli
Rossi P (2022) La compatibilità con la Costituzione italiana e il diritto internazionale dell'invio di armi all'Ucraina. SIDIBlog 8 March 2022
Salvatore A (2025) Political philosophy and the problem of war: mapping the battlefield. In: Cavaggion G (ed) The 'Pacifist Principle' in the Italian and Japanese constitutions in the wake of the war in Ukraine. Springer Nature Switzerland, Cham
Scuto F (2025) Una questione epocale per l'Unione europea: il processo di adesione dell'Ucraina tra guerra e incerta evoluzione costituzionale del Paese. Rassegna di diritto pubblico europeo 1:77–104
Ventura L, Pupo V (2022) Osservazioni sui problemi internazionali e interni conseguenti alla guerra in Ucraina. Forum di Quaderni costituzionali rassegna 3:1–32
Villone M (2022a) Armi, risoluzione discutibile. Adesso il Parlamento vigili. Il Fatto Quotidiano 3 March 2022
Villone M (2022b) La Costituzione tra difesa legittima e ripudio della guerra. Il Manifesto 8 April 2022
Volpi M (2022) La guerra in Ucraina e il costituzionalismo democratico. Costituzionalismo.it 1:XI–XIII
Zappa M (2025) The "Pacifist Integralism" Myth: Japan's evolving national security approach since the 1992 peacekeeping law and the Japan socialist party's narrative and political shift. In: Cavaggion G (ed) The 'Pacifist Principle' in the Italian and Japanese constitutions in the wake of the war in Ukraine. Springer Nature Switzerland, Cham

Japan

Six Faces of Article 9: Japan's Constitutional Pacifism and the World Order

Akihiko Kimijima

We, the Japanese people, desire peace for all time and are deeply conscious of the high ideals controlling human relationship, and we have determined to preserve our security and existence, trusting in the justice and faith of the peace-loving peoples of the world. We desire to occupy an honored place in an international society striving for the preservation of peace, and the banishment of tyranny and slavery, oppression and intolerance for all time from the earth. We recognize that all peoples of the world have the right to live in peace, free from fear and want. (Second paragraph of the Preamble to the Constitution of Japan of 1946).

(1) *Aspiring sincerely to an international peace based on justice and order, the Japanese people forever renounce war as a sovereign right of the nation and the threat or use of force as means of settling international disputes.* (2) *In order to accomplish the aim of the preceding paragraph, land, sea, and air forces, as well as other war potential, will never be maintained. The right of belligerency of the state will not be recognized. (Article 9 of the Constitution of Japan of 1946).*

1 Introduction

1.1 Global and Structural Understanding of Article 9

The purpose of this article is to examine the 80-year trajectory of Article 9, the peace provision of the Japanese Constitution of 1946. Constitutional reform was one of the major issues of the Allied Powers' occupational reform of defeated Japan,

---

A. Kimijima (✉)
Ritsumeikan University, Kyoto, Japan
e-mail: kimijima@ir.ritsumei.ac.jp

G. Cavaggion (ed.), *The 'Pacifist Principle' in the Italian and Japanese Constitutions in the Wake of the War in Ukraine*,
https://doi.org/10.1007/978-3-032-23108-6_7

and Article 9 of the new constitution has been the most important element for demilitarization of Japan. It has had deep impacts domestically, regionally, and globally. The dynamics of Article 9 have often been driven by changes in international relations and the world order, to which this article pays particular attention. In addition, the Japanese word "heiwa shugi" (pacifism) is used extremely loosely, and clarification of this concept is indispensable. In any case, in order to clearly grasp the trajectory of Article 9 and the concept of constitutional pacifism, it is necessary to go beyond the boundaries of constitutional studies and consult with the insights of peace research and international relations. This article aims at the global and structural understanding of the pacifism of the Japanese constitution. It is still a rough sketch of ideas and a working hypothesis that needs to be developed further.

1.2 How to Grasp the Complexities of Article 9

The important point in capturing Article 9 of the Constitution of Japan is to distinctively and clearly capture its contradictions, polysemy, multifacetedness, and potential. Article 9 of the Constitution appears to different people as different things. In order to clearly distinguish these complexities, this article presents a way of thinking: "Article 9 as a hexahedron." This way of thinking has been influenced by ideas such as Masayasu Hasegawa's "two legal systems" theory,[1] Ichiyo Muto's "three legitimacy principles of the post-war Japanese state,"[2] and Naoki Ṣakai's understanding of "double-tongued or triple- tongued nature of the Japanese Constitution."[3] "Article 9 as a hexahedron" modifies and strengthens the spirits of those ideas. This way of thinking is an "anatomy chart" that looks at Article 9 from six viewpoints: from Washington DC and San Francesco, from the Japanese Empire, from the Japanese people, from Okinawa, from East Asia, and from all the peoples of the world. Article 9 is an aggregation of these six aspects. A hexahedron, that is. At the same time, it can be said that these six viewpoints are theoretical—merely ideal types—posited for analysis. But in reality they are intertwined and far from clearly separated.

[1] Hasegawa (1960).
[2] Muto (2016).
[3] Sakai (2008).

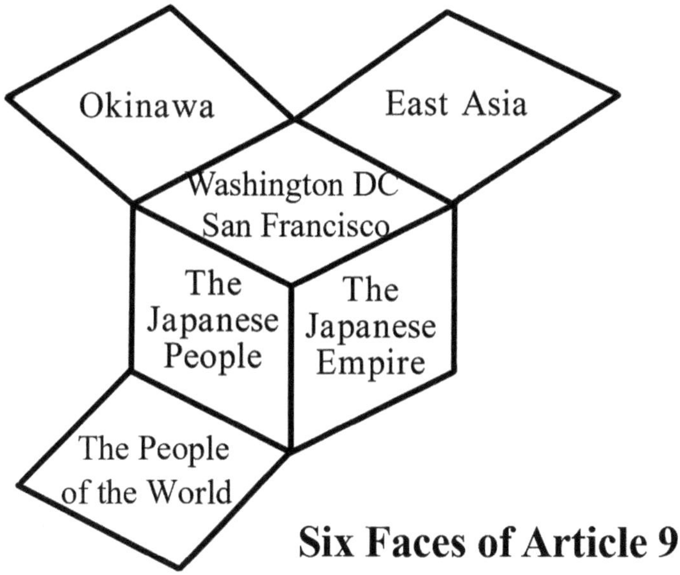

2 Article 9 as Seen from Washington DC and San Francisco

2.1 Occupational Reform and Demilitarization of the Axis Power

The postwar world order can be seen as Pax Americana, a world order that takes the United States as a hegemon. The Pax Americana's foundation of value was established mainly by the United States and the United Kingdom during World War II. Documents such as the "Four Freedoms" of US President Roosevelt (January 1941) and the Atlantic Charter, signed by US President Roosevelt and British Prime Minister Churchill (August 1941), indicated the direction of the postwar world order. This direction will lead to the postwar UN Charter (June 1945) and the Universal Declaration of Human Rights (December 1948).

The key to understanding Article 9 in this context is the eighth section of the Atlantic Charter. It says that "since no future peace can be maintained if land, sea, or air armaments continue to be employed by nations which threaten, or may threaten, aggression outside of their frontiers, they believe, pending the establishment of a wider and permanent system of general security, that the disarmament of such nations is essential." Here, "nations which threaten aggression" refer to the Axis Powers. This can be said to be one of the origins of Article 9 clause 2.

Article 9 clause 2 refers to the disarmament of Japan, as an Axis Power, by the Allied Powers. It is meant to totally dismember Japan's armed forces because of its aggression in the Asia-Pacific War. In that sense, Article 9 contains an aspect of "punishment." At the time of 1945–1946, the major issue of world peace was demilitarization and democratization of the Axis Powers. This was pursued by the Allied Powers' occupation reforms of the Axis Powers. Constitutional reform was inevitable in this occupation reform, and, as a result, the new constitutions of Japan, Italy, and Germany all have these demilitarization/peace clauses: Article 9 of Japan, Article 11 of Italy, and Article 26 of West Germany. The origin of Article 9 is the Second Principle of the so-called MacArthur's Three Principles. These were the basic principles of constitutional reform determined by the Supreme Commander for the Allied Powers. But as to where the basic idea behind those principles came from, there has been a serious difference of opinion among many researchers.

2.2 *"Peace of San Francisco": Japan Incorporated Into the Western Alliance*

Beginning in 1947 and 1948, the confrontations developed within the Allied Powers—what came to be called the "Cold War." As a result the relationship between the Allied Powers and the Axis Powers changed. In particular, within Pax Americana the position of the Axis Powers changed. In San Francisco in September 1951, during the Korean War, Japan signed the Peace Treaty with the Allied Powers—though without the Soviet Union and China. At that time Japan also signed the Japan-US Security Treaty. This "Peace of San Francisco" set the basic framework of the postwar Asia-Pacific regional order. The original assumption that the security of a disarmed Japan would be provided by the United Nations had been changed. Japan had decided to rely on the Japan-US Security Treaty for its protection. In addition, in order to supplement the Western alliance confronting the Soviet Union, rearmament of Japan was pursued.

On the other hand, the US forces which had been stationed to occupy and rule the Axis Powers continued to remain in place even after the end of the occupation period. Consequentially there are to this day many US military bases in Japan, Germany, and Italy. The US military presence in the Axis Powers was said to play a role of "double containment"—containing its former enemies and at the same time containing the Soviet Union. Although Article 9 clause 2 says that "land, sea, and air forces, as well as other war potential, will never be maintained," the presence of the US forces in Japan was considered as constitutional by Japan's Supreme Court in its 1959 decision of the Sunagawa case.

The United States nonetheless promoted and pursued Japan's rearmament. The United States did so by seeking the revision of Article 9, but it did not succeeded because of the resistance of the Japanese people. As a result, the process of Japan's rearmament has been accomplished by changes of interpretation of Article 9—sometimes called "interpretative constitutional revision." Japan's conservative politicians also utilized Article 9 as a "shield" to counter the US demands of military burden sharing.[4]

[4] Sakai (1991).

2.3 *Article 9 in the Post-Cold War Era: Japan in the Twilight Years of Pax Americana*

During the Cold War years the Japan-US security system was operated for the most part stably. But with the conclusion of the Cold War in 1989, the system has been changing. After the Cold War ended, and since Japan had become an important economic power, there was a growing call for Japan's international contributions. In the 1990s a decision was made to dispatch the Self-Defense Forces (SD F) overseas even though they were not originally intended for such service. They were sent as part of many UN PKO humanitarian missions as well as one that provided "rear area logistical support" for the US forces.

Since the year 2000, a Washington DC-based think tank has issued policy recommendations that Japan should lift its self-imposed ban on the exercise of the right of collective self-defense. According to the third Armitage-Nye Report published in August 2012, the change—to institute the right of collective self-defense—should be done by constitutional interpretation, not by changing the text of the Constitution.

In line with the intention of Washington DC, the New National Security Laws enacted in 2015 expanded the scope allowed to the SDF's activities—including the limited exercise of the right of collective self-defense. Pax Americana had already entered a period of decline, and the Trump administration accelerated that decline by disrespecting internationalism and multilateralism.

In relation to this, I would like to touch on the Abe administration's idea of "proactive contribution to peace based on the principle of international cooperation." In the National Security Strategy decided by the Cabinet on December 17, 2013, the Abe administration has launched "proactive contribution to peace based on the principle of international cooperation" as the basic principle of Japan's security policy. It should be noted that the idea of "proactive contribution to peace" is not derived from the pacifism of the Japanese Constitution but from the post-Cold War, post-Gulf War discussions of the Liberal Democratic Party and the Ministry of Foreign Affairs. This is intended to supplement the declining US power by further utilization of the SDF in the twilight years of Pax Americana, and it has a direction to prepare revising Article 9.

After the outbreak of the Russia-Ukraine War in 2022, the geopolitical change in Europe influenced the East Asian security environment. Partly responding to this change, the Japanese government adopted three national security policy documents in December 2022: National Security Strategy, National Defense Strategy, and Defense Buildup Program. These security policy documents contain major changes of interpretation of Article 9. With these documents, the Japanese government interprets that Article 9 allows Japan's maintenance of counterattack capabilities as part of self-defense capabilities. This change has been justified as a necessary measure for deterrence to the Taiwan contingency.

3 Article 9 as Seen by the Japanese Empire

3.1 The Emperor and Article 9 in Pax Americana

After defeat, Japanese ruling elites were incorporated into Pax Americana while secretly preserving the values of the Japanese Empire. Emperor Hirohito also survived being incorporated into Pax Americana. For them, Article 9's dismantling of the Japanese military forces—and the Japanese militarism itself—would be understood as "lightning rods" to save the Emperor and his government. It was not the Emperor but the Japanese military forces that were sacrificed. The First Principle of the MacArthur's Three Principles (the survival of the Emperor) and the Second Principle (renunciation of war and military forces) are closely linked. In February 1946 the Shidehara Cabinet was presented with a draft of the Constitution of Japan, the so-called MacArthur draft. The Shidehara Cabinet initially resisted but finally accepted it in order to "save the imperial family." Emperor Hirohito himself recognized that the Japanese government's draft Constitution was excessively conservative and inadequate. Hirohito highly valued the MacArthur draft.

For the Japanese ruling elites the protection of the Emperor and the acceptance of Article 9 are related, but there is another interpretation, namely, that the US government had decided upon the preservation of a postwar Emperor system at a very early stage. According to Tetsuro Kato, a document by the US Department of Army in June 1942 already proposes a strategy of "separating the Emperor from the military and using him as a symbol of peace." As early as this time, there may have been groups within the US government that had designed the symbolic Emperor system in postwar Japan. In addition, a memorandum on policy toward Japan secretly sent to the Department of Army in September 1942 by Edwin Reischauer, who was a young scholar at Harvard University, said that "to keep the Emperor available as a valuable ally or puppet in the postwar ideological battle we must keep him unsullied by the present war."[5] In order to use the Emperor as an ally or a puppet after the war, it would be necessary to prevent the argument that the Emperor was responsible for the war of aggression and its atrocities. That was exactly what MacArthur did.

3.2 "Postcolonial Situation" in Postwar Japan

The Constitution of Japan of 1946 is the "postwar Constitution," and at the same time it is the "postcolonial Constitution." The postcolonial nature of the Japanese Constitution however has been largely overlooked, especially in contrast to the widely recognized character of the postwar constitution. The Japanese Empire decolonized its colonies heteronomously or passively along with the defeat. As a result, the topic of overcoming colonialism was very weak in postwar Japan. In the Tokyo

---

[5] Sakai (2008).

Tribunal in which the Allied Powers ruled on Japanese war crimes, the military's responsibilities were adjudicated, but the colonial responsibilities were not. In the San Francisco Peace Treaty as well, the pursuit of colonial responsibilities was weak.

Remaining colonialism in postwar Japan is most easily seen in the status of resident Koreans and the inadequate protection of their rights. They were deprived of Japanese nationality in 1952 when, by the notice of the Japanese government, the San Francisco Peace Treaty came into force. They still have no Japanese citizenship and no voting right. They are excluded from "popular sovereignty." This also indicates the inadequacy of the decolonization of the Japanese Empire.

3.3 *Current Stage of "Imperial Consciousness"*

Naoki Sakai's analysis of the postcolonial situation in postwar Japan is sharp.[6] According to Sakai, postwar Japan was incorporated into Pax Americana and became the "empire under subcontract" to the United States' world domination. Although postwar Japan has a subordinate position in relation to the United States, it has maintained its sense of superiority and discrimination toward the former colonies and has kept its "imperial consciousness."

However, with the decline of Pax Americana, the power shift in East Asia is happening (declining Japan and rising China). Moreover, the gap between the Japanese people's "imperial consciousness" and the reality of power shift is so clear that that imperial consciousness is heading for "reclusion" (praising itself for escaping from reality) and xenophobic "exclusivity" (hate speech). This remaining "imperial consciousness" is demonstrably connected to the present anti-Korea and anti-China sentiments that tend to support the Japanese government's militarization policies.

4 Article 9 as Seen by the Japanese People

4.1 *Article 9 as Liberation from Militarism*

Article 9 liberated the Japanese people from militarism. Unlike the case in which the Korean democratization movement defeated the military dictatorship, the Japanese popular movement did not defeat militarism. The people were liberated from militarism as a result of the defeat of the Japanese military forces. Although there were thoughts and practices of anti-war, disarmament, and peace in prewar Japan, it was principally the military defeat that made Article 9.

[6] Sakai (2017).

4.2 Internalization of Article 9 by the Japanese People and Constitutional Scholars

The Japanese people have come to accept Article 9 as their own through various means and methods. The majority of the Japanese people has opposed several attempts to revise the article. They have supported lawsuits challenging the constitutionality of the US military forces stationed in Japan as well as lawsuits challenging the very existence of Japan's Self-Defense Forces. Japanese constitutional scholars have located Article 9 in the history of humanity's various efforts to abolish war itself—such as France's 1791 Constitution with its peace provisions; Immanuel Kant's theory of peace (*Toward Perpetual Peace*, 1795); and the development of international law (the 1928 Kellogg-Briand Pact, the 1945 United Nations Charter). They also provided theoretical supports to numerous constitutional lawsuits. And they discovered the idea of "the right to live in peace" in the Preamble of the 1946 Japanese Constitution. They also developed the theory of "peace as a human right." These pioneer efforts have been avidly followed by theorists and practitioners around the world.

These understandings of Article 9 and the Preamble were not reached at the time of the enactment in 1946 but were gradually developed by the postwar Japanese people and constitutional scholars. Many years of acceptance by the Japanese people and constitutional scholars matter. Article 9—now zealously embraced by the Japanese people and constitutional scholars—is no longer a passive disarmament clause imposed upon an Axis Power by an Allied Powers. Nor is it a "lightning rod" to save the Emperor System. Article 9 has been widely reconstructed by the people as a provision aimed at "peace by peaceful means." If we borrow the words of Eiji Oguma, "in postwar Japan, a representative example of the text that was given a reading beyond the intention of the original author was the Japanese Constitution. The Constitution given by the United States has become a medium for resisting the US Cold War strategy and expressing Japanese nationalism."[7] Oguma creates the term "Article 9 nationalism."

4.3 Article 9 as "the Core of a Comprehensive Peace Policy Package"

Postwar Japan's peace movement, peace research, and peace education have been overwhelmingly affected by the presence of Article 9 as a constitutional provision. Article 9, combined with the judicial review system of constitutionality, has become the most important source for criticizing Japan's militarization on popular initiatives. Because there is Article 9 in postwar Japan, peace issues have immediately become constitutional issues. Peace movements have often taken the form of constitutional lawsuits or movements opposing Article 9 revisionism. However, there is a downside to this. In postwar Japan, peace issues have instantly become legalistic

[7] Oguma (2002).

constitutional arguments (interpretations, revisions, and preservations). As a consequence, comprehensive peace and security discussions have been weak. Discussions tend to concentrate on criticism against government policies. Proposing alternative visions and policies true to the spirits of Article 9 has been extremely weak. Constitutional norms are of course important, but the agenda for overcoming war and creating long-lasting peace spans a vast area beyond constitutional norms. Article 9 should be treated as "the core of a comprehensive peace policy package" and that "comprehensive peace policy package" needs to be vigorously developed and presented. This aspect has been tragically weak.

5 Article 9 as Seen from Okinawa

5.1 *Article 9, the Emperor, and the US Military Forces in Okinawa*

For General MacArthur, Article 9 and the US bases in Okinawa were a set. One month after the Constitution came into force, in June 1947, MacArthur stated that "it is important for Japan to put the US Air Force in Okinawa, and it will be a clear guarantee for Japan's security."[8] For MacArthur the US military bases in Okinawa made Article 9 possible. At the same time, in September 1947, Emperor Hirohito sent the so-called Okinawa message to William J. Sebald, the political adviser to MacArthur, by way of Hidenari Terasaki, an adviser to Emperor Hirohito. In that message Hirohito said he would like the US forces to stay in Okinawa for an extended period of time (25–50 years). The Emperor thought that this occupation would be beneficial to the United States as well as that it would also protect Japan.[9] Under these circumstances, Article 9, Emperor Hirohito, and the US forces stationed in Okinawa are all mutually connected.

5.2 *Okinawa's Struggle for Peace: "Return to the Peace Constitution" and Thereafter*

Okinawa fell under US military rule at the end of March 1945. The Japanese Constitution, which came into force on November 3, 1946, and implemented on May 3, 1947, was not applied to Okinawa. In addition, Okinawa was separated from administration by mainland Japan. Governance continued by the US military under the terms of Article 3 of the San Francisco Peace Treaty, which came into force on April 28, 1952. Okinawa, to which Article 9 was not applied, however, had a

[8] Koseki (2002).

[9] Toyoshita (2015).

tradition of living by an anti-war theory. Okinawans also have had, since the end of the Asia-Pacific War, the rich experience of a 50-year-long nonviolent resistance movement as led by Shoko Ahagon.

People in Okinawa who suffered from the oppressive US military occupation pursued the policy of "return to the peace constitution." However, after Okinawa was returned to Japan in 1972 and the Japanese Constitution entered into force there, the number of US bases and servicemen in Okinawa did not decrease. In September 1995, triggered by the case of a girl kidnapped and brutally raped by US soldiers, Governor Masahide Ota refused to sign a proxy for the continued imposition of US military bases. Furthermore, the Okinawan people's anti-base sentiment increased. This incident developed into a major administrative lawsuit between the Governor of Okinawa and the Japanese government. In this lawsuit, Governor Ota argued that Okinawan residents' property rights and rights to live in peace were infringed—disproportionate to the rest of Japan—due to the concentration of US military bases in Okinawa. The Supreme Court, however, decided that the existing situation was constitutional. This case sent a message to the people of Okinawa, namely, that the Japanese Constitution would not bring peace to Okinawa.[10] After this lawsuit, it seems that the people of Okinawa prefer to use international human rights law and international human rights organizations for their pursuit of human rights and the right of self-determination.[11] There are also different forms of aspiration for peace that have arisen—such as an argument that mainland Japan should share the burden of US bases (by relocating US bases to mainland Japan). Some also argue that Okinawa should become independent from Japan.

6 Article 9 as Seen from East Asia

6.1 Article 9 as a Provision for the Security of East Asian People

Article 9 of the Japanese Constitution is not a provision for the security of Japan. Article 9 is the provision of the "security against the threat of Japanese militarism," the provision of security of the Allied Powers, and the provision of security of East Asian people who suffered under Japanese imperialism and militarism.[12] Japan's security is mentioned in the Preamble of the Constitution ("we have determined to preserve our security and existence, trusting in the justice and faith of the peace-loving peoples of the world"). The original intention of the Japanese Constitution of 1946 was that Japan would rely on the United Nations for its security. However, the Cold War made that impossible to do. It was not disarmament but rearmament of

[10] Komatsu (2015).

[11] Abe (2015).

[12] Lee (2017).

Japan that was demanded by the United States. The process of Japan's rearmament started in 1950. And in 1954 the government's constitutional interpretation established that the Self-Defense Forces were the minimum necessary capabilities for self-defense—based on Japan's right to self-defense—and therefore did not violate Article 9. From that time on, Article 9 has been transformed into the provision of security for Japan. Accordingly, the original intention of the Constitution (that Japan relies on the UN's collective security arrangements) receded into the background.

It was Rokuro Hidaka, sociologist at the University of Tokyo, that understood the meaning of Article 9 in the context of East Asia in the deepest sense and at the earliest time. Hidaka writes as follows, reflecting on the time when he read the "Outline of a Draft for a Revised Constitution" published in the newspaper on March 7, 1946.

"I wondered how people across Asia who experienced war and massacres would read the Constitution of Japan and understand Article 9. For them, Article 9 should be an international guarantee that Japan would never again employ cruel use of force, self- righteous political behavior, and human rights violations and discriminations. It was obvious for them that Article 9 contained the meaning of punishment. What is essential for us is to remember the Fifteen Years' War, keep it as history, and link it with the feeling of regret and link it with our ethical thinking. It is embarrassing to talk about the 'pioneering nature of Article 9' without being able to do these things."[13]

6.2 *Theory of "Donut-Shaped Alternative Militarism"*

During the Cold War, the Self-Defense Forces were established, but Article 9 of the Constitution was maintained. Article 9 was maintained due to various factors such as politics in Japan (the presence of pro-Article 9 opposition parties; the use of Article 9 by conservative politicians), peace movements, efforts of constitutional scholars, etc. However, international relations in East Asia also should not be ignored. Korean scholar Kwon Heok-Tae says that because South Korea, Taiwan, and Okinawa have been heavily militarized and served as a frontline of confrontation during the Cold War, mainland Japan enjoyed the luxury of being lightly armed while also holding onto Article 9. He emphasizes this structural relationship.[14]

Yoshikazu Sakamoto, political scientist at the University of Tokyo, had already made a sharp analysis of this "structural relationship." Sakamoto had pointed out that during the Cold War the relative light armament of mainland Japan and the militarization of the surrounding countries were a set and that there was "something like a donut-shaped alternative militarism structure" in which Japan's economic aid

[13] Hidaka (2010).

[14] Kwon (2016).

supported the militarized neighboring governments.[15] It is important, therefore, to see the peace in postwar Japan in relation to the militarization of its East Asian neighbors.

6.3 Preparing a "Conference on Security and Cooperation in Asia:" Common Security in East Asia

The second paragraph of the Preamble of the Japanese Constitution provides that "we have determined to preserve our security and existence, trusting in the justice and faith of the peace-loving peoples of the world." This meant that Japan would rely on the United Nations for its security. But because of the Cold War, the United Nations security mechanism had not been realized. The Japanese government turned to the US-Japan Security Treaty instead of the United Nations.

But if we respect the original idea of Japan's security in the Japanese Constitution—not the idea of miliary alliance but the idea of common security—we should prepare an inclusive common security mechanism in East Asia such as a Conference on Security and Cooperation in Asia (CSCA).[16] I think this is an evolutive interpretation of the Preamble of the Japanese Constitution. Policy documents prepared by International Peace Bureau and other NGOs proposed common security mechanisms in East Asia.[17]

In addition, if the Japanese government is not interested in preparing a common security mechanism in East Asia, then other actors should act first. Diamond and McDonald, a peace researcher and a retired US diplomat, have been proposing the theory of multitrack diplomacy.[18] According to them, peacebuilding is the system orchestrated by nine tracks: government, nongovernment expert, business, private citizen, university, social movement (civil society organizations), religion, funding organization, and media. I include local governments into government (track 1). These various actors can prepare for a common security mechanism in East Asia.

[15] Sakamoto (1990).
[16] Tokola (2018).
[17] Common Security 2022 and Common Security in the Indo-Pacific Region (2024).
[18] Diamond and McDonald (1996).

7 Article 9 as Seen from the People of the World

7.1 *Interaction Between Global Civil Society and a Law for Peace*

It is often pointed out that the Kellogg-Briand Pact of 1928 (General Treaty for Renunciation of War as an Instrument of National Policy) is one of the origins of Article 9 clause 1 of the 1946 Constitution of Japan. One thing that should not be overlooked here is that there was a peace movement called the "outlawry of war" movement in the United States in the 1920s as one of the driving forces that made the Kellogg-Briand Pact possible. On the other hand, ever since the Hague Appeal for Peace Conference was held in the Netherlands in May 1999, global peace movements have often cited Article 9 of the Japanese Constitution as a law for peace. This interaction is extremely interesting. Peace movements instigated the Kellogg-Briand Pact in the 1920s. That Pact influenced Article 9 clause 1 in 1946. Then from the 2000s forward, it has been Article 9 that is most often cited by peace movements. Here we observe two interactions: one is between global civil society and the search for a universal law for peace, and the other is between the demands of international law and the strictures of national constitutional law.

7.2 *Article 9 to Prepare the Next World Order*

As mentioned earlier, it is well known that Article 9 is derived from the Second Principle of MacArthur's Three Principles. Here, I would like to focus on the expression in that Second Principle: "war as a sovereign right of the nation." This same expression was used in Article 9 clause 1: "The Japanese people forever renounce war as a sovereign right of the nation." This statement is extremely important. It means that Article 9 is a self-restraint on Japan's military sovereignty. Two directions emerge from here.

For a sovereign state, as long as it is justified under international law, the use of force is a possible option. Since Article 9 is a "severe restraint," it is understandable that a desire to revise Article 9 and become an "ordinary state" emerges. By revising Article 9 and regaining military sovereignty, Japan will return to a normal sovereign state. This is one direction.

The other direction is to take it as an "advantage" that Japan—being a "semi-sovereign state" with self-restraint on military action and working with global civil society organizations—could prepare for the next world order. This would be a world where military forces are reduced and strictly regulated and where international cooperation is strengthened. There seems to be an "alliance of Article 9 and global civil society organizations" because both of them need to overcome the current "realistic" order of international relations.

The history of Article 9 and our experiences with it may have shown the way to a transitional period of human history. We have been asked which way to go between returning to the modern sovereign state system or to pursuing the next world order (still ambiguous). It has been a period of transition and ambivalence. Global civil society organizations seek to create a next world order, and they resonate with the direction of Article 9. In that sense, it can be said that Article 9 stands with the people of the world. Article 9 of the Constitution is the supreme law of Japan, but the thought of Article 9 is for humanity.

8 Conclusion

8.1 Clarification of the Concept of Pacifism

The word "heiwa shugi" (pacifism) in the Japanese Constitution has been used without any widely agreed definition. Its meaning needs to be clarified. We will start by consulting the typology of ideas on war and peace, for which the typology of British political scientist Martin Ceadel is the most elaborate and informative.[19]

In Ceadel's typology five positions are located in the spectrum of war and peace, ranging from the most pro-war to the most anti-war. The most pro-war is militarism; then comes crusading; in the center is defensism; then the moderate anti-war position of pacificism; and finally the most anti-war, pacifism. Linearly, it is like this:

Militarism—crusading—defensism—pacificism—pacifism

One of the advantages of Ceadel's typology is the distinction between "pacifism" and "pacificism."[20] Pacifism does not allow the maintenance and use of any military force at all. In contrast, although pacificism does not abandon the long-term goal of abolishing war, it does provisionally maintain military force to be used for defensive purposes. Historically, both pacifism and pacificism have mutually coexisted, often without great distinction between them. It can further be said that pacificism, rather than pacifism, has been the mainstream among peace movements. But it seems that this dynamic was not noticed before Ceadel. When I translate "pacificism" from English into Japanese, I use "gradual pacifism" because pacificism tries to realize the abolition of war and military force gradually, emphasizing fundamental long-term institutional reform and the transformation of international order.

[19] Ceadel (1987).

[20] Ceadel (2010).

8.2 *Constitutional Pacifism as a Dynamic Process*

A closer look at postwar Japan's pacifism suggests that both absolute pacifism and gradual pacifism (Ceadel's "pacificism") have existed. The original intention of Article 9 seems to have been an absolute pacifist position that does not allow the maintenance and use of any military force. But during the Cold War and especially after the Korean War, Japan could not rely on the United Nations collective security system. As a result, a gradual pacificist position arose alongside of, and in addition to, absolute pacifism. The Cabinet Legislation Bureau's interpretation of Article 9 is that the Self-Defense Forces are the minimum necessary capabilities for self-defense and therefore they are not military forces—which are prohibited by Article 9—and that they may exercise the right of self-defense if Japan were to be attacked. This governmental interpretation, a gradual pacificist position, is the result of debates between the ruling party and the opposition parties. The latter are pacifist positions (the Self-Defense Forces are unconstitutional), and the former are more realistic defensist positions. In postwar Japan, it should be said that both absolute pacifism and gradual pacifism have coexisted complementarily.

Unlike absolute pacifism, gradual pacifism takes a long-term perspective. Gradual pacifism is a dynamic process in which we approach the final goal of overcoming military forces and war through our active engagement toward transformation of the international order.

Assuming that pacifism of the Japanese Constitution has elements of gradual pacifism in addition to absolute pacifism, our actions to create a more just and peaceful world order become crucially important. At the same time, from the standpoint of gradual pacifism aiming at long-term demilitarization, we are required to endure the contradiction between Article 9 and existence and activities of the Self-Defense Forces. Article 9 imposes responsibility on the Japanese government to explain the constitutionality and legitimacy of the Self-Defense Forces' existence and actions. No matter how large the contradiction between Article 9 and the Self-Defense Forces will become, the significance of Article 9 clause 2 as a provision imposing this responsibility will not diminish.

References

Abe K (2015) Okinawa and international protection of human rights. In: Shimabukuro J, Abe K (eds) Revisiting Japan's security from Okinawa. Iwanami Shoten

Ceadel M (1987) Thinking about peace and war. Oxford University Press

Ceadel M (2010) Pacifism versus Pacificism. In: Young NJ (ed) The Oxford international Encyclopedia of peace, vol 3. Oxford University Press

Common Security 2022: For Our Shared Future (2022) Olof Palme International Center, International Peace Bureau, and International Trade Union Confederation

Common Security in the Indo-Pacific Region (2024) International Peace Bureau, PEACEMOMO, and the Campaign for Peace, Disarmament, and Common Security

Diamond L, McDonald J (1996) Multi-track diplomacy: a systems approach to peace, 3rd edn. Kumarian Press

Hasegawa M (1960) The Ampo struggle and constitutional problems. Horitsu Jiho 32(11) (September Issue)

Hidaka R (2010) My experience on constitution. Chikuma Shobo

Komatsu H (2015) Postwar Okinawa and the peace constitution. In: Shimabukuro J and Abe K (eds) Revisiting Japan's security from Okinawa. Iwanami Shoten

Koseki S (2002) Re-examining Japan as peaceful state. Iwanami Shoten

Kwon HT (2016) Peaceless 'pacifism': thought and behavior in postwar Japan. Hosei University Press

Lee KJ (2017) The Japanese constitution in Asia: Japan-Korea relations and constitutional revisionism. Nihon Hyoron Sha

Muto I (2016) Postwar regime and constitutional pacifism. Shobo Shinsha

Oguma E (2002) <Democracy> and <Patriotism>: nationalism and the public in postwar Japan. Shinyosha

Sakai N (2008) Hope and the Japanese constitution. Ibunsha

Sakai N (2017) Nationalism of the withdrawal. Iwanami Shoten

Sakai T (1991) The end of the <Article 9--Security Treaty> regime: postwar Japan's diplomacy and party politics. Kokusai Mondai No. 372

Sakamoto Y (1990) The role of Japan in the World. In: International politics in the earth age. Iwanami Shoten

Toyoshita N (2015) Emperor Showa's postwar Japan: the road to <constitution-security treaty regime>. Iwanami Shoten.

Tokola M (2018) Dream big - a peace conference to end the Korean War and what it could become, on the Korea Economic Institute of America's website, https://keia.org/the-peninsula/dream-big-a-peace-conference-to-end-the-korean-war- and-what-it-could-become/

E. H. Norman, C. L. Kades, and the "Feudal Remnants" in Postwar Japan

Filippo Dornetti

1 Introduction

There is a blind spot in the drafting process of the Japanese constitution. It is common knowledge that Supreme Commander for the Allied Powers (GHQ/SCAP)'s Government Section (GS) staff wrote the draft that became the basis of the current Japanese constitution, after being amended and approved by the Japanese Diet. The constitution drafting, completed over the course of 6 days in February 1946, was the result of an initiative by General Douglas MacArthur. The General directed GS chief Brigadier General Whitney to have the GS prepare a draft. Whitney handed GS deputy chief Colonel Charles Kades a three-point set of handwritten provisions, commonly known as the "MacArthur Notes." The "Notes" were intended to be guidelines for the constitution draft. Point II called for the renunciation of the war and armed forces. To this day, it remains unclear who the actual author of these notes was—whether MacArthur himself or Whitney after obtaining MacArthur's assent to its content. All the more, it remains uncertain who originally conceived point II (McNelly 1982; Kades 1989, p. 224; Williams 1979, p. 42).

This chapter explores the intellectual connection between the Canadian historian and diplomat E. Herbert Norman and Kades. The latter repeatedly acknowledged his intellectual debt to the Canadian historian (Bowen 1986, p. 130; Dower 1975: LIII). However, scholarly literature has yet to thoroughly examine the precise terms of this intellectual debt—both in terms of its content and its chronological development. What may appear to be a marginal issue actually has implications that go far beyond mere biographical interest. Kades undoubtedly played a key role in the drafting of the constitutional text, since he was part of the standing committee

F. Dornetti (✉)
University of Milan, Milan, Italy
e-mail: filippo.dornetti@unimi.it

G. Cavaggion (ed.), *The 'Pacifist Principle' in the Italian and Japanese Constitutions in the Wake of the War in Ukraine*,
https://doi.org/10.1007/978-3-032-23108-6_8

directing the drafters and, more importantly, being in charge of reworking point II. If, as McNelly (1982, pp. 7–9) has suggested, he was also instrumental in the early discussions that led to the idea of abolishing Japan's armed forces, then it becomes all the more important to reconstruct the intellectual milieu in which he operated. McNelly (1982, p. 17) cited the influence exerted on Kades by the Paris Peace Pact and the interwar disarmament policies during his formative years as a lawyer and federal official. Far less is known, however, about the intellectual resources he drew upon during the hectic months when he served as deputy chief of SCAP's Government Section. As Kades himself admitted, he had no prior knowledge of Japan when he was first sent there (Gibney 1996, p. 75). On the other hand, various documented testimonies and studies have pointed out the considerable weight Norman's views carried within SCAP—most notably with General Douglas MacArthur himself—as evidenced by the decision to indict Konoe Fumimaro for war crimes (Price 2001, pp. 391–395; Bowen 1986, pp. 122–123).

It is therefore legitimate to ask at what stage of his work within SCAP Kades met Norman, to what extent he was inclined to accept and assimilate Norman's vision of Japan, and to what degree he sought to translate that vision into his own work.

To answer these questions, I consulted not only secondary sources in English and Japanese but also a number of primary sources preserved in the archives of the University of British Columbia (E. H. Norman Papers; Norman Family Fonds), Amherst College (Charles L. Kades Papers), and the National Archives of Canada.

In the pages that follow, I will consider Norman's studies on Japan prior to his encounter with Kades, highlighting the novel aspects of his work within the historiographical context of the time. I will also aim to demonstrate how Norman projected his historical interpretation onto an analysis of power structures in Meiji Japan—an analysis he still regarded as valid during the occupation years. In subsequent sections, I will attempt to reconstruct the relationship between Kades and Norman in the months preceding the drafting of the constitutional text by the GS, discussing the available testimonies on the subject and describing the work environment they shared. I will focus on the period preceding the constitution drafting, between 1945 and 1946. Finally, I will seek to assess the intellectual debt Kades owed to Norman by offering an internal analysis of some of Kades's writings; I will attempt to show how this debt was received and translated into political action, particularly in the matter of dismantling the oyabun-kobun system.

2 Norman's Historical Studies on Meiji Japan (1940–1944)

During his lifetime, Herbert Norman enjoyed significant prestige and attention, both as a historian specializing in Japan and as a political analyst. After his premature death, however, his intellectual legacy was quickly forgotten in the Cold War-era United States—partly due to the dominance of modernization theory in area studies but especially because of the infamous accusation of Soviet espionage (Bowen 1984, pp. 46–71; Pyle 1984, pp. 92–98; Dower 1975, pp. 9–102). In contrast,

Norman's reputation persisted in Japan and Canada, as demonstrated by the scholarly works dedicated to him, published intermittently even over the past 30 years (Price 2001, pp. 383–386).

Norman can be seen as a successor to the British tradition of Asian studies, represented by historians and analysts such as his mentor George B. Sansom (Bowen 1986, p. 112; Dower 1975, p. XLIII) and other prominent figures like Arnold Toynbee (Castellin 2016, pp. 95–110). Born in Nagano, a rural area in Japan, Norman spent the first 16 years of his life there. Nonetheless, he came to the study of Japanese history relatively late, after pursuing an education in classical studies and in European medieval history. Between 1935 and 1938, he earned his M.A. and Ph.D. in Japanese history at Harvard, supported by a Rockefeller Foundation scholarship.

After the doctoral completion, Norman preferred a diplomatic career over an academic one, but he still managed to publish several significant historical studies between 1939 and 1945. The core of his research during this period was the volume *Japan's Emergence as a Modern State* (1940), based on his doctoral dissertation. This was followed by two essays that further developed topics already addressed in the book: "Soldiers and Peasants in Japan: The Origins of Conscription" (1943) and "The Genyōsha: A Study in the Origins of Japanese Imperialism" (1944), both published in *Pacific Affairs*, the journal of the Institute of Pacific Relations (IPR). The first essay examines the 1873 introduction of military conscription, which Norman interpreted as a governmental tool for suppressing the numerous peasant uprisings that marked the Restoration years. The second focuses on the patriotic society Genyōsha, offering a concrete example of samurai opposition to the government following the defeat of Saigō Takamori's armed rebellion in early Meiji (229–230). In January 1945, Norman presented a "data paper" titled *Feudal Background of Japanese Politics* at the ninth IPR conference. Published posthumously, this work develops many of the themes found in his book (Norman 1975b). That same year, he also published a short article titled "Mass Hysteria in Japan" in Far Eastern Survey, where he interprets the Eejanaika movement as a violent reaction to feudal oppression (Norman 1945d).

In *Japan's Emergence*, Norman analyzes the formation of the modern state during the Meiji period (1868–1912), giving equal weight to short-term political and institutional developments ("the design lay with the Meiji architects") and medium-term socioeconomic structural changes ("a legacy of the preceding age") (Norman 1975a, p. 111). Across six dense chapters, Norman covers the crisis of the Tokugawa socioeconomic system (Ch. 1); the political developments of the Restoration (Ch. 2); and a detailed analysis of the social groups driving the transformation and the policies aimed at dismantling feudal structures (Ch. 3). Chapter 4 explores the early phases of Japanese capitalism, focusing on the origins of economic concentration via the zaibatsu and the roles of the state and international pressure in that process. The fifth chapter deals with land tax reform and its effects on rural classes, particularly in relation to the emergence of a labor market. The final chapter addresses the rise of anti-government parties in the 1870s and 1880s and the political configuration that followed the promulgation of the 1889 constitution. In this chapter, Norman identifies seeds of democracy and liberalism in the Popular Rights Movement (*Jiyū minken undō*) of the 1870s and 1880s. According to his account, this movement, "betrayed" by liberal parties, was ultimately stifled by the authoritarian and absolutist framework of the new constitutional regime.

In Norman's narrative, the Restoration occurred within a dual context of internal and external pressures: on the one hand, Western powers demanding Japan's opening to trade and diplomacy, and, on the other, a domestic crisis rooted more in social tensions than institutional failure—specifically, the rise of the merchant class, empowered by the growth of a monetary economy and credit networks, which eroded the Confucian social order of Tokugawa Japan to the detriment of the lower classes. In discussing the contextual elements that encompassed the Restoration, Norman's portrayal of Tokugawa society significantly differs from that of his friend and leading Japan historian, Edwin O. Reischauer. The latter emphasized the proto-modern features of Tokugawa Japan, such as the formation of a national consciousness and a commercial economy masked by feudal appearances. On the other hand, Norman describes it as an oppressive regime based on the exploitation and repression of the peasantry (Reischauer 1947, pp. 106–107; Packard 2010, p. 252).

Norman presents the Restoration as a "revolution from above," i.e., the result of an alliance between low-ranking samurai and merchants, who manipulated growing peasant discontent toward feudal institutions through the mobilization of armed peasant bands (*kiheikai*). A revolution it certainly was, as the political institutions and social order of Tokugawa Japan were abolished. Yet it remained incomplete, lacking a Jacobin phase. Norman writes:

> Once the crumbling bastions of the Tokugawa rule had been stormed in the war for the Restoration (1867–8) [...] the new Government set itself as firmly against any demand for further reform on the part of the lower order as it did against attempts to restore the old regime. (Norman 1975a, p. 111)

This quotation encapsulates a core thesis of Norman's research: Meiji authoritarianism was not the result of a political culture shaped over centuries by non-Western religious or cultural values, as argued then by some American scholars, like Robert K. Reischauer (1939, pp. 17–19). Rather, for Norman, it was a continuation of feudal forms that originated in the Tokugawa period and persisted into Meiji due to the revolution's incompleteness.

The question of feudal remnants in modern Japan had long been a topic of debate among Japanese Marxists. The most orthodox view within the Japanese Communist Party, represented by the Kōza school, was rooted in Comintern theses of 1927 and 1932. According to this perspective, the 1920s Japan was still semifeudal—legally and economically—dominated by tenancy and an absolutist institution as the imperial system. Notably, the discussion included the political institutions of Japan, an original aspect that stood in contrast to Marxist orthodoxy, which identified feudalism primarily with agrarian relations of production, similar to serfdom (Dower 1975, pp. 34–39; Dobb 1970, p. 35; Tōyama 1984, p. 125).

Norman was undoubtedly familiar with this debate. Yet in *Japan's Emergence*, he identifies feudal residues not only in economic relations and state organs but more broadly in a cultural system and social practices shared both by elite and subordinate classes. He writes:

> The ideal of feud loyalty, the patriarchal system, the attitude toward women, the exaltation of the martial virtues, these have acquired in Japan all the garish luster of a tropical sunset. [...] In Japan there has been a time-lag between the adoption of the new mode of life and the full maturing of its cultural and psychological expression. (Norman 1975a, pp. 116–117)

These traces of feudalism were not merely the result of a rushed or incomplete modernization process. Norman emphasized that it was the Meiji "bureaucrats" who actively preserved this tradition, as it served to sustain their own power. The Canadian historian never clearly defined "bureaucracy," neither in the book nor in other documents. He refers to state officials appointed—rather than elected—due to their prestige and influence in political circles (Price 2001, p. 394). In the volume he rejected a sharp distinction between civil and military bureaucrats, as their political networks spanned both domains (Norman 1975a, p. 312). Ultimately, in Norman's research, bureaucracy was defined more by its political function than its composition. As the direct inheritors of the samurai-merchant alliance, bureaucrats maintained power through political mediation—not only absorbing popular discontent, but also maneuvering behind the scenes

> the conflicts between the military and financial or industrial groups, shifting their weight now to one side and now to the other in order to prevent the complete domination of the military clique and to check big business from controlling politics in its exclusive interest. (Norman 1975a, p. 313)

In Meiji Japan the major conflict between the military forces and the government was the armed insurrection led by Saigō Takamori in 1877. As is well known, after being dismissed from the government for his position in favor of an invasion of Korea, Saigō led an anti-government revolt of his loyalists from Satsuma to enforce his idea. In "Soldiers and Peasants," Norman delves into this episode from the Meiji period, linking it to the introduction of mandatory conscription in 1872–1873. Unlike the more common interpretation, which analyzes conscription in the framework of national security policy as one of the many steps in the construction of the modern state, this essay presents conscription as a governmental tool primarily for internal political purposes. Introduced to suppress democratic and liberal movements, it had the effect of absorbing "the most aggressive militaristic elements of Japan," who, after Saigō's defeat, "preferred to work within the government to achieve and win their goal of aggression abroad and of stifling, militarist reaction at home" (Norman 1943, p. 156). Norman's judgment on the military forces of his time, heirs to this reactionary policy, was scathing:

> Far from not mixing in politics, as admonished in one of the Meiji Emperor's rescripts, the Japanese army has been the spearhead of fascism in Japan, and by its manifold political and propagandist activities has virtually obviated the need for a single fascist party as in Germany or Italy. (Norman 1943, p. 165)

Feudal Background was a conference paper originally composed of five chapters that shares the common goal of unraveling "the mechanism of Japanese reaction and particularly the role of chauvinism in strengthening the reaction" (Norman

1975b, p. 320). These chapters revisited and expanded on some of the arguments from the volume, also including the results from the article on the patriotic society Genyōsha. However, unlike the book, this text more clearly highlights the author's need to apply historical knowledge to the study of Japanese politics of the time. The context in which it appeared had changed. It was 1945, by which time the Pacific War was clearly headed toward an American victory, and a debate was emerging about Japan's future after defeat.

In the paper, we find a definition of feudalism in Tokugawa Japan based on several general characteristics: the presence of a dominant class based on land control, peasants bound to their condition living in misery, low productivity, decentralization of institutions, a politics of intrigue, and the destinies of individuals governed by social status (Norman 1975b, p. 323). The feudal structures of the Tokugawa regime were maintained by a set of oppressive institutions, namely, the police apparatus and mutual surveillance organizations, which served as precursors to the police state of the wartime era. Indeed, *Feudal Background* overlooks the formation of Japanese capitalism, emphasizing instead the autocratic consolidation of the Meiji state. In this process, the 1889 constitution functioned as the "bulwark of autocracy": positioned at the core of bureaucratic power, it replaced the former prestige of Satsuma and Chōshū, the regions that led the Restoration, with the cult of the Emperor.

Norman first applied the results of his research to the debate on Japan's future in 1944. In that year, the public opinion in the United States and in other allied countries engaged in an intense discussion about Japan's fate after the war. The terms of the debate centered on the Emperor's responsibility in the Japanese expansionism. In the American public opinion, the idea prevailed that the Emperor was responsible for the war and that the institution should be abolished once the occupation was completed. "Until the Japanese imperial dynasty is rooted out of Japan, it will apparently be impossible to make the Japanese a people for the company of civilized men" (Takeda 1988, p. 10). This view, published in *Chicago News* on January 31, aligned with similar editorials in the *New York Herald Tribune* and *The Nation*. The call by Sun Fo (1944), "The Mikado must go," was shared by most area experts of the time. For example, Owen Lattimore in *Solution in Asia* considered the Emperor to be an integral part of Japan's militaristic and economic expansionism and, therefore, should be eliminated (Lattimore 1945, pp. 47–48).

On the other hand, in the US State Department, a more conciliatory stance toward the Emperor's fate prevailed. Advocate for this position was Undersecretary Joseph C. Grew, who argued that it was necessary to use the imperial system to make the process of pacification easier and more durable (Grew 1943, p. 28; Takeda 1988, p. 11).

What positions emerged within the IPR, with which Norman was collaborating at the time? T. A. Bisson initiated the debate with an article published in *Pacific Affairs* in March 1944, entitled "The Price of Peace in Japan." In this article, Bisson offered an original perspective on the debate about Japan's future. He emphasized that the sources of Japanese authoritarianism should be detected not only in the Imperial Court but in a broad power bloc consisting of landowners, zaibatsu, and the armed forces. It was this alliance that had built the imperial myth that underpinned the aggressive nationalism of the Japanese people. Therefore, efforts to achieve a pacified Japan in the long run should not be limited to the abolition of the imperial system; they should also target the sources of authoritarianism through demilitarization, the fight against economic concentration, and land reform. This set of radical reforms, and particularly the abolition of the imperial system, if not carried out spontaneously by the population, should be imposed by the occupying forces (Bisson 1944, pp. 5–25).

Norman took up Bisson's arguments, aligning himself with the American commentator's positions. However, he emphasized that Japan's demilitarization should not be limited to the officers of the army and navy. It should also extend to the civilian sphere, particularly the police, a tool for political persecution and the heir of the Meiji-era police system he had studied (Norman 1975b, p. 458). He broadened the circle of responsibility to include the political police (*tokkōka*), the military police (*kenpeitai*), and the patriotic societies that had shaped the country's foreign policy, citing groups such as Genyōsha and Kokuryūkai, to whom he had dedicated a paper and discussed in *Feudal Background* (Bates and Latourette 1944, pp. 194–196). Regarding the responsibilities of the Emperor, Norman offered a cautious judgment, lacking sufficient elements to form a definitive opinion. However, he clearly stated that "even a disarmed Japan, if it is left with the Emperor system, will continue to be an unsolved and dangerous problem for the rest of the world" (Ivi: 202–203).

The cautious stance toward the Emperor question is reiterated in a report for External Affairs from September 1944, addressed to H. L. Keenleyside. In this report, Norman wrote: "It is not necessary for us to decide now whether or not we should permit the Emperor Institution to continue after Japan's defeat. [...] What is necessary is a scientific and objective enquiry into the historical role of the Emperor institution, its relation to the different cliques in Japan [...] One of the great objectives of weakening the forces of aggression in Japan will be in the first instance, to drive a wedge between the Emperor institution and the military clique" (Norman 1944, pp. 7–8; Bowen 1986, p. 130; Price 2001, pp. 389–390). According to Norman, the responsibility for Japanese expansionism lies more heavily with the power bloc, and allied forces should prioritize breaking the relation between the latter and the Imperial Court.

The judgment on the military forces, however, was much clearer: in the same document, he wrote: "not even a skeleton army should be permitted with a General Staff. [...] If Japan is left without any army, and, needless to say, a General Staff organization would be equally forbidden, even should Japanese of military ambition dream and plan another war, without a common center or organizational structure their daydreams would hardly menace the rest of the world" (Norman 1944, pp. 5–6). Thus, the historical and political judgment on the armed forces, already expressed in "Soldiers and Peasants," was reaffirmed, calling for drastic measures. However, it should be emphasized that Norman considered the armed forces, as well as the other power block elements, as parts of a broader alliance that should be addressed in its entirety.

3 Norman as a SCAP Official (1945)

Norman's commitment with the Department of External Affairs of Canada led him to reside in Tokyo almost continuously from 1945 to 1950. In 1939, he began his collaboration with the Department of External Affairs, and the following year he was employed as a language expert at the Canadian Embassy in Tokyo. After the attack on Pearl Harbor, Norman was interned at the Embassy for 7 months. From his repatriation in 1942 until 1945, he continued his collaboration with the Department of External Affairs, this time with the Examination Units, focusing on counterintelligence. In the summer of 1945, after Japan's surrender, he was in Manila, engaged in the repatriation of Canadians. In September, he returned to Tokyo, where, for 4 months until December, while maintaining his position as a Canadian Embassy official, he worked with the SCAP's Civil Intelligence Section (CIS), which was then led by General Eliot R. Thorpe. In February 1946, he returned to Ottawa. From March to July, he was in Washington as the deputy representative of Canada in the Far Eastern Commission (FEC), collaborating with Ambassador Lester Pearson. In the summer of 1946, he returned to the Canadian Embassy in Tokyo, where he served as the head of the liaison mission until March 1949, after which he was promoted to extraordinary envoy and plenipotentiary minister, holding this position until October 1950 (Bowen 1986, pp. 114–115, 117; Nakano 1990, pp. 108–109). From that month, back to Canada, he became the head of the Far Eastern Division at the Department of External Affairs in Ottawa.

Norman left Manila on a flight to Okinawa on September 8, 1945. On the same day, he met General MacArthur for the first time in Yokohama, where the headquarters of the Supreme Command of the Allied Powers (SCAP) was still located. MacArthur, who had been in Japan for just over a week, had been appointed by President Truman as the head of SCAP. As Supreme Commander, MacArthur was the highest political and military authority in the territory between Kyūshū and Hokkaidō.

According to the United States Initial Post-Surrender Policy for Japan, published on September 6, SCAP was not meant to replace the Japanese government but "use the existing form of Government of Japan" (The State-War-Navy Coordinating Committee: 1945). SCAP, therefore, upon receiving policy guidelines from Washington, was to translate them into specific directives for the Japanese government.

The Japanese government of the time, led by Prince Higashikuni, was not particularly inclined to this change. Formed after the declaration of surrender, the government's priority was to protect the imperial system and prevent the democratization envisaged in the Potsdam Declaration from undermining the established order. As a result, about 3000 political prisoners remained in custody, and more than 7,000 individuals continued to be under police surveillance (Yui 1987, p. 37).

In the unconditional surrender, the Emperor had committed to accepting the joint declaration of Potsdam, which included the removal of all obstacles to the development of "democratic tendencies among the Japanese people" (point 10 of the joint declaration) (Heads of Governments, the United States, China, and the United Kingdom 1945). Norman, just days after his arrival in Japan, was immediately aware that, after the surrender, the authoritarian system that had led Japan to war remained intact. In a letter to his wife Irene on September 25, 1945, he wrote: "The whole structure of bureaucracy is still unchanged—even down to the tokkōka (political police) whom I am informed are quietly watching Japanese suspected of being 'too democratic' or friendly toward Russia."[1] In his diary dated September 13, he jotted down a few notes, bitterly critical of the political class of the time, too compromised by the recent war: "Too many old men Ozaki, Abe Isoo, Hatoyama etc, deep resentment of people vs. their former leaders, but no way to show it."[2]

From October 2, the SCAP staff was reorganized into several special sections: among them, the Government Section, where Kades was placed, and the Civil Intelligence Section (CIS), where Norman began collaborating. In a letter dated October 26, he described his work to his wife Irene: "You have no idea how terribly busy I have been the last two weeks. Yet never so excitingly busy in my life. My present position is head of the Research and Analysis branch of the Counter-Intelligence of GHQ—and it is every bit as interesting as it sounds. (…) Incidentally, here are some of the jobs I've got into. Interviewing political prisoners and leaders—collecting books and magazines on politics."[3]

Under the leadership of General Thorpe, the CIS was primarily tasked with gathering information on individuals responsible for war crimes and arresting them. The first to be arrested was Tōjō, on September 11, along with his collaborators (Masuda and Yamamoto 2012, p.202; Emmerson 1978, pp. 253–254). In addition to this activity, the CIS was involved in gathering information on political prisoners, targets of purges, and ongoing political trends.

According to the authoritative testimony of Kades, it was the CIS that handled the preparatory documentation for the significant directive of October 4, known as the Civil Liberties Directive (Yui 1987, p. 40). This directive called for the immediate suspension and repeal of all regulations that obstructed freedom of thought in political and religious matters, as well as freedom of association and speech. It also called for the elimination of the police apparatus that had been a tool of political repression, particularly the tokkōka, the secret police. Finally, it ordered the release of political prisoners, including communists. Ōkubo Kenji, a friend and collaborator of Norman, who also edited the Japanese editions of his works, argued that Norman himself participated in drafting the directive (Katō 2002, p. 305).

At the end of September, Norman was engaged in a series of meetings with Suzuki Yasuzō, one of the promoters of the Constitution Study Society (*Kenpō Kenkyūkai*) (Nakano 2019). The association, consisting of prominent figures from the academic world and public opinion, presented a constitutional draft in December

[1] Herbert Norman to Irene Norman, 25 September 1945 (Howard and Gwen Norman Papers, Special Collections Division, Main Library, University of British Columbia, Box 1, File 1-8) p. 3.

[2] Norman (1945a).

[3] Herbert Norman to Irene Norman, 26 October 1945 (Howard and Gwen Norman Papers, Special Collections Division, Main Library, University of British Columbia, Box 1, File 1-8) p. 5.

that was highly appreciated by SCAP officials. This draft was used as a source by the Government Section committees involved in drafting the new constitution (Kades 1989, p. 227).

On October 5, Norman visited the Fuchū prisons together with John K. Emmerson, an official from the Political Adviser's Office, a political advisory body of the State Department that supported MacArthur's activities. During this visit, he was able to conduct interviews with Tokuda Kyūichi and Shiga Yoshio, who would later lead the Japanese Communist Party in the postwar period (Emmerson 1978, pp. 256–261; Bowen 1986, pp. 118–119). Between October and December, Norman was engaged in gathering intelligence relevant to the operations of purging suspected war criminals. In November, he submitted a memorandum on Konoe Fumimaro to the director of the Political Adviser's Office, which was forwarded to the State Department on November 17. Konoe had been the prime minister during Japan's 1937 attack on the Republic of China, and the memorandum provided documentation supporting his indictment as a war criminal. In October, Konoe had been tasked by the Imperial Minister of Justice to prepare a reform of the constitution. As already stated, his proposed constitutional draft, submitted in late November, was abandoned when Konoe was indicted in December (Bowen 1986, p. 122; Price 2001, pp. 393–394; Nakano 1990, pp. 115–116). Norman's intelligence-gathering efforts continued with a memorandum on Kido Kōichi, who was closely allied with Konoe and had held the position of Imperial Minister of Justice. The memorandum on Kido was presented to the State Department by Atcheson on November 19. Based on the memorandum, Kido was indicted for war crimes and sentenced to life imprisonment by the Tokyo Tribunal (Bowen 1986, pp. 123–124; Nakano 1990, p. 116). Finally, Norman produced a third memorandum, submitted to the Political Adviser's Office of the State Department in December 1945. This memorandum focused on Izawa Takio, a figure described as the "gray eminence" of Japanese politics. A member of the Privy Council since 1940, Izawa maintained a significant political role in the postwar period, though largely behind the scenes. Although he was not indicted by the International Military Tribunal, he was barred from holding public office in 1947.

During this intense period of work, between the autumn and winter of 1945–1946, the Canadian historian took the opportunity to revisit his studies on the Meiji-era Japanese bureaucracy, refining his analysis and critically applying its findings to the situation he observed daily. An unpublished memorandum titled "Japanese Politics," which according to Ōkubo was written in December 1945, provides a clear picture of Norman's perception of Japan under occupation during these tumultuous months (Ōkubo 1977, pp. 450–452). It is noteworthy that, at the time, the Higashikuni government, which had resigned after receiving the Civil Liberties Directive on October 4, had been replaced by the much more cooperative Shidehara government. Furthermore, following the aforementioned directive, the political police had already been disbanded. In the memorandum, Norman proposed a synthesis of the power system during the war period. He identified as the main characteristic of

Japanese politics "its anonymity of leadership and decision by inner circle."[4] Norman confirmed the composition of the political oligarchy that already presented in precedent writings: the military, the Imperial Court, the zaibatsu (large industrial conglomerates), and the bureaucracy. These groups had been able to maintain a balance of power based on a common interest, which centered around three key points: "the need for continuing the oligarchy's dictatorship over the people of Japan," "the desirability of Japanese expansion," and "the necessity of the Emperor system as the linchpin of the system."[5] Norman bitterly observed that the bureaucracy had managed to maintain the status quo, despite the efforts of the occupation forces to facilitate the transition to democracy. He commented: "Efforts of the bureaucracy to maintain its traditional position. Its attempt to act as a buffer between SCAP and the people of Japan. Higashikuni and the present government are relatively unchanged in political quality. The government, while not necessarily sabotaging GHQ directives, does as little as possible to implement them vigorously."[6] He further noted the centers of the "old bureaucracy" that still controlled Japanese politics: at the governmental level, officials from the Ministry of the Interior, including the clique surrounding Izawa, and in local politics, the "traditional Japanese 'boss' system."(*Ibidem*) The reference here is to the *oyabun-kobun* system, which, as will be clarified in the next section, Kades attempted to dismantle.

In his memorandum on Izawa, Norman delved more specifically into the political maneuvers orchestrated by the Japanese officials. After various regional appointments, Izawa built a career within the Ministry of the Interior, where he obtained the position of head of the police department (*keimu kyokuchō*) in 1914. He was elected to the upper house in 1916, appointed Governor-General of Taiwan in 1924, and became the Mayor of Tokyo in 1926. A supporter of the First Konoe Cabinet and its decision to attack China, he also played a significant role in the establishment of the Shidehara's cabinet (1945–1946). According to Norman's gathered testimonies, "Izawa is now contemplating a move to change the present government, replacing it with one which will inspire the fullest confidence of GHQ, but by trading on this confidence will be permitted to maintain intact as much of the old Japanese political structure as possible."[7] Izawa's clique consisted of "senior bureaucrats within the Home Office, prefectural governors (most of whom rose to high positions through Home Office careers), and influential members of the House of Peers."[8] The memorandum provides profiles of 15 officials who were part of this clique. In the 1930s, Izawa's network, through the *Kokuikai* association, played a significant role in connecting the military forces with civilian officials. Another association orchestrated by Izawa, the *Asameshikai*, sought to strengthen the ties between the military and the Imperial Court in the 1930s, after the Kwantung Army's invasion of Manchuria.

---

[4] Unsigned (1945?), p. 1.

[5] Ivi, p. 2.

[6] Ivi, p. 4.

[7] Norman (1945a), p. 9.

[8] Ivi, p. 3.

This political network of civil officials, already active in the 1930s, continued to exert considerable influence even after the war. The network was not tied to any particular political faction: Izawa had close ties with Hamaguchi and the Minseitō party in the late 1920s and early 1930s, but he had also built strong relationships with the opposition party, the Seiyūkai.[9]

Through the study of the Izawa case, Norman was able to confirm the eminent political role of the bureaucracy, which took on a more tangible form than in his previous works. Political networks of state officials, led by "gray eminences" like Izawa, extended to the military, the court, and large economic interests. This clique was certainly conservative and reactionary in orientation but lacked a clear political agenda. The goal seemed to be merely to reinforce cohesion between the various branches of the state through personalist relations, maintaining the status quo and their political preeminence. It was ultimately based on personal loyalty to the leader, according to Norman, in forms not dissimilar to the feudal relationships between samurai during the Tokugawa era. In a report presented at Yale in March 1945, before the war had ended, Norman had written: "The samurai tradition of feudal Japan has been preserved and transformed so that in its modern guise it has been the driving force in public affairs, steadily thrusting the nation towards more flagrant aggressions. The exponents of this tradition have well adapted their activities to the peculiarities of the Japanese institutional and political system, obviating the need for a single fascist party."[10] By the time of Japan's unconditional surrender 4 months later, Colonel Charles L. Kades of the Government Section was acutely aware of this enduring tradition.

4 Kades and the *Oyabun-Kobun* System

As previously mentioned, the GS was one of the sections that constituted the SCAP, established on October 2, 1945. The primary function of the GS was to provide advice to the Supreme Commander regarding the state and policies of the Japanese government, as well as the Korean military government. In practice, it translated the directives from Washington into concrete and actionable political guidelines to achieve the ultimate goal of democratizing Japan. The scope of the GS included policies on demilitarization, decentralization of government, the elimination of "feudal or totalitarian practices which tended to prevent government by the people," and the severance of ties between the government and the business world. These tasks were assigned to the Public Administration Division, led by Colonel Charles L. Kades (Supreme Commander for the Allied Powers 1949b, pp. 790–795; Kades 1989, p. 219).

[9] *Ibidem.*

[10] Norman (1945b), p. 2.

Kades arrived in Japan on August 30, the same day as General MacArthur. Like the general, Kades resided in Yokohama's Grand Hotel for the first half of September, before the SCAP was organized at the Daiichi Hotel in Tokyo. Upon his arrival, Kades began working within the GHQ on implementing the initial directives arriving from Washington before being assigned to the GS (Kades 1961, pp. 30–39). The GS was led by Brigadier General W. E. Crist until December 13, when Brigadier General Courtney Whitney took over the direction of the section. Kades and Whitney shared a strong determination to strictly implement the directives outlined in the Joint Declaration, particularly the elimination of any remnants of the military regime that had pursued a reckless foreign policy of aggression. US directives to SCAP implied the purging of individuals directly and indirectly responsible for militarism. The task of preparing the implementation directives for the purges was assigned to the GS, which produced an initial memorandum in early December 1945. The purging program was concretely applied through SCAPIN directives 550 ("Abolition of Certain Political Parties, Associations, Societies, and Other Organizations") and 548 ("Abolition of Certain Political Parties, Associations, Societies, and Other Organizations") (Political Reorientation, vol. 1: 10–17). Kades played a significant role in the drafting of these directives in the final months of 1945 (Williams 1979, p. 38). These were the main tasks he was involved in before the drafting constitution in February 1946.

When and how did Norman and Kades meet? I do not possess direct testimony regarding their relationship. However, it is not difficult to imagine that their first meeting occurred on the day Norman arrived in Yokohama, September 8, 1945. Norman left evidence that he met several military officials in the Yokohama Custom House, which was designated as the headquarters of the Eighth Army.[11] Following the establishment of SCAP at the Daiichi Hotel in Tokyo in mid-September, the likelihood of an encounter between the two increased, as they were working within the same building. A documented meeting between the two dates back to September 27, 1945. Kades recalls learning of the conversation between Hirohito and MacArthur from Norman himself. Norman had received this news directly from MacArthur on the day of the meeting, September 27, and that same evening, Norman revealed it to Kades (Sodei 1979, pp. 89–90; Bowen 1986, p. 136).

It is also noteworthy that in the archive of Charles L. Kades, preserved at Amherst College Library, within the series dedicated to documentation related to the Japanese constitution, under the subseries "Reports and Briefings," there is a typed document titled "Genyosha."[12] This is Chapter 5 of the paper *Feudal Background*, presented by Norman in January 1945 in the United States and never published (Norman 1975b, p. 317). One can imagine that Kades received this typed manuscript directly from its author between the end of 1945 and the beginning of 1946, during the preparations for the two purging directives, which also addressed the patriotic society studied by Norman.

---

[11] Norman (1945a), pp. 1–2.

[12] Unsigned (undated).

To what extent was Kades influenced by Norman's historical-political perspective? On January 17, 1946, a delegation from the newly formed Far Eastern Commission visited Tokyo to assess the activities of the GS, specifically inquiring about the section's role in the constitutional reform process. Among the members of the commission was Norman, who had concluded his assignment with SCAP to represent Canada on the international commission. Kades was called upon as the representative of the GS to report on the activities of the section he led. The representative of the Philippines to the FEC, Tomas Confessor, asked Kades whether the GS was studying a constitutional reform plan. Kades denied it and explained the relationship between the constitution and the GS's efforts to democratize Japan in the following terms: "In Japan, you cannot turn to the written constitution for everything you may wish to know about the governmental system. The written constitution is important in understanding the Japanese constitutional system. But the actual working constitution in Japan is a constantly changing complex of principles, usages, statutory elaborations, executive supplements, and extra-constitutional bodies. These changes occur from day to day" (GHQ SCAP 1946, p. 32). Kades seems to draw a distinction between the formal and the material constitutions of the country. For the latter, he refers to the "constantly changing complex of principles, usages [...] extra-constitutional bodies" (GHQ SCAP 1946, p. 32). It is not difficult to discern a veiled reference to the power cliques that permeated the Japanese political world above and beyond the rule of law, a topic that Norman had been investigating in Tokyo until just a few weeks earlier.

The pervasiveness of the "rule of men" as opposed to the "rule of law," which hindered the democratic progress of the country, was directly confronted by Kades in his battle against the *oyabun-kobun* system, from the summer of 1947 to the following year. The *oyabun-kobun* system refers to the complex of ritual kinship relationships characteristic of traditional Japanese social system. Ishino (1953, p. 696) defines it as an institution "in which persons usually unrelated by close kin ties enter into a compact to assume obligations of a diffuse nature similar to those ascribed to members of one's immediate family." Between the oyabun, in the role of the parent, and the kobun, in the role of children, there exists a paternalistic relationship in which the protection offered by the former is reciprocated by loyalty and reverence from the latter. In Japan, this system provided the framework for integrating the activities of a group engaged in the same endeavor, not only within political organizations or public administration but also in the labor market. The oyabun acted as an intermediary between companies seeking labor and workers, who were considered kobun. This institution had its origins in corporate organizations and the behavioral rules of the samurai during the Tokugawa period.

The SCAP began to study the oyabun-kobun system closely following scandals related to the hoarding and black-market sale of goods belonging to the Japanese armed forces. After the surrender, the Japanese government ordered the confiscation and custody of all goods possessed by the army and navy, including food, clothing, and vehicles. In early 1946, it was discovered that some of these goods had been illegally sold on the black market. In the summer of 1947, an independent investigation revealed that the proceeds from the illegal sales were used to finance the 1946 general election campaign. The investigation also exposed the key role played by police officers in these operations. These officers, part of cliques infiltrating the Ministry of the Interior and certain political parties, facilitated these illicit activities on behalf of public officials with whom they maintained ties of loyalty through the oyabun-kobun system. While MacArthur viewed this system of relationships as part of Japanese culture, and thus considered any intervention in this matter beyond the scope of SCAP's authority, Kades believed that every effort should be made to investigate and eradicate this phenomenon. He considered it a "feudal and totalitarian" practice that prevented the full democratic development of the country (Williams 1979, p. 45; Supreme Commander for the Allied Powers 1949a, pp. 307–313). It was not merely a matter of political morality: Kades suspected that Yoshida Shigeru, the leader of the Liberal Party—at that time one of the largest parties in parliament—acted as a "pipeline between their political group and some persons behind the scenes on a lower level" (Guascoigne 1947). There was a suspicion that some of these "persons behind the scenes" included purged individuals, who continued to exert influence over politics (Gayn 1989, pp. 472–475).

It is worth noting that in his December 1945 memorandum "Japanese Politics," Norman had already identified one of the key centers of political power at the time as a clique within the Ministry of the Interior. He also observed the pervasiveness of such relationships: "on the lower levels, contact with people maintained through traditional Japanese 'boss' system…cf. Also procurators and bosses of gamblers' groups."[13]

Norman would return to the issue in more detail in a dispatch to Ottawa on December 5, 1947. Contrary to descriptions in some newspapers, Norman did not believe that the cliques operated as a unified "secret government." Moreover, he commented that the oyabun-kobun system in the postwar period was far from in decline: "Since the end of the war […] the Oyabun system has been considerably strengthened by the flood of purgees and repatriated soldiers in search of some economic and social security, many of whom were able to find a niche for themselves in an Oyabun-dominated organization." According to Norman, given the nonexistence of a shadow Japanese government, the system required the attention of the occupying forces, as "this feudalistic system… quite patently acted as a potential or, in some cases, active opposition to the democratic reforms currently being carried out."[14]

Kades had the opportunity to explain the rationale of his crusade against the oyabun-kobun system in the Introduction of the 1949 book *Political Reorientation of Japan*. According to the Colonel, corruption in Japan stemmed from an attitude of impunity and a lack of civic responsibility among public officials, with deep historical roots. "The axiom of the Tokugawa Shoguns that 'punishment shall not be administered to the gentleman, nor courtesy to the commoner,' has not been repudiated" (Supreme Commander for the Allied Powers 1949a: xxxii). The system,

---

[13] Unsigned (1945?), p. 4.

[14] Norman (1947), p. 4.

which Kades referred to as "feudalistic corruption," (*Ibidem*) was nothing more than "another hangover of the Meiji era, rooted like the bureaucracy in the rule of men rather than the rule of law" (*Ibidem*). This, according to Kades, stemmed from the Meiji Restoration, which he presented as a "failed revolution":

> Unlike the English Revolution of 1688 and the American and French Revolutions in the eighteenth century, the Japanese 'Restoration of 1868' had not been a revolution directed against despotism, family privilege, and a stratified society. On the contrary, it entrenched more firmly the forces of tyranny and caste. (Ivi: xxxi)

As a consequence of this "failed revolution," "feudalism had technically ceased to exist. However, except for this centralization of the source of political authority and the concentration in the hands of a dozen family groups of monarchical capitalism, the feudal forces in Japan continued to exert strong influence on the morals and manners of people. These forces of extremes find a willing and powerful ally in a traditional Japanese bureaucratic clique which holds to the belief that the people are unable to judge for themselves that which is best for them" (Ivi: xxxiv, xxxxi). It is evident from these excerpts the imprint of Norman's analysis on the historical origins of the political configuration in postwar Japan.

5 Conclusions

The term "feudalism" was frequently associated with Japan by members of the occupation forces. Herbert Norman's studies on the history of Meiji Japan undoubtedly contributed in providing a precise meaning to its usage. In many cases, "feudal" was used as a synonym for premodern, obsolete, and ethnocentrically defined: for example, General MacArthur, in his memoirs, wrote, "Supposedly, the Japanese were a twentieth-century civilization. In reality, they were more nearly a feudal society, of the type discarded by Western nations some four centuries ago" (MacArthur 1964, p. 283).

Norman highlighted the persistence of aspects of feudalism during the Meiji period not only in agricultural labor relations and the imperial system as it was established in the Meiji constitution but also in an elitist and reactionary political culture, kept alive by the bureaucracy as a strategy for maintaining power. This feudalistic culture was perpetuated during wartime period by a system of clientelist and paternalistic relationships (the *oyabun-kobun* system) pervading the bureaucracy that contributed, he thought, to stifling the democratic seeds in the country. During his permanence in Tokyo, in the course of the occupation period, Norman further solidified his study of the Japanese bureaucracy, contributing to a deeper understanding of the cliques that retained their ability to influence Japanese politics.

This particular analysis of modern Japanese history was deeply internalized by Colonel Charles L. Kades. The two men lived in Tokyo during the American occupation years, from September 1945 to October 1950. More importantly, they worked closely together for the SCAP from September to December 1946. In those intense and decisive months, immediately preceding the drafting of the SCAP's constitutional draft, they likely had the opportunity to exchange ideas about the future of Japan.

Kades interpreted the application of point 10 of the joint declaration—the strengthening of democratic tendencies in the Japanese people—"somewhat the way the British change their constitution gradually, through directives and through reorganization of the government," without thinking, at least until February 1946, about rewriting the constitution (Kades 1961, p. 62). For Kades, the reform of the country's material constitution should include the elimination of paternalistic relationships within the police forces, which he believed were a concrete remnant of the Tokugawa feudal culture, still kept alive by the authoritarianism of modern Japanese state power. The perception of the complexity of Japanese politics, so tied to the unique historical development of the country, was perfectly aligned with Norman's studies and writings.

Can Kades' debt to Norman, as proposed in these pages, be extended to their shared interest in the elimination of the military? I was unable to find any direct evidence for this. However, it can be stated with certainty that Norman, whose opinions were highly valued by Kades, had expressed such views even before arriving in Tokyo. Moreover, disarmament, as a radical interpretation of the goal of destroying Japan's "war-making power" expressed in the joint declaration, was a goal that aligned with the postwar analysis of Japanese politics that they both shared. Specifically, a political world permeated by cliques and hidden factions, extending from the civil to the military sector, which would be difficult to eradicate solely through the rewriting of the constitution. A network linking disparate elements—politics, public administration, and economic interests—that would have represented a threat to international peace if it had been able to access military power.

References

Primary Sources

Bowen RW (1984) E. H. Norman: His Life and Scholarship. University of Toronto Press, Toronto

Bowen RW (1986) Innocence Is Not Enough: The Life and Death of Herbert Norman. M. E. Sharpe, Armonk, N.Y

GHQ SCAP (1946) Report of Government Section to Far Eastern Commission, 12 January. https://www.ndl.go.jp/constitution/e/shiryo/03/061/061_001l.html

Grew J (1943) Address at the Annual Banquet celebrating the 90th Anniversary of the Illinois Education association, Chicago, at 8:00 pm, December 29. https://www.ndl.go.jp/constitution/e/shiryo/01/003/003_028l.html

Guascoigne A (1947) Alleged "hidden government" in Japan, F 15227/15/23, 19 December (National Archives of Canada, Record Group 25, Vol. 3342, File 4606-40)

Heads of Governments, United States, China, and the United Kingdom, Potsdam Declaration (1945). https://www.ndl.go.jp/constitution/e/etc/c06.html

Norman EH (1944) Japan and the Japanese Empire: General Considerations, 22 September (National Archives of Canada, Record Group 25, Vol. 3342, File 4606-40)
Norman EH (1945a) A Japanese Eminence Grise: Izawa Takiwo, 19 December 1945. In: Ōkubo G (ed) Historical and Political writings by Herbert Norman, No publisher, privately mimoed by Ōkubo, 1978 (E. Herbert Norman Fonds, Special Collections Division, Main Library, University of British Columbia)
Norman EH (1945c) Notes from Tokyo visit (E. Herbert Norman fonds, Special Collections Division, Main Library, University of British Columbia, Box 7 File 2)
Norman EH (1945d) Samurai tradition in Japanese politics (E. Herbert Norman Fonds, Special Collections Division, Main Library, University of British Columbia, Box 7 File 3)
Norman EH (1947) Despatch to the Canadian Liaison Mission Secretary of State for External Affairs, despatch n. 304, 5 December, Department of External Affairs, Ottawa, 5/12/1947 (National Archives of Canada, Record Group 25, Vol. 3342, File 4606-40)
McNelly T (1982) General MacArthur and the Constitutional Disarmament of Japan. Transactions of the Asiatic Society of Japan (17):1–34
Pyle KB (1984) E.H. Norman and the New Stage in Western Studies of Japan. In: Bowen RW (ed) E.H. Norman: His Life and Scholarship.University of Toronto Press, Toronto: 92-98
The State-War-Navy Coordinating Committee (1945) Summary of United States Initial Post-Defeat Policy relating to Japan, SWNCC 150/3. https://www.ndl.go.jp/constitution/shiryo/01/022/022tx.html
Tōyama S (1984) The Appreciation of Norman's Historiography. In: Bowen RW (ed) E.H. Norman: His Life and Scholarship.University of Toronto Press, Toronto: pp. 122–138.
Unsigned (1945?) Japanese politics. In Ōkubo G (ed) Historical and Political writings by Herbert Norman, No publisher, privately mimeographed by Ōkubo, 1978 (E. Herbert Norman fonds, Special Collections Division, Main Library, University of British Columbia)
Unsigned (undated) The Genyosha of Fukuoka (Charles L. Kades Papers, Amherst College Archives and Special Collections, series 5, sub-series C, Box 2, Folder 44)

Secondary Sources

Bates MS, Latourette KS (1944) The future of Japan. Pac Aff 17(2):194–203
Bisson TA (1944) The price of peace for Japan. Pac Aff 17(1):5–25
Castellin L. G. (2016) Toynbee on trial: sul rapporto tra storia e relazioni internazionali. In Leonardi F, Maggioni L (eds) Arnold J. Toynbee. Il mondo oltre le civiltà, Edizioni Unicopli, Milano, pp 95–110
Dobb MH (1970) Studies in the development of capitalism. International publisher, New York
Dower JW (1975) E. H. Norman, Japan and the uses of history. In: Norman EH (ed) Origins of the modern Japanese state. Pantheon Books, New York
Emmerson JK (1978) The Japanese thread: a life in the U.S. Foreign Service, Holt, Rinehart and Winston, New York
Fo S (1944) The Mikado Must Go. Foreign Aff 23(1):17–25
Gayn M (1989) Japan Diary. Tuttle Publishing, New York
Gibney A (1996) Six days to reinvent Japan. Wilson Quart 20(4), 72(80):72–80
Ishino I (1953) The Oyabun-Kobun: a Japanese ritual kinship institution. Am Anthropol 55(5):695–707
Kades CL (1961) Reminiscences of Charles Louis Kades, Columbia Center for Oral History, Columbia University
Kades CL (1989) The American role in revising Japan's imperial constitution. Polit Sci Quart 104(2):215–247
Katō S (2002) Habāto Nōman, hito to gyōseki. Iwanami shoten, Tokyo

Lattimore O (1945) Solution in Asia. Atlantic Monthly Press, Boston
MacArthur A (1964) Reminiscences. McGraw Hill, New York
Masuda H, Yamamoto R (2012) MacArthur in Asia: the general and his staff in the Philippines, Japan, and Korea. Cornell University Press, Ithaca
Nakano M (2019) E. H. Nōman, Suzuki Anzō no sengo hatsukaidan, sono igi to jijitsukankei ni tsuite, Kanada kenkyū nenpō 59(76):57–74
Nakano T (1990) H. Nōman, aru demokuratto no tadotta unmei, Riburopōto, Tokyo
Norman EH (1943) Soldier and Peasant in Japan: the origins of conscription (Part II). Pac Aff 16(2):149–165. https://doi.org/10.2307/2751956
Norman EH (1945b) Mass Hysteria in Japan. Far Eastern Surv 14(6):65–70
Norman EH (1975a) Japan's emergence as a modern state. In Norman EH. Origins of the modern Japanese state. Pantheon Books, New York, pp 109–316
Norman E. H. (1975b) Feudal background of Japanese politics. In: Norman EH (ed) Origins of the modern Japanese state. Pantheon Books, New York, pp 317–464
Ōkubo G (1977) Hābāto Nōman zenshū, vol 2. Iwanami shote, Tokyo
Packard GR (2010) Edwin O. Reischauer and the American Discovery of Japan, Columbia University Press, New York
Price J (2001) E. H. Norman, Canada and Japan's postwar constitution. Pac Aff 74(3):383–405
Reischauer EO (1947) Japan past and present. Duckworth, London
Reischauer RK (1939) Japan government politics. Thomas Nelson and Sons, New York
Sodei R (1979) Makkāsā no nisen nichi. Chūōkōronsha, Tokyo
Supreme Commander for the Allied Powers (1949a) Political Reorientation of Japan, September 1945 to September 1948: Report of Government Section, Supreme Commander for Allied Powers, vol 1. United States Government Printing Office, Washington, DC
Supreme Commander for the Allied Powers (1949b) Political Reorientation of Japan, September 1945 to September 1948: Report of Government Section, Supreme Commander for Allied Powers, vol 2. United States Government Printing Office, Washington, DC
Takeda K (1988) The dual-image of the Japanese emperor. New York University Press, New York
Williams J (1979) Japan's political revolution under MacArthur: a participant's account. University of Georgia Press, Athens
Yui D (1987) Democracy from the ruins: the first seven weeks of the occupation in Japan. Hitotsubashi J Soc Stud 19(1):31–45

Whither Pacifism in Cold War Japan? An Interpretive Path (1947–1990)

Oliviero Frattolillo

1 Introduction

Japan's transformation, in the aftermath of the Second World War, from an unconditionally surrendered and catastrophically devastated country to a pacifist parliamentary democracy, should be analyzed in the framework of a series of "developments" that took place both nationally and internationally. The development, or crucial phases, of this process concerned the formulation of its pacifist identity and its institutionalization as state policy. Imposed on Japan by the Americans as a binding constitutional principle, pacifism served functionally and effectively so that the country could focus its resources and energies on economic reconstruction, while the national security was delivered into the hands of the United States. This strategy then sublimated a few years later in the so-called Yoshida Doctrine which, however, had its costs in the long-term.

This contribution analyzes the historical trajectory of pacifism as a state policy in Japan during the Cold War years, contextualizing it in the framework of the trans-Pacific alliance. Specifically, the analysis focuses on the institutionalization and development of Japanese pacifism in the period between 1947 (with the entry into force of the current Japanese constitution) and 1991, when Japan had to deal with the effects produced internationally by the First Gulf War.

The text is structured into three sections. The first analyzes historically the origins of pacifism in Japan by focusing on the idea that it was a heteronomous principle forcibly introduced and non-negotiable, instrumental to the broader political strategy that the United States aspired to in the region. The second outlines the trajectory of "pacifism as politics", identifying within the years of the Cold War a few

O. Frattolillo (✉)
Roma Tre University, Rome, Italy
e-mail: oliviero.frattolillo@uniroma3.it

G. Cavaggion (ed.), *The 'Pacifist Principle' in the Italian and Japanese Constitutions in the Wake of the War in Ukraine*,
https://doi.org/10.1007/978-3-032-23108-6_9

sub-periods or phases that highlight how pacifism in Japan has progressively taken root although the conditions of the international system have ended up weighing against its own application. The third and final section examines the implementation of Japan's pacifist policy at its "crisis" point, when the country had to face pressure from the international community (basing on the principle of the "burden-sharing") following the new needs for international cooperation in the security field that arose in the early 1990s.

2 The American Occupation and the Invention of Japanese Pacifism

The political, economic, and social consequences of Japan's occupation continue to fuel intellectual debate today. As Mark E. Caprio and Sugita Yoneyuki clearly stated in the introduction to their groundbreaking work, this has generated different interpretations of the historical significance of this process. In their words:

Some scholars credit this occupation with producing a pluralist and democratic Japan, which remained one of the United States' most loyal allies in the post-Cold War period. Others focus on the limitations that U.S. forces have faced, limiting their efforts to achieve the goals of the occupation. Still others focus their discussions on the effects that international crises, particularly world capitalism and Cold War politics, have had on this experiment. Finally, several studies consider the influence of employment policies on the "miraculous" economic growth that Japan enjoyed for much of the postwar period. More recent studies have considered this story from the Japanese perspective.[1]

The U.S. occupation of Japan, with the support of the British Commonwealth, began two weeks after its surrender on 2 September 1945, and lasted until early 1952. The Americans felt invested with the task of returning political sovereignty to the Japanese people, far from a reactionary tradition that celebrated the emperor (*Tennō*) as a real divinity. Postwar governments focused on rebuilding a nation completely devastated by war, traumatized by two nuclear attacks and an economic crisis that had deprived it of even basic needs. The belief behind the occupation was the universality of American values, which could help the Japanese curb militarism and adopt democratic and liberal values. The main changes promoted by the occupiers were political and made explicit in the constitutional reform. In addition to political and economic reforms, the occupiers also sought to inculcate the idea of American democracy in the Japanese people, placing magazines and newspapers under their control.[2] The American model of democracy would be the one to emulate. Similarly, the rules governing the family were also subjected to scrutiny, as was the school system, from which the country had to begin to educate young people in

[1] Caprio and Sugita (2007), p. 1.

[2] Kushner and Satō (2005), p. 28.

these democratic values. The United States soon asked Japan to provide war reparations to the victims of its military occupation; they also decided that the industrial apparatus considered unnecessary for the economic recovery of the country be demolished. In January 1946, the SCAP (The Supreme Commander for the Allied Powers) drew up a plan to dismantle most of the steel, shipbuilding, and related facilities, but the plan soon proved too difficult to be implemented: the victors could not agree on the division of resources and the equipment was in such poor condition that its value did not cover the costs of the transport elsewhere. Moreover, the Japanese economy would never survive such deprivation.[3]

2.1 *Yoshida Shigeru and the Transition to a Pacifist Democracy*

During the first phase of the occupation, the Americans instead of worrying about economic reconstruction, considered the demilitarization of the country and the democratization of its political institutions to be fundamental. They devoted most of their energies promulgating social, political, and above all economic reforms, which would make Japan a new Western-style democracy. In this regard, the United States considered it was essential, through the contribution of both the SCAP and Japanese politicians, to focus on drafting a new constitution. The members of the Japanese Cabinet were shocked, not only by the war renunciation clause resulted in the draft but also by the intimidation that the SCAP General Headquarters could not answer for whatever might happen to "the person of the Emperor if the draft were not accepted".[4] The new "Shōwa constitution", drafted by a team of U.S. officials, was soon considered the most promising outcome of the reforms accomplished during the occupation period. The text, approved by the Diet on 3 November 1946, radically reformulated the Japanese political-institutional structure: it extended the powers of the Diet and subordinated the institutional acts of the *Tennō* to the opinion and approval of the parliament. The occupiers' goal of acquiring popular sovereignty was fully achieved. The constitutional reform was aimed primarily at preventing the re-emergence of militarist forces in Japan, and to this end the "renunciation of war" was clearly prescribed in Article IX. This would become the epicenter of foreign policy choices in the future, the premise of bilateralism with the United States, and the push for Japan to become a civilian power. Japan had renounced its sovereign right to war. The approval process went through numerous parliamentary questions and protests from members of the Diet, who complained about the ambiguity of this article, especially regarding the issue of the right to self-defense, which was not mentioned in either paragraph of the article.[5]

---

[3] Fukunaga (2014), p. 51.

[4] Yoshida (1961), p. 133.

[5] Iokibe (1985), p. 43.

The Security Treaty clearly reflected the asymmetric character of the U.S.–Japan balance of power in those years. This, however, did not prevent protests from within the Diet, from both those who supported a strong U.S. engagement in the defense of Japan and those who opposed it. In the months before the signing of the Treaty, the idea that the country could question its anti-militarist pacifism and sign a security treaty with the United States, excluding both the USSR and China from the negotiating table, had fueled an extremely tense climate between the government and political opposition, religious associations, and social groups. Socialist leaders Asanuma Inejirō and Suzuki Mosaburō defended the idea of a "positive neutrality" that would make the country impervious to the Cold War and promote trade relations with the two Communist powers, averting dangerous military repercussions. The Communist Party, for its part, accused Yoshida of turning Japan into an outpost of international imperialism and fueling war against the Soviet Union in various ways.[6] Rearmament was the most sensitive issue (and would remain so throughout the Cold War and beyond) in Japan-U.S. relations. Moreover, it was thought that the USSR "could launch an attack on any of the many areas of the world".[7] The prospect was terrifying: an attack on Japan would mean the beginning of a nuclear war between the two superpowers, and their direct confrontation would occur in Asia. But the Americans feared that, if that happened, North Atlantic Treaty Organization (NATO) allies might reject the confrontation and then withdraw. At that point, it would have been inevitable to leave the Korean battlefield. The only way to prevent this from happening was to build a solid defensive line in Japan that would deter any feared Soviet initiative.[8]

Faced with this scenario, Yoshida showed skepticism and, while not in favor of radical neutralism, the prime minister had consistently maintained a pacifist stance, obstructing any talk of rearmament. In particular, he avoided any interpretation of Article IX that was not restrictive. In addition, Yoshida argued that economic recovery was a priority for Japan.[9] As a result, pacifism developed less organically and more forcefully during the years of occupation. From the American point of view, a constitutionally enshrined pacifist position for Japan was non-negotiable. The fact that Japan could not possess or maintain an adequate army for its defense due to the peace clause and, therefore, had to depend on the United States for its security, also served to legitimize a continued military presence on Japanese soil after the end of the occupation. This allowed the Americans to remain within the Asian continent, with a considerable force ready to be deployed anywhere in the continent when needed, just as was the case with the Korean War. American interests had therefore de facto imposed not only the inclusion of the peace clause, but also severe constitutional limitations on its amendment.

[6] Iokibe (2006), pp. 66–67.

[7] Heuser (1991), p. 18.

[8] Takemae and Sodei (1992), p. 67.

[9] Hoshiro (2022), p. 110.

Since there was no choice but to accept the imposition of a pacifist constitution, Yoshida continued to interpret and implement it in a way that would set the tone for Japanese politics for decades to come. Beginning with Yoshida's mandate as Japan's prime minister in the immediate postwar years, the concept of pacifism imposed and enshrined in the 1947 Constitution was exploited for Japan's nation-building and development efforts, while relying on the United States for its security needs.[10]

The new system established by the Americans was centered on an imposed pacifist ideal, which was accepted more for the gravity of the circumstances than for a choice. The same was then followed by Japanese leaders who took the helm after the occupation ended. Yoshida, of course, was at the forefront, and his interpretation and application of pacifism developed into a path that leaders would later take, either voluntarily or with a slight hint of reluctance.[11]

The development model that allowed the affirmation of pacifism as a policy in postwar Japan was analyzed using the methodology adopted by Iokibe Kaoru, in which the postwar years are divided into sub-periods, that are understood as "integral components of a whole".[12] Iokibe breaks down the first postwar decades according to the mandates of prime ministers Yoshida Shigeru, Satō Eisaku, and Nakasone Yasuhiro. Although the subdivision facilitates an understanding of historical memory and political developments after the Second World War, it has been specifically used here to trace the development of pacifism as a policy. Also, for a more complete understanding, I believed that the cabinets of prime ministers Kishi Nobusuke and Ikeda Hayato cannot be ignored. Thus, the trajectory of pacifism and the Yoshida Doctrine have been analyzed from 1947 to 1991, through the following sub-periods: Yoshida (1948–1954), Kishi (1957–1960), Ikeda (1960–1964), Satō (1964–1972), and Nakasone (1982–1987).

2.2 *The Kishi Effect: Realism Versus Pacifism*

One factor that attracted greater attention during Kishi Nobusuke's mandate as prime minister was the push to revise the Security Treaty with the United States to obtain less subordinate conditions to the Americans. As argued by the well-known Japanese historian Togo Kazuhiko in his study of Japanese foreign policy, by the 1951 treaty Americans were under no obligation to protect Japan.[13] At that time, threats were considered common, and the Americans would come to Japan's aid when necessary. However, there was still a degree of uncertainty. This aspect found a fundamental place in the negotiations for the amendment at that time, led by Kishi. Nonetheless, the amended treaty did less to alleviate Japan's position vis-à-vis the

[10] Hosaka (2009), p. 78.

[11] Takahashi (2014), p. 43.

[12] Iokibe et al. (2020).

[13] Togo (2005), p. 58.

United States and more to ensure that the Americans would now protect Japan from the treaty's binding obligations. Despite Kishi's penchant for rearmament, Japan maintained ambiguity through an implicit invocation of the Article IX. While this may seem like an added benefit, Kishi highlighted concerns about Japan's "unintended involvement" in the U.S. war efforts elsewhere, in case the Americans demanded reciprocity from the Japanese.[14] This situation, therefore, eliminated one level of uncertainty, but ended up creating a new one. Kishi's attempt to improve Japan's position, especially in terms of military capabilities, evidently did not achieve its rather ambitious goals. The overhaul and renewal of the Security Treaty led to a series of major pacifist protests across Japan, which eventually led to Kishi's resignation from office in 1960.[15] We can glimpse here a new element linked to the role played by the pacifism in Japan's historical-political path: Kishi was able to force the Americans to protect Japan through the Security Treaty, regardless of the common perception of the threat. And this happens although Kishi was inclined toward a radical revision of the Japanese constitution: it should be enough to consider that the "Commission on the Constitution" (*Kenpō chōsakai*)[16] wanted by his predecessor Hatoyama Ichirō and chaired by Takayanagi Kenzō—as part of the program of the Liberal Democratic Party (LDP)—started to work in 1957, under Kishi Cabinet. It is significant that, as argued by Kenneth J. Ruoff, both Takayanagi and the vice-chair Yabe Teiji "were inclined against revision" and adopted "a policy that effectively served to limit the commission's political power".[17] The Commission's work proved to be a useful exercise in clarifying and validating the interpretation of the no-war clause which justified the maintenance of a force that had solely defensive purposes. However, the firm opposition from the Japan Socialist Party (JSP) and the Japan Communist Party (JCP) within the Parliament dampened any potential enthusiasm, leaving the Commission to work for several more years without having a decisive impact on the internal political debate. Kishi will continue tirelessly for several years after his term to advocate for Japanese constitutional revision, both inside and outside the Commission.[18] As it can be read in the declassified Central Intelligence Agency (CIA) documents published in 1981:

The LDP's Commission on the Constitution which was established simultaneously with the merger of conservative has, throughout the past 25 years, reflected the ups and down of the arguments within the party; that is, although it has directly

---

[14] Togo K., *cit.*, p. 61.

[15] Perkins (2023), pp. 19–63.

[16] The National Diet Library, *Kenpō Kaisei Chōsakai Kansei*, NDL, Tokyo, 1955: https://www.ndl.go.jp/constitution/e/shiryo/02/058d/058d_001l.html (accessed 27 April 2025).

[17] Kenneth (2001), p. 80.

[18] In 1980 Kishi promoted a new campaign for collecting signatures across the country to start the process of constitutional revision under the slogan *Jidai o isshin* (for a complete renewal of the age) to indicate the radicalism of his ideas. See McCormack (1986), p. 59.

taken up the argument of the revision in the first half of its existence, thereafter, it has consciously avoided the issue.[19]

Kishi tried to further institutionalize the Yoshida Doctrine, as the United States would now play an even more deliberate role in protecting Japan, while Article IX continued to be invoked, ostensibly protecting Japan from mutual involvement. This shows that although there was resistance to Japanese submission under the Security Treaty, Yoshida's successors were willing to follow a similar framework, with renegotiations, where possible.

2.3 *Ikeda's "Three Pillars Theory" and the Pacifism Constraints*

On 19 July 1960, Ikeda Hayato became prime minister. Japan was emerging from the extremely chaotic and frenetic period due to the Anpo (Anzen Hoshō Jōyaku) protests for the renewal of the Security Treaty with the United States. His weighted positioning based on "Tolerance and patience" (*Kanyo to nintai*), however, did not exclude Japan from undertaking initiatives in pursuit of its national interest and stability, based primarily on Japan's economic growth (for which Ikeda is generally remembered in history books). The figure of Ikeda himself seemed that of an independent-minded individual, inclined to follow ambitious objectives, without fear of risk and not completely aligned with imposed rules: the rhetoric on the undertaking of a policy mainly conciliatory and his "low profile" appeared as an expedient to better address the needs of the moment.[20]

The search for such initiatives had necessarily to be built against the background of the international system that from the Japanese perspective was based on a solid pre-eminence of the relationship with Washington, and upon its belonging to the "Free World" as opposed to the communist bloc (which at that time was moreover in crisis due to the Sino-Soviet Split). In such scenario, an equally Japan-Western Europe axis was inexistent, mainly due to trade disputes between the two parts. Ikeda adopted a proactive diplomatic approach, leveraging on the common belonging to the Western block and proposing his "Three Pillars theory" (*Sanbon bashira*). In Ikeda's eyes, the international system was in those years made up of three pillars: the United States, Western Europe, and Japan. To strengthen this system, it was necessary to consolidate the Eurasian axis, strengthening relations with Western European countries. The *Sanbon bashira* approach therefore seemed to be not only a lens for observing the geopolitical structure of the "Free World", but also a persuasive rhetoric useful for convincing European actors that trade discrimination against

[19] Central Intelligence Agency, *Japan Report (FOUO 40/81)*, JPRS L/9840, 13 July 1981, p. 16: https://www.cia.gov/readingroom/docs/CIA-RDP82-00850R000400030021-1.pdf (accessed 27 April 2025).

[20] Tadokoro (2011), pp. 81–82.

Japan could have been functional to the interests of Moscow and Beijing, willing to take advantage of every crack to wedge themselves into the internal strife of the liberal democracies and compromise them.[21] In November 1962 Ikeda went on diplomatic missions to Berlin, London, Paris, Brussels, The Hague, and Rome. The prior support assured in Washington by the American President John F. Kennedy in 1961 was fundamental, as he didn't agree with the idea that Japan, now a fully industrialized country, was not part of the OECD as this exclusion made a neutralist Japanese drift more possible. In his own words, "Western Europe, U.S. and Japan if tied closer and closer together can serve as a basis to expand the cause of freedom in the world".[22]

Against the backdrop of such dynamics, it is easy to understand that the Ikeda government had seriously considered the possibility of revising the pacifist clause that could allow the country to fully play its leading role as the third pillar of the free world, even in the military field. From the evidence of a CIA archive document, this thesis is fully confirmed:

Ikeda thinks of Japan as one of the three pillars of the free world, along with Western Europe and the United States. If he could have it his way, he would probably move rapidly toward his military goals, and in so doing he would like to take advantage of the renewed sense of national self-confidence and independence inspired by the nation's spectacular economic revival.[23]

Likewise, Ikeda had accepted the "Final Report of the Commission on the Constitution" produced in 1964, then submitted to the Diet. In September of the same year, the Cabinet Bureau of Legislation established a special section to make further recommendations on the conclusions reached and suggestions that had been expressed. It was hoped that the debate could continue within the Diet, considering starting a possible process of constitutional revision based on the Commission's report.[24] As the Americans themselves have acknowledged, Ikeda's government "appears to be taking an increasingly positive attitude toward defense" and "the revision of Article IX as part of a larger program of constitutional revision has been discussed tentatively".[25] However, the socialist opposition strenuously opposed any attempt at revision, fearing that Japan might return to a pre-1945 style of militarism and that it was accommodating the interests of a certain business community for a

---

[21] Ikeda (2007), p. 19.

[22] Kennedy Presidential Library, *Visit of Prime Minister Ikeda to Washington, June 20–23, 1961. Policy Toward Communist China*, Declassified E.O. 12356, Sec. 3.4, NLK-92-138; Diplomatic Archives of the Ministry of Foreign Affairs of Japan, "Ikeda sōri Ōshū hōmon", 29 October 1962, Ō-A-kyoku, *Sōri hōhō kaidan yōchōsho* (A'0365).

[23] Central Intelligence Agency, *Special Report. Shifting Japanese Attitudes on Defense*, OCI No. 0334/64A, 5 June 1964, p. 56: https://www.cia.gov/readingroom/docs/CIA-RDP79-00927A004500020002-1.pdf (accessed 28 April 2025).

[24] Ward (1965), p. 425.

[25] Central Intelligence Agency, *Special Report. Shifting Japanese Attitudes on Defense*, *cit.*, p. 3.

full rearmament of the country. As stated by the CIA itself, "Ikeda nevertheless sees ample evidence that Japan is not ready for any substantial or speedy remilitarization".[26]

2.4 Satō and the Making of Japan's Non-Nuclear Policy

Satō Eisaku took office immediately after the 1964 Summer Olympics, which marked a symbolic, if not political, affirmation of Japan's full return to the international community of nations. The Olympics also took place during a decade of massive economic growth in Japan. However, post-revision protests by the Anpo erupted across the country, with Tokyo turning into a melting pot of voices from different sides and Japanese pacifism finding renewed relevance.[27]

These protests revealed the underlying tensions within the U.S.-Japan Alliance and focused on two main fronts. First, there were concerns about Japan's "unintended involvement" in war theaters.[28] Now that the Americans were obliged to defend the Japanese, fears arose that Japan might be called upon to help the Americans in their endeavors as the Cold War evolved, particularly in terms of military assistance. This did not fit well with Japan's now entrenched pacifist position, among both political leaders and the population, and thus fueled the renewed relevance of pacifist principles. The Japanese analyst Izumikawa Yasuhiro argued that this fear of "entrapment" was an integral element of Japan's pacifism.[29]

Satō belonged to Yoshida's school of thought, given his long collaboration with the former prime minister, and was in favor of continuing in a broad sense with the Yoshida Doctrine.[30] At the same time, he felt that the time had come for Japan to be more assertive, albeit in line with its modern pacifist identity. This became increasingly relevant in the wake of the turmoil that had shaken the nation in those years. Pacifism as a policy was further developed during Satō's mandate through both the return of Okinawa to Japan, thus guaranteeing complete territorial sovereignty, and the withdrawal of nuclear weapons from the Japanese soil. Moreover, if the domestic policy focused on upholding peace and prosperity, Satō's international political agenda was characterized by the adoption of an "omnidirectional peaceful diplomacy" (*zenhōi heiwa gaikō*), striving toward a "friendly approach" to all countries. The premier was facing a new international scenario as the world order was no longer merely a reflection of flexible bipolarism. The emergence of new conflicts that were not necessarily global but linked to local antagonisms, produced by ideological issues and imbalances in the regional geopolitical contexts, had determined new strategic scenarios. Although the multipolarization process was still under

---

[26] Central Intelligence Agency, *Special Report. Shifting Japanese Attitudes on Defense*, *cit.*, p. 4.

[27] On this subject see: Hasegawa (2019); Miller (2019), pp. 953–986.

[28] Togo K., *cit.*, p. 61.

[29] Izumikawa (2010), pp. 123–160.

[30] See Nakakita (2020); Kawai (2022), pp. 422–451.

development, it suggested that the stability of the international system could no longer depend solely on the peaceful coexistence of the two blocks.[31]

With the return of administrative sovereignty over Okinawa to Japan, Satō had managed to "carry out Yoshida's peace diplomacy" and, through the maintenance of American forces in the Ryūkyū, had also ensured the continuation of the Yoshida Doctrine.[32] Moreover, Satō's invocation of the "Three Non-Nuclear Principles" in 1967 gained more credibility.[33] With Okinawa back under Japanese control, the Americans gradually withdrew all nuclear weapons from Japanese territory. Satō was thus able to interpret and use pacifism as a policy in a way that played into Japan's favor. Although the Okinawans did not achieve their goals, the broader Japanese aim of a complete administrative sovereignty was achieved. Thus, despite Satō's government seeing another round of protests by the Anpo in 1970, when the treaty was automatically renewed, his use of pacifism as policy to regain control over Okinawa and convince Americans to withdraw nuclear weapons from the island played in his favor.

Nevertheless, the Commission on Constitution had not abandoned its revisionist goals and in 1972, under Tanaka Kakuei's government (1972–1974), a "Draft of the outline of the revision" which followed the 1956 interim report was released. Compared to the latter, which emphasized how the constitution had been a "forced" text for the country, explicitly exposing its most critical aspects, the new draft minimized "these problematic points and used less bold language".[34]

From what we learn from some archive documents:

The same can be said for the League of Dietmen for Realization of Autonomous Constitution, regarded as the "head temple" of the hawk faction within the LDP. Young Dietmen tend to shy away from the League as if to imply that the "Constitution issue is not a vote-getter".[35]

The time, once again, was not ripe. However, it was announced on 8 October 1974, that Satō would be awarded the Nobel Peace Prize, becoming the first Japanese to receive it. The Norwegian Nobel Committee named his efforts toward peace in the Pacific and stopping the proliferation of nuclear weapons as the reasons for the choice.[36]

---

[31] See Satō (1999).

[32] Hattori (2021), p. 113.

[33] "Three Non-Nuclear Principles"—Statement by Prime Minister Eisaku Satō at the Budget Committee in the House of Representatives (11 December 1967): https://www.mofa.go.jp/policy/un/disarmament/nnp/index.html#:~:text=My%20responsibility%20is%20to%20achieve,line%20with%20Japan's%20Peace%20Constitution (accessed 19 April 2025).

[34] Central Intelligence Agency, *Japan Report (FOUO 40/81)*, *cit.*, p. 16.

[35] Central Intelligence Agency, *Japan Report (FOUO 40/81)*, *cit.*, p. 16.

[36] See Hattori (2021), pp. 234–245.

2.5 *Nakasone, Pacifism, and the Defense Dilemma*

If Yoshida had paved the way for Japan's later leaders, Kishi had attempted a renegotiation, Ikeda struggled against the anti-militarist constraints, and Satō had resorted to pacifism to regain full administrative sovereignty, Nakasone Yasuhiro raised the question of Japan's greater role in security, while remaining a pacifist nation. While Satō was proceeding with the "Non-Nuclear Principles" announced in 1967, it was Nakasone who suggested the addition of a third principle, namely that the Japanese government would not permit their introduction into Japan, despite its well-known propensity for the country's rearmament.[37] This underscored the political importance he initially gave of staying within the confines of pacifism, while supporting a better-armed Japan.

Nakasone had served as Director General of the Japan Defense Agency (reorganized as the Ministry of Defense after 2006) in the early 1970s, and his views on Japan's role in security had evolved significantly during this Cabinet. According to the Japanese scholar Komine Yukinori, Nakasone "was frustrated by Japanese citizens' aversion to acquiring solid self-defense skills, an aversion he believed stemmed from post-1945 Japanese pacifism", and was "particularly critical of the so-called Yoshida Doctrine".[38] Given his strong views on a renegotiation of the security and defensive posture for Japan when he assumed power in 1982, it is necessary to frame both Nakasone and his vision for a rearmed Japan in the broader context of developments before and during his premiership.

During a historic visit to Guam in 1969, the U.S. President Richard Nixon announced a radical change in U.S. foreign policy, which is known as the "Nixon Doctrine": each ally nation was in charge of its own security, but the United States would act as a nuclear umbrella when requested. The President's statements came at a time when the Americans were engaged in a strategic withdrawal from the war in Vietnam. Responding to a question about potential concerns from Asian nations about how the United States intended to continue to play a significant role in security in Asia considering its disengagement in Vietnam, Nixon stated that the United States would provide military assistance to nations that requested it, but would not undertake all the defense of the free nations of the world.[39] This strategic redirection served to cast doubt on Japan's security posture within its alliance with the United States. Would the Americans intervene to help Japan only in the event of a nuclear threat? How could Japan then have defended itself in the event of a conventional threat, other than a nuclear war, given the pacifist clause that the Americans themselves had imposed within the constitution? Was the White House attempting to shirk its obligation to defend Japan under the revised Anpo by making such an

---

[37] Hattori (2023), p. 91. See also Komine (2016).

[38] Komine Y., *cit.*, p. 98.

[39] The American Presidency Project, *Richard Nixon - Address to the Nation on the War in Vietnam*, November 03, 1969: https://www.presidency.ucsb.edu/documents/address-the-nation-the-war-vietnam (accessed 25 April 2025); Hanhimäki (2008), p. 39.

announcement? The Japanese found themselves in a dilemma regarding the constraints of the pacifist clause, as well as the Yoshida Doctrine, which had embraced a limited scope of operation for the *Jieitai* (or Self-Defense Forces).[40] Nakasone, who took over the leadership of the Japan Defense Agency in 1970, was faced with these questions, especially about Japan's self-defense capabilities, rearmament, and a greater security role for Japan, not only for its own defense but also, ultimately, for the defense of the neighboring countries. For Nakasone it was crucial to bridge any potential gap between the United States and Japan, especially in the security field. As prime minister, he deliberately attempted to develop a relationship of mutual understanding and cooperation, with a personal touch, between himself and the then U.S. President, Ronald Reagan—the so called Ron-Yasu relationship which found its leverage in a common and strong anti-communist orientation.[41] In doing so, Nakasone also intended to pursue his desire for a more independent Japan with greater self-defense capabilities, while promoting deeper relations with Washington.[42]

During Nakasone's mandate and given Reagan's tacit recognition of his goals for a more security-oriented Japanese position, his critics, both domestically and internationally, expressed their fears about what they saw as an attempt to repeal the peace clause entirely. This could have potentially led to a "resurgent Japanese militarism", which according to Chalmers Johnson can be understood as the "first horn of the current Japanese defense dilemma".[43] On the other hand, the second horn emerged in the form of a persistent accusation that Japan is "playing its cards open" on the backs of Americans, Koreans, Taiwanese, and all other peoples of the Pacific basin who take seriously their responsibilities in trying to maintain a stable and secure environment. Concerns about a return of Japan to prewar "militarism", however hyperbolic the claim, nevertheless existed among nations that had experienced Japanese occupation. Given these developments, Nakasone found himself with more limited room for maneuvering. In a letter addressed to Nakasone dated 2 September 1985, Reagan wrote about the future of the relationship between the two countries, emphasizing the need to protect liberal trade.[44] The only option left to him was to continue within the framework of the Yoshida Doctrine, regardless of how it was perceived by other Asian nations. Accusations of not contributing to security weighed much less than those of renewed militarism. Despite Nakasone's attempts to increase the prestige and relevance of the Japanese military and its role,

[40] Edström (2025), p. 240.

[41] Dickinson (2021), p. 153.

[42] Ministry of Foreign Affairs of Japan, *Nakasone Sōri Daijin no hōbei kanren bunsho*, 1985: https://www.mofa.go.jp/mofaj/gaiko/bluebook/1985/s60-shiryou-407.htm (accessed 18 April 2025).

[43] Johnson (1986), pp. 558–559.

[44] Wilson Center Digital Archive, Diplomatic Archives of the Ministry of Foreign Affairs of Japan, *Letter, Ronald Reagan to Yasuhiro Nakasone*, September 2, 1985, File No. 2017-0631: https://digitalarchive.wilsoncenter.org/document/270633 (accessed 25 April 2025).

he eventually had to return and continue to adopt pacifism as a policy.[45] His contributions, however, are not without legacy, as it was Nakasone's legacy that informed and, to some extent, influenced the policies of Japanese leaders in the twenty-first century.

3 The "End of History" and the First Turmoil in Japanese Pacifist Identity

After the fall of the Berlin Wall and the upheaval of the international order, political circumstances often exceeded the goals of the Japanese leaders (as they had been until then), leading to compromises of one kind or another. "Pacifism as politics", therefore, did not remain unscathed, and in 1991 it recorded a first breaking point.

On 2 August 1990, Iraq invaded Kuwait. After its annexation to the *status* of an Iraqi province, the United Nations condemned the invasion and demanded the unconditional withdrawal of Iraqi troops from the Kuwait's territory. The subsequent negotiations did not lead to significant breakthroughs, or to a withdrawal of Iraqi troops from the occupied lands and, when there was a real risk that Iraq would invade Saudi Arabia (with its huge oil reserves) on 16 January 1991, the United States began the military invasion of the country. Five weeks later, on 27 February, Iraq was forced to sign the surrender. Meanwhile, the Japanese collaborated with U.S. diplomats, freezing all Kuwaiti assets held in Japan.[46]

That September, moreover, Japanese government submitted to the Diet an "Act on Cooperation for United Nations Peacekeeping Operations and Other Operations", as to provide non-military support and aid to multilateral forces and not to send its own Self-Defense Forces into war theaters.[47] The Act included provisions about the "five principles of participation in UN PKOs", and following a difficult debate in the Diet, the "PKO Act" was approved in June 1992 and enacted in August. This policy would also involve the deployment of the Self-Defense Forces in response to requests from the U.S. government.[48]

Upon explicit request from the U.S. President George H.W. Bush to join in sanctions on Iraq, Misoji Sakamoto (chief Cabinet Secretary in the government of Japanese Prime Minister Toshiki Kaifu—1989–1991) announced a set of sanctions against Iraq on August 5 "that included such measures as a ban on oil imports from

[45] Hattori R., *Fighting Japan's Cold War: Prime Minister Nakasone Yasuhiro and His Times*, *cit.*

[46] Ministry of Foreign Affairs of Japan, *Diplomatic Bluebook 1991*, "Section 2. Japan's Response to the Gulf Crisis": https://www.mofa.go.jp/policy/other/bluebook/1991/1991-2-2.htm (accessed 5 April 2025).

[47] Ministry of Foreign Affairs of Japan, *Special Feature: 20th Anniversary of Japan's Participation in the United Nations Peacekeeping Operations*: https://www.mofa.go.jp/policy/other/bluebook/2013/html/chapter3/cp3_sf1.html (last access on 21 April 2025).

[48] Inoguchi (1991), p. 258.

Iraq and a freeze on all ODA to that country".[49] The same did the Western allies, imposing economic sanctions on Iraq before mobilizing their troops in the area. Japan, on the other hand, was in trouble perceiving its role in this realm. The main constraint felt was the lack of non-economic options that could be adopted by the *Kantei* (the Prime Minister's Office). Thus, the inaction on the part of the Japanese government began to lead to resentment from the White House. As a result, within the LDP, a debate arose on whether to go beyond Japan's traditional "checkbook diplomacy".[50] Within the government and the LDP, criticism and dismay were expressed regarding Japan's helpless and passive behavior toward such an international emergency.

Meanwhile, at a press conference held on 31 August 1990, the Minister of Finance Hashimoto Ryutarō publicly responded to the plan drawn up by the Minister of Foreign Affairs, Nakayama Tarō, by increasing the financial contributions to the maximum amount possible for that year.[51] Despite their efforts, the economic and trade measures launched by Tokyo were criticized by the Bush administration, as they were considered aimed at maximizing private profits and minimizing risks of Japanese lives.[52] Furthermore, some criticism arose in the U.S. Congress on Tokyo's perceived foot-dragging on the issue and its refusal to dispatch Self-Defense Forces to the Middle East.[53] Since the financial commitment was of paramount importance to demonstrate Japan's role alongside the United States during this crisis, an additional financial aid was announced on 14 September. The commitment of an additional four billion dollars was therefore arranged and the government decided to allocate these aids to multinational forces and emergency loans for the damaged areas.[54]

In addition, the *Kantei* had to deal with the compatriot hostages stranded in Iraq and Kuwait. In fact, approximately 500 Japanese citizens were in that territory during the conflict. However, Japan was very cautious, in the face of this crisis, not to take unilateral actions so as not to harm the Allies. The financial proceedings and sanctions issued by Japan were also criticized by Iraq itself, as it accused Japanese diplomacy of being too dependent on the White House. These accusations and criticisms also led, in an already politically delicate situation, to internal tensions in

[49] Sadō (2015), p. 28.

[50] Purrington (1991), p. 309.

[51] Bochorodycz (2017), pp. 30–31.

[52] Inoguchi T., *cit.*, pp. 309–310.

[53] Doi T., "Diplomatic Documents: Hefty Host Nation Payments Legacy of '90 Persian Gulf Crisis", *The Asahi Shimbun*, December 23, 2021: https://www.asahi.com/ajw/articles/14508829 (accessed 21 April 2025).

[54] The Washington Post, *Japan Offers New Gulf Aid. $4 Billion to Help Economies, US-Led Force*, 14 September 1990: https://www.washingtonpost.com/archive/politics/1990/09/14/japan-offers-new-gulf-aid/fa293995-3284-488d-846d-24969d6defc4/ (accessed 21 April 2025).

Japan, where many citizens accused the government of underestimating its primary importance in protecting the lives of the 261 Japanese hostages.[55]

In addition, in a memorandum of telephone conversation between Bush and Kaifu we learn that the U.S. President thanked the Japanese premier for supporting sanctions against Iraq but pressed a new request for support with military operations. Kaifu's reply underscored the difficult political bind such a request places him in: "With respect to the military side that you have touched upon, because of our constitutional constraints and Diet resolutions, it is almost a national policy in this regard so it would be next to unthinkable to participate directly in the military sphere". Bush responded as follows: "My bottom line is that when this chapter of history is written, Japan and the U.S. and a handful of other countries will have stood side-by-side".[56]

The ruling coalition stalled over the decision to be made regarding the *status* of Self-Defense Forces members who would be sent abroad during the crisis.[57] In detail, the Ministry of Foreign Affairs argued that, given the constitutional limitations and Kaifu's pacifist political statements, the members of the Self-Defense Forces deployed abroad should be separated from the other Self-Defense Forces in the form of "secondment" or "leave". Instead, the Defense Agency insisted that the military personnel receive a "double commission" and maintain their position within the Self-Defense Forces apparatus.[58] It should be noted that the formation of a multinational force during the Gulf War offered an option to exercise the collective security function of the United Nations at a time when circumstances would have made the formation of a UN force extremely difficult.

However, Japan responded only to the use of military force, and the tone of the argument was remarkably critical toward Washington. This, in effect, erased the existing taboo that Japan's international cooperation should not only be financial, including also personal contributions and, depending on the circumstances, provide for the deployment of the Self-Defense Forces.

During the crisis, the Kaifu government was deeply influenced by the public opinion. Both within the political elite and civil society, debates began regarding the position of government within this crisis. As stated by the *Asahi Shimbun* newspaper, 33% of Japanese citizens considered the financial measures launched by the *Kantei* to be appropriate. On the other hand, 40% of the Japanese population found

[55] Ministry of Foreign Affairs of Japan, *Diplomatic Bluebook, Section 4. The Hostage Problem*: https://www.mofa.go.jp/policy/other/bluebook/1991/1991-2-4.htm (accessed 21 April 2025).

[56] National Security Archive, Washington D.C., *Memorandum of Telephone Conversation (C) between President George H. W. Bush and Japanese Prime Minister Toshiki Kaifu, ca. August 13, 1990*: https://nsarchive.gwu.edu/document/23940-memorandum-telephone-conversation-c-between-president-george-h-w-bush-and-japanese (accessed 21 April 2025).

[57] The Japan News (by Yomiuri Shimbun), *Bush demanded Japan send 'forces' for 1990 Gulf crisis, declassified documents confirm*, 29 September 1990: https://japannews.yomiuri.co.jp/politics/defense-security/20211222-8210/ (accessed 21 April 2025).

[58] C. Purrington, *cit.*, p. 309.

little enthusiasm about government measures.[59] However, despite the divisions, the LDP strongly supported the centrality of the UN Charter of Peace and Cooperation in resolving this conflict.

Although Japan found itself on the sidelines and struggling to understand its role in the Persian Gulf War, the same cannot be said for the *peace-building* efforts achieved within the Cambodian crisis (1990–1992). On the one hand, Japan took responsibility for building peace in a war-torn country, and on the other, the International Charter for Peace and Cooperation made it possible for it to be involved alongside the United Nations.[60] The conflict in Cambodia was the very first occasion in which Japan had a positive and active political role in the international arena.

The first step taken by the Japanese in this direction was to host the Tokyo Conference on 4 and 5 June 1990. The purpose of the Conference was to overcome the military stalemate that occurred after the withdrawal of the Vietnamese armed forces in 1989 and to rebalance the political situation "in the light of the need for the continued wide support of the international community for a comprehensive political settlement in Cambodia".[61] To overcome the stalemate in peace talks, the Japanese presented their own modified peace plan in February 1991. This plan was intended to overcome Cambodian objections to the peace-building plan proposed by the United Nations. Under this proposal, the United Nations Transitional Authority in Cambodia (UNTAC) verified the conditions proposed by Japan.[62] These military conditions provided four points: the ceasefire, the quartering of the forces, the discovery of the armament's depots, and the disarmament of the troops with consequent demobilization.[63] The United Nations launched Operation UNTAC in Cambodia in March 1992, and Japan moved quickly, on the basis of the experience gained during the Gulf War, and played a key role in the peacebuilding operation. A Japanese PKO unit was sent to the city of Kure in September. The mission and conditions set by UNTAC were unprecedented if compared to previous peacebuilding operations, restoring peace to a country torn apart by civil war and reestablishing the political situation in the area. In terms of quantitative outcome, the performances of the Self-Defense Forces were highly praised by the UNTAC, the local government, and the Cambodian people.[64]

Peacekeeping operations in Cambodia also caused divisions in domestic public opinion. It took almost two years for the implementation of the PKO Law that the government submitted to the Diet in October 1990. In a public opinion poll

[59] *Asahi Shimbun* (morning), 5 February 1991.

[60] Takeda (1998), p. 555.

[61] United Nations, General Assembly, *Report of the Ad Hoc Committee of the International Conference on Kampuchea on its Activities during 1989/90*, A/CONF.109/16, 12 September 1990, p. 3.

[62] Ministry of Foreign Affairs of Japan, *Kanbojia wahei oyobi fukkō e no Nihon no kyōryoku*, January 2007: https://www.mofa.go.jp/mofaj/area/cambodia/kyoryoku.html (accessed 24 April 2025).

[63] Akashi (1992), p. 34.

[64] Takeda (1998), p. 561.

conducted in June 1992, 56% of people opposed the overseas dispatch of the Self-Defense Forces.[65]

Following these two internal debates in Japanese politics and society in the early 1990s, discussions began for the first time about a possible revision of the Article IX of the constitution. However, as shown by the abovementioned polls, aversion to Japan's intervention in military operations remained very strong in Japan. The political establishment, fearing a possible resurgence of nationalism within the country and a U.S. withdrawal in terms of security, decided to postpone any discussion on constitutional reform until certain extreme right-wing sentiments had been completely contained.[66] However, with the onset of a multipolar system, the rise of new actors and alliances on the world stage, Japan began to undertake new approaches and strategies which suggested the country's intention to play a new international role.

4 Conclusive Remarks

Three final points can be deduced from what has been discussed in this contribution. First, political pacifism can be considered a heteronomous principle, introduced from the outside (in this specific case, imposed) by the Western world, undermining its *kokutai* (the "essence of the State").[67] The experience of the Second World War and Japan's atomic holocaust ended up shaping a forced receptivity within the country of this principle that supplanted the idea of a possible "positive neutralism". A disarmed Japan was essential for the strategic interests of the United States in the Asia-Pacific area in the Cold War period. Secondly, through an analysis of the premierships that have marked the fundamental stages of postwar Japan's foreign policy, it has become clear that external systemic variables at the international level have exerted a decisive weight on the attitudes and will of the single governments which were somehow entangled in the pacifist constraint of the national constitution. The construction of national identity in Japan, indeed, seemed to evolve in close correlation with the actions of the political leaders who have ruled the country since the end of the Pacific War.[68]

Finally, the fall of the Berlin Wall, the redefinition of the world order, and the need to thoroughly rethink the logic of international engagement in the face of so-called fault-line conflicts have led to a radical change in the political agendas of the single states and Japan was not immune to this. Washington found itself changing the course and appealing to Japan's duty to participate in the burden-sharing of responsibilities in a world that was now looking toward globalization of political

[65] *Yomiuri shimbun*, 28 June 1992.
[66] Michael (1996), pp. 314–322.
[67] Hidaka (2015), p. 136.
[68] Ezaki (2018), p. 212.

processes. Tokyo thus had to deal with external pressures by rethinking, to the possible extent, its international contribution that had to go beyond its checkbook diplomacy and get involved operationally by deploying overseas its Self-Defense Forces. The Gulf War and the Cambodian crisis of the early 1990s represented a testing ground for the country in this sense, paving the way for a debate that, with alternating phases of intensity, has characterized the way of Japan's internal political history up to the present day.

In short, Japan's postwar path is defined by two decisive elements that are the Article IX of the 1947 Constitution and the U.S. occupation of Japan, which culminated in the creation of the U.S.-Japan alliance. The former has been an integral part of Japan's foreign policy decisions, while the latter exerted a fundamental influence on its evolution. In this regard, this contribution tried to frame the pacifism as a notion imposed by the United States, adopted by the Japanese prime minister Yoshida Shigeru, and interpreted in a way that allowed Japan to focus on reconstruction, outsourcing its security needs to the United States. This paradigm, known as Yoshida Doctrine, became in turn an integral part of pacifism as a policy. The trajectory of pacifism is then examined as a policy under prime ministers Yoshida, Kishi, Ikeda, Satō, and Nakasone. Here it was possible to outline a framework within which Yoshida established the system, Kishi tried to modify it, Ikeda struggled against its constraints, Satō used it to Japan's advantage, and Nakasone tried to surpass it. However, as has been discussed, the prevailing conditions of the time often weighed against them, and each of these leaders had to maneuver around pacifism. Although the "pacifism as politics" evolved over the decades, it has changed form according to prevailing conditions and, therefore, has not remained intact. In 1991, a breaking point was reached. Growing U.S. pressure, which gave substance to Japanese fears of being trapped in U.S.-led wars since the Anpo amendment in 1960, peaked during the First Gulf War in 1990–1991. The historical contingencies of that time profoundly shook the foundations of "pacifism as politics", leaving Japan with little choice but to consider options outside of this framework. This development also gave rise to the concept of a "normal Japan" and laid the foundations for a new interpretation, in the form of the "proactive pacifism", which emerged in the twenty-first century.[69] Pacifism as a policy played a pivotal role in Japanese foreign policy throughout the period from 1947 to 1991, and its relevance at all major turning points can be easily highlighted.

---

[69] On this subject see: Mochizuki (1990), pp. 121–37; Sato (1991), pp. 145–79; Katzenstein and Okawara (1993), pp. 84–118; Segal (1993); Brown (1994), pp. 430–46; Yomiuri shinbun sengo-shi han-hen (2015), Satō (2015); Shiota (2023).

References

Akashi Y (1992) To build a new country: the task of the UN transitional authority in Cambodia. Harv Int Rev 15(2):34

Bochorodycz B (2017) Policy entrepreneurs and policy proposals: gulf war experience and foreign policy change in Japan after the cold war. Silva Iaponicarum 52-55:30–31

Brown E (1994) Japanese security policy in the post-cold war era: threat perceptions and strategic options. Asian Surv 34(5):430–446

Caprio ME, Sugita Y (2007) The U.S. occupation of Japan – innovation, continuity and compromise (Introduction). In: Caprio ME, Sugita Y (eds) Democracy in occupied Japan. The U.S. occupation and Japanese politics and society. Routledge, Abingdon, p 1

Dickinson FR (2021) Nichibunken and me: from 'Nihonjinron' to visions of the world through a Japanese prism. Sekai no naka no nihonkenkyū: Hihanteki teigen o motomete - Sōritsu 30 shūnenkinen kokusai shinpojiumu:153

Edström B (2025) Japan's evolving foreign policy doctrine. The long postwar. Palgrave Macmillan, Cham, p 240

Ezaki M (2018) Nihon senryō to 'haisen kakumei' no kiki. PHP Kenkyūjo, Tokyo, p 212

Fukunaga F (2014) Nihon senryō shi, 1945-1952. Tōkyō, Washinton, Okinawa, Tokyo, Chūō Kōronsha, p 51

Hanhimäki JM (2008) An elusive grand design. In: Logevall F, Preston A (eds) Nixon in the World: American foreign relations, 1969-1977. Oxford University Press, Oxford, p 39

Hasegawa K (2019) Student radicalism and the formation of postwar Japan. New Directions in East Asian History. Palgrave MacMillan, Singapore

Hattori R (2021) Eisaku Sato, Japanese Prime Minister, 1964-72: Okinawa, foreign relations, domestic politics and the Nobel Prize. Routledge, New York, p 113

Hattori R (2023) Fighting Japan's cold war: prime minister Nakasone Yasuhiro and his times. Routledge, London and New York, p 91

Heuser B (1991) NSC 68 and the soviet threat: a new perspective on western threat perception and policy making. Rev Int Stud 17(1):18

Hidaka Y (2015) Amerika ga Nihon ni 'Shōwa kenpō' o ataeta shinsō. PHP Kenkyūjo, Tokyo, p 136

Hosaka M (2009) Senryō-ka Nihon no kyōkun. Asahi Shinbun Shuppan, Tokyo, p 78

Hoshiro H (2022) Deconstructing the 'Yoshida Doctrine'. Jap J Polit Sci 23(2):110

Ikeda S (2007) Ikeda seiken no Yōroppa gaikō to Nichibei-Ō sanbon no hashira ron. Hiroshima kokusai kenkyū XIII:19

Inoguchi T (1991) Japan's response to the gulf crisis: an analytic overview. J Jap Stud 17(2):258

Iokibe K et al (eds) (2020) History, memory and politics in postwar Japan. Lynne Rienner Publishers, Boulder CO

Iokibe M (1985) Beikoku no Nihon senryō seisaku. Sengo Nihon no sekkeizu. Chūō Kōronsha, Tokyo, p 43

Iokibe M (2006) Sengo Nihon gaikō-shi. Yūhikaku, Tokyo, pp 66–67

Izumikawa Y (2010) Explaining Japanese antimilitarism: normative and realist constraints on Japan's security policy. Int Secur 35(2):123–160

Johnson C (1986) Reflections on the dilemma of Japanese defense. Asian Surv 26(5):558–559

Katzenstein PJ, Okawara N (1993) Japan's national security: structures, norms, and policies. Int Secur 17(4):84–118

Kawai K (2022) Mission unaccounted: Japan's shift of role in US extended nuclear deterrence. Journal for Peace and Nuclear Disarmament 5(2):422–451

Kenneth JR (2001) The People's Emperor: democracy and the Japanese Monarchy, 1945-1995. Harvard University Press, Cambridge, p 80

Komine Y (2016) Negotiating the U.S.-Japan alliance: Japan confidential. Routledge, London and New York

Kushner B, Satō M (2005) Digesting postwar Japanese media. Dipl Hist 29(1):28

McCormack G (1986) Beyond economism: Japan in a state of transition. In: McCormack G, Sugimoto Y (eds) Democracy in contemporary Japan. Sharpe, New York, p 59

Michael Y (1996) The international politics of the Asia-Pacific. Routledge, London and New York, pp 314–322

Miller JM (2019) Fractured alliance: anti-base protests and postwar U.S.–Japanese relations. Dipl Hist 38(5):953–986

Mochizuki MM (1990) Japan after the cold war. SAIS Rev 10(2):121–137

Nakakita K (2020) The liberal democratic party of Japan: The realities of 'power'. Routledge, London and New York

Perkins C (2023) The Tokyo University trial and the struggle against order in postwar Japan, New directions in East Asian history. Palgrave Macmillan, Singapore, pp 19–63

Purrington C (1991) Tokyo's policy response during the gulf crisis. Asian Surv No. 31:309

Sadō A (2015) Reisen shūketsu to PKO e no sanka — Jieitai no kaigai haken. Kokusai mondai, Nihon Kokusai mondai kenkyūjo, 638(1–2):28

Satō E (1999) Satō Eisaku nikki, vol I. Tokyo, Asahi shibunsha

Sato H (1991) Japan's role in the post-cold war world. Curr Hist 90(555):145–179

Satō M (2015) Keisatsu yobi-tai to sai gunbi e no michi: Dai ichi-kisei ga mita soshiki no jitsuzō. Tokyo, Fuyōshobō shuppan

Segal G (1993) Adjusting to the new international order. In: Matthews R, Matsuyama K (eds) Japan's military renaissance? Palgrave Macmillan, London

Shiota U (2023) Bōei seisaku kettei no uchimaku. Tokyo, Tōyō keizai shinpōsha

Tadokoro M (2011) The model of an economic power: Japanese diplomacy in the 1960s. In: Yokibe M (ed) The diplomatic history of postwar Japan. Routledge, London and New York, pp 81–82

Takahashi S (2014) Nihon ga nido to tachiagarenai yōni Amerika ga senryōki ni itta koto. Chichi Shuppansha, Tokyo, p 43

Takeda Y (1998) Japan's role in the Cambodian peace process. Diplomacy, manpower, and finance. Asian Surv 38(6):555

Takemae E, Sodei R (1992) Sengo Nihon no genten, vol 1. Yūshisha, Tokyo, p 67

Togo K (2005) Japan's foreign policy, 1945-2003: The quest for a proactive policy. Brill, Leiden, p 58

Ward RE (1965) The Commission on the constitution and prospects for constitutional change in Japan. J Asian Stud 24(3):425

Yomiuri shinbun sengo-shi han-hen (2015) Shōwa sengo-shi. 'Sai gunbi' no kiseki, Tokyo, Chūkō bunko

Yoshida S (1961) The Yoshida memoirs: the story of Japan in crisis. Heinemann, London, p 133

Japanese Pacifism and Constitutional Misalignment

Elisa Bertolini

1 Premise

The current war in Ukraine has prompted countries belonging to the so-called Western bloc to rethink their relationship with defence, military spending and conscription. In Japan, it has had an additional repercussion, namely bringing to the surface the ongoing debate regarding the constitutionality of the entire defence architecture of the country, which ranges from the existence of Self-Defence Forces (SDF), to the high percentage of GDP allocated to military spending,[1] to the presence of US military bases on Japanese soil (such as the Futenma base in Okinawa) and participation in international operations, both through the deployment of troops (peacekeeping operation under the UN umbrella, participation in the war on terror launched by the United States in the Indian Ocean) and arms supply (the Ukrainian case).

The constitutional issues arise due to Article 9, which marks Japan's rejection of war as a mean of resolving international disputes and prohibits the country from maintaining land, sea and air forces.

This misalignment between the factual situation and the Constitution has been, since the late 1940s, the elephant in the room of the Japanese constitutional debate,

[1] According to the data from the Stockholm International Peace Research Institute (SIPRI), Japan's military spending rose by 21% to $55.3 billion in 2024, the largest annual increase since 1952. Its military burden reached 1.4% of GDP, the highest since 1958 and 2% of the world's spending. See https://www.sipri.org/sites/default/files/2025-04/2504_fs_milex_2024.pdf.

E. Bertolini (✉)
Bocconi University, Milan, Italy
e-mail: elisa.bertolini@unibocconi.it

G. Cavaggion (ed.), *The 'Pacifist Principle' in the Italian and Japanese Constitutions in the Wake of the War in Ukraine*,
https://doi.org/10.1007/978-3-032-23108-6_10

which has essentially settled around two well-identified positions: the doctrine and some lower courts (albeit with rather outdated case-law) that see the SDF and the US stationing as a violation of the Constitution, specifically Article 9, on the one hand, and the Supreme Court and the government on the other hand, although their positions are articulated differently; the Supreme Court has always declared its incompetence on the matter, given its purely political nature, while the government, with an evolving and expansive interpretation of Article 9, has affirmed its constitutionality.[2]

It is evident that the interpretation of Article 9 transcends the constitutional debate in a strict sense, as it is strongly ideologically oriented. Indeed, different stakeholders make Article 9 say different things. The genesis of Article 9, as well as the creation of the SDF, are products of a specific historical moment, in which the desire to reshape the Japanese constitutional order was accompanied by geopolitical and ideological considerations.[3] The same can be said for the subsequent interpretative evolutions.

This chapter aims to clarify the constitutional implications of Article 9 in the country's relationship with its defence and rearmament, discussing how its interpretation, with the constitutional text unamended,[4] has changed over the decades and how the different branches of government, civil society and the United States, which is responsible for the country's defence by virtue of the 1951 San Francisco Peace Treaty and the 1960 Japan-US Mutual Cooperation and Security Treaty (hereinafter Anpo, according to the contraction of the name in Japanese),[5] have positioned themselves in relation to it; without forgetting the key role played by the geopolitical framework in shaping Japan's security policy. A brief discussion of the genesis of Article 9, the reasons that inspired it and the specific choices regarding its formulation, complicated by the fact that the original English had to be translated into Japanese, is essential for understanding the debate.[6]

---

[2] It could be possible to argue that there is a significant misalignment between the formal and the material Japanese constitution. On material constitution, see *ex multis* Romeo (2025 forthcoming).

[3] For this reason, the SCAP (Supreme Commander for Allied Powers, an acronym that refers both to MacArthur himself and the entire team that supports him) General MacArthur was certain of an amendment following the end of the occupation in 1952, after the Peace Treaty signed in San Francisco the year before it came into effect. A logical consequence of this belief was the decision made by the SCAP itself in October 1946, before the Constitution was promulgated, to proceed, within two years, with a revision of the text by the Diet, with the collaboration of the Constitution Popularization Commission, to prevent a revision that was too conservative once the occupation was over.

[4] The Japanese Constitution has not been subject to any amendment since its entry into force on May 3, 1947. Instead, it has undergone a revision through the interpretation of provisions deemed less respectful of the indigenous translation (notably Article 9 and Chapter I, devoted to the emperor). See Higuchi (1993).

[5] This is a renewed version of the 1951 Treaty.

[6] It is noted that the Charter was drafted in English and only later translated into Japanese. Regarding the translation work of the Charter and especially the subtle use of translation as a tool for 'Japanisation' (and alteration) of the text, see Inoue (1991).

2 Article 9: Genesis and Interpretations

The rationale behind Article 9 can be traced back to the militarism that characterized the fascism of the imperial system (*tennōsei fashizumu*) in the 1930s, which led to the Pacific War,[7] and the subsequent desire of the Allied Forces to prevent Japan from once again posing a threat to the stability of the Asia-Pacific region and, more generally, to world peace. In this context, Article 9 is just one piece of the dismantling of the totalitarian state and the construction of a democratic regime, in application of the Potsdam Declaration (particularly points 10 and 12) of July 1945.[8]

There is an extensive literature on the genesis of the constitutional text and especially on the debate regarding the nature of the imposed Charter (so-called *oshitsuke Kenpō*) or the result of collaboration between the Supreme Commander for Allied Powers (SCAP) and the Japanese government (so-called collaborative theory),[9] as well as on the legitimacy of the procedure followed,[10] which does not seem necessary to dwell on here again. However, it remains essential to frame the genesis of the

[7]To which must be added the ten years of undeclared war against China, which began with the gradual invasion of Manchuria starting in 1931 and continued the following year with the creation of the puppet state of Manchukuo, headed by the last Emperor of the Celestial Empire, Pu Yi. See Calman (1992) and Beasley (1987).

[8]Douglas MacArthur arrived in Japan in September 1945 as SCAP, tasked with implementing the Potsdam Declaration of July 26, 1945 (point 12 of the same). In point 10, it states, 'The Japanese government will remove all obstacles to the revival and strengthening of democratic tendencies in the Japanese people. Freedom of speech, religion, and thought, as well as respect for fundamental human rights, must be ensured.' On the occupation, see Oppler (1976); Kawai (1960); Whitney (1956). General Whitney, a lawyer, was one of MacArthur's closest collaborators and Chief of the Government Section of the General Headquarters (GHQ), as well as one of the drafters of the new Constitution. The Japanese government, as well as part of the doctrine, did not consider a revision of the Meiji Constitution (1889) necessary to implement the Potsdam Declaration, emphasizing that it delegated to ordinary law the implementation of much of its provisions. On this point and on the possible continuity of the current constitution with respect to the Meiji one, see Ofuji (2004).

[9]Takayanagi (1968).

[10]Formally, in fact, the procedure followed is the one prescribed by Article 73 of the Meiji Constitution, in force until May 2, 1947. On the Meiji Constitution, see Beckmann (1975). This is the only constitutional revision procedure in Japanese constitutional history. However, the qualification of constitutional amendment remains controversial, as the amendment changed the holder of sovereignty, usually considered non-negotiable; see Moore (1979). Certainly, however, the recourse to Article 73 allowed for a formal legality to be conferred on a measure that military defeat had made necessary to complete as quickly as possible; see Kiyomiya (1979), p. 51. It can be argued that imperial sovereignty had actually already been abandoned with the acceptance of the Potsdam Declaration. Certainly, the process was, in fact, of a constituent nature. See Beer and Maki (2002); Hellegers (2001); Koseki (1997); Kades (1989); Tanaka (1976); Ward (1956); Whitney (1946).

pacifist vocation of the Charter, which is embodied in the Preamble[11] and in Article 9.[12]

The second principle, after popular sovereignty, which the new Constitution affirms, is therefore the pacifist principle and renunciation of war.[13] The attempt to prohibit war of any kind (so-called absolute pacifism) constitutionally was entirely unprecedented until that moment, because an absolute interpretation of renunciation implies renouncing even the right to self-defence. In favour of the absolute interpretation, one should read the constitutional prohibition on maintaining armed forces, which would make even self-defence impossible. It could be argued that self-defence can be exercised not exclusively by armed forces, but also, for example, by police forces. However, even if it is the latter, the type of equipment they have remains relevant in terms of war potential.

However, it is undeniable that the desire to banish war emerges incontrovertibly from the Preamble, and that this was one of the reasons behind the adoption of the new constitutional text, as a reaction to the devastation caused by war, which the country had well experienced during the Pacific conflict.

Another consequence of the Preamble and Article 9 is the absence of any constitutional provision devoted to defence or armed forces, except for Article 61, paragraph 2, which states that all members of the government must be civilians. The reference to civilians is quite peculiar, considering that the Constitution prohibits armed forces. Therefore, it could be interpreted as the Constitution does not fully prohibit armed forces—as the government will argue.

The starting point should be the identification of the author of the two provisions. The American imprint in the formulation of the Preamble emerges with certainty—the "un-Japanese," but very American "we, the Japanese people"—while it is more difficult to identify a clear hand behind the formulation, and especially the inspiration, of Article 9. Even Colonel Kades, who played a leading role in drafting the current constitutional text, is unable to deliver to history the author of Article 9; he indeed considers that the idea of its introduction into the Constitution can be traced back to MacArthur, to then-Prime Minister Shidehara, or even to Emperor Hirohito

[11] "We, the Japanese people, acting through our duly elected representatives in the National Diet, determined that we shall secure for ourselves and our posterity the fruits of peaceful cooperation with all nations and the blessing of liberty throughout this land, and resolved that never again shall we be visited with the horrors of war through the action of government, do proclaim that sovereign power resides the people and do firmly establish this Constitution. We, the Japanese people, desire peace for all time and are deeply conscious of the high ideals controlling human relationship, and we have determined to preserve our security and existence, trusting in the justice and faith of the peace-loving peoples of the world."

[12] "Aspiring sincerely to an international peace based on justice and order, the Japanese people forever renounce war as a sovereign right of the nation and the threat of force as means of setting international disputes.

In order to accomplish the aim of the preceding paragraph, land, sea, and air forces, as well as other war potential, will never be maintained. The right of belligerency of the state will not be recognized."

[13] Chinen (2005).

himself.[14] The reason for the impossible identification must be traced, according to Kades, in the fact that all the major parties involved agreed that renunciation of war was indispensable. MacArthur himself has further complicated the issue by repeatedly attributing, although his assertion remains disputed and, according to many scholars, even somewhat unbelievable,[15] authorship to Shidehara since 1951.[16] However, MacArthur remains the most likely "suspect," and this is based on two considerations. First, the instrumental use he made of the renunciation of war to mitigate the hostility of other allies towards the imperial institution. Secondly, the renunciation of war as a sovereign right of the nation is one of the three principles (along with the abolition of the feudal system and the preservation of the imperial institution) that he indicates on February 3, 1946, to General Whitney as the pillars of constitutional reform.

Even though the incorporation of pacifism and the renunciation of war in the draft Constitution presented by SCAP to the Japanese government is initially considered unacceptable, during the debate in the Diet,[17] Article 9 is not a subject of discussion (which does not mean a lack of interest),[18] and the government itself presents it as an essential provision for the future of Japan. It is thus approved with only the opposition of the Communist Party, an opposition that must be understood considering the opportunity to renounce the use of military force even in cases of self-defence.

Although, as mentioned, it is not a subject of much discussion, the article is, however, the subject of an amendment, the so-called Ashida amendment, with implications that are far from negligible, consisting of two small additions to the beginning of both paragraphs.[19] In paragraph 1, the phrase "Aspiring sincerely to an international peace based on justice and order" is added; while in paragraph 2, "In order to accomplish the aim of the preceding paragraph." Although nothing emerged in this direction from the parliamentary debates, Ashida years later claims to have proposed the amendment with the intent of allowing the country to have military

---

[14] Kades (1989), p. 223. For the complete text of MacArthur's Three Principles from February 3, refer to Koseki (1997), p. 79.

[15] Similarly, Hellegers (2001), p. 576. In support of MacArthur's authorship, there is the precedent of the 1935 Constitution of the Philippines, which in Article II, Section 3 renounces war as an "instrument of national policy." This reference is not trivial, as in 1935 MacArthur, prior to the constitutional process, was a military advisor to the (semi-independent) Philippine government, and his father had been the governor-general. However, it should be noted that the Philippine provision did not imply disarmament.

[16] McNelly (2000), p. 106; Koseki (1997), p. 83.

[17] As previously mentioned, the procedure follows that of constitutional revision under Article 73 of the Meiji Constitution.

[18] Opinions and comments on the article are reported in Koseki (1997), pp. 192–195.

[19] See also Koseki (1997), pp. 192–211 and Kades (1989), pp. 236–238. Also see Röhl (1963), p. 98. For a comprehensive contribution on Article 9, McNelly (1962); Auer (1990); and Southgate (2003).

forces for self-defence purposes.[20] Certainly, it remains that paragraph 2 is a highly ambiguous constitutional standard when talking of war potential.

However, the original governmental interpretation (up until the very early 1950s), conveyed on behalf of the entire government by the minister for constitutional revision, Kanamori, is different from Ashida's alleged intent. In presenting the provision to the House of Peers, Kanamori clearly states that paragraph 1 does not deny Japan the right to self-defence, but that it is paragraph 2 that does so, as it prohibits the maintenance of any type of armed forces (war potential), even for self-defence purposes.[21] Even Shidehara's successor at the head of the government, Yoshida, in the passage of the text to the House of Representatives in May 1946, emphasizes the prohibition of self-defence war, highlighting the danger that allowing it would pose, considering that all recent wars had been started under the pretext of self-defence. This initial interpretation is certainly not unrelated to the governmental will to channel all available resources into reconstruction and economic development rather than defence.

The decisive turning point is represented by the outbreak of the Korean War and the establishment of the National Police Reserve in 1950, that become the Self-Defence Forces (SDF) in 1954, which the government considers not to be assimilable to the prohibited war potential.

As for the doctrine, the majority aligns with the original governmental interpretative line and focuses its analysis on the interpretation to be assigned to the term "war," specifically regarding which type of war Article 9 concretely refers to. The resolution of this interpretative knot is essential to settle the issue of legitimacy of self-defence warfare. Now, if one interprets the war referred to in paragraph 1 as illegitimate war, that is, the invasion of another country, it follows that paragraph 2, which expressly recalls the purpose of paragraph 1, prohibits the maintenance of war potential only for the purposes of aggression, but not for defensive purposes (this will also be the interpretation of the Mito District Court in the *Hyakuri case* in 1977). A second interpretative line, however, while agreeing on the interpretation of paragraph 1, diverges on that of paragraph 2, believing that it prohibits the right of belligerence in an absolute sense (an interpretation accepted by the Sapporo District Court in the *Naganuma case* in 1973). More precisely, what paragraph 2 would prohibit is self-defence through military forces, but not through the existing police forces or at an individual level. Finally, a third interpretative line considers that paragraph 1 prohibits all wars, thus not distinguishing between aggressive and defensive wars; this interpretation can be classified as absolute pacifism. Therefore, it is only this last interpretation that does not consider the exercise of the right to self-defence as constitutionally legitimate. This interpretation would be confirmed by the fact that the Constitution does not contain a section dedicated to a state of emergency or, more generally, to the potential invasion by a third country.

[20] On Ashida's role and the real intentions of the amendment, see also Koseki (1997), pp. 195–202.

[21] Dower (1999), p. 396.

The 1950s represent a turning point as they mark the rearmament of Japan and the birth of the Liberal Democratic Party (LDP), still today the dominant political force in the country. Given the circumstances in which the current Constitution was born, since its formation, the LDP has aimed to significantly amend the Constitution, starting with Article 9, to make it truly Japanese. Despite various attempts made since the 1950s, no amendment has yet been approved or even discussed by the Diet. The impossibility of proceeding with an amendment has led to implicit changes to the Constitution, particularly Article 9, through interpretation.

In any case, the legitimacy of a potential amendment to Article 9 and the pacifist principle of the Preamble remains debated.[22] The Constitution does not, in fact, provide for any explicit limits. The majority doctrine holds that the possibility of proceeding with a total revision should be excluded; in particular, popular sovereignty, fundamental rights and pacifism, as fundamental principles of the legal system, would be unamendable. More precisely, regarding Article 9, two theories oppose each other: the first sees it as unamendable in its entirety, as it is instrumental to the pacifist principle, while the second considers only paragraph 1 as unamendable, believing that the country can still contribute to maintaining peace while possessing military forces.[23]

In this context the evolutionary interpretation of Article 9 must be read, which, after the pivot of the early 1950s, sees the government resolution of July 1, 2014, as another crucial moment.[24] Regarding the interpretation of paragraph 1, the resolution did not change the now "peaceful" interpretation that allows for the possession of numerically reduced military forces with limited offensive capability, but capable of ensuring a minimum defence of the country. The focal point is therefore paragraph 2 and the debated issue of self-defence.[25] The pre-2014 interpretation, developed mainly since 1954, admits the so-called individual self-defence, meaning the possibility of defending oneself against attacks from third countries, but not the so-called collective self-defence,[26] which is the possibility for Japan to intervene militarily in support of allied third countries under attack,[27] expressly considered as not permitted since 1981.[28] This prohibition implies, broadly, that Japan's participation in international missions must be limited to support actions not involving the use of force.

The new interpretation is based on the supplementary opinion of Supreme Court Justice Tanaka, who in 1959 (*Sunagawa case*) stated Japan's obligation to defend

---

[22] Ejima (2024), p. 15.

[23] Matsui (2011b).

[24] A panel of 14 advisors presented the new interpretation to the Prime Minister, which then had to receive the approval of the entire government (1-7-2014). See Lee (2015).

[25] Tokuchi (2019).

[26] This right is recognized for the country based on international law, pursuant to Article 51 of the United Nations Charter.

[27] The denial of collective self-defence is also the basis of the Anpo, as will be discussed below.

[28] It should be noted that the revision of the interpretation on collective self-defence has met with the approval of President Obama.

third countries. It is interesting to note how the New Kōmeitō, an ally of the LDP,[29] and the opposition parties have denied that this supplementary opinion referred to collective self-defence, emphasizing that this concept was not clearly defined at the time of the ruling; thus, according to the New Kōmeitō's interpretation, the reference would have been to self-defence in general. In order to overcome the resistance of its government ally, the LDP proposed very strict conditions for the use of collective self-defence: a threat to Japan's security; an attack on third countries that have close ties with Japan; an explicit request for help to Tōkyō; the internal security of allies' defence not compromised; and final approval from the Diet for the use of troops.

However, the conditions just outlined are anything but strict. They are formulated in a vague manner and lack the degree of precision necessary to limit the government's interpretative margin. It is by no means clear what is meant by the expression "close ties with Japan" and on what parameters the relationship should be evaluated. It goes without saying that the intensity of a relationship varies based on the parameters considered, whether they are historical, economic or political-diplomatic. Similar doubts arise regarding the notion of a threat to internal security.

Finally, considering the blurred division of powers that characterizes the Japanese legal system and the lack of an effective system of checks and balances, one cannot regard the necessary approval of the Diet for the deployment of troops as a moment of actual scrutiny over the government's activities. Nor can one think that the Supreme Court will abandon its decades-long deference to the executive to becoming a real watchdog. Consequently, the interpretation that the government will attribute to the six conditions will be the official one and universally accepted by the other two branches of government.

3 The Creation of the Reserve Forces and the Self-Defence Forces (SDF)

The communist victory in China and the outbreak of the Korean War generated a significant shift in SCAP's policy, aimed at countering the growing red threat. Regarding defence, it is evident that the original absolute pacifism does not any longer keep up with the times. The relocation of some US armed forces stationed in Japan to Korea raises the issue of defending the archipelago. Consequently, with US blessing, in July 1950, the Diet approved the law establishing the Reserve Forces, composed of 75,000 men and equipped with heavily armed vehicles. In 1952, they were renamed Security Forces, and in 1954, they took on their current name of Self-Defence Forces (SDF). The SDF, according to the SDF Act, are land, air and sea forces and are placed under the control of the Defence Agency, which was elevated to the rank of Ministry of Defence in 2007.

[29] Political section of the Sōka Gakkai.

According to the SDF Act, Article 76, the Prime Minister orders the deployment of troops in the event of an attack or a real risk of attack; he must, however, obtain the approval of the Diet, as per Article 9, Section 7 of the Armed Attack Act, in the absence of which he is required to order the withdrawal of troops (Article 9, Section 11). Furthermore, as the commander-in-chief of the SDF on behalf of the government (Article 7), he can order their intervention to prevent potential actions against private property and the lives of citizens (Article 82); similarly, the Minister of Defence can order the interception and destruction of missiles intended to strike the country (Article 82-2, Section 1), an order that, in the absence of time to obtain the Prime Minister's agreement, can still be issued based on guidelines approved by the head of government (Article 82-2, Section 3).

While the international political context that allowed for the reconstitution of armed forces is clear, their constitutional compatibility has not been entirely peaceful, both then and now. Since their establishment, the government has maintained that the SDF are not comparable to military forces and therefore do not constitute the war potential prohibited by Article 9; rather, they are police forces, whose purpose is merely to maintain public safety, even intervening in situations of natural disaster.[30]

As briefly noted earlier, since 1950 there has been a gradual change in the government's interpretation of Article 9, which accompanies a similar progressive (re) militarization of the country. Already in 1951, Yoshida stated that the Constitution does not actually impose a perpetual demilitarization of Japan;[31] by 1954, the Charter would not even prohibit the establishment of defence military forces, a stance that in 1957 even embraced nuclear armaments, provided they are used for defensive purposes.[32]

The doctrine has approached the issue differently, based on whether it concerns the Reserve Forces or the SDF. In the case of the former, it evaluated their compliance with the constitution, not considering them comparable to the prohibited war potential. The opposite interpretation, however, "strikes" the SDF, precisely because they fall into the category of war potential that goes well beyond mere self-defence purposes, even though their equipment is always of a defensive type.

Despite the pacifism that civil society has always demonstrated, there is little criticism directed towards the SDF, and the reason can be traced to their deployment in rescue missions during natural disasters that cyclically affect the country.

The aspect that encounters resistance, even from the New Kōmeitō, the junior coalition party, is the expansion of the SDF's role, especially regarding their deployment in foreign missions, which will be discussed shortly.

[30] Thus, Yoshida in 1950 stated the non-military nature of the Reserve Forces in the House of Councillors.

[31] Similarly, in the House of Councillors on September 29, 1951.

[32] Likewise, Prime Minister Kishi in the House of Councillors on May 7, 1957.

3.1 The SDF and the Case-Law

The debate on the constitutionality of the SDF has not been limited to doctrine alone but has also involved the judiciary. However, it should be clarified that the case-law on this matter is sporadic and rather dated. There are several reasons contributing to this situation; among them, one can mention the traditional deference of the courts, especially higher courts, towards the executive, which, in this specific case, manifests itself in the recourse to the political question doctrine; the application of the principle of stare decisis; and the frequency with which courts deny standing to the petitioners. Furthermore, there remains a growing perplexity in the face of a reasoning from the Supreme Court that is rarely articulated.

The constitutionality of the SDF has proven to be, from the very beginning, and especially in the eyes of public opinion, highly questionable.

The first case that addressed their constitutionality is the 1952 *National Police Reserve case*.[33] Suzuki, a socialist MP, had proposed a direct appeal to the Supreme Court, arguing that the National Police Reserve was unconstitutional. The Court did not examine the issue, considering itself incompetent to judge in the absence of a real and current controversy, as it is not a constitutional court.[34] Actually, this will be a constant of the Supreme Court: the refusal to examine the constitutionality of the SDF on the merits, even when the controversy is characterized by concreteness.

The first relevant case on the matter is the *Eniwa case*, decided by the Sapporo District Court in 1967. The Court did not substantially rule on the issue, as the SDF Act could not be applied to the specific case, and thus did not consider the constitutionality of the SDF.[35]

The second case is the *Naganuma case*.[36] In 1973, the Sapporo District Court,[37] after affirming the standing of the petitioners,[38] declared the SDF unconstitutional as they represent the war potential expressly prohibited by Article 9, paragraph 2. Therefore, the Court continued, the petitioners (who had contested the decision to

---

[33] Supreme Court, Grand Bench, 8-10-1952, 6 Minshū 783.

[34] Conversely, Suzuki interprets Article 81 of the Constitution in favour of the competence to decide on abstract issues.

[35] Wada (1976).

[36] The petitioners contest the government's decision to build a missile defence base in a forest reserve near Naganuma, arguing that the abolition of the reserve would harm their agricultural activities as well as their constitutional right to live in peace. This case confirms the general trend that district courts are more progressive and "brave" compared to higher courts. The most relevant passages from the judgments of the three levels of jurisdiction can be found in Beer and Itō (1996), p. 83.

[37] *Ito et al. v. Minister of Agriculture, Forestry and Fisheries*, Sapporo District Court, 7-9-1973, Hanrei Jihō 712, 24.

[38] This is emphasized because it is not uncommon for courts to deny standing to avoid addressing thorny issues, without an express legislative provision, which is almost always absent, and therefore courts decide on the existence of standing on a case-by-case basis.

reclassify a forest as a missile launch site for the SDF) enjoy a constitutional right to live in peace.[39] Even more importantly, the Court rejected the government's position that it should not examine the merits of the case, as the issue would be highly political and thus exclusively within the government's competence; in this regard, the Court expressly stated that the doctrines of *acte de gouvernement* and political question arose in different contexts (and are therefore not applicable to Japan) and that Article 81 provides for judicial review of all laws and acts of the government, a provision that makes the judiciary superior to the other two branches of government. Here, there is a direct reference to the *Sunagawa case*, and the Court emphasizes that exceptions, i.e., excluding matters from judicial review must be very limited. Moreover, the Court does not fail to point out that the expression "highly political nature" used by the government to qualify the issue is vague and ambiguous and thus subject to various (and extensive) interpretations. In any case, and this is a crucial point of the reasoning, the Court clearly states that it is neither its competence nor intention to review the appropriateness of the establishment of the SDF, but to verify its constitutional compatibility; it is on the basis of this consideration that the Court does not believe it should exclude the matter from judicial review. The Court then inextricably links pacifism to popular sovereignty and protection of fundamental rights, and therefore it must be effectively applied. To establish the unconstitutionality of the SDF, the decision expressly recalls the original interpretation of the government, that of absolute pacifism, clearly expressed by Kanamori and Shidehara before the Diet in 1946. The Court then addresses the issue of self-defence in a very interesting way, emphasizing that it does not necessarily have to be based on military force; on the contrary, diplomacy, but above all individual commitment to peace, is its pillar. In 1976, the Sapporo High Court[40] completely overturned the first instance ruling, rejecting the constitutional right to live in peace and refusing to decide on the constitutionality of the SDF. The pacifism of the Preamble is characterized by the Court as a general aspiration of the Japanese people and, therefore, not concretely defined (thus it is not enforceable). As a result, the right to live in peace makes no sense as a legal norm precisely because it lacks a clear and identifiable content. Finally, the Court denies, contrary to what the petitioners claim, that Article 9 "gives substance" to the pacifism of the Preamble and thus makes it a right like any other. Unsurprisingly, the Supreme Court in 1982[41] confirmed the second instance ruling, thus not entering the merits of the issue.

The third fundamental case is the *Hyakuri Base case*.[42] Without going into the details of the matter, the issue was the constitutionality of the sale of land to the government for the purpose of constructing a SDF base (it was therefore a private contract). In 1977, the Mito District Court stated that the Constitution does not

[39] On this right, see Sasaki (2012). Although older, Slomanson (1975).

[40] *Minister of Agriculture, Forestry and Fisheries v. Ito et al.*, Sapporo High Court, 5-8-1976, 27 Gyōsai Reishū 8, 1175.

[41] Supreme Court, 1st petty bench, 9-9-1982, 36 Minshū 9, 1679.

[42] *Ishizuka et al. v. Japan et al.*, Supreme Court, 3rd petty bench, 20-6-1989, 43 Minshū 6, 385. For the text of the decision, see Beer and Itō (1996), p. 130.

prohibit self-defence, but that the judgment on the appropriateness of having self-defence forces belongs to the government and not to the court. In 1981, the Tōkyō High Court considered that, since the subject of the dispute was a private contract,[43] it was unnecessary to discuss the constitutionality of the SDF, a position reaffirmed by the Supreme Court in 1989. The Supreme Court thus denied the applicability of Article 9 to a private contract, even if one of the parties is the State, emphasizing the abstract and ideal nature of pacifism and the right to live in peace that derives from the constitutional mandate.[44]

3.2 SDF and the Peacekeeping Operations

It has previously been noted that the extensive interpretation of the prohibition for the country to exercise collective self-defence has resulted in a substantial disengagement, at least initially, of Japan in the context of international police operations, which has sparked general criticism from the international community for inadequate support for peace.

Certainly, in response to this criticism, coinciding with the Gulf War, the government decided to present initial legislation allowing the Self-Defence Forces to participate in peacekeeping operations. The involvement of the legislative body proved necessary as this type of operation did not fall within the objectives of the SDF under the former SDF Act. After an initial failure due to opposition from the Diet, it was approved in 1992, the International Peace Cooperation Act (Act on Cooperation with International Peacekeeping Operations of the United Nations). The law thus authorizes the government to send troops to provide humanitarian support and conduct monitoring operations during elections. More specifically, for the deployment of the SDF, five conditions must be met: a ceasefire must be agreed upon between the warring parties; participation must be supported by the major countries involved in the conflict; the SDF must remain neutral in the conflict; the SDF must withdraw if any of the previous conditions are not met; the use of weapons is only permitted to defend SDF personnel.

With this legal basis, the SDF has participated in numerous peacekeeping operations under the UN sponsorship, including those in Cambodia, Mozambique, Rwanda, Golan Heights and East Timor.

In this context, the 9/11 attacks and the war on terror under the Bush Administration arrive, for which Japan lacks a legal basis for participation. The Diet thus approves the Anti-Terrorism Special Measures Act (Special Measures Act concerning Measures to be Adopted by our Country Regarding Activities of Foreign Countries in order to Accomplish the Aims of the United Nations Charter in Response to the

[43] See Beyer (1993).

[44] Matsui argues that one of the reasons for the very low rate of declarations of unconstitutionality can be traced to the fact that the Supreme Court refuses to consider the Constitution as a source of positive law that must be enforced. See Matsui (2011a).

Terrorist Attack in the United States of America on September 11, 2001, and Related Humanitarian Measures to be Adopted Based on Resolutions of the United Nations), under which the MSDF, that is, the maritime forces, can provide fuel to allied forces in the Indian Ocean. The Act is intended to remain in effect for only a limited number of years, until 2007. Upon the expiration of the term, the Diet approves the New Anti-Terrorism Special Measures Act (Special Measures Act Concerning the Implementation of Fuel Supply to Anti-Terrorism Maritime Activities), which authorizes refuelling for the year 2008 as well. It is worth noting that in this instance, the Diet is practically divided, as the Lower House, with a two-thirds majority, had to overcome the opposing vote of the Upper House.[45] Only the change of government in 2010[46] puts an end to the practice of annual renewal (2008 and 2009).

Japan does not fail to provide its support to the United States even during the invasion of Iraq in 2003, for which participation the Diet approves the Iraq Special Measures Act (Special Measures Act Concerning the Implementation of Humanitarian Reconstruction Support Activities and Security Maintenance Support Activities in Iraq).

It should also be noted that the 2007 amendment to the SDF Act included participation in peacekeeping operations among the objectives of the SDF, thus eliminating the need for specific legislation whenever there is a political will to participate in these operations.

It seems almost redundant to emphasize that the participation of the SDF in such operations has also raised constitutional concerns; and it is equally redundant to state that the courts have always refused to address the issue. In response to petitions filed in the early 1990s requesting injunctions to block the dispatch of troops to the Gulf, the courts have always denied locus standi.

In response to these objections, the government argues that participation is not unconstitutional due to the lack of involvement in active combat, the limited use of weapons for the defence of personnel (which cannot therefore be equated to a real use of force) and the fact that the deployment is subject to the five conditions mentioned above.

The current war in Ukraine falls into a completely different context from what has been discussed so far, being an ongoing war in which Western support mainly consists of supplying specific types of weapons. While Japan's participation in sanctions does not present issues from a constitutional law perspective, as does humanitarian assistance or the sending of electric generators, the situation is different when it comes to sending technology and non-lethal military defence equipment (mainly drones).

---

[45] The Japanese bicameralism is not perfect and is characterized by the predominance of the Lower House, the House of Representatives, as per Article 59, paragraph 2.

[46] The years 2009–2012 are essentially the only ones in which the LDP was neither in government nor providing external support.

According to the Three Principles on Transfer of Defence Equipment and Technology developed by the government in 2014,[47] it is not possible to send military equipment, such as weapons, to a country that is actively involved in an armed conflict. Now, the Japanese government has classified Ukraine as a country that is not part of a conflict, an interpretation made possible based on the definition assigned to the phrase "part of the conflict," meaning a country against which the United Nations Security Council has adopted a resolution. This is obviously not the case for Ukraine.

Furthermore, the operational guidelines of the Three Principles provide for assistance to countries with which Japan has close ties and that are geographically nearby; these guidelines were waived in April 2022 to allow shipments to Ukraine, as Ukraine is neither geographically close nor in particularly close relations with Japan. The government has therefore hastened to assert that this deviation from the official line would be a one-time occurrence. A year later, however, the government's stance has changed; it is indeed reflecting on modifying the principles underlying that greater flexibility is desirable to help all countries that are victims of aggression. Additionally, regarding the supply of drones sent, the government has emphasized that this is not a transfer of technology, as they are commercially available products, thus not falling under the prohibition of the Three Principles. The government has therefore based the sending of equipment, and especially drones, on Article 116, paragraph 3 of the SDF Act, which allows for the transfer of "equipment no longer in use for the purpose of aiding a developing country."[48] The use of this provision as the legal basis for the transfer has also allowed the government to avoid involving the Diet.

However, it is important to clarify that the Japanese approach to the war in Ukraine must be understood within the framework of a broader anti-China strategy.

4 The Anpo

The last profile to be analysed concerns the stationing of US troops on Japanese soil and its compliance with Article 9. Within the framework of the Peace Treaty, the Security Treaty between the United States and Japan of 1951 provides for the maintenance of US bases on Japanese soil even after the conclusion of the occupation (1952). The interest in the Treaty is quite evident for both parties: Japan needs the protection of the United States (especially the nuclear umbrella) against communist threats from the USSR, China and the Korean Peninsula; the United States, for their part, would benefit from additional military bases in the Pacific.

[47] This corresponds to the new interpretation of Article 9. For the text of the *Principles* and operational guidelines, see https://www.mofa.go.jp/fp/nsp/page1we_000083.html.

[48] The paragraph came into effect in 2017, and it is on this base that Japan provided materials to the Philippines, which at the time were not part of any conflict.

In 1960, despite violent opposition from the left and students, the 1951 Treaty was renewed and made permanent[49] under the name of the Treaty of Mutual Cooperation and Security, referred to as Anpo. Compared to the 1951 text, Anpo introduces a fundamental change regarding reciprocity, meaning that Japan also has the obligation to defend the United States in the event of an attack on Japanese soil, and not just vice versa. This limitation (an attack on the United States on Japanese soil) must be understood in the context that at the time, the legitimacy of exercising collective self-defence was not widely accepted.

As was the case with the Self-Defence Forces and would also be for peacekeeping operations, the constitutionality of Anpo, specifically the stationing of US troops, was not peacefully accepted by public opinion. The famous case that provided the opportunity for the courts to address the issue is the *Sunagawa case*.[50]

In 1959, the Tōkyō District Court ruled on the unconstitutionality of the stationing of US troops, as it was contrary to Article 9. What the Court essentially noted was that, although the Constitution recognizes a right to self-defence, it does not permit war under the pretext of self-defence, nor does it allow for the maintenance of military forces for that purpose. The defence of Japan, the Court continued, is ensured by the United Nations. However, US troops are not under the control of the United Nations, and they are stationed in Japan with the purpose of intervening whenever peace and security in the Far East are threatened, and thus not only in Japan; consequently, these two elements make them military forces prohibited by Article 9. The Supreme Court intervened immediately in the same year, upon direct appeal from the government, overturning the first instance ruling. It noted that the security of the country does not actually depend solely on the United Nations, but that Japan has the authority to choose how to provide for its own security based on international balances, including the use of force. In other words, according to the Court's reasoning, the Constitution would not prohibit Japan from seeking support from a third state to ensure its defence. The prohibition under Article 9, paragraph 2, according to the Court, only affects Japan and not the armed forces of a third country. Regarding the violation of paragraph 1, the Court considers the issue to be highly political and therefore not within its jurisdiction, except in cases of manifesting unconstitutionality, and it does not consider this to be such a case. Nevertheless, the Supreme Court does not declare Anpo constitutional but limits itself to refusing to enter the merits of the issue.

The Court had the opportunity to revisit the stationing of US troops in another case, the Land Lease Dispute Case (1996),[51] which specifically concerned the US bases in Okinawa and marks a further step beyond Sunagawa. The issue at stake here is the use of land owned by local residents by the US bases; the governor of Okinawa refuses to grant permission, despite the government's order; the governor

[49] There is always the possibility for the parties to withdraw after ten years, with notification to the other party one year in advance.

[50] Supreme Court, Grand Bench, 16-12-1959, 13 Keishū 3225.

[51] Supreme Court, Grand Bench, 28-8-1996.

challenges the order before the Supreme Court, which rules on the legitimacy of the order based on the *i*, a law adopted under Anpo that must be considered constitutional as it is not manifestly unconstitutional. Here, therefore, the Court goes beyond Sunagawa, although it does not satisfactorily articulate the reasons why Anpo should not be considered manifestly unconstitutional.

5 Concluding Remarks

The Japanese experience is characterized as a unique case in comparative law, starting from the Meiji Restoration of 1868, which initiated the modernization (Westernization) of the country. If we look at Japanese constitutional history, we see how the two pivotal moments—the adoption of the Meiji Constitution in 1889 and the current Constitution of 1946–1947—both represent cases of legal transplant, albeit with a significant distinction: in the first case, it can be said that it was voluntary, "sought" by Japan, whereas the second was not. The 1947 Constitution, even if one accepts the theory of collaboration proposed by Takayanagi, retains a strongly heterodirected imprint; yet, contrary to all expectations (especially those of SCAP), it has not been subject to any modifications, at least at a formal level.

That a constitution undergoes implicit changes, an amendment by interpretation, is certainly not an exclusive trait of Japan, nor is it limited to the nature of Article 9 and the pacifist principle. What is decidedly more peculiarly Japanese, thus connecting back to its uniqueness, is the way the change in interpretation of Article 9 has occurred. There has been no input from courts, no shift in public opinion nor of the political-party system that would have required an adjustment of the formal constitution to the material one; on the contrary, there is a top-down process, where only the will of the government—discretionary and arbitrary and not subject to the control of the Diet or the judiciary—provides the legitimacy for the revision by interpretation.

However, aside from this reconstruction that depicts a government completely free to interpret Article 9 as it pleases and to rearm the country without the control of any effective counterpower, at least two considerations can be made. First, the resort to amendment by interpretation is a defeat for the government, as it marks the impossibility, at least until now, of proceeding with a constitutional amendment. The LDP, despite being the dominant party since 1955, has not even managed to present an amendment proposal to the Diet for deliberation. The constitutional referendum law was only approved in 2007 (in effect since 2010).[52] Secondly, it cannot be overlooked that Article 9, although not concretely implemented by the courts, may still have served as a brake and limited government policy in defence matters. Furthermore, its highly symbolic value—also in terms of foreign policy towards Japan's neighbours—is far from negligible.

[52] Ejima (2024)

Certainly, it has become more and more evident that major changes in the Japanese security strategy may come from the new approach to security issues of the Trump administration. It is indeed too early to try to appraise this impact on Japan's security policies and diplomacy, although a small shift since 2024 can be identified. In April 2024, in the context of the Japan-US Summit Meeting,[53] the then Prime Minister Kishia delivered a speech at a Joint Meeting of the United States Congress entitled For the Future: Our Global Partnership,[54] in which he stressed the importance of the Japan-US partnership in front of the growing threats of China and North Korea in the Far East. The 2025 Summit Meeting between then Prime Minister Ishiba[55] and President Trump, despite still mentioning the cooperation between the two countries, does not insert anymore the US-Japan relationship within the international order.[56] It is also the lack of any reference to common values such as the rule of law that questions the future of the alliance. A further concern is connected to the fact that the very same day he had been elected president of the LDP, Ishiba had the Hudson Institute, a US think tank, publish his paper The Future of Japan's Foreign Policy,[57] whose opening line refers to an Asian NATO,[58] a proposal seeming to have vanished into thin air, and not just because of the US disengagement. Nevertheless, it seems worth to discuss whether and how this proposal fits in the architecture of the Japanese defence system. First, Ishiba considers that the Japan-US alliance is the only existing asymmetrical alliance in international relations; hence, the only way to reduce the imbalance and the presence of US troops on Japanese soil is for Japan to exercise collective self-defence. Second, Ishiba considers collective self-defence as a deterrent to wars' breaking out and thus the lack of any agreement on collective self-defence at Asian scale is problematic. Third, an Asian NATO is the only way to maintain a regional balance. The feasibility of this proposal is very low, the reasons being the peculiarity of the Japanese collective self-defence doctrine, the US disengagement, the divergence of the security policies in the area and fore and foremost the negative perception many Asian countries have towards Japanese rearmament. Furthermore, marines starting to leave Okinawa must not be interpreted in the light of the recent trends in the US security policy. The downscaling of the US troops in Okinawa in favour of a military base in Guam was agreed 12 years ago, after negotiations that had started in 1995.

---

[53] An account of the discussion is available at https://www.mofa.go.jp/na/na1/us/pageite_000001_00256.html.

[54] The text of Kishida's speech is available at https://www.mofa.go.jp/pageite_000001_00262.html.

[55] It seems convenient to recall that Ishiba served as Minister of Defence in Fukuda's Cabinet in the years 2007–2008.

[56] The *Leaders' Statement* is available at https://www.mofa.go.jp/mofaj/files/100791691.pdf.

[57] Available at https://www.hudson.org/politics-government/shigeru-ishiba-japans-new-security-era-future-japans-foreign-policy. For a comment, see Jinbo (2025).

[58] Kishida also wanted to tighten the relations with NATO; nevertheless, the opening of a *liaison office* in Tōkyō was ruled out by NATO leaders.

However, it seems that for the moment neither the United States nor Japan is ready to abandon their alliance and completely reshape their security strategy in Far East Asia. And the erosion of the normative value of the constitution continues.

References

Auer JE (1990) Article Nine of Japan's Constitution: from renunciation of armed force "Forever" to the third largest defence budget in the world. Law Contemp Probl 53(2):71–187
Beasley WG (1987) Japanese Imperialism, 1894-1951. Oxford University Press, Oxford
Beckmann GM (1975) The making of the Meiji constitution. Greenwood, Westport
Beer LW, Itō H (1996) The constitutional case law of Japan, 1970 through 1990. University of Washington Press, Seattle
Beer LW, Maki JM (2002) From imperial myth to democracy: Japan's two constitutions, 1889-2002. University Press of Colorado, Boulder
Beyer L (1993) The Hyakuri Base Case: Article 9 of the constitution and the public law/private law dichotomy in Japan. Jap Stud 13(3):4–19
Calman D (1992) The nature and origins of Japan imperialism. Routledge, New York
Chinen MA (2005) Article 9 of the constitution of Japan and the use of procedural and substantive heuristics for consensus. Mich J Int Law 27:55–114
Dower JW (1999) Embracing defeat: Japan in the wake of World War II. WW Norton & Company, New York
Ejima A (2024) Constitutional amendment in Japan - 'Unfeasable amendments versus 'Unnoticed' amendments. In: Bui NS, Malagoldi M (eds) Asian comparative constitutional law, vol. 2., constitutional amendments. Hart, Oxford, pp 7–27
Hellegers DM (2001) We, the Japanese people: World War II and the origins of the Japanese constitution. Stanford University Press, Stanford
Higuchi Y (1993) The constitution and the emperor system: is revisionism alive? In: Luney PR Jr, Takahashi K (eds) Japanese constitutional law. University of Tōkyō Press, Tōkyō, pp 57–68
Inoue K (1991) MacArthur's Japanese constitution: a linguistic and cultural study of its making. The University of Chicago Press, Chicago
Jinbo K (2025) Asian NATO is not viable: the seriousness of a "Security Expert" politician's lack of basic understanding, in diplomacy n. 86. https://www.japanpolicyforum.jp/diplomacy/pt2025012700591215045.html
Kades CL (1989) The American role in revising Japan's imperial constitution. Polit Sci Quart 104(2):215–247
Kawai K (1960) Japan's American Interlude, 1945-1952. The University of Chicago Press, Chicago
Kiyomiya S (1979) Droit constitutionnel. Yuhikaku, Tōkyō
Koseki S (1997) The Birth of Japan's postwar constitution. Westview Press, Boulder
Lee J (2015) Collective self-defence or collective security: Japan's reinterpretation of Article 9 of the constitution. J East Asia Int Law 8(2):373–392
Matsui S (2011a) Why is the Japanese Supreme Court so conservative. Wash Univ Law Rev 88(6):1375–1423
Matsui S (2011b) The constitution of Japan: a contextual analysis. Hart, Oxford and Portland
McNelly TH (1962) The renunciation of war in the Japanese constitution. Polit Sci Quart 77(3):350–378
McNelly TH (2000) The Origins of Japan's democratic constitution. University Press of America, Lanham
Moore RA (1979) Reflections on the occupation of Japan. J Asian Stud 38(4):721–734

Ofuji N (2004) Tradition constitutionnelle et supra-constitutionnalité: y a-t-il une limite à la révision constitutionnelle? L'exemple de la Constitution japonaise. Revue Française de Droit Constitutionnel 59:619–631

Oppler AC (1976) Legal reform in occupied Japan: a participant looks back. Princeton University Press, Princeton

Röhl W (1963) Die japanische Verfassung. Metzner, Frankfurt

Romeo G (2025 (forthcoming) Unveiling the constitution: why and how material constitution doctrines matter in constitutional theory?. In: Vienna lectures in legal theory. Hart, Oxford

Sasaki T (2012) Whose Peace? Anti-military litigation and the right to live in peace in Postwar Japan. Asia-Pac J Jap Focus 10(29):1–17

Slomanson WR (1975) Judicial review of war renunciation in the Naganuma Nike case: juggling the constitutional crisis in Japan. Cornell Int Law J 9(1):24–49

Southgate EJL (2003) From Japan to Afghanistan: the US-Japan joint security relationship, the war on terror, and the ignominious end of the pacifist state? Univ Pa Law Rev 151(4):1599–1638

Takayanagi K (1968) Some reminiscences of Japan's commission on the constitution. In: Henderson DF (ed) The constitution of Japan: its first twenty years, 1947–1967. University of Washington Press, Seattle, pp 71–88

Tanaka H (1976) A history of the constitution of Japan of 1946. In: Tanaka H (ed) The Japanese legal system. University of Tōkyō Press, Tōkyō, pp 653–668

Tokuchi H (2019) Implications of revision of Article 9 of the constitution of Japan on the defence policy of Japan. Columbia J Asian Law 33:83–93

Wada H (1976) Decisions under Article 9 of the constitution - the Sunakawa, Eniwa, and Naganuma decisions. Law Japan 9:117–128

Ward RE (1956) The origins of the present Japanese constitution. Am Polit Sci Rev 50(4):980–1010

Whitney C (1946) Memorandum regarding constitutional reform, February 1, 1946. In SCAP Files of Commander Alfred R. Hussey, Doc. n. 3, Tōkyō, National Diet Library

Whitney C (1956) MacArthur: His Rendezvous with history. Knopf, New York

The "Pacifist Integralism" Myth: Japan's Evolving National Security Approach Since the 1992 Peacekeeping Law and the Japan Socialist Party's Narrative and Political Shift

Marco Zappa

1 Introduction

The prohibition on the Japan Self-Defense Force (JSDF)'s participation in conflicts abroad constitutes one of the pillars of Japan's hegemonic security identity, still influenced by Japan's postwar pacifism and antimilitarism. And yet, after the end of the Cold War, this pillar of Japan's long-standing security posture has been, at least in principle and in its more integralistic interpretation, challenged and stretched by subsequent dispatches of the JSDF abroad in the context of UN-led peacekeeping operations (PKOs).

Together with a series of incremental changes to, particularly, the institutional framework (the upgrade of the Defense Agency to the Defense Ministry and the creation of a joint chief of staff the JSDF in the late 2000s) and JSDF equipment, these events have enabled what Oros defines Japan's "gradual security awakening" (Oros 2017, p. 47).

This incremental and gradual change can be traced in the evolution of the concept of "comprehensive security" whose foundations were laid at the end of the 1970s by Liberal Democratic Party (LDP) and government leaders such as Ōhira Masayoshi (Hattori 2019; Zappa 2022; Hughes 2004; Oros 2008). Since the 1980s, subsequent LDP-led administrations have stretched the boundaries set by domestic antimilitarism and centered on three key pillars (no traditional armed forces, no use of force except in self-defense, and no Japanese participation in wars abroad) and, particularly since the late 1990s, have gone as far as to replace old policies and expand the reach of the country's security policies (Oros 2008, p. 34).

M. Zappa (✉)
Ca' Foscari University of Venice, Venice, Italy
e-mail: marco.zappa@unive.it

G. Cavaggion (ed.), *The 'Pacifist Principle' in the Italian and Japanese Constitutions in the Wake of the War in Ukraine*,
https://doi.org/10.1007/978-3-032-23108-6_11

The adoption of new institutional and legislative frameworks allowing for the emergence of a "normalized" Japan in the security arena was attained through a continuous renegotiation of the abovementioned pillars of Japanese antimilitarism. In 1992, the LDP-led Miyazawa cabinet pushed a piece of legislation, the Act on Cooperation with United Nations Peacekeeping Operations (PKO law), through the Diet and paved the way for the first dispatch of members of the JSDF abroad since the end of WWII in the context of UN-led PKOs overseas. Subsequent cabinets have built on this measure to promote further incremental changes leading, among other things, to the recognition of the right for Japan to exercise collective self-defense in 2015, under the second Abe cabinet, and to a further broadening of the scope of Japan's international security activities under the Kishida cabinet.[1] In this regard, central to the shifts in Japan's security identity has been the narrative surrounding Japan's international contribution (*kokusai kōken*).

Making Japan "normal" by revising its postwar constitution has been a long-time political aim of multiple Japanese politicians. In 1955, constitutional revision was listed among the six core missions of the newly founded LDP (Fukui 2023). Kishi Nobusuke, one of the founders of the LDP and PM between 1957 and 1960, was among the earliest proponent of a constitutional revision and even discussed the issue with US ambassador to Japan at the time, Douglas MacArthur II (MacArthur 1957). Despite sections of the LDP continued holding the conviction that constitutional revision was necessary, it was only in the early 1990s, at the end of the Cold War, that the topic re-emerged in the public debate. Among the most prominent supporters of a constitutional revision was former LDP Secretary-General Ozawa Ichirō (Ozawa et al. 1994). In Ozawa's political bestseller he significantly referred to the need to renegotiate Japan's antimilitarist stance embodied by the Art. 9 of the country's postwar constitution in the face of mutated international conditions. With the benefit of hindsight and notwithstanding Ozawa's own political fate, nearly all cabinets since the 1990s have contributed to the comprehensive renegotiation of Japan's security policies and identity.

It might be misleading however to focus on the LDP as the only political actor in Japan which contributed to said shifts in Japan's security identity, or at least on the

[1] Among these changes it might be worth listing the dispatch of the Maritime and Air Self-Defense Force in the Indian Ocean to offer rear-area support to US operations in Afghanistan and Iraq in 2001 and 2004 on top of the Ground Self-Defense Force's dispatch for humanitarian assistance and infrastructure reconstruction (Oros 2008, p. 34). Furthermore, in 2009, against the backdrop of Japan's continuing effort alongside UN and NATO in the fight against international terrorism and piracy in the Indian Ocean, the Asō cabinet brokered a deal with the Republic of Djibouti for the acquisition of a lot of land where to set up a JSDF base overseas, again, in a first since the end of WWII. Particularly, the Kishida administration has provided non-lethal military assistance to Ukraine in the context of the 2022 war against Russian attempted invasion and launched the revision of three major documents constituting the cornerstone of Japan's defense and security posture and pledged to increase the country's defense spending to put it on a par with partners and allies in Europe and North America. Furthermore it has created a framework for enhanced security cooperation with partners and allies through its Official Security Assistance (OSA). For a more detailed discussion see Pugliese and Wallace (2023) and Pugliese and Zappa (2024).

narratives surrounding it. Short-lived non-LDP administrations since the early 1990s, when the party's monopoly on power briefly ceased to exist, have basically acted in continuity with the LDP administrations. Significant are the 1994–1996 Murayama cabinet, which was led by Murayama Tomiichi, the then-chairperson of the Japan Socialist Party (JSP), historically critical of the LDP's moves to re-interpret the constitution since the founding of the JSDF in 1954. This chapter reviews the context of the passing of the 1992 Peacekeeping Law and discusses the shift in the JSP's posture and narratives regarding PKOs from its time at the opposition and apex of its political influence domestically to its time in power. How have these administrations contributed to the establishment of a new enhanced role of the JSDF and a de facto interpretation of the Art. 9? How have they narratively justified these policies in the face of growing disaffection from their own electorate?

Through the close reading of articles published on the JSP's monthly newsletter *Seisaku shiryō* (*Policy and Legislation*) between 1991 and 1995, political memoirs (*kaikoroku*) and secondary literature based on recently declassified diplomatic documents, this chapter aims to contribute to a deeper understanding of the role that opposition parties may play in non-competitive democratic settings (Scheiner 2005) and of the ideological evolution within the JSP, which had been, until 1996, the main opposition party in Japanese politics.

2 The Dispatch of JSDF Abroad: Dealing with a Historical and Bipartisan Cautiousness

The surprising nomination of Murayama Tomiichi as Prime Minister (PM) in 1994 was a comeback of the socialists to a cabinet leadership position, almost 50 years after the appointment of Katayama Tetsu and after 39 years of almost continuous LDP dominance (Yakushiji 2012). Murayama's tenure was characterized by unprecedented contingencies (the January 1995 Hanshin earthquake and the March 1995 sarin gas attack in the Tokyo subway system) both domestically and on a global level (the Rwandan genocide, the North Korean nuclear crisis, and the third Taiwan strait crisis between 1994 and early 1996). Under its cabinet, relevant decisions concerning Japan's security posture in the context of the Japan-US alliance and the dispatch of JSDF were taken. First, under Murayama, the 1995 National Defense Program Outline (NDPO) was adopted. Maintaining the principle of the "Basic Defense Force Concept" (*kibanteki bōeiryoku kōsō*) as the linchpin of the JSDF's capacities, the document reaffirmed the "indispensable" nature of Japan-US security arrangement for Japan's own security and peace and stability in the surrounding regions. Moreover, the document stressed Japan's desire to "Contribute to efforts for international peace through participation in international peace cooperation activities" (Ministry of Foreign Affairs of Japan 1995). Later, in November 1995, the Murayama cabinet finally ordered the dispatch of JSDF to the Golan Heights, on the border between Israel and Syria, in the context of the UN Disengagement

Observer's Force (UNDOF). Despite the divisive nature of such issues for Murayama's own party, the JSP, in the context of the party's waning influence on domestic politics, the PM's "pragmatic" approach appeared a trade-off of sorts. As clearly illustrated by George Mulgan, the configuration of the Murayama cabinet as a coalition government formed by the JSP, the LDP, and New Party Sakigake members was a key factor in the JSP's renegotiation of its key tenets with regard to the Constitution, the JSDF, and Japan's international contribution (George Mulgan 1995, pp. 1105–1106).

Nonetheless, the JSP in power could nevertheless see part of its stances (particularly its cautious approach to the dispatch of JSDF abroad) integrated in the broad political platform of the coalition government and of successive cabinets. Despite various attempts at reinterpreting or diluting it in recent years, the Murayama statement on the 50th anniversary from the end of the Pacific War is still upheld today as an integral part of Japan's own diplomatic identity (Gustafsson 2013).

Leaving this consideration aside, it might be worth noting that the JSP's reluctance to dramatically change Japan's security identity and existing policies after the passing of the 1992 PKO Law (which was harshly criticized by elements within the JSP) was shared by sectors of the LDP. As it will be shown below, the path between the emergence of a debate on Japan's international contribution in the late 1980s and the passing of the 1992 PKO Law has been fraught with difficulties, indecisiveness, and contradictions stemming from internal divisions within the LDP, particularly between dovish (which have held the balance of power in the early and mid-1990s) and hawkish nationalist-realist factions. Similar patterns can be identified in the internal debate within the JSP before and after its rise to executive power. As poignantly observed by Aurelia George Mulgan, "International peacekeeping [presented] both a policy dilemma and opportunity for Japan" (George Mulgan 1995, p. 1103).

Since the mid-1980s, Japan had enhanced its international presence through financial means (FDIs) and through its Official Development Assistance (ODA) programs (Söderberg 1996; Yennie Lindgren 2021; Inada 1989). With political instability emerging particularly in the Middle East, a key region for Japan's and the world's most developed economies of the time's energy supply, Japanese leaders had to manage external pressures, coming particularly from the US in a context of trade disputes between the two allies. In Washington's view, Japan had to contribute more to the international endeavor to maintain peace and stability globally (Islam 1993). As clearly illustrated by Shōji (2024), in the 1980s the Japanese cabinets upheld a conservative interpretation of the constitution's Article 9, barring Japan from sending troops overseas to contribute to UN-sanctioned operations (such as PKOs) as far as these involved the use of military force.

Under these circumstances, PM Nakasone Yasuhiro opted for offering financial support to the installation of a hyperbolic radio navigation system (Decca) in the Persian Gulf, and to neighboring countries possibly affected by the inflow of migrants and refugees from the war zone. The Nakasone cabinet also increased its contribution to the "courtesy budget" for US bases in Japan and to the UN General Secretariat for the solution of the Iran-Iraq conflict, but fell short of dispatching

JSDF minesweepers to the Persian Gulf in the final phases of the Iran-Iraq war in 1987 despite a request from the US Defense Department and UN Security Council resolution 598 establishing a Military Observer Group (UNIIMOG) tasked with monitoring the cessation of hostilities. Particularly, sending minesweepers would have meant breaking Japan's neutrality toward the Iraq-Iran dispute and sending a message of hostility to Iran, which was then a key trade partner (Shōji 2024, p. 30; United Nations Peacekeeping Peace and Security n.d.).

As pressures from allies and international partners grew in the context of simmering Cold War-era tensions, the ensuing Takeshita administration proved to be more proactive on the issue of Japan's "contribution" (*kōken*) to the world. This would constitute the narrative backbone of Japan's changes in security policies first and renegotiation of its postwar identity. In his initial policy address to the Diet, PM Takeshita Noboru stressed his willingness to turn Japan into a country that could contribute to the peace and stability on a global scale (*Sekai ni kōken suru Nihon*), including by dispatching unarmed members of JSDF personnel around the globe as electoral observers, transport and communication lines coordinators, and military doctors. Takeshita made similar pledges at summit meetings with US and European allies after tasking Ministry of Foreign Affairs (MOFA) with the draft a framework for Japan's international contribution which he articulated in three pillars: (1) Japan's ODA; (2) strengthening of Japanese cultural institutions abroad (Japan Foundation), and (3) Japan's cooperation for peace (*heiwa no tame no kyoryoku*) (Shōji 2024, pp. 31–32).

Eventually, the Takeshita administration succeeded in dispatching a group of civilian electoral observers to Namibia in 1989, but corruption and sex scandals leading to the demise of both Takeshita and Uno administrations that year further hindered deliberations on Japan's future approach to UN PKOs (Shōji 2024, pp. 40–41).

3 The "Gulf Trauma" and the Fear of International Stigma

Renewed international pressures around Japan's defense normalization materialized soon after the appointment of a new PM, Kaifu Toshiki. Kaifu rose to the premiership in August 1989 at a time of political crisis within the LDP which had fallen short of obtaining the majority at the Upper House election of that year (see below). In addition, hailing from a minor moderate faction within the party, he could not enjoy a strong support from within his own party. Most relevantly, Kaifu did not appear to have a strong stance on Japan's security posture as opposed to other LDP heavyweights such as Ozawa Ichirō and Hashimoto Ryūtarō (Tadokoro 2021, p. 102). Ozawa, particularly, saw with favor the dispatch of JSDF abroad as a first decisive step leading to Japan's security normalization through constitutional revision (Ozawa et al. 1994; George Mulgan 1995, pp. 1105–1107; Oros 2008, p. 78).

Despite these facts, Kaifu's tenure (1989–1991) represented a watershed moment for Japan's participation in UN PKOs as it constituted a precedent upon which the

1992 PKO Law was established. In August 1990, Saddam Hussein's Iraq launched an "unexpected" attack against neighboring Kuwait (Kaifu 2022). In the face of Iraq's refusal to withdraw immediately, the Japanese cabinet joined the international community in imposing economic sanctions to Iraq, froze Iraqi assets in Japan, and, among other measures, ordered a halt on the nation's oil purchase from the country.

In his memoir, Kaifu recalled how, amidst resistances from the Ministry of International Trade and Industry (MITI) concerned that this could cause in turn the halt of Iraq's repayments on Japanese loans, he maintained that Japan had to act in coordination with the international community for the sake of "international confidence" in Tokyo (*kokusai shin'yō kizu tsukeru*) (Kaifu 2022). He also detailed how he resisted US pressures, coming directly from the then-US President George H. W. Bush, to send equipment and Maritime Self-Defense Force (MSDF) minesweepers in support of a possible multinational military mission to the Persian Gulf stressing that based on Art. 9 of the Constitution, Japan could not exert the right of belligerency. Hence, based on its pacifist constitution, the JSDF could not take part directly in US-led multinational military expeditions. However, he pledged to further examine the issue (Kaifu 2022; Shōji 2024, p. 44). Finally, at the end of August 1990, the government opted for a USD 4-billion-worth financial contribution to the US-led multinational mission to the Gulf. In subsequent meetings involving Japan's MOFA and US State of Department officials, the US government's disappointment for the Japanese refusal to make a "human contribution" (*jinteki kōken*) emerged clearly. Moreover, the figure offered by the Japanese government after strenuous negotiations between the MOFA and the Minister of Finance led by Hashimoto Ryūtarō was deemed insufficient. The US reaction is aptly summarized by the expression "too little too late" popularized by US and international media (Shōji 2024; Tadokoro 2021; Kitaoka et al. 2021; Kaifu 2022).

Particularly, the Bush administration expressed contempt for Japan's refu sal to provide logistical support using private carriers to ship goods to the war front. Civil disobedience played a part in this: in September 1990, the All-Japan Seamen's Union blocked a shipment of 800 four-wheel-drive trucks at the port of Nagoya until it received reassurances from the government that the shipment could be stopped at any time in case of "anticipated danger." External pressures on the Japanese cabinet further mounted when the PM was shown by US embassy officials aerial pictures of Japanese tankers continuing their operations in the Persian Gulf (Kaifu 2022).

If on the one hand, Japan's budgetary restraints in the aftermath of the end of the asset bubble were putting the stability of US-Japan alliance from MOFA officials' standpoint (Tadokoro 2021), on the other, Kaifu's inaction created frictions within the ruling LDP where "security hawks" such as the then-LDP Secretary-General Ozawa Ichirō's were pushing for the government to allow the JSDF's participation in the US-led multinational expedition (Shōji 2024, p. 45). Under these circumstances, a first MOFA-drafted UN Peace Cooperation bill aimed at allowing the dispatch of civilian personnel to support the multinational military expedition to Iraq was submitted to the Diet for deliberations but was sunk in November 1990 due to opposition from the JSP and other minority parties and sectors of the LDP, forcing the cabinet to relinquish its plans (Inoguchi 1991; Kaifu 2022).[2] It is worth noting that, according to Kaifu’s memoir, the PM himself was reluctant to proceed with the dispatch of the JSDF abroad also in the light of the public opinion’s “deeply rooted allergy” (*kokumin no arerugī ga nezuyokatta*) to such changes to Japan’s security identity (Kaifu 2022).

As Kaifu’s attempt to pass the UN cooperation bill failed, in November 1990, the UN Security Council adopted resolution 678 which paved the way for air and land operations by the US-led multinational forces.[3] Faced with renewed request to contribute to the US-led military effort in early 1991, the Japanese government agreed to allocate an additional 9 billion USD in financial support (Inoguchi 1991). To finance this new aid package to the US-led military operation, Kaifu opted for a temporary tax increase (corporate and petrol taxes) and negotiated a spending review (including reducing the Defense budget for FY 1991) with Kōmeitō and the Democratic Socialist Party who voted in favor of the cabinet’s proposal (Kaifu 2022, p. 7; Burrell 1991).

Hostilities in the Persian Gulf ended on February 28, 1991, after Iraq agreed to withdraw from Kuwait in the face of the US-led multinational forces’ military superiority, and in April the UN Security Council adopted Resolution 687 formally declaring the ceasefire (Ministry of Foreign Affairs of Japan 1992). Against this backdrop, and after consultations with the diplomatic offices of Saudi Arabia and Kuwait, the Kaifu cabinet ordered the dispatch of a squadron of six minesweepers to the Gulf. The decision was not subject to parliamentary debate but nonetheless attracted criticism from both the opposition and within the LDP. Art. 3 and 99 of the SDF Law provided the legal basis for the dispatch of minesweepers. The government’s rationale was that the dispatch did not constitute use of military force prohibited by the Japanese constitution, as it served the purpose of guaranteeing the safe passage of vessels “related to Japan” (*wagakuni kankeisuru senpaku*)[4] through the Persian Gulf (Shōji 2024, pp. 68–69). During a press conference following the decision, Kaifu specified that a stable import of crude oil to Japan was essential to the very existence of Japan as a nation and to sustain the livelihood of the Japanese stressing Japan’s dependence on raw materials imported from the Middle East (Yomiuri Shinbun 1991).

[2] With the House of Councillors in control of the JSP as a result of the July 1989 election, the JSP could actually have an effective political leverage blocking the cabinet’s draft legislation. Kaifu was eventually elected PM, due to the House of Representative’s constitutionally sanctioned preeminince over the appointment of the head of the government.

[3] This measure allowed UN member-states participating in the US-led multinational forces expedition to Iraq to use “all necessary means” (including force) to implement resolution 660 demanding Iraq’s immediate and unconditional withdrawal and subsequent resolutions, in case of non-compliance by the Iraqi forces by January 15, 1991 (UN Security Council 1990).

[4] The government’s decision in April 1991 received the praise of the Keidanren, Japan’s major business federation, as a “natural and timely decision.” Other business associations, including the Petroleum Association of Japan (*Sekiyu renmei*) and All Japan Seamen’s Union (*Zen Nihon Kaiin Kumiai*) had asked the government to guarantee the safety of their operations (Shōji 2024, p. 68).

In addition, the squadron would not be exposed to hostile fire as the end of the conflict was institutionalized at the UN-level. Public opinion polls also showed that, with the war over, contrary to the previous year, the public opinion was "mature" enough for a sea change in Japan's security posture. As Kaifu recounted in his memoir, "had there been victims, that operation would not have been remembered in the same way" (Kaifu 2022, p. 9). The dispatch of minesweepers by West Germany ahead of the Japanese government's decision and the absence of Japan from the official statement of the government of Kuwait thanking the international community for its endeavor to defend it from Hussein's invasion contributed to changing the popular sentiment and, consequently, the political debate, laying the foundations of the so-called Gulf Trauma (*wangan torauma*) (Shōji 2024; Satō 2022; Kaifu 2022). This expression summarizes the emotional baggage of stigmatization which provided the backdrop for a coerced adoption of a new set of norms and institutions which became integral to the new post-Cold War arrangements (Zarakol 2011, 2014).

4 The 1992 Momentum and the Approval of the PKO Law

As shown above, Kaifu's breakaway from Japan's long-standing security posture materialized without any sensible change to the legislative framework due to the PM's own reticence[5] and to the structural constraints imposed by the Diet gridlock and internal divisions within the majority. Nonetheless, the 1991 Gulf trauma was the turning point leading, in June the following year, to the approval of Act on Cooperation with United Nations Peacekeeping Operations and Other Operations (or International Peace Cooperation Act). The subsequent LDP leadership of Miyazawa Kiichi set out to change the international image of a country that contributed to the international order without shedding "blood nor sweat."

After months of debates and negotiations between the LDP government and the opposition parties, a three-party agreement (LDP, Democratic Socialist Party (Minshatō), and Kōmeitō) was reached in late May 1992 on a draft bill, based on the earlier version submitted by the Kaifu administration.

The draft legislation allowed the JSDF to participate in UN-led PKO under five principles: (a) the existence of an agreement on a ceasefire between the parties involved in the conflict; (b) the consent of host countries as well and/or fighting parties to the UN PKO and to the participation of JSDF in it; (c) the impartiality of the PKO toward any of the parties involved in the conflict; (d) the termination of the peace cooperation assignment by the JSDF in case of the absence of the above

[5] Contributing to the PM's indecisiveness may have been the possible reaction from Asian neighbors. Recently declassified documents showed that the MOFA actively contacted the foreign ministries of the PRC and ROK to notify about the cabinet's intention to dispatch the minesweepers. Both expressed understanding but asked Japan to act carefully as sending Japanese troops overseas was an "extremely sensitive issue" given the historical tensions between the three countries (Kyodo News 2022).

conditions; (e) limitations to the use of weapons to the minimum necessary (*hitsuyōna saishōgen*) to protect the lives of JSDF personnel involved in the mission. The use of small weapons was allowed in specific conditions in accordance to the local PKO command's directives (Hironaka 1998, p. 82; Ministry of Foreign Affairs of Japan 2024; Shōji 2024, p. 71). The leaders of the three parties also agreed upon a series of items, including the freeze on the JSDF participation in PKF "core duties" (*PKF hontai gyōmu*) further limiting JSDF's participation to UNPKO to rear support (*kōhō shien*) (medical care, logistics, communication and military engineering, and the review of the implementation of the law after 3 years from establishment (Hironaka 1998, pp. 160–161; George Mulgan 1995, p. 1103). The law became effective in August that year and the PM took on the role of chair of the headquarters for International peace cooperation established in the Cabinet Office (Hironaka 1998, p. 200). In September, a group of 683 people (600 JSDF soldiers, 75 civilian police officers, and 8 electoral observers) was finally dispatched to Cambodia in response to the UN's request. The Japanese government asked in turn the UNTAC Command to assign the Japanese contingent to a "relatively stabilized area," as any incident could have raised the concern of the Japanese public opinion, hence the assignment of JSDF personnel in Takeo province (Hironaka 1998, p. 214).

The timing of the negotiations is worth analyzing. In March 1992, Akashi Yasushi, a Japanese diplomat working with the UN, landed in Cambodia as Chief of Mission of the UN Transitional Authority in Cambodia (UNTAC) whose task was guiding the country's transition to a civil administration years of war, favoring the disarmament of the fighting faction (particularly the remaining followers of former Khmer Rouge leader Pol Pot), and monitoring the country's first democratic election in 1993.

The appointment of Akashi was far from being the result of Tokyo's machinations at the UN level, but rather a coincidence (Hironaka 1998, p. 154). Nonetheless, the fact that a Japanese diplomat was assigned to such an important UN mission served as a political leverage for Miyazawa in his search for a convergence with parties from the opposition camp. Moreover, 2 years after another conference which paved the way for the 1991 Paris Peace Agreements, Tokyo hosted another ministerial conference on the reconstruction of Cambodia in June 1992 which ended with a pledge of 800 million USD-worth package to Cambodia.

Within the newly established legal framework, the Miyazawa cabinet and subsequent administrations were able to dispatch JSDF in several UN-led missions. After Cambodia, Mozambique (ONUMUZ, 1993), Rwanda (1994), The Golan Heights (UNDOF, 1996), East Timor (1999–2000; UNMISET 2002–2003; UNMIT 2010), Afghanistan (2001), Iraq (2003), Nepal (UNMIN 2007), Sudan (2008), Haiti (MINUSTAH 2010), South Sudan (2011), and Egypt (2019), which are currently the only two PKOs with active (though residual) Japanese participation (Ministry of Defense of Japan n.d.; Suzuki 2017).

5 The JSP Surge and the Check on the LDP's Assertiveness

As illustrated above, before entering a coalition government and having its chairman elected as PM in 1994, the JSP had been critical of the LDP's moves to allow the JSDF to participate in UN PKOs. Until then, the JSP, in fact, upheld an "integralist" view of the Art. 9 of the postwar constitution that barred the country from (a) having an army, including for self-defense and, consequently, (b) dispatching its troops abroad.

Historically, the JSP had defended the need for Japan to adopt neutrality as its main foreign policy posture going as far as to defend neutrality as key to national security in the context of the Cold War. The JSP posture until the mid- and late 1980s centered on the denial of the utility of the JSDF which were in turn seen as a potential danger to democratic governance in the country. On top of this, the JSP mainstream position on the Japan-US alliance was very critical toward the Japan-US Security Treaty. Allowing the US troops into Japanese soil was a factor of tension with the rest of Asia and the USSR, could expose Japan to nuclear attacks from foreign powers, and hindered the solution of territorial disputes. For these reasons, according to this view, Japan should abolish the Japan-US Security Treaty and negotiate a peace treaty with the USSR, thus removing US bases, and regaining sovereignty over Okinawa and part of the Kuriles (Stockwin 1962, pp. 35–36).

In the context of an LDP legitimacy crisis at the end of the 1980s, the JSP was under heavy pressures to modernize, as its major support base, the unions, faltered and its image ceased to be on a par with the voters' expectations. With the appointment of Doi Takako at the party's helm in 1986, the JSP took the opportunity to renegotiate several of its major political tenets, thus reforming its domestic image. In particular, rather than focusing on the Japan-US alliance and issues related to the 1946 Constitution, the JSP started focusing on issues such as fighting political corruption and working for a reform of the political funding system, amidst revelations on the involvement of LDP heavyweights in a major corruption scandal in 1988, and highlighted its opposition to the LDP's fiscal and trade policies (Kabashima and Steel 2012, p. 37). On top of the influence peddling scandals which had tarnished the party's reputation since the Lockheed scandal in the early 1970s, the LDP had significantly lost consensus in favor of the largest opposition party after the passing of an unpopular 3% consumption tax in April 1989. Concomitantly, the LDP had temporarily lost ground in its traditional constituencies in rural Japan which felt threatened by the advance of trade negotiations between Japan and the US in the context of subsequent disputes surrounding Japan's compliance with GATT obligations concerning food and agricultural goods trade policies.[6] After Tokyo announced

[6] Particularly, the US accused Japan of applying food import restrictions that were inconsistent with the GATT's regulations and pushed Japan to reform its agricultural sector accordingly. At the Lower House election of 1990, after pledging to protect the domestic rice industry, the LDP obtained a stable majority, as the opposition divided on the issue, with Kōmeitō turning in favor of a gradual liberalization of Japan's rice market. See Meyerson (2003).

its decision to end import quotas on beef and citrus by the early 1990s, the JSP sided with Japanese farmers and contributed with other opposition parties to the introduction of a series of amendments to the 1988 budget granting compensations to farmers affected by the end of import quotas. Later in 1989, the government, led by Uno Sosuke, succeeded to the embattled Takeshita Noboru, timidly pledged to cooperate during the Uruguay Round to partially liberalize its agricultural goods and food market, including rice (Meyerson 2003).

Trying to seize the opportunity entailed in the LDP's decline, the newly elected JSP leadership moved to review its posture on the JSDF and US presence in Japan in an attempt to build an anti-LDP front with the opposition, excluding the Japanese Communist Party (JCP). In August 1989, the party's Secretary-General Yamaguchi Tsuruo laid out a series of new policy directives indicating a first "pragmatist" turn in the JSP postwar history. He declared that the party would "accept the existence of the JSDF" and work to reduce the US military presence in Japan but will not seek the abolition of the Japan-US Security Treaty. However, the party would keep on advocating for peace and disarmament globally (Associated Press 1989). The said pragmatist turn happened as a result of debates within the party on the role that it should shoulder in the possibility that the LDP was ousted from power, whether one of direct control of the cabinet or one of LDP watchdog (Hyde 2009).

Against this backdrop, the evolution of the party's position on the JSDF role and Japan's participation in UN PKOs between 1991 and 1996 offers an interesting case-study of how structural constraints of the international system and stigma operate at the domestic level forcing former opposition parties to embrace certain policies and renegotiate key items in their political agendas.

As emerged from the close reading of the articles published on *Seisaku shiryō* (*Policy and Legislation*), with regard to the PKO draft law and the possible reform of the JSDF, the JSP accused the LDP of "wanting to cut an opening in the legislation allowing for the dispatch of troops (*hahei*)," despite the abovementioned hesitation by the Kaifu government. The JSP would support cooperation with UN PKO on a "non-military and civilian dimension (*higunji, minseimen de no kokuren no heiwa iji katsudō*)" and "oppose any draft law where the possibility of JSDF participation, which is forbidden by our Constitution, remains" (JSP 1991b, p. 2).

One of the JSP's key proposals before the passing of the PKO Law under the Miyazawa administration was to create a separate organization a "Peace cooperation corps" that would undertake non-military and civilian tasks such as disaster relief and rescue operations under the UN PKO framework. Such a proposal was, according to the then-JSP chairwoman Doi Takako, aligned with the directive of UN Secretary-General of the time, Javier Perez De Cuellar, who indicated his intention to expand the role of civilians instead of the military in UN PKOs (Doi 1991). On the same January 1991 issue of *Seisaku shiryō*, an article authored by the JSP internal working group on the PKO issue, further highlighted the fact that for Japan to cooperate with the UN under the UN PKO framework, it was crucial for the government to, first, build consensus and support among the Japanese people; second, to obtain unanimity in the Diet or a substantial majority; and finally to have the decision understood by neighboring countries (Kokusai heiwa kyōryoku mondai purojekuto 1991).

In ensuing issues of its publication, when the Kaifu administration's intention toward the dispatch of JSDF became clearer in early 1991, the JSP leadership continued criticizing the LDP government for trying to force the country's postwar constitution and reacting hastily and fuzzily to pressures from the US. The JSP's criticism emerges clearly in the March 1991 issue of the bulletin, where the proposed 1991 budget is analyzed. Here, the increase in defense spending was analyzed against the backdrop of the cabinet's efforts to allow the JSDF to take part, though in the conditions specified above, in the US-led multinational mission in the Gulf. Particularly, the introduction of thc M270 Multiple Launch Rocket System (MLRS), along with the Aegis integrated naval weapons system and airborne radar early warning system, was elicited as illustrative of the government's plan to make the JSDF deployable abroad (*jieitai no kaigai tenkai*), as they were being employed in the Gulf (JSP 1991a, pp. 6–7). Instead of abiding by US pressures finalized at sharing the burden of the war in the Middle East and opening new markets for its arms export, Japan should make more efforts for an immediate non-violent resolution of the conflict rather than pursuing a path which would lead to more war and violence (JSP 1991a, p. 7). In January 1991, highlighting the JSP autonomous diplomatic efforts, JSP Secretary-General Yamaguchi demanded that all efforts were made to avoid the military intervention in Kuwait and the end of Japan's all financial support of military operations (Yamaguchi 1991b, p. 61; 1991a, p. 64). Echoing the words of Chairwoman Doi who addressed PM Kaifu after the approval of the nine billion extra financial contribution to the US-led military expedition in the Persian Gulf, Yamaguchi further clarified:

> our country should make the utmost effort for an immediate ceasefire and for the materialization of peace rather than for war cooperation (*sensō kyōryoku*). To this aim, it should pursue adequate policies and implement them. These are the most urgent of all measures. (Yamaguchi 1991c)

On top of the above, the JSP prepared a roadmap for Japan's engagement in postwar Middle East. Besides providing humanitarian aid to war refugees and displaced communities through bilateral aid and UN agencies in war-hit areas, Japan should take steps to guarantee the access to food and basic goods for communities in the Palestinian territories of Gaza and the West Bank, where Israel had been implementing a blockade since the start of the Gulf War, through continuous support to the UNRWA. Furthermore, the proposal included, among other measures, the creation of a UN Fund dedicated to the monitoring of ceasefires, and the creation of an international framework for the environmental restoration of the Persian Gulf, heavily affected by crude oil spills and environmental decay related to the military operations in the area; and increased contributions on rebuilding housing, welfare, and healthcare across the region (JSP Headquarters for Emergency Measures in the Middle East 1991, pp. 5–6).

6 The JSP Crisis, the Anti-LDP Coalition, and the Experience of the "Water and Oil Cabinet"

The 1991 local elections signaled a crisis in the JSP's domestic popularity and led to Doi's resignation as JSP chairwoman. The approval of the PKO Law under Miyazawa's leadership further contributed to sinking the JSP's popularity while deepening internal divisions. The JSP's decision to filibuster the vote on the 1992 PKO law by adopting the "cow walk" strategy after the LDP scrapped the hypothesis of a separate organization tasked with the participation in UN PKOs put the JSP alongside the JCP and made further electoral cooperation with Kōmeitō and DSP impossible, having these two parties voted in favor of the legislation (Hironaka 1998; Hyde 2009). This resulted in a progressive isolation of the JSP on the matter, although the party succeeded in retaining its position as the largest opposition party in the Upper House election of 1992.

In addition to domestic factors, the JSP's approach to Japan's evolving security posture came to be further at odds with the international discourse at the very UN level as opposed to 1991. The selection of Boutros Boutros-Ghali as the new UN Secretary-General from January 1992 coincided with the consolidation of a new narrative on preventive deployment, peacebuilding, and peacekeeping centered around the notion of proactive military contribution by UN member states (Boutros-Ghali and Secretary-General 1992). In response to this new vision, JSP Chairman Yamahana Sadao penned a letter to the UN Secretary-General in which he expressed concern that "if the United Nations' military activities continue to expand gradually eroding previous barriers (*nashikuzushi teki kakudai*), it will undermine trust in the UN as an international mediation body" (Yamahana 1993a).

Nonetheless, *Policy and Legislation* continued hosting JSP leaders and members' criticism of the government's action. Particularly, after the dispatch of the JSDF to Cambodia, the newsletter featured commentaries and analyses on the relationship between the principles established by the postwar constitution and Japan's strive for international contribution (particularly on the issue of the use of force for personnel involved in UN PKOs) and statements by JSP officials denouncing the deteriorating security situation in the Southeast Asian country, particularly after the killing of a Japanese member of a UN volunteer group (Amatatsu 1993; Shimazaki 1993). After the killing of a Japanese civilian police officer involved in UNTAC operations, the JSP leadership, particularly Secretary-General Akamatsu Hirotaka, renewed their calls for an immediate withdrawal of the JSDF from Cambodia, as the ceasefire in the country was clearly undermined by the Khmer Rouge's refusal to participate in the peace process (Akamatsu 1993). In the light of these events, in his political manifesto on "constitutional (re)building" (*sōken*), Yamahana reiterated, among other items, the traditional JSP view on the constitutional prohibition of the dispatch of troops abroad and Japan's non-exertion of the right to collective self-defense, arguing for a reform of Japan's defense that would establish the JSDF as a mere territorial defense force while creating a separate organization to participate in UN PKOs (Yamahana 1993b, pp. 13–14).

A shift in the JSP's official narrative on the JSDF and PKOs emerged after the formation of a coalition government in 1993. In the aftermath of the July 1993 general election the JSP had emerged as the second largest (though declining) party after the LDP and the linchpin of a non-LDP coalition government led by Hosokawa Morihiro. The administration's political program was based on the so-called eight-party agreement and foresaw a series of reforms in Japan's political, fiscal, and administrative system. JSP Chairman Yamahana was appointed minister in charge of the political reform, a position he retained until Hosokawa's resignation in April 1994. Against this backdrop, on the JSDF's role in the UN PKOs, Hosokawa received the JSP's proposal to create a separate organization that would deal with the UN's request to collaborate to PKOs, though the PM himself remained unclear whether this would be created within or without the JSDF. This conflicted however with the views held by Ozawa, who quit the LDP along with Hata Tsutomu in 1993 to form the Japan Renewal Party (Shinseitō) and joined the non-LDP coalition government. In fact, he viewed the JSDF's participation in UN PKO as instrumental for Japan to acquire "normal statehood" (Shōji 2024, p. 127; George Mulgan 1995, p. 1107).

A few months after Yamahana's cabinet appointment, the JSP held internal elections to select its new leadership. Long-standing tensions between more conservative and progressive sectors of the party re-emerged when Yamahana and others' plans to break away from the JSP to form a new party emerged. In this context, the JSP held an election for its new chairman won by Murayama Tomiichi who took over as party chief. Following Hosokawa's resignation in April 1994, taking the initiative to form a new cabinet, Ozawa and Hata marginalized the JSP proceeding with cabinet appointments without consulting with Murayama. In response, the JSP chairman decided to withdraw the party's support to the short-lived Hata cabinet (Yakushiji 2012, p. 151). In so doing, Murayama paved the way for the formation of a third coalition government formed by the JSP, the New Party Sakigake—a moderate reformist internationalist party born out of the initiative of former LDP lawmakers Takemura Masayoshi and Hatoyama Yukio—and the LDP. Particularly, the formation of a JSP-LDP cabinet struck observers as an attempt at mixing "water with oil" due to historical divergences between the two groups (Shōji 2024, p. 138). The new administration, inaugurated on June 30, 1994, would be led by Murayama himself. The composition of the cabinet reflected the internal balance of political power: six ministers out of 21 were allocated to the JSP, while a majority of ministers, including the vice-PMs, Foreign Minister Kōno Yōhei, and Trade and Industry Minister Hashimoto Ryūtarō, hailed from the LDP.

7 Changing Paradigms

Under the aforementioned circumstances, the Murayama-led JSP had to compromise on its long-standing policies regarding (a) the role of the JSDF and (b) Japan's participation in UN PKOs after the introduction of the 1992 legislation. First, the idea to create separate organization that could take part in UN PKOs thus upholding the JSP's long-standing interpretation of the constitution was included in a JSP policy paper published on *Policy and Legislation* in the immediate aftermath of Murayama Tomiichi's Diet nomination as PM in June 1994 and formation of a new coalition cabinet (JSP 1994, p. 6). However, this item is absent from the text of the agreement with the New Party Sakigake which reads as follows:

> Recognizing that the Constitution of Japan is founded on the ideal of universal security under the United Nations, we will actively (*sekkyoku tekini*) participate in UN peacekeeping operations to ensure global peace and our own national security. Regarding UN peacekeeping operations (PKO), we will cooperate in accordance with the principles governing PKO deployment and within the framework of the Constitution (*kenpō no han'inai de kyōryoku suru*). Our country places importance on 'contribution to coexistence' (*kyōzon e no kōken*) —contributing to global peace and coexistence without relying on military power—by addressing global issues such as environmental protection in the region and human rights, which are essential to humanity's coexistence. The new administration [...] will work toward reforming the United Nations aiming to build a global peace order centered on the UN. (JSP and New Party Sakigake 1994, p. 11)

Against this backdrop, the JSP seemed to scrap its own proposal of creating a new separate entity that could take part in UN PKOs. Faced with this trade-off, as shown in the party's 1995 Upper House Election manifesto, the JSP pledged to keep working for a scale-down of the JSDF from its Cold War arrangements and a revision of its equipment and management (particularly to enhance its readiness in case of a large-scale natural disaster in Japan) and reiterated the need to expand its international contribution in the non-military area (JSP 1995a, p. 13). In this regard, it may be worth noting that the Murayama administration was successful in reining in the increase of the defense spending below the 1% of GDP on an annual basis while maintaining, despite the country's tight finances, the annual expenditure on the country's ODA on a par with the previous year (JSP 1995b, pp. 44–51).

With regard to the UN PKOs, however, Murayama's margins for action were much more limited. Since 1993 the Ministry of Foreign Affairs (and particularly its newly established Foreign Policy Bureau (*sōseikyoku*)) had been in talks with the UN on a possible new PKO assignment for the JSDF. When Finland announced its withdrawal from UNDOF on the Golan Heights, a new window of opportunity for Japan opened up at the end of 1993. In particular, Canada, which had the command of the UNDOF saw favorably Japan's forthcoming engagement (Shōji 2024, pp. 128–132). Against this backdrop, Japan's participation in UNDOF was no longer a matter of "if," but of "when" and "how."

Soon after taking office, in fact, the Murayama cabinet was busy responding to international and domestic contingencies. First, despite it being relatively more dangerous than the Golan Heights, the government decided to prioritize the humanitarian crisis in Rwanda, by dispatching JSDF to provide medical assistance and fresh water supplies to refugee camps on the border with Zaire and Tanzania throughout 1994 and early 1995 (Shōji 2024, p. 142). Moreover, in early 1995, the Japanese government had to respond to two unprecedented major emergencies: the Hanshin-Awajishima earthquake of January 1995 and the Aum Shinrikyō terror attack on the

Tokyo subway in March that year. In addition to these, the JSP was facing a deep internal crisis with former chairman Yamahana and other party heavyweights threatening to leave the party in view of the July 1995 Upper House election (Shōji 2024, p. 144; Yakushiji 2012, p. 176).

In light of these facts, any political decision on the dispatch of a Japanese contingent to the UNDOF stalled until after the vote. Meanwhile, two survey missions composed by lawmakers of the majority and government parties that were sent to the area to gather information and verify the applicability of the aforementioned five principles for JSDF PKO deployment confirmed that, in spite of a few minor incidents, the area of dispatch was safe. In addition, the two missions were instrumental to receiving the support of the international community. As recounted by JSP lawmaker Taguchi Kenji, a member of one of the survey missions, "it was impressive to meet with so many key figures, from foreign minister al-Sharaa of Syria, to Prince Hassan of Jordan, to Israel's PM Rabin, to PLO's Arafat, and hear that every one of them had great expectations toward Japan" (Taguchi 1995).

The Upper House election ended in a dramatic loss for the JSP which lost nearly half of the seat which were up for renewal therefore reducing the JSP's stake in the cabinet. Nonetheless, political divisions within the JSP on the issue of the JSDF participation to UN PKOs remained. Particularly problematic was the relation between JSDF's rear-area support operations and the core duties of the UN peacekeeping forces to which the PM himself was opposed. Finally, a consensus within the JSP emerged. On top of barring the JSDF from the PKF core duties, the JSDF were prohibited from transporting weapons of foreign militaries and armed personnel and participating in live fire military exercises (Shōji 2024, pp. 153–154). As with earlier peacekeeping deployments ordered by LDP-governments, a cautious approach to PKO-related seemed to prevail. Nonetheless, further incremental changes to the PKO Law which were favored by sectors of the MOFA and by conservative fringes within and without the LDP were avoided.

8 Conclusion

In his September 1995 policy speech, following a diplomatic tour of the Middle East, during which he made stops in Saudi Arabia, Egypt, Syria, Israel and the Gaza Strip, and Jordan, Murayama reiterated Japan's intention to continue proactively contributing (*hikitsudzuki sekkyokutekini kōken suru*) the peace process in the region through economic assistance and the dispatch of military personnel in the context of UN-sanctioned operations contributing to the reconciliation between Israel and Syria (*Shiria-Isuraeru aida no wahei ni kiyo*) (Murayama 1995). In this manner, the socialist PM, in continuity with his predecessors, showed Japan's commitment to peace and stability globally.

As noted above, Japan's increased international presence, especially through its involvement in UN PKOs has been accompanied by ongoing internal debates and contradictions between pacifist and nationalist views within Japanese politics.

Narrative shifts at the domestic and international level anticipated actual policy changes that were favored, mainly, by mounting international pressure for Japan to take a more active role in global security. The fear of being *stigmatized* by the international community and hereby losing access to a set of common goods (trade, security, etc.) at a time of dramatic changes in the international order was a major factor in Japan's adoption of a set of new norm which inevitably contributed to a paradigm shift in its postwar security posture. This is particularly evident in the Kaifu cabinet's approach to Iraq's invasion of Kuwait in 1990 and in the run-up to the approval of the 1992 PKO Law.

This law allowed the Japanese Self-Defense Forces (JSDF) to participate in UN peacekeeping missions under strict conditions: agreement between conflicting parties, host country consent, ceasefire, impartiality, and limits on weapon use. The law also restricted JSDF involvement in combat and required periodic reviews. Within Japan, political divisions deepened, with security "hawks" pushing for a more active military role.

Against this backdrop, putting the brakes on Japan's security normalization and reasserting Japan's promotion of the ideals of peace (*heiwa no rinen*) and democracy were the major legacies of the Murayama cabinet. Before joining a coalition government in 1994, JSP was strongly critical of the LDP's attempts to allow the dispatch of JSDF abroad. As shown above, the JSP interpreted Article 9 of the constitution strictly, opposing both the existence of an army and the deployment of troops abroad. The party even criticized the Japan-US Security Treaty, described as a threat to Japan's security and sovereignty. By the late 1980s, facing a decline in support and changes in leadership, the JSP leadership started reviewing its long-standing policies and reconsidered its stance on the JSDF and US presence, though it continued to advocate for peace and disarmament. The JSP opposed the PKO Law on the grounds that they contradicted Japan's pacifist constitution. Despite electoral setbacks and internal disagreements, the JSP could briefly influence government policy as part of the 1993–1994 non-LDP coalition and later the 1994–1996 coalition with the LDP.

In the latter cabinet, under Murayama, the JSP endorsed the continuation of the policy inaugurated in 1992 with the JSDF dispatch to Cambodia, for the sake of Japan's "international contribution." As illustrated above, the JSP maintained a cautious approach to the shift of Japan's security identity and acted as a bulwark against more radical revisions of the five principles of PKO, particularly that concerning the use of weapons during PKO deployment. Despite its historical posture, the JSP-led cabinet acted in a manner which is consistent with the policies initiated under the LDP. To put it differently, international contingencies and domestic political changes pushed the JSP to renounce its traditional integralist interpretation of the 1946 Constitution, and to embrace a new interpretation of Japan's pacifism, one with a global projection. Hence, the narrative shift, during its tenure in government, toward a discourse centered on Japan's "proactive contribution to peace" (*sekkyokuteki heiwashugi*) discourse, which has gained strength since the early 2010s (Hughes 2017; Maslow 2015; Fujishige et al. 2022).

Concomitantly, while keeping the level of defense spending stable, it did not endorse the "normalization of statehood" endorsed by conservative lawmakers as Ozawa Ichirō, nor supported radical breakaways from previous decisions, including the 1992 PKO Law. As recounted by Murayama in his memoir about his January 1995 meeting with then-US President Bill Clinton, in fact, previously determined policies concerning Japan's diplomacy and security, including the Japan-US Security Treaty, could not be renounced single-handedly by his administration. Nonetheless, existing arrangements could and should be improved through discussion and negotiations (Yakushiji 2012, pp. 196–197).

References

Akamatsu H (1993) Kanbodia Jōsei Ni Tsuite (Danwa). Seisaku Shiryō/Policy and Legislation, July 1993

Amatatsu T (1993) Kokusai Kyōryoku to Kenpō Rongi. Seisaku Shiryō/Policy and Legislation, April 1993

Associated Press (1989) Japan's socialists ease stand on defense issues, 22 August 1989

Boutros-Ghali B, UN Secretary-General (1992) An agenda for peace: preventive diplomacy, peacemaking and peace-keeping: report of the Secretary-General pursuant to the statement adopted by the Summit Meeting of the Security Council on 31 January 1992: Boutros Boutros-Ghali. https://digitallibrary.un.org/record/145749

Burrell S (1991) Kaifu trims tax package in trade-off for $9 bn war aid. Australian Financial Review, 18 February 1991. https://www.afr.com/politics/kaifu-trims-tax-package-in-trade-off-for-9bn-war-aid-19910218-k49e5

Doi T (1991) Kokuren Heiwa Kyōryoku No Arikata Ni Tsuite (Danwa). Seisaku Shiryō/Policy and Legislation, January 1991

Fujishige HN, Uesugi Y, Honda T (2022) Japan's peacekeeping at a crossroads: taking a robust stance or remaining hesitant? Sustainable development goals series. Springer International Publishing, Cham. https://doi.org/10.1007/978-3-030-88509-0

Fukui H (2023) 8. Constitutional revision. In: Party in power. University of California Press, pp 198–226. https://www.degruyterbrill.com/document/doi/10.1525/9780520329423-012/html

George Mulgan A (1995) International peacekeeping and Japan's role: catalyst or cautionary tale? Asian Survey 35(12):1102–1117

Gustafsson K (2013) Japanese Prime Minister Abe's U-Turn on the Murayama Statement. East Asia Forum (blog), 31 May 2013. https://eastasiaforum.org/2013/05/31/japanese-prime-minister-abes-u-turn-on-the-murayama-statement/

Hattori R (2019) Zōhohan Ōhira Masayoshi Rinen to gaikō. Zōhohan. Bungei Shunju, Tokyo

Hironaka Y (1998) Miyazawa Seiken: Roppyaku Yonjū Yonichi. Gyōken shuppan kyoku, Tokyo

Hughes CW (2004) Japan's security agenda: military, economic and environmental dimensions. Lynne Rienner Publishers, Boulder. http://webcat.warwick.ac.uk/record=b1735132~S1

Hughes CW (2017) Japan's strategic trajectory and collective self-defense: essential continuity or radical shift? J Japanese Stud 43(1):93–126

Hyde S (2009) The transformation of the Japanese left: from old socialists to new democrats. Routledge, London. https://doi.org/10.4324/9780203874356

Inada J (1989) Japan's aid diplomacy: economic, political or strategic? Millennium 18(3):399–414. https://doi.org/10.1177/03058298890180030701

Inoguchi T (1991) Japan's response to the Gulf crisis: an analytic overview. J Japanese Stud 17(2):257–273

Islam S (1993) Foreign aid and burdensharing: is Japan free riding to a coprosperity sphere in Pacific Asia? In Regionalism and rivalry: Japan and the United States in Pacific Asia. The University of Chicago Press, pp 321–390. https://www.nber.org/books-and-chapters/regionalism-and-rivalry-japan-and-united-states-pacific-asia/foreign-aid-and-burdensharing-japan-free-riding-coprosperity-sphere-pacific-asia
JSP (1991a) 1991 Nendo Seifu Yosan an No Bunseki to Hihan. Seisaku Shiryō/Policy and Legislation, March 1991
JSP (1991b) Kokuren Heiwa Kyōryoku Mondai: Tō Senmei. Seisaku Shiryō/Policy and Legislation, January 1991
JSP (1994) Aratana Renritsu Seiken Juritsu Ni Attatte. Seisaku Shiryō/Policy and Legislation, August 1994
JSP (1995a) 95 Nen Sangiin Senkyo Seisaku Taikō. Seisaku Shiryō/Policy and Legislation, July 1995
JSP (1995b) 95 Nendo Yosan No Seika No Pointo. Seisaku Shiryō/Policy and Legislation, February 1995
JSP and New Party Sakigake (1994) Atarashii Renritsu Seiken No Juritsu Ni Kansuru Gōi Jikō. Seisaku Shiryō/Policy and Legislation, August 1994
JSP Headquarters for Emergency Measures in the Middle East (1991) Takokusekigun Tsuika Shien 90 Oku Doru No Zaigen Taisaku No Kettei Ni Tsuiite (Danwa). Seisaku Shiryō/Policy and Legislation, April 1991
Kabashima I, Steel G (2012) Changing politics in Japan. Cornell University Press
Kaifu T (2022) Kaifu Toshiki Kaikoroku 海部俊樹回想録. Chūnichi Shinbun, 14 January 2022. https://www.chunichi.co.jp/article/400147
Kitaoka S, Miyake K, Nakamitsu I (2021) Ogata Sadako Shi Ga Mezashita Kokusaishakai, Okamoto Yukio Ga Mezashita Nihon Gaikō. Kokusa Mondai, no. 700 (April). https://www2.jiia.or.jp/kokusaimondai_archive/2020/2021-04-002.pdf?noprint#page=1.00
Kokusai heiwa kyōryoku mondai purojekuto (1991) Kokuren Chūshin No Kokusai Heiwa Kyōryoku No Suishin Ni Tsuite. Seisaku Shiryō/Policy and Legislation, January 1991
Kyodo News (2022) Japan sought China, South Korea's views before 1991 SDF Gulf dispatch. Kyodo News+, 21 December 2022. https://english.kyodonews.net/news/2022/12/5db227f25ec2-japan-sought-china-s-koreas-views-before-1991-sdf-gulf-dispatch.html
MacArthur II D (1957) Telegram from the Embassy in Japan to the Department of State. US Department of State. 794.00/9–2057. Department of State, Central Files. https://history.state.gov/historicaldocuments/frus1955-57v23p1/d226
Maslow S (2015) A blueprint for a strong Japan? Abe Shinzō and Japan's evolving security system. Asian Survey 55(4):739–765. https://doi.org/10.1525/as.2015.55.4.739
Meyerson C (2003) Domestic politics and international relations in US-Japan trade policymaking: the GATT Uruguay Round agriculture negotiations. International political economy series, 1st edn. Palgrave Macmillan UK, London. https://doi.org/10.1057/9780230512078
Ministry of Defense of Japan (n.d.) Kokuren Heiwa Iji Katsudō (Kokuren PKO) Nado e No Kyōryoku. https://www.mod.go.jp/j/approach/kokusai_heiwa/pko/index.html
Ministry of Foreign Affairs of Japan (1992) How the Gulf crisis began and ended. In: Diplomatic Bluebook 1991. Tokyo. https://www.mofa.go.jp/policy/other/bluebook/1991/1991-2-1.htm
Ministry of Foreign Affairs of Japan (1995) National Defense Program Outline 1995. https://www.mofa.go.jp/policy/security/defense96/capability.html
Ministry of Foreign Affairs of Japan (2024) Outline of Japan's International Peace Cooperation. Ministry of Foreign Affairs of Japan. https://www.mofa.go.jp/fp/ipc/page22e_000683.html
Murayama T (1995) Murayama Shushō No Shoshin Hyōmei Enzetsu. Asahi Shimbun, 29 September 1995. Asahi Shimbun CrossSearch - Asahi News Database
Oros A (2008) Normalizing Japan: politics, identity, and the evolution of security practice, Studies in Asian security. Stanford University Press, Stanford

Oros AL (2017) Japan's security renaissance: new policies and politics for the twenty-first century. Columbia University Press

Ozawa I, Rubinfien L, Ozawa I (1994) In: Gower E (ed) Blueprint for a new Japan: the rethinking of a nation, 1st edn. Kodansha International, Tokyo

Pugliese G, Wallace C (2023) Japan 2022: Putin and Abe shocks Thwart Kishida's enjoyment of three golden years despite major defence overhaul. Asia Maior XXXIII/2022

Pugliese G, Zappa M (2024) Japan 2023: still walking in Abe Shinzō's footsteps. Asia Maior XXXIV:65–124

Satō M (2022) Kokusai heiwa kyōryoku hō ga seiritsu suru made 国際平和協力法が成立するまで - 内閣府. Cabinet Office, Government of Japan, 26 July 2022. https://www.cao.go.jp/pko/pko_j/organization/researcher/atpkonow/article116.html

Scheiner E (2005) Democracy without competition in Japan: opposition failure in a one-party dominant state. Cambridge University Press, Cambridge. https://doi.org/10.1017/CBO9780511610660

Shimazaki Y (1993) Kambodia de No Nihonjin Senkyo Kanshiin No Satsugai Jiken Ni Tsuite (Danwa). Seisaku Shiryō/Policy and Lcgislation, June 1993

Shōji T (2024) Nihon No PKO No Seisaku: Kattō to Kunō No 60 Nen. Chikuma Shobō, Tokyo

Söderberg M (ed) (1996) The business of Japanese foreign aid: five cases from Asia. Routledge, London. https://doi.org/10.4324/9780203035665

Stockwin JAA (1962) "Positive Neutrality" – the foreign policy of the Japanese Socialist Party. Asian Survey 2(9):33–41

Suzuki K (2017) Twenty-five years of Japanese peacekeeping operations and the self-defense forces' mission in south Sudan. Asia-Pacific Rev 24(2):44–63. https://doi.org/10.1080/13439006.2017.1407534

Tadokoro M (2021) Nihon Gaikō Ni Totte Dai-Ichi Wangan Sensō. Sensō-Shi Kenkyū Kokusai Forum Hokokusho, no. Reiwa 3 nen, 99–107

Taguchi K (1995) Hajimete No Chūtō No Tabi. Seisaku Shiryō/Policy and Legislation, July 1995

UN Security Council (1990) Resolution 678 (1990) adopted by the Security Council at Its 2963rd Meeting, on 29 November 1990. S/RES/678(1990). https://digitallibrary.un.org/record/102245?ln=en&v=pdf

United Nations Peacekeeping Peace and Security (n.d.) Iran-Iraq UNIIMOG background. https://peacekeeping.un.org/mission/past/uniimogbackgr.html

Yakushiji K (2012) Murayama Tomiichi Kaikoroku. Iwanami Shoten, Tokyo

Yamaguchi T (1991a) Chūtō Wangan Sensō Shien No Tame No Seifu Hōshin No Kettei Ni Tsuite. Seisaku Shiryō/Policy and Legislation, March 1991

Yamaguchi T (1991b) Danwa. Seisaku Shiryō/Policy and Legislation, March 1991

Yamaguchi T (1991c) Takokusekigun Tsuika Shien 90 Oku Doru No Zaigen Taisaku No Kettei Ni Tsuiite (Danwa). Seisaku Shiryō/Policy and Legislation, March 1991

Yamahana S (1993a) Butorosu Butorosu-Gari Kokuren Jimu Sōchō Kakka. Seisaku Shiryō/Policy and Legislation, April 1993

Yamahana S (1993b) Watashi No Sōkenron. Seisaku Shiryō/Policy and Legislation, July 1993

Yennie Lindgren W (2021) WIN-WIN! With ODA-man: legitimizing development assistance policy in Japan. Pacific Rev 34(4):633–663. https://doi.org/10.1080/09512748.2020.1727552

Yomiuri Shinbun (1991) Sōkaitei Haken Kettei No Kakugigo No Kaifu Shushō No Kisha Kaiken Yōshi 掃海艇派遣決定の閣議後の海部首相の記者会見要旨, 25 April 1991. Yomidas - Yomiuri Database Service

Zappa M (2022) Tracing the roots of the free and open Indo-Pacific strategy: anxiety and opportunism in foreign policy narrative construction in Japan from the late 1970s to the mid-2000s. Quaderni Di Scienze Politiche 2022(21):51–70

Zarakol A (2011) After defeat: how the east learned to live with the west, Cambridge studies in international relations, vol 118. Cambridge University Press, Cambridge

Zarakol A (2014) What made the modern world hang together: socialisation or stigmatisation? Int Theory 6(2):311–332. https://doi.org/10.1017/S1752971914000141

The Tragic Demise of Japan's Constitutional War Constraints

Craig Martin

The Constitution of Japan is famous for imposing constraints on the government's use of armed force and the maintenance of armed forces. These restrictions are contained in Article 9, the so-called peace clause, which has been a source of national identity as well as a cause of passionate political activism and controversy for decades. Paragraph one of Article 9 imposed a prohibition on the use of force, while paragraph two imposed a prohibition on the maintenance of armed forces and "other war potential."[1] While these provisions were effectively imposed on a defeated Japan by its American conquerors, Article 9 was proclaimed by Japanese politicians during the ratification debates as setting Japan at the vanguard for a new way of thinking about international peace and security, and it was subsequently embraced by the Japanese people. And though conservative forces and factions of the ruling party had sought to revise these provisions of Article 9 from the moment Japan regained its full sovereignty, for almost seven decades Article 9 operated to effectively constrain successive Japanese governments from engaging in any use of

I would like to thank Giovanni Cavaggion and the other organizers from the University of Milan for their kind invitation to participate in the symposium that gave rise to this book. I would also like to thank all the participants of the symposium, and particularly Giovanni Cavaggion and Akihiko Kimijima, for their comments and feedback; and, as well, I would like to thank Takamasu Nishihara, Mark Levin, and Lawrence Repeta, for their helpful comments and input at various stages of the research and writing of this chapter. I am of course responsible for any errors.

[1] There is a third element in paragraph two, being the non-recognition of the rights of belligerency, as is discussed in more detail below, but this chapter focuses on the two core elements.

C. Martin (✉)
Washburn University School of Law, Topeka, KS, USA
e-mail: craig.martin@washburn.edu

G. Cavaggion (ed.), *The 'Pacifist Principle' in the Italian and Japanese Constitutions in the Wake of the War in Ukraine*,
https://doi.org/10.1007/978-3-032-23108-6_12

force or participating in any armed conflict, and to significantly moderate Japan's defense spending, military posture, and national security policy.

This all began to change in 2014 when the government of Prime Minister Shinzo Abe purported to "reinterpret" Article 9 through an executive branch fiat, making permissible uses of force that had long been understood to be prohibited by Article 9. This reinterpretation focused on weakening the clear and effective prohibition on the use of force in paragraph one of Article 9. The move was widely considered illegitimate and ultimately unconstitutional, on both grounds of procedure and substance—it circumvented the formal constitutional amendment process entirely, and imposed a radical new understanding that was outside of the range of reasonable constitutional interpretation. Yet this reinterpretation has not been overturned. Time has served to entrench it, and the government has slowly moved to extend it. Then, with the Russian invasion of Ukraine in February 2022, the government seized the opportunity to issue a new national security strategy that fundamentally reoriented Japanese military capability, posture, and doctrine. This new national security strategy not only extended some elements of the reinterpretation, but it focused on overturning the prohibition on the maintenance of armed forces and other war potential that was imposed by paragraph two of Article 9, and thereby completed the transformation of both core elements of Article 9.

This chapter examines this process of constitutional transformation, explaining briefly why and how it represents an arguably illegitimate process of eviscerating long-established constitutional constraints on executive power, which has undermined the rule of law in Japan, and eroded the pacifist principles that have constituted a defining element of Japan's post-war constitutional identity. It also suggests that this process of constitutional transformation has significance that extends far beyond Japan's borders. This is of course true for the evolving geopolitics and foreign relations in the region—but I am here speaking of the legal theory implications. As I have written about this elsewhere, this transformation has implications for how so-called informal constitutional amendments should be understood; and the transformation is also significant for the relationship between domestic constitutional law and international legal constraints on the use of force. Article 9's incorporation of *jus ad bellum* principles from international law represented a pioneering attempt to create mutually reinforcing legal regimes—using domestic constitutional mechanisms to strengthen international law's often tenuous grip on state use of force. The provision's erosion thus represents a loss not only for Japan's constitutional order but for the broader project of subjecting the use of force to meaningful legal constraints in an increasingly weak international system. In short, and as will be explored further in the conclusion, the demise of Article 9 is tragic in the true sense of the word.

Section 1 explains the traditional understanding and operation of Article 9 from its first authoritative interpretation in 1954 through to 2014, demonstrating how its provisions, and particularly the prohibition on the use of force, created meaningful and effective constraints on Japanese security policy and fostered a distinctive pacifist constitutional culture. Section 2 provides a detailed analysis of the "reinterpretation" undertaken by the Abe administration in 2014–2015, which gutted the prohibition on the use of force in paragraph one of Article 9, and argues that this represented neither legitimate constitutional interpretive development or informal amendment as that concept is understood in constitutional theory, but rather an illegitimate circumvention of the formal amendment procedure provided for in Article 96 of the Constitution. Section 3 examines the dramatic acceleration of this constitutional transformation following the Ukraine invasion, with particular focus on the revolutionary changes embodied in Japan's December 2022 National Security Strategy documents. These effectively completed the reinterpretation of Article 9 by gutting the paragraph two constraints on the maintenance of armed forces and other war potential. The chapter concludes by reflecting on why this transformation should be understood as tragic in the Classical Greek sense, in terms of the loss of something great, due in part to inherent flaws—explaining what was great about Article 9, which flaws contributed to its fall, and why its loss is so significant.

1 The Traditional Understanding and Operation of Article 9

To fully comprehend the nature and significance of the demise of Article 9, one requires some understanding of its origins, the traditional interpretation, and its operation for close to 70 years after its promulgation.

1.1 The Origins of Article 9

It is not possible in this short essay to really capture the remarkable and dramatic nature of the story of the making of the 1947 Constitution of Japan.[2] It began with four simple points on a one-page memo from Douglas MacArthur to a small group of his staff in the Supreme Commander Allied Powers (SCAP), with instructions to urgently prepare a full draft constitution to present to the government of Japan as a replacement for the pre-war Meiji Constitution. The idea of constraining Japan's war-making ability—what was to become Article 9—was one of the four points on that memo. The subcommittee of the drafting team that undertook the work on this provision incorporated language from the 1928 Kellogg-Briand Pact, which was the first treaty to prohibit the use of force, as well as language from Article 2(4) of the United Nations Charter, which had just been concluded weeks earlier. This provision was, and remains, one of the few examples of a constitutional provision directly and explicitly incorporating principles on the prohibition of the use of armed force

[2] For the best full accounts of this history in English, see Moore, Robinson (2002) and Shōichi (1997); for my own account of the history of Article 9, see Martin (2008); there is a massive literature in Japanese, but see, e.g., Hara (2004); Takayanagi (1972).

from the modern *jus ad bellum* regime in international law.[3] This is, indeed, one of the features that makes Article 9 so significant.[4] The post-war German Basic Law and Italian Constitution, which were being drafted with American input during the same period, also contained provisions that constrained uses of force that would constitute acts of aggression, but they did not go as far as the Japanese provision, or as directly incorporate international treaty language.[5]

The draft constitution prepared by the SCAP team was presented to the Japanese government in dramatic fashion, and after some deliberation and considerable pressure from MacArthur, the government accepted it as the basis for a new constitution.[6] But the draft was nonetheless subject to extensive negotiation, debate, and considerable revision over the course of the next year, with a final version finally being formally promulgated in 1947. The provision that became Article 9 itself underwent significant revision during the constitutional adoption process, with language being added that arguably strengthened its pacifist orientation.[7] The final text of Article 9 in English is as follows:

> Aspiring sincerely to an international peace based on justice and order, the Japanese people forever renounce war as a sovereign right of the nation and the threat or use of force as means of settling international disputes.
>
> In order to accomplish the aim of the preceding paragraph, land, sea, and air forces, as well as other war potential, will never be maintained. The right of belligerency of the state will not be recognized.[8]

It is important to keep in mind as the analysis proceeds that the provision contains three distinct elements, which have operated with lesser and greater effectiveness over the history of the provision. The first paragraph contains a renunciation of "war as a sovereign right of the nation" and a renunciation of "the threat or use of force as means of settling international disputes." This is the part of the provision that borrows language from the international law *jus ad bellum* treaties.[9] The second paragraph contains two distinct elements: a prohibition on maintaining "land, sea, and air forces, as well as other war potential" and a denial of recognition of "the

[3] For a full analysis of this process, and the significance of this incorporation of *jus ad bellum* principles, see Martin (2008), pp. 297–299, 309–318. There are some who argue that the origin of Article 9 was then-Prime Minister Shidehara, but this is not widely accepted—for discussion of the evidence and sources, see Martin (2008), p. 296 and fn. 76. For more on the broader theoretical analysis of constitutional incorporation of *jus ad bellum* principles, see Martin (2011), pp. 662–704.

[4] For a full analysis of the significance of this feature, see Martin (2008), pp. 309–318; Martin (2011), pp. 655–658, 705–715.

[5] Basic Law of the Federal Republic of Germany, 1949, Article 26, para. 1; and Constitution of the Italian Republic, 1947, Article 11; for detailed discussion of these, see Martin (2011) pp. 649–661.

[6] Moore, Robinson (2002).

[7] Martin (2008), pp. 291–299, 301–308; Moore, Robinson (2002), chaps. 12–14, 16.

[8] Constitution of Japan, 1947. Article 9.

[9] It also resembles language in the 1933 Constitution of the Philippines, Article 11, § 3, with which MacArthur would have been familiar. See, Martin (2008), p. 278.

right of belligerency." Both elements were quite unique and were at the time unprecedented.[10] As will be discussed below, the meaning and operation of the first of these elements has been controversial, while the second element has been the subject of far less attention and is typically considered far less significant, yet has also been frequently misunderstood.

Before turning to the formal interpretation and operation of the provision, it is worth noting that Article 9 quickly transcended its origins as an "imposed constraint" to become what has been termed a "constitutive constitutional norm"—a provision that not only regulates government behavior but helps constitute that national identity of a country.[11] This process began in the debates in the Diet over the draft constitution even before it was promulgated, with members of the government touting Article 9 as setting Japan in the vanguard of nations creating new ideas about international security.[12] The Japanese people almost immediately embraced the idea of Japan as a pacifist country, and continuing strong public support for and identification with Article 9 was a major factor in making any formal amendment of the provision politically impossible.[13] This popular and political power of the provision, quite apart from its narrower legal normative authority, is important for understanding both the provision's remarkable durability and the significance of its recent erosion. Similarly, it is important to recognize the extent to which Article 9 represented a unique experiment in the constitutional incorporation of the principles of international law on the use of force to operate as a pre-commitment device to bind the government's ability to engage in armed conflict.[14]

1.2 The Established Interpretation of Article 9

During the initial deliberations in the Diet on the draft constitution there was considerable debate in the Diet regarding how Article 9 should be interpreted, how it would operate, and what the implications of its limitations might be. Much has been made of the fact that none other than Prime Minister Yoshida Shigeru stated during the ratification debates that the provision would preclude Japan from maintaining

[10] In 1949 the Constitution of Costa Rica also abolished the army as a permanent institution of the state, and permitted military forces only to be organized temporarily for national defense purposes. Constitution of Costa Rica, 1949, Article 12.

[11] Peczenik (1989), pp. 276–281; Waldron (2006); on Article 9 as constitutive norm, see, Katzenstein (1996), pp. 4–5, 40–44, 116–118.

[12] For full discussion of these debates, see Martin (2008), pp. 305–307; Moore, Robinson (2002), pp. 270–290.

[13] Martin (2008), pp. 299–308; Moore, Robinson (2002), pp. 170–214; see also, Port (2005), Inoue (1991), and Ashida (1946).

[14] Martin (2008), pp. 280–291, 309–318; and on pre-commitment devices, Elster (1979); Elkins (2009).

any armed forces sufficient for any exercise of self-defense.[15] But it is important also to note that not only is there some fluidity and uncertainty in constitutional interpretation during the period immediately following promulgation, but that Japan's sovereignty was not even fully restored until 1952. The interpretive framework that would govern Article 9's application and operation for nearly six decades was established through a series of government statements in the 1950s, culminating in the authoritative interpretation issued by the Cabinet Legislation Bureau (the CLB) in 1954. The CLB is an administrative agency attached to the Cabinet Secretariat that, at least up to 2014, enjoyed significant independence and authority, and which among other things reviewed draft legislation for consistency with other laws and the constitution.[16] It was initially modelled on the *Conseil d'État* in France, and in some ways is similar to the Office of Legal Counsel in the American Department of Justice. Over time the CLB played the primary role in interpreting and enforcing Article 9, as the Supreme Court in 1959 effectively blessed the CLB's interpretation but abdicated its role in enforcing the constitutional provision.[17] It is worth examining the CLB's 1954 interpretation in some detail, particularly since its understanding of the meaning of the prohibition on the use of force would be consistently maintained by successive governments for six decades.

First and most significantly, the CLB interpretation held that while Article 9 renounced war and the threat or use of force "as a sovereign right of the nation" and as "a means of settling international disputes," it did not deprive Japan of the inherent right of individual self-defense recognized under international law. But the interpretation drew a crucial distinction between individual and collective self-defense. While Japan retained the right to use force in individual self-defense when directly attacked, the CLB held that Japan had explicitly renounced both the right to exercise collective self-defense—that is, the right to use force in defense of another state that was the subject of armed attack in accordance with Article 51 of the U.N. Charter—and the right to use force in collective security operations authorized by the U.N. Security Council pursuant to Article 42 of the U.N. Charter.[18] These were the "sovereign rights of the nation" under international law being renounced

---

[15] Moore, Robinson (2002), p. 212; Nishi (1987), pp. 100–102; Yasuzawa (1981), pp. 156 and 186 (dismissing Yoshida's comments as irrelevant).

[16] For a detailed analysis of the CLB, and its role in interpreting Article 9, see Nishikawa (2000, 2013), Nakamura (1996), Samuels (2004), and Sakata (2014); for my discussion of its role, see Martin (2017b), pp. 469–470.

[17] In the famous *Sunakawa* case in 1959, in which the constitutionality of U.S. forces based in Japan under the U.S.-Japan Security Treaty were at issue, the Supreme Court confirmed that Japan had a right of individual self-defense under Article 9, but also held that most claims regarding government action in relation to Article 9 would be non-justiciable unless "obviously unconstitutional and void." For detailed analysis of the judicial treatment of Article 9, see Martin (2008), pp. 337–342.

[18] Nishikawa (2000), p. 46; Nishikawa (2013), pp. 63–66; Sakata (2014), pp. 145–146; Martin (2017b), pp. 471–472; for further discussion of the relationship between Article 9 and the *jus ad bellum* regime under the U.N. Charter, see Martin (2008), pp. 309 *passim*.

by Japan in Article 9. This distinction would become the critical fault line in subsequent constitutional debates.

Turning to the second paragraph's prohibition on maintaining armed forces and "other war potential," the CLB concluded that because Japan was entitled to exercise the right of individual self-defense in response to an armed attack, paragraph 2 of Article 9 could not be interpreted as precluding a "minimum necessary defense capability." In 1957 the CLB further clarified that the maintenance of the "minimum necessary force" for purposes of individual self-defense did not constitute the kind of "war potential" prohibited by Article 9.[19] This implied both quantitative limits (force size and defense spending, relative to perceived threats) and qualitative restrictions (types of weapons systems and operational capabilities). As will be discussed next, both of these purported limitations were both extremely contingent and very difficult to define.

Regarding the second element in paragraph two of Article 9, it can be noted in passing that there have long been scholarly debates regarding the proper meaning of this clause—that is, the denial of rights of belligerency. This element has not been much affected by either "reinterpretation" or the more recent changes to national security policy, and so we need not dwell on the debate here—but as I have explained at some length elsewhere, the clearly better view, and one supported by CLB advice regarding military deployment laws enacted in 2005, is that the clause was designed to deny any Japanese military forces the rights of belligerency under the international law of armed conflict, which governs the rights, authority, obligations, crimes, and legal defenses of members of the armed forces engaged in armed conflict.[20] It was designed to be, in essence, a third mechanism to ensure that Japan never again waged war.

1.3 The Historical Operation of Article 9

I have elsewhere written at some length on the dynamic process by which this established interpretation, particularly that of the prohibition on the use of force, became entrenched in Japanese foreign and national security policy.[21] There is not room to do so here, but a few words on this historical operation of the provision is necessary. It will be argued below that the effort to "reinterpret" Article 9 in 2014 was unprecedented, illegitimate, and a significant weakening of the normative power of the constitutional constraints on the use of force. This requires, however, that we establish that the interpretation of Article 9 remained fairly constant, and that it operated to effectively constrain government policy. In order to do that, it is quite important to distinguish between the two main elements of the provision, because too often

[19] Nishikawa (2000), pp. 48–51.

[20] See my analysis, and supporting authorities, in Martin (2008), pp. 314–318.

[21] See Martin (2008), pp. 329–350.

debate about Article 9 conflates, confuses, or entirely fails to distinguish between the two very different clauses. The first clause, the prohibition on the threat or use of force, functioned as a relatively clear constitutional rule, and operated to significantly constrain government policy; while the other, the prohibition on the maintenance of armed forces and other war potential, was defined more as a flexible and contingent standard, the meaning of which necessarily shifted over time, and which therefore exercised a far less clear and effective influence on national security policy.

To expand on this, the CLB interpretation that the first paragraph prohibited any use of force for either collective self-defense or collective security operations authorized by the U.N., functioned as a clear rule that provided little room for interpretive manipulation. When faced with specific scenarios, policymakers and legal advisors could apply the rule with reasonable clarity. This was demonstrated during various international crises. During the 1991 Gulf War, for instance, the United States exerted enormous pressure on the government of Japan to contribute forces to the "coalition of the willing" to help liberate Kuwait—an operation that was both authorized by the U.N. Security Council and a valid exercise of collective self-defense under Article 51 of the U.N. Charter.[22] The CLB advised the Cabinet that any Japanese participation would constitute a violation of Article 9's prohibition on the threat or use of force, and the government very reluctantly declined to do more than contribute money to the effort and impose economic sanctions on Iraq.[23] What is important to emphasize is that both the government and analysts at the time viewed Japan's inability to contribute militarily to this effort as having caused irreparable harm to Japan's alliance with the United States and to its standing in the world, and yet the government complied with the CLB's guidance that it could not do so without violating Article 9.[24] The clear and binding nature of the constitutional rule in paragraph one of Article 9 thus operated to constrain government policy even when the government was under enormous pressure to act.

Similarly, during the Afghanistan and Iraq conflicts of the early 2000s, when the Japanese government was again under great pressure to contribute to America's "global war on terror," paragraph one of Article 9 operated to limit Japan's participation. While the Japanese government enacted laws that allowed Japan to deploy the Self-Defense Forces (SDF) for purposes of providing rear-area logistical support and engage in humanitarian reconstruction efforts after the initial conflict and during the occupation phases, the CLB ensured that there were clear restrictions in place to ensure that Japanese troops could not participate in combat operations or

[22] S.C. Res. 661, U.N. Doc. S/RES/0661 (Aug. 6, 1990). There are differences of opinion among international law scholars over the question of whether the Gulf conflict was an exercise of collective self-defense, a Chapter VII collective security operation, or both. See, e.g., Dinstein (2005), pp. 273–277; Franck (2002), pp. 24–30; de Wet (2018), pp. 459–465.

[23] For a full discussion see Pyle (2007), pp. 290–291; Togo (2005), pp. 77, 305–306, 386–387; Samuels (2004), p. 7; Fukushima (1999), pp. 69–70; Martin (2008), pp. 344–346.

[24] Togo (2005), p. 77.

even provide direct operational support to other forces engaged in combat.[25] The geographic and functional limitations placed on SDF deployments—keeping them away from combat zones and restricting them to non-combat activities—reflected careful efforts to avoid any possibility of any SDF conduct that might constitute collective self-defense. And even then, the Nagoya High Court opined, in dismissing a legal challenge to the deployments (on the basis of lack of standing), that the SDF's operations in support of the coalition's belligerent occupation of Iraq were so integral to the use of force by coalition forces, that they constituted a use of force by Japan in violation of Article 9. This decision made famous the *ittaika* or "integration" doctrine related to Article 9's prohibition on the use of force.[26]

In contrast to the effective operation of the clear rule provided by paragraph one of Article 9, the interpretation of the second paragraph as only limiting the SDF to a "minimum necessary force" functioned more as a loose and ambiguous standard than a rule. This is because, as mentioned earlier, it was very much contingent and relative, being entirely dependent on the current threat perception, technological developments, and regional security dynamics; and because the distinction between offensive and defensive capability has very little meaning in practical terms, and is, again, very contingent upon intentions. This ambiguity allowed for both evolutionary adaptation and the gradual expansion of military capabilities. While its policy white papers and national security strategies continued to emphasize the "minimum necessary force" principle and "purely defensive capability," Japan nonetheless developed an increasingly sophisticated and capable military force.[27] This evolution not only fueled increasingly vociferous critiques of the government's disregard for Article 9, but it created a growing gulf between the plain text and common understanding of paragraph two on the one hand, and on the other hand, the practical reality that the SDF represented, all of which further added to the controversy and debate regarding Article 9's effectiveness.[28] It is these criticisms and controversies that have tended to obscure both the consistent interpretation of paragraph one and its effective operation as a policy constraint.

Notwithstanding the less defined and weaker constraint that paragraph two created, it must be said that it nonetheless operated to restrain Japanese military development to some extent. It was certainly the origin of three important conventions or principles that took on quasi-constitutional stature over time: (1) the non-nuclear principles (that Japan would not possess, manufacture, or allow the introduction into its territory, any nuclear weapons); (2) the 1% of GDP ceiling on defense

[25] For full discussion and analysis of these laws, see Tamura (2008), pp. 483–486; Hatake (2006), p. 258; Martin (2008), pp. 350–356.

[26] Nagoya High Court, 2056 *Hanrei-jiho* 74 (2008), a translation of which is available in Hamilton (2010).

[27] See, e.g., Hughs (2006).

[28] There is an enormous literature on just this aspect of Article 9, but in English, see, e.g., Auer (1993); Port (2005); see Nishikawa (2013), pp. 132–147, rejecting claims that this evolution constituted a form of informal amendment.

spending; and (3) the prohibition on the export of military arms.[29] As I and others have argued, even with the weak and ambiguous interpretation of paragraph two, Article 9 as a whole not only exercised specific legal constraints, but served to influence policy in ways that were self-reinforcing, strengthening, and entrenching the constitutive norms that Article 9 created, which in turn helped to shape policies and political dynamics that further strengthened the authority of the constitutional provision.[30] The growth and development of military capability was in tension with these norms, which created political conflict, but the norms prevailed until 2014.

Against this backdrop, it should be noted that there were political forces in Japan that sought to amend Article 9, or otherwise "free" Japan of the constraints that it imposed, which were viewed as keeping Japan from being a "normal" country. Factions within the Liberal Democratic Party (LDP) had made this their objective from even before the CLB interpretation of 1954, but due to complex political dynamics and the strong public support for the provision, conservative forces seeking to undermine Article 9 were held at bay for decades[31]—until the era of Shinzo Abe.

2 The "Reinterpretation" of Article 9

The so-called reinterpretation of Article 9 in 2014–2015 was the first grievous blow in the process of gutting Article 9 of its normative power. Some appreciation of the context, substance, and ramifications of this effort are important for purposes of a fuller understanding of the arc of the provision's decline. In this section I will explain both the process and substance of this reinterpretation, explore how significantly it altered the scope and power of Article 9's constraints, and briefly consider the broader implications for the constitutional rule of law.[32]

2.1 Laying the Foundation

Prime Minister Shinzo Abe, beginning during his first term in 2007, made revision of Article 9 one of his primary objectives. While continuing longstanding LDP efforts to finally table concrete constitutional amendment proposals and initiate

[29] Katzenstein (1996), pp. 117–118; Pyle (2007), pp. 273–276; Togo (2005), p. 63; Hughes (2006), ch. 3; Hughes (2005), ch. 4.

[30] Martin (2008), pp. 226–237; more generally, see Boyd and Samuels (2005).

[31] For detailed analysis of these political dynamics, see Boyd and Samuels (2005); Hook and McCormack (2001).

[32] I have elsewhere considered the reinterpretation in much more detail, including an analysis of it from the perspective of theories regarding the legitimacy of so-called informal constitutional amendments: see, Martin (2007, 2016, 2017a). This section draws on these works.

formal amendment procedures under Article 96, he simultaneously pursued a strategy to entirely circumvent such formal revision by way of a "reinterpretation" of Article 9. He established an ad hoc "Advisory Panel on the Reconstruction of the Legal Basis for Security" under chairmanship of former Ambassador Shunji Yanai with a mandate to recommend how—not whether—Article 9 should be reinterpreted. The panel was criticized at the time for being stacked with national security hawks, having few lawyers, and only one constitutional scholar.[33] The panel produced a report in 2008,[34] and while it was shelved after Abe resigned on health grounds, it would later provide the intellectual framework for predetermined conclusions regarding the necessity for reinterpretation, wrapped in expert legitimacy.

Upon returning to power in 2012, Abe immediately revived his efforts to revise Article 9. The LDP published a new comprehensive constitutional amendment proposal, which included substantial proposed revisions to Article 9,[35] and Abe reconstituted the Advisory Panel with a broadened mandate and a new Chair. When the formal amendment process once again looked likely to fail due to significant political and public opposition, Abe proposed amending the constitutional amendment formula itself, reducing the super-majority requirements to a simple majority in each chamber of the Diet, and a majority in a national referendum. This transparent attempt to facilitate subsequent Article 9 revision drew heavy criticism from scholars who argued it would undermine constitutional supremacy—the very principle that enables constitutions to constrain government power.[36] The proposal was finally shelved in 2013, and Abe pivoted to once again pursue his reinterpretation strategy through the Advisory Panel, which duly issued a new report recommending reinterpretation in 2014.[37]

To pave the way for his reinterpretation effort, in yet another move that reflected the illegitimacy of the entire process, Abe pressured the CLB Director to resign, and appointed in his place a former Foreign Ministry diplomat who was known to support revision.[38] This unprecedented interference with the CLB, and departure from appointing internal legal experts or former judges, arguably represented a fundamental assault on the institutional independence and integrity of the CLB.[39] Though Komatsu resigned in 2014 due to illness, he had laid the groundwork for the CLB's acquiescence to the Cabinet issuing a reinterpretation of Article 9.

---

[33] For details, see Martin (2007); Martin (2017a), p. 49.

[34] The Advisory Panel on Reconstruction of the Legal Basis for Security, Report of the Advisory Panel on Reconstruction of the Legal Basis for Security (June 24, 2008).

[35] *Jimintō, Kenpō Kaisei Sōan* [Liberal Democratic Party, Constitutional Amendment Proposal], 2012. For my analysis of the dangers this amendment proposal posed, see Martin (2017a).

[36] Martin (2017a), pp. 51–52.

[37] *Anzenhoshō no hōtekikiban no kōchiku ni kansuru kondankai* [Report of the Advisory Panel on Reconstruction of the Legal Basis for Security], May 15, 2014.

[38] Abe to Pick Backer of Collective Self-Defense as Head of Legislation Bureau, *Asahi Shimbun*. Aug. 2, 2013.

[39] Nishikawa (2013), ch. 2; Hasebe (2017), p. 128.

2.2 *The 2014 Cabinet Decision: Constitutional Amendment by Executive Branch Fiat*

In July 2014 the Cabinet passed a resolution, which was then issued in form of a "Cabinet Decision," as the mechanism that purported to unilaterally change the meaning of Article 9.[40] This Cabinet Decision provided a rationale for the reinterpretation, and more importantly, provided an outline of how key laws would be revised to enable an expanded national security posture in accordance with the new understanding of the constitutional constraints. The rationale was primarily in line with the explanations of the Advisory Panel, namely that the strategic environment around Japan had become more threatening, and that the government's obligation to guarantee the security of the Japanese people required a more robust national security posture, particularly within the context of the US-Japan security arrangements. It was a transparently result-oriented argument that the situation had changed, which required greater latitude in the use of military force, and therefore the meaning of Article 9 must be understood and interpreted in a manner that would allow such a use of force.[41]

Substantively, the Cabinet Decision suggested three main areas of change, or categories of policy for which laws would be revised to achieve new policy objectives, and which require a revised understanding of the constraints imposed by Article 9. Each of these posed serious issues from both a constitutional law and an international law perspective. The first "category" related to the use of the SDF in "grey zone operations." The decision authorized force against "infringements not amounting to armed attack" in situations there were "neither pure peacetime nor contingencies"—with "contingencies" being the word somewhat euphemistically used in the unofficial English translation for the word *yūji*, which arguably means something closer to "hostilities" in this context. It goes on to provide that the use of force would be permissible in circumstances that do not involve an armed attack, such as in response to "infringements" that occur in the areas "surrounding remote islands," and in other circumstances in which the police would not be capable of responding effectively.[42] As will be discussed in more detail below, this would appear to authorize military action that would be in violation of the international law prohibition on the use of force.[43]

The second category of policy that the Cabinet Decision addressed was in relation to Japan's contribution to "the peace and stability of the international community." In order for Japan to play a more meaningful role, legislation would be required to permit an expansion of the scope and nature of support to be provided to

---

[40] Cabinet Decision on Development of Seamless Security Legislation to Ensure Japan's Survival and Protect Its People (provisional English translation) (July 1, 2014), available at: http://www.cas.go.jp/jp/gaiyou/jimu/pdf/anpohosei_eng.pdf.

[41] Id., and see Martin (2017a), pp. 51–52.

[42] Cabinet Decision, 2014.

[43] For detailed analysis of the international law implications, see Martin (2016).

allied armed forces engaged in armed conflict.[44] This was specifically aimed at overturning the *ittaika* or "integration" doctrine, pursuant to which it was understood that excessively close support for belligerents engaged in a use of force could constitute a use of force by Japan as well, in violation of Article 9. Under the new guidance in the Cabinet Decision Japanese support for allied states' armed forces would only risk constituting a use of force by Japan if the support was provided directly to forces operating at the time in active theatres of hostilities.[45]

The final category was in many ways the most consequential, and the most controversial, as it related to the long-time objective of expanding Article 9 to permit the use of force in the exercise of collective self-defense. The category itself was titled "measures for self-defense permitted under Article 9," and it noted, in a result-oriented manner, that "sufficient responses would not necessarily be possible if the constitutional interpretation to date were maintained."[46] In so stating the Cabinet Decision explicitly acknowledged that it was departing substantially from the established understanding of Article 9 paragraph one—though it gestured at a justification for this by misquoting the "right to live in peace" in the preamble, and referencing the "right to life, liberty and the pursuit of happiness" as a supreme consideration of government in Article 13, and suggesting that Article 9 could not be interpreted in a manner that would prohibit Japan from taking measures "necessary to maintain its peace and security and to ensure its survival." What had changed, it argued, was that now collective self-defense was necessary in some circumstances to ensure the survival of Japan and preserve the people's right to life, liberty, and pursuit of happiness.

In accordance with this logic, however, the Cabinet Decision articulated a concept of collective self-defense that is markedly different from the concept as it is understood as part of the *jus ad bellum* regime in international law. The latter, codified in Article 51 of the U.N. Charter and fleshed out in state practice in the form of customary international law, as well as articulated in the jurisprudence of the International Court of Justice (ICJ), is a use of force by one state in response to an armed attack on another state, when that second state has declared itself the victim of such attack and has explicitly requested such assistance.[47] In contrast, the Cabinet Decision developed some *sui generis* concept under the name of collective self-defense, acknowledging its departure from established international legal concepts with the statement that the "legal basis in international law and constitutional interpretation need to be understood separately."

The newly coined concept would permit Japan to use force in response to an armed attack against "a foreign country that is in a close relationship with Japan," and when that attack is one that "threatens Japan's survival and poses a clear danger

---

[44] Cabinet Decision, 2014.

[45] Id.

[46] Id.

[47] For the most complete discussions of this, see Green (2024), and on the scope and conditions for self-defense more generally, Ruys (2010).

to fundamentally overturn [the] people's right to life, liberty, and pursuit of happiness, and when there is no other appropriate means available to repel the attack."[48] This could be construed as creating much stricter conditions for the use of force than the actual concept of collective self-defense in international law, and indeed it was argued by the government at the time that this was precisely its intent. But there were many who questioned this intent at the time, and raised many questions about how the concept would operate in practice, noting that in any event, how precisely it would be implemented would be entirely up to perceptions and interpretations of future governments.[49] And leaving aside the consistency with international law, the Cabinet Decision purported to explicitly make permissible a use of force that had been understood for decades to be unconstitutional. I will return to these issues below in an exploration of the legitimacy of these moves.

2.3 *Implementation: International Commitments and Legislative Revision*

In a move that has considerable significance to questions regarding the legitimacy of the reinterpretation, the government next sought to implement the revised understanding of Article 9 within international commitments prior to submitting any draft legislation to the Diet for approval. Immediately following the issuance of the Cabinet Decision, the government undertook discussions with the United States to revise a set of guidelines that provided more particularity regarding the mutual obligations, expectations, and responsibilities under the Japan-U.S. Security Agreement. These guidelines had last been updated in 1997, and they articulated a shared understanding of the limitations on Japan's ability to use force, provide logistical support, or deploy the SDF in accordance with treaty obligations.[50] In April 2015 a revised Guidelines for Japan-U.S. Defense Cooperation was formally agreed to by the two countries, without any input from the Diet.[51] The 2015 Guidelines incorporated the salient elements of the reinterpretation, including an entirely new section to implement the new concept of collective self-defense, using precisely the same language as the Cabinet Decision.

Finally, in May 2015, almost a year after issuing the Cabinet Decision, and after implementing the reinterpreted constitutional understanding into international

[48] Cabinet Decision, 2014.

[49] See, e.g., Blurry Limits on SDF Missions, Japan Times, Apr. 24, 2015; Conditions for Exercising Right to Collective Self-Defense Open to Interpretation, Asahi Shimbun, May 12, 2015; and see Martin (2016); Martin (2017b), pp. 481–482 and 497–499.

[50] American Society of International Law (1997), pp. 1621–1638. For analysis of the 1997 Guidelines see Togo (2005), pp. 80–85; Hughes (2006) pp. 100–101; Tamura (2008), ch. 10; Drohan (2007), pp. 143–151; Fisher (1999).

[51] Japan Ministry of Defense, The Guidelines for Japan-U.S. Defense Cooperation (2015), https://www.mofa.go.jp/files/000078188.pdf.

commitments, the government tabled an omnibus bill in the Diet that would revise ten existing security laws, as well as introduce one new draft bill, for an International Peace Support Law.[52] This package implemented the changes called for in the Cabinet Decision, and effectively operationalized the broadened scope of operations made possible by the reinterpretation of Article 9, while avoiding explicit constitutional acknowledgment or requesting explicit approval of the reinterpretation.[53] The new law created permanent authority for the government to deploy the SDF with simple Diet approval, displacing the established convention that required specific authorizing legislation with detailed operational limits for each and every deployment.

The legislation provoked unprecedented opposition. By the time the laws were finally passed in the Diet on September 19, in a vote that involved actual physical confrontations in the Upper House, tens of thousands of people had protested nationwide. Polls consistently reflected majority opposition to the new legislation.[54] This was likely influenced in part by a surprising and unprecedented degree of professional protest. Three former CLB Directors and a former Supreme Court Chief Justice declared the bills unconstitutional. Most dramatically, three prominent constitutional scholars—including the LDP's own nominee, Professor Yasuo Hasebe—testified in the Diet that the new and revised laws were unconstitutional. Over 200 constitutional scholars publicly supported this position while the government struggled to find two supportive voices.[55] Notwithstanding the opposition and criticism, the laws passed, and the following summer the LDP was re-elected with an even larger majority—though the reinterpretation, national security laws, and constitutional issues more generally, were decidedly absent from the topics raised in the election campaign.[56]

2.4 *The Illegitimacy of the Reinterpretation*

In thinking about the extent to which the reinterpretation contributed to the demise of Article 9, and more broadly to a weakening of the normative authority of the constitution as a whole, questions regarding the validity and legitimacy of the reinterpretation take on considerable significance. It may be noted at the outset that

---

[52] The bills, the short titles of which are *Heiwa Anzenhosei Seibiho* [Law for the maintenance of the peace and security legal system] (2015), and *Kokusai Heiwa Shijiho* [International peace support Law] (2015) are available online at: http://www.cas.go.jp/jp/gaiyou/jimu/housei_seibi.html.

[53] For analysis of the laws, see, e.g., Hasebe (2015); Martin (2017b), pp. 284–286.

[54] See, e.g., Yoshida and Aoki (2015), Osaki (2015), and Mori (2015).

[55] Ono (2015); Former Justice Brands Security Bills as Unconstitutional, Slams Abe for Sophistry, *Japan Times*. Sept. 16, 2015; Constitutional Law Scholars Lash Out at Government Criticism, Insults, *Asahi Shimbun* June 16, 2015. Sakata (2014), p. 140.

[56] On the significance of this, see Martin (2017b), pp. 487 and 502–505; Dixon and Baldwin (2019), pp. 156–157.

most constitutional scholars in Japan were quite outspoken in their condemnation of the reinterpretation as being illegitimate and unconstitutional, both on grounds of process—that is, the reinterpretation process entirely and quite intentionally circumvented the formal amendment procedure provided for in the Article 96 of the Constitution; and on grounds of substance—in that the reinterpretation was so radically inconsistent with text, founding intention, spirit, and long-established understanding of Article 9.[57] In this section we will briefly explore this issue further.

I have elsewhere, in a long law review article, analyzed these issues within the framework of theories on informal constitutional amendment.[58] Such theories recognize that the understanding and operation of constitutional provisions can be transformed over time, without the benefit of formal amendment, and yet such changes may be considered legitimate. This is most obviously the case where these changes result from incremental judicial interpretation. Such interpretive development is considered quite normal in most constitutional systems. But the concept of informal amendment typically refers to more dramatic and sudden changes (though not rising to the level of complete revolutionary transformation), often resulting from the action of one or both of the political branches of government, yet not produced through the formal constitutional amendment process. An example of this is the significant constitutional transformation brought about in the New Deal and the development of the modern administrative state in the United States in the 1930s. There is a substantial theoretical literature on when and under what specific conditions such amendments may be considered legitimate,[59] and indeed there are many who reject the idea of legitimate informal amendments altogether.[60] There is, unfortunately, not room here to delve into the particulars of that theoretical debate, but I will briefly explain how I assessed the legitimacy of the Abe government's reinterpretation through the lens of informal amendment theory.

As mentioned above, an initial question is whether the reinterpretation can be characterized as a normal interpretive development in constitutional meaning rather than an informal amendment, in the way, for instance, the scope of the equal protection clause of the 14th Amendment of the U.S. Constitution was expanded over time to encompass gender equality. But for reasons of both process and substance the answer to that question is quite definitively negative. Reasonable interpretive development is more typically the result of incremental judicial decision. Even when change may be initiated by one of the political branches and later acquiesced to by the courts, it is typically incremental in nature and within what may be called a reasonable range of constitutional interpretation. As will be explained in more detail below, and as argued by the vast majority of Japanese constitutional scholars at the time, the reinterpretation was neither incremental, nor did it propose a revised

57 See, e.g., Hasebe (2017) and Sakata (2014).

58 Martin (2017a).

59 See, e.g., Ackerman (1998); Levinson (1995); Balkin and Levinson (2001); Lutz (1995); and see my review of the debate in Martin (2017b), pp. 437–458.

60 See, e.g. Griffin (1995).

understanding that fell within a reasonable range of constitutional interpretation. It made permissible that which had long been clearly unconstitutional, and did so in ways that were arguably inconsistent with the international law principles that Article 9 had been founded on.[61] What is more, normal interpretive development does not include unilateral efforts by one of the political branches of government to relax a provision that was specifically designed to bind that very branch—and in the case of the reinterpretation, the executive sought to reduce the constraints of a provision that was specifically intended to limit executive branch action.[62] Finally, in addition to the Prime Minister and others frankly acknowledging that the reinterpretation constituted a dramatic break from past interpretations, the rationales provided were not in the form of accepted constitutional argumentation, but rather result-oriented claims couched in strategic and foreign relations terms.

If not a normal interpretive development, the question then is whether it can be characterized as a legitimate informal amendment. In my synthesis of the theoretical work on informal amendments, I suggested that there are three key features to consider in assessing the legitimacy of a purported informal amendment: (1) the extent to which it was or was not supported or ratified by the popular will; (2) the extent to which it was or was not an act of deliberate agency in circumventing the formal amendment procedure; and (3) the extent to which it stands the test of time. To reduce a rather complex analysis to a nutshell, the argument is that the more an informal amendment is the product of deliberate and self-conscious efforts by a government to circumvent the formal constitutional amendment process, the more it is *prima facie* illegitimate, and the more it will require a very explicit and genuine expression of consent by the popular will (through, for instance, referendum, or an election fought on the issue), to gain legitimacy, but also, that it may nonetheless be gradually legitimated by the passage of time if not repudiated—though the more blatantly illegitimate it is, the more time it may take.[63]

It will be clear from the discussion thus far that the reinterpretation was precisely an intentional, deliberate, and self-conscious circumvention of the formal amendment process when that process proved too difficult. The very fact that the formal procedure was too difficult, due to public opposition that translated into political opposition, is evidence enough that the reinterpretation was undertaken in defiance of the popular will, rather than it being any expression of public desire.[64] But in addition, in the elections that followed the reinterpretation, for both the lower and upper houses of the Diet, the LDP quite conspicuously avoided any and all discus-

[61] See Martin (2016); also, on the requirement that Article 9 be interpreted in a manner that is consistent with the *jus ad bellum* regime, see, e.g., Fujii (2005), ch. 12–14; Sakamoto (2007), p. 56; Nasu (2016).

[62] See Martin (2017b), p. 508.

[63] See Martin (2017b), pp. 517–520.

[64] It should be noted that while the Constitution of Japan has never been amended, and it is often said to be too difficult to do so, in a study of many liberal democratic constitutional systems, Japan's constitution was determined to be procedurally less difficult to amend than that of the United States and many other countries: Lutz (1994), pp. 362–364.

sion of not only the reinterpretation and the national security legislation, but its pet topic of constitutional amendment altogether. Indeed, days before the election, members of the government publicly denied the prospect of constitutional amendment. Thus, while the party did win those elections and expand its hold on both chambers, this has been shown to have been the result of other factors, and cannot be considered a popular ratification of the reinterpretation as informal amendment.[65]

Of course, the third element of my proposed framework is time, with the suggestion that even blatantly invalid and illegitimate efforts to reinterpret a constitution may over time become entrenched, accepted, and eventually, legitimate. One might argue that this is where we are today. The LDP failed once again to pass new amendment proposals that were informally tabled in 2018, which were designed to subtly entrench many aspects of the reinterpretation, but the reinterpretation itself has largely become the accepted understanding of Article 9 for policy purposes. There were many lawsuits challenging the national security legislation, and in 2023 it was reported that at least 25 were still ongoing, but none have been successful thus far, nor are they likely to be.[66] The reinterpretation's entrenchment, notwithstanding its stark illegitimacy, reveals troubling truths about constitutional democracy's vulnerability. Through strategic appointments, extra-constitutional advisory bodies, international commitments preceding domestic debate, and legislative packaging, governments can fundamentally eviscerate constitutional constraints while maintaining procedural facades.

It is worth noting, in closing our discussion of the reinterpretation, that it was focused almost entirely on hallowing out the clear constitutional rule on the use of force provided for in Article 9 paragraph one. It had little impact on the understanding of Article 9 paragraph two, and the maintenance of armed forces. Indeed, this was why constitutional amendment proposals immediately before and after the reinterpretation focused on legitimating the SDF. But if time served to entrench and legitimize the reinterpretation of the constraint on the use of force, developments in the 2020s would catalyze the gutting of paragraph two's constraints, thus completing the full transformation of Article 9.

3 The Final Blow to Article 9

As will have been apparent from the foregoing account, the normative power of Article 9 was already badly compromised by the end of the 2010s. The most effective and clear constraint in Article 9, the prohibition on the use of force, had been severely weakened by the reinterpretation. Sights then turned to undermine the already weak constraints that paragraph two exercised on the maintenance of armed forces and other war potential. As will be discussed below, these efforts began very

[65] See Dixon and Baldwin (2019).

[66] Japan High Court Rules 2015 (2023).

soon after the reinterpretation was in place. But the process was galvanized and massively boosted by the Russian war of aggression against Ukraine.

3.1 The Acceleration: Pre-Ukraine

After the reinterpretation, the government continued to characterize Japan's security environment as "severe" and "uncertain," due primarily to perceptions of the threat posed by North Korea, which had launched a spate of missiles in 2016 and 2017, and China, which was viewed as becoming increasingly proactive in the area militarily.[67] As mentioned earlier, in 2018 the LDP again issued a constitutional amendment proposal, which took aim at the paragraph two constraints on armed forces, though it was never formally tabled. More concretely, in 2018 the government issued the 2018 National Defense Program Guidelines (NDPG), and the Mid-Term Defense Program (MTDP).[68] These called for a fundamental strengthening of Japan's defense structure, and the development of a defense capability "that does not lie on a linear extension of the past."[69] In particular it called for the development of a "multi-domain defense force," which would include forces operating in space, cyber, and the electromagnetic spectrum. The SDF was also to develop "stand-off defense capability."[70] Despite his muscular formulation of defense capability, the Defense White Paper issued in 2019 reaffirmed the reinterpreted understanding of Article 9, but included the traditional view that Japan's defense capability was limited to the minimum necessary for self-defense, and that Japan adhered to an exclusively defense-oriented defense policy.[71]

Notwithstanding those assertions, in 2020 the government unexpectedly cancelled the Aegis Ashore missile defense program, which precipitated renewed discussion about developing a "strike capability against enemy bases."[72] That is, the development of missile capability to strike assets within foreign territory, which would involve a projection of power capability that had long been thought inconsistent with the "purely defensive" posture. The government dredged up statements made by Prime Minister Hatoyama in 1956 suggesting that Article 9 did not prevent Japan from possessing and using long range missiles for purposes of self-defense, and it was careful to emphasize that any development of such a capability would not be for preemptive use, but would be solely for "counterattack."[73] It was also argued that the development of such capability would be beneficial for interoperability with

[67] See, e.g., Ministry of Defense White Paper, Defense of Japan (2019).

[68] National Defense Program Guidelines (2018).

[69] Id.

[70] Id.

[71] White Paper: Defense of Japan, 2019.

[72] Akimoto (2020) and Basu (2020).

[73] Basu (2020).

U.S. forces. Nevertheless, these discussions did not progress to actual practical policy change or the implementation of any weapons procurement and development. All that would change in 2022.

3.2 The Ukraine Shock and the 2022 National Security Documents

Russia's full-scale invasion of Ukraine on February 24, 2022, sent shockwaves through the entire international system, but they reverberated with particular intensity in Japan. The spectacle of a permanent member of the U.N. Security Council launching an unprovoked war of territorial aggression against a neighboring state, in violation of the fundamental prohibition on the use of force and with apparent impunity, shattered comfortable assumptions about the stability of the post-Cold War international order, and even the reliability of the U.S. security assurances.[74] For Japan, a country that had premised its security strategy on faith in international law and institutions, and on American security guarantees, the implications were profound and unsettling—particularly in the context of ongoing concerns about China's increasingly assertive conduct, and the perceived risk of a Chinese invasion of Taiwan.[75]

While there is no doubt that the invasion of Ukraine was a genuine shock, and that it fostered legitimate concerns about Japanese security in the region, the Ukraine crisis also created a permissive political environment for dramatic policy changes. It provided an opportunity. Public opinion, previously resistant to ideas of expanding military capability, shifted markedly. Media coverage too tended to emphasize Japan's vulnerability and the need for stronger national defense. Opposition parties found it difficult to argue against enhanced capabilities in the face of graphic evidence of military aggression.[76] The crisis thus provided political cover for changes that had long been contemplated but deemed politically impossible.

On December 16, 2022, the Kishida government released three interrelated strategy documents that are widely viewed as representing the most dramatic shift in Japanese security policy since the establishment of the Self-Defense Forces. The National Security Strategy (NSS),[77] the National Defense Strategy (NDS),[78] and the Defense Buildup Program (DBP)[79] (collectively, the Security Documents) articulate

---

[74] This had, of course, happened to some extent in 2003, albeit without the territorial acquisition component, but for obvious reasons the U.S. invasion of Iraq was less troubling for Japan.

[75] Fujimoto (2025) and Tatsumi (2023).

[76] Tokuchi (2023).

[77] The National Security Strategy of Japan (2022).

[78] The National Defense Strategy (2022).

[79] The National Defense Buildup (2022).

changes that would have been politically unthinkable absent the Ukraine shock. They not only reflect a seismic shift in both policy regarding the development of military capability and the reformulation of doctrine regarding national security policy[80]—which is how they have been generally characterized in the policy and academic discourse to date—but in many respects they serve as a second reinterpretation of Article 9, this time targeting the remaining weak constraints imposed by paragraph two of the provision.

The Security Documents' rhetoric emphasizes continuity and adherence to defensive intent, repeatedly invoking Japan's commitment to "exclusively defense-oriented policy" and "peaceful development." Yet this rhetorical packaging cannot obscure the fundamental departures from established constraints. The changes can be analyzed along three dimensions: capability expansion, operational doctrine, and strategic posture.[81] Beginning with the expansion of capability, the NSS provides a new commitment to increase defense spending to 2% of GDP within 5 years. This represents more than a radical quantitative expansion and abandonment of the 1% principle, which, it will be recalled, was a quasi-constitutional convention that was understood to have its source in Article 9's paragraph two. This doubling of the defense budget enables significant qualitative transformation in military capabilities. In addition, the documents explicitly embrace the development of "counter-strike capability" (the new term for the decades old debate over "strike capability against enemy bases")—requiring the acquisition and deployment of long-range precision weapons capable of attacking targets deep within foreign territory. While framed as defensive, these capabilities are inherently offensive in nature, designed for power projection rather than territorial defense.

In addition to establishing the development of counter-strike capability, the Security Documents articulate a broader need for "standoff defense capabilities," which would require not only the development or acquisition of long-range missiles, but also hypersonic weapons, enhanced cyber warfare capabilities, possible capabilities in space, and expanded intelligence, surveillance, and reconnaissance assets. The National Defense Buildup allocates ¥43 trillion (approximately $315 billion) over 5 years,[82] with specific line items for extensive power-projection capabilities that would have been categorically prohibited under the traditional interpretation of Article 9.

Equally significant is the abandonment of longstanding restrictions on defense industrial policy. The Security Documents call for strengthening Japan's defense industrial base through relaxed export controls, increased international collaboration, and government support for defense technology development. This, of course, overturns the second quasi-constitutional convention that arose from Article 9's paragraph two, being the prohibition on arms exports, and reverses decades of

[80] Tokuchi (2023) and Oguma (2025).

[81] The National Security Strategy of Japan (2022); see Tokuchi (2023), Fujimoto (2025), and Oguma (2025).

[82] The National Defense Buildup (2022).

policies designed to prevent Japan from becoming a major arms exporter or developer of offensive military technologies. The NSS does explicitly state that the non-nuclear principles—the third of the quasi-constitutional conventions—remain in place, but there has been increasing discussion within the political discourse about whether Japan should begin to explore a nuclear program as well.[83]

Turning to the dimension of doctrinal innovation, the operational concepts articulated in the 2022 Security Documents represent a radical departure from traditional "exclusively defense-oriented policy." Most importantly, as already mentioned, the embrace of a "counter-strike capability" reflects an abandonment of the foundational distinction between defensive and offensive weapons—as ambiguous and tenuous as that distinction may have always been. Indeed, there is the explicit adoption of deterrence theory as the foundation for defense policy. While Japan had previously emphasized "defensive defense"—maintaining only capabilities necessary to repel attack—the new documents embrace the concept of deterrence based on establishing sufficient military capability to impose severe costs on adversaries within their own territories, fundamentally changing the nature of Japanese military power from shield to sword. This also suggests a departure from a very strict adherence to principles of necessity and proportionality that are integral to the international law doctrine of self-defense, which had long constrained Japanese security policy and military development.[84] The government's assertions that these capabilities remain "defensive" because they would only be used after and in response to an actual armed attack, places all the stress on intent, whereas the long-established understanding had been that constraint on capability was essential.

The Security Documents also articulate new concepts regarding a "seamless response" to situations that fall below the threshold of armed attack. This includes working toward greater integration between the Self-Defense Forces and Coast Guard, preparation for military responses to "gray zone" situations, and the development of capabilities for "swift and persistent" operations in response to various "contingencies." This reflects a practical policy implementation of the ideas initially articulated in the 2014 Cabinet Decision regarding the use of force in response to "contingencies that do not rise to the level of armed attack"—and constitute a concrete lowering of the threshold for military action and a blurring of the distinctions between law enforcement and military operations in ways that risk violations of the international law on the use of force.[85] As discussed earlier, the legitimate use of force in the exercise of self-defense is contingent upon the use of force being in response to an armed attack, a concept that is understood to encompass the most

[83] Chang (2024) and Miki and Kobara (2025).

[84] See, e.g., Hatake (2006), ch. 6; Fujii (2005), chs. 12–14.

[85] Martin (2016); Martin (2017b), pp. 499–501; Tokuchi (2018).

grave forms of the use of force, and thus creating a significantly higher threshold than mere border skirmishes or minor maritime incursions.[86]

Finally, on the dimension of strategic transformation, the way the Security Documents characterize regional security relationships reveals a seismic shift in strategic orientation. Taiwan is explicitly identified as a critical security concern, with stability in the Taiwan Strait described as "indispensable" to Japan's security. Moreover, Taiwan is defined as a nation with which Japan has a close relationship, thus ostensibly bringing it within the scope of the three conditions for the exercise of Japan's concept of collective self-defense in the reinterpretation. This formulation, combined with the embrace of Japan's uniquely defined collective self-defense and new counter-strike capabilities, signals the possibility of direct Japanese military involvement in response to a Chinese attack on Taiwan—a scenario that would have been unthinkable under the traditional interpretation of Article 9.

The deepening of alliance integration with the United States also goes far beyond the traditional understanding, which focused primarily on joint operations in defense of Japan, to now encompass joint planning for counter-strike operations, combined deterrence strategies, and "seamless operational coordination." The Security Documents envision Japanese forces not merely supporting U.S. operations but serving as integral components of combined operations potentially far from Japanese territory, even in the context of U.S. operations in an armed conflict to which Japan is not a party. This is entirely inconsistent with the traditional understanding of the prohibition on the use of force in Article 9, and the established idea that close support of other states' use of force would constitute an "integration" with their use of force, and thereby be in violation of Article 9, as discussed earlier.

3.3 The Implications: Final Blow to Article 9 and Beyond

The 2022 Security Documents, while professing fealty to constitutional constraints, effectively completed the process of hollowing out Article 9 that had begun with the 2014 reinterpretation. In addition to implementing more directly into policy and doctrine some of the concepts relating to the use of force in the 2014 reinterpretation, it tackled what the reinterpretation had failed to address altogether—the constraints on the maintenance of armed forces and other war potential in paragraph two. In dismantling those prohibitions, the Security Documents effectively concluded the radical weakening of every meaningful constraint that Article 9 traditionally imposed.

The rapid transformation of security policy following the invasion of Ukraine has also been accompanied by significant shifts in public opinion and political discourse, which suggest deeper changes in Japanese society's relationship with military power. Understanding these societal dynamics is crucial for assessing whether

[86] See Ruys (2010), pp. 138–140, citing *Nicaragua v. United States of America*, (1986), para. 191.

recent changes represent a temporary response to crisis or a more permanent transformation. The evidence would tend to suggest the latter. Public opinion polling reflects dramatic shifts in attitudes toward defense policy. Support for increased defense spending jumped from a minority to majority position following the Ukraine invasion. Acceptance of "counter-strike capabilities"—weapons that would have been politically unthinkable just years earlier—now commands plurality support. Perhaps most strikingly, discussion of nuclear weapons, long taboo in Japanese politics, has entered mainstream discourse with prominent politicians, including Prime Minister Ishiba himself, suggesting the need to consider not only "nuclear sharing" arrangements, but even the development of Japan's own nuclear weapons capability.[87] Media coverage has both reflected and reinforced these shifts. Major newspapers that traditionally served as guardians of pacifist principles have adopted more accommodating stances toward military expansion. Television coverage emphasizes threats and vulnerabilities while downplaying constitutional concerns. The framing of security issues has shifted from "whether" military capabilities should expand to "how much" and "how quickly."[88]

The political dynamics surrounding security policy have also been transformed. The traditional pattern of LDP governments pushing against pacifist opposition has given way to broader consensus on need for enhanced capabilities. Opposition parties, weakened by electoral defeats and shifting public opinion, have largely abandoned principled opposition to militarization in favor of tactical criticism of specific policies. The political costs of opposing defense increases have risen while benefits have diminished.[89] These societal shifts suggest that the normative constraints Article 9 once imposed through political and cultural mechanisms have significantly weakened. The "constitutional culture of antimilitarism" that reinforced legal constraints appears to be giving way to acceptance of military power as a normal tool of statecraft. Together with the passage of time, this normative transformation reflects the acceptance and de facto legitimation of the reinterpretation, and the real demise of Article 9—which is tragic notwithstanding such acceptance.

4 Conclusion: The Tragedy

The word "tragic" is used here in the true sense of the word, not merely to denote misfortune but to capture the deeper sense of loss from the once-great brought low, typically through some inherent flaw, that is a feature of classical Greek tragedy. As many of the members of the Diet proclaimed in the ratification debates in 1946, there was something great about Article 9—the incorporation of *jus ad bellum*

[87] Chang (2024).

[88] Ishizuka (2019) and Oguma (2025).

[89] Oguma (2025).

principles, and indeed constraints that went beyond those principles in international law, to force the country onto a peaceful path. As they noted in lofty speeches, this put Japan in the vanguard of states that would rely on the new international collective security system rather than engage in the traditional security dilemmas of the past.[90] And it served Japan well for close to 75 years, during which time Japan did not once participate as a belligerent in any armed conflict. But like a Greek drama, the demise of Article 9 contained elements of inexorability—forces set in motion by earlier decisions playing out to their logical conclusion, and caused in part by some intrisic flaw. What were the flaws? There were many, but not least were some of the ambiguities created by the CLB interpretations in the early 1950s, and a complete reliance on the United States for its security, while the U.S. consistently pressured Japan to rearm and use force notwithstanding a constitutional provision that the U.S. had itself imposed upon it. And like a Greek tragedy, academics like myself can only play the part of the chorus, commenting on and lamenting the tragic downfall.

The negative consequences of this tragic fall operate on multiple planes. At the most immediate level, it represents the loss of effective constitutional constraints on the use of military force. Article 9 once imposed meaningful limitations that shaped policy, constrained options, and forced creative approaches to security challenges. These constraints have been systematically dismantled through reinterpretation and policy changes that render the constitutional text virtually meaningless. Future Japanese governments will face fewer domestic legal obstacles to using military force, and will be constrained only by an increasingly feeble international law regime and domestic political calculations. This in turn will mean that Japan may become embroiled in armed conflict, and regional neighbors will now view Japan as more of a threat, potentially contributing to regional security dilemmas and an escalating arms race.

At a deeper level, the tragedy lies in the corruption of constitutional democracy itself. The methods used to circumvent Article 9—constitutional reinterpretation through executive fiat, manipulation of advisory processes, and implementation through international agreements before any legislative debate or approval—all establish precedents that threaten constitutional governance more broadly, and certainly weaken the normative power of the Constitution of Japan more specifically. If fundamental constitutional provisions can be reversed through creative interpretation when they prove politically inconvenient, then constitutionalism itself loses meaning. The rule of law depends on the bindingness of legal constraints exactly when they prove inconvenient. Current events in the United States, the world's oldest modern democracy, strikingly illustrate these dangers.

There are also international dimensions of this tragedy. Article 9 represented a unique experiment in using domestic constitutional law to incorporate and reinforce international legal constraints on the use of force. Its incorporation of *jus ad*

[90] For the details of such debates, see Moore, Robinson (2002), ch. 20; for a summary on this issue, see Martin (2008), pp. 304–305.

bellum principles created a model for how states might bind themselves to the prohibition against the use of force, and the core concept of peaceful resolution of disputes. Japan's Constitution was quite unique in this regard, and there was a degree of greatness in its successful operation for over seven decades—and so the failure of this experiment, particularly at a time when the international law regime constraining the use of force is itself in increasing disarray, is indeed tragic. It tends to suggest rather pessimistic conclusions about the possibility of maintaining effective legal constraints on state violence. Japan represented a practical implementation of the ideals that initially inspired the collective security system of the United Nations—and its failure in the midst of the war of aggression against Ukraine among other unlawful conflicts in motion today may reflect the final death of those ideals altogether.

While the curtain appears ready to drop on this tragedy, the story may not, of course, end with Article 9's demise. Japan's future trajectory still remains contested, with voices still calling for restraint and respect for constitutional limitations. The formal text of Article 9 remains unchanged, creating at least a theoretical possibility for renewed enforcement. The international law prohibition on the use of force remains operative, even as recent actions and postures by Russia, the United States, Israel, and others have done significant violence to it. One may hope that the tragedy of Article 9's demise may contribute to the growing sense within the international legal community that renewed efforts are urgently required to subject the use of force to meaningful legal constraints.

References

Ackerman B (1998) We the people, vol 2: Transformations
Akimoto D (2020) Explaining debate on Japan's strike capability. The Diplomat, 7 August 2020
American Society of International Law (1997) Japan-United States: Joint Statement on Review of Defense Cooperation Guidelines and Defense Cooperation Guidelines, pp 1621–1638
Anzenhoshō no hōtekikiban no kōchiku ni kansuru kondankai [Report of the Advisory Panel on Reconstruction of the Legal Basis for Security], May 15, 2014
Ashida H (1946) Kenpō no kaishaku [Interpretation of the constitution]
Auer JE (1993) Article Nine: renunciation of war. In Luney PR Jr, Takahashi K (eds) Japanese constitutional law, p 69
Balkin JM, Levinson S (2001) Understanding the constitutional revolution. Virginia Law Rev 87:1045
Basu T (2020) Will Japan pursue first strike capability? The Diplomat, 28 July 2020
Boyd JP, Samuels RJ (2005) Nine lives?: The politics of constitutional reform in Japan
Cabinet Decision on Development of Seamless Security Legislation to Ensure Japan's Survival and Protect its People (provisional English translation) (July 1, 2014). http://www.cas.go.jp/jp/gaiyou/jimu/pdf/anpohosei_eng.pdf
Chang GG (2024) Japan's new leader wants nuclear weapons. Newsweek, 13 October 2024
Constitutional law scholars lash out at government criticism, insults, Asahi Shimbun, 16 June 2015
De Wet E (2018). The Gulf war-1990-91. In: Ruys T, Corten O (eds) The use of force in international law, pp 456–468
Dinstein Y (2005) War, aggression and self-defence

Dixon R, Baldwin G (2019) Globalizing constitutional moments? A reflection on the Japanese Article 9 debate. Am J Comp Law 67:145
Drohan TA (2007) American-Japanese security agreements, past and present
Elkins Z, Ginsburg T, Melton J (2009) The endurance of national constitutions
Elster J (1979) Ulysses and the Sirens: studies in rationality and irrationality
Fisher RA (1999) The erosion of Japanese pacifism: the constitutionality of the 1997 U.S.-Japan Defense guidelines. Cornell Int Law J 32:393
Former Justice Brands Security Bills as Unconstitutional, Slams Abe for Sophistry, Japan Times, 16 September 2015
Franck TM (2002) Recourse to force: state action against threats and armed attacks
Fujii T (2005) Kenpō to kokusai shakai [The constitution and international society]
Fujimoto T (2025) Strengthening Japan's defense in response to Russia's aggression against Ukraine
Fukushima A (1999) Japanese foreign policy: the emerging logic of multilateralism
Green JA (2024) Collective self-defence in international law
Griffin S (1995) Constitutionalism in the United States: from theory to politics. In: Levinson S (ed) Responding to imperfection, p 37
Hamilton H (2010) Mōri v. Japan: The Nagoya High Court recognizes the right to live in peace. Pacific Rim Law Policy J 19:549
Hara H (2004) Nihonkoku Kenpō seitei no keifu [The origins of the Japanese constitution]
Hasebe Y (2015) Kensho – Anpohōan: Doko ga kenpōihanka [Examined – national security laws: where are they unconstitutional?]
Hasebe Y (2017) The end of constitutional pacifism? Wash Int Law J 26:125
Hatake M (2006) Kenpō 9 jō: kenkyū to giron no saizensen [Article 9 of the constitution: the vanguard on research and arguments]
Heiwa Anzenhosei Seibiho [Law for the maintenance of the peace and security legal system] (2015)
Hook GD, McCormack G (2001) Japan's contested constitution: documents and analysis
Hughes CW (2005) Japan's security agenda: military, economic & environmental dimensions
Hughes CW (2006) Japan's re-emergence as a 'normal' military power
Inoue K (1991) MacArthur's Japanese constitution: a linguistic and cultural study of its making
Ishizuka N (2019) Constitutional reform in Japan. Columbia J Asian Law 33:5
Japan High Court Rules 2015 (2023) Security laws don't violate constitution. Mainichi Shimbun, 6 December 2023
Katzenstein PJ (1996) Cultural norms and national security: police and military in postwar Japan
Kokusai Heiwa Shijiho [International peace support Law] (2015)
Levinson S (1995) How many times has the United States constitution been amended? (A) > 26; (B) 26; (C) 27; (D) > 27: accounting for constitutional change. In: Levinson S (ed) Responding to imperfection: the theory and practice of constitutional amendment
Lutz DS (1994) Toward a theory of constitutional amendment. Am Polit Sci Rev 335
Lutz DS (1995) Toward a theory of constitutional amendment. In: Levinson S (ed) Responding to imperfection, p 237
Martin C (2007) The case against revising interpretations of the Japanese constitution. Asia-Pacific J: Japan Focus 5:5
Martin C (2008) Binding the dogs of war: Japan and the constitutionalizing of Jus ad Bellum. Univ Pa J Int Law 30:267–357
Martin C (2011) Taking war seriously: the case for constitutional constraints on the use of force in compliance with international law. Brooklyn Law Rev 76:611–730
Martin C (2016) Jus ad Bellum implications of Japan's new national security laws. Asia-Pacific J Jpn Focus 14:10
Martin C (2017a) Change it to save it: why and how to amend Article 9. Ritsumeikan J Peace Stud 18
Martin C (2017b) The legitimacy of informal constitutional amendments and the 'reinterpretation' of Japan's war powers. Fordham Int Law J 40:427
Miki R, Kobara J (2025) Is it time for Japan to have nuclear arms? Trump uncertainty sparks debate. Nikkei Asia, 30 April 2025

Military and Paramilitary Activities in and Against Nicaragua (Nicaragua v. United States of America), Merits Judgment, 1986 I.C.J. Rep. 14
Ministry of Defense White Paper, Defense of Japan (2019). https://www.mod.go.jp/en/publ/w_paper/wp2019/pdf/index.html
Moore RA, Robinson DL (2002) Partners for democracy: crafting the new Japanese State under MacArthur
Mori S (2015) The new security legislation and Japanese public reaction. Tokyo Foundation, 2 December 2015
Nakamura A (1996) Sengoseiji ni yureta kenpō kyūjō – naikaku hōsiekyoku no jishin tsuyōsa [Article 9 of the constitution rocked by post war politics: the strength and self-confidence of the Cabinet Legislation Bureau]
Nasu H (2016) Japan's 2015 security legislation: challenges to its implementation under international law. Int Law Stud 92:249
National Defense Program Guidelines (2018). https://www.mod.go.jp/en/d_act/d_policy/national.html
Nishi O (1987) The constitution and the National Defense Law System in Japan
Nishikawa S (2000) Shirarezaru kanchō: naikaku hōseikyoku [The unknown agency: the Cabinet Legislation Bureau]
Nishikawa S (2013) Korede Wakatta! Naikaku Hōseikyoku [Here understood! The Cabinet Legislation Bureau]
Oguma S (2025) Bōei senryaku no henka to keizokusei - 2022-nen 'kokka bōei senryaku' to shin jidai no bōeiryoku [Changes and Continuity in Defence Strategy: The 2022 'National Defence Strategy' and defence capabilities in a new era], Anzen Hoshō Senryaku Kenkyū, 5:175
Ono K (2015) Former legislation bureau chiefs criticize security bills as placing citizens in danger. Asahi Shimbun, 22 June 2015
Osaki T (2015) Thousands protest Abe, security bills at diet rally. Japan Times, 30 August 2015
Peczenik A (1989) On law and reason
Port KL (2005) Article 9 of the Japanese constitution and the rule of law. Cardozo J Int Comp Law 13:127
Pyle KB (2007) Japan rising: the resurgence of Japanese power and purpose
Ruys T (2010) 'Armed attack' and Article 51 of the UN Charter: evolutions in customary law and practice
Sakamoto M (2007) Buryokukōshi ihōka gensoku no naka no kyūjōron [The Article 9 debate within the criminalization of the use of armed force]. Juristo 1334:50
Sakata M (2014) Hō no Banjin: Naikaku Hōseikyoku no Kyōji: Kaishyaku Kaiken ga Yurusanai Riyū [The law's gatekeeper – the dignity of the Cabinet Legislation Bureau: reasons why the reinterpretation is unacceptable]
Samuels R (2004) Politics, security policy, and Japan's Cabinet Legislation Bureau: who elected these guys, anyway? Japanese Policy Research Inst., Working Paper No. 99. http://www.jpri.org/publications/workingpapers/wp99.html
Shōichi K (1997) The birth of Japan's Postwar Constitution
Takayanagi K et al (eds) (1972) Nihon-koku kenpō seitei no katei [The making of the Constitution of Japan]
Tamura S et al (2008) Nihon no Bōeihōsei [The National Defense Legal System of Japan]
Tatsumi Y (2023) How Russia's invasion of Ukraine changed Japan's approach to national security. Stimson.org
The Advisory Panel on Reconstruction of the Legal Basis for Security, Report of the Advisory Panel on Reconstruction of the Legal Basis for Security (June 24, 2008)
The National Defense Buildup (2022). https://www.mod.go.jp/en/d_policy/index.html
The National Defense Strategy (2022). https://www.mod.go.jp/en/d_policy/index.html
The National Security Strategy of Japan (2022). https://www.mod.go.jp/en/d_policy/index.html
Togo K (2005) Japan's Foreign Policy 1945–2003

Tokuchi H (2018) Implications of revision of Article 9 of the Constitution of Japan. Columbia J Asian Law 33:84
Tokuchi H (2023) Japan's new national security strategy: background and challenges. Policy paper: Robert Schuman Centre for Advanced Global Governance
Waldron J (2006) Are constitutional norms legal norms? Fordham Law Rev 75:1697
Yasuzawa K (1981) Kenpō daikyūjō no kaishaku [Interpretation of Article 9 of the Constitution]
Yoshida R, Aoki M (2015) Amid angry scenes, ruling parties force security bills through Lower House Committee. Japan Times, 15 July 2015

The Comparative and Transnational Perspective

The Constitutions of Japan, Italy and Germany Reject War: And the Current Non-Wars?

Mario G. Losano

1 The Origin of International Law of War and Humanitarian Law

A date can perhaps be set for the beginning of international law of war and humanitarian treaties: 24 June 1859, the date of the Battle of Solferino in the Second Italian War of Independence, with thousands dead and tens of thousands wounded and missing on both sides.[1] The sight of the thousands of wounded left to themselves left an impression on a Swiss businessman, the Calvinist Henry Dunant (1828–1910), who described his horror in a book—*Un Souvenir de Solférino*. At the same time, he emphasised the participation of the local women: "But the women of Castiglione [dello Stiviere] seeing that I make no distinction of nationality, follow my example by showing the same benevolence to all those men of such different origins and who are all equally foreign to them. "All brothers", they repeated, moved. Honour to these charitable creatures, honour to the women of Castiglione!"

The horror of the massacre and the example of the women of Castiglione led Dunant to create an institution to remedy these inhuman situations, in which, after bloody battles, the wounded were left to themselves: he founded the Red Cross for this purpose and was awarded the Nobel Peace Prize in 1901.[2] One of the funda-

[1] On the French-Piedmontese side, 1622 dead; 8530 wounded; 1518 missing or prisoners. On the Austrian side, 2292 dead; 1807 wounded; 8638 missing or prisoners: Pieri (1962), p. 619 (with numerous re-editions).

[2] Enrico Dunant, *A Memory of Solferino*. Con un appendice sulla formazione permanente di istituzioni internazionali pel servizio sanitario degli eserciti in tempo di guerra [With an appendix on

M. G. Losano (✉)
Accademia delle Scienze, Turin, Italy

G. Cavaggion (ed.), *The 'Pacifist Principle' in the Italian and Japanese Constitutions in the Wake of the War in Ukraine*,
https://doi.org/10.1007/978-3-032-23108-6_13

mental principles of the Red Cross is impartiality: "It makes no distinction of nationality, race, religion, social status or political affiliation. It devotes itself exclusively to helping individuals according to the gravity and urgency of their suffering".

These humanitarian principles took shape in various international meetings, alongside which an international law of war and humanitarian law were developed.

Before the Second World War, between 1864 and 1929, six Geneva Conventions were signed. Dunant's influence is already evident in the title of the 1864 convention: "Convention for the Amelioration of Military Wounded in War". The aims pursued by these international meetings are summarised by the First International Peace Conference, held in The Hague in 1899, which proposes "the general maintaining of peace", "the amicable settlement of international conflicts", the "extension of law and the strengthening of the feeling of international justice", and—as a means to realise these ends—"the permanent establishment of an arbitral jurisdiction accessible to all": thus the "Permanent Court of International Arbitration" is born. In closing, the Final Act attached three declarations regarding the law and customs of war: (1) the prohibition of launching projectiles and explosives from the height of balloons or by other similar new means; (2) prohibition of the use of projectiles whose sole purpose is to spread asphyxiating or deleterious gases; (3) prohibition of the use of bullets that expand or crush easily in the human body. To sum up, there are three prohibitions: to bomb from the air; to use gas; to use anti-personnel mines.[3] What has been happening on a daily basis since 2022 in the Russian invasion of Ukraine and what has been happening in the Gaza Strip since well before that attests to the fact that reality is far removed from these ideals.

International treaties and international courts have also generated an intense legal-scientific activity, developing the branch of the law of war and humanitarian law: an activity that has, however, waned in recent decades, as we shall see. Limiting ourselves to a few examples, studies on the law of war were published during the Second World War, or immediately after.[4] In 1957, the internationalist Giorgio Cansacchi summarised the situation as follows: "The international law of war is but a 'particular law' in relation to the common international law, also called 'law of peace'. This law, formed almost entirely by custom, has been, since the nineteenth century, successively codified, clarified and modified by various conventions": the main ones have been quoted above. However, Cansacchi emphasises a problem that has worsened to the present day: "Unfortunately, it cannot be said that the rules of international law of war are scrupulously observed by the belligerents: the last two great wars of 1914–1918 and 1939–1945 documented the contrary. These conflicts

the permanent formation of international institutions for the medical service of armies in time of war]. Italian version by Zanetti (1863), 222 pp.; Firpo (1979), XLII–117 pp.; also contains: Dunant (1862a), b).

[3] A summary is in the paragraph *Le convenzioni contro la guerra*, in Stassi (2024), pp. 148–155; the quotation is on p. 150. Furthermore technical-legal data can be found in the international law texts cited in footnotes 4 and 5.

[4] Serra et al. (1941), 218 pp.; Vedovado (1946), 221 pp. ("Edizione provvisoria ad uso degli studenti"); Pallieri (1954), XI–464 pp. (2nd edition. entirely revised).

on a global scale have, on the contrary, ascertained that the greater power gradually assumed by the offensive means is usually accompanied by a greater indiscrimination of targets, so much so that hostilities have affected civilians more than combatants".[5] Since then, the situation has worsened, as evidenced by the current spate of wars in Ukraine, the Middle East and Sudan, to name but three representative examples of a much more generalised situation: there are more than 50 conflicts currently taking place in the world.

It is in this context that the three post-war constitutions prohibiting the use of war other than in defence are in force. We shall now examine how these constitutions were arrived at (Sect. 2); what the "pacifist" articles contained in them contain (Sect. 3) and, finally, what situation of legal-political anomie the current development of offensive weapons in the context of ongoing conflicts and the increasingly frequent practice of what will be called "non-wars" (Sect. 4) have generated.

2 From National Socialism to Post-War Parliamentary Democracies

On 27 September 1940, Germany, Italy and Japan signed the aggressive "Tripartite Pact" in Berlin,[6] which consecrated the territorial expansion of the three states according to the "Great Spaces" concept founded by the geopolitician Karl Haushofer.[7]

> Karl Haushofer proposed the creation of several large continental-sized areas that, from north to south, would each include an Arctic, a temperate and a tropical zone. [...] These amalgamations would allow each pan-region to be self-sufficient. Here the inseparable companion of the Great Spaces makes its appearance: 'autarky', economic self-sufficiency. [...] Each pan-region would consist of peripheral states, suppliers of raw materials, and a leading state: in the American pan-region, the United States; in the Asian one, Japan; in the Western European one, Germany; in the Eastern European one, the USSR.[8]

In Italy, that pact was personified with the initials of the three capitals Rome, Berlin and Tokyo, and when faced with the difficulties of war, people exclaimed:

[5] Cansacchi (1957), 159 pp.; the quotation, taken from the *Preface*, is on p. 5. This is the volume which I myself have studied: [a] volume that reached its 6th edition in 1973. The first edition (Arti grafiche Castello, Turin 1953, 94 pp.) stated on the title page 'Scuole di applicazione d'Arma - Ed. f. c.'.—"whose didactic programme served as an outline for the drafting of the text" (p. 6).

[6] This treaty recognised the three signatory states' right to realise the 'Great Spaces' (*Großräume*) theorised by the geopolitics of dictatorships: Art. 1. Japan recognises and respects the leading task of Italy and Germany for the establishment of a new order in Europe. Art.2. 'Italy and Germany recognise and respect the steering task of Japan in establishing a new order in greater East Asia'.

[7] Losano (2009), pp. 275–284; Losano (2008a), pp. 281–290; Losano (2008b), pp. 275–284.

[8] Losano (2011), 336 pp.; the quotation is on pp. 12 f.

"Ro-Ber-To will take care of it".[9] But "Ro-Ber-To" lost the war: the Italian and German dictatorial regimes disappeared, while the Japanese militarist regime underwent a drastic transformation. These institutional changes found expression in the new constitutions with which the three states of the former "Tripartite Pact" faced the post-war period.

As the Second World War had arisen from the bellicose policy of the three states of that pact, the victorious powers wanted each of the post-war constitutions of the three defeated states to contain an article explicitly rejecting war as an instrument for resolving international conflicts. This provision was already present in the 1931 constitution of the Spanish Republic and was taken up by several other constitutions.[10] In the following subsection, attention will focus on the "pacifist" articles in the constitutions of the three former Tripartite Pact states.

Each of these three states is a medium power that—as an Italian constitutionalist writes referring to Italy (but this is also true for Germany and Japan)—"is included in a system of alliances hegemonised by a single great power and is by definition confined in a situation of limited sovereignty that originates from the disastrous outcomes of the Second World War, from which it emerged as a defeated state that had a peace treaty imposed between victors and therefore not open to question"; thus the pacifist articles "have behind them a congenital limitation of sovereignty and certainly not free choices of the constitutional organs".[11]

2.1 The Anti-War Constitutional Articles

The articles of the three pacifist constitutions are briefly referred to below: for an analysis of their genesis and content, I refer to my more extensive discussion and the literature cited there: see footnote 19.

In the Japanese Constitution of 1947, the rejection of war is contained in Article 9: "*Renunciation of War.* (1) Aspiring sincerely to an international peace based on justice and order, the Japanese people forever renounce war as a sovereign right of the nation and the threat or use of force as means of settling international disputes. (2) In order to accomplish the aim of the preceding paragraph, land, sea, and air

[9] 'Ro-Ber-To', although defeated, was not forgotten and is also mentioned in recent works; for example: 'On the eve of the Second World War [Ettore] Conti is appointed ambassador extraordinary and minister plenipotentiary' for Japan and Manchukuo. "His was a purely commercial mission, aimed at opening a triangulation between the puppet state of Manchukuo, Japan and Italy. The Ro-Ber-To axis, Rome-Berlin-Tokyo, which was to be formalised with the tripartite pact of 27 September 1940 between Italy, Germany and Japan, was at its dress rehearsal" (Righi 2013, p. 110).

[10] "Artículo 6. España renuncia a la guerra como instrumento de política nacional" (Spain renounces war as an instrument of national policy); in addition, Art. 77 established the principle of the peaceful settlement of disputes. A detailed list of other constitutions with pacifist clauses is in De Vergottini (2004), pp. 28 f.

[11] De Vergottini (2004), pp. 9 f.

forces, as well as other war potential, will never be maintained. The right of belligerency of the state will not be recognised".[12]

In the Italian Constitution of 1948 this principle is contained in Article 11, which has no title but is one of the 12 "Fundamental Principles" of the republic: "Italy rejects war as an instrument of aggression against the freedom of other peoples and as a means for the settlement of international disputes. Italy agrees, on conditions of equality with other States, to the limitations of sovereignty that may be necessary to a world order ensuring peace and justice among the Nations. Italy promotes and encourages international organisations furthering such ends".[13]

In the Basic Law of the Federal Republic of Germany of 1949 (extended in 1990 to the unified Germany[14]) this principle is contained in Article 26: "*Ban on preparing a war of aggression.* (1) Activities tending and undertaken with the intent to disturb peaceful relations between nations, especially to prepare for aggressive war, are unconstitutional. They shall be made a punishable offence. (2) Weapons designed for warfare may be manufactured, transported or marketed only with the permission of the Federal Government. Details will be regulated by a Federal Law".[15]

---

[12] Official translation of the Japanese text. English translation: Chapter II—*Renunciation of War*. Article 9. [I] In sincere aspiration to international peace based on justice and order, the Japanese People forever renounce war as the sovereign right of the nation and the threat or use of force as a means of settling international disputes. [II] For the purpose of achieving the goal set forth in the preceding paragraph, land, sea and air forces, as well as other war potential, shall never be maintained. The right of the state to war shall not be recognised. Chapter III, *Rights and Duties of Persons*, follows.

The English text of the Japanese Constitution can be found on the website of the Prime Minister of Japan: <http://japan.kantei.go.jp/constitution_and_government_of_japan/constitution_e.html>

The French text of the Japanese Constitution can be found at: <http://mjp.univ-perp.fr/constit/jp1946.htm>.

The Italian text of the 1947 Japanese constitution can be found at: <http://www.filodiritto.com/articoli/2006/08/costituzione-del-giappone/>.

[13] "Art. 11. Italy shall repudiate war as an instrument of offence against the freedom of other peoples and as a means of settling international disputes; it shall consent, on equal terms with other States, to the limitations of sovereignty necessary for an order that ensures peace and justice among Nations; it shall promote and favour international organisations directed to this end".

The text of the Italian Constitution can be found on the website of the Chamber of Deputies not only in Italian, but also in the French and English translations: Historical Italian constitutions can be found at: <http://dircost.di.unito.it/index.shtml>.

[14] On 3 October 1990, the five Länder that formed the DDR became part of the Federal Republic of Germany, so that the unification of Germany was actually the inclusion of the GDR into the FRG, with the consequent extension of the Basic Law to the new territories. The German text of the Basic Law, also in the English and French translations, can be found on the website of the German Parliament: <https://www.bundestag.de/grundgesetz>. The German text of the Basic Law and the historical German constitutions can be found on the website: <www.verfassungen.de> (which also contains, in German and often in English, the current constitutions of many states in the world). The Italian text of the Basic Law can be found at: <http://dircost.di.unito.it/cs/paesi/germania.shtml> Finally, the German text with the Italian translation opposite is at <http://www.consiglioveneto.it/crvportal/BancheDati/costituzioni/de/zGermania_sin.pdf>.

[15] "Art. 9. (1) Handlungen, die geeignet sind und in der Absicht vorgenommen werden, das friedliche Zusammenleben der Völker zu stören, insbesondere die Führung eines Angriffskrieges vorzu-

Such a radical rejection of war was not only the imposition of the victors, but was shared by almost the entire population. Those who were leaving behind the worst conflict in world history—especially among Europeans—lived in dread of a new war, fuelled also by the growing tension between the two blocs that pitted former allies against each other and the possibility that a new war would be an atomic one. Natalia Ginzburg sums up this widespread state of mind by describing the weariness of life of the writer Cesare Pavese in post-war Turin: he "continued to be afraid of war, even after the war had long since ended: as, moreover, did we all. Because this happened to us, as soon as the war was over, we immediately began to fear a new war again, and to think about it all the time".[16] In this climate, any guarantee of peace was therefore welcome.

Decades later, the pacifist constitutional norms of the immediate post-war period had to be interpreted in light of a new type of armed interventions, called "peace missions" (or similar), which have been multiplying since the 1990s. A crucial point was undoubtedly the Kosovo War of 1996–1999, because NATO states intervened without prior UN authorisation.

In general, a progressive weakening of the international institutions is consolidating, as in the Kosovo conflict: "In it, we see a weakness in the UN comparable to that of the League of Nations in the late 1930s. Indeed, the UN was unable to prevent either the "ethnic cleansing" in Kosovo or the NATO attacks. And the legal problem remains the same: that is, the prevalence of the law of the individual state over international law".[17]

The debate provoked by the intervention in Kosovo exemplarily reveals the difficulties of coordinating pacifist constitutional dictates with military interventions defined as "humanitarian" or similar. A volume collects the opinions of various members of the Italian Association of Constitutionalists, who met in 1999 at the request of the Association of Yugoslavian Constitutionalists, on this issue; these interventions are accompanied by 15 international documents referring to the Kosovo War.[18] An equivalent book could be prepared for each of the subsequent

bereiten, sind verfassungswidrig. Sie sind unter Strafe zu stellen. (2) Zur Kriegsführung bestimmte Waffen dürfen nur mit Genehmigung der Bundesregierung hergestellt, befördert und in Verkehr gebracht werden. Das Nähere regelt ein Bundesgesetz". Translation: "Art. 26 (1) Acts that are suitable and performed with the intention of disturbing the peaceful coexistence of peoples, and specifically of preparing a war of aggression, are unconstitutional. They must be punished. (2) Weapons intended for the conduct of war may only be manufactured, transported and put into circulation with the authorisation of the federal government. A federal law shall regulate the details.

[16] Ginzburg (1963), p. 205 (also: Ginzburg 2016, p. 299).

[17] From my interview with Conradin Wolf: *Völkerrecht. Die UNO konnte den Kosovo-Krieg nicht verhindern*, 'Berner Zeitung', 14 April 1999, Fortsetzung auf Seite 43 (my translation).

[18] Dogliani and Sicardi (1999), 287 pp. The volume refers to the Kosovo crisis of 1998–1999 (summarised therein in the footnote on pp. 95 f.) and contains 15 essays by Italian constitutionalists, with an appendix of 15 international documents (pp. 139–287), mostly in English and French. For the Italian context: Cavino and Malvicini (2023), 250 pp. (in particular: *The Kosovo War (1999)*, pp. 194–198; bibliography, pp. 229–250).

armed interventions, as has in part been done in a growing number of volumes and journal articles.

I refer the examination of the genesis, content and current application of these constitutional articles in the context of the description of the geopolitical situation during the Second World War, the transition from dictatorship to democracy in the three Tripartite Pact states and the emergence of their renewed armed forces in the context of the Cold War to a more extensive discussion of mine;[19] the debate on the unrealised "European Defence Community" of the 1950s[20] is repeated in 2025, regarding the project of a European, i.e. supranational, army. It is also necessary to analyse the debates of the constituent bodies that led to the approval of those articles in their final formulation, their interpretation and application up to the present day, the current compatibility of those articles with the conflicts of the immediate post-war period and, above all, with the asymmetrical conflicts, the "hybrid wars" and the "peacekeeping" or "policing" missions of the last two decades.

3 The Current "Non-War": "Ceci n'est pas une guerre"?

Conflicts of the twenty-first century tend not to be referred to as "wars", not only for propaganda reasons, but also because the governments involved do not want to incur the sanctions provided for in international treaties (mostly theoretical condemnations, as international bodies have no coercive force to sanction those who do not respect the treaties they have signed) and also because these are not traditional conflicts between states, since often at least one of the parties is a "mercenary force" or an independence movement, i.e. a non-state structure, even if in fact supported and financed by a state, which however prefers not to act itself.

Some of these military operations are regulated by the UN Charter and are carried out by the "Blue Helmets", the United Nations Peacekeeping Forces, founded in 1956 because of the Suez crisis. They are actual military operations, in which UN troops prevent a possible conflict (*peacekeeping*) or interpose themselves between two contending states (*peace restoring* or *peace enforcement*). However, the UN forces' rules of engagement limit their intervention, as seen in Srebrenica in July 1995, during the war in Bosnia and Herzegovina (1 March 1992–14 December 1995):

> The Netherlands will have to compensate the families of 300 of the more than eight thousand victims of Srebrenica. 19 years after the massacre, the Hague Tribunal has found that the blue helmets of the Duchbat III (Dutch UN battalion) stationed in Potočari did not do enough to protect civilians from deportation by the Bosnian Serbs, exposing them to a real risk of death, as was later the case. However, the responsibility of the UN soldiers proved

[19] Losano (2020), 403 pp. (Institute for European Legal History, Frankfurt am Main, https://doi.org/10.12946/gplh14). Full text online: <https://www.rg.mpg.de/publikationen/gplh-14>.

[20] In Italy, on 6 April 1954, the Scelba government presented a bill to the Chamber of Deputies for the 'Ratification and Execution of the Agreements for the European Defence Community', which was however withdrawn on 22 June 1955.

> by the Court is limited to the victims who were at the base at the time of the massacre, and not to all the other inhabitants of Srebrenica who tried to save themselves between 10 and 13 July [1995].[21]

3.1 The Evolution of Weapons

In conflicts, the function of weapons is also to keep the adversary at a distance: the spear, the bow, the crossbow, the catapult are the first steps in an evolution that—passing through firearms—reaches more modern times with the use of aviation[22] and, more recently, missiles and drones: "aerial surveillance devices that have become killing machines, the best definition of drones is undoubtedly this: flying high-resolution cameras armed with missiles".[23]

A quick review of the evolution of weapons used in warfare provides a better understanding of the difficulties international law is encountering in its application. Born in fact to regulate a certain context, it should now be applied to a totally different situation. A comparison drawn from the material history of flight may be illuminating.

In 1910, the Frenchman Louis Paulhan won the flight competition from London to Manchester by covering the distance of 296 km with a Farman biplane in a flight time of 4 h and 18 min: roughly 70 km/h, the speed of a small car; but the journey lasted around 12 h in total, because he had to stop for supplies 117 miles from London. Today, the military drone *Predator* and its successor *Reaper* have a speed of around 700 km/h, a range of 24 h and a flight time of approximately 1000 km from the take-off base. Therefore, the Italian base at Sigonella, 1000 km from Libya, would prove irreplaceable in a possible conflict against Libya in perpetual tension.

The prospects for the future are even more alarming. China is testing "Jiu Tian" (Ninth Heaven),

> a kind of "flying aircraft carrier". The robot aircraft, in fact, can carry and launch from its capacious cargo hold as many as 100 small kamikaze drones, for 'swarm' attack actions, as an alternative to a more traditional war load, such as cruise missiles aimed at land and sea targets, or air-to-air missiles for self-defence against enemy fighters. [...] It is a drone of strategic range, being able to fly for 12 hours and with a range of 7000 km. It is ideal for long armed patrols over waters and archipelagos of the boundless Pacific Ocean, a further challenge to US hegemony, especially in the event of a war over Taiwan. Such a 'flying aircraft carrier', although its mini-drones are small, could overwhelm the air defences of an American aircraft carrier or base, e.g. the island of Guam. Among the 100 mini-drones that can be dropped by the Jiu Tian, many could act as decoys to saturate anti-aircraft. After all,

---

[21] Ilaria Romano, *Srebrenica, 19 years later: the responsibility of the Dutch blue helmets*, 'Reset', 28 July 2014 <https://www.reset.it/reset-doc/srebrenica-19-anni-dopo-la-responsabilita-dei-caschi-blu-olandesi>.

[22] Annati and Scovazzi (2012), XII–399 pp.

[23] Chamamayou (2014), p. 14. On the use of drones for targeted killings, see the chapter Chamamayou (2018), pp. 369–388.

> if at least ten of these large drones took part in a large attack action, it would mean a total swarm of a thousand mini-drones.[24]

In short, the internationalist standards designed for the first decades of aviation are obsolete (and inapplicable) in the face of today's technology.

It has been seen (footnote 3) that one of the three prohibitions of the original law of war concerned the then innovative "bombardment from the sky" with tethered balloons or dirigibles (as opposed to classic land or naval artillery bombardment). Italy particularly distinguished itself in this field. The first aerial bombardment in history was in fact carried out in the 1911 Italian-Turkish War by the Italian aviation pioneer Giulio Gavotti. Gabriele D'Annunzio, impressed by this warlike action, celebrated it in verse in the "Canzone della Diana":

> and you, Gavotti, from your slight height
> stooped in the danger of the winds
> On the enemy who ignores the new assault!
>
> Then as the weaver throws the spool
> Or as the slinger casts the snout
> (the astonished the great wing flies over)
>
> Even Death now has his seed.
> You must with one hand
> Pull, and tear the spring with your teeth.[25]

The last triplet describes the technique by which the first aerial bombardment took place: Gavotti, pilot of a single-engine monoplane Etrich Taube, holds the *stick* with one hand and with the other picks up a hand grenade and tears off its safety tab with his teeth, before throwing it.

These still individual exploits were followed by squadron bombings, as in 1937 against the Basque City of Guernica, which was jointly bombed by the German Condor Legion and the Italian Legionary Air Force.

Also during the Italian-Turkish War, officer Giulio Douhet wrote a report in which he theorised for the first time about the use of high-altitude bombing. In 1912, the Italian Air Force was founded, which owed a strong impetus to Douhet. In 1914, Douhet promoted the construction of the Ca31 three-engine bomber at the Caproni company (contravening his superiors' instructions and thus coming into conflict with them). In 1921, Douhet published *Il dominio dell'aria*,[26] a work that made him the international theoretician of strategic bombing and that found practical implementation in the carpet bombing of the Second World War. A character as

---

[24] Mirko Molteni, *China plans Ninth Heaven, the mother of all kamikaze drones*, 'Libero', 21 May 2025, p. 8; 'Libero' takes the news from one of the Chinese regime's 'newspapers, the *South China Morning Post*'.

[25] These are verses 184–195 of the 'Song of Diana': <https://it.wikisource.org/wiki/Merope_(D%27Annunzio)/La_canzone_della_diana>. Gavotti himself described the course of that operation in detail in a letter to his father <https://it.wikipedia.org/wiki/Giulio_Gavotti>.

[26] Douhet (2002), LXIII–447 pp.

appreciated as he was criticised, the "Giulio Douhet Air Force Military School" in Florence, which prepares future Italian military aviation officers, has been named after him since 2006.

In order to avoid the direct involvement of a state in a conflict, in recent decades some states have resorted to using non-state forces in warfare operations: mercenary troops have thus reappeared and become established, on which we need only mention a few words here, although there is a vast literature on the subject.[27]

3.2 *The Return of the Mercenaries*

Mercenaries are generally dependent on private companies, so they do not rely on international treaties and act outside the rules of international law of war. A modern-day definition of "mercenary" is contained in a protocol of the Geneva Conventions:

> 1. A mercenary has no right to be a combatant or prisoner of war. - 2. A mercenary is a combatant: (a) expressly recruited in the country or abroad to fight in an armed conflict; (b) in fact takes a direct part in hostilities; (c) takes part in hostilities essentially with a view to gaining personal advantage and to whom has actually been promised, by or on behalf of a Party to the conflict, material remuneration substantially in excess of that promised or paid to combatants of similar rank and function in the armed forces of that Party; (d) who is not a national of a Party to the conflict or a resident of territory controlled by a Party to the conflict; (e) who is not a member of the armed forces of a Party to the conflict; (f) who has not been sent by a State other than a Party to the conflict on an official mission as a member of the armed forces of that State.[28]

All these criteria must be fulfilled for a combatant to be considered a mercenary. Since the mercenary stands outside the legal rules, he is treated outside the legal rules in the event of capture: he is equated de facto with a saboteur, and therefore the rules of the international rules on the treatment of prisoners of war (who must be regular soldiers of one of the belligerent parties, or equivalent) do not apply to him. Nevertheless, the mercenary must—or should—be treated humanely and subjected to due process; but he is not entitled to repatriation.

Individual states have enacted rules to regulate or prevent the use of mercenaries. In particular, Italy does not allow the participation of persons not belonging to its armed forces in conflicts on the territory of another state: the prohibition is enshrined in Law No. 21 of 12 May 1995, which ratified the 1989 UN Convention.

Recourse to mercenaries is destabilising, because it indicates that the state that resorts to them does not have sufficient armed forces to guarantee its aims: Machiavelli already mentioned this in *The Prince*. In Milan at the end of the 1400s, after the rule of the Visconti family, Francesco Sforza, commander of a mercenary company in the service of the Sforza family, took power. More recently, in June

---

[27] Vecchioni (2024), 289 pp. (with bibliography).

[28] The 47th Article of the Additional Protocol of 8 June 1977 (APGC77) to the Geneva Conventions on the Protection of Victims in International Armed Conflicts has been ratified by 167 states.

2023, in Russia, the "Wagner Private Military Company" attempted and failed a coup against President Vladimir Putin. We find the "musicians" (as the Wagner mercenaries are called) with other private militias in the wars that have been destabilising Africa for years:

> The world of private military companies (PMCs), or 'mercenaries', is invading Africa. While the international press continues to focus on Russia's Wagner, numerous Western, Middle Eastern and Asian security companies, far more powerful than Wagner, have managed to sign contracts with dozens of African states. A trend that, after the abandonment of Afghanistan and Iraq, will only intensify. The PMCs on the black continent provide the highest bidder with military, logistical, intelligence and computer security capabilities, as well as propaganda tools. It is a complex sector where PMCs of different nationalities can clash by training the military forces of a given African country or fight side by side in another. The identity of a PMC can also be concealed by another company or investment fund, or by a simple name change. This is the case of the infamous 'Blackwater', founded in 1996, which became 'Xe Services' in 2009, and then 'Academi' since 2011.[29]

3.3 *Paramilitary Groups*

In order to avoid falling under the prohibitions of international conventions, states undertake military actions without calling them wars: the most obvious example is the "special military operation" with which Russian President Vladimir Putin, in a televised speech on 24 February 2022, announced aggression against a sovereign and internationally recognised state such as Ukraine. An unintentional reference to René Magritte's "Ceci n'est pas une pipe"? The lexical *ploy* and political justifications for the aggression were debated to no practical avail and, as Pope Bergoglio stated, the world is now in the presence of the Third World War in pieces.

Other times, direct confrontation between states is avoided—even in the presence of clashes of war—by resorting to para-military forces, financed and equipped by a state which, however, does not operate itself and thus avoids conflict through treaties (which it has not always signed). Just one example: the Houti rebels attack merchant ships in the Red Sea to counter supplies to Israel, and they can be traced back to the state of Yemen. The latter, however, does not figure prominently, but because of this connection it has been heavily bombed by Israel's allies the United States and Great Britain. The dreaded three "Hs" of international terrorism are, in addition to the Houthis, Hamas (whose attack on Israel on 7 October 2023 started the current Israeli carnage in the Gaza Strip) and Hezbollah,[30] which can be traced

[29] Matteo Fraschini Koffi, Mercenari. Dagli eserciti privati in Africa il rischio di una nuova colonizzazione, "L'Avvenire", 13 gennaio 2023 https://www.avvenire.it/opinioni/pagine/dagli-esercitiprivati-in-africa-il-rischio-di-una-colonizzazione. Blackwater was taken to court for its extremely violent practices, which caused casualties not only among civilians, but also among its own affiliates, whose relatives brought the lawsuits that led the company to change its name several times: Pelton (2007), 358 pp.

[30] Di Donato (2015), 221 pp.

back to Iran; the Pasdaran (the "Guardians of the Revolution": a state within a state in Iran); Islamic Jihad, linked to the Muslim Brotherhood; and finally al-Qaeda,[31] best known for the 11 September 2001 attack in the United States, which caused three thousand deaths.

As an example of conflict between the state and paramilitary groups, Peru in the years of terrorism (1980–2000) was troubled by internal guerrilla warfare due to the "Sendero Luminoso" movement (linked to the Communist Party) and the "Túpac Amaru Revolutionary Movement".[32] How difficult life had become in that context can be illustrated by an example. Among the South American states, Peru was the first to sign an equal treaty with Japan in 1873; a strong emigration from Japan to Peru followed, where the large Japanese-Peruvian community also backed the Peruvian President Alberto Fujimori. Internal guerrilla warfare and the economic crisis caused a return emigration of Japanese-Peruvians to Japan.

The story of the Nippo-Peruvian Augusto Higa Oshiro (1946–2023) is exemplary: he was already an established writer, but in 1990 the economic and social crisis forced him to emigrate to Japan that same year. He returned to Peru in 1992, after 18 months as a factory worker in various Japanese factories: from this experience came the novel-testimony *Japón no da dos oportunidades*, from which the following testimony is taken:

> In 1990 I was a professional specialising in the Ministry of Education's journals and publications and my salary was no more than 80 dollars a month. My wife's income, a doctor in a Ministry of Health hospital, came to $100, and we were both supporting a family with two children studying in the school 'La Unión'. I would add that in 1988 I had finished my third book, a novel about the working-class neighbourhood 'El Porvenir', which I never managed to publish despite contacts with two publishers. We were experiencing Peru's deep crisis, when inflation was rising at 60 per cent a month, businesses were failing like a whirlwind, legions of workers were being laid off, and chaos and delinquency were spreading like wildfire. In this explosive situation, the unconventional war of subversion[33] with its twenty thousand dead ran through all social classes and all corners of the country. From 1988-1989 the migratory avalanche among the descendants of Japanese was unleashed: a logical response and providential solution to a crisis that was showing clear signs of collective delirium.[34]

Equally dramatic was the situation in Colombia, where (after a series of civil wars in the nineteenth century) an internal war had been raging since 1960, which escalated between 1988 and 2002 between extreme left-wing groups, extreme right-wing paramilitary formations, organised crime and drug traffickers.[35] Attempts were

---

[31] Gerges (2011), X–259 pp.

[32] Walker (2014), 347 pp.

[33] [Augusto Higa refers to the armed struggle of the 'Sendero Luminoso' and 'Túpac Amaru' revolutionary movements: see *supra*, footnote 32.]

[34] Oshiro (2019), pp. 111 f. On this circular migration from Japan to Latin America, and back: Losano (2025), XIX–414 pp. (on Augusto Higa Oshiro, pp. 33–115).

[35] For initial information, see the detailed Wikipedia entry <https://it.wikipedia.org/wiki/Conflitto_armato_colombiano>, containing two appendices: Anexo 1: *Bibliografía sobre el Conflicto armado interno de Colombia* (lista de los principales libros); Anexo 2: *Obras sobre el Conflicto*

made to remedy these violent internal clashes, going so far as to amend the constitution in 2017 with the introduction of Article 22A, which prohibits paramilitary organisations:

> ARTÍCULO 22A. [Artículo adicionado por el artículo 1 del Acto Legislativo 5 de 2017. El nuevo texto es el siguiente:] Como una garantía de No Repetición y con el fin de contribuir a asegurar el monopolio legítimo de la fuerza y del uso de las armas por parte del Estado, y en particular de la Fuerza Pública, en todo el territorio, se prohíbe la creación, promoción, instigación, organización, instrucción, apoyo, tolerancia, encubrimiento o favorecimiento, financiación o empleo oficial y/o privado de grupos civiles armados organizados con fines ilegales de cualquier tipo, incluyendo los denominados autodefensas, paramilitares, así como sus redes de apoyo, estructuras o prácticas, grupos de seguridad con fines ilegales u otras denominaciones equivalentes. - La ley regulará los tipos penales relacionados con estas conductas, así como las sanciones disciplinarias y administrativas correspondientes.[36]

3.4 *Prisoners and Hostages*

After the First World War, the status of prisoners of war was regulated by the Geneva Conventions: *The Convention Relating to the Treatment of Prisoners of War* (1929), reformed by the Third Geneva Convention of 12 August 1949, which took into account the experience of the Second World War. In particular, the rules for the treatment of prisoners of war were also extended to partisan forces, provided certain conditions were met. The characteristics of this regulation, which was very articulate but in fact often not respected, are illustrated and discussed by a large body of internationalist literature.

With the advent of "non-wars", the situation of prisoners has become more complicated, because the belligerents are also non-state structures, thus not signatories to the Geneva treaties, and therefore not bound by their requirements. The capture of military personnel has been accompanied by the capture of civilians. But the capture of hostages, in order to obtain a ransom in monetary or other terms, is an act proper to crime, especially so-called organised crime; if practised during a war conflict, it is a war crime.[37] We can recall the Second World War in Italy and the numerous cases of civilian hostages shot in retaliation by National Socialist troops (such as the hostages killed at the Fosse Ardeatine); or—in the case of hostages taken by groups not formally part of an army traceable to a state—to the Israeli hostages captured by Hamas on 7 October 2023, many of whom are dead or not yet released;

armado interno en Colombia (el Conflicto armado "ha inspirado gran cantidad de obras, manifestaciones culturales y representaciones artísticas en diversos campos como la literatura, la música, el teatro, las artes plásticas, el grafiti, el muralismo, la poesía, la caricatura, la escultura, la cinematografía, televisión e incluso en el deporte").

[36] <http://www.secretariasenado.gov.co/senado/basedoc/constitucion_politica_1991.html>.

[37] Labanca (2024), 311 pp.; Amirante (1970), multiple volumes.

meanwhile, Israel's reaction has involved the Gaza Strip in a war that continues to this day.

From a legal point of view, the common Article 3 of the Geneva Conventions of 1949 punishes hostage-taking in an internal conflict as a war crime; hostage-taking in an international conflict is regulated by the Fourth Geneva Convention (Art. 34, 147) and some additional protocols. Finally, on 17 December 1979, the UN General Assembly approved (except for 24 states) the "International Convention Against the Taking of Hostages".[38] But in this field, the discrepancy between legal prescriptions and their actual application is greatest.

4 Hybrid Warfare and the Civil Population

The techniques of warfare in recent decades have also been radically transformed by the rapid evolution of information technology and networks, coupled with innovations in aeronautics and rocketry, and above all, with the advent of drones, i.e. "remotely piloted aircraft": by this term it is meant an aircraft that does not have a human pilot on board, even though it is guided by a human pilot thousands of kilometres away (assisted by an observer-weaponman, in military drones). Combining several advanced technologies, drones are capable of performing interventions that are defined as "surgical" due to their high degree of precision: they have been used in the fight against terrorism and for targeted interventions against individuals in the enemy camp. The use of drones (also increasingly relevant in the humanitarian and civil spheres) would require a separate discussion. Suffice it here to mention their use in warfare.[39]

Today's war includes traditional techniques, aided by computer and airborne techniques: for example, drones, using cameras, inspect the terrain and detect enemy units on which traditional ground units will have to intervene. It is a *hybrid war*, because it merges various technologies. It no longer corresponds to classical warfare, characterised by the declaration of war, by armies distinguished by their uniforms, by the front line distinguished from the rear and, above all, by the distinction between warring armies and the civilian population, which had to be touched as little as possible by the war. Everything was regulated, as far as possible, by the legal rules of the international law of war and by the military codes of the individual belligerent states. This classical view of war no longer applies to the conflicts that characterise the twenty-first century: they are described as "hybrid wars" because, in armed conflicts, new actors and new instruments have been added to the elements that characterised classical wars.[40]

---

[38] The text of the '5th International Convention Against the Taking of Hostages' is in: <https://treaties.un.org/Pages/ViewDetails.aspx?src=TREATY&mtdsg_no=XVIII-5&chapter=18&clang=_en#1>.

[39] Losano (2018), pp. 19–38.

[40] For the now vast literature on hybrid wars: Romeo (2021), 220 pp.; see also the article cited in the following footnote.

The actors are no longer only states in conflict with each other, but also entities that are not states in the legal or internationalist sense of the term, such as ISIS (or Islamic State). It is not only regular armies that clash with each other, but armed groups of various origins and mercenaries (now called *contractors*), with the external (i.e. economic and propagandistic) support of states in the traditional sense of the term, which can, however, claim not to be belligerents. This is what happened in Ukraine with Russian support for the separatists and with the occupation of Crimea in 2014 by the "little green men" officially not identifiable with the Russian state army.[41] Thus, all delimitation of time and space disappears: the hybrid war can start at any time and in any place, because there is no longer a state declaring it, nor is there a front line. Consequently, hybrid war also directly involves the civilian population.

According to Clausewitz, classical war is the continuation of the duel: that is, it is the clash between two belligerents. The evolution of war technology has always aimed at increasing the distance between the two belligerents to ensure the safety of one against the other. In hybrid warfare, this separation has become total, thanks to the spread of information technology in today's societies and, therefore, also in the armed forces and their combat instruments: for instance, the course of drones can be altered with a *brouillage*[42] that alters the communications from the base to the drone.

It is also possible to alter or destroy a vital element of the enemy, without knowing from whom the cyber attack originates: it is possible to covertly penetrate and alter databases of all kinds, to block or destroy railway, military, civil networks (e.g. electricity or water distribution networks), causing damage as serious as that of a traditional bombing: this is *cyberwar*, which has now become a fundamental ingredient in the heterogeneous mixture of instruments of hybrid warfare. The most typical instrument of atypical warfare today is the drone, the remotely piloted aircraft.[43]

The fusion of information technology and atypical conflicts is so close that the term "cyberwar" often ends up becoming synonymous with the whole "hybrid war". A senior US security official has summarised the set of tools that converge in today's hybrid warfare under the name "cyberwar", because information technology is the common element in all the techniques of this new conduct of war. The central chapters of his book therefore describe cyberwar in the strict sense, as well as economic warfare, economic espionage, the evolution of command techniques and psychological warfare: all hostile activities that would be unthinkable today without information technology.

A computer specialist, on the other hand, distinguishes "network wars" (which aim to sabotage or block government or private, transport or communication

---

[41] Gardner (2015), 16 pp. (online).

[42] *Comment brouiller un drone: guide complet et détaillé*: "Le brouillage d'un drone implique l'interruption intentionnelle des communications entre le drone et sa télécommande. Cette technique utilise un signal de brouillage pour bloquer les transmissions radio ou GPS" <https://www.mondrone.net/drones/comment-brouiller-un-drone-guide-complet-et-detaille>.

[43] For the literature on drones, *see § 6. Drones: remotely piloted covert assassins* in Losano (2018), pp. 19–38.

networks) from "cyberwar" (understood as operations that aim to make false but destabilising news credible, i.e. psychological operations, "Psyop").[44] As there is no standardised terminology, comparing various authors, it is prudent to check what the definition of cyberwar and related practices is in each one.

Moreover, a cyber attack can be carried out by anyone and anywhere: so war no longer seems to be "soldier's business", it is "outside their domain", they no longer have control over it; and, in fact, in a book on cyberwar, the chapter "A Military Left Out" opens with the words: "Militaries, and their supporting contractors, have difficulty defining a role for themselves in modern war because much of it is outside their domain. In all but a few cases, military capability is not as relevant in war as it once was".[45]

The success of hybrid warfare is due as much to its effectiveness (not least because with it numerous legal constraints resulting from international law or signed treaties fall away) as to the favour it enjoys among decision-makers. Politicians like hybrid warfare because it is decided almost secretly in the governmental context, outside of parliamentary debate; because it limits the deaths of soldiers of the national armed forces as much as possible, thus avoiding criticism from the political opposition and from the media; the military establishment does not dislike it, because the expenses of hybrid warfare are added to those for the traditional military structure, without replacing them. Finally, it allows a constitutional ploy for the three states whose constitutions include a ban on the use of war.[46] Germany, Japan and Italy do not participate in wars (to be decided in parliament, where the question of unconstitutionality would arise), but contribute to international police operations, *peacekeeping*, *peace restoring*: euphemisms for military actions outside national borders, atypical or hybrid wars. In short, "low-intensity conflicts", i.e. non-wars, even if war armaments are used in them.

One thing is certain: the hybrid war heavily involves the civilian population. Almost a library has now been written about the relentless slaughter of children and minors in the Gaza Strip: in vain.[47] To the numerous deaths among journalists and medical personnel[48] must be added the sick who have died as a result of the lack of proper care.

---

[44] Hofstetter (2016), 511 pp.; "Netzkriege unterscheiden sich von Cyberkriegen" (p. 395).

[45] Poindexter (2015), 221 pp.; the citation is on p. 130. By this author see also: Poindexter (2013).

[46] Cf. Losano (2017b); also in <http://observare.autonoma.pt>.

[47] Onlus (2009), 84 pp., with a presentation by the scientist and astrophysicist Margherita Hack (1922–2013); (2023), 142 pp.; Gentile (2024), 92 pp.

[48] *Gaza, more journalists killed than in World War II: NGO complaint and The Intercept investigation*, 25 June 2024, <https://www.lanotiziagiornale.it/giornalisti-a-gaza-ne-sono-morti-piu-che-durante-lintera-seconda-guerra-mondiale/>. Marie-Aure Perreaut Revial, Médecins Sans Frontières emergency coordinator in Gaza, recounts what she saw in November and December 2023: 'In four months of war, 339 health workers have been killed in Gaza. Medical personnel are bearing an incredibly heavy burden: doctors and nurses work day and night to save lives, while bombs continue to fall on them and their families. No hospital is able to provide life-saving medical care anymore' <https://www.medicisenzafrontiere.it/news-e-storie/news/guerra-gaza-opera-

Women are directly affected, and unfortunately in more ways than one, by this new type of conflict. As a passive subject (as part of the civilian population), they suffer the attacks of hybrid warfare right into their own homes; moreover, since hybrid warfare is a gang war, collective violence against women has also become a weapon. As an active subject, women combatants—limiting ourselves to the Middle East today—can be found in all fighting forces. In particular, they are present in the fighting parties that refer to Islam with differing interpretations of the position of women. To cite but a few examples, the armed forces of Turkey, as a bastion of secularism, included women but banned the Turkish Islamic veil, which has been reinstated since the beginning of 2017. Women are also present in the armed forces of the Islamic Republic of Iran. In the Kurdish army the "Women's Defence Units" have been fighting since 2012, and they are women soldiers as well as officers. The Islamic State has also enlisted women.[49]

In 2017, *El País* in Spain devoted an entire insert to *cyber attacks, conflicts that neither begin nor end, lethal technologies, Jihadists, Mafia: welcome to the new wars*, and *Die Zeit* in Germany described *Germany in the crosshairs* in the three-page article "Bloodless Wars: Unknown Hackers Try Every Day to Paralyse Businesses, Phone Networks or Government Offices, or Influence Public Opinion. It seems that the actors are led by Russia"[50] (some subsequent quotes will be taken from this article). These are but two examples of a daily trickle.

The techniques of cyber intervention have become more refined, state and parallel organisations using them have increased and, in 2017, alongside the wars in the Middle East, a "hybrid" intervention in three general elections—in Germany, France and the Netherlands—could have destabilised the European Union: an outcome consistent with Russia's current expansionist goals. *Die Zeit* quotes the Chancellor's Office: "The real test of Russian strategy is the Bundestag elections". And more and more often Russia is (or is suspected of being) behind these cyber attacks "Aggressive Russian cyber attacks boosted Romania's pro-Moscow presidential candidate Europe Calin Georgescu, the pro-Russian outsider candidate now leading in Romania's presidential elections, was 'aggressively' promoted on social media platform TikTok through coordinated accounts and paid promotion, according to documents declassified Wednesday from Romania's security services".[51] In short, "cyberwar" is now a widespread practice globally.[52]

---

tori-sanitari-uccisi/>. Also: *Doctors and health workers killed in Gaza* <https://www.informazione.it/a/732AD039-88C3-4794-94FD-373AE4345B16/Medici-e-sanitari-uccisi-a-Gaza>.

[49] On the position of women in a fundamentalist Islamic state: Losano (2017a), 169 pp.

[50] *Guerra 3.0*, 'El País', 12 February, pp. 1–4; *Deutschland in Visier - Krieg ohne Blut*, '*Die Zeit*', 23 February 2017, pp. 2 f.

[51] <https://www.france24.com/en/europe/20241204-romania-targeted-by-aggressive-russian-cyber-attacks-during-elections-security-reports-say>. Also: <https://www.ilmessaggero.it/mondo/russia_attacchi_ibridi_europa_romania_antiterrorismo_50_attacchi_cosa_succede-8652906.html>.

[52] Losano, *ChatGPT in court, from Colombia a paradigmatic ruling*, 'MicroMega' online, 31 December 2024, 14 pp. <https://www.micromega.net/chatgpt-in-tribunale-sentenza-colombia>;

The doctrine of information warfare was formulated by the commander of the Russian General Staff, Valerij Vasiljevič Gerasimov in February 2013 in an article in the *Military-Industrial Courier* (*Voenno-Promyšlennyi Kur'er*): the new war is undeclared and resorts to non-military means, primarily communication. This is the first step in the hybrid warfare discussed so far.

In the following year, in 2014, the practical application of this doctrine took place in an operation that, until now, can be considered the model of a hybrid war: the destabilisation of Ukraine, which began with the occupation of Crimea. "That military operation became the example of the Gerasimov Doctrine: a mixture of political deception, secret military interventions, cyber attacks and disinformation campaigns". The Ukraine campaign was interpreted in the West as a sudden decision by the Russian government; instead, it had behind the Gerasimov Doctrine, which drew inspiration from guerrilla warfare and envisaged the possible intervention of regular armed forces only as a last resort.[53]

On 7 January 2015—while the Ukrainian Prime Minister, Arsenij Jazenjuk, was flying to Berlin to obtain German support—the pro-Russian hacker group CyberBerkut attacked German government computers for 48 consecutive hours, hacking from several sides and heading for different points in the German computer system. Angela Merkel's spokesman to *Die Zeit*: "Several groups took turns, so it must have been a large and strictly organised group". The attack ended on 8 January, when the Ukrainian president returned home.

In the autumn of 2016, an even more extensive attack blocked Internet servers in the United States. From 2017, the German government (but actually all governments) is strengthening its cyber defences.

In summary, the hacker's process consists of identifying a weakness in a computer's software and using it to surreptitiously enter the system and insert a "malware" (or *malicious software*, e.g. a Trojan virus) contained in an attachment. Through this "malware", the hacker launches thousands of messages: if an attachment is opened by the recipient, the malware is installed on their computer and from that moment on, the messages will come from that (unsuspecting) computer, and not from the hacker. When the operation is successful, the hacker has thousands of computers under their control, from which they can launch their attacks on, for instance, a government computer. In the 2015 attack on the Germans, 35,000 computers were involved, and in the 2016 attack against the United States, one million. From each of the captured computers, the hacker bombards the target computer with messages, until the targeted system crashes due to the excess of messages it receives.

Id., *The Constitutional Courts of Romania and Colombia on computer interference and artificial intelligence*, 'Comparative and European Public Law' (Dpce), 2025, (in press).

[53] Thomas Gutschker (*Putins Schlachtplan*, 7 September 2014, 'Frankfurter Allgemeine Zeitung', www.faz.net) quotes Gerasimov's (alarming) speech in January 2013 to the Russian Academy of Military Sciences, describing the new conduct of the war: 'Breit gestreuten Einsatz von Desinformationen, von politischen, ökonomischen, humanitären und anderen nichtmilitärischen Maßnahmen, die in Verbindung mit dem Protestpotential der Bevölkerung zum Einsatz kommen'.

This is the attack technique used in the cases just examined and known as Distributed Denial of Service (DDoS).[54] It corresponds to a traditional military attack, but does not take place in a declared war context and the hacker is not detectable.

Hacker groups such as the pro-Russian CyberBerkut are organised by intelligence services or government structures and can also carry out disinformation actions. In Crimea, a hundred people operated in the pro-Russian hacker group of the NewsFront news agency. Directly or by means of enslaved computers, this agency disseminated partly or completely false news, for instance, to stir up internal tensions (as in the case of the non-existent rape of a minor by German soldiers in Latvia) or to interfere in political life and especially in elections (as was the case in the United States during the election of Donald Trump).

A DDoS attack was launched against French candidate Emmanuel Macron (liberal and pro-European, therefore not liked by Russia), blocking his election campaign on the Internet in February 2017. The bombardment of messages from hundreds of thousands of enslaved computers prevents any contact between Macron and his voters. The Russian agencies RT and Sputnik News launch “fake news” about Macron, the most widespread of which describes him as a homosexual: on 4 February 2017, a campaign involving social networks, blogs and the online media is launched, until in approximately ten days, the debate shifts from the candidate’s non-existent homosexuality to the attempt to identify the person who put the fake news into circulation.

In Turkey, after the coup attempt on 15 July 2016, the enemy of President Recep Tayyip Erdoğan was the preacher Fethullah Gülen, at the head of an important political and religious movement.[55] In this struggle, a speech by Gülen was manipulated to attribute to Gülen an anti-Kurdish position that is alien to him.[56] The media and computer path of this manipulation offers a clear example of how fake news circulates, not least because Karakoyun’s volume reconstructs the chronological sequence of the news in detail. However, the reality was more complex than this linear sequence, because the individual sources often referred back to the news not immediately preceding it, or to several news items in no particular order, thus transforming the linear sequence into a complex network. A non-existent anti-Gülen attitude has thus been credited.[57]

---

[54] Meggiato (2016), pp. 123–140, explains ‘what a DDoS, the most classic of attacks used in cyberwar, consists of’. On Computer Networks Attack (CNA) and Computer Network Exploitation (CNE) in the US: Poindexter (2015), pp. 157–160.

[55] Karakoyun (2017), 224 pp.: an instructive read, bearing in mind, however, that Karakoyun is a representative of the Gülen movement in Germany.

[56] Cf. the chapter *Ins Gegenteil verkehrt: Gülen* Aufruf *zur Gewaltlosigkeit* [Transformed into its opposite: Gülen’s appeal against violence], in Karakoyun, *Die Gülen Bewegung*, cit., pp.

[57] The reconstruction of the circulation of the texts and the entire controversy is in Bultmann (2013), 105 pp. The second, expanded edition has a slightly different title: *Gut gefälscht. Zitatfälschung als Normalfall beim Nachrichtenmagazin “Der Spiegel” und für den Landtag von Baden-Württemberg*, Ulenspiegel-Verlag, Erfurt 2016, 205 pp.

The spread of fake news through numerous media and social networks makes it difficult to determine whether a piece of news is true or false. Since news agencies often take news from each other, the fact that several sources assert the same fact does not mean that that fact is true. Moreover, even when it is established that it is fake news, it has been stored by thousands of private users and continues to circulate, even if only to reaffirm that it is fake news.

Indeed, falsehood or slander continues to have an influence even after it has been proven to be unfounded. Psychologists are studying how to combat this persistence of the unmasked lie ("belief perseverance"[58]), but have not so far indicated how to get to the bottom of it. Beaumarchais' maxim in the "Barber of Seville" is thus confirmed: "Calomniez, calomniez; il en restera toujours quelque chose".

Thus, the final dilemma in the chain of disinformation arises: is it appropriate for the media to critically disseminate the news of the falsehood, or by doing so do they contribute to spreading it further? A similar debate had accompanied the Islamic State videos. In all these cases, a difficult choice has to be made: is the duty to inform (and the right to be informed) prevailing, or the duty not to contribute to the spread of the propaganda to be countered? As hybrid warfare aims to generate fear and disorientation, it can be said that it is also achieving its goal in the field of disinformation.

Since the new conflicts are less and less military and cyber attacks have even more devastating potential than hitherto known, it must be admitted that the cold war is back, albeit a hybrid one.

5 War or Neutrality? The Rapacki Plan of 1957

In 2025, the Russian-Ukrainian conflict enters its 4th year with an unsustainable balance for both sides, which cannot even be summarised here.[59]

Instead of continuing the "special military operation", the hybrid war, the non-war, would it not be more humane to think of "neutrality"? Already in the sixteenth century, Francesco Guicciardini suggested: "Neutrality in the wars of others be a laudable thing, and for which one flees many molestations and expenses".[60] In the case of Ukraine, however, possible neutrality is controversial because it would entail its obligation not to join NATO and thus would not guarantee its security against possible future attacks. Ukraine would become a state with limited sovereignty, guaranteed only by the treaty signed in this way: but unfortunately, we live in an era in which international treaties are not respected, the decisions of interna-

[58] Baumeister *et al.* (2007) under *Belief Perseverance*.

[59] Among the hundreds of titles listed by the Italian National Library System: *Il mondo cambia l'Ucraina: riscopriamo la diplomazia per pensare il dopoguerra e ricostruire un paese distrutto*, Gedi, Rome 2024, 275 pp. (corresponds to "Limes", no. 7, 2024); Alfieri and Barbieri (2022), XVI–208 pp.; Pubusa and Rossi (2022), 192 pp.

[60] Francesco Guicciardini, *La historia d'Italia*, lib. X, chap. VIII.

tional courts are disregarded by signatory states and individual states leave international organisations, which are thus progressively weakened:

> Even if Kiev received a security guarantee from NATO or an ad hoc coalition in the West, could it really count on the intervention of its allies in the event of further Russian aggression? The US foreign policy establishment likes to assume so. However, judging from the past three years, such confidence is unproven. The US, Germany, France, the UK and other NATO members have armed Ukraine to the teeth, but arming a country remotely to resist Russia is not the same as deploying your own troops and going to war on behalf of Ukraine. NATO has shown time and again that while it is willing to do the former, it has no intention of doing the latter.[61]

A direct intervention by a western state, moreover, could collide with its constitutional rules repudiating war: we need only recall the discussions that have arisen on the occasion of interventions in the Balkans or in the Middle East. But, above all, the current anti-institutional attitude of many states would not guarantee respect for neutrality (which obviously should not be unarmed neutrality).

The current neutrality proposal for Ukraine is reminiscent of the plan for the creation of a demilitarised and denuclearised area in the centre of Europe, presented on 2 October 1957 to the UN General Assembly by the then Polish Foreign Minister Adam Rapacki (1909–1970). It proposed the creation of a buffer zone consisting of the two Germanies, Poland and Czechoslovakia, wedged between the Soviet bloc and the Western European powers.[62] Even today, the analysis of both the debate on the Rapacki Plan and its failure can be instructive with respect to the complex situation in the European East today, with the problematic areas of Transnistria, Moldavia and Romania itself, so close to Ukraine.

References

Alfieri M, Barbieri F (eds) (2022) Ucraina 24.02.2022: l'invasione russa e le conseguenze della guerra in Europa. Il Sole-24 Ore, Milan

Amirante L (1970) Prigionia di guerra, riscatto e postliminium. Lectures. Jovene, Naples

Annati M, Scovazzi T (eds) (2012) Diritto internazionale e bombardamenti aerei. Università degli studi Milano Bicocca—Giuffrè, Milan

Baumeister RF et al (eds) (2007) Encyclopedia of social psychology. Sage Publications, Thousand Oaks

Bultmann C (2013) Gut gefälscht. Besichtigung einer Zitatfälschung im Nachrichtenmagazin 'Der Spiegel'. Ein Vademecum für den Deutschen Presserat. Ulenspiegel-Verlag

Cansacchi G (1957) Nozioni di diritto internazionale bellico, Third edition revised and updated. Giappichelli, Torino

---

[61] Daniel R. DePetris, *Why Neutrality is the Best Way Forward for Ukraine*, 10 January 2025 <https://italiaeilmondo.com/2025/01/15/perche-la-neutralita-e-la-strada-migliore-per-lucraina_di-daniel-r-depetris/>.

[62] In ascending chronological order: *Le Plan Rapacki: documents, declarations*, Warsaw 1962, 31 pp. (excerpt from No. 4 of "Perspectives polonaises"); Rapacki (1963), pp.; Stefancic (1987), pp. 401–412; Ozinga (1989), V–193 pp.; Wandycz (1994), pp. 289–318 (also: online resource).

Cavino M; Malvicini M (2023) Le guerre dell'Italia repubblicana. Il Mulino, Bologna
Chamamayou G (2014) Teoria del drone. Principi filosofici del diritto di uccidere. DeriveApprodi, Rome
Chamamayou G (2018) Robots y drones. In: Freedman L (ed) La guerra futura. El estudio sobre el pasado y el presente. Crítica, Barcelona
De Vergottini G (2004) Guerra e Costituzione. Nuovi conflitti e sfide alla democrazia. Il Mulino, Bologna
Di Donato M (2015) Hezbollah: Storia del Partito di Dio; introduction by Massimo Campanini. Mimesis, Milan
Dogliani M, Sicardi S (eds) (1999) Diritti umani e uso della forza. Profili di diritto costituzionale interno e internazionale. Profili di diritto costituzionale interno e internazionale. Giappichelli, Turin
Douhet G (2002) Il dominio dell'aria e altri scritti. Edited and with an introductory essay by Luciano Bozzo, Ufficio storico dell'Aeronautica militare, Rome
Dunant H (1863a) L'avvenire sanguinoso, Italian edition edited by Luigi Zanetti. Tipografia Guglielmini, Milan
Dunant H (1863b) Un ricordo di Solferino. In Dunant H (1863a)
Firpo L (ed) (1979) Henry Dunant e le origini della Croce Rossa. UTET, Turin
Gardner H (2015) Hybrid warfare: Iranian and Russian versions of 'Little Green Men' and contemporary conflict. NATO Defence College, Rome (online)
Gentile C (2024) Bambini all'inferno: da Gaza ai Territori occupati. Undici storie d'infanzia nel cuore di un conflitto che colpisce prima di tutto gli innocenti. Pages, Rome (first edition: Salani, Milan 2012)
Gerges FA (2011) The rise and fall of al-Qaeda. Oxford University Press, Oxford
Ginzburg N (1963) Lessico famigliare. Einaudi, Turin
Ginzburg N (2016) Le piccole virtù. Lessico famigliare. La Stampa, Turin
Hack M (2023) La strage dei bambini: giustizia per Gaza. EditorialeNovanta, Roma
Hofstetter Y (2016) Das Ende der Demokratie. Wie die künstliche Intelligenz die Politik übernimmt und uns entmündigt. Bertelsmann, München
Karakoyun E (2017) Die Gülen Bewegung. Was sie ist, was sie will. Herder, Freiburg i.B.
Labanca N (ed) (2024) Ostaggi della guerra: vittime civili civili del secondo conflitto mondiale. Viella, Rome
Losano MG (2008a) Le affinità elettive: geopolitica tedesca e italiana nei viaggi di Karl Haushofer. Limes. Rivista italiana di geopolitica 3:281–290
Losano MG (2008b) Tra storia e biografia: le frequentazioni italiane di Karl Haushofer. Limes. Rivista italiana di geopolitica 5:275–284
Losano MG (2009) Il testamento geopolitico di Haushofer. Limes. Rivista italiana di geopolitica 2:275–284
Losano MG (2011) La geopolitica del Novecento. Dai Grandi Spazi delle dittature alla decolonizzazione. Bruno Mondadori, Milan
Losano MG (2017a) La Rete e lo Stato Islamico. The Internet and women's rights in Islamic fundamentalism. Mimesis, Milan
Losano MG (2017b) The rejection of war in the post-war constitutions of Japan, Italy and Germany. In: Moita L, Pinto LV (eds) Espaços económicos e espaços de segurança. Observare Universidade Autónoma de Lisboa, Lisboa (in press)
Losano MG (2018) Hybrid wars, targeted killings, drones: conflicts without borders and without law. In: Forni L, Vettor T (eds) Security and freedom in times of global terrorism. Giappichelli, Turin 2017 [but 2018], pp 19–38
Losano MG (2020) The three Pacifist constitutions. The rejection of war in the constitutions of Japan, Italy and Germany. Max-Planck-Institut für Europäische Rechtsgeschichte, Frankfurt a.M.
Losano MG (2025) L'America latina e i primi trattati paritetici del Giappone moderno. I trattati con Perù, Messico e Brasile, 1873-1895. Accademia University Press, Turin

Meggiato R (2016) Cyberwar. Lo sapevi che un computer può uccidere? Preface by Raoul 'Nobody' Chiesa. Hoepli, Milan, pp 123–140
Gazzella Onlus (2009) I bambini di Gaza. Edizioni Q, Roma
Oshiro AH (2019) Japón no da dos oportunidades. Animal de Invierno, Lima
Ozinga JR (1989) The Rapacki Plan: the 1957 proposal to Denuclearize Central Europe, and an analysis of its rejection. McFarland, Jefferson
Pallieri GB (1954) Diritto bellico. CEDAM, Padua, XI–464 pp. (2nd edition. entirely revised)
Pelton RY (2007) Licensed to kill: hired guns in the war on terror. Three Rivers Press, New York
Pieri P (1962) Storia militare del Risorgimento. Einaudi, Turin
Poindexter DF (2013) The Chinese information war. Espionage, cyberwar, communications control and related threats to United States interests. McFarland, Jefferson
Poindexter DF (2015) The new cyberwar. Technology and the redefinition of warfare. McFarland, Jefferson
Pubusa F, Rossi C (2022) Ucraina, 2022: un'analisi storica giuridica e politica. Jovene, Naples
Rapacki A (1963) The Polish plan for a nuclear-free zone today. International Affairs
Righi S (2013) La città illuminata. L'intuizione di Giuseppe Colombo, la Edison e l'elettrificazione dell'Italia. Rizzoli, Milan
Romeo G (2021) Hybrid wars: the new faces of conflict. Preface by General Fabio Mini, Diana, Frattamaggiore
Serra E et al (1941) Dizionario di diritto internazionale bellico. Istituto per gli studi di politica internazionale, Milan
Stassi F (2024) Bebelplatz. Sellerio, Palermo
Stefancic D (1987) The Rapacki Plan: a case study of European diplomacy. East Eur Q 21(4):401–412
Vecchioni D (2024) Mercenari. Il mestiere della guerra dall'antica Grecia al Gruppo Wagner. Diarkos, Santarcangelo di Romagna
Vedovado G (1946) Diritto internazionale bellico. Tre studi: la legislazione tedesca nei territori occupati d'Occidente; la protezione internazionale dei monumenti storici contro le offese aeree; la punizione dei crimini di guerra. Sansoni, Firenze
Walker CF (2014) The Tupac Amaru rebellion. The Belknap Press of Harvard University Press, Cambridge
Wandycz P (1994) Adam Rapacki and the search for European security. In: Craig GA, Loewenheim FL (eds) The diplomats, 1939–79. Princeton University Press, Princeton, pp 289–318
Zanetti L (1863) Typography Guglielmini. Milan

Umberto Campagnolo, the European Society of Culture and the Atomic Threat: A Peace Proposal from Intellectuals During the Cold War

Fabio Guidali

1 Opening Remarks

After World War II, the role of writers, artists, scientists and scholars underwent a profound transformation. The rise of totalitarian regimes and the massification of society had challenged the traditional function of intellectuals as moral and cultural leaders. At the same time, global conflicts had heightened political consciousness, while the Cold War further polarised the intellectual world along ideological lines and around opposing visions of freedom, truth and progress (Scott-Smith and Krabbendam 2003; Mikkonen et al. 2018).[1] In this context, several intellectual associations, movements and events emerged, including the World Congress of Intellectuals for Peace organised in Wrocław, Poland, aligned with communist propaganda (Łaptos 1993), and the anti-communist Congress for Cultural Freedom (Stonor Saunders 1999; Scott-Smith 2002).

The Société européenne de culture (European Society of Culture, SEC), founded in 1950, was part of this broader intellectual ferment, but, unlike other organisations, did not aim to steer intellectuals politically (Jachec 2015). Its founder, the philosopher Umberto Campagnolo (1904–1976), was driven by a desire to address what was regarded as the "European problem", with the aim of safeguarding the

[1] Within the vast bibliography on the Cold War, we refer here to key works, such as Westad (2005); Gaddis (2007); Leffler and Westad (2010).

Translations from French are by the author.

F. Guidali (✉)
University of Milan, Milan, Italy
e-mail: fabio.guidali@unimi.it

G. Cavaggion (ed.), *The 'Pacifist Principle' in the Italian and Japanese Constitutions in the Wake of the War in Ukraine*,
https://doi.org/10.1007/978-3-032-23108-6_14

autonomy of culture from political interference and, as a result, fostering peace on the continent.

This chapter looks at Campagnolo's work and puts it in the framework of the SEC, which was joined by hundreds of intellectuals from all over Europe, regardless of their political beliefs. Campagnolo's thinking will be highlighted, along with his relationship to European federalism and the lack of connection between his association and the Partisans for Peace, to show the original perspective from which the Italian philosopher and the SEC viewed the pacifist question and the atomic threat in the early 1950s.

2 Campagnolo, Kelsen, the Crisis of the League of Nations and the Federalist Solution

Campagnolo (Guidali 2023) studied philosophy at the University of Padua, graduating in 1931. However, after refusing to join the National Fascist Party—which had become a requirement for anyone wishing to teach in schools—he decided to leave Italy, and moved to Switzerland at the end of 1933. In Geneva, a city that was the seat of the League of Nations during the interwar period and virtually the capital of Wilsonian internationalism, he met the jurist Hans Kelsen, also an expatriate, and became his student at the Institut de hautes études internationales (von Bernstorff 2010; Schuett 2021). The resulting decision to specialise in the philosophy of law for his doctorate was another significant turning point in his life.

Campagnolo's relationship with Kelsen was marked by deep respect, but he did not hesitate to express clear and well-argued disagreement with his mentor's ideas (Kelsen and Campagnolo 1999; Campagnolo 2010). Kelsen believed that supranational law was superior to national law and advocated a future federation of states; Campagnolo, on the other hand, believed that perpetual peace could never be achieved as long as sovereignty remained in the hands of states. Halfway through the 1930s, when the League of Nations system was definitively in crisis, Campagnolo argued, with remarkable realism, that sovereign states would never agree to abolish themselves. In his opinion, the supranational order that had emerged from World War I would never have ensured peace, because it was based on the legal sovereignty of individual states that were irreconcilable with each other, that is, on a mere balance of power (Campagnolo 1938a, b).

Campagnolo therefore advocated dismantling the system that had arisen from World War I: the protagonists should not be governments but other entities, which he identified as the peoples. Campagnolo's affinity with federalist thinking flowed from his natural attraction to the limitation of national sovereignty and the idea of creating a single state capable of nullifying the sovereignty of its components. Although the theme of peace was not explicitly mentioned in Campagnolo's writings, it emerged from beneath the veil of philosophical and legal issues and became increasingly urgent during World War II.

This took place at a time when Campagnolo's personal situation had also changed after the outbreak of the conflict. Returning to Italy in 1940 so as not to evade possible general mobilisation, Campagnolo first collaborated with the Olivetti family in Ivrea (Guidali 2023, pp. 41–50), then, in 1943, he began teaching the history of political doctrines at the University of Padua, continuing to develop his ideas in an original way. He could be counted among federalist authors, although not labelled politically as a liberal or a socialist, as can be deduced from his book *Repubblica federale europea* (European Federal Republic), published at the end of the war (Campagnolo 1945).

Campagnolo was convinced that states would never accept limitations to their sovereignty and argued that diplomatic efforts were futile unless peoples themselves desired national unification—an aim he saw as the only way to prevent future wars. He envisaged treaties between governments being replaced by representatives of the peoples adhering directly to the federation. Secondly, his emphasis on the complete transfer of sovereignty to a federal entity implied the cooperation of all the continent's peoples, including the British and the Soviets. Thirdly, Campagnolo was persuaded that cultural activity should be directed towards stimulating the necessary awareness and participation among the masses, to be achieved through non-ideological cultural work. Political parties should only serve to channel the will of the people and initiate a European constituent process at the service of the masses.

Campagnolo was actively involved in the Movimento federalista europeo (European federalist movement, MFE), an Italian anti-fascist political group that aimed to unify the continent (Preda 1995; Pistone 2013), becoming its national secretary for a few months between 1946 and 1947 (Guidali 2023, pp. 75–92). Nevertheless, his positions differed markedly from those of Altiero Spinelli (Spinelli 1988; Graglia 2020)—the movement's leader and one of the authors of the celebrated *Ventotene Manifesto*—whose vision ultimately prevailed (Spinelli and Rossi 2017; Lacchè 2021). Campagnolo's line appeared utopian compared with Spinelli's more pragmatic approach; while Spinelli refused to abandon an institutional project based on relations between states, Campagnolo imagined a broader union that included the Russian people—an idea that the Cold War soon rendered unfeasible.[2]

3 The Birth of the SEC and the "European Spirit"

At that point, once his militant commitment to the MFE waned, Campagnolo concentrated on a project he had previously fielded in September 1946 (Benda et al. 1947, pp. 343–348), namely the creation of an intellectual association. This plan

[2] For the geopolitical and cultural situation in Europe after World War II, see Mazower (1999); Judt (2010); Gilbert (2015); Jarausch (2015), pp. 399–584.

aligned with his goal of raising awareness of the need to transform the legal structure of European society through culture. In his view, only intellectuals were capable of grasping the underlying unity of culture, therefore it was essential to guarantee their autonomy from politics that continued to uphold the old system of state power and its legal structures. This would allow intellectuals to reveal beneath the surface of nationalism and state egoism the matrix that bound the European peoples together.

Once again, the goal of peace was not explicitly mentioned, but was implied when Campagnolo defended the "European spirit" as "the essential reason for European civilisation, that is, the measure by which its scale of values is constructed, the criterion by which the works and actions of European man and their very principles are judged" (Campagnolo 1950a, b, p. 24). In order to be defended, the "European spirit" required peace. In fact, Campagnolo combined his idea of legal change led by peoples seeking peace with the conviction, reiterated a few years later, that "a truly peaceful movement must [...] be popular: it cannot be promoted or directed by states or governments, nor by organisations that are in any way dependent on them, but by free associations" (Campagnolo 1950a, b, p. 43), such as the SEC, in his opinion. Campagnolo's pacifism was not merely opposition to war, but was part of a structural rethinking of the relationship between culture, law and power.

However, it was not until 1948 that he was able to put his innovative idea into practice. He secured funding and indirect support from the Italian government (though the SEC always remained independent), thanks to the mediation of Giovanni Ponti, then Special Commissioner of the Venice Biennale. After some delays, the SEC's founding meeting was held in Venice between 28 May and 1 June 1950—just days before the Korean War broke out—with the aim of establishing intellectuals as the driving force behind a peaceful and culturally united Europe (Guidali 2023, pp. 141–155).

The SEC had already begun attracting members—mainly Italian, French and Swiss—who represented a variety of political ideas. The association did not seek to compete with the party affiliations of intellectuals, and thus could promote the possibility of coexistence within a single cultural institution (Campagnolo 1950b). According to Campagnolo, this was possible because an intellectual's primary concern should be the conditions that allow culture to flourish, while political or ideological convictions must always remain secondary. He referred in particular to the concept of the "auto-disposition" of culture, that is, the right and duty of culture to regulate itself autonomously. This implies a refusal to adapt one's work to external demands, even when the intellectual in question had chosen to join a party, which remained their legitimate right.[3]

In line with this approach, Campagnolo was open to progressive intellectuals and made early efforts to recruit influential Italian communist scholars—such as Umberto Terracini and Antonio Banfi—to the SEC, although they only became

[3] Première séance tenue au Palais des doges Salle du Piovego le 29 mai à 9 h. 30. Comprendre 2, 1950: 29.

involved at a later date. In Campagnolo's view, the presence within the association of members with ideas that are even opposed to each other could be achieved by focusing on individuals' pre-political dispositions and their desire to "save, in the current crisis in Europe, the conditions necessary for the development of that universal culture which is the raison d'être of our civilisation".[4] The SEC's objective was defined as "safeguarding the possibility of a dialogue, so essential among men of culture, that is threatened by the frustration of political struggles that are tending to divide Europe into two camps increasingly closed to one another" (Campagnolo 1950b, p. 9). For this reason, according to Campagnolo, inspiration came from the growing awareness that "at the heart of the current crisis in Europe lies the problem of its unity, that is, the elimination of the divisions that fragment it into pieces" (Campagnolo 1950b, p. 13). Peace, then, may have been at the origin of the SEC project, but it was a precondition rather than an explicit aim, a prerequisite for resuming dialogue, with the real focus placed on the cultural and legal reconstruction of Europe.

4 The SEC's Relationship with the Partisans for Peace

The fact that peace was a secondary objective is one reason why the SEC cannot be confused with pacifist movements, but it is not the only one.[5] Another reason was its relationship with organisations that declared themselves pacifist, at least on paper, as became apparent during the first ordinary general assembly in November 1951. On that occasion, the painter Gabriele Mucchi, a Communist activist, complained that the SEC had not yet expressed a clear position "on the problems of East-West relations, the possibility of peaceful coexistence and cooperation between peoples".[6] Mucchi used expressions adopted by pro-Soviet propaganda, such as "peaceful coexistence", which was quite different from mere neutralism; he cited the World Peace Council—the Partisans for Peace movement—which had been founded in 1949 shortly after the signing of the North Atlantic Treaty had prompted the Cominform (Information Bureau of the Communist and Workers' Parties) to focus on the struggle for peace. In particular, the Stockholm Appeal against atomic weapons (Holloway 1994) initiated by the Partisans for Peace was gaining widespread support in civil society (Guiso 2007; Cerrai 2011); the collection of signatures had accelerated sharply after the outbreak of the Korean War, because, faced with the danger of the conflict becoming global, the mobilisation for peace went beyond the limits of Communist support for the first time since World War II (Gozzini and Martinelli 1998, pp. 166–184).

[4] Projet des Statuts de la Société européenne de culture. Comprendre, 1, 1950: 50, 52.

[5] For an overview, see Ziemann (2008) and, specifically on Italy, Martellini (2006).

[6] Deuxième séance tenue en la salle de l'Ateneo Veneto le 9 novembre - matin, Comprendre 5–6: 41.

Although the Partisans for Peace achieved significant results, it would be inaccurate to describe it as a genuinely pacifist movement. Its campaigns, unbeknownst to many of its members, leveraged popular support for peace to advance specific foreign policy objectives, namely détente between the blocs, which served to strengthen Soviet influence in Eastern Europe. Furthermore, according to the classification proposed by April Carter, two essential elements were missing in order to speak of pacifism, namely independence from parties or governments ("non-alignment") and the rejection of violent or destructive methods of protest (Carter 1992). In fact, the Partisans for Peace did not deny the use of armed violence in certain situations and did not oppose the Soviet Union when the atomic balance was finally achieved.

In early 1950, Campagnolo had already privately expressed to Umberto Terracini—an influential figure in the Italian Communist Party—his opposition to the nascent SEC declaring its sympathy for the Partisans for Peace. He believed that each member of the association should remain free to adopt whatever political stance they wished (Guidali 2023, pp. 119–122). The role of the SEC was not to take collective political positions, but rather to overcome the kind of individualism among intellectuals that, in Campagnolo's view, rendered them subservient to political power.[7] When Mucchi asked him to officially express his sympathy for the Partisans for Peace, which he did publicly almost two years after Terracini had made the same request privately, Campagnolo responded in the only way he could: the SEC could not endorse a specific political line, since it operated on a pre-political level. Furthermore, in his report at the beginning of the SEC general assembly in November 1951, Campagnolo stated that "the word 'peace' for the Partisans for Peace claims to embrace the idea of peace in general, peace-tranquillity, peace-rest, whereas in reality, given the political nature of this organisation, it aims at a particular international balance. [...] It is a trap that must be avoided".[8] Finally, Campagnolo could not support a vision of peace based on international equilibrium achieved through traditional political treaties since he firmly rejected the notion, as previously discussed. His response to the Communist appeals, in fact, stemmed from a deep intellectual conviction that dated back to before the outbreak of World War II.

Nevertheless, Campagnolo was not criticising the World Peace Council: rather, his aim was to involve Communist representatives in the SEC to foster a genuine dialogue between intellectuals with differing political positions. This goal began to materialise shortly thereafter, following a statement by the association (Jachec 2011) affirming its commitment to culture and open dialogue and rejecting the logic of mutual exclusion that characterised the Cold War—without explicitly mentioning peace. Campagnolo stated, "Our society was founded to pursue a struggle aimed at

---

[7] Extraits des procès-verbaux des séances organisées par le centre français et tenues à Paris en la salle des commissions de la Direction générale des arts et des lettres. Du 29 juin au 1er juillet 1951. Comprendre, 4, 1951: 15.

[8] Débats de la première Assemblée générale ordinaire de la Société européenne de culture, Venise 8–11 novembre 1951. Comprendre, 5–6, 1952: 49.

ensuring the autonomy of culture, and only indirectly addresses the issue of war and peace, in that its solution is a necessary condition for the autonomy of culture".[9]

5 The SEC and the Atomic Threat

At this point, the organisational and theoretical construction of the SEC became increasingly entangled with the issue of peace. Yet peace was never addressed as a topic in its own right, either during the association's meetings during those years, nor in Campagnolo's writings. This omission reflected a mature awareness that such a complex issue could not be reduced to slogans or abstract positions. Before speaking of peace, it was necessary to redefine the role of the intellectual and to safeguard the autonomy of culture. Only within such a framework could peaceful coexistence be achieved—on a continent finally united, first and foremost, from a legal point of view.

This is why the second issue of the SEC journal *Comprendre* is so significant. Published in October 1950, it included a monographic section entitled *Enquête sur la responsabilité dans la construction et l'usage de la bombe atomique* (Investigation into responsibility for the construction and use of the atomic bomb). It was preceded by a brief unsigned introduction (undoubtedly written by Campagnolo), which insisted that the SEC could never commit itself to a collective political statement, but that its aim was to encourage discussion among intellectuals, giving them a platform for exchange that was sufficiently independent from politics to guarantee an authentic dialogue.[10] The authors who agreed to contribute essays to this survey came from different cultural backgrounds and were clearly interested in current affairs. They were presented in *Comprendre* in strict alphabetical order, although this did not hide the prevalence of progressive authors. This was not Campagnolo's choice: the invitation had been extended to a much larger number of members, but only a few had accepted.

It is evident that the SEC did not intend to settle the question of intellectuals' responsibility in the face of atomic weapons, nor to frame it in categorical terms. The debate in the journal did not seek to compare contrasting positions, but merely to establish a common starting point. On the other hand, the issue was already widely discussed at the time: for existentialists, in particular, reflection on nuclear weapons was central (van Munster 2023; Bousquet 2024), and the world of culture in general had not remained silent faced with what was immediately seen as a break in the history of humanity.[11] The debate in *Comprendre* was therefore just a frag-

[9] Extraits des procès-verbaux des séances du Conseil exécutif tenues à Paris en la salle des Commissions de la Direction générale des arts et des lettres du 5 au 7 janvier 1952. Comprendre, 5–6, 1952: 101.

[10] Avant-propos. Comprendre, 2, 1950: 5.

[11] Consider for instance Andren (2022). For a vast though non-comprehensive bibliography, see https://ahf.nuclearmuseum.org/ahf/history/debate-over-bomb-annotated-bibliography/ (accessed

ment of a wider conversation, but Campagnolo's goal went beyond the nuclear issue: his aim was to encourage SEC members not to withdraw from contemporary society, but to engage with it critically. Political positions—diverse, yet all legitimate within the SEC—were secondary to the emergence of a shared understanding of the core values to be defended. The nuclear question thus served more as a catalyst than as the central focus of discussion.

The Swiss Hellenist André Bonnard praised Communist society and the supposed fraternity that existed within it. In the Soviet Union, he wrote, one could witness "science fertilised by brotherhood" (Bonnard 1950, p. 87). He spoke of the need to conduct science in a moral manner, but also of the need to take responsibility for the lack of conscience in others, and therefore openly supported the Partisans for Peace (already largely superseded by the SEC, as we have seen, thought its members were free to join it). Theodor Brugsch, an influential doctor from East Berlin, proposed an "absolute cultural veto" on the use of atomic weapons on civilian populations, but as a scientist, he distinguished between the military and peaceful uses of atomic energy (Brugsch 1950). The Australian archaeologist Vere Gordon Childe acknowledged the relative and transitory nature of the values and integrative processes produced by European culture. Yet he identified the atomic bomb as a turning point—a rupture so profound that war, which had been a driver of technological progress throughout history, now threatened the survival of the human species. For this reason, he regarded the Stockholm Appeal by the Partisans for Peace, however politically problematic, as a legitimate attempt to express the widespread desire for peace and compel governments to listen (Childe 1950).

These initial three essays were followed by one from Karl Jaspers, who would later break with the SEC due to his connections with the pro-Atlantic Congress for Cultural Freedom (Jachec 2011; Guidali 2022). The German philosopher reflected on the qualitative and not just quantitative significance of the atomic bomb. In his view, "From the point of view of quality, it is equally despicable to torture an individual to death or to inflict this fate on millions of human beings", as happened in Hiroshima and Nagasaki (Jaspers 1950a, p. 103). Jaspers' focus, therefore, was on conscience, with his famous distinction between criminal, political, moral and metaphysical guilt (Jaspers 1946). He emphasised that, even in an era of technology and large-scale destruction, every individual remains responsible for the world they help to build or destroy.[12] The theme of responsibility was also central to the Swiss biologist Adolf Portmann, for whom, in a scientific landscape where individual researchers increasingly work in collaboration with others, responsibility is by its nature social and collective (Portmann 1950).

The political economist Sergei Prokopovich (writing under the francized name Serge N. Prokopovicz), a Marxist and social democrat who had been exiled from the Soviet Union for over 30 years, retraced the various attempts and peace conferences

30 May 2025). To contextualise the dropping of the atomic bomb, see Overy (2025). For discussions about the bomb see Rotter (2008); Rubinson (2016).

[12] See also Jaspers (1950b), p. 375. His most definitive statement on nuclear war is seen in Jaspers (1958).

over the recent past to conclude that humanity was incapable of putting an end to the horrors of war (as had been most recently demonstrated by the atomic bomb). Thus, he argued that the only solution was the resistance of the civilian population, for which mass humanitarian education was necessary (Prokopovicz 1950). The Czechoslovak Marxist philosopher Ladislav Rieger openly attacked capitalism, calling it a sorcerer's apprentice no longer able to control the forces it had summoned. According to the classic Leninist interpretation, he believed that wars were not accidental events but stemmed from the essence of modern capitalism, which had become imperialist in its final phase. This view inevitably led to a call for a profound change in the political and economic order, capable of breaking the warlike dynamics inherent in the capitalist system at their roots (Rieger 1950).

Before the final contribution by Jean Wahl, another progressive philosopher (Wahl 1950), the French legal scholar Georges Scelle expressed a different perspective. He advocated for a federalist solution as the only salvation against the arbitrariness of centralism and emphasised that, while men of culture bore a general responsibility, science and discovery could not be constrained. At the same time, he maintained that it was the duty of politicians to establish the necessary rules (Scelle 1950).

The *Comprendre* essays, although politically diverse, showed that their authors all shared a keen awareness of the intellectual's role in public life, typical of the post-war period, and of their direct or indirect responsibility for the use of atomic weapons. Less evident, however, was the question of peace and pacifism, a knot that was impossible to untangle: while it was easy to declare oneself against the atomic bomb, it was paradoxically much more difficult to declare oneself in favour of peace, especially while the Cold War was at its height. "Traditional" pacifism could be associated with neutralism, which the SEC had rejected from a political point of view (Guidali 2023, p. 161), since it was seen in the West as playing into Soviet hands. Furthermore, the point was to define how peace could be not only the absence of war, but also a redefinition of world order—an issue that required a purely political discussion that many preferred to avoid. In any case, Campagnolo, well aware of these complexities, sought to initiate a dialogue rather than offer definitive answers: for him, peace was only one piece of the larger puzzle he was trying to assemble.

6 "Politics of Culture" as Politics of Peace: An Indirect Outcome

The history of the SEC is complex, marked by evolving needs, moments of rupture and difficulty, and diverse national perspectives.[13] In this context, it is worth noting how Campagnolo, who consistently led the association with determination, developed his thinking in continuity with his earlier reflections. He demonstrated not

[13] At present, the only national milieu studied is the German one (Guidali 2022).

only coherence and imagination, but also a keen awareness of the pressing issues of the time and the profound complexity of the issue of peace.

Campagnolo placed dialogue at the centre of his philosophy. He believed that, at that moment in history, "The dilemma is clear: either talk to each other or kill each other. Dialogue is a source of knowledge, understanding and therefore peace". For him, however, dialogue was not merely an exchange of views, but rested on a moral foundation, namely respect for the human person—a value explicitly rooted in Christianity (though not in a dogmatic sense). He believed that this principle was broadly acceptable, as "none of the political or ideological trends currently present are considering challenging" it. Dialogue "implies a common spiritual reality, that unity in diversity which is the very essence of humanity": not, therefore, peace as the mere absence of war or as a balance between states, but as a relational condition, based on the mutual recognition of human dignity, and in this case of fellow intellectuals. For Campagnolo, only this authentic dialogue, rooted in a common spiritual reality, could constitute the true foundation of lasting peace: not a compromise between powers, but a moral commitment between consciences,[14] as he had made clear at the 1951 SEC assembly.

Campagnolo continued to explore this issue throughout the 1950s and early 1960s with increasing intellectual rigour. In his words, dialogue is based on "the notion of the unity of man, regardless of his particular conditions of existence, his personal or ethnic situation" (Campagnolo 1952, p. 152), and this was clearly a concept of philosophical origin. When contextualised within the Cold War and the broader search for dialogue between the opposing blocs—an effort also pursued at the time by Norberto Bobbio, also an active member of the SEC (Bobbio 1955)—it becomes clear why Campagnolo assigned such a crucial role to dialogue, which he did not see as a mere exchange of opinions or a form of intellectual courtesy, but an exercise in profound responsibility: "This is not just any dialogue that touches on abstract theories, but one that engages the moral and political conscience of the participants, compelling them, if necessary, to change their convictions and attitudes" (Campagnolo 1955, p. 235). It was therefore a transformative practice and a historical creation, since he defined it as "the instrument that human reason invents and constructs to solve the problems that present themselves to humanity, either as a whole or within the groups that constitute it at certain moments in history".[15] In this sense, if tolerance merely "appeals to a sense of indulgence towards human weakness", dialogue, understood as respect for differences, "implies that opposing opinions contain a positive element for historical development" (Campagnolo 1955, pp. 234–235), that is, they have at their core a set of values that can be traced back to a common interest in humanity and culture.

Campagnolo defined this solution as "politics of culture" ("politique de la culture" in the original French)—a concept extensively elaborated in the early years of

[14] Rapport du Secrétaire général, M. Umberto Campagnolo. Vers une prise de conscience du rôle politique de la culture. Comprendre, 5–6, 1952: 29–30.

[15] Neuvième assemblée générale ordinaire. Tenue à Rome au Palais du Banco di Roma, du 10 au 12 octobre 1963. Comprendre, 26–27, 1964: 279.

the SEC, with Bobbio's support (Bobbio 1952, 1955, pp. 61–74). This "politics of culture" was not to be confused with cultural policy, that is, the planning of culture by political authorities, nor with the mere promotion of the free circulation of cultural products. Rather, it referred to action aimed at defending the conditions necessary for the existence and development of culture. The "politics of culture" was conceived as the search for shared values and positions in order to restore to culture its vital function of understanding and synthesis—one which intellectuals committed themselves to and which served society as a whole. Indeed, Campagnolo wrote that, "The aim of this policy is to contribute to creating the conditions necessary for the full development of human creativity. It affirms the autonomy of culture against conformism, totalitarianism, moralism, opportunism and all other *-isms* that a society in crisis can invent" (Campagnolo 1957). This was the only way that culture could "continue this dialectical development thanks to which society progresses and civilisation is able to create" (Campagnolo 1952, p. 152).

The "politics of culture", therefore, should not be confused with pacifism. In fact, it "is not based on hypothetical goodwill and does not appeal to ideals of equality and brotherhood among men"; the "politics of culture" does not naively believe that it can "create a climate favourable to peace", but rather "is based on a calculation of forces, on the assessment of trends, pressing demands and incoercible aspirations" (Campagnolo 1962–1963, pp. 84–85). Campagnolo's assertions were a continuation of his legal thinking, according to which "peace and war are merely two methods of struggle, almost two modes of war", as he repeated again in the early 1960s; in fact, states establish relationships through agreements, which are the precondition for peace, but peace endures only as long as those agreements hold (Campagnolo 1962–1963, pp. 67–68). A change in international structures was urgently needed, a principle he had long upheld: based on relations between peoples founded on law, not relations of power.

In this context, according to Campagnolo, atomic weapons had clarified that the existing system of nation-states was incapable of guaranteeing genuine peace (Campagnolo 1968, p. 93). By contrast, the "politics of culture", grounded in rational and relational dialectics, could serve as a safeguard against war (Campagnolo 1955, p. 240). Philosophically, this approach implied an aspiration not merely to unity, but to universality. It was for this reason that, from the early 1950s onwards, Campagnolo began to articulate a new concept: the "civilisation of the universal" ("civilisation de l'universel"), understood as a civilisation of progress that actively seeks connection and dialogue with all other civilisations (Campagnolo 1953).[16]

[16] On the problematic nature of this concept, see mainly Jachec (2015), pp. 146–176; Guidali (2023), pp. 171–202.

7 Conclusion: Unrecognised but Necessary Efforts

With the benefit of hindsight, Campagnolo's vision may appear naively optimistic or even unrealistic. Yet, at the time, his thinking possessed undeniable strength. Many of his insights—particularly those concerning the value of dialogue and the profound meaning of the "politics of culture"—remain surprisingly relevant. The real issue lies in how distant such reflections seem from the dominant concerns and sensibilities of today's intellectual and public discourse.

Over the course of its first decade, the SEC grew to encompass around 1200 members (though not all of them still active), representing the elite of European intellectual life. This does not mean, however, that all of them closely followed Campagnolo's ideas or fully endorsed his vision. Some joined for reasons of prestige; others (particularly the Communists in the early years) with the aim of exploiting the association; others simply out of a herd mentality. Yet many genuinely saw the SEC as a meaningful forum for discussion and embraced the dialogue it promoted. Campagnolo had succeeded in building a significant international network, even extending beyond Europe. For this reason, despite never working directly in the field of peace, he was nominated several times for the Nobel Peace Prize, starting in 1960 following a recommendation from Albert Schweitzer, himself a recipient of the prize and a fellow member of the SEC.

Campagnolo could count on the fact that the SEC and its "politics of culture" had managed to build bridges between intellectuals with different ideologies and backgrounds at the height of the Cold War. This was achieved through discussions of principle that helped to reawaken a sense of responsibility among writers, scholars and artists regarding the role of culture. Not a party or a movement, but a moral force; not a rhetorical appeal to harmony, but a demanding exercise in critical self-awareness and a willingness to question one's own convictions and acknowledge the reasons of one's opponents.

In light of these considerations, and although the SEC lost momentum as the international context and the cultural landscape evolved, Campagnolo believed that the Cold War and even the advent of the atomic age should be seen primarily as symbols of a deeper, unresolved issue: the sovereignty of nation-states. From the 1960s onwards, both his attention and that of the SEC increasingly shifted towards the theme of human rights (Campagnolo 1968), in the awareness that culture implied not only a political responsibility, but also the material capacity for intellectuals to influence reality. This conception of culture—not as erudition, but as a method—undoubtedly remains his most significant legacy.

References

Andren M (2022) Atomic war or world peace order? Karl Jaspers, Denis de Rougemont, Bertrand Russell. Global Intellect Hist 7(4):784–800. https://doi.org/10.1080/23801883.2020.1830494

Benda J et al (1947) L'esprit européen. Textes in-extenso des conférences et des entretiens organisés par les Rencontres internationales de Genève 1946. Éditions de la Baconnière, Neuchâtel

Bobbio N (1952) Politica culturale e politica della cultura. Rivista di filosofia 43(1):61–74
Bobbio N (1955) Politica e cultura. Einaudi, Turin
Bonnard A (1950) Les universités et la paix. Comprendre 2:80–88
Bousquet A (2024) Nuclear existentialism: on the philosophical response to life and death under the bomb. Rev Int Stud. https://doi.org/10.1017/S0260210524000512
Brugsch T (1950) Notre responsabilité envers l'emploi de l'énergie atomique à des fins pacifiques et belliqueuses. Comprendre 2:89–97
Campagnolo U (1938a) Nations et droit. Le développement du droit international entendu comme développement de l'État. Alcan, Paris
Campagnolo U (1938b) La paix, la guerre et le droit. Revue générale de droit international publique 45:436–456
Campagnolo U (1945) Repubblica federale europea. Unificazione giuridica dell'Europa. L'Europa Unita, Milan 1945 (republished with an introduction by Cedroni L in 2004, Rubbettino, Soveria Mannelli)
Campagnolo U (1950a) Introduzione. In: Benda J et al (eds) Spirito europeo. Edizioni di Comunità, Milan
Campagnolo U (1950b) Origines de la Société européenne de culture. Comprendre 1(1):11–12
Campagnolo U (1952) La civilisation du dialogue. Comprendre 5–6:147–153
Campagnolo U (1953) Responsabilités européennes. Comprendre 9:78–83
Campagnolo U (1955) Rapport du secrétaire général, M. Umberto Campagnolo. Le devoir politique de l'homme de culture. Comprendre 13–14:231–240
Campagnolo U (1957) Essence de la culture. Comprendre 17–18:308–309
Campagnolo U (1962–1963) Guerre froide, désarmement et politique de la culture. Comprendre 25:65–85
Campagnolo U (1968) La paix, une idée révolutionnaire. L'O.N.U. et le Congrès mondial des peuples. Comprendre 31–32:90–118
Campagnolo U (2010) Conversazioni con Hans Kelsen. Documenti dell'esilio ginevrino 1933-1940. Edited by MG Losano. Giuffrè, Milan
Carter A (1992) Peace movements. International protest and world politics since 1947. Longman, London-New York
Cerrai S (2011) I partigiani della pace in Italia. Tra utopia e sogno egemonico. Libreriauniversitaria edizioni, Padua
Childe G (1950) La fin de la culture? Comprendre 2:98–101
Gaddis JL (2007) The Cold War: a new history. Penguin Books, London
Gilbert M (2015) Cold War Europe: the politics of a contested continent. Rowman & Littlefield, Lanham
Gozzini G, Martinelli R (1998) Storia del Partito Comunista Italiano. Dall'attentato a Togliatti all'VIII congresso. Einaudi, Turin
Graglia PS (2020) Altiero Spinelli. il Mulino 6:994–1000
Guidali F (2022) Kultur and its Ambiguities: West German Intellectuals and the Société Européenne de Culture in the early 1950s. Contemp Eur Hist 32(3):327–338. https://doi.org/10.1017/S0960777321000552
Guidali F (2023) Un intellettuale europeo. Umberto Campagnolo tra antifascismo e guerra fredda. Pacini, Ospedaletto-Pisa
Guiso A (2007) La colomba e la spada. "Lotta per la pace" e antiamericanismo nella politica del Partito comunista italiano (1949-1954). Rubbettino, Soveria Mannelli
Holloway D (1994) Stalin and the Bomb: The Soviet Union and Atomic Energy, 1939–1956. Yale University Press, New Haven
Jachec N (2011) The Adresse aux Intellectuels de l'Europe et du Monde (1952) and its Aftermath: Some Comparative Perspectives on the Intelligentsia's Response to the Partitioning of Europe. In: Feldner H, Gorrara C, Passmore K (eds) The lost decade? The 1950s in European history, politics, society and culture. Cambridge Scholars Press, Newcastle upon Tyne, pp 84–100
Jachec N (2015) Europe's intellectuals and the Cold War. The European society of culture, post-war politics and international relations. I. B. Tauris, London-New York

Jarausch KH (2015) Out of Ashes: a new history of Europe in the twentieth century. Princeton University Press, Princeton
Jaspers K (1946) Die Schuldfrage. Lambert Schneider, Heidelberg
Jaspers K (1950a) La conscience devant la menace de la bombe atomique. Comprendre 2:102–106
Jaspers K (1950b) Das Gewissen vor der Bedrohung durch die Atombombe, in Rechenschaft und Ausblick: Reden und Aufsätze. R. Piper & Co. Verlag, Munich
Jaspers K (1958) Die Atombombe und die Zukunft der Menschheit. R. Piper & Co., Munich, translation The Atom Bomb and the Future of Man, University of Chicago Press, Chicago 1963
Judt T (2010) Postwar: a history of Europe since 1945. Vintage, London
Kelsen H, Campagnolo U (1999) Diritto internazionale e Stato sovrano. Con un inedito di Hans Kelsen e un saggio di Norberto Bobbio. Edited by MG Losano. Giuffrè, Milan
Lacchè L (2021) Agli albori dell'Europa libera e unita. Per gli ottant'anni del Manifesto di Ventotene (1941-2021). Quaderni costituzionali 41(4):987–997
Łaptos J (1993) Le pacifisme apprivoisé: le Congrès mondial des intellectuels pour la Défense de la Paix à Wroclaw en 1948. In: Vaïsse M (ed) Le Pacifisme en Europe des années 1920 aux années 1950. Bruxelles, Bruylant, pp 325–338
Leffler MP, Westad OA (eds) (2010) The Cambridge history of the Cold War. Vol. 1. Origins. Cambridge University Press, Cambridge
Martellini A (2006) Fiori nei cannoni. Nonviolenza e antimilitarismo nell'Italia del Novecento. Donzelli, Rome
Mazower M (1999) Dark Continent: Europe's twentieth century. Penguin Books, London
Mikkonen et al (eds) (2018) Entangled East and West. Cultural diplomacy and artistic interaction during the Cold War. De Gruyter Oldenbourg, Munich-Vienna
Overy R (2025) Rain of Ruin. Tokyo, Hiroshima, and the Surrender of Japan. WW. Norton, New York
Pistone S (2013) Settant'anni di vita del Movimento federalista europeo (1943-2013). Il Federalista 40:2–3. https://www.thefederalist.eu/site/index.php/it/saggi/1404-settantanni-di-vita-del-movimento-federalista-europeo-1943-2013. Accessed 28 May 2025
Portmann A (1950) Le problème de la responsabilité. Comprendre 2:107–112
Preda D (1995) Declino e rilancio del MFE tra fine della guerra e Piano Marshall. In: Dumoulin M (ed) Plans des temps de guerre pour l'Europe d'après-guerre 1940-1947/Wartime Plans for Postwar Europe 1940-1947. Bruylant, Bruxelles-Milan-Paris-Baden Baden, pp 489–525
Prokopovicz SN (1950) Les dangers de la bombe atomique sous l'angle social et culturel. Comprendre 2:113–122
Rieger L (1950) La situation actuelle, la responsabilité et le futur de l'humanité. Comprendre 2:123–130
Rotter AJ (2008) Hiroshima: The World's Bomb. Oxford University Press, Oxford
Rubinson P (2016) Redefining science: scientists, the national security state, and nuclear weapons in Cold War America. University of Massachusetts Press, Amherst
Scelle G (1950) Responsabilité éventuelle des hommes dans l'invention et l'utilisation des moyens de destruction massive et de la bombe atomique en particulier. Comprendre 2:131–139
Schuett R (2021) Hans Kelsen's political realism. Edinburgh University Press, Edinburgh
Scott-Smith G (2002) The politics of apolitical culture. The congress for cultural freedom, the CIA, and postwar American hegemony. Routledge, London
Scott-Smith G, Krabbendam H (eds) (2003) The Cultural Cold War in Western Europe, 1945–1960. Cass, London-Portland, OR
Spinelli A (1988) Come ho tentato di diventare saggio. il Mulino, Bologna
Spinelli A, Rossi E (2017) Il Manifesto di Ventotene. Foreword by Colorni E. Facsimile edition edited by Pistone S with an essay by Bobbio N. CELID, Turin
Stonor Saunders F (1999) Who paid the Piper? The CIA and the Cultural Cold War. Granta, London
van Munster R (2023) Nuclear weapons, existentialism, and international relations: Anders, Ballard, and the human condition in the age of extinction. Rev Int Stud 49(5):813–831

von Bernstorff J (2010) The public international law theory of Hans Kelsen: believing in universal law. Cambridge University Press, Cambridge
Wahl J (1950) La bombe atomique, situation limite? Comprendre 2:140–142
Westad OA (2005) The Global Cold War: third world interventions and the making of our times. Cambridge University Press, Cambridge
Ziemann B (ed) (2008) Peace movements in Western Europe, Japan and the USA during the Cold War. Klartext, Essen

War and Peace in Poland's Constitutional Framework: Past and Present

Piotr Podemski

The purpose of this paper is to present the issue of war and peace as addressed in the Polish Constitution, i.e., the Constitution of the Republic of Poland (Third Republic), of 2 April 1997.[1]

Firstly, the provisions of the current Constitution—which vest the principal authority in this regard in the Sejm (historically also referred to in English as the Seym or the Diet)—will be analysed within the broader context of Polish constitutional traditions, ranging from the so-called *nobles' democracy* of the 16th–18th centuries, through the partition era of foreign domination (1795–1918), to the constitutions of twentieth-century Polish statehood, both sovereign and non-sovereign.

Secondly, the analysis of the contemporary Polish Constitution will not be limited to the conditions governing the decision to declare a state of war or peace but will also extend to the legal consequences thereof, including the states of emergency, the restrictions of civil liberties and human rights, and the principles governing the deployment of Polish armed forces beyond national territory.

Thirdly, the article will address the practical application of the relevant provisions of the 1997 Constitution in matters relating to war and peace, particularly in the context of Poland's accession to the North Atlantic Treaty Organization in 1999, the participation of Polish armed forces in military interventions led by the United States in Afghanistan (2002–2021) and Iraq (2003–2011), as well as in light of the ongoing Russian aggression against Ukraine (post-2014).

[1] Constitution of the Republic of Poland (1997).

P. Podemski (✉)
University of Warsaw, Warsaw, Poland
e-mail: p.podemski@uw.edu.pl

G. Cavaggion (ed.), *The 'Pacifist Principle' in the Italian and Japanese Constitutions in the Wake of the War in Ukraine*,
https://doi.org/10.1007/978-3-032-23108-6_15

The paper demonstrates that the decisive role of the Sejm in matters concerning war—conceivable solely in circumstances requiring individual or collective defence—derives from the spirit of Polish constitutional traditions, the traumatic twentieth-century wartime experiences, and the historical moment in which the Constitution was adopted (1997). While the constitutional provisions clearly reflect the lawgivers' commitment to upholding—even in wartime—the standards of a democratic state governed by the rule of law, military interventions of Polish armed forces abroad may have resulted in circumstances that could be interpreted as violations of principled constitutional norms in this respect.

1 *Nihil Sine Consensu*: War and Peace in Poland's Constitutional Traditions

The problems of war and peace have long been at the core of Poland's struggle for power between the king and the country's nobles. Although the hereditary rulers of the Piast dynasty (966–1370), within the concept of patrimonialism, were as a rule allowed to arbitrarily wage war and conclude peace, already under the Jagiellonians (1385–1572), the nobility would voice their objections to the point that, in 1454, a formal privilege was issued guaranteeing that Polish monarchs would require the nobles' approval prior to calling them to arms. This tendency was strengthened in the historic *Nihil Novi* Constitution of 1505, which formulated (in Latin) a general principle according to which "quoniam jura communia et constitutiones publicae non unum, sed communem populum afficiunt" (since common laws and constitutions bind not one person but the entire people), "nihil novi constitui debeat […] sine communi Consiliariorum et Nuntiorum Terrestrium consensu" (nothing new should be decided without the common approval of counsellors [i.e., senators] and landed gentry deputies).[2]

If the *Nihil Novi* Constitution laid the foundations for the system of nobles' democracy, it was ultimately sealed by a more extensive document—namely, the Henrician Articles of 1573. Among the systemic principles submitted for signature to the newly elected king of the Polish-Lithuanian Commonwealth (1569–1795), Henry of Valois—chosen by the entirety of the nobility—was a provision (now expressed in the Polish vernacular) stating: "as for war or a general levy, nothing are we [the king] to undertake, save with the permission of the Sejm of all Estates, nor are we to lead across the Crown's borders the Knighthood of both nations [i.e. Poles and Lithuanians] in martial custom in any manner whatsoever".[3]

Similarly, influenced by the American and French revolutions, the first Polish Constitution in the modern sense—namely, the Government Act of 3 May 1791, more widely known as the Constitution of 3 May, entitled by its London publishers

[2] Volumina legum (1859), vol. 1, p. 137.

[3] Volumina legum (1859), vol. 2, p. 898.

as "The New Constitution of the Government of Poland, established by the revolution",[4] reserved the matters of war and peace to the Diet (Sejm). Discussing the prerogatives of the king and his council within the overarching idea of the three pillars of government, it specified that "this executive power cannot assume the right of making laws, or their interpretation. [...] It is expressly forbidden [...] to declare war; to conclude definitively any treaty, or any diplomatic act, [which should happen] always in reference to the Diet."[5]

The foregoing three examples indicate that within the earliest constitutional traditions of Poland, the elite then forming the political nation—the nobility—attached considerable importance to securing for themselves the authority to decide matters of war and peace, refusing to vest such powers in the hands of the monarch or any executive power. It seems safe to argue that this specific form of pacifism, frequently criticized in contemporary historiography as leading to passivity, stemmed not primarily from moral reservations regarding the conduct of war but rather from a jealous defence of a wide-ranging scope of political liberty, as well as a desire to remain focused on the management of one's own estates and subjects.[6]

By contrast, during the period of the partitions (1795–1918), successive Polish constitutions were shaped by foreign powers—typically militaristic and expansionist empires—imposing frameworks that reflected their strategic and ideological agendas rather than earlier Polish constitutional traditions.

The first significant constitutional experiment for post-partition Poland—though welcomed with genuine enthusiasm by many members of the Polish elite as a hopeful blueprint for restoring the national sovereignty lost in 1795—was the octroyed Constitution of the Duchy of Warsaw, granted by Napoleon Bonaparte on 22 July 1807 in Dresden. The document, devised for what was effectively a satellite polity of the French Empire, bore many hallmarks of Napoleonic political design. From the outset, the subordinated constitutional order was made explicit by a notable clause: the French-language text of the Constitution would take precedence over the Polish translation, underscoring the imposed and non-deliberative character of the legal act. Although styled a "duchy"—a term reflective of its designation in the Treaties of Tilsit (1807)—the institutional arrangements outlined in the Constitution firmly anchored executive authority in the person of the king. This is reflected with particular force—in line with Bonapartist centralism—in Article 6, which states that "Le Gouvernement réside dans la personne du Roi. Il exerce dans toute sa plénitude les fonctions du pouvoir exécutif."[7]

The monarch in question, Frederick Augustus I of Saxony, was appointed by Napoleon as the Duke of Warsaw—an arrangement that mirrored in spirit the earlier Polish Constitution of 3 May 1791 while, in practice, situating the restored Polish statehood as a subordinate element within a personal union with Saxony under

[4] New Constitution of the Government of Poland (1791).

[5] New Constitution of the Government of Poland (1791), pp. 20–21.

[6] Stone (2001), p. 133; Butterwick (2001), p. 188.

[7] Statut constitutionnel du Duché de Varsovie (1808), p. V.

French patronage.[8] While no constitutional article explicitly enumerates the power to declare war or make peace, the combined effect of Article 6 and Articles 79 to 81, concerning "la force Armée", renders it clear that full command over military affairs was formally vested in the king. Yet this sovereignty was hollow: the substantial armed forces of the Duchy were deployed at the Emperor's discretion across Europe, from Russia to the Iberian Peninsula; even today, a striking consequence of this dynamic remains a Polish diaspora as far as Haiti, formed by the descendants of Polish troops sent by Napoleon to suppress a local uprising in 1801–1804 against French rule in what was then the colony of Saint-Domingue.[9]

The authority to decide on matters of war and peace was even more explicitly secured by the next emperor ruling Poland, Alexander I Romanov, in the 1815 Constitution of the Kingdom of Poland. Paradoxically, despite being octroyed by an autocrat, the constitutional monarchy it introduced has often been regarded as notably liberal—running counter to the prevailing political tendencies in Europe in the aftermath of the Congress of Vienna (1814–1815). Some scholars even argue that the so-called Congress Kingdom, established after the fall of the Napoleonic Duchy of Warsaw and placed under Romanov rule, functioned as a constitutional experiment—a laboratory for regime reform—that Alexander I contemplated extending to the wider Russian Empire.[10]

Nevertheless, the Constitution of the new kingdom made it unambiguously clear that "The kingdom of Poland is for ever united to the Empire of Russia" (Article 1) and that "The external political relations of our empire shall be common to the kingdom of Poland" (Article 8). Most significantly, it stipulated that "The sovereign alone shall have the power to determine the participation of the kingdom of Poland in the Russian wars, as well as in the treaties of peace which that power may conclude" (Article 9). Conversely, in an attempt to underscore the new regime's alleged liberalism—particularly in contrast to the Bonapartist model—the Constitution also included a meaningful pledge in Article 10, stating that "The Polish army shall never be employed out of Europe".[11] Nevertheless, the same Polish society, which had earlier acquiesced to the mobilization of an army numbering nearly 100,000, or roughly one-sixth of the entire Grande Armée, for Napoleon's 1812 Russian campaign—a commitment that also entailed significant fiscal costs—rose in armed revolt against Russian rule in 1830. One of its immediate triggers was the planned deployment of Polish troops by the Russian authorities to suppress liberal revolutions in Belgium and France.[12] It was self-evident which of the two imperial patrons, French or Russian, the Poles were more eager to fight and die for.

Poland's constitutional traditions in the twentieth century—prior to the adoption of the current Constitution of 1997—should be examined in relation to two distinct

[8] Czubaty (2016).

[9] Girard (2011), p. 325.

[10] O'Meara (2019), p. 156.

[11] Constitutional Charter of the Kingdom of Poland (1831), Articles 1, 8–10.

[12] Kostantaras (2020), p. 150.

periods: the Second Polish Republic (1918–1939) as a sovereign state (with the March Constitution of 1921 and the April Constitution of 1935) and the Polish People's Republic (1944–1989) as a satellite state subordinated to the USSR.

The first Constitution of a reborn Polish state in the post-partition era, adopted on 17 March 1921, already in its preamble expressed gratitude "to Providence for setting us free from a servitude of a century and a half" and a commitment "to taking up the glorious tradition of the memorable Constitution of the Third of May", as well as to "establish her [Poland's] independent existence, power, safety, and social order on the eternal principles of right and liberty" and "for the good of the whole of renascent humanity".[13] The document thus echoed Poland's deep-rooted traditions of liberty, a sense of universal solidarity of mankind, and the democratic optimism inspired by the Wilsonian progressivism of the era while also bearing the imprint of a bitter wartime experience—the trauma of the First World War and the Polish-Soviet War, which formally concluded only the following day after the Constitution's adoption. In keeping with this context, Article 50 of the March Constitution explicitly provided: "The President of the Republic may declare war and conclude peace only after obtaining the consent of the Seym."[14] This clause institutionalized a robust framework for parliamentary oversight in decisions concerning war and peace, affirming the primacy of the legislature in exercising sovereign authority.

Equally telling was Article 46, shaped by the foundational political conflict of the Second Republic—namely, the rift between the principal architect of Polish independence, Marshal Józef Piłsudski, and his political adversaries. The article stated: "The President of the Republic is at the same time the supreme head of the armed forces of the state, but he may not exercise the chief command in time of war." This provision both enshrined the civilian command structure and reflected political anxieties over the concentration of military power in the hands of the executive, setting clear limits on presidential authority during wartime. It was not only the quoted Article 46—which effectively forced Piłsudski to choose between holding the state's presidency in peacetime and serving as Commander-in-Chief during war—but also the broader marginalization of the presidency in favour of the Sejm and political parties that led the Marshal to adopt an increasingly critical stance towards the March Constitution. Ultimately, this dissatisfaction contributed to his decision to overthrow the existing government—operating under that very Constitution—by means of the so-called May Coup of 1926.[15]

The resulting April Constitution, enacted on 23 April 1935 to replace its predecessor, marked a fundamental departure in Poland's constitutional design. Drafted in an authoritarian and romantic spirit, it envisioned a centralized architecture of state power centred on the presidency. Already in Article 2, the President's role was expressed with pronounced clarity and ideological weight: "The President of the

[13] Constitution of the Republic of Poland (1921), Preamble.

[14] Constitution of the Republic of Poland (1921), Article 50.

[15] Plach (2006), p. 82.

Republic stands at the head of the State. The responsibility before God and history for the destinies of the State rests on him. His supreme duty is to care for the welfare of the State, for its readiness to meet attack and for its position among the nations of the world. The one and indivisible authority of the State is united in his person."[16] Accordingly, Article 12 provided: "The President of the Republic [...] is the Supreme Head of the Armed Forces; [...] represents the State abroad [...], decides on war and peace; [...] concludes and ratifies treaties with other States." These provisions underscored the emergence of a personalist and Bonapartist model of governance, in line with the tendencies then dominant in interwar Europe, contrasting sharply with the earlier parliamentary framework and effectively institutionalizing a presidential republic with authoritarian features.

Following the unprecedented and unmatched trauma experienced by the populations of the Polish territories—those "Bloodlands", as termed by Timothy Snyder[17]—during the Second World War, the country's new political regime was forged under the bayonets of the Red Army. Its foundation can be traced to the Manifesto of the Polish Committee of National Liberation, established in Moscow under Stalin's direct supervision, published on 22 July 1944. Only after a prolonged period of struggle for and consolidation of power was a new Stalinist constitutional framework adopted: the Constitution of 22 July 1952, which formally introduced the name "Polish People's Republic". Within the broader context of the systematic Sovietization of post-war Poland, this Constitution incorporated numerous provisions directly transplanted from Soviet models—among them the Potemkin-like (i.e., façade-like) quality of many constitutional guarantees, which, on paper, proclaimed broad civil liberties and citizen rights. In practice, however, these guarantees clashed profoundly with the reality of life under a totalitarian regime, exemplifying what Orwell famously described as doublethink.[18]

This contrast was especially apparent in the constitutional provisions concerning war and peace. Article 28 of the 1952 Constitution stated that "a decision concerning the declaration of a state of war may be adopted only in the event of armed aggression having been committed against the Polish People's Republic, or if, in pursuance of international agreements, the necessity of common defence against aggression should arise. Such a decision is voted by the Seym".[19] Taken literally, these provisions could suggest that Stalinist Poland had not only revived the early modern Polish tradition of parliamentary oversight over declarations of war and peace but had also formally prohibited offensive warfare, limiting the use of military force exclusively to individual or collective self-defence against foreign aggression. As we shall see, this language would subsequently influence the constitutional arrangements of the Third Republic.

[16] Constitution of the Republic of Poland (1935), Article 12.

[17] Snyder (2012).

[18] Brooks (2021), pp. 9, 66.

[19] Constitution of the Polish People's Republic (1952), Article 28.

Nevertheless, one must bear in mind that the slogans of peace defence and—paradoxically—"the struggle for peace" constituted central pillars of Eastern Bloc propaganda in its ideological confrontation with alleged Western "imperialists" and "warmongers".[20] In practice, the authorities of the Polish People's Republic demonstrated their readiness to deploy the Polish Army—alongside other Warsaw Pact forces—for military interventions, such as the one in Czechoslovakia in 1968, shrewdly labelling such operations "brotherly help" rather than acts of war.[21]

In summary, when in the aftermath of the collapse of real socialism the leaders of the Third Republic of Poland undertook the task of constructing its modern constitutional framework, they did so under the influence of a rich legacy of national constitutional traditions. These conveyed some solid pacifist inclinations or, at the very least, the normative claim for civic or parliamentary oversight over decisions concerning war and peace. This demand stemmed both from the collective trauma of wartime experience deeply embedded in society and from a political habitus inherited from the People's Republic of Poland—a practice that permitted the deployment of armed forces without the need for a formal declaration of war.

2 *Et in Terra Pax Hominibus*: The Ideals of Poland's Constitution

From today's perspective, the current Polish Constitution may be regarded as a relatively late product of the "liberal revolution", to adopt Bruce Ackerman's well-known term.[22] In his book published as early as 1992, Ackerman—an analyst of systemic transitions in Central and Eastern Europe in the making—repeatedly criticized the hasty pace and consequent superficiality of constitutional reforms undertaken in post-communist countries. Rather than swift constitutional engineering, he advocated for a process of deeper deliberation, capable of producing durable legitimacy for the new democratic political regimes born of the 1989 "Autumn of Nations". However, as Tomasz Słomka has rightly observed, Poland's systemic transformation was, as a matter of fact, marked by a compromise between the forces of the old (socialist) and the new (liberal) orders and, thus, proceeded through a multi-stage process involving repeated amendments to the 1952 Constitution of the Polish People's Republic, prior to its eventual replacement by the Constitution of the Third Republic on 2 April 1997, subsequently ratified via a nationwide referendum,[23] thus largely in line with Ackerman's precepts.

In its solemn preamble, the new Constitution expressly acknowledged the specific historical context in which it was adopted, with its framers "recalling the best

[20] Barghoorn (1964), p. 97.

[21] Pazderka (2019), p. 185.

[22] Ackerman (1992).

[23] Słomka (2015), p. 18.

traditions of the First and the Second Republic, obliged to bequeath to future generations all that is valuable from our over one thousand years' heritage, […] aware of the need for cooperation with all countries for the good of the Human Family, mindful of the bitter experiences of the times when fundamental freedoms and human rights were violated in our Homeland, desiring to guarantee the rights of the citizens for all time".[24] It seems evident that this very spirit of desired constitutional continuity, human solidarity, and respect for human rights also shaped Article 116 defining the Polish constitutional order with regard to the state of war and peace.

The first paragraph of Article 116 of the Constitution of the Republic of Poland provides that "The Sejm shall declare, in the name of the Republic of Poland, a state of war and the conclusion of peace".[25] This provision harks back to the roots and long-standing traditions of the Polish constitutional order, wherein such competences had been claimed, already in the sixteenth century, by the nobility as citizens of the Commonwealth, often in conflict with monarchical authority. The second paragraph adds that "if the Sejm cannot assemble for a sitting, the President of the Republic may declare a state of war". The rationale of this clause is clear: it anticipates scenarios—likely especially under conditions of contemporary total or asymmetric warfare—in which an adversary might effectively paralyse the operations of state organs, particularly those of a collective character. Under such circumstances, the machinery of the state must not rest paralysed, and thus the Constitution entrusts the President with this power as a matter of necessity.

Of particular interest is the latter part of the second paragraph, which specifies: "The Sejm may adopt a resolution on a state of war only in the event of armed aggression against the territory of the Republic of Poland or when an obligation of common defence against aggression arises by virtue of international agreements." As noted by the distinguished Polish constitutional scholar Ryszard Piotrowski, while the Constitution of the Republic of Poland of 1997 does not reproduce verbatim the phrasing of Article 11 of the Italian (Republican) Constitution, which proclaims the rejection of "war as an instrument of aggression against the freedom of other peoples and as a means for the settlement of international disputes",[26] the substantive intent behind both provisions is markedly similar. Piotrowski contends that, under Poland's constitutional framework, "a democratic state governed by the rule of law may engage in war only in response to an act of aggression against its own territory or in the execution of obligations arising from international treaties".[27]

It must nevertheless be noted that while Article 116 refers to the "state of war" (Polish: *stan wojny*), that is, essentially, the declaration of war on a foreign state in response to its aggression against Poland or its treaty allies, the similarly worded Polish term *stan wojenny*—traditionally translated into English as "martial

[24] Constitution of the Republic of Poland (1997), Preamble.

[25] Constitution of the Republic of Poland (1997), Article 116.

[26] Constitution of the Italian Republic (1948), Article 11.

[27] Piotrowski (2022), p. 303.

law"—denotes a significantly broader concept.[28] Its legal contours are outlined in Chapter XI of the Constitution, entitled "Extraordinary measures". Already the opening paragraph of Article 228 therein stipulates that martial law (Polish: *stan wojenny*), alongside a state of emergency (Polish: *stan wyjątkowy*) or a state of natural disaster (Polish: *stan klęski żywiołowej*), may be introduced "in situations of particular danger, if ordinary constitutional measures are inadequate". The subsequent provision, Article 229, specifies that martial law may be introduced by the President of the Republic "on request of the Council of Ministers", either "in a part of or upon the whole territory of the State", "in the case of external threats to the State, acts of armed aggression against the territory of the Republic of Poland or when an obligation of common defence against aggression arises by virtue of international agreement". The Constitution thus allows for the imposition of martial law even absent—or merely in anticipation of—a state of war.

Although, due to the typically urgent circumstances accompanying its introduction, martial law, as has been shown, may be enacted by the President at the request of the Council of Ministers, Article 231 establishes a mechanism to guard against the abuse of executive power in this respect. This takes the form of a requirement "to submit the regulation on the introduction of martial law [...] to the Sejm within 48 hours of signing such regulation" while simultaneously vesting in the Sejm the authority to annul it "by an absolute majority of votes taken in the presence of at least half the statutory number of Deputies". Similarly, as stated in Article 234, "whenever, during a period of martial law, the Sejm is unable to assemble for a sitting, the President of the Republic shall, on application of the Council of Ministers, [...] issue regulations having the force of statute. Such regulations must be approved by the Sejm at its next sitting", which implies that, for the duration of martial law, upon the President rests both the right and the duty to issue regulations having the force of statute on the motion of the Council of Ministers.[29] However, the Sejm retains its constitutionally guaranteed oversight role, as such presidential regulations must be submitted for approval or rejection at the earliest opportunity.

Therefore, the imposition of martial law, although not necessarily or directly linked to the declaration of a state of war, nonetheless gives rise to extraordinary legal consequences for the general population. Article 233, paragraph 1, delineates—by means of a negative clause—the scope of the limitation of the freedoms and rights of persons and citizens in times of martial law, stipulating that such limitations may not affect "the freedoms and rights specified in Article 30 (the dignity of the person), Article 34 and Article 36 (citizenship), Article 38 (protection of life), Article 39, Article 40 and Article 41, para. 4 (humane treatment), Article 42 (ascription of criminal responsibility), Article 45 (access to a court), Article 47 (personal rights), Article 53 (conscience and religion), Article 63 (petitions), as well as Article 48 and Article 72 (family and children)". Moreover, paragraph 2 prohibits any limitation of rights on the basis of discriminatory criteria, such as "race, gender,

[28] Nowińska (2018), p. 224.

[29] Nowińska (2018), p. 234.

language, faith or lack of it, social origin, ancestry or property". Solely the judiciary-focused Article 175, paragraph 2, stating that "extraordinary courts or summary procedures may be established only during a time of war" makes reference neither to martial law (*stan wojenny*), introduced by the President under Article 229, nor to a state of war (*stan wojny*), declared by the Sejm according to Article 116, but to a time of war (*czas wojny*) or a period of actual fighting taking place on Polish territory, as defined by the doctrine.[30]

The legal consequences of declaring martial law—thus far considered and which may but need not derive from a state of war—have primarily pertained to the internal legal order of the state. However, the Polish Constitution also addresses another issue situated within the framework of international law that may arise from the initiation of a state of war: namely, the deployment of Polish troops abroad. Article 117, which directly follows Article 116 concerning the state of war, stipulates that both the deployment of the Armed Forces beyond the borders of the Republic of Poland and the presence of foreign troops on the territory of the Republic of Poland require specification in the form of a ratified international agreement or statute. Piotrowski emphasizes, however, that Articles 116 and 117 must be interpreted jointly—i.e., the use of Polish armed forces in combat operations beyond national borders is constitutionally permissible only, even if based on ratified international agreements or statutes, within the framework of a state of war declared by the Sejm pursuant to the procedure laid down in Article 116, since beyond a state of war, there can logically only be a state of peace, with no legal middle ground.[31] It is within this context that Polish military interventions alongside the United States in Afghanistan and Iraq are frequently subject to criticism from constitutional scholars.

Since Article 91 of the Constitution stipulates in paragraph 1 that "a ratified international agreement shall constitute part of the domestic legal order and shall be applied directly" and in paragraph 2 that "an international agreement ratified upon prior consent granted by statute shall have precedence over statutes", it follows that in matters of war and peace, Poland is bound by, inter alia, the Charter of the United Nations (already binding at the time of the adoption of the 1997 Constitution), the North Atlantic Treaty (since Poland's accession to the North Atlantic Treaty Organization (NATO) on 12 March 1999), and the Treaty on European Union (since its accession to the EU on 1 May 2004).

Among these, the Charter of the United Nations, in particular, imposes on Poland obligations "to save succeeding generations from the scourge of war" (Preamble) and "to maintain international peace and security" (Article 1) and, more specifically, "to refrain in [her] international relations from the threat or use of force against the territorial integrity or political independence of any state" (Article 2). At the same time, it reserves for signatory states "the inherent right of individual or collective self-defence if an armed attack occurs against a Member of the United

[30] Piotrowski (2022), p. 305; Nowińska (2018), pp. 227–228.

[31] Piotrowski (2022), p. 308.

Nations" (Article 51).[32] Frequently—though somewhat simplistically—invoked, Article 5 of the North Atlantic Treaty of 1949 provides that "an armed attack against one or more of [the signatories] in Europe or North America shall be considered an attack against them all", thereby authorizing any NATO member state "individually and in concert with the other Parties, [to take] such action as it deems necessary, including the use of armed force, to restore and maintain the security of the North Atlantic area".[33] Comparatively speaking, the Treaty on European Union speaks least explicitly about war, omitting the term altogether; however, it repeatedly affirms that peace is among the fundamental values of the European Union (e.g., Preamble, Articles 3 and 21).[34]

3 *Ex Iniuria Ius Oritur*?—Practices of War in Afghanistan and Iraq

In the context of the wars in Afghanistan and Iraq, the legal justifications most frequently invoked were, naturally, the right to collective self-defence guaranteed under Article 51 of the Charter of the United Nations, as well as Article 5 of the North Atlantic Treaty, which permits "the use of armed force" in response to an armed attack against a member state. Both organizations issued official statements regarding the terrorist attacks on the World Trade Centre on 11 September 2001 as early as the following day. The United Nations Security Council, in Resolution 1368 (2001), emphasized its determination "to combat by all means threats to international peace and security caused by terrorist acts" and recognized "the inherent right of individual or collective self-defence".[35] That same day, the North Atlantic Council—for the first time in the Alliance's history—invoked the principle of Article 5, acknowledging the attack against the United States as an attack against all NATO members. The NATO statement crucially recalled, in its final words, that under Article 5, "each Ally will assist the Party that has been attacked by taking such action as it deems necessary. Accordingly, the United States' NATO Allies stand ready to provide the assistance that may be required as a consequence of these acts of barbarism."[36] Nonetheless, individual Allies responded to this obligation in different ways, reflecting varying national approaches to collective defence implementation.

From the outset, Poland was among the states that strongly supported the United States in its plans to carry out a military campaign in Afghanistan. On 22 November 2001, President Aleksander Kwaśniewski, acting pursuant to the Act of 17 December

[32] United Nations Charter (1945), Preamble, Articles 1, 2, and 51.

[33] The North Atlantic Treaty (1949), Article 5.

[34] Consolidated Version of the Treaty on European Union (2012), Preamble, Articles 3 and 21.

[35] UN Security Council Resolution 1368 (2001).

[36] Statement by the North Atlantic Council (2001).

1998 on the Principles of the Use or Stay of the Armed Forces of the Republic of Poland Outside the Country and upon the request of the Council of Ministers, issued a decision authorizing the deployment of a Polish military contingent (comprising up to 300 personnel) within allied forces stationed in the Islamic State of Afghanistan, the Republic of Tajikistan, the Republic of Uzbekistan, and the Arabian Sea and Indian Ocean, as part of Operation Enduring Freedom.[37] It seems crucial to point out that Article 2 of the aforementioned statute stipulates that Polish armed forces may be used abroad, inter alia, for the purpose of "participation in an armed conflict or in order to strengthen the forces of an allied state or states".[38] However, the term "armed conflict" (Polish: *konflikt zbrojny*), as used in the statute, was not synonymous with the constitutional notion of a "state of war" (Polish: *stan wojny*). As such, it functioned—according to critics in constitutional law—as a kind of legal loophole, allowing combat operations without a formal declaration of a state of war by the Sejm of the Republic of Poland.[39] Nonetheless, a degree of international legal sanction for the mission in Afghanistan was provided by United Nations Security Council Resolution 1386 (2001), adopted on 20 December 2001, which authorized "the establishment for 6 months of an International Security Assistance Force [ISAF] to assist the Afghan Interim Authority in the maintenance of security".[40] Furthermore, on 11 August 2003, command of ISAF was transferred to NATO, providing a further legitimization and institutionalisation of the mission.

The initial size of the Polish military contingent in Afghanistan was set at a maximum of 300 soldiers, with the mission to last until 30 June 2002. However, at its peak, the deployment expanded to approximately 2600 personnel, stationed notably at Bagram Airfield near Kabul and Camp White Eagle in Ghazni. The final withdrawal of Polish troops was completed only on 30 June 2021.[41] It is noteworthy that the initial decision to deploy Polish forces to Afghanistan was taken by a left-leaning (post-communist) government and President, whereas subsequent decisions to increase military presence were made by right-leaning politicians (originating from the former anti-communist opposition). Nevertheless, regardless of ideological orientation, the opposition of the day consistently criticized successive governments for expanding Poland's involvement in the war in Afghanistan.[42] Although the Polish public initially expressed cautious support for the deployment (with the highest approval rating reaching 57% in April 2002), over time—and likely in connection with a growing recognition that the mission in Afghanistan had evolved from a stabilization effort into a full-fledged armed conflict—public sentiment

[37] Postanowienie Prezydenta Rzeczypospolitej Polskiej z dnia 22 listopada 2001 r.... (2001).
[38] Ustawa z dnia 17 grudnia 1998 r.... (1998).
[39] Piotrowski (2022), p. 303.
[40] UNSC Resolution 1386 (2001).
[41] Koniec misji w Afganistanie (2021).
[42] Zalewski (2014), p. 22.

became increasingly sceptical. For instance, by December 2007, 83% of respondents in opinion polls expressed opposition to the continued engagement.[43]

Two highly publicized incidents may have had a marked influence on the shift in Polish public opinion regarding the country's military engagement in Afghanistan: the Nangar Khel incident and the Central Intelligence Agency (CIA) black site at Stare Kiejkuty. On 16 August 2007, Polish soldiers shelled the village of Nangar Khel in Afghanistan, resulting in the deaths of six civilians and serious injuries to three others, including women and children.[44] As a consequence, from 2007 to 2016, a war crimes trial—the first of its kind in Poland since World War II—was conducted across successive judicial instances. Ultimately, the proceedings concluded with convictions for the improper execution of orders, though not for the crime of war itself.[45] Meanwhile, the training centre of the Polish intelligence services in Stare Kiejkuty became notorious as one of the CIA's secret detention and interrogation sites, allegedly operating from 2002 to 2005. In July 2014, the European Court of Human Rights (ECHR) ruled that Poland was complicit in the CIA secret detention and torture programme. The Court found that Poland had violated the rights of two detainees—Abu Zubaydah and Abd al-Rahim al-Nashiri—by enabling their secret imprisonment and torture and by failing to investigate or prevent these abuses.[46] The case became a national scandal in Poland, especially after global media outlets began to report on it, and left-wing officials governing in 2002–2005 initially denied any involvement. It was only years later that President Aleksander Kwaśniewski acknowledged: "It was not us who arrested the terrorists and interrogated them. We assumed that our allies respect the law. If something was not in accordance with the law, this is the Americans' responsibility and they should be accountable."[47] However, the Court did not accept this as an adequate explanation and, on 24 July 2014, formally found Poland in violation of the rights of the detainees.

A markedly different international atmosphere accompanied the US's decision to invade Iraq under the banner of Operation *Iraqi Freedom* (2003–2008). As aptly observed by Marek Madej, in its attempt to replicate the pattern of intervention used in Afghanistan, the United States failed to convince global public opinion and parts of its own alliance of any credible link between the terrorist network al-Qaeda—responsible for the 2001 attacks on the World Trade Centre — and Saddam Hussein's regime in Iraq, nor could it substantiate claims that Iraq possessed weapons of mass destruction threatening the West. As a result, Washington squandered much of the trust and goodwill accumulated in the aftermath of 11 September, fuelling a rise in anti-American sentiment globally and causing rifts among its closest allies.[48] When

43 Centrum Badania Opinii Społecznej (2007a), p. 1.

44 Wasiński (2008).

45 Sąd Najwyższy (2016).

46 Amnesty International (2014).

47 European Court of Human Rights (2014), para 130.

48 Madej (2004), p. 417.

Poland—one of the staunchest supporters of US policy—joined the United Kingdom, Italy, and others in signing the so-called Letter of Eight in support of the impending invasion, it met with sharp criticism from French and German elites, who went so far as to label Warsaw not only "America's Trojan horse" but also a "Trojan donkey" within Europe.[49] French President Jacques Chirac publicly asserted that Poland and other Eastern European EU candidate states had "missed a good opportunity to remain silent" on the matter (fr. *perdu une bonne occasion de se taire*).[50]

In line with the approach taken in Afghanistan, a decision to deploy a Polish Military Contingent as part of the Multinational Joint Operational Forces of the international coalition—across a vastly extended geographic area encompassing the Kingdom of Saudi Arabia, the Kingdom of Bahrain, the Hashemite Kingdom of Jordan, the State of Qatar, the State of Kuwait, and the Republic of Iraq, as well as the Persian Gulf, the Red Sea, and the Indian Ocean—was made on 17 March 2003 by President Aleksander Kwaśniewski, upon the request of the post-communist government of Prime Minister Leszek Miller.[51] Initially, a modest contribution of no more than 200 soldiers, to be deployed from 19 March to 15 September 2003 only, was envisaged. However, as with the Afghan mission, these assumptions evolved over time: Polish forces remained deployed in the Euphrates and Tigris valleys until October 2008 as part of Operation *Iraqi Freedom*, reaching a peak of around 2500 troops. During this period, Poland assumed command of the Multinational Division Central-South (MND-C-S) and, thereby, responsibility for one of the four NATO-controlled sectors—the Centre-South Zone, located south of Baghdad. The division's headquarters was first located at Camp Babylon and then, from 2004 onwards, at Camp Echo. A small number of Polish military personnel remained in Iraq under the auspices of the NATO Training Mission-Iraq (NTM-I) until 2011, this time under the mandate of UN Security Council Resolution 1546 (2004).[52] Polish forces returned yet again post-2016 as part of renewed NATO advisory efforts in Iraq, in the context of the expansion of the Islamic State (ISIS) in Syria and Iraq.[53]

According to the official portal of the Polish Armed Forces, "the nature of the Iraqi Freedom mission—as well as the tasks carried out under its framework—underwent significant changes over time. Initially, the primary focus was placed on stabilization operations, which were of critical importance given that the country, following the cessation of combat activities, required the restoration of order and improved security conditions. As the mission evolved, its mandate was redefined: training became the central priority, followed by training-and-advisory functions. Toward the end of the operation (during rotations IX and X), it became necessary to intensify stabilization efforts once again, partly due to the gradual reduction in the

[49] James (2003).
[50] Chirac do Polaków: milczeć! (2003).
[51] Postanowienie Prezydenta Rzeczypospolitej Polskiej z dnia 17 marca 2003 r…. (2003).
[52] NATO's assistance to Iraq (2004–2011).
[53] NATO Mission Iraq (2025).

strength of Multinational Division Central-South (MND C-S), which in turn contributed to heightened insurgent activity."[54] One of the most emblematic moments of the Polish military presence in Iraq was the defence of the Karbala City Hall, which took place between 3 and 6 April 2004. During this engagement, 34 Polish and 20 Bulgarian soldiers held off an assault by militants from the Mahdi Army. The same official source characterizes the event as a "heroic battle", recognized as "one of the most significant episodes in the modern history of the Polish Armed Forces".[55] From these descriptions, it can be inferred that the military command, within the official discourse, regarded the mission in Iraq as purposeful and successful, portraying it as aligned with the proud traditions of the Polish Armed Forces.

A strikingly divergent sentiment regarding the war in Iraq prevailed among the Polish public opinion and many respected voices, including legal authorities. From the outset in 2003, a majority of Poles opposed the involvement of Polish troops in the Iraq operation (with the highest recorded support at 40% in September, compared to 53% of those opposed), and this trend only intensified over time (by January 2007, support had dropped to just 20%, while 77% expressed opposition).[56] This scepticism might have been strengthened by the firm stance taken by the Polish Pope, John Paul II, who, in an address to the diplomatic corps on 13 January 2003, proclaimed: "NO TO WAR! [...] It is always a defeat for humanity. International law, honest dialogue, solidarity between States, the noble exercise of diplomacy: these are methods worthy of individuals and nations in resolving their differences. [...]. And what are we to say of the threat of a war which could strike the people of Iraq, the land of the Prophets, a people already sorely tried by more than twelve years of embargo? War is never just another means that one can choose to employ for settling differences between nations. As the Charter of the United Nations Organization and international law itself remind us, war cannot be decided upon, even when it is a matter of ensuring the common good, except as the very last option and in accordance with very strict conditions [...]."[57]

Largely similar to the Pope's pronouncement were the views expressed within Polish scholarship on international law. The above-mentioned distinguished scholar, Ryszard Piotrowski, cited numerous respected authorities who argued that "the actions undertaken by the coalition led by the United States constituted a serious violation of the Charter of the United Nations", that "resorting to military force contrary to the UN Charter without an appropriate resolution of the Security Council [...] under a false pretext leads to the erosion of international law", and that "the arguments advanced by the states initiating military action in Iraq are insufficient to render the intervention lawful".[58] According to Roman Kwiecień, the "political triumph of interventionism has revealed itself as yet another defeat for international

---

[54] Matuszak (2020).

[55] Matuszak (2020).

[56] Centrum Badania Opinii Społecznej (2007b), p. 2.

[57] John Paul II (2003), para 4.

[58] Piotrowski (2022), p. 309.

law, exposing the fragility of its internal structure. In the face of the intervention in Iraq, we are once again confronted with the necessity of accepting the principle of *ex iniuria ius oritur*."[59]

Piotrowski's own assessment of Poland's military involvement in Afghanistan and Iraq is even more severe. He concludes that "participation in both wars posed a threat to the security and axiological identity of the state—stemming both from the circumstances in which the decisions were made and from the disregard for constitutional values, which proved weaker than clandestine negotiations and informal arrangements".[60] One might claim that according to those critics, participation in what they candidly defined as "wars", and not "armed conflicts" or "missions", in Afghanistan and Iraq marked no less than Poland's own "end of the innocence" and failure to live up to the high moral standards proclaimed in the Constitution.

***

Whoever today writes from a Polish perspective on war, peace, and international law inevitably turns their attention to the war unfolding just beyond Poland's border, in Ukraine. For Poles—historically scarred by Russian imperial expansionism—the series of aggressions against Ukraine (from the annexation of Crimea in 2014, through the seizure of Donetsk and Luhansk, to the full-scale invasion beginning in February 2022) served less as a surprise and more as a confirmation of their deeply rooted anxieties. Once again, it exposed the weakness of international law and its retreat in the face of raw force and propaganda (Russian sources, until as late as March 2024, persistently avoided referring to the events in Ukraine as "war", opting instead for the euphemism "special military operation").[61] For Poland, it also brought to the forefront two pressing matters: in the short term, the provision of military assistance to Ukraine and, in the long term, Poland's own defence preparedness.

Poles frequently emphasize that they have provided substantial military assistance to Ukraine, amounting to approximately 350 tanks, 14 fighter jets, 12 helicopters, around 350 armoured combat vehicles and personnel carriers, and over 100 self-propelled artillery pieces, with a total estimated value of approximately €3.23 billion (as of autumn 2024).[62] According to international sources, however, this figure is not considered exceptionally high in light of contributions made by other NATO countries, such as the United States ($69 billion), Germany ($13.6 billion), the United Kingdom ($10.8 billion), Denmark ($8.1 billion), or the Netherlands ($6.3 billion).[63] Public opinion research in Poland nonetheless indicates a steady decline in support for accepting refugees from war-affected territories (from 96% support in March 2022 down to only 40% in March 2025 r.). An increasing number of Poles also anticipate that the war will end with Ukraine having to relinquish some

---

[59] Kwiecień (2004), p. 93.

[60] Piotrowski (2022), p. 311.

[61] Solmaz (2024).

[62] Defence24 (2024).

[63] BBC (2025).

occupied territories (67% in March 2025 compared to 34% in April 2022 r.), a solution that is gaining broader acceptance (58% in favour in March 2025 r. compared to 26% in April 2022). A clear majority of Poles (68% among the general public, but as many as 80% among the youth) also oppose the deployment of Polish troops to Ukraine—even after a peace agreement with Russia and in coordination with other European countries.[64]

The context of the war in Ukraine has also prompted Poland to undertake intensified defensive measures. A symbolic manifestation of this is the Statute on Defence of the Motherland (Polish: *Ustawa o obronie Ojczyzny*), adopted on 11 March 2022, i.e., shortly after the onset of the full-scale war and still under the conservative rule of the Law and Justice (PiS) Party.[65] On a rhetorical level, the statute reinforced the governing party's image as patriotic leaders resolute in confronting any potential aggressor; in practical terms, it systematized previously dispersed regulations (with the legislator having formerly regarded an all-out war as essentially unrealistic), increased funding for the national defence effort, and improved the processes of military recruitment and training. According to the official NATO website, "Poland has quickly established itself as a burden-sharing champion within NATO, increasing its defence spending from 2.7% of GDP in 2022 to 4.2% in 2024",[66] with a projected rise to 4.7% in 2025, amidst public opinion support for this policy still reaching 72.9% in November 2024.

According to another recent opinion poll, these attitudes may be linked to the still widely held belief among many Poles that an attack by Russia on NATO member states within the next 3–8 years is "very probable or rather probable" (59% in April 2025 compared to 65% in April 2024), accompanied by a slightly diminished readiness to actively participate in the defence of the country in the event of a Russian assault (27% in April 2025, down from 31% one year before) and a growing number of individuals acknowledging that they would attempt to flee to a safer location within Poland or abroad (28% in April 2025 compared to 24% one year before).[67] A noteworthy comparison emerges from the global data reported by Gallup International: with 45% of its citizens willing to fight for their country if invaded, Poland ranks between Sweden (47%) and the United States (41%), in contrast to the striking results recorded for Ukraine (62%) and Russia (32%), as well as for the United Kingdom and Germany (each at 33%) and Italy (14%).[68]

A reasonable conclusion of reflections on war and peace within Poland's constitutional tradition and contemporary legal framework may be sought in the principled tone of the resolution adopted by the Sejm on the very eve of Russia's invasion of Ukraine in February 2022. In that resolution, Polish deputies wrote, inter alia: "The principle of sovereignty and the right to self-determination of nations are

---

[64] Centrum Badania Opinii Społecznej (2025a), pp. 2–3, 5, and 7.

[65] Ustawa z dnia 11 marca 2022 r. o obronie Ojczyzny (2022).

[66] Oleksiejuk (2025).

[67] Centrum Badania Opinii Społecznej (2025b), pp. 2–3.

[68] Gallup International (2024).

among the fundamental values of the Western civilization. [...] The Sejm of the Republic of Poland once again condemns in the strongest possible terms all actions by the Russian Federation aimed at attacking Ukraine's sovereignty. The international community must do everything possible to prevent war. [...] We call on the EU and NATO governments and the entire international community to stand in solidarity on the side of freedom and the right of the Ukrainian people to live in an independent state."[69]

In these words, the Polish Sejm bore witness to a deep commitment to the ideals of Western civilization—such as liberty and solidarity—the principle of respect for the sovereignty of nation states, and a steadfast belief in the capacity of NATO and the European Union to prevent war through collective strength. These values are firmly rooted in Poland's centuries-long constitutional tradition and are reflected in the provisions of the current Constitution, adopted in the somewhat naïve and idealistic spirit of Fukuyama's "end of history"[70] at the close of the twentieth century, which regards war as unthinkable except in cases of individual or collective self-defence against aggression. Critics—or perhaps sober-minded realists—might argue, however, that Poland, excessively eager to endear itself to its new American allies, did not in fact uphold these declared ideals, having engaged—in violation of its own Constitution—in the wars in Afghanistan and Iraq. And it may be that now, too, Poles watch helplessly as the law of force prevails over the force of law, in the form of Russia's aggression against Ukraine, deeply concerned over whether or not they may become the next victim of such an aggression in the following years.

References

Ackerman B (1992) The future of liberal revolution. Yale University Press, Yale

Amnesty International (2014) Landmark Rulings Expose Poland's Role in CIA Secret Detention and Torture - https://www.amnesty.org/en/latest/news/2014/07/landmark-rulings-expose-poland-s-role-cia-secret-detention-and-torture/. Accessed 3 July 2025

Barghoorn F (1964) Soviet foreign propaganda. Princeton University Press, Princeton

BBC (2025) Jakie uzbrojenie otrzymała Ukraina od swoich sojuszników? - https://www.bbc.com/polska/articles/cwy62lxl3eno Accessed 3 July 2025

Brooks J (2021) Thank You, Comrade Stalin!: Soviet public culture from revolution to Cold War. Princeton University Press, Princeton

Butterwick R (2001) The Polish-Lithuanian Monarchy in European Context, c.1500-1795. Palgrave-Macmillan, London

Centrum Badania Opinii Społecznej (2007a) Stosunek do obecności polskich żołnierzy w Afganistanie i ostatnich wydarzeń związanych z tą operacją. Komunikat z badań - https://cbos.pl/SPISKOM.POL/2007/K_188_07.PDF. Accessed 3 July 2025

Centrum Badania Opinii Społecznej (2007b) Stosunek do obecności żołnierzy polskich w Iraku i Afganistanie. Komunikat z badań - www.cbos.pl/SPISKOM.POL/2007/K_162_07.PDF. Accessed 3 July 2025

[69] Resolution of the Sejm of the Republic of Poland of 23 February 2022 (2022).

[70] Fukuyama (1992).

Centrum Badania Opinii Społecznej (2025a) Polacy o potencjalnym zakończeniu wojny w Ukrainie. Komunikat z badań, Fundacja CBOS, Warszawa
Centrum Badania Opinii Społecznej (2025b) Czy wojna rozszerzy się na państwa NATO? Jak postąpilibyśmy w takiej sytuacji? Komunikat z badań, Fundacja CBOS, Warszawa
Chirac do Polaków: milczeć! (2003) - https://www.wprost.pl/kraj/40681/chirac-do-polakow-milczec-aktl.html Accessed 3 July 2025
Consolidated Version of The Treaty On European Union (2012) - https://eur-lex.europa.eu/resource.html?uri=cellar:2bf140bf-a3f8-4ab2-b506-fd71826e6da6.0023.02/DOC_1&format=PDF. Accessed 3 July 2025
Constitution of the Italian Republic (1948) - https://www.senato.it/documenti/repository/istituzione/costituzione_inglese.pdf. Accessed 3 July 2025
Constitution of The Polish People's Republic (1952) - https://biblioteka.sejm.gov.pl/tek01/txt/kpol/e1952a.html. Accessed 3 July 2025
Constitution of the Republic of Poland (1921) - https://biblioteka.sejm.gov.pl/tek01/txt/kpol/e1921.html. Accessed 3 July 2025
Constitution of the Republic of Poland (1935) - https://biblioteka.sejm.gov.pl/tek01/txt/kpol/e1935.html. Accessed 3 July 2025
Constitution of the Republic of Poland (1997) – https://www.sejm.gov.pl/prawo/konst/angielski/kon1.htm. Accessed 3 July 2025
Constitutional Charter of The Kingdom of Poland (1831). Ridgway, London - https://en.wikisource.org/w/index.php?title=File:Constitutional_Charter_of_the_Kingdom_of_Poland,_In_the_Year_1815.pdf&page=7. Accessed 3 July 2025
Czubaty J (2016) The Duchy of Warsaw, 1807-1815: A Napoleonic Outpost in Central Europe. Bloomsbury, London
Defence24 (2024) Prezydent powiedział, ile sprzętu Polska dostarczyła Ukrainie - https://defence24.pl/wojna-na-ukrainie-raport-specjalny-defence24/prezydent-powiedzial-ile-sprzetu-polska-dostarczyla-ukrainie. Accessed 3 July 2025
European Court of Human Rights (2014) Application no. 28761/11, Abd Al Rahim Hussayn Muhammad Al Nashiri against Poland, lodged on 6 May 2011 - https://hudoc.echr.coe.int/eng?i=001-112302. Accessed 3 July 2025
Fukuyama F (1992) The end of history and the last man. The Free Press, New York
Gallup International (2024) Fewer people are willing to fight for their country compared to ten years ago - https://www.gallup-international.com/fileadmin/user_upload/surveys_and_news/2024/Fewer_people_are_willing_to_fight_for_their_country_compared_to_ten_years_ago/Fighting_for_the_country.pdf. Accessed 3 July 2025
Girard PR (2011) The slaves who defeated Napoleon. The University of Alabama Press, Tuscaloosa
James B (2003) Action by 8 countries reveals deep breach: Iraq letter splits Europe. The New York Times Feb 1, 2003 - https://www.nytimes.com/2003/02/01/news/action-by-8-countries-reveals-deep-breach-iraq-letter-splits-europe.html. Accessed 3 July 2025
John Paul II (2003) Address of His Holiness Pope John Paul II to The Diplomatic Corps, 13th January 2003 – https://www.vatican.va/content/john-paul-ii/en/speeches/2003/january/documents/hf_jp-ii_spe_20030113_diplomatic-corps.html. Accessed 3 July 2025
Koniec misji w Afganistanie (2021) - https://www.wojsko-polskie.pl/dgrsz/articles/aktualnosci-w/koniec-misji-w-afganistanie/. Accessed 3 July 2025
Kostantaras D (2020) Nationalism and Revolution in Europe, 1763-1848. Amsterdam University Press, Amsterdam
Kwiecień R (2004) Interwencja zbrojna a naruszenie suwerenności państwa w prawie międzynarodowym. Sprawy Międzynarodowe 2004(1):79–94
Madej (2004) Wojna w Iraku a walka z terroryzmem międzynarodowym – jak kulą w płot?. Rocznik Strategiczny 2003/2004:416–424
Matuszak J (2020) Operacja międzynarodowych sił stabilizacyjnych w Iraku - https://www.wojsko-polskie.pl/weterani/articles/historia-misji-n/2020-05-12a-operacja-miedzynarodowych-si-stabilizacyjnych-w-iraku/. Accessed 3 July 2025

NATO Mission Iraq (2025) - https://www.nato.int/cps/en/natohq/topics_166936.htm. Accessed 3 July 2025
NATO's assistance to Iraq (2004–2011) - https://www.nato.int/cps/en/natohq/topics_51978.htm. Accessed 3 July 2025
New Constitution of the Government of Poland (1791). Debrett, London - https://polona.pl/item-view/659c2b21-1cfc-4165-8a2c-4b00c8f5ee2a?page=7. Accessed 3 July 2025
Nowińska M (2018) Stan wojny i stan wojenny w Konstytucji Rzeczypospolitej Polskiej. Biuletyn SAWP KUL XIII 15(2):223–238
O'Meara P (2019) The Russian Nobility in the Age of Alexander I. Bloomsbury, London
Oleksiejuk M (2025) Sharing the burden: how Poland and Germany are shifting the dial on European defence expenditure - https://www.nato.int/docu/review/articles/2025/04/14/sharing-the-burden-how-poland-and-germany-are-shifting-the-dial-on-european-defence-expenditure/index.html. Accessed 3 July 2025
Pazderka J (2019) The soviet invasion of Czechoslovakia in 1968: the Russian perspective. Lexington Books, London
Piotrowski R (2022) Wojna i pokój w Konstytucji RP. Studia Iuridica 91:300–319
Plach E (2006) The clash of moral nations: cultural politics in Piłsudski's Poland, 1926-1935. Ohio University Press, Athens
Postanowienie Prezydenta Rzeczypospolitej Polskiej z dnia 22 listopada 2001 r. o użyciu Polskiego Kontyngentu Wojskowego w składzie Sił Sojuszniczych w Islamskim Państwie Afganistanu, Republice Tadżykistanu i Republice Uzbekistanu oraz na Morzu Arabskim i Oceanie Indyjskim (2001) - https://isap.sejm.gov.pl/isap.nsf/download.xsp/WMP20010420674/O/M20010674.pdf. Accessed 3 July 2025
Postanowienie Prezydenta Rzeczypospolitej Polskiej z dnia 17 marca 2003 r. o użyciu Polskiego Kontyngentu Wojskowego w składzie Wielonarodowych Połączonych Sił Operacyjnych Koalicji Międzynarodowej w Królestwie Arabii Saudyjskiej, Królestwie Bahrajnu, Jordańskim Królestwie Haszymidzkim, Państwie Kataru, Państwie Kuwejtu I Republice Iraku oraz w Zatoce Perskiej, na Morzu Czerwonym I Oceanie Indyjskim (2003) - https://isap.sejm.gov.pl/isap.nsf/download.xsp/WMP20030140200/O/M20030200.pdf. Accessed 3 July 2025
Resolution of the Sejm of the Republic of Poland of 23 February 2022 on the aggression of Russia against Ukraine (2022) - https://www.sejm.gov.pl/media9.nsf/files/ASEA-CBXDCN/%24File/uchwała_en.pdf. Accessed 3 July 2025
Sąd Najwyższy (2016) SN utrzymał w mocy wyrok w sprawie ostrzelania afgańskiej wioski Nangar Khel - https://www.sn.pl/aktualnosci/SitePages/komunikaty_o_sprawach.aspx?ItemSID=91-271e0911-7542-42c1-ba34-d1e945caefb2&ListName=Komunikaty_o_sprawach&rok=2016. Accessed 3 July 2025
Słomka T (2015) Między dwiema konstytucjami: kilka uwag o specyfice polskiej ciągłości i zmiany systemowej. In: Materska-Sosnowska A, Słomka T (eds) Konstytucje polskie z 1952 i 1997 roku: tradycja, instytucje, praktyka ustrojowa. Elipsa, Warszawa, pp 11–20
Snyder T (2012) Bloodlands: Europe between Hitler and Stalin. Hachette, London
Solmaz T (2024) Why Russia has only now declared war on Ukraine - https://www.lowyinstitute.org/the-interpreter/why-russia-has-only-now-declared-war-ukraine. Accessed 3 July 2025
Statement by the North Atlantic Council (2001) - https://www.nato.int/docu/pr/2001/p01-124e.htm. Accessed 3 July 2025
Statut constitutionnel du Duché de Varsovie (1808) Drukarnia Zawadzkich, Warszawa - https://bbc.mbp.org.pl/dlibra/publication/9994/edition/9043/content. Accessed 3 July 2025
Stone D (2001) The Polish-Lithuanian State, 1386-1795. University of Washington Press, Seattle
The North Atlantic Treaty (1949) - https://www.nato.int/cps/en/natohq/official_texts_17120.htm. Accessed 3 July 2025
United Nations Charter (1945) - https://www.un.org/en/about-us/un-charter/full-text. Accessed 3 July 2025
UNSC Resolution 1368 (2001) - https://digitallibrary.un.org/record/448051?ln=en&v=pdf. Accessed 3 July 2025

UNSC Resolution 1386 (2001) - https://digitallibrary.un.org/record/454998?v=pdf. Accessed 3 July 2025

Ustawa z dnia 11 marca 2022 r. o obronie Ojczyzny (2022) - https://isap.sejm.gov.pl/isap.nsf/download.xsp/WDU20220000655/O/D20220655.pdf. Accessed 3 July 2025

Ustawa z dnia 17 grudnia 1998 r. o zasadach użycia lub pobytu Sił Zbrojnych Rzeczypospolitej Polskiej poza granicami państwa (1998) - https://isap.sejm.gov.pl/isap.nsf/download.xsp/WDU19981621117/T/D19981117L.pdf. Accessed 3 July 2025

Volumina legum (1859), vols. 1-2. Ohryzko, St. Petersburg

Wasiński M (2008) Odpowiedzialność prawna Polski za incydent w Nangar Khel. Państwo i Prawo 2008(8):26–40

Zalewski J (2014) Polska w Afganistanie – doświadczenia i wnioski dla polityki bezpieczeństwa. Studia Bezpieczeństwa Narodowego 4(5):17–46

The Pacifist Principle in Germany: Between Established Constitutional Constants and Unprecedented Military Expansionism

Andrea De Petris

1 Introduction: From the Demilitarisation of Nazi Germany to the Rearmament of the *Bundesrepublik*

After the end of World War II, at the Potsdam Conference in 1945, the Allies had decided on the complete demilitarisation of Germany, and in fact, in its original version of 23 May 1949, the Basic Law (BL) contained no provision for the establishment of German armed forces: for the newly formed Federal Republic, no armed forces of its own were planned. Subsequently, the Paris Treaties signed in 1954 created the preconditions for the accession of the Federal Republic of Germany (FRG) to the Western European Union (WEU) and NATO (*North Atlantic Treaty Organisation*), paving the way for West German rearmament.

The Basic Law Amendment Act of 19 March 1956[1] created the so-called Military Constitution (*Wehrverfassung*).[2] It includes, inter alia, Article 87a, which states that 'The Federation shall establish armed forces for defence', and Article 87b, which provides for the establishment of an independent civil defence administration. The power of command-and-control rests in peacetime with the Minister of Defence,[3] while in the case of defence, it passes to the Federal Chancellor.[4] The declaration of

[1] Gesetz zur Ergänzung des Grundgesetzes, Gesetz über die Rechtsstellung der Soldaten, BGBl. I, p. 111, of 21.3.1956.

[2] Roemer (1956), pp. 193–198.

[3] Art. 65a, para. 1 BL.

[4] Art. 115b BL.

A. De Petris (✉)
Università degli Studi Internazionali (UNINT), Rome, Italy
e-mail: andrea.depetris@unint.eu

G. Cavaggion (ed.), *The 'Pacifist Principle' in the Italian and Japanese Constitutions in the Wake of the War in Ukraine*,
https://doi.org/10.1007/978-3-032-23108-6_16

the state of defence is the responsibility of the Bundestag,[5] while the determination of the state of defence is promulgated by the Federal President in the *Bundesgesetzblatt* (Federal Law Gazette).[6] The Federal President appoints and dismisses officers and non-commissioned officers[7] and also holds the right to determine the ranks of soldiers and decide on the uniform, as well as to award orders and honours, thus exercising the so-called formal supreme command in the military.

In addition to the aforementioned articles, the so-called Emergency Constitution (*Notstandsverfassung*) was added in 1968,[8] which, among other things, regulated the power of the armed forces to protect civilian objects in the event of defence and tension, as well as the deployment of the armed forces in support of the police and federal border police in the protection of civilian objects and in the fight against militarily organised and armed insurgents.[9] Apart from this addition, the Military Constitution has remained practically unchanged since 1956.[10]

2 Peace in West German Constitutional and Political Discourse

When speaking of the 'requirement of peace', the 'state of peace' or the pacifist principle in the Basic Law (BL), reference is made to a series of normative elements on which this is based. In reality, the normative datum represents an attempt to translate, at a constitutional level, a sentiment that characterised the political climate in West Germany after the end of World War II and the Nazi dictatorship, which for German history were necessarily perceived as interconnected and essentially inseparable. The Nazi regime had led the German state and the German people not only to a world war but also to the cessation of its existence and to a state of *Debellatio*, from which the reconstruction of whatever came next would have to start.

In the constituent phase of 1948–1949, therefore, even talking about rearmament appeared extremely dangerous, considering the proximity and vividness of the memories present not only in the memories of the German survivors. This explains the numerous references to peace that the BL contains, in order to clear the field of any doubt as to the fact that the indispensable condition in respect of which the reconstitution of a German state order could be admissible was that of a state marked by the realisation of peace.

At the same time, however, it was also clear to the German political class of 1949 that it was necessary to prepare a scenario in which some kind of German

---

[5] Art. 115a BL.

[6] Art. 82 para. 2 BL.

[7] Art. 60 para. 1 BL.

[8] Siebzehntes Gesetz zur Änderung des Grundgesetzes of 24 June 1968, BGBl. I, p. 709.

[9] Art. 87a (2) and (3) BL.

[10] Epping (2000), pp. 183–208.

rearmament policy was acceptable and practicable in the more or less near future, because a state can only be considered sovereign if it has a constitutionally regulated, but nonetheless existing, faculty for the legitimate use of force, including military force.

The rules of the BL are therefore intended to respond to this twofold need: to guarantee respect for the pacifist principle and, at the same time, provide a way of access to rearmament and the use of military force, which, as we shall see, is declined purely within a framework of supranational alliances. Probably in order to reassure its Allies first and foremost, who until shortly before its birth had been its most implacable enemies—as well as among the greatest victims of Nazi Germany's barbaric violence—the *Bundesrepublik* made it clear that it only conceived of a military policy within supranational defensive alliances aimed at protecting peace. The Allies, therefore, would have drawn from a (more or less) rearmed Germany the advantage of an associate capable of contributing to eventual war efforts, while at the same time warding off any hypothesis of a 'rush forward' by the institutional leadership in Bonn, in the event of any ambition to use force in some way classifiable as aggressive, in itself already inadmissible from an internal constitutional point of view, even before having to verify its compatibility with the constraints of the Alliances in which the Federal Republic had been admitted to contribute.

In the course of this contribution, the salient points of the constitutional dictate of the BL that deal with the issues of the pacifist principle and the use of force in the military sphere will be illustrated. This will be followed by a reference to a number of Bundesverfassungsgericht (BVerfG) rulings that have clarified the sense in which the German Constitutional Charter understands the correct declination of these two elements. Finally, some considerations will be presented with respect to the future developments of this interpretation, in view of the possible changes of scenario that are increasingly affecting the defence policies of the European continent and the North Atlantic space, of which Germany remains a fundamental component and whose role must also necessarily be rethought.

3 Preamble and Article 1 BL

A first programmatic but nevertheless pregnant reference to the theme of peace can already be found in the preamble of the Basic Law, which states that the 'German people [...] inspired by the will to serve the peace of the world as an equal member of a united Europe' has 'adopted this Basic Law by virtue of its constituent power'. In the same vein, the subsequent Article 1 paragraph 2 declares that the German people 'recognises [...] the inviolable and inalienable rights of man as the foundation of all human community, peace and justice in the world'.

The two provisions, in conjunction, establish not only a normative but almost a teleological obligation for all German state authorities to recognise and commit to 'peace', without, however, specifying further details. In particular, it is not made clear to what extent and in what respect peace is to be understood as 'something more' than at least the absence of war (*pax absentia belli*): probably the most correct interpretation of the point suggests that commitment to the realisation of peace represents an end that should inspire the entire action of the institutions of the FRG as a complementary and indispensable element of the other founding objectives of the BL, such as the protection of the democratic principle and the intangibility of human dignity, for which the realisation of peace, or at least the commitment of the order to realise it, is an indispensable condition.

4 The Pacifist Principle in Practice: Sections 24 and 26 BL

Some articles of the Grundgesetz contain provisions that concretely call for the realisation of peace, albeit declined within the commitment of the German state to operate within international organisations.

A first example comes from Article 24 BL, which is a crucial provision with regard to the transfer of sovereign rights to interstate bodies, being part of the context of international cooperation and constituting the legal basis that allows Germany to participate in supranational organisations and cede its state sovereignty in certain areas. Paragraph 1 of Article 24 BL allows the Federation to 'transfer sovereignty rights to supranational organisations by law', opening up the German state to international cooperation. It permits Germany's participation in supranational organisations, ceding its state sovereignty in certain areas while respecting the inviolable fundamental core enshrined in the so-called eternity clause of Article 79 paragraph 3 BL.[11]

The concept of sovereignty is to be understood here in a broad sense, encompassing all powers pertaining to the state monopoly of force: the transfer of such rights must, however, always be compatible with the principles of democracy, the rule of law, the welfare state and the federal state, as referred to in the aforementioned *Ewigkeitsklausel*, whereby only those rights may be transferred that do not affect the fundamental core of the Constitution, in particular the fundamental rights and structural principles of the Constitution. In the jurisprudence of the Federal Constitutional Court (BVerfG), it has been repeatedly emphasised in this regard that the transfer of sovereignty rights by the German state is to be regarded as permissible in the context of European integration only as long as democratic legitimacy and control of the standards of protection of rights enshrined in the Basic Law remain guaranteed.[12]

---

[11] 'No amendment of this Basic Law that concerns the division of the Federation into Länder, the principle of the participation of the Länder in legislation or the principles set out in Articles 1 and 20 shall be permissible.'

[12] V. BVerfGE 89, 155, of 12.10.1993 (Maastricht Urteil), for which see Frowein (1994), pp. 1–16, and BVerfGE 123, 267, of 30.6.2009 (Lissabon Urteil), for which see the Special Section: The Federal Constitutional Court's Lisbon Case in No. 8/2009 of the German Law Review.

Interstate bodies are to be understood as organisations established by interstate treaties in which several states participate, such as the United Nations (UN), the European Union (EU) or NATO. In any case, Article 24 paragraph 1 BL speaks only of the transfer of sovereignty, without giving any specifications as to the purposes for which this transfer would be permitted—a peculiarity that distinguishes it from the content of the subsequent paragraph 2, which will be discussed more shortly.

A formal reservation of law stipulates that the transfer of sovereignty rights must take place by means of a formal federal law, which requires the approval not only of the Bundestag but, when the competences of the Länder are affected, also of the Bundesrat,[13] emphasising the need to respect both the federal principle and broad democratic legitimacy.

Article 24 paragraph 2 then allows the Federation to adhere to systems of mutual collective security for the protection of peace 'that realise and ensure a peaceful and lasting order in Europe and among the peoples of the world': the possible devolution of sovereignty is conditioned in this case by the specific aim of realising an order permanently marked by the search for peace. The definition of 'peaceful coexistence of peoples' includes all forms of friendly relations between states as recognised by international law; therefore, not only preparations directed towards war but also political or economic measures that foment international tensions may constitute a breach of the peace.

A mutual collective security system is to be understood as an interstate alliance that serves to ensure the peace and collective defence of its members, with NATO being the most prominent example in this regard. Only later was the further controversial question of constitutional scope clarified as to whether the Bundesverfassungsgericht also considered the European Union to be a collective security system. In 1994, the judges in Karlsruhe expressly classified the WEU, which was dissolved in 2011 as such, but in the 'Lisbon' judgment[14] of 2009, the Federal Constitutional Court did not consider the Common Security and Defence Policy (CSDP) of the EU as a mutual collective security system, justifying this decision, among other things, by the lack of power of the CSDP bodies over the *Bundeswehr* and the lack of binding effect of the mutual assistance obligation of the EU member states. According to the BVerfG in its *Lisbon Treaty* judgment, the EU has not yet taken the step towards a common defence, but the Treaty only set the conditions for such a shared system to be realised in the future.[15]

In any case, the transfer of sovereignty rights in these areas must be regarded as limited to defence measures and may not lead to the involvement of Germany in actions contrary to international law. In addition, it follows that the security systems to which sovereignty may be transferred are not neutral but only permitted if they are aimed at the protection of peace and the realisation of a peaceful and lasting

[13] See Art. 24 para. 1 BL in conjunction with Art. 50 BL.

[14] BvE 2/08, 2 BvE 5/08, 2 BvR 1010/08, 2 BvR 1022/08, 2 BvR 1259/08 and 2 BvR 182/09, Decision of 30.6.2009.

[15] Näbig (2025), Einsatz ohne Mandat? Was das Grundgesetz über ‚Out-of-Area'-Missionen sagt, 11.5.2025.

order in Europe and internationally. In other words, the purpose of the realisation of peace is an indispensable condition for the legitimacy of the transfer of sovereignty as understood by the article in question.[16]

Article 26 BL contains both an individual prohibition and a legislative obligation to protect peace, acting as a legal barrier against the preparation and execution of wars of aggression. Paragraph 1 prohibits 'actions that are liable to disturb the peaceful coexistence of peoples and carried out with that intention, in particular with a view to preparing a war of aggression', which are unconstitutional and 'must be prosecuted under criminal law'. The prohibition must be understood as universally applicable and is aimed not only at institutions but also at individuals. In addition, the prohibited acts must not only be capable of disturbing the peace but also be carried out with the intention of doing so: the provision ensures that only acts aimed at actually disturbing the peace are covered.

The subsequent Section 26(2) provides that 'weapons intended for the conduct of war may only be manufactured, transported and marketed with the authorisation of the Federal Government'. In this regard, it must first be clarified that 'weapons of war' are to be understood as weapons not intended for individual self-defence but used primarily for combat operations in armed conflicts, such as tanks, combat aircraft or artillery.

The regulation at the constitutional level in the BL finds a final, decisive reference in Article 87a, introduced in 1968, which in paragraph 1 gives the Federation the competence to organise armed forces for the defence of the country, specifying that their manpower and the basic regulation of their organisation must be set out in the Bund budget; paragraph 2 then goes on to stipulate that, outside of defence, the armed forces may 'be engaged only to the extent that this Basic Law explicitly allows', imposing a constitutional reservation to regulate the practical conditions for exercising this power.[17]

5 The BVerfG's Narrow but Significant Jurisprudence on the Pacifist Principle and the Employment of Armed Forces

Whereas during the Cold War the German armed forces had been established exclusively for the purpose of military deterrence and defence of the territory and alliances to which the FRG adhered, with the new phase of international relations following the fall of the Berlin Wall and the end of the division between the two great East-West blocs, the *Bundeswehr* was to actively participate in armed peacekeeping missions in crisis zones throughout the world, within the framework of the military alliances to which the Federal Republic was (and still is) a member.

---

[16] Deiseroth (2020).

[17] Bagnato and Piccolo (2024), pp. 85–96.

In the early 1990s, Germany participated for the first time in armed peacekeeping operations, in Cambodia and Somalia in 1991 and 1992, under a UN mandate,[18] but without the prior consent of the Bundestag. On this occasion, the question arose as to whether the BL permitted military missions abroad and what rights the Bundestag had in this respect. In 1990, during the debate on military participation in the UN sanctions against Iraq's occupation of Kuwait, the Bundestag heatedly debated this question. While the governing coalition of the time, consisting of the Christian Democratic Union of Germany (CDU), the Christian Social Union in Bavaria (CSU) and the Free Democratic Party (FDP), considered possible in principle the deployment of the German army 'out of area' under a UN mandate, the Social Democratic Party of Germany (SPD) and Green parties, then in opposition, had spoken out against this hypothesis.

In 1992, with the 'Petersberg Turn', the SPD initiated a thorough revision of its foreign policy and declared possible its consent to *Bundeswehr* interventions under UN mandate: this, however, had not resolved the dispute over the interpretation of the Basic Law. Whereas Article 87a paragraph 1 of the Basic Law states that it is the task of the Federation to establish armed forces for defence, Article 24 paragraph 2 of the Basic Law, as seen, provides for the possibility of the Federation to join a 'system of mutual collective security' to 'safeguard peace' and, in doing so, accept limitations on its sovereign rights. The wording itself did not make it clear whether this made military operations permissible under both UN and NATO mandates and whether the Bundestag was responsible for taking a decision on the conduct of such operations.

In order to settle this issue, the FDP and SPD parliamentary groups appealed to the Federal Constitutional Court in 1994 in a so-called *Organstreitverfahren*—a conflict between organs. Both plaintiffs saw a possible violation of the Constitution in the participation of German soldiers in the NATO surveillance flights over Bosnia-Herzegovina in 1992; in addition, the SPD questioned the German navy's intervention in the Adriatic and Germany's military participation in the UN mission in Somalia. The main argument put forward by both parliamentary groups was the same: the federal government had violated the parliament's right of co-decision by deciding alone on the deployment of German soldiers abroad.

On 12 July 1994,[19] the Karlsruhe Court ruled that 'out-of-area' missions are constitutionally compliant provided that the Bundestag gives its prior approval, thus establishing the existence of a parliamentary reservation in this matter. According to

[18] More precisely, in the very early 1990s, the German armed forces were sent to various external conflict scenarios and in very different capacities on different occasions: naval mine-clearing units in Operation 'Southern Flank' in the Mediterranean and in the Persian Gulf (August 1990–September 1991) as part of the Second Gulf War: an anti-aircraft missile squadron in Diyarbakir, Turkey, in support of Operation Desert Storm (January–March 1991); navy ships in the Adriatic (Operation Sharp Guard, June 1993–October 1996); two United Nations (UN) missions in Phnom Penh, Cambodia (UNAMIC and UNTAC, October 1991–November 1993); one in Somalia (UNOSOM II, March 1993–March 1994); see Zimmermann (2019).

[19] 2 BvE 3/92, 2 BvE 5/93, 2 BvE 7/93, 2 BvE 8/93 of 12.7.1994. For a commentary on the judgment, see Heintschel von Heinegg and Haltern (1994), pp. 285–311.

the constitutional judges, the Basic Law not only authorises the Federation to adhere to a collective security system but also provides the constitutional basis for any subsequent military intervention by the *Bundeswehr*. Not only the UN but also NATO represent defensive systems of this kind; however, in the military interventions carried out up to that point, according to the *Bundesverfassungsgericht*, the federal government had violated the constitutional principle that requires it to obtain the approval of the parliament before deploying armed forces. In particular, the parliamentary reservation is derived from the fundamental constitutional principle that the Bundestag has always been obliged to approve the deployment of armed forces in the case of defence (Article 115a paragraph 1 BL[20] and Article 59a paragraph 1 BL,[21] later repealed). This principle is therefore also applicable to missions abroad in accordance with Article 24 paragraph 2 Auslandseinsätze (AOA). According to the courts, only in the case of 'imminent danger' can a preventive mandate be dispensed with, but even then, the Bundestag must be consulted afterwards, with the obligation to withdraw the armed forces if the Bundestag refuses its consent.

Despite the Constitutional Court's ruling, the parliamentary reservation was initially treated as a practice with no formal legal basis. In December 1998, the Bundestag voted in favour of the deployment of German fighter planes in the Kosovo war,[22] for which there was no UN mandate, as approval by the UN Security Council was lacking—a circumstance that raised quite a few legal controversies as to the legitimacy of the military action taken.[23] In November 2001, the Members of Parliament (MPs) voted, within the NATO alliance, in favour of the participation of German soldiers in the war in Afghanistan,[24] but again without the approval of an authorising legislation in this regard. It was only in 2005 that the parliamentary reservation was implemented in a special legislative provision: the current Act on Parliamentary Participation in Decisions on the Deployment of Armed Forces Abroad[25] of 18 March 2005 states in Article 1 paragraph 2: 'The deployment of German armed forces outside the scope of the Basic Law requires the approval of the Bundestag.' Since the ruling of the Federal Constitutional Tribunal in 1994, the

[20] 'The Bundestag, with the consent of the Bundesrat, determines that federal territory is being attacked by force of arms or that such an attack is imminent (state of defence). The determination is made at the instance of the Federal Government and requires a two-thirds majority of the votes cast, equal to at least a majority of the members of the Bundestag.'

[21] 'The declaration of the state of defence is the responsibility of the Bundestag.'

[22] In the roll-call vote, in addition to the left-wing PDS party, some MPs from Bündnis 90/Die Grünen, SPD, FDP and CDU/CSU did not approve the government's motion. In total, 500 MPs voted in favour of the federal government's motion, 62 were against and 18 abstained; see Vor 25 Jahren: Bundestag stimmt erstmals für Kriegseinsatz der Bundeswehr, bundestag.de.

[23] Schwabach (1999), pp. 405–418.

[24] Münch (2021), pp. 151–171.

[25] Parlamentsbeteiligungsgesetz of 18 March 2005 (BGBl. I S. 775). On the observance of the Bundestag's prerogatives by the law in question, see Wagner (2010).

number of the *Bundeswehri's* armed missions abroad has increased considerably:[26] among the most significant places of deployment are Kosovo and Afghanistan, but the German armed forces have also been or are currently active in Mali, Iraq, Syria, South Sudan, Sudan, Lebanon, the Mediterranean and the Horn of Africa, with a mandate from the Bundestag.[27]

The most controversial aspect has remained the question of under which conditions the deployment of the *Bundeswehr* should be considered an 'armed deployment'. In 2003, during the Iraq war, the red-green German government (SPD-Gruenen) argued that the deployment of German soldiers to secure the airspace over Turkey by NATO was not subject to approval, since the aircraft deployed were not armed; specifically, Chancellor Gerhard Schröder stated: 'German soldiers will participate in anything that serves the protection of the alliance's territory, but not in anything that implies participation in war.' Meanwhile, the then President of the Greens Reinhard Bütikofer confirmed: 'we have drawn a very clear line of demarcation: participation in AWACS (*Airborne Warning & Control System*) flights for the defence of the alliance is allowed. Participation in AWACS flights acting as a fire control centre for attacks in Iraq is not permitted'.[28]

In its judgment of 7 May 2008,[29] however, the Second Chamber of the Federal Constitutional Court contradicted this thesis, stating that the mere existence of concrete indications of a possible involvement of German soldiers in armed conflicts justified a parliamentary reservation, which would have meant that the Bundestag would have been obliged to pass a legislative measure authorising the military commitment as early as 2003. The ruling stated that in order to legitimately deploy German soldiers in NATO's Airborne Warning and Control System (AWACS) aircraft for airspace surveillance over Turkish territory in the spring of 2003, the federal government would have to obtain the Bundestag's approval. The decision made it clear that the parliamentary reservation in the Basic Law on Defence for the use of armed forces applies whenever, based on the context of the operation and the individual factual and legal circumstances, the involvement of German soldiers in armed conflicts is concretely foreseeable. By intervening in the surveillance of Turkish airspace by NATO AWACS aircraft, according to the Karlsruhe judges, German soldiers had participated in a military operation in which there were concrete and tangible indications of imminent involvement in armed clashes.[30]

The 2008 decision was essentially based on a number of considerations: firstly, in the aforementioned judgment of 12 July 1994 ('Out-of-Area'), the Karlsruhe judges, basing themselves on the general context of the constitutional provisions on

---

[26] Merziger (2018), pp. 40–67.

[27] Bundeszentrale für politische Bildung, Vor 25 Jahren: Bundesverfassungsgericht billigt Auslandseinsätze, 8.7.2019.

[28] Pflüger (2003) Zwiespältiges Die deutsche Rolle im Irakkrieg, Wissenschaft und Frieden 02/2003.

[29] 2 BvE 1/03, 7.5.2008.

[30] On the problematic nature of the notion of 'employment of armed military units', see Daum (2013).

defence and in the light of the German constitutional tradition, deduced from the Basic Law a general principle according to which any deployment of armed forces requires the binding and, in principle, prior approval of the Bundestag. The authorisation contained in Section 24 paragraph 2 of the Basic Law to participate in a mutual collective security system thus constitutes the constitutional basis for the participation of the German armed forces in operations outside federal territory, insofar as these take place within the framework and according to the rules of that system. Pursuant to Section 59(2) sentence 1 of the Basic Law, there is a reservation of the law in favour of the Bundestag, which must approve the legal basis of a mutual collective security system,[31] whereas the implementation of the treaty and the implementation of the integration programme laid down therein are the responsibility of the federal government. German involvement in the overall strategic orientation and the formation of will on concrete missions of the alliance is thus predominantly in the hands of the federal government.

The federal government's freedom of action in matters of alliance policy does not, however, include the decision as to who, at the national level, should determine whether *Bundeswehr* soldiers participate in a concrete intervention adopted within the alliance. According to the ruling, given the political dynamics that characterise alliance systems, it is all the more important that the main responsibility for the deployment of the armed forces lies in the hands of the people's representative body. The constitutional parliamentary reservation on defence constitutes in this respect an essential corrective to the limits of parliamentary accountability in the area of foreign security policy. The Bundestag is thus called upon to take the fundamental and constitutive decisions on the employment of the armed forces and holds responsibility for the armed deployment of the *Bundeswehr* abroad. Given the function and importance of the parliamentary reservation under the Federal Defence Act, its scope cannot be determined restrictively. In doubtful cases, the parliamentary reservation must rather be interpreted favourably. In cases in which a competence of the German Bundestag in the form of a right of co-decision in defence matters can be deduced from the Basic Law, there is no autonomous decision-making margin in favour of the federal government: the parliamentary reservation must be regarded as an integral part of the principle of the separation of powers, not a violation of it.

According to the Basic Law, therefore, the use of armed forces is only admissible on the basis of the Bundestag's consent if German soldiers are involved in armed operations: for the application of the parliamentary reservation of defence, it is not relevant that armed clashes have already taken the form of an actual conflict, but it is sufficient that, on the basis of the context of the intervention and the individual legal and factual circumstances, the involvement of German soldiers in armed clashes is concretely foreseeable. The decision makes it clear, however, that the mere possibility of armed clashes occurring during a mission is not sufficient: only the concrete foreseeability of involvement in armed clashes necessitates the

[31] 'Treaties regulating the political relations of the Federation or relating to matters of federal legislation require the favourable opinion or federal participation in the form of a federal law.'

parliamentary approval of a mission abroad by German soldiers. For this, on the one hand, concrete and sufficient indications are required that an operation may result in the use of armed force, depending on its purpose, the concrete political and military circumstances and operational powers. On the other hand, a particular proximity to the use of armed force is required, and the involvement of German armed forces must therefore be directly foreseeable: an indication of this exists when they carry weapons abroad and are authorised to use them. The question of whether there is involvement of German soldiers in armed operations is, on the other hand, fully subject to judicial review: in this case, the federal government has no margin of appreciation, nor is any aspect of foresight excluded, in whole or in part, from the Federal Constitutional Tribunal's power of review.[32]

According to this yardstick of assessment, the participation of German soldiers in the surveillance of Turkish airspace by NATO from 26 February to 17 April 2003 constituted a deployment of armed forces, which, in accordance with the parliamentary defence reserve, required the approval of the Bundestag. By conducting a surveillance of Turkish airspace with NATO AWACS aircraft, German soldiers participated in a military operation in which there were real and concrete indications of imminent involvement in armed conflict. The AWACS reconnaissance aircraft deployed formed part of a system of concrete military protection measures against a feared attack on NATO alliance territory. From the outset, Turkish airspace control held a specific reference to a military conflict with Iraq, which was considered possible on the basis of concrete circumstances. NATO had been seriously preparing for such a conflict since at least 18 March 2003, as the start of military operations in Iraq was widely anticipated, making it clear that it was not merely an abstract possibility of an armed conflict, but rather there were concrete and tangible indications that NATO's involvement in a military conflict was foreseeable. The immediate involvement of German soldiers in armed clashes was also foreseeable. At the latest, with the extension of the rules of engagement linked to the deteriorating situation, the involvement of German soldiers in armed clashes depended only on whether Iraq would attack Turkey and when it would do so. In conclusion, all conditions were in place to make the parliamentary reservation on the employment of German soldiers binding, which the federal government could not order without the prior authorisation of the Bundestag.

[32] Concurs with the BVerfG's decision and the view that in the case of German participation or involvement in an international armed conflict, the prior consent of the Bundestag is still required, Dreist (2004), pp. 1001–1043.

6 Conclusion: The Pacifist Principle to the Test of the New German Defence Policy

Up to now, the Federal Constitutional Court has not provided interpretations on the requirements laid down in Article 26 BL, as cases on this subject have only rarely been submitted to it. However, in light of the constitutional jurisprudence that has emerged in other articles related to the pacifist theme, it would be appropriate to discuss whether, in certain situations, an intensive rearmament policy can already be considered to increase tensions between states and thus endanger peaceful coexistence.

In recent years, German executives have tried, on several occasions, to increase spending in the military sector, departing from the constitutional limits on the subject. Following the Russian invasion of Ukraine in February 2022, on 3 June of that year, the government, led by then Social Democratic Chancellor Olaf Scholz, succeeded in obtaining a two-thirds majority vote in the Bundestag, which is needed to change the public debt ceiling and allow Germany to set up a EUR 100-billion defence fund that would not be subject to the restrictions[33] by adding the aforementioned Article 87a to the Basic Law.[34] The amendment was approved by the Bundestag with 568 votes in favour, 96 against and 20 abstentions[35] and was then also endorsed by the Bundesrat on 10 June.[36] The loosening of constitutional budgetary constraints raised a substantial public debate on whether these constraints should be kept intact in light of the need for public investment not only in the defence sector but also in the overall infrastructure networks and services of the German system.[37]

The most recent developments in the German rearmament policy also deserve to be assessed in the light of the existing constitutional constraints on the pacifist principle:[38] on 18 March 2025, in fact, in the last useful session of its 20th Legislature,

---

[33] According to an official communication from the Berlin government, 'The amendment of Article 87a of the Basic Law creates the constitutional basis for the establishment of the fund. This gives the federal government the power to establish a special fund with its own one-off credit authorisation of up to EUR 100 billion in order to strengthen Germany's alliance and defence capability. The one-off authorisation is exempt from the credit limit that normally applies under constitutional debt regulations. The amendment of the Basic Law constitutionally guarantees that the special fund is intended for the strengthening of alliance and defence capabilities.' 100 billion euros for a powerful Federal Armed Forces, bundesregierung.de, 3.6.2022.

[34] Id.

[35] Peltzer (2023).

[36] Bundesrat billigt Gesetzesänderung zum Sondervermögen für die Bundeswehr, Bundesrat.de, 10.6.2022.

[37] Hellermann (2022).

[38] On March 25, 2025, a landmark bill stated that defence spending above 1% of Germany's gross domestic product will be effectively exempt from the country's 2009 'debt brake'; see Paternoster T (2025), Germany's upper house clears historic defence spending bill. In: euronews.com 21.3.2025.

the Bundestag approved several constitutional amendments allowing the Federation and the Länder to contract new debts amounting to several hundred billion euros. The original bill submitted by the SPD and CDU/CSU parliamentary groups was substantially amended following an agreement with the party and the Bündnis90/ Die Grünen parliamentary group, in order to achieve the qualified majority of two-thirds of the Bundestag members required to amend the Basic Law, which the SPD and CDU/CSU members alone could not have achieved.[39]

These constitutional amendments have led to an extension of the exemption from the debt brake (*Schuldenbremse*),[40] with a focus on defence spending, to which the debt brake will in future only apply to the extent of 1% of gross domestic product (GDP), whereas expenditure exceeding this limit will not be counted towards the debt brake. As a result, German defence expenditure that will continue to be subject to the debt limit should amount to approximately EUR 40 billion. In return for voting in favour of the aforementioned constitutional revision, Bündnis 90/Die Grünen obtained a significant expansion of the expenditure areas: in addition to traditional defence expenditure, the exemption will also extend to civil protection and security for the population, intelligence services, protection of computer systems, and assistance to states that are victims of aggression contrary to international law.[41] In the form now approved, the exception to the *Schuldenbremse* is based on a broader concept of defence policy, in the belief that external security is guaranteed not only by national and allied defence capabilities but also by protection against cyberattacks and by the work of intelligence services, while aid to Ukraine is also partly covered by the exemption from the obligations of the debt brake.

In the debate in the Bundestag on the occasion of the vote, Friedrich Merz—then President of the CDU/CSU parliamentary group and, since 6 May 2025, German Chancellor,[42] stated that in light of Putin's war of aggression in Ukraine, the international and security situation in Europe calls for a 'paradigm shift in defence policy', which envisages a gradual move towards an independent European defence and a European defence community.[43] Even then Defence Minister Boris Pistorius (SPD), confirmed in the new Merz Cabinet, emphasised the need for the changes envisaged by the reform in question on that occasion, stating that he was faced with a decision of historic importance, on which the security and future of the country depended,

---

[39] 512 MPs voted in favour of the constitutional revision bill, while 206 voted against, and there were no abstentions.

[40] The debt brake is a constitutional provision approved by the Commission on Federalism in early 2009 to limit German public debt, which, since 2011, has imposed binding targets on the federal government and the states to reduce the budget deficit. With this measure, regulated by Section 109 paragraph 3 and Section 115 BL, the new 'structural' net borrowing, i.e. independent of the economic situation, of the federal government and the states is limited to a maximum of 0.35%—thus a total of 0.7%—of the nominal gross domestic product (GDP), Kinkartz S (2025), What is Germany's debt brake?, dw.com, 3.5.2025.

[41] Bundeszentrale für politische Bildung, Grundgesetzänderung für Verteidigung und Sondervermögen, 28.3.2025.

[42] Friedrich Merz is German Chancellor, deutschland.de, 6.5.2025.

[43] Mehrheit für Reform der Schuldenbremse: 512 Abgeordnete stimmen mit Ja, bundestag.de.

and that it would imply an obligation for Europe to grow in security policy, warning that in the future, defence policies would have to be managed by prioritising the need to defend against possible threats over the current economic and financial constraints.[44]

It is therefore appropriate to ask how what can rightly be considered an epoch-making strategic change in the defence policy of the Federal Republic will impact on the well-established constitutional doctrine of the pacifist principle hitherto observed in the German legal system: developments are likely to follow.

References

Bagnato S, Piccolo C (2024) Pacifist constitutions and humanitarian protection: the deliberative processes of missions in Italy, Germany and Japan through the prism of constitutional bodies. In: dpce online, special issue, pp 85–96

Daum O (2013) Was bedeutet 'Einsatz bewaffneter Streitkräfte' nun wirklich?, juwiss.de

Deiseroth D (2020) Das Friedensgebot des Grundgesetzes und der UN-Charta. In: Friedensforum 2/2010

Dreist P (2004) AWACS-Einsatz ohne Parlamentsbeschluss? In: Zeitschrift für ausländisches öffentliches Recht und Völkerrecht (ZaöRV), pp 1001–1043

Epping V (2000) Wehrverfassung: Entmilitarisierung - Wiederbewaffnung - Leistungsfähigkeit. In: Pieroth B (Hrsg) Verfassungsrecht und soziale Wirklichkeit in Wechselwirkung. Duncker & Humblot, Berlin, pp 183–208

Frowein J (1994) Das Maastricht-Urteil und die Grenzen der Verfassungsgerichtsbarkeit. In: Zeitschrift für ausländisches öffentliches Recht und Völkerrecht (Zaörv), pp 1–16

Heintschel von Heinegg W, Haltern UR (1994) The Decision of the German Federal Constitutional Court of 12 July 1994 in Re Deployment of the German Armed Forces 'Out of Area'. In: Netherlands International Law Review, pp 285–311

Hellermann J (2022) Das Sondervermögen Bundeswehr, der Bundeshaushalt und die Schuldenbremse. In: Verfassungsblog.de, 3.6.2022

Merziger P (2018) Out of area. Humanitäre Hilfe der Bundeswehr im Ausland (1959-1991). In: Zeithistorische Forschungen, 2018, 40–67

Münch P (2021) Ein paradoxer Krieg. Der Einsatz der Bundeswehr in Afghanistan. In: Maurer J, Rink M (Hg.) Einsatz ohne Krieg? Die Bundeswehr nach 1990 zwischen politischem Auftrag und militärischer Wirklichkeit, Vandenhoeck & Ruprecht, Göttingen, pp 151–171

Näbig R (2025) Einsatz ohne Mandat? Was das Grundgesetz über 'Out-of-Area'-Missionen sagt. In: Europäische Sicherheit und Technik, 11.5.2025

Peltzer F (2023) Kreative Sondervermögensgestaltung: Die Kritik des Bundesrechnungshofs an der Zweckerweiterung des Sondervermögens Bundeswehr. In: Verfassungsblog, 18.12.2023

Pflüger T (2003) Zwiespältiges Die deutsche Rolle im Irakkrieg. In: Wissenschaft und Frieden, vol 2

Roemer W (1956) Die neue Wehrverfassung. Juristen Zeitung (JZ):193–198

Schwabach A (1999) The Legality of the NATO Bombing Operation in the Federal Republic of Yugoslavia. In: Pace International Law Review, pp 405–418

[44] Id.

Wagner TM (2010) Parlamentsvorbehalt und Parlamentsbeteiligungsgesetz. Die Beteiligung des Bundestages bei Auslandseinsätzen der Bundeswehr. Beiträge zum Parlamentsrecht (BPR), vol 66. Duncker & Humblot, Berlin

Zimmermann J (2019) 25 Jahre Rechtsprechung des Bundesverfassungsgerichts zu 'Out of area'-Einsätzen der Bundeswehr, bundestag.de, 4.7.2019

Pacifist Clauses, Euro-Atlantic Integration Clauses and Neutrality in the Constitutions of the Former Soviet Republics of Ukraine, Georgia and Moldova

Arianna Angeli

1 'Foreign Policy Clauses' in the Constitutions of the Former Soviet States: The Cases of Ukraine, Georgia and Moldova

This chapter aims to investigate 'foreign policy clauses' in the constitutions of the countries of the former Soviet space, focusing in particular on the cases of Ukraine, Georgia and Moldova. Reference is made to constitutional provisions, endowed with an external dimension,[1] that put precise constraints on State institutions in foreign policy decisions, among which it is possible to include renunciation of war and the peaceful resolution of international controversies (the so-called 'pacifist clauses'), international cooperation clauses, Euro-Atlantic integration clauses and neutrality clauses, which can be combined in different ways.[2]

Foreign policy clauses can be more generally framed within the so-called foreign relations law, *i.e.* norms 'of each nation that govern how that nation interacts with the rest of the world'.[3] Even if strictly related to norms of international law that regulate relations among States, for the purpose of this chapter, we make reference only to norms of domestic law.

[1] On the external dimension of the Constitution as a tool to proclaim independence and allow other nations to recognize a legitimate government, express the commitment of the State to comply with customary international law or specific international treaties and provide information on the procedure for the adoption of treaties (through a monist or dualist approach), as well as on war, see Henkin (1996); Ginsbourg (2017), pp. 326 ss.; Ginsbourg (2018), pp. 63 ss.

[2] Ibrido (2022, 2025).

[3] See Bradley (2018), pp. 4–5.

A. Angeli (✉)
University of Milan, Milan, Italy
e-mail: arianna.angeli@unimi.it

G. Cavaggion (ed.), *The 'Pacifist Principle' in the Italian and Japanese Constitutions in the Wake of the War in Ukraine*,
https://doi.org/10.1007/978-3-032-23108-6_17

Foreign policy clauses—which can be identified both in consolidated democracies and in constitutional systems based on autocratic principles, as well as in hybrid regimes among which it is possible to classify Ukraine, Georgia and Moldova[4]—can be considered specific techniques of 'rationalisation' of foreign policy.[5]

Reference to war and to the conditions for its legitimate exercise originally appeared in the constitutions adopted in the context of the French Revolution.[6] The desire of domination over other nations was deemed to be enshrined in the *ancient régime* system and had to be overcome, according to the Revolution ideology. Pacifist clauses—or better 'the renunciation to the *war of conquest* and to the use of force against the freedom of other peoples'—were included in almost all French constitutions and, in particular, in the 1791 Constitution, the 1793 Jacobin Constitution (with a partially different formula), the 1848 Constitution and the 1946 Constitution, which in turn is mentioned in the Preamble to the 1958 Constitution.[7]

In the twentieth century, the contemporary notion of 'war of aggression' appeared in international documents, and first attempts were made, within the dimension of the League of Nations, to restrict the right to engage in war. However, it was the Briand-Kellogg Pact that radically innovated the *ius ad bellum* discipline, codifying the principles of renunciation of war 'as an instrument of national policy' and the settlement of disputes 'by pacific means'. Such international innovations paved the way for the constitutionalisation of the renunciation of war of aggression in the Spanish Constitution (1931) and in the Irish Constitution (1937).[8]

Principles stated in the Briand-Kellogg Pact were reaffirmed and strengthened in the Charter of the United Nations, in Article 2 on the 'renunciation to the threat or use of force in international relations' and Article 33 on the 'pacific settlement of international disputes'. Accordingly, only 'individual or collective self-defence' would have been considered legitimate (Article 51, Charter of the United Nations).

Pacifist clauses were added to the constitutions adopted from that moment on, following WWII (with reference, in particular, to defeated countries, *i.e.* Japan 1946, Italy 1948 and Germany 1949), in the 1970s (Greece 1975, Portugal 1976 and Spain 1978), in the 1990s (in Central and Eastern Europe, in the aftermath of the fall of communist regimes), up to the most recent texts, adopted in Montenegro (2007), Kosovo (2008) and Hungary (2011).[9]

As already said, there is a wide range of formulas codifying opposition to war, from the less binding ones, expressing the commitment of the State to promote peace in international relations, to the strictest ones, prescribing disarmament (Article 9, Japanese Constitution 1946; Article 12, Costa Rican Constitution 1949).

---

4 Di Gregorio (2019a), b, c), pp. 1–29; Di Gregorio (2023), p. 2023.

5 Cfr. Mirkine-Guetzévitch (1937, 2009).

6 Vedaschi (2008), pp. 91 ss.

7 De Vergottini (2004), p. 27.

8 Vedaschi (2008), p. 101.

9 Di Gregorio (2019a), b, c).

Pacifist clauses are often combined with other foreign policy clauses, among which international cooperation clauses expressing the *favour* for peace and cooperation in international relations.[10] Such clauses, endowed with cogent nature, do not entail a complete 'abstention from conflict' or from the deployment of armed forces abroad but subordinate their use to obligations under international law.[11] Some constitutions, in particular, mention the possibility for the Armed Forces of the State to participate in collective defence, peacekeeping or humanitarian operations abroad, in compliance with obligations under international law (*e.g.* Portugal 1976, Slovakia 1992, Czech Republic 1992, Hungary 2011).

Pacifist clauses do not coincide with neutrality clauses, which entail a specific legal regime defined by international law, regulated by international agreements (Switzerland 1815), unilaterally declared at the constitutional level (Austria: Constitutional Law 1955, Malta: Amendment Act 1987, Moldova: Constitution 1994) or introduced *de facto* (Ireland; Finland and Sweden up to 2022).[12]

Finally, Euro-Atlantic integration clauses express the commitment of a State—or more frequently the intention or the aspiration—to become part of an international or supranational organisation, namely the European Union, the North Atlantic Treaty Organization (NATO) or both.

In the countries of the former Soviet space, the definition of foreign policy clauses was conditioned by a multitude of factors, among which the desire to overcome the previous system. Prior to independence, in the Soviet period, foreign policy was regulated by the 1977 USSR Constitution, which was endowed with 'supreme legal force' (Article 173, para. 1). All the constitutions of the Soviet Socialist Republics (SSRs) had to comply with the USSR Constitution (Article 76, para. 3). Particularly relevant from a procedural—and also substantial—perspective was the attribution to the Communist Party of the competence to determine USSR's 'domestic and foreign policy' (Article 6).

Two sections of the 1977 USSR Constitution were dedicated respectively to foreign policy and the defence of the Socialist Homeland (Sections 4 and 5). In Section 4, reference to peace, based on the Leninist doctrine,[13] was combined with cooperation among Socialist countries (Articles 28 and 30). Wide references were made to principles agreed in the Helsinki Final Act[14] (Article 29).[15] In Section 5, defence of

[10] Ibrido (2022).

[11] De Vergottini (2004), p. 41.

[12] Vedaschi (2008), pp. 129 ss.; Ronzitti (2023); Haider-Quercia (2024).

[13] See the Decree on Peace, adopted by the Second All-Russia Congress of Soviets of Workers' and Soldiers' Deputies on 26 October (8 November) 1917.

[14] As Brezhnev pointed out during his visit to France in July 1977, the Soviet Constitution - or better, the 'project' - would have been the first constitutional text to incorporate all the fundamental principles set out in the Helsinki Final Act. Biscaretti di Ruffia, Crespi Reghizzi (1979), pp. 132–133.

[15] According to Article 29, 'The relations of the USSR with other States are built on the basis of observance of the principles of sovereign equality; mutual refusal to use force or the threat of

the Homeland was defined as one of the most prominent functions of the State (Article 31). Finally, war propaganda was prohibited (Article 28, para. 3).

The amendments to the USSR Constitution approved on 1 December 1988 marked the transition from a 'Socialist' State system to a Socialist State system 'under the Rule of Law' and introduced the 'co-determination' of the internal and foreign policy, divided among the Communist Party, the Congress of Deputies and the President of the Supreme Soviet.[16] Then with USSR Law No. 963-I of 20 December 1989, the SSRs started autonomous constitutional reform paths and to develop autonomous foreign policies.

Following independence, all the countries of the area distanced themselves from the previous system. Compared to the constitutions adopted in the aftermath of WWII, in the 1970s, and in the 1990s in former Socialist States that are now members of the EU, which regulate foreign policy with great detail, the constitutions of the countries of the former Soviet space—and in particular the Constitutions of Moldova 1994, Georgia 1995 and Ukraine 1996— originally included laconic foreign policy clauses, which followed long sections dedicated to self-determination, independence and sovereignty.

Such choice was conditioned by the complexities of the region—and in particular the late acquisition of statehood, difficulties in State-building and nation-building processes, non-homogeneous populations, the destabilising presence of non-autochthonous Russian-speaking minorities, secessionist pressures and the re-emergence of border disputes with neighbouring countries[17]—the instability caused by the dissolution of the Soviet Union and the Warsaw Pact military alliance, and, above all, the fear of renovated forms of cooperation with Russia.

Faced with the increasing 'assertiveness' of the Russian Federation at the international level, these three countries of the former Soviet space had to rethink provisions dedicated to foreign relations. This chapter therefore intends to investigate how foreign policy clauses have been reinterpreted or amended within the context of the large-scale aggression of the Russian Federation against Ukraine.

2 Peace, Cooperation and Euro-Atlantic Integration Clauses in the Constitutional Acts of Independent Ukraine

Ukraine started to develop—or better to manifest the intention to develop—an autonomous foreign policy as part of the independence process. Compared to Georgia and Moldova, Ukraine was endowed with a peculiar international status.

---

force; inviolability of borders; territorial integrity of States; peaceful settlement of disputes; non-interference in internal affairs; respect for human rights and fundamental freedoms (…)'.

[16] Ganino (1989), p. 181.

[17] Di Gregorio (2023), p. 4. Cfr. Giannini (1946–1947), pp. 500–540; Kuzio (1998, 2007); De Stefano (2015); K. Wolczuk and R. Dragneva, *Russia's Longstanding Problem with Ukraine's Borders*, in *Chatham House*, 24.08.2022; Lami (2022).

The Ukrainian SSR was not an independent State, but—like the Belorussian SSR—it was a founding member of the United Nations.[18] The participation in the UN of the two SSRs was due to political considerations, to strengthen the position of the USSR.[19]

With USSR Law No. 963-I of 20 December 1989, Ukraine started an autonomous constitutional reform path, which led to independence in 1991. Between 1989 and 1991, eight constitutional amendments were approved. After independence, 16 further amendments were added. Due to the difficulties in the approval of a new constitution, a so-called Small Constitution was adopted on 18 May 1995 (*i.e.* the Law 'On the Principles of Organisation of State Power and Local Self-Government'). The text was incorporated into a Constitutional Agreement—signed by the President of the Republic, the President of the *Rada*, *i.e.* the unicameral parliament of Ukraine, and the deputies who had approved it—which replaced the conflicting sections of the 1978 Constitution. The *interim* constitutional regime that resulted from this process was extremely complex, and foreign policy clauses were revised several times.

With the approval of the Declaration on State Sovereignty of Ukraine on 16 July 1990 and the amendments to the Ukrainian SSR Constitution on 24 October 1990 (which followed the amendment of the 1977 USSR Constitution, approved in March 1990), foreign policy clauses were radically reformed, both from substantial and from procedural points of view.

In particular, with the Declaration of 16 July 1990, the SSR solemnly proclaimed the 'State sovereignty' of Ukraine—defined as 'the supremacy, independence, completeness and indivisibility of the power of the Republic within its territory and independence and equality in foreign relations' (Preamble)—and 'the inalienable right to self-determination' of the Ukrainian nation (Section I). The Declaration would have represented the foundations for the new Constitution and for the definition of new international agreements (Concluding Section).

The text realised a peculiar combination of foreign policy clauses, balancing neutrality and international cooperation with pacifist and pan-European aspirations (sic!), as well as with the recognition of the supremacy of *jus cogens*. In particular, the Ukrainian SSR solemnly proclaimed its intention to become 'a permanently neutral State, that does not participate in military alliances and adheres to the three non-nuclear principles: not accepting, not producing and not acquiring nuclear weapons'. For Ukraine, neutrality had more political rather than military significance: by declaring the neutral status, Ukraine wanted first and foremost to distance itself from the USSR, become independent and exclude the possibility of a new alliance with Russia or a closer political-military union with other Soviet Republics.

The Ukrainian SSR committed itself to participating in international cooperation organisations, to actively contribute to the strengthening of peace and international security and to participate directly in the pan-European process and European

[18] https://research.un.org/en/unmembers/founders.

[19] Filippini (1995); Ganino (2020).

structures (Section X, paras. 1–2). Ukraine also reaffirmed its right to have its own armed forces and to regulate military service (Section IX).

Contradicting the principles of socialism, the Ukrainian SSR recognised the superiority of universal human values over class values and the superiority of universally recognised norms of international law over norms of domestic law (Section X, para. 3). Finally, the relations of the Ukrainian SSR with the other Soviet Republics would have been based on the principles of equality, mutual respect and non-interference in internal affairs.

Additionally, the amendments to the Ukrainian SSR Constitution adopted on 24 October 1990—through which Ukraine transposed into its Constitution the amendments to the USSR Constitution approved on 14 March 1990—repealed Article 6 on 'the Communist Party's leading role in shaping foreign policy' (Article 6) and removed references to the USSR Constitution from Articles 28 and 29 of the Ukrainian Constitution.

On 25 February 1991, the Warsaw Pact Organization—the military branch of the Treaty of Friendship, Co-operation and Mutual Assistance (TFCMA), created in the Eastern Bloc as a counterweight to the North Atlantic Treaty Organization (NATO)—ceased to exist.[20]

That same year, shortly after the *coup d'état* against President Gorbachev, the *Verkhovna Rada* of the Ukrainian SSR adopted the Declaration of Independence on 24 August 1991,[21] ratified by a referendum on 1 December 1991.

Compared to other Soviet Republics, the Ukrainian Declaration was a really short text, in which the *Verkhovna Rada*—after recalling the millennial tradition of Ukrainian statehood, affirming the right to self-determination as set out in the Charter of the United Nations and seeking to implement the Declaration of Sovereignty—proclaimed the independence of the country. Reference to neutrality disappeared from the text. After independence, attempts were unsuccessfully brought about to introduce neutrality, which failed in the face of the security needs of the country.[22]

Representatives from Ukraine participated in the Novo-Ogaryovo meeting, along with representatives from other Soviet Republics, with the aim of negotiating a renovated Treaty of Union. Nevertheless, Ukraine refused to sign an agreement on the establishment of a confederation that retained elements of continuity with the previous system (with a common military, foreign policy, market, currency and space activity). This led to the failure of negotiations.[23]

On 8 December 1991, representatives from Russia, Belarus and Ukraine convened in Belovezhskaya Pushcha (Minsk), where they reached an agreement on the dissolution of the Soviet Union and the establishment of the Commonwealth of

---

[20] Stucchi (1995), p. 531.

[21] On 1 December 1991, a republican referendum was held to confirm Declaration of Independence.

[22] In particular, in 2007, I.A. Shufrych, deputy of the Party of Regions—who is now in detention—presented a draft law in Parliament on the neutrality of Ukraine. In https://babel.ua/en/news/118006-the-court-extended-the-preventive-measure-for-nestor-shufrych.

[23] Filippini (1995), pp. 91–92 ss.

Independent States (CIS). The High Contracting Parties committed themselves to respecting each other's territorial integrity and the inviolability of existing borders (Article 5), cooperating in ensuring international peace and security (Article 6, para. 1), as well as recognising each other's aspirations to achieve the status of a nuclear-weapon-free zone and neutrality (Article 6, para. 2). Member States would have preserved, under a unified command, a common military-strategic space, including unified control over nuclear weapons (Article 6, para. 3), developed coordinated activities in foreign policy, and cooperated in the definition of a common economic space, environmental policies, migration policies and the fight against organised crime (Article 7). Moreover, the High Contracting Parties, as successor States of the USSR, committed themselves to the fulfilment of international obligations arising from treaties and agreements of the former USSR (Article 12), formally renouncing the principle of *tabula rasa* in matters of succession in international relations. A few weeks later, the Minsk Agreement was extended from the three original members to 11 former Soviet Republics through the Alma-Ata Protocol. Originally framed as an association of sovereign States, with a limited level of institutionalisation, the CIS's evolution has been characterised by the hegemonic role of Russia.[24]

Soon afterwards, tensions emerged between Russia and Ukraine with reference to Crimea and the fleet in the Black Sea, and they became blatant in the context of the START I and START II negotiations on the non-proliferation of nuclear weapons.[25] Such tensions partially found a solution 3 years after, on 5 December 1994, with the Budapest memorandum,[26] in which the Russian Federation, the UK and the USA reaffirmed their commitment to respect the independence, sovereignty and existing borders of Ukraine and their obligation to refrain from threat or use of force and economic coercion against Ukraine (Section 1–3, Budapest memorandum). In turn, Ukraine agreed to transfer nuclear warheads to Russia. That same year, Ukraine signed the Partnership and Cooperation Agreement (PCA) with the European Union and entered into the NATO Partnership for Peace. Both agreements were part of neighbourhood policies specifically designed to fill the void in regional security generated by the collapse of the Soviet Union, and they were not intended as a first step towards accession processes.[27]

Due to a series of difficulties experienced by the country, as already said, Ukraine adopted a new Constitution only in 1996. The Fundamental Law, in its original

[24] Di Gregorio (2019a).

[25] Tensions between Russia and Ukraine have already emerged within the context of the START I negotiations. The Lisbon Protocol, signed on 23 May 1992, represented a partial solution to the problem, identifying Russia, Belarus, Ukraine and Kazakhstan as successor States to the Soviet Union, assuming all obligations in connection with the treaty. The Protocol was immediately ratified by the USA, Belarus and Kazakhstan, while Ukraine opted for a partial ratification on 6 November 1993. The same difficulties emerged within the SALT II negotiations. Stucchi (1995), pp. 535–536. Cfr. Larrabee and Lynch (1994).

[26] Memorandum on Security Assurances in Connection with Ukraine's Accession to the Treaty on the Non-Proliferation of Nuclear Weapons, in treaties.un.org/doc/Publication/UNTS/Volume%20 3007/Part/volume-3007-I-52241.pdf. Cfr. Cella (2021).

[27] Lami (2022).

version, introduced a laconic pacifist clause combined with an equally laconic international cooperation clause, whose interpretation has radically changed over time. According to Article 18, 'The foreign policy activity of Ukraine shall be aimed at ensuring its national interests and security, maintaining peaceful and mutually beneficial cooperation with members of the international community, in accordance with the generally recognised principles and norms of international law'. Such a provision should have been interpreted in light of the Charter of the United Nations, as well as according to the Declaration of Independence (Preamble).

In 2010, President Viktor Yanukovych—the leader of the pro-Russian Party of Regions—presented a bill in Parliament 'On the Principles of Domestic and Foreign Policy'. The latter was approved by the *Verkhovna Rada* soon afterwards and introduced a new controversial interpretation of Article 18 of the Constitution. In particular, the 2010 Law on the Principles of Domestic and Foreign Policy repealed provisions on Ukraine's 'integration Euro-Atlantic security space', contained in the 2003 Law on National Security, thereby excluding the possibility of Ukraine joining NATO.

According to Article 11 of the Law on the Principles of Domestic and Foreign Policy, Ukraine's foreign policy would have been based on the principle of 'non-alignment', defined as 'non-participation in military-political alliances'. In a quite contradictory way, however, Article 11 confirmed the intention of the country to contribute 'to the improvement and development of the European system of collective security', to prosecute 'the constructive partnership with the North Atlantic Treaty Organization and other military-political blocs on all issues of mutual interest' and to obtain the full membership of the European Union.[28]

It was on the issue of economic integration that the contradictions of the Yanukovych presidency emerged most dramatically. Ukraine, in fact, was negotiating both with Russia and with the European Union a strengthened economic partnership.[29] When in November 2013 President Yanukovych declared its intention not to ratify the Association Agreement with the EU, protests erupted in Kyiv (the so-called Euromaidan). President Yanukovych was forced to leave the country and found refuge in the Russian Federation (confirming suspicions of Russian influence on his presidency).

Those events were followed by the proclamation of independence of the Crimean Peninsula in March 2014 (not internationally recognised)—which completed its accession to the Russian Federation that same year—and the proclamation of

[28] As stated in Article 11, Ukrainian foreign policy would have ensured national interest and security as well as the protection of the sovereignty and territorial integrity of the State, strengthened the authority of the State, promoted 'international peace and security in the world, participating in a comprehensive political dialogue to increase mutual trust among States, overcoming traditional and new security threats', adhered to the policy of non-alignment, strengthened the role of international law, prevented conflicts in neighbouring regions, protected the rights and interests of the citizens and of Ukrainians living outside the borders and ensured Ukraine's integration into the European Union as a full member.

[29] Cfr. Di Gregorio (2019a).

independence of the Republics of Donetsk and Luhansk (not internationally recognised)—which joined the Russian Federation 8 years later, in 2022.

The new President, Petro Poroshenko—elected in May 2014—immediately signed the Association Agreement with the EU.[30] On 23 December 2014, the *Verkhovna Rada*—on the initiative of the President Poroshenko—approved the amendments to the legislation regulating the principles of domestic and foreign policy and the principles of national security, repealing the provisions on non-alignment and affirming the intention of the country to become a member of NATO.[31]

Five years later, such an aspiration was codified at the constitutional level. In 2019, the Ukrainian Parliament passed an amendment to the Constitution that repositioned the country in the international arena.

The bill 'On Amendments to the Constitution of Ukraine (on the Strategic Course of the State towards Ukraine's Full Membership in the European Union and the North Atlantic Treaty Organization)' was introduced by President Petro Poroshenko, bypassing the preliminary check of the Constitutional Commission. After the control of the Constitutional Court, it was approved by the *Verkhovna Rada* in a first session on 22 November 2018 and in a second session on 7 February 2019.

The constitutional amendment modified the Preamble, adding a reference to the European identity and the irreversibility of the European and Euro-Atlantic paths of the country. Provisions on the competences of the State institutions in defining foreign policy were amended accordingly. In particular, Article 85, para. 5, assigns to the *Verkhovna Rada* the competence to 'implement the strategic course of the State for the acquisition of full membership of Ukraine in the European Union and in NATO'. Article 102 defines the President as 'the guarantor of the implementation of the strategic course of the State for Ukraine's full membership in the European Union and the North Atlantic Treaty Organization'. Finally, as set out in Article 106, the Cabinet of Ministers 'ensures the implementation of the strategic course of the State for the acquisition of full membership of Ukraine in the European Union and in the North Atlantic Treaty Organization'.

With a view to avoiding any confrontation with Russia, Section 14, Transitional Provisions—which affirmed that 'The use of existing military bases on the territory of Ukraine for the temporary stay of foreign military formations is possible in accordance with the procedure determined by international treaties ratified by the *Verkhovna Rada* of Ukraine'—was deleted.[32] In the meantime, in 2018, Ukraine—which was a CIS founding member, with a non-participant status not having ratified the CIS Charter—withdrew from the Commonwealth of Independent States.

[30] Association Agreement between the European Union and its Member States, of the one part, and Ukraine, of the other part, in eur-lex.europa.eu/legal-content/EN/ALL/?uri=CELEX%3A22014A0529%2801%29.

[31] The bill, submitted to Parliament by Ukraine's President Petro Poroshenko, was supported by 303 deputies. The document's explanatory note stated that the non-aligned status proved ineffective in terms of maintaining the country's security.

[32] Filippini (2019), p. 596.

On 14 September 2020, President Zelenskyy adopted Decree No. 392/2020, which provided for the development of a strengthened special partnership with NATO, with the aim of obtaining the full membership.[33] Aspirations of the country to join both NATO and the EU have started to materialise in the months following the full-scale aggression of the country.

On 28 February 2022, Ukraine applied for EU membership, asking for a fast-tracking procedure considering wartime circumstances.[34] On 17 June 2022, the Commission presented its Opinion on the accession of Ukraine, and that same month, the EU Council granted the country the candidate status, together with Moldova. On 25 June 2024, the European Union formally opened accession negotiations with Ukraine.[35] It is worth noting that one of the six clusters of accession negotiations is devoted to external relations and, in particular, to foreign, security and defence policy, which will require a realignment of the country.

Full-scale aggression has produced a real change in the foreign policy of Ukraine, which has always been divided between pro-Russia and pro-Western positions. War, in fact, has excluded any accommodating solution—including the possibility to proclaim the neutral status[36]—and pushed, for the first time, the country out of Russia's sphere of influence.

3 The Euro-Atlantic Integration in the Georgian Constitution

Georgia has followed a constitutional path parallel to that of other SSRs. Nevertheless, the country has always presented distinctive features. After the fall of the Tsarist Empire, even if in an extremely unstable context, the country was able to acquire full statehood. Indeed, following the short-lived experience of the Transcaucasian Democratic Federative Republic, on 26 May 1918, the National Council of Georgia (led by Mensheviks) proclaimed the independence of the Democratic Republic of Georgia, and Noah Jordania was elected President. It is worth noting that the Act of Independence declared the 'permanent neutrality' of

---

[33] Cfr. J. Frosini, V. Lapa, *Would Ukraine Breach its own Constitution if it Dropped its NATO Bid?*, in *Verfassungsblog*, 18.02.2022.

[34] S. Lashyn, *Fast-Tracking Applications for EU Membership*, in www.europeanlawblog.eu/pub/6i9a35im/release/1.

[35] EU Opening Statement on Accession Negotiations, www.consilium.europa.eu/media/hzmfw1ji/public-ad00009en24.pdf.

[36] President Zelenskyy's stance on neutrality has radically changed over time, and it seems now, after more than 3 years of war, that neutral status—which would require a constitutional amendment forbidden in wartime—is no longer an option in peace negotiations. See 'Ukraine's Zelenskyy to offer neutrality declaration to Russia for peace "without delay"', in www.pbs.org/newshour/world/ukraines-zelensky-to-offer-neutrality-declaration-to-russia-for-peace-without-delay, 28.03.2022; 'Zelenskyy on Ukraine's neutral status: In 2014, it didn't stop the war', in news-ukraine.rbc.ua/news/zelenskyy-on-ukraine-s-neutral-status-in-1750085957.html, 16.06.2025.

the country (para. 3).[37] On 7 May 1920, Bolshevik Russia recognised Georgia's independence and committed itself to non-interference in Georgian domestic affairs.

On 21 February 1921, the Constituent Assembly, elected in 1919 through *universal suffrage*, adopted the Constitution. However, the first modern fundamental law in the nation's history, the result of a 3 years' work, remained in force for only 4 days.[38] On 25 February 1921, the Red Army occupied Tbilisi, and it took 70 years for Georgia—which became a founding member of the Soviet Union as part of the Transcaucasian SSR—to restore its independence.

Georgia started to develop an autonomous constitutional path once again in an extremely unstable context, which made it almost impossible to rethink its external relations. On 9 April 1989, protests for independence erupted in the capital city, Tbilisi, which were rapidly suppressed by Soviet forces.

The following year, on 9 March 1990, the Georgian SSR adopted the Declaration of Sovereignty. The text denounced the occupation and *de facto* annexation of Georgia by Soviet Russia in 1921. Accordingly, Georgia considered the Treaty on USSR as 'illegal and invalid' with reference to Georgia.

After the approval of the 1990 Amendments to the USSR Constitution, on 28 October 1990, the first multi-party elections of the Supreme Council of the Georgian SSR were held. Only 16 days later, the Supreme Council amended the 1978 Georgian SSR Constitution. The words 'Soviet Socialist' were removed from the country's name, the State was renamed 'Republic of Georgia', State symbols were changed, the leading role of the Communist Party was abolished and political pluralism was introduced.

Georgia—like Moldova—opposed the referendum on a renovated USSR,[39] and on 31 March 1991, it organised the referendum on State independence. In particular, Georgian citizens were asked if they agreed to restore statehood 'in accordance with the Declaration of Independence of 26 May 1918'. With 98% of the votes and a voter turnout of 90%—*i.e.* 3,295,493 votes in favour of independence out of 3,672,403 citizens entitled to vote—Georgians expressed their will to regain independence.

On 9 April 1991, Georgia adopted the Act of Restoration of State Independence, which solemnly proclaimed the independence of the country; defined the Constitution as the supreme law of the land; and affirmed the primacy of international law over domestic legislation. Moreover, the document declared the firm intention of the State to 'observe the universally recognised principles of political, economic and cultural cooperation with other States'. There were no foreign policy clauses in the Constitution.

---

[37] *The 1921 Constitution of the Democratic Republic of Georgia*, Constitutional Court of Georgia and Noe Jordania Institute, Batumi, 2012, pp. 8 ss.

[38] *The 1921 Constitution of the Democratic Republic of Georgia*, cit., pp. 33 ss. Cfr. M. Matsaberidze, *The 1921 Constitution of Georgia: A Symbol of the Independence of Georgia*, in constcourt.ge/files/4/3)%20JCL%20-%201-2(2021)%20-%20Matsaberidze%20ENG.pdf.

[39] Filippini (1995), p. 90.

In the first years following independence, Georgia experienced civil war and escalating tensions with the separatist regions of Abkhazia and South Ossetia. With the dissolution of the Soviet Union—perceived as a threat by these separatist regions, which had benefited from a high degree of autonomy during the Soviet period—the situation became even worse. In December 1991, the Supreme Council, the President of the Republic and the government were revoked and replaced by the Military Council. The latter repealed the amended 1978 Constitution and, on 21 February 1992, adopted the Declaration on the Restoration of the 1921 Constitution, which actually did not enter into force.

To solve the crisis, Eduard Shevardnadze returned to Georgia, and soon afterwards, the Military Council was dissolved and the State Council re-established. In this context, on 6 November 1992, the newly elected Parliament adopted the Law on State Power, known as the 'Small Constitution'.

The following year, in 1993, after initial reluctance, due to pressure from the Russian Federation and to the 'dire' situation of the country, Georgia adhered to the Commonwealth of Independent States. However, the country did not entirely renounce Western integration: in 1994, Georgia entered into the NATO Partnership for Peace (following Ukraine and Russia), and in 1996, the country signed the Partnership and Cooperation Agreement (PCA) with the EU. As already stated with reference to Ukraine, such agreements were not intended as a first step towards the accession processes. Finally, in 1999, the country became a member of the Council of Europe.

On 24 August 1995, the Parliament adopted the new Constitution of Georgia, which included a truly laconic pacifist clause on the commitment of the State to enhance 'independence and peaceful relations with other peoples' (Preamble). In Article 98, 'defence war' is defined as a 'sovereign right of Georgia', and the Armed Forces are put in charge of defending the independence, sovereignty and territorial integrity of the country, as well as honouring the international obligations of the State. Article 98 could be barely defined as a pacifist clause: the tenor of the provision makes it comparable to a 'deterrent on' rather than a 'limitation to' the use of force. In the original version of the text, there were no other provisions dedicated to foreign policy, except for the procedural dimension.

The 2001 constitutional amendments have added references to *jus cogens* and treaties in the Constitution. In particular, according to the new Article 6, legislation of Georgia should comply with universally recognised principles and rules of international law, and international treaties—unless they contradict the Constitution of Georgia—prevail over domestic normative acts.

Constitutional amendments approved in the aftermath of the 2003 Revolution introduced only new procedural rules on the definition of foreign policy.[40] One year after, however, on 15 May 2005, the Parliament adopted the first National Security

[40] Georgia's Constitution of 1995 with Amendments through 2004, in www.constituteproject.org/constitution/Georgia_2004.pdf?lang=en.

Concept.[41] The document was extremely cautious: it just vaguely mentioned separatism and conflicts in Abkhazia and South Ossetia as a potential threat for the country, together with conflicts in neighbouring States (Chechenia), the presence of Russian military bases in the country, organised crime and terrorism. Only a general reference to Euro-Atlantic integration was included among the major directions of the Georgian national security policy, which also mentioned a strategic partnership with Russia.

In April 2008, at the NATO Summit in Bucharest, the Allies agreed that Georgia (and Ukraine) would have eventually become NATO members, 'provided they would have met all necessary requirements'.[42] No clear path or time frame was defined at that time for both States. A few months later, in August 2008, the separatist regions of Abkhazia and South Ossetia proclaimed their independence, and after a 5-day conflict, they were recognised as sovereign States by Russia. That same year, Georgia withdrew from the CIS, and in 2009, it adhered to the Eastern Partnership of the EU, together with Moldova and Ukraine.[43]

On 23 December 2011, the Parliament adopted a new National Security Concept,[44] which, compared with the previous version, extensively codified the aspirations of the country to complete integration into NATO and EU structures. Moreover, the document identified the threat posed by Russia to the very existence of the country and its attempts to derail the Georgian path towards Euro-Atlantic integration.

In the following years, Georgia's foreign policy goals have also been defined in a series of resolutions adopted by the Parliament. The restoration of territorial integrity has been defined as a matter of utmost importance in all of them. In particular, the Resolution of 7 March 2013[45] formalised the new strategic course of the country and defined 'the integration into the European and Euro-Atlantic structures' as a priority (§3).

In the Resolution adopted on 29 December 2016, the Georgian Parliament reaffirmed the intention of Georgia to join the EU and NATO (§3 and §4), and for the first time, it expressed its commitment 'to support international peace and to share its duties in the fight against the challenges that the civilized world faces' (§7).

In the meantime, in 2014, Georgia signed the Association Agreement, including the Deep and Comprehensive Free Trade Area (DCFTA), with the EU, which, however, did not constitute a first step towards negotiations on accession, nor obviously was it endowed with a military dimension.

In continuity with previous resolutions, in 2018, the Georgian Parliament codified, at the constitutional level, the new strategic path of the country. The

---

[41] National Security Concept Finalized, https://old.civil.ge/eng/article.php?id=9887.

[42] Relations with Georgia, in www.nato.int/cps/en/natohq/topics_38988.htm.

[43] Eastern Partnership, in www.eeas.europa.eu/eeas/eastern-partnership_en.

[44] Georgia's New National Security Concept, in https://civil.ge/archives/186158.

[45] Resolution on Basic Directions of Georgian Foreign Policy [unofficial translation], in www.clingendael.org/sites/default/files/2016-02/Parlementsresolutie%20Georgie.pdf.

Constitutional Law of 23 March 2018 added to the Constitution a clause on integration into European and Euro-Atlantic structures. In particular, Article 78 states: 'The constitutional bodies shall take all measures within their competences to ensure the full integration of Georgia into the European Union and the North Atlantic Treaty Organisation'.

In 2020, a Draft Resolution on the Integration in the European Union was presented in Parliament, in which the EU integration was defined as 'the driving force for Georgia's democratic development'. In the document, the Government was required to 'step up its efforts towards Georgia's European integration (…), in order to prepare Georgia for membership of the European Union'. The text was approved only 2 years later, after the large-scale aggression of Russia against Ukraine.

That same year, on 3 March 2022, Georgia applied for EU membership, and on 14 December 2023, it was granted candidate status by the European Council. However, in that latter year, the country experienced severe democratic weaknesses, which, on 24 November 2024, finally led Prime Minister Irakli Kobakhidze to announce the suspension of the country's EU membership application process until the end of 2028.[46]

4 The Neutral Status of Moldova

Moldova started to develop an autonomous foreign policy in the context of the dissolution of the Soviet Union. On 23 June 1990, the Supreme Soviet of the Moldovan SSR adopted the Declaration of Sovereignty and, after the *coup d'état* against President Gorbachev, on 27 August 1991, the Declaration of Independence. The documents elaborated by Moldova were probably the most articulated of this constitutional cycle, compared to those of the other SSRs.

The 1990 Declaration of Soveregnity combined pacifist and cooperation clauses, affirming the commitment of the country to comply with the Charter of the United Nations and the norms of unanimously recognised international law, its intention to live 'in peace and good understanding with all countries and peoples' and its strong opposition to 'confrontations in international, interstate and interethnic relations' (para. 11). Moreover, the Moldovan SSR declared itself a 'demilitarized zone', which intended to actively contribute 'to the strengthening of world peace and security' and participate in 'the European process for cooperation and security' (para. 12). The term 'demilitarisation' was intended as an indirect call for the withdrawal of Soviet armed forces from the territory of the Republic. Finally, the Declaration of Sovereignty would have served as a basis for the new Constitution (para. 13).

[46] Georgia, in www.consilium.europa.eu/en/policies/georgia/#EaP.

In the Declaration of Independence—after a systematic reconstruction of the country's history[47] and the solemn proclamation of the country's independence—Moldova expressed its desire to 'establish political, economic, cultural and other relations of common interest with European countries and with all other States of the world' and to be admitted to the United Nations.

Compared with the indirect formulation of the Declaration of Sovereignty, the Declaration of Independence openly called on the USSR government to start negotiations on the termination of the illegal occupation and the withdrawal of Soviet troops from the national territory of the Republic of Moldova.

Despite that, Moldova, together with other former Soviet Republics except the Baltics, signed, on 21 December 1991, the Alma-Ata Protocol as a founding member of the Commonwealth of Independent States (CIS), which was ratified 3 three years later.[48] Moreover, Moldova—like Ukraine—did not sign international commitments in the military dimension of the CIS (the short-lived CIS Joint Armed Forces) and later refused to enter the Collective Security Treaty Organization (CSTO).

In the winter of 1991–1992, clashes occurred between Russian-backed Transnistrian forces and the Moldovan police. Between 2 March and 26 July 1992, the conflict escalated into an open military confrontation. The war ended with a ceasefire and the establishment of a security zone under the surveillance of tripartite (Russian, Transnistrian and Moldovan) peacekeeping forces.[49]

Moldova experienced severe troubles in the State-building process, and it had to struggle for its territorial integrity. Even if not mentioned in the founding documents, neutrality—which cannot be assimilated to demilitarisation—was discussed in the constituent process as a way to overcome the consequences of the war in Transnistria, to ensure domestic tranquillity and keep an equal distance between the major geopolitical actors in the region.[50]

---

[47] The Moldovan State finds its roots in the principality of Moldova, a tributary entity of the Ottoman Empire. As mentioned in the Declaration of Independence, the Moldovan national territory was 'dismembered' between the neighbouring countries from 1775 to1812, with the annexation of Bukovina by the Habsburg Empire and the occupation of Bessarabia by the Tsarist Empire. The following period, leading to the creation of the Romanian State, was not mentioned. The Declaration of Independence considered the Molotov Ribbentrop Pact as null and void *ab initio*. Indeed, the document remembered that without consulting their respective populations, Bessarabia, northern Bukovina and Hertsa County were occupied by Soviet troops on 28 June 1940 and annexed to the Moldavian SSR (Transnistria). The latter was formed on 12 October 1924 by the Supreme Soviet of the USSR as part of the Ukrainian SSR. The document also contained a valuable reconstruction of the transition to democracy, which started in 1989. Cfr. Di Gregorio (2019a), b, c).

[48] The Alma-Ata Protocol was signed by Moldovan President Mircea Snegur on 21 December 1991, but it was ratified by Parliament only on 8 April 1994, after the pro-Russian Agrarian Democratic Party won the parliamentary elections. Kunert-Milcarz and Herbut (2023).

[49] Judgment on the Interpretation of Article 11 of the Constitution (permanent neutrality), Complaint no. 37b/2014), 2 May 2017, in www.rulac.org/assets/downloads/Cst_Court_of_Moldova_Judgment_Neutrality.pdf.

[50] Cojocaru (2001); Grosu (2017).

Original plans for unification with Romania were abandoned, and a new Constitution was adopted on 29 July 1994,[51] granting autonomy to Transnistria—which was not under the control of the State—and Gagauzia.

An evocative pacifist clause is included in the Preamble of the Constitution, stating that the country devotes itself to 'the general-human values, and expresses its the desire to live in peace and good understanding with all the peoples of the world, according to the unanimously recognized principles and norms of international law' (Preamble).

Neutrality is enshrined in Article 11 and regulated by the Decision of the Parliament n. 482 of 6 June 1995 on the Military Doctrine of the Republic of Moldova. A special procedure is set out in Article 142 to revise provisions on the sovereign, independent and unitary character of the State, as well as those on permanent neutrality, which should be approved by a referendum—'by the majority of citizens entitled to vote'.

Similarly to Ukraine and Georgia, Moldova also joined NATO's Partnership for Peace[52] and entered in the EU Partnership and Cooperation Agreement, both in 1994. Moreover, in 1995, the country became a member of the Council of Europe. Moldova, together with Ukraine, Georgia and Azerbaijan, is also a founding member of the Organization for Democracy and Economic Development-GUAM, whose role is, however, marginal in the region.[53] In the following years, Moldova strengthened its cooperation with both NATO and the EU. In particular, in 2014, the country signed the Association Agreement, including the DCFTA.[54] It is worth remembering that none of these agreements, however, were intended as first steps towards accession processes to the EU or NATO.

With its pivotal Judgment of 2 May 2017, the Constitutional Court provided an interpretation of Article 11 of the Constitution on Moldova's permanent neutrality, both in peace and war times. In the judgment, the Court reconstructed with great detail the historical circumstances that led the country to proclaim permanent neutrality. According to the Court, from a constitutional and historical point of view, neutrality has never been considered a goal in itself but rather an instrument to meet specific objectives, among which the end of the occupation of the Eastern part of the Republic's territory, the consolidation of its independence and the restoration of its territorial integrity.

The Court explicitly stated that neutrality could not be interpreted in such a way as to limit the defence capacity of the country or entail its isolation. Accordingly, Moldova's participation in collective security systems, such as the United Nations

[51] https://www.constcourt.md/public/files/file/Actele%20Curtii/acte_en/MDA_Constitution_EN.pdf.

[52] https://www.nato.int/cps/en/natolive/topics_82584.htm.

[53] https://guam-organization.org/en/about-the-organization-for-democracy-and-economic-development-guam/.

[54] Commission Opinion on the Republic of Moldova's Application for Membership of the European Union, in https://enlargement.ec.europa.eu/opinion-moldovas-application-membership-european-union_en.

security system, peacekeeping operations, humanitarian operations, etc., should not be considered in contradiction with the neutrality status of the country.[55]

In 2022, Russia's unprovoked invasion of Ukraine led Moldova to reconsider its national security strategy and the interpretation of the country's neutral status. Strategic issues (a common border with Ukraine, the refugee crisis, tensions with separatist regions, Russian hybrid warfare), combined with the economic crisis, hyperinflation and shortages in energy supplies, exposed the country's vulnerabilities.[56]

Moreover, the conflict resurfaced deep political, linguistic and ethnic fractures in Moldovan society, which is divided between supporters of neutrality and those who believe that Moldova should strengthen its military forces, apply for NATO membership or even become part of Romania.[57]

On several occasions, the Moldovan government denied the intention of the country to join NATO but reaffirmed that neutrality did not entail international isolation.[58] At the same time, it opted to strengthen its relations with the EU, and on 3 March 2022, it submitted a formal application for EU membership. On 23 June 2022, the country was granted candidate status by the European Council, and in December 2023, accession negotiations were opened.[59]

Soon afterwards, President Maja Sandu asked the Parliament to plan a 'constitutional referendum'—which is not explicitly regulated by the Constitution—on the 'irreversibility' of the European integration path of Moldova. Based on the request of the Head of State, 46 members of the presidential majority—corresponding to one-third of the members of the body, as prescribed by the Constitution to initiate a constitutional amendment process (Article 141, para. 1b)—submitted to the Constitutional Court a draft decision of the Parliament on holding a 'Republican constitutional referendum', together with a draft law amending the Constitution.

The amendment would have reformed the Preamble and added a new Article 140^{I} on the procedure for accession to the EU. In particular, amendments to the Preamble would have added a reference to the European identity of the people of the Republic of Moldova, the irreversibility of the European path of the country and confirmed its integration into the EU as a strategic goal. According to the new Article 140^{I} the accession to the EU would have been regulated by organic law. Moreover, following the accession, EU law would have prevailed over domestic legislation (primacy of EU law).

[55] Judgment on the Interpretation of Article 11 of the Constitution (permanent neutrality), Complaint no. 37b/2014), 2 May 2017, in www.rulac.org/assets/downloads/Cst_Court_of_Moldova_Judgment_Neutrality.pdf.

[56] Molis and Jardan (2023).

[57] Kunert-Milcarz and Herbut (2023).

[58] Moldova Not Pursuing NATO Membership But Aims to Strengthen Cooperation with Alliance, in www.rferl.org/a/moldova-nato-membership-cooperation-alliance/32155800.html.

[59] *EU-Moldova Relations*, in https://enlargement.ec.europa.eu/european-neighbourhood-policy/countries-region/moldova_en#moldovas-eu-path.

On 16 April 2024, the Constitutional Court expressed a favourable opinion on the possibility of holding a constitutional referendum on procedural, temporal and material grounds.[60] With reference to the latter, the Court did not consider the draft amendment as falling within the special procedure set out in Article 142, requiring the majority—instead of one-third—of citizens entitled to vote to amend provisions on the sovereign, independent and unitary character of the State and on permanent neutrality (§30).[61] The Court evaluated whether the accession to the EU was compatible with sovereignty, but it avoided any consideration related to the country's permanent neutrality status. Finally, the referendum was scheduled the same day as the presidential elections, on 20 October 2024.

The referendum was highly criticised by oppositions and law scholars on several grounds. In particular, scheduling the referendum the same day as the presidential elections was interpreted as a populist move.[62] Moreover, the compatibility between the question submitted to the electorate (modified shortly before the referendum) and the text of the amendment was contested. Finally, questions arose about the necessity to call a referendum before concluding the accession negotiations.[63]

The amendment was approved by the referendum, with 50.35% of the votes and a voter turnout of 50.56% (corresponding to 749,719 votes out of 3,020,814 citizens entitled to vote), and entered into force on 5 November 2024.[64]

Several violations of international standards on electoral consultations were reported on both sides, among which disinformation campaigns, vote-buying schemes and cyberattacks.[65]

Instead of a plebiscite reconfirming the President and the European path of the country, the referendum showed weaknesses and multiple fractures—along political, linguistic and ethnic lines—existing in Moldovan society.

---

[60] Danielciuc-Colodrovschi and Spatari (2024).

[61] Aviz privind proiectul de lege pentru modificarea Constituției prin referendum (aderarea la Uniunea Europeană) (sesizarea nr. 84c/2024), 16 aprilie 2024, constcourt.md.

[62] Danielciuc-Colodrovschi and Spatari (2024).

[63] R. Secrieru, *Anchoring European Integration in Moldova's Constitution: A Critical Victory Amid Unprecedented Hybrid War*, in constitutionnet.org.

[64] M.R. Corman, *Three Takeaways from the Nearly Failed EU Referendum in Moldova*, in *VerfassungsBlog*, 01.11.2024.

[65] R. Secrieru, *Anchoring European Integration in Moldova's Constitution: A Critical Victory Amid Unprecedented Hybrid War*, in constitutionnet.org/news/voices/anchoring-european-integration-moldovas-constitution.

5 Closing Remarks

The full-scale aggression against Ukraine in 2022, as well as the reactions that it generated, is destined to produce deep and long-term consequences on the international relations system and on the functioning of the institutions operating both at the global and regional levels.[66]

The threat posed by Russia to the world order led to a rethinking of security alliances, in particular NATO, which reacted by asking its members to increase defence expenditures.[67] An analogous process has been brought about within the European Union, aimed at strengthening defence capabilities (ReArm Europe Plan—Readiness 2030), based on a new approach to security and defence (White Paper for European Defence).[68]

At the national level, the war in Ukraine has totally reshaped constitutional provisions regulating foreign policy, from both procedural and substantial points of view. As for the first dimension, the conflict altered the relations among State institutions, strengthening the role of executives and marginalising legislative bodies in both belligerent and non-belligerent States.[69] As for the second dimension, the war has contributed to reshaping the interpretation of foreign policy clauses. In particular, the very essence of the pacifist principle, or better of the idea of renunciation of war, has been progressively eroded.

In the countries of the former Soviet space—which experienced difficulties in State-building and nation-building processes, struggling for their own existence—references to peace were already weak compared to clauses dedicated to independence/self-determination and compliance with international law.

Georgia and Ukraine originally opted for weak pacifist and cooperation clauses, while Moldova chose neutrality. Faced with the increasing 'assertiveness' of the Russian Federation at the international level, the three countries of the former Soviet space first reinterpreted and then amended constitutional provisions dedicated to foreign relations.

Euro-Atlantic integration clauses have progressively been introduced—first in normative acts and then in constitutions—first in Georgia, then in Ukraine, repositioning the two former Soviet States in the international scenario and codifying their pro-Western aspirations. In the only country that had originally opted for neutrality—*i.e.* Moldova—this concept has been progressively reinterpreted and then combined with integration into the European Union.

The full-scale aggression of Ukraine has produced a *caesura*, a real change in the foreign policy orientations of the countries of the former Soviet space, which have always been divided between pro-Russia and pro-Western positions. In Ukraine,

[66] Pedrazzi (2022). Cfr. Giblin et al. (2026).

[67] The Hague Summit Declaration, in www.nato.int/cps/en/natohq/official_texts_236705.htm.

[68] Introducing the White Paper for European Defence and the ReArm Europe Plan-Readiness 2030, defence-industry-space.ec.europa.eu. Cfr. Cafaro (2025).

[69] Vedaschi (2024).

war has, for the first time, pushed the country out of the Russian sphere of influence and led Georgia and Moldova—even if with great difficulties—to withdraw from/ reduce any form of cooperation with Russia and the Commonwealth of Independent States, the last vestige of the Soviet Empire.

References

Biscaretti di Ruffia P, Crespi Reghizzi G (1979), La Costituzione sovietica del 1977. Un sessantennio di evoluzione costituzionale nell'URSS. Giuffrè, Milano

Bradley CA (2018) What is foreign relations law. In: Bradley CA (ed) The Oxford handbook of comparative foreign relations law. OUP, Oxford

Cafaro S (2025) Il Libro bianco della Commissione e dell'AR e la sicurezza europea. Diario di diritto pubblico

Cella G (2021) Storia e geopolitica della crisi ucraina. Carocci, Roma

Cojocaru EG (2001) Foreign policy of the Republic of Moldova. Publishing House Civitas, Chişinău

Danielciuc-Colodrovschi N, Spatari M (2024) Le parcours européen instrumentalisé au profit des ambitions électoralistes de la présidence: risques et intérêt de l'initiative de réviser la constitution moldave. Lettre de l'Est

De Stefano C (2015) Dissoluzione e ristrutturazione statuale sullo spazio ex-sovietico. DPCE (2)

De Vergottini G (2004) Guerra e costituzione. il Mulino, Bologna

Di Gregorio A (2019a) The Eurasian Economic Union: origin and development of a new integration format compared with that of the EU. In: Di Gregorio A, Angeli A (eds) The Eurasian Economic Union and the European Union: moving towards a greater understanding. Eleven, the Hague

Di Gregorio A (2019b) I fenomeni di degenerazione delle democrazie contemporanee: qualche spunto di riflessione sullo sfondo delle contrapposizioni dottrinali. Nuovi Autoritarismi e Democrazie 1(2)

Di Gregorio A (2019c) I sistemi costituzionali dei paesi dell'Europa centro-orientale, baltica e balcanica. Cedam, Padova

Di Gregorio A (2023) Lo spazio ex sovietico tra "costituzionalismo" euroasiatico e condizionalità europea, DPCE (1)

Filippini C (1995) L'evoluzione del sistema sovietico fino alla sua dissoluzione e i riflessi internazionali. In: Sacerdoti G (ed) Diritto e istituzioni della nuova Europa. Giuffè, Milano

Filippini C (2019) Rigidità costituzionale e riforme in Ucraina tra diritto interno e diritto internazionale. DPCE (4)

Ganino M (1989) La riforma costituzionale in Unione sovietica. La legge di revisione del 1° dicembre 1988. Giappichelli, Torino

Ganino (2020) Tempi e modi rituali della revisione costituzionale di Putin. Continuità e varianti? Nuovi Autoritarismi e Democrazie 2(1)

Giannini A (1946–1947) La "grande Ucraina". Rivista di Studi Politici Internazionali 13/14(3–4)

Giblin J, Chub O, Butchard P, Senatorova O (forthcoming) International law after the Ukraine war. Routledge, London-New York

Ginsbourg T (2017) Constitutions and foreign relations law: the dynamics of substitutes and complements. Am J Int Law 111

Ginsbourg T (2018) Comparative foreign relations law: a national constitutions perspective. In: Bradley CA (ed) The Oxford handbook of comparative foreign relations law. OUP, Oxford

Grosu R (2017) The Concept of the Permanent Neutrality of the Republic of Moldova from the Point of View of Discrepancies between Judicial Norms and Geopolitical Uncertainties. Cross-Border Journal for International Studies, 2 (2).

Haider-Quercia U (2024) La neutralità permanente in tempi di guerra: Irlanda e Austria e il sostegno militare europeo all'Ucraina. DPCEonline, Sp. 1
Henkin L (1996) Foreign affairs and the constitution. OUP, Oxford
Ibrido R (2022) I "fattori costituzionali condizionanti" della politica estera tra diritto e geopolitica. DPCE (2)
Ibrido R (2025) Geopolitica costituzionale. Il Mulino, Bologna
Kunert-Milcarz R, Herbut M (2023) Neutralność Mołdawii w kontekście rosyjskiej inwazji na Ukrainę. East Rev 12(1)
Kuzio T (1998) Ukraine: state and nation building. Routledge, London – New York
Kuzio T (2007) Ukraine, Crimea, Russia. A triangle of conflict. Ibidem, London
Lami G (2022) L'Ucraina in 100 date. Dalla Rus' di Kyiv ai nostri giorni. DellaPorta, Pisa
Larrabee FS, Lynch A (1994) Ukraine, Russia, and European security: implications for western policy. RAND, Santa Monica
Mirkine-Guetzévitch B (1937) Le technique parlementaires des relations internationales. Recueil Sirey, Paris
Mirkine-Guetzévitch B (2009) Comparazioni teoriche e razionalizzazioni costituzionali. Pensa, Lecce
Molis A, Jardan I (2023) Moldova on the Brink: Safeguarding Against Russian Aggression. Lith Annu Strateg Rev 21
Pedrazzi M (2022) L'aggressione russa all'Ucraina, l'Europa e la comunità internazionale. EuroJus
Ronzitti N (2023) Neutralità e non belligeranza nel conflitto russo-ucraino, in Percorsi costituzionali (1)
Stucchi A (1995) Dallo smantellamento dei blocchi armati ai conflitti locali in Europa. In: Sacerdoti G (ed) Diritto e istituzioni della nuova Europa. Giuffrè, Milano
Vedaschi A (2008) À la guerre comme à la guerre? La disciplina della guerra nel diritto costituzionale comparato. Giappichelli, Torino
Vedaschi A (2024) Costituzionalismo, declinazioni del principio pacifista e conflitti armati. Dpceonline, Sp. 1

The Philosophical and Political Perspective

Contingent or Principled? On the Philosophical Distinctiveness of Pacifism

Giulia Bistagnino

1 Why Defining Pacifism Matters

The ongoing conflict in Ukraine, the humanitarian crisis in Gaza, and the escalating violence in the Middle East have once again brought war to the forefront of political discourse. Ukraine's military resistance against Russia's full-scale invasion in February 2022, in particular, was widely regarded as a paradigmatic instance of a just war: the defence against an act of aggression and the violation of a sovereign political community's borders. While the goal of achieving a just peace was broadly affirmed, few voices responded to the war's outbreak with a pacifist stance. On the contrary, the invasion seemed to underscore the limits—if not the implausibility—of pacifism, echoing the familiar challenge often posed by references to the Second World War. To many, pacifism appears unrealistic and politically irrelevant, a noble ideal at best, but one offering little practical guidance in the real world.

In response to this challenge, some political philosophers—primarily in the years preceding Russia's invasion—have articulated a revised conception of pacifism they call "contingent pacifism" (Bazargan 2014; Fiala 2014, 2018a; May 2012, 2015a; Morrow 2018), which they argue is better suited to grapple with the realities of modern warfare. In general, pacifists maintain that war is always unjustifiable. Contingent pacifists, by contrast, accept that war may be justifiable in principle, as per just war theory.[1] However, they argue that in practice, very few wars meet the

[1] Traditionally, there are three main views on the morality of war. On one end of the spectrum is political realism, which holds that moral principles do not apply to the realm of politics or war. On the other end is pacifism, which maintains that no plausible moral theory could justify the excep-

G. Bistagnino (✉)
University of Milan, Milan, Italy
e-mail: giulia.bistagnino@unimi.it

G. Cavaggion (ed.), *The 'Pacifist Principle' in the Italian and Japanese Constitutions in the Wake of the War in Ukraine*,
https://doi.org/10.1007/978-3-032-23108-6_18

necessary moral standards and that most, if not all, recent, current, and foreseeable wars are likely to be unjust. Curiously, this position has found greater consonance among theorists working within the just war tradition[2] than among those aligned with more traditional accounts of pacifism.[3] At first glance, this might seem paradoxical: if all identify as pacifists, should they not be allies? Yet the tension between contingent pacifists and what I refer to as "principled pacifists" is a revealing one. It reflects not merely a rhetorical divergence but also a deep and philosophically robust disagreement. My aim in this contribution is precisely to clarify this disagreement. While both contingent and principled pacifists may appear aligned when viewed through the lens of just war theory—a perspective centred on the question "Can war be justified?"—their positions diverge sharply when assessed through other criteria. In particular, distinctions regarding the relation between means and ends, as well as differing conceptions of politics itself, reveal a radical cleavage between the two perspectives. In this sense, if my analysis is correct, contingent pacifism is better understood as a radical and pessimistic account of just war theory rather than a genuinely pacifist philosophical position. In this respect, my contribution aligns with Cheyney Ryan's (2018, p. 279) critique of what he terms "just war pacifism"[4] and seeks to build upon his insights by further unpacking the philosophical foundations of both principled and contingent pacifism. The reason for using the term "principled" rather than the more commonly used "absolute" is to emphasise that, if my argument is correct, contingent pacifism is a pragmatic approach to peace. This contrasts with principled pacifism, which is an absolutist position that does not allow for any circumstances in which war can be justified, and it is also a genuinely principled stance based on a philosophical understanding of political violence and politics.

Addressing the definition of pacifism is important not only from a theoretical perspective but also from an evaluative one. On the one hand, the emergence of contingent pacifism within recent philosophical debates calls for a broader inquiry into the nature of pacifism itself, specifically, whether contingent pacifism can genuinely be considered a pacifist position. On the other hand, the term "pacifist" is widely used in public discourse, often imprecisely or inconsistently. One of the aims of this discussion is to show that pacifism refers to a distinctive set of philosophical commitments and not merely to a general aspiration for peace. To illustrate this

---

tional horrors and destruction wrought by war. Positioned between these two is just war theory, which argues that war can be morally justified under certain conditions, specifically when normative constraints are observed concerning the reasons for going to war (*jus ad bellum*), the conduct of war (*jus in bello*), and the establishment of a just peace afterwards (*jus post bellum*). Contingent pacifism seeks to occupy a space between just war theory and pacifism, acknowledging the theoretical possibility of just war while denying its practical feasibility under current conditions.

[2] McMahan (2010, p. 44) states that "the most plausible form of pacifism, in my view, is based on a non-absolute prohibition of knowingly killing an innocent person".

[3] Contingent pacifism is criticised, for example, by Ryan (2024); Hutchingson (2018); and Parkin (2018).

[4] Such a label was used first by Sterba (1998).

point, I examine the so-called pacifist principles enshrined in the Italian and Japanese Constitutions,[5] assessing whether the pacifist label is justified in each case. I argue that the Italian Constitution, with its (qualified) rejection of war and reference to peace, operates firmly within the framework of just war theory and thus cannot be accurately described as pacifist. By contrast, the Japanese Constitution embodies a genuinely pacifist orientation.[6] However, this orientation does not align with contingent pacifism, despite claims to the contrary by some of its proponents (May 2015, p. 2; Chan 2023). Moreover, if contingent pacifism is best understood as a pessimistic account of just war theory, as I argue here, then the contrast between the two Constitutions also reveals the broader philosophical divide examined in this chapter.

The structure of the paper is as follows. Section 2 offers some preliminary remarks about pacifism and war. Section 3 examines how principled pacifism and contingent pacifism are typically presented and defended, highlighting how these positions are often distinguished in terms of their scope—whether they concern the moral integrity of individuals or the political and institutional dimensions of international relations—and the reasons they offer for endorsing pacifism. I argue, however, that while these distinctions are illuminating, they fail to capture the core commitments of pacifism. In Sect. 4, I propose a different analytical framework for comparing principled pacifism and contingent pacifism, focusing on their respective interpretations of the means-ends distinction and their underlying conceptions of politics. This analysis reveals that the disagreements between the two are fundamental and irreconcilable: they represent distinct philosophical positions. Section 5 brings the discussion into a concrete context by examining the so-called pacifist principles in the Italian and Japanese Constitutions. Finally, Sect. 6 concludes with reflections on pacifism's philosophical contributions and its ongoing dialogue with just war theory.

2 Some Preliminary Remarks on Pacifism and War

Before delving into the diversity of positions defending the non-justifiability of war, an important caveat must be introduced. Here, I focus specifically on views that engage directly with the practice of war. While it is true that "pacifism" is a relatively recent term, it encompasses a long and complex tradition involving both theoretical approaches and political movements (Fiala 2018b). As such, the term can be used broadly to denote a renunciation of all forms of violence, including personal self-defence, as famously advocated by Leo Tolstoy. However, my concern here lies

[5] For a comprehensive historical and legal analysis of the so-called pacifist principles in the Italian, Japanese, and German Constitutions, see Losano (2020).

[6] As is well known, interpretations of Article 9 of the Japanese Constitution range from strongly pacifist to more realist readings. In this paper, I adopt a strongly pacifist interpretation as a conceptual tool to illustrate my argument. I expand on this point in section 5.

with those arguments labelled "pacifist" insofar as they reject the justification and practice of war. In this sense, I am here interested in accounts of pacifism that consider their core commitment as that of "anti-warism" (Teichman 1986) rather than an opposition to violence in all its forms. The reasons for focusing specifically on conceptions of pacifism that oppose war are twofold. First, it helps narrow the scope of the debate, thereby making the discussion more precise and analytically manageable. Second, it enables a clearer comparison with just war theory, which serves as both the primary counterpart to contingent pacifism and the key framework that pacifists engage with critically.

To better understand what it means to reject war, it may be useful to spend a few words on the definition of war. Traditionally, war has been considered a formally recognised condition of enmity between territorially defined political groups with clear and formally recognised limits with respect to who is involved, in what capacity, over what period of time, and in what part of the world. This is evident not only in Jean-Jacques Rousseau's view (1762/2004), which considers war as a relation between states, specifically a symmetrical war and so a clash between organised armies, but also in Carl von Clausewitz's conviction (1832/1976, p. 75) that war is "a duel on a larger scale". According to him, war is a clash between states, which are moved by their interests and compelled to wage war to pursue them. For Clausewitz (1832/1976, p. 95), combat is a contest not between individuals but between soldiers who are "recruited, clothed, armed and trained" to be able to "fight at the right place and the right time". Building on these traditional views about the definition of war, contemporary pacifists tend to define war not merely as a clash of armies or a legal state of conflict between states but also as a complex social and institutional phenomenon. Rather than focusing exclusively on combat or military engagement, they highlight war's broader structure as an organised, large-scale, and politically sanctioned practice of violence. For Fiala (2018c), war is a systemic expression of coercive force that reflects political and diplomatic failure. Similarly, Ryan (2024) defines war as an entrenched political and institutional practice, not simply a violent episode but a sustained framework of organised, legitimised killing. Moreover, May (2015b) emphasises war's status as a regulated and collective form of violence pursued for political ends, typically carried out by organised agents such as states or coalitions. While these authors offer different emphases, they share a broad, reflective understanding of war that focuses on its institutional nature and political character, rather than reducing it to episodic combat or physical confrontation.[7]

[7] In this respect, pacifists oppose revisionist accounts of just war theory that broaden the concept of war to encompass a moral continuum: from individual acts of violence to large-scale, coordinated conflict (McMahan 2004). Pacifist accounts often align more closely with political realism and traditional accounts of just war theory in maintaining that the principal actors in war and international relations are states, political groups, and international organisations rather than individuals. It is important to note that although pacifists generally agree that war is primarily a practice involving states, they typically reject the "domestic analogy" famously advanced by Walzer (1977), which is central to traditional just war theory.

As a final remark, I want to stress that pacifism is best understood as a commitment against war, not as a general commitment to peace. This clarification matters because just war theorists also regard peace as a central normative aim, often justifying war precisely as a means to secure or restore peace (Walzer 1977; Orend 2016). Of course, just war theory rejects political realism's conception of peace as a mere *modus vivendi*, intended as a balance of power in which conflicting parties refrain from war while underlying hostilities persist and remain unresolved. By contrast, just war theory understands peace as a form of stability that is normatively grounded. As John Rawls (1999, p. 47) writes, "there is true peace among them because all societies are satisfied with the status quo for the right reasons". Peace is achieved when a legitimate international order is established, one that secures sovereignty and self-determination for political communities and the respect for human rights.[8]

3 Pacifism from Different Angles

As already noted, principled and contingent pacifists may appear aligned when considered in relation to the question: "Are wars justified?" Principled pacifism maintains an absolute and unconditional opposition to war as such, while contingent pacifism holds that no actual war meets the moral standards required for justification. Moreover, principled and contingent pacifists may also overlap in the scope of their perspectives and the reasons underpinning their positions. In what follows, I will explore both of these aspects in greater detail.

Pacifist positions can be generally distinguished with respect to their scope and focus in two broad categories: individual and institutional forms of pacifism.[9] Individual pacifism is a normative perspective centred on the moral agency of individuals. It emphasises personal refusal to participate in war and advocates for individual and social transformation to foster peace among individuals and political communities. At its core lies the principle of individual moral responsibility. The central question guiding individual pacifism is: Should I be complicit in actions that contribute to a specific war or support a political system that regards war as a

[8] Interestingly, just war theorists often give limited attention to the concept of peace, as their primary concern lies with identifying the normative conditions under which war may be justified. There is a division of labour: just war theory focuses on the ethics of war, while the task of theorising peace is often taken up by scholars in the ethics of international relations, whether internationalist or cosmopolitan in orientation. In contrast, pacifists typically engage more directly with both war and peace.

[9] The individual/institutional distinction roughly parallels the personal/political distinction discussed by Ryan (2018, 2024, pp. 81–121). However, I adopt the former primarily to clarify that my focus is limited to questions of scope, specifically the standpoint from which the issue of war is approached (i.e. individual moral responsibility versus the public or institutional domain). By contrast, Ryan's personal/political distinction is more nuanced and also addresses other dimensions, such as the underlying reasons for adopting personal or political pacifism.

legitimate means of resolving conflict? A well-known example is Henry David Thoreau's conscientious refusal to support war and slavery, grounded in his commitment to personal moral integrity. In "Resistance to Civil Government", Thoreau writes (2004, p. 71):

> It is not a man's duty, as a matter of course, to devote himself to the eradication of any, even the most enormous wrong; he may still properly have other concerns to engage him; but it is his duty, at least, to wash his hands of it, and, if he gives it no thought longer, not to give it practically his support. If I devote myself to other pursuits and contemplations, I must first see, at least, that I do not pursue them sitting upon another man's shoulders. I must get off him first, that he may pursue his contemplations too.

This passage makes it evident that Thoreau's central concern lies with the individual conscience. His refusal stems from a personal unwillingness to be complicit in what he perceives as injustice, such as war. While there may be differing interpretations of whether Thoreau's stance qualifies as genuinely political,[10] what matters here is that his objection to war is framed as a moral issue grounded in the integrity and conscience of the individual. Accordingly, individual pacifism's emphasis is not on structural reform or collective mobilisation but on the ethical responsibility of the individual to remain morally untainted by participating in or enabling unjust practices.

What I have referred to as individual pacifism can encompass both principled and contingent forms of pacifism. As Ryan argues in *Pacifism as War Abolitionism* (2024), individual pacifism often takes the form of principled pacifism, grounded in the moral conviction that participation in war necessarily involves actions that violate one's conscience and integrity, such as killing. From this perspective, the refusal to participate in war is not primarily a judgment about the justice of particular conflicts but a first-personal ethical stance: a categorical rejection of killing as incompatible with one's moral commitments.

A contingent pacifist can also adopt an individual perspective by concluding, based on a moral assessment of historical and empirical realities, that participation in actual wars will almost certainly involve wrongdoing. Larry May (2015a) exemplifies this position when he argues that the structural features and empirical conditions of modern warfare make it exceedingly unlikely that individuals can fight justly, thus grounding his pacifism in the moral risks that war poses to personal responsibility. According to May, several factors contribute to the conclusion that just wars cannot be fought in practice: the high likelihood that, under current conditions, innocent people will be killed; the difficulty of satisfying the requirements of last resort and proportionality; and other practical constraints. Crucially, these considerations must be evaluated from the perspective of individual soldiers, who

[10] It could be argued that Thoreau's actions, being grounded in individual conscience, remain confined to the private rather than the public sphere and therefore do not qualify as properly political (Arendt 1972). However, one might also contend that individual pacifists aim to influence public attitudes towards peace by exemplifying its moral importance through their conduct and personal example (Ryan 2024).

should not assume the moral "risk of violating the rights of civilians as well as of fellow soldiers" (May 2015a, p. 80).

Paul Morrow (2018) makes a similar argument by drawing on Laurie Ann Paul's (2014) concept of a "transformative experience". In deciding whether to undergo a transformative experience, for example becoming a parent, it is difficult to rely on rational decision-making because the changes in knowledge and values brought about by such experiences cannot be predicted in advance or fully evaluated afterwards. Morrow argues that the decision to enlist or accept conscription into the armed forces is likely to be such a transformative decision, particularly with respect to one's moral outlook. As he notes, a key difficulty lies in grasping, ahead of time, what it means to live in circumstances where it is possible to kill and be killed. These circumstances fundamentally alter a person's moral relationships: "enlisting for or accepting conscription into the armed services transforms an individual's moral relationships; it establishes new moral responsibilities, and exposes individuals to new moral risks" (Morrow 2018, p. 148). Importantly, in line with contingent pacifism, Morrow does not deny that a just war may be possible in principle. Rather, he contends that the actual conditions under which individuals are asked to fight typically fail to meet the moral thresholds required for justification. As such, the moral risks involved in military participation are sufficiently grave to make abstention or conscientious objection not only prudent but also morally justified.

The target of institutional pacifism differs from that of individual pacifism. While the latter is concerned with the conscience of individuals, the former is concerned with ending war as a social practice. Thus, it calls for the radical reform of political institutions and international relations. Institutional pacifism is therefore concerned with social and political structures, particularly what is sometimes termed "militarism" (Fiala 2014): the social, economic, and political systems devoted to standing armies; the production of armaments; and the constant preparation for military defence and war. Institutional pacifists believe that constant preparation for war and the threat of military force in various scenarios should be rejected. It is the system that allows for the preparation and building of war that must be changed.

Similarly to individual pacifism, institutional pacifism can encompass both principled and contingent forms. Institutional pacifism can be articulated as a form of principled pacifism when it rests on the foundational moral conviction that war, as a systemic and institutionalised practice, is inherently unjust and must be categorically rejected. From this perspective, the wrongness of war stems not solely from its consequences or contingent features but also from its structural role in perpetuating violence, inequality, and dehumanisation. As Ryan (2018, pp. 286–289) argues, war can be rejected as a social practice, one that is deeply embedded in political life and state structures.[11] Institutional principled pacifists maintain that militarism is

[11] Interestingly, principled pacifists tend to be sceptical of states because they are considered key institutions that enable war. As Ryan (2024, p. 11) puts it, "modern war has been an enterprise of states, empires, and nations. But understanding war is not just a matter of what those institutions do. It is more fundamentally a matter of what they are. They are artifacts and enablers of war, specifically of what I term war building. Historically, states, empires, and nations prevailed over

fundamentally incompatible with moral commitments to justice and peace. They argue that the very existence of standing armies, military-industrial complexes, and war-oriented foreign policies represents a morally corrupting force. As such, this form of pacifism calls for the radical transformation of institutions that sustain the war system, aiming to replace them with structures oriented towards non-violent conflict resolution and global cooperation. In this way, institutional principled pacifism reflects a systemic moral critique of the justification of war and the political order that normalises it.

Contingent pacifism can adopt an institutional perspective when based on the premise that, while war may be morally permissible in principle, the current political, institutional, and historical context makes it almost impossible for wars to fulfil the moral criteria for justification. As Fiala (2014) argues, contingent pacifism is based on a sceptical view of real-world institutions: states are often motivated by national self-interest, influenced by propaganda and part of militaristic cultures. These systemic features erode the moral reliability of decisions to go to war and of conduct within war. From an institutional perspective, then, contingent pacifism advocates reform or restraint at the structural level, calling for resistance to militarism and deep scepticism towards standing armies and war-making institutions. It also supports non-violent means of conflict resolution. According to Fiala (2014, p. 468), "what makes a social system militaristic is its commitment to military solutions and the structure of military power". This commitment is not to an abstract moral principle that forbids all war but rather to the practical judgment that, given the current conditions, war is profoundly morally hazardous and should be rejected until the political and institutional frameworks that support it have been transformed. From the perspective of contingent pacifism, working at the institutional framework, militarism pushes towards injustice and away from peace; thus, because of reasonable probabilistic considerations, a system of preparing for and making war should be dismantled.

As previously mentioned, principled and contingent forms of pacifism may overlap with respect not only to their scope but also to the normative reasons grounding each position. While principled and contingent pacifism differ in their stance on whether war could ever be justified in principle, the normative reasons that support them may nonetheless converge. These reasons can be broadly grouped into two categories: moral and epistemic.

Moral reasons focus on the immorality of war, particularly in relation to the violation of human dignity, the unjustifiable nature of killing, and the corrupting influence of violence. Principled pacifists categorically reject war, asserting that no cause can justify participation in organised violence. Principled pacifism can be either deontological or consequentialist. Following Kantian thinking, it can be argued that war is inherently wrong and that one should never engage in it,

---

other political forms by their success at mobilizing the human and material resources for war—to the point that their very identities are constituted by war". This is one of the reasons why pacifism can be considered closely related to both anarchism (Fiala 2018d) and cosmopolitanism (Reader 2007).

regardless of the possible consequences. Conversely, it can be argued that there are good consequentialist reasons for opposing war. Adopting a rule-consequentialist framework, one could argue that a rule banning wars would be the most beneficial for the greatest number of people on the planet.[12]

Those who advocate for contingent pacifism on moral grounds accept that war may be justifiable in theory, but they argue that wars, in practice, invariably involve severe moral failings, such as indiscriminate harm or the exploitation of combatants, which render them unjust. According to May, soldiers face the serious moral risk of violating the rights of civilians and fellow combatants, even when acting in good faith. As he writes (2015a, p. 81), "the major moral risk of participating in war has always been that one will unjustifiably kill innocent people. The killing of the innocent is a moral wrong, and the intentional killing of the innocent without justification or excuse is the paradigmatic moral wrong." Thus, contingent pacifism can be embedded in deep moral commitments, such as concern for human dignity and respect for individuals, judging war as inevitably failing to meet the normative standards that would otherwise permit its use.

Epistemic reasons may also support pacifism. Although principled pacifists usually prefer to appeal to moral reasons and devote more space to them in their arguments, they also refer to epistemic reasons. For example, they state that "if we can be confident of anything, it is that war will not be ended by more war" (Ryan 2024, p. ix). Recognising that war actually causes more war leads to the adoption of pacifist views, maintaining that there is no sense in waging war with the objective of ending war, as standard just war theory retains.

Contingent pacifists are more explicit about the epistemic reasons underlying their position, arguing that there is uncertainty and structural limitations to their ability to determine when, if ever, war is morally permissible. One of the most prominent examples of epistemically grounded contingent pacifism is that defended by Bazargan (2014), who argues that there is a strong presumption against the permissibility of waging and supporting wars because individual agents (especially soldiers) typically lack access to all the facts needed to determine whether their side is fighting a just war. This includes information about historical grievances, political motivations, and the justification for the opponent's resort to war. Consistent with the contingent nature of the argument, Bazargan concedes that just wars are theoretically possible. However, in practice, combatants operate under epistemic conditions that make it impossible, or at least highly improbable, to be confident that their participation is morally justified.

[12] Reader (2000) argues that pacifism might follow from a widely held and fundamental intuition about the moral status of persons, which is shared by both utilitarianism and Kantianism.

4 Means, Ends, and Different Conceptions of Politics

The previous section attempted to show that some usual distinctions employed to categorise the different types of pacifism, with respect to their scope and underlying reasons, do not distinguish between principled and contingent pacifism. Indeed, in many respects, there is overlap and convergence between these two approaches to the morality of war. In this section, I will argue that, when considering two different elements—the relationship between means and ends and the conception of politics—it becomes apparent that principled and contingent forms of pacifism are fundamentally different. Despite agreeing on justificatory reasons and on whether pacifism can be a matter of individual conscience or institutional practice, principled and contingent forms of pacifism disagree fundamentally about deep philosophical commitments concerning the justification of using controversial means to achieve positive ends and, more generally, about the nature of politics.

The relationship between means and ends is a long-standing problem in political philosophy, and it is commonly analysed through three conventional views. The "anti-morality view"[13] holds that moral concerns are inappropriate in politics, meaning that no means can be ruled out in advance, even if they are morally controversial. If a certain end is worthy of pursuit and there are available means to achieve it, they should be employed. The "morality-as-seamless view", on the other hand, holds that moral considerations are of fundamental importance when evaluating and assessing political actions. From a deontological perspective, for example, if certain ends require immoral means, they should either be pursued differently or not at all. The argument is that if immoral means are employed to achieve a desirable end, this ultimately renders the end immoral and undesirable. Finally, the "political morality view" acknowledges the possibility of so-called "dirty hands" scenarios: sometimes it is necessary to use controversial means to achieve desirable ends because, in politics, there are unavoidable clashes between political responsibilities and moral convictions.

It is important to introduce the relationship between means and ends into the discussion about pacifism because, as previously noted, if there is a significant conceptual distinction between pacifism and just war theory, it cannot lie within the realm of ends. The end of just war theorists is undoubtedly that of establishing just and durable peace. Conversely, if there is a significant conceptual distinction between pacifism and just war theory, it must regard the means available within the political realm. Principled pacifists reject war as a means because they believe it is always wrong and cannot produce any moral good. This idea is particularly clear in the arguments defended by Ryan (2024, p. 82, italics in the text), who draws a parallel between the abolition of war and that of slavery, arguing that pacifists should adopt a similar stance to that of abolitionist supporters. "An abolitionist [...] did not distinguish between good and bad instances of slavery; they condemned it

[13] The labels "anti-morality view", "morality-as-seamless view", and "political morality view" are adopted from De Wijze (2012).

unreservedly. An abolitionist was someone whose actions towards slavery were ones of unconditional opposition. They opposed it, as it were, without reservation". Moreover, within principled pacifism, war is also rejected because of its consequences, as it contributes to militarism and the perpetuation of further wars. According to principled pacifists (Ryan 2023), it is a mistake and a contradiction to believe that war can be used to achieve peace because only means of the same moral nature as the desired end can lead to its realisation.

Conversely, with respect to the distinction between means and ends, contingent pacifism aligns with just war theory in accepting the "political morality view". While political realists consider war to be a means that can be evaluated not in moral terms but rather in terms of its success in delivering desirable ends, just war theorists consider war to be a highly controversial and morally problematic means. However, they argue that when certain conditions are met (e.g. if it is used in response to an aggression, if it successfully discriminates between combatants and non-combatants, etc.), it is permissible to wage war. Contingent pacifists do not reject this basic moral framework. Rather, they express deep scepticism about whether the conditions for justified war—those concerning *jus ad bellum*, *jus in bello*, and *jus post bellum*—can ever realistically be met. Their disagreement with just war theory, then, is pragmatic rather than principled. The core issue is not with resorting to war as such, but with the belief that morally defensible wars are feasible in the contemporary world. At the same time, contingent pacifism diverges philosophically, though not necessarily pragmatically, from principled pacifism, in that it rejects the "morality-as-seamless view". As Michael Neu (2011, p. 428) writes, "just war theorists will always insist that war can be a justified means to protect the rights of innocents [...]; and pacifists [...] will always insist that such a justification misses out on a fundamental moral truth, namely, that allegedly justified wars necessarily involve acts that cannot be justified". In this sense, contingent pacifism may be best understood as a pessimistic interpretation of just war theory.

A second area of philosophical disagreement between principled and contingent pacifism concerns the underlying conception of politics they each presuppose. Drawing on Hannah Pitkin's formulation (1972, p. 205), one can characterise the political domain through the question: "What shall we do?" This framing emphasises that the domain of the political concerns making collective decisions about which actions are appropriate under specific circumstances, and it inherently involves groups, not merely individuals. Within this framework, various theories of politics offer different answers to what politics entails. Political realists, for instance, often conceive of politics as fundamentally rooted in conflict. A paradigmatic example is Carl Schmitt's definition of the political in terms of the friend-enemy distinction. For Schmitt, this opposition is irreducible to other dichotomies, such as good versus evil, and it derives its force from the existential possibility of war. That is, the political is constituted by the potential for groups to view one another as enemies in the most literal sense: capable of and willing to kill each other. As he famously writes (2007, p. 26), "the distinction of friend and enemy denotes the utmost degree of intensity of a union or separation, of an association or dissociation". While just war theorists and contingent pacifists clearly reject Schmitt's view that war is the foundation of politics, they nonetheless take the political reality of conflict seriously. In this respect, they treat war not as a desirable outcome but as a central and inescapable problem that must be addressed within political life. Moreover, they consider political violence an inevitable and sometimes necessary part of the toolkit of politicians: violence and the possibility of its use are inherently political.

Now, I am not suggesting that principled pacifists do not regard war as a central issue that politics must address. Rather, their understanding of politics diverges fundamentally from that of just war theorists. In my view, principled pacifists view violence [14] as *anti-political* in the Arendtian sense. As is well known, Hannah Arendt conceptualises politics as a form of action in which the capacity for speech plays a foundational role. Although speech is only one type of action, it is central to the political realm. As Arendt (1998, p. 26) writes, "most political action, in so far as it remains outside the sphere of violence, is [...] transacted in words". Authentic politics, on this view, is marked by deliberation, dialogue, and persuasion among equals and stands in opposition to coercion and violence. Accordingly, given that speech is the most vivid and relevant form of action, and since it is an activity that inherently requires others, Arendt understands politics as a fundamentally public activity: politics is about doing things together. For Arendt, political action arises not from isolated individuals but from a plurality of people engaging collectively in deliberation. In contrast to traditional accounts centred on coercion or command, Arendt emphasises that genuine political power emerges when individuals act in concert towards a shared goal they have discussed and endorsed. As she puts it (1970, p. 44), "power corresponds to the human ability not just to act but to act in concert. Power is never the property of an individual; it belongs to a group and remains in existence only so long as the group keeps together".

For principled pacifists,[15] then, the political project is not about managing violence but about transforming political life in ways that displace it altogether. This project can be seen as rooted in a vision of politics as freedom, the freedom to begin anew and to interrupt what seems inevitable. Indeed, Arendt describes freedom as the capacity to initiate the unexpected, to act in ways that defy pre-determined roles or mechanical responses. Principled pacifists argue that, although war appears entrenched in contemporary political life, it is neither necessary nor inescapable. Their goal is to challenge its normalisation and imagine alternatives. This transformative ambition is especially evident in those who integrate pacifism with other critical traditions, such as feminism: "as a feminist and a pacifist, feminist pacifism is a collective political project dedicated to transforming a world in which the

[14] Here, I use the terms "war" and "violence" somewhat interchangeably. While the forms of pacifism discussed in this contribution are primarily concerned with the rejection of war, the conception of politics adopted here is framed in terms of violence, in line with the broader philosophical literature. This shift in terminology reflects a difference in analytical focus rather than a substantive change in the object of critique.

[15] Jonathan Schell (2005) explicitly draws on Arendt in arguing that, within pacifism, non-violence should be understood not merely as a tactic but also as a way to fundamentally rethinking and transforming the nature of political power itself.

structures, practices, and discourses of gender and war reinforce each other" (Hutchings 2018, p. 185). In this way, principled pacifism offers not just a critique of war but also a re-imagining of political life itself. It invites us to envision a politics grounded not in violence but in cooperation, plurality, and the shared human capacity to begin anew. Principled pacifists show that resisting war is not merely a matter of abstaining from violence but also an active, collective endeavour to reshape our institutions, values, and political imagination.

5 The "Pacifist" Principles in the Italian and the Japanese Constitutions

In this final section, I examine Article 11 of the Italian Constitution and Article 9 of the Japanese Constitution, both of which articulate their respective countries' stances on war and are often described as "pacifist". My aim is not to provide a detailed constitutional analysis or to assess these provisions from a legal or political standpoint. Nor will I engage with the extensive and important debates surrounding their interpretation and application. Rather, I will consider these articles as expressions of underlying philosophical positions on war and peace. I argue that Article 11 of the Italian Constitution reflects the principles of just war theory, whereas Article 9 of the Japanese Constitution embodies the ideals of principled pacifism.

Article 11 of the Italian Constitution sets out key principles concerning Italy's role in the international community and its commitment to the promotion of peace and justice among nations. The text reads as follows:

> Italy rejects war as an instrument of aggression against the freedom of other peoples and as a means for the settlement of international disputes. Italy agrees, on conditions of equality with other States, to the limitations of sovereignty that may be necessary to a world order ensuring peace and justice among the Nations. Italy promotes and encourages international organizations furthering such ends.[16]

The first interesting element to consider is the "rejection of war". In this context, of interest is the Italian Constitution's extremely clear normative stance on the means of war which is considered morally controversial and problematic; otherwise, there would be no need for the verb "reject". On the other hand, war as a political means is not rejected in all circumstances. Rather, according to the Italian Constitution, war can never be used to aggress against the freedom and sovereignty of other peoples or to settle international disputes. Yet it admits the use of armed force in order to safeguard the territorial integrity of a state suffering unjust aggression. In this sense, Article 11 clearly aligns with just war theory, denouncing aggressive warfare while acknowledging the possibility of war as a means of defence. In

[16] Official translation by the Senato della Repubblica (Italian Senate), available at https://www.senato.it/documenti/repository/istituzione/costituzione_inglese.pdf.

this sense, the rejection of war is not absolute.[17] Moreover, given that Article 11 does not explicitly consider the conditions that make a war just in the present circumstances, nor does it state that we should be sceptical about the morality of wars fought today, it should not be considered an instance of conditional pacifism. However, it is interesting to note that if such a specification were added, Article 11 could be considered to align with contingent pacifism.

Article 9 of the Japanese Constitution differs from Article 11 of the Italian Constitution in that the former rejects war in an absolute sense:

> Aspiring sincerely to an international peace based on justice and order, the Japanese people forever renounce war as a sovereign right of the nation and the threat or use of force as means of settling international disputes.
>
> In order to accomplish the aim of the preceding paragraph, land, sea, and air forces, as well as other war potential, will never be maintained. The right of belligerency of the state will not be recognized.[18]

Article 9 outlaws war as a means of settling international disputes and formally renounces the right of sovereign belligerency. The aim is to establish international peace based on justice and order. In fact, Japan renounces the right to wage war altogether, which prevents it from maintaining any armed forces. A radical interpretation of Article 9 could argue that Japan should not be permitted to maintain a military force, even for self-defence purposes. This could be interpreted as giving up the right to national defence.[19] Moreover, it is important to note that Article 9 does not deny the right of individual self-defence; rather, it rejects the moral justification of war at the level of the state. In this sense, Article 9 aligns closely with forms of principled pacifism that are political in nature. The dismantling of armed forces represents precisely the kind of radical and transformative change to the global order envisioned by principled pacifists, who oppose militarism as an entrenched social practice. If principled pacifism seeks to abolish war by dismantling the systems that prepare for and sustain it, then Article 9 can be seen as a clear expression of anti-militarism in constitutional form. The rejection of war and militarism is absolute and unconditional.

Of even greater interest in this context is the consideration and evaluation of Article 9 in conjunction with the Preamble to the Japanese Constitution, which states:

> We, the Japanese people, desire peace for all time and are deeply conscious of the high ideals controlling human relationship, and we have determined to preserve our security and existence, trusting in the justice and faith of the peace-loving peoples of the world. We desire to occupy an honored place in an international society striving for the preservation of

[17] To further corroborate this point, it can be noted that Article 78 of the Italian Constitution provides: "The Parliament has the authority to declare a state of war and vest the necessary powers into the Government."

[18] Official document available at https://japan.kantei.go.jp/constitution_and_government_of_japan/constitution_e.html.

[19] The Japanese Supreme Court has already ruled that the Constitution still retains a fundamental right of self- defence, and that Japan can enter into treaties for mutual security (Haley 2017). Yet such an interpretation is debated (Chen and Wada 2017).

> peace, and the banishment of tyranny and slavery, oppression and intolerance for all time from the earth. We recognize that all peoples of the world have the right to live in peace, free from fear and want.
>
> We believe that no nation is responsible to itself alone, but that laws of political morality are universal; and that obedience to such laws is incumbent upon all nations who would sustain their own sovereignty and justify their sovereign relationship with other nations.

The Preamble can be interpreted in line with the conception of politics emphasised in the previous section. Not only is there a clear reference to human relations as the focus of moral concern, but the Preamble also sets out an ideal of world order composed of "peace-loving peoples" who strive for "the preservation of peace and the banishment of tyranny, slavery, oppression and intolerance for all time from the earth". In this sense, the Preamble rejects the view that conflict among states is inevitable. Instead, it offers an ideal of peaceful coexistence that must be realised collectively, peacefully, and respectfully. The Japanese Preamble presents itself as the first step towards constructing a war-free world, which can only be achieved through a deliberative process in which all states recognise the existence of a universal moral law that rejects war.

The conception of peace building set out in the Preamble appears to be more demanding and to carry more normative weight than that set out in the Italian Constitution. Indeed, in line with just war theory, Article 11 promotes the idea of peace as more than just a *modus vivendi* or balance of power. Peace is fundamentally linked to the concept of justice in international relations. The idea here is that in order to ensure a long and lasting period of peace among peoples, Italy is willing to submit to international rules and build peaceful, reciprocal relations with other states. In this sense, the Italian Constitution considers peace to be an integral part of a legitimate international order in which political communities respect each other's sovereignty, self-determination, and human rights. However, contrary to the Preamble of the Japanese Constitution, Article 11 neither mentions a "right to live in peace" nor appeals to the notion of "trust among peoples", which seems to constitute building blocks for a form of political life in which war can actually be eradicated.

6 Conclusion

In this contribution, I have discussed principled and contingent accounts of pacifism to show that, despite both answering in an affirmative sense to the question of whether war is justified, these two positions fundamentally diverge on key philosophical issues. In particular, I have shown that they sharply disagree on how to approach the means/ends problem and the conception of politics on which their respective positions are based. In essence, my argument concludes that contingent pacifism is a pessimistic interpretation of just war theory. In this sense, contingent pacifism is pacifist only in practice, being grounded in pragmatic rather than principled considerations. To better explain their differences, I have examined the "pacifist principles" of the Italian and Japanese Constitutions. Article 11 of the Italian Constitution can be understood as a principle aligned with just war theory and could be considered a form of contingent pacifism if further specified in this direction. Conversely, the Japanese Constitution's absolute rejection of war and ideal of a war-free global order reflect the philosophical tenets of principled pacifism.

Of course, the reflections offered here tell us nothing about which position should be considered preferable and desirable in addressing and tackling contemporary problems, nor it answers the question whether pacifism in general is coherent and convincing. Rather, I hope that my reflections will encourage further consideration of pacifism and just war theory. In particular, I suggest that the normative question of which position is preferable cannot be answered without a thorough analysis of their differences and their diverging philosophical commitments.

References

Arendt H (1970) On violence. Harcourt Brace Jovanovich, San Diego

Arendt H (1972) "Civil disobedience", in Crises of the Republic. Harcourt Brace Jovanovich, New York

Arendt H (1998) The human condition. The University of Chicago Press, Chicago

Bazargan S (2014) Varieties of contingent pacifism in war. In: Frowe H, Lang G (eds) How we fight. Oxford University Press, Oxford, pp 1–17

Chan BS (2023) Utilitarian contingent pacifism and Article 9 of the Japanese constitution. Philosophia 51:635–657

Chen PL, Wada JT (2017) Can the Japanese Supreme Court overcome the political question hurdle? Wash Int Law J 26:349–379

De Wijze S (2012) The means/ends problem in politics. In: Besussi A (ed) Philosophy and politics: methods, tools and topics. Ashgate, Surrey, pp 135–148

Fiala A (2014) Contingent pacifism and contingently pacifist conclusions. J Soc Philos 45:463–477

Fiala A (2018a) Transformative pacifism: critical theory and practice. Bloomsbury, New York

Fiala A (2018b) Pacifism. In: Zalta EN, Nodelman U (eds) The Stanford Encyclopedia of Philosophy (Fall 2023 Edition). URL = <https://plato.stanford.edu/archives/fall2023/entries/pacifism/>

Fiala A (2018c) Pacifism: a philosophy of nonviolence. Cambridge University Press, Cambridge

Fiala A (2018d) Anarchism and pacifism. In: Jun NJ (ed) Brill's companion to anarchism and philosophy. Brill, Leiden

Haley J (2017) Article 9 in the Post-Sunakawa World: continuity and deterrence within a transforming global context. Wash Int Law J 26:1–16

Hutchings K (2018) Pacifism is dirty: towards an ethico-political defence. Crit Stud Secur 6:176–192

Losano MG (2020) Le tre costituzioni pacifiste: Il rifiuto della guerra nelle costituzioni di Giappone, Italia e Germania. Max Planck Institute for Legal History and Legal Theory

May L (2012) Contingent pacifism and selective refusal. J Soc Philos 43:1–18

May L (2015a) Contingent pacifism: revisiting just war theory. Cambridge University Press, Cambridge

May L (2015b) The morality of defensive war. Cambridge University Press, Cambridge

McMahan J (2004) War as self-defence. Ethics Int Aff 18:75–80

McMahan J (2010) Pacifism and moral theory. Diametros 23:44–68

Morrow P (2018) Contingent pacifism. In: Fiala A (ed) The Routledge handbook of pacifism and nonviolence. Routledge, New York, pp 142–153
Orend B (2016) The morality of war. Broadview, Peterborough, Ontario
Parkin N (2018) Conditional and contingent pacifism: the main battlegrounds. Crit Stud Secur 6:193–206
Paul LA (2014) Transformative experience. Oxford University Press, New York
Pitkin H (1972) Wittgenstein and justice: on the significance of Ludwig Wittgenstein for social and political thought. University of California Press, Berkeley
Reader S (2000) Making pacifism plausible. J Appl Philos 17:169–180
Reader S (2007) Cosmopolitan pacifism. J Global Ethics 3:87–103
Rousseau J-J (1762/2004) The social contract. Penguin, London
Ryan C (2018) Pacifism. In: Lazar S, Frowe H (eds) The Oxford handbook of the ethics of war. Oxford University Press, New York, pp 277–293
Ryan C (2023) Why pacifism now. J Pacifism Nonviolence 1:65–75
Ryan C (2024) Pacifism as war abolitionism. Routledge, New York
Schell J (2005) The unconquerable world: power, nonviolence, and the will of the people. Penguin, London
Schmitt C (2007) The concept of the political. Expanded edition. The University of Chicago Press, Chicago
Sterba J (1998) Justice for here and now. Cambridge University Press, Cambridge
Teichman J (1986) Pacifism and the just war. Basil Blackwell, Oxford
Thoreau HD (2004) Resistance to civil government. In: Glick W (ed) The higher law: Thoreau on civil disobedience and reform. Princeton University Press, Princeton
Von Clausewitz C (1832/1976) On war (M. Howard & P. Paret, Eds. & Trans.). Princeton University Press, Princeton
Walzer M (1977) Just and unjust wars. Basic Books, New York

Political Philosophy and the Problem of War: Mapping the Battlefield

Andrea Salvatore

The connection between political philosophy and war has always been, and continues to be, intricate and multifaceted and frequently paradoxical. For a long time, philosophers have wrestled with the causes, ethics, significance and consequences of war, and their views span a wide spectrum—from justifying it under certain conditions to condemning it outright. This chapter aims to map this bi-millennial tradition in its essentials, on the basis of the fundamental question of whether war can be justified. Needless to say, this is just one possible starting point for exploring the problem of armed conflict, which is in turn one of the most profound and contested questions in ethics, politics and history. Furthermore, the answer (or the set of answers) significantly depends on the adopted perspective—practical, moral or legal. That said, taking a generally normative standpoint and limiting our analysis to outlining the key distinctive features of each of them, we can identify five possible answers (i.e. five fundamental theories) to the question raised above: *just war theory*, *pacifism*, *political realism*, *bellicism* and what can be labelled as *holy war theory*. As with any mapping exercise, the aim is to produce the most precise and comprehensive cartography possible (which, of course, is always an exercise in abstraction). However, exploring the normative justifiability and argumentative cogency of the approaches we are going to consider, as well as their historical roots and development over time, is beyond the scope of this contribution. The only relevant question to which a comprehensive answer will be attempted is the following: How many philosophical approaches exist to the issue of the legitimacy of war?

A. Salvatore (✉)
Sapienza Università di Roma, Rome, Italy
e-mail: andrea.salvatore@uniroma1.it

G. Cavaggion (ed.), *The 'Pacifist Principle' in the Italian and Japanese Constitutions in the Wake of the War in Ukraine*,
https://doi.org/10.1007/978-3-032-23108-6_19

1 Just War Theory

Perhaps the best known and certainly the most controversial answer to the question of whether or not war can be justified is the so-called just war theory. Rather than being an accomplished theory, it is actually a philosophical and ethical framework used to outline and evaluate the morality of initiating and conducting war. Rooted in both Roman jurisprudence (particularly in the *ius fetiale*) and Christian theology, the theory seeks to balance the need for security and justice with the moral costs of war.[1] Just war theory asserts the possibility of distinguishing between permissible (whether admissible or commanded) and impermissible wars (a) on the basis of a normative criterion (whether moral or legal) (b) based on a concept of justice as fairness (c). In this view, legitimate wars are justified if and insofar as they meet certain criteria of justice (variously outlined and assembled by the different theories sharing the conceivability of a permissible war) and are, therefore, regarded as 'just'. As we can see, it resorts to a minimal concept of justice. According to this view, justice is fulfilled when specific conditions are met that legitimise the use of force. To put it differently, a just war is simply (or, at least, is not necessarily other than) a *justifiable* war.

Despite the immediate success of the term 'just war' (*iustum bellum*) and the widely held need for an argumentative strategy that combines (or proves to combine) war and morality, there has never been, nor is there now, a generally accepted conception among scholars of what constitutes a just war nor a common understanding of its constituent elements. Consequently, each version of the theory accounts for and defends its own specific set of criteria that must be met for a war to be considered just. This means that a war may be permissible according to one theory and impermissible according to another—with both theories (rightly) claiming to be an inherent part of the just war paradigm, if not the only possible substantiation. Just war theory can therefore be considered a continuum embracing an extraordinarily wide spectrum of philosophical positions on the legitimacy of war, with pacifism (no war is just) and bellicism (all wars are just) as the two polar extremes. Accordingly, the two extreme positions within the range are as follows: on the one hand, one might argue from a quasi-pacifist standpoint that no war is justifiable except one (type); on the other hand, one might argue from a quasi-bellicist standpoint that all wars are justifiable except one (type).

Starting from this definition, all alternative positions can be derived *e contrario*, i.e. by reasoning from the opposite. Denying A, i.e. the possibility of distinguishing between permissible and impermissible wars, leads to pacifism if the denial moves towards an absolute prohibition of all wars or to bellicism if the denial moves towards an absolute permissibility. Denying B, i.e. admitting the possibility of a distinction but not according to a normative criterion, results in political realism. Finally, denying C leads to what can be termed a 'holy war theory', which admits the

[1] For an overview of the history and doctrinal development of just war theory, see Bellamy (2006), Johnson (1975), Regout (1934) and Robinson (2003).

possibility of distinction according to a normative criterion but not in relation to a conception of justice as fairness (for the purpose of our map, justice as fairness implies that all parties involved in war deserve equal consideration and treatment of their interests and rights, regardless of their affiliation).

Just war theory is generally, but not unanimously, divided into three main parts, with each part identifying a different set of criteria: one part (*jus da bellum*) states the criteria of justice relevant before war, another (*jus in bello*) states the criteria relevant during war, and a more recently added part (*jus post bellum*) states the criteria relevant after war. Each theory comprises at least one of the following parts, and each part comprises at least one of the following criteria[2]:

1. *Jus ad bellum* (justice before war) comprises the criteria that must be met for a war to be considered just at the time of its initiation: (a) just cause—war must be a response to a real, certain and immediate danger, typically in the form of self-defence or defence of others against aggression; (b) legitimate authority—only duly constituted public authorities may wage war; (c) right intention—the primary motive must be to promote peace and justice, not self-interest or vengeance; (d) probability of success—there must be a reasonable chance of success; otherwise, war is futile; (e) last resort—all non-violent options must have been exhausted, not only in advance and before the war but also during it and at any other relevant time; and (f) proportionality: the anticipated benefits of waging war must be proportionate to the expected harms.
2. *Jus in bello* (justice during war) comprises the criteria that must be met for a war to be considered just in its conduct, regardless of whether the war itself is just: (a) discrimination—combatants must distinguish between combatants and non-combatants and must avoid attacking, causing damage to or offending the latter; (b) proportionality—the force used must be proportional to the military objective; and (c) military necessity—actions must be intended to achieve a legitimate military objective and be necessary for its success.
3. *Just post bellum* (justice after war) comprises the criteria that must be met for a war to be considered just in its conclusion. These criteria are particularly important for justice of peace agreements and post-war rebuilding: (a) restoration of rights—victims must have their rights restored and their wrongs redressed as far as possible; (b) fair treatment of prisoners and civilians: retributive justice should be avoided; and (c) rehabilitation: all possible efforts should be made to restore infrastructure, political order and reconciliation.

As with any other normative theory whose principles are both multiple and gradual (i.e. there is no unique or exhaustive principle of justice, and the different principles of justice can be satisfied to a greater or lesser extent), just war theory faces two main problems, which we refer to here as being relevant to its formulation. (A) Under what conditions can the normative demands implied by a criterion be said to

[2] Please note that while the above lists cover the most relevant and frequently debated criteria, other criteria are also mentioned occasionally.

be fulfilled, thereby satisfying the principle underlying it? For example, can the death of *some* civilians ever be justified? (B) What weight should be given to each criterion when forming a final judgement on the legitimacy of the war as a whole, and how should the outcomes resulting from applying the individual criteria be combined? For example, can the infringement of *some* criteria ever be justified? In other words, with reference to what might be called gradualism, the question is precisely to what extent a criterion must be met (and thus whether and to what extent it can be violated without *completely* unacceptable consequences). With reference to normative pluralism, the question is whether a war must *necessarily* meet all the indicated criteria to be considered just, or whether it is rather a question of approximating the ideal as closely as possible. These two issues lead to a meta-theory of just war that is, at least partly, inevitable. This meta-theoretical level aims to establish stringent criteria for evaluating the criteria of justice on the basis of their combined results rather than as single, partial and unrelated steps in the evaluation of the overall morality of the war under scrutiny.

Given its complexity, it is unsurprising that just war theory has led, and continues to lead, to different, and even conflicting, judgements about the legitimate use of violence—both generally and in specific contexts.

2 Pacifism

Pacifism is the belief that violence, including war, is never justifiable and that all disputes should be resolved by non-violent means, regardless of their nature or the parties involved. Those who adhere to this belief typically oppose military force and refuse to support or participate in armed conflict. The lowest common denominator of every definition of pacifism is opposition to violent conflict in all its forms. According to this broadest possible interpretation, pacifism is essentially an *anti-war* stance: wars are (largely and mostly, at least) unjust and (thus) unjustifiable.

There are several varieties of pacifism, each with different views on what constitutes violence and how to eliminate it most effectively. As with just war theory, there is no reference paradigm as the variants depend on the variable being considered.[3] By considering the degree of absolutism, one can distinguish between absolute pacifism (where violence is always unacceptable), conditional pacifism (where violence is wrong but allowed in exceptional cases) and selective pacifism (where only certain wars or forms of violence are opposed). Considering the belief foundation allows one to distinguish between religious pacifism (based on divine command, sacred texts or spiritual principles, such as the well-known concept of ahimsa in Jainism and Gandhi's philosophy), philosophical pacifism (based on abstract principles or mundane ethics) and pragmatic pacifism (based on political strategy or the

[3] For more information on the different types of pacifism, including their historical context, see Ackerman and DuVall (2000), Brock (1998), Brock and Young (1999) and Cortright (2008).

belief that violence is ineffective, unpredictable or counterproductive). Considering the context of application or the scale of implementation reveals personal pacifism, which applies only to an individual's actions and/or interpersonal relations; political pacifism, which applies to state or group behaviour; and global pacifism, which advocates universal non-violence and world (or at least international) peace.

As we are interested in the relationship between political philosophy and the problem of war, it is necessary to define pacifism by identifying the distinctive features of an armed conflict and deriving the essential characteristics of pacifism as anti-warism from these features. The most general and least restrictive definition of war is as follows: war is an act, or a series of acts, of physical violence against people (and/or the things on which their immediate survival depends), with the intention of imposing one's will on the adversary. Therefore, for our purposes, pacifism can be essentially characterised as the use of *non-violence against things and/ or people* in the aforementioned sense. It is important to note that it is possible to conceive of a non-nonviolent pacifism; in fact, most forms of pacifism reject absolute non-violence, even in cases of self-defence (for example, legal pacifists argue that the use of force in international relations should be legalised rather than abolished). However, it seems absolutely necessary to identify pacifism with non-violence here since, when contrasted with the theory of just war—a theory for which resorting to armed force is always unacceptable—pacifism must necessarily be characterised as a theory for which resorting to armed force is *always* unacceptable.

Therefore, any distinction between absolute or unconditional pacifism and contingent or conditional pacifism loses all relevance. The comparison between just war theory and pacifism implies a complete identification between pacifism and non-violence. In fact, conditional (or selective) pacifism would be nothing more than a theory of just war characterised by particularly restrictive criteria regarding the use of force. Ultimately, it would be a theory of just war defined by what it prescribes rather than what it allows. And as is well known, one can view the glass as half empty or half full. Therefore, rejecting certain types of war (e.g. those not dictated by legitimate defence) or aspects of war (e.g. the use of nuclear weapons), as well as any other restrictions (in terms of means, objectives, time or recipients), are necessary but not sufficient conditions for calling such a version a variant of pacifism. This is because both the refusal and limitation in question can be constitutive parts of a just war theory. Once again, therefore, it is worth reiterating that pacifism is either absolute or not, at least when compared with the latter. Therefore, by pacifism, it is meant here a total rejection of violence in favour of absolute non-violence. Unlike the theory of just war, pacifism holds that resorting to violence to counteract violence is always and unconditionally unacceptable (*vim vi repellere non licet*).

Two final remarks on the comparison between just war theory and pacifism. Firstly, for there to be a real difference, pacifism must be prescriptively universal, affirming that *everyone is obliged* not to engage in violence. The reason is straightforward here, too, and it is related to the required specificity of the perspective being considered. Regardless of the question of the possible constitutive relationship between morality and universality, limiting the number of people to whom the rule applies (whether through conscientious objection or otherwise) is, once again, entirely consistent with just war theory. In fact, just war theory affirms the permissibility of recourse to violence rather than its obligatory nature (in most cases, at least). Furthermore, even when it permits the use of violence, nothing prevents conscientious objection from being granted (Osiel 1999; Walzer 1970, pp. 120–145). In other words, one has the right, but not the duty, to resort to force (Holmes 1973; Narveson 1965). Thus, again, to be a valid alternative from a theoretical point of view (i.e. in outlining the different positions on the problem of war as mutually exclusive and jointly exhaustive), pacifism must assert that one has a duty, rather than simply a right, not to resort to force and that this duty must apply to everyone involved, without exception.

In a sense, there are two particular perspectives halfway between pacifism and just war theory: epistemological (or fallibilist) pacifism and historical (or technological) pacifism. The former recognises the legitimacy of war in principle, but not in practice, as it believes that the conditions required for legitimacy can never be met in reality. The latter, on the other hand, maintains that these conditions can no longer be met due to changes in historical and factual conditions (primarily technological), which in the past permitted their normative cogency. These positions are two particular forms of conditional (or contingent: May (2015)) pacifism. By distinguishing the different domains to which they refer, it is possible to isolate a moment of absolute pacifism (the practical domain in the case of epistemological pacifism and the temporal domain prior to change in the case of historical pacifism) from a moment that can be traced back to the potential legitimacy of war (the ideal domain in the case of epistemological pacifism and the temporal domain subsequent to change in the case of historical pacifism. To highlight this ambivalence, Teichman speaks of 'just war pacifisms' (Teichman 1986, pp. 1–9). Clearly, both moments are equally constitutive of each perspective; therefore, preference for one or the other is a stipulative choice. Can someone who loves travelling still call themselves a travel lover if they no longer travel because they consider all destinations to be excessively touristy nowadays?

3 Bellicism

Like pacifism, bellicism starts from the impossibility of distinguishing between different wars. However, rather than claiming that all wars are inadmissible, as pacifism does, bellicism claims that all wars are desirable. This idea is summed up perfectly in an extraordinarily telling maxim from Nietzsche. *Thus Spoke Zarathustra* (part 1, Chap. 10): 'You say that it is the just cause that sanctifies war? I say to you: it is the just war that sanctifies every cause.' According to this view, war is not an object created by justice but rather the creator of justice. It is no longer considered evil (whether a lesser evil, as in the theory of just war and realism, or a greater evil, as in pacifism) but rather a positive good, since it is the only thing that can bring about certain benefits and advantages (whether or not these are the greatest is irrelevant here), which are necessary for society. These goods would either not be achieved, not be fully developed, or become worn out as a result of a prolonged period of peace, even if they were ideally conceived. However decisive, Norberto Bobbio rightly points out that the distinction between bellicism and pacifism is not absolute:

> No war advocate has ever been so radical as to regard lasting and universal war as a highly desirable goal for humanity. While the pacifist aims to eliminate war, the bellicist does not seek to abolish peace. Rather, for the latter, peace is the negative moment and war the positive moment of history. Unlike the political realist, who denies that lasting and universal peace is possible, the bellicist denies that it is desirable. He opposes the pacifist by denying that war is an absolute evil, and by denying that peace is always a sufficient good. The bellicist believes that, in certain circumstances, war can be good and peace can be evil. He also believes that a world without war would be spiritually, morally and materially poorer. The bellicist therefore not only denies that war is eliminable, as the political realist does, but also believes that even if its elimination were possible, it would not be desirable (Bobbio 1997, p. 140).

When considering just war theory and pacifism, the bellicist paradigm is almost always omitted and, as if for the sake of symmetry, replaced by political realism. This substitution has contributed to generating quite a few misunderstandings by attributing to political realism characteristics proper to bellicism, often distorting both positions.

Firstly, it is bellicism, not realism, that claims the primacy of war over peace. Therefore, the commonality between pacifism and just war theory, as identified in the literature as the presumption against violence and the corresponding obligation (at least prima facie) not to resort to it, is only relevant when opposed to bellicism, not realism. Political realism, albeit according to different criteria of judgement, shares this presumption. Secondly and in a similar vein, bellicism, not political realism, is the only theory for which war *can* be an end in itself rather than a means to an end.[4] This different understanding of the intrinsic purpose of war gives rise to the two main declinations of political realism, which have been termed 'fulfilment' and 'hegemony' bellicism (Ceadel 1987, pp. 21–42). Fulfilment bellicism, which concerns the individual level more, affirms that war is the activity that realises the authentic expressive potential of the individual to a greater extent than any other activity. Consequently, the individual can only find full fulfilment and realisation in it. Therefore, the end is constituted by the war action as such (particularly its

[4] This is relevant for including, in such a theory, all those philosophies of history that view war as either an apparent or a necessary evil (Bobbio 1997, pp. 66–75). For these philosophies, war is a necessary means, not an end in itself, for achieving an equally necessary end. As can be seen from the terminology employed, these teleological perspectives lie somewhere between just war theory and bellicism. Specifically, their inclusion in bellicism depends on two main variables: (1) whether their ultimate goal justifies any war and (2) whether this end, if pursued without recourse to armed force, would be either inconceivable or drastically reduced (in this view, war would still be a positive good in that it increases the value of the outcome pursued). Since the presence of even one of these conditions is sufficient for a position to be considered bellicist, the absence of both is required for a philosophy of history to be considered as belonging to a different theory, which will be either that of just war or holy war.

existential and totalising dimension), regardless of the outcome. In contrast, hegemony bellicism, which focuses more on the collective level, argues that war is the only instrument capable of establishing who is legitimised to dominate others and how this dominion should be organised in practice. Here, the end is not the experience of war itself but the state of affairs that follows.

Despite apparent similarities with other theories that will be referred to, the specificity of bellicism remains decisive. Unlike them, the post-war scenario is not justified on the basis of a criterion external to the war that the conflict is supposed to realise (and in view of which the war is merely a means) but by virtue of the principle that the final condition determined by the war itself is just. All wars are thus justified and even glorified because they provide the only real proof and incontrovertible evidence of supreme human values (the Hegelian world history as a court of judgement of all values, political and human)—a testbed that becomes the ultimate justification of the entire process. Although they can occur separately, fulfilment bellicism and hegemony bellicism are usually considered complementary. However, it should be noted that both types of bellicism claim to fulfil specific demands for justice. In both cases, war is said to reflect a just hierarchy ingrained in the natural order and, above all, to benefit primarily those who are defeated. For hegemony bellicism, this is because the experience of war is said to enrich both the victor and the vanquished spiritually. For the second type, this is because, due to its supposed inherent civilising power, hegemony realises and recognises the right of the victor to dominate and enables the development of the potential of those who would otherwise be prevented from flourishing by their minority status.

While bellicists and pacifists are absolutely opposed to each other on every aspect and from every point of view, bellicists and advocates of just war theory have different but not entirely incompatible ideas about the relationship between the end that justifies recourse to armed force and the outcome of war. Bellicists equate the ideal and real outcomes of war, meaning that the two can never contradict each other: from this perspective, the ideal outcome is simply that which war gives rise to. Conversely, just war theory considers this dialectic to be highly problematic because contradiction is not only possible but also probable: the actual outcome may be the opposite of what is desired. This is enough to invalidate one of the most widespread and misleading analogies: that between war and judicial procedure. As Bobbio clearly formulates it,

> What guarantee does armed conflict offer that evil, or at least the greatest evil, is inflicted on the wrongdoer? War is a judicial procedure in which the greater evil is inflicted not on those who are in the right, but on those who have the greater force. This results in a situation where it is not force that is at the service of right, but rather right that is at the service of force. In summary, any judicial procedure is instituted with the aim of *ensuring that the right person wins*. But the result of war is just the opposite: *making the winner right.* Regarding the analogy between war and sanction, war is not a judicial procedure, but a judgement of God (Bobbio 1997, p. 59).

4 Political Realism

For the purposes of this investigation, political realism is the theory that some wars can be justified, not by a normative criterion that encompasses all parties but by a logic that maximises one's own strategic interests. In other words, wars are categorised not as just or unjust but as either convenient or inconvenient—for and by each party involved.

However, this does not imply, as many argue, that political realism generally denies the applicability of moral discourse to war. Assuming this perspective would not account for a wide range of realist theories. Similarly unconvincing is the thesis that still purports to respond to the reductionism of the previous one, namely that there are two types of realism: a descriptive one and a prescriptive one. By focusing exclusively on this dichotomy, it would still be necessary to identify a defining feature that is common to both types. Actually, political realism only denies that the criterion for discriminating between various wars can be normative—here, a minimalist, albeit contestable, conception of normativity is adopted, which implies the rejection of a purely self-interest vision. However, such an exclusion can be justified from a normative point of view rather than merely a factual one. For example, it could be argued that rulers have obligations only towards those they rule and are, therefore, not only allowed to disregard other stakeholders but are obliged to do so. Therefore, the decisive alternative is between the autonomy of morality and its dependence on totally self-interested considerations, not between the normative and factual domains, as is often assumed. As a consequence, neither pacifism nor political realism can be confined to one of the two domains. In fact, both pacifism not based on normative reasons and political realism centred on them are conceivable (hence the choice to categorise the various theories concerning the problem of war based not on their normative characterisation but on the much more cogent criterion of the admissibility of recourse to war). Thus, while they both share the criterion of strategic rationality for discriminating between various conflicts, there are two variants of political realism depending on the reasons given in support of the principle of self-interest: descriptive (or factual) realism and prescriptive (or normative) realism.

4.1 *Descriptive Realism*

The basic argument is as follows: it is impossible to distinguish between just and unjust wars because moral considerations have no place in interstate relations. This non-existence can be understood as either a logical impossibility (strong descriptive realism) or a factual impossibility (weak descriptive realism). In the former case, a distinction based on moral character would be nonsense; in the latter, it would be an illusion. However, the fundamental premise that states act exclusively in their own interest is a prerequisite, but not a sufficient condition, for formulating an alternative realist theory, for two reasons. Firstly, this assumption can also be made by theories other than political realism. Secondly, it does not necessarily imply the basic argument of descriptive realism.

According to *strong descriptive realism*, applying moral parameters to war would be akin to judging a scientific theory based on aesthetic criteria or a surgical operation based on the elegance of the surgeon's gestures. However, it should be noted that this approach is limited to denouncing these alleged paralogisms without providing reasons to defend a thesis that is counterintuitive, to say the least. The fact that war is informed by a strategic logic does not prove that it is the only relevant logic, nor does it mean that this logic cannot be judged from a normative point of view—or regulated by the legal system, even if only to legitimise it, as supporters of the extra-legal or meta-juridical nature of war claim (Dinstein 2005, pp. 73–75). To assert the impossibility of moral judgement on the basis of the irrelevance of the underlying categories is a circular argument. In light of this, one could argue that the strong descriptive variant constitutes a radicalisation of other forms of realism rather than an autonomous declension. Conversely, *weak descriptive realism* denies the factual possibility of moral alternatives that are still theoretically possible. In this case, it is not the relevance of morality that is lost but the actual freedom of choice, which is a necessary condition of the former. The strategic logic that dominates the interstate domain is such that it removes any possibility of authentic self-determination from the actors within it. It imposes specific behaviour on them that cannot be declined without risking their own self-preservation. In this context, it makes no sense to speak of normative criteria since moral freedom, which is their condition of possibility, is denied by the constitutive determinism that characterises the supranational sphere.

4.2 Prescriptive Realism

The basic thesis is as follows: it is not possible to distinguish between just and unjust wars because moral considerations *must* be excluded from interstate relations. Considering the determinism of the descriptive variant to be unfounded, prescriptive realism does not deny the possibility of morality having a relevant and conditioning influence within the international domain; rather, it questions the desirability of such an outcome. It does so on the basis of several reasons, which allow a distinction to be made between prudential and moral prescriptive realism. For *prudential descriptive realism*, acting strategically is the best way to maximise one's own interests, while for *moral descriptive realism*, it is the best way to maximise the interests of the greatest number of international actors. Conversely, acting morally is the worst way to maximise interests in both variants. While this is intuitive in the case of prudential prescriptive realism, in the case of moral prescriptive realism, the strategic option is justified by the belief that it achieves the moral goals it sets itself through a kind of heterogenesis of ends. For moral prescriptive realism, the best moral intentions can lead to outcomes that are unacceptable even to those with the best of intentions (whether due to the dehumanising Manichaeism of morality, its imperialistic particularism or its reckless erosion of precarious geopolitical balances). It is worth noting that this view leads to conclusions that are, in some ways, similar to those of pacifism:

> Pacifism in its pure or 'absolute' form shares with realism a deep moral scepticism about war. Both deny that war can ever be subject to moral limitation. Moreover, both regard the attempt to subject war as dangerous or counterproductive, increasing rather than decreasing the likelihood of war, adding to its ferocity, and obscuring the moral degradation and corruption that war inevitably brings about (Coates 1997, p. 82).

However, on closer inspection, moral prescriptive realism is simply the reverse of the parasitic critique of weak descriptive realism. Just as achieving the strategic goal required moral action as a means in the former case, achieving the moral goal now requires strategic action as a means. The fundamental difference is that, in this case, strategic action is subordinate to moral action, unlike in the previous case. Therefore, while it is formally possible to speak of a realist variant, the thesis of moral prescriptive realism is merely a strategic declination of just war theory. This is because moral prescriptive realism lacks the specific hierarchical relationship between the two types of action on which the formal criterion of self-interest is based. The principle of self-interest is merely a means to the normative end that characterises the realist variant under scrutiny. In any case, it is a different matter for prudential prescriptive realism, which is usually referred to when realism is defined as a theory based on the amorality of political action. As should now be clearer, the amoral characterisation of realism does not make explicit the decisive difference between descriptive and prescriptive realism.

5 Holy War Theory

Contrary to the almost universal claim of scholars that it is a specific internal variant of just war theory, holy war theory presents a normative logic that is completely incompatible with it. Therefore, it is not a possible (or necessary, depending on the approach) degeneration of just war theory but rather a completely alternative historical and doctrinal standpoint.[5] The absolutism, both theoretical and practical, that characterises the holy war theory is actually a potential outcome of any position based on the lawfulness of recourse to armed force.

In literature on the subject, the two defining features of holy war are typically identified as either the transcendent cause that justifies or motivates it (e.g. Yoder 1991) or the obligatory nature of recourse to it as a commanded action (e.g. Bobbio 1991). In my opinion, neither of these is diriment.

[5] Attempts to include holy war within the theory of just war have always met with strong resistance in medieval treatises (and beyond): see Bainton (1960), Russell (1975) and Walters (1973). For an analysis of the distinctive features of holy wars, see Canto-Sperber (2005), pp. 280–301; Johnson (1981), pp. 229–277; and Yoder (1996), pp. 12–14, 130–135.

The transcendent nature of the cause can be understood in two main ways: in a religious sense, harking back to the historical phenomenon of the Crusades and religious wars, or as an absolutisation of the end of war itself, rendering the previous historical distinction ideal-typical. In the former case, holy war would essentially be a variant of just war, determined by the specification of just cause. As such, it would not be an independent case in its own right since the religious nature of the cause is neither a necessary nor a sufficient condition for the unrestricted exercise of violence, which distinguishes a holy war from a just war. Limiting the analysis to Christianity, both just wars and holy wars have occurred (broadly speaking, and limited to the respective theoretical formulations, reference to wars of religion and crusades may correspond to the bi-partition recalled here). The same argument applies when holy war is considered a conflict waged in the name of a cause, religious or otherwise, that is considered inalienable and absolute for whatever reason. Even in this case, the limitlessness of recourse to violence in degree and extent does not necessarily follow from the premises. Proof of this can be seen in the practice of interventions in defence of human rights. Regardless of one's opinion on their legitimacy and/or appropriateness, the inalienability of these rights is not necessarily accompanied by indiscriminate and systematic violence against human and non-human targets, even though they are now recognised as an integral part of *jus cogens*.

The criterion of compulsory action, which dates back to the Jewish concept of *milchemet mitzvah* (i.e. commanded or obligatory war), is also not decisive. While the deontological character is a necessary feature of the concept of holy war, there are often good reasons to demand the same moral restraint from cases that are usually included in the list of just wars (above all, humanitarian interventions, according to some of their supporters). Limiting oneself to pointing out the lawfulness of resorting to armed force reduces just war to a macro-phenomenon of individual self-defence. In this light, it seems to be left to the individual to decide on an action that is merely declared non-prohibited. However, when one considers one's responsibilities towards those who, for whatever reason, are unable to defend themselves, the same arguments in favour of permissibility can *prescribe*, or compulsorily require, the use of force.

Therefore, an alternative definition is needed. A holy war can be usefully understood as a conflict characterised by the denial of the normative reciprocity inherent in the criteria that legitimise recourse to violence, whether they are borrowed from just war theory or not. This denial can be either de facto or *de jure*. The former constitutes an ever-possible degeneration of any conflict, independent of other factors, precisely because it is freed from any normative reference. On the other hand, the second case characterises the theory of holy war itself since all alternative theories recognise the reciprocity of the norms that regulate (or invalidate) armed conflict. Unlike the theory of just war, holy war theory imposes respect for the rules of war, or more generally the criteria legitimising recourse to violence, exclusively on the enemy. This unidirectional obligation is justified by implicitly or explicitly referring to a presumed moral superiority over the enemy, who is rejected not so much for what they do or do not do but primarily for who they are and/or what they represent.

The distance between the theories of holy war and just war is therefore as insurmountable as the difference between unilateralism and reciprocity, legal-moral equality and legal-moral inequality, general and abstract norms and particular and concrete norms, and war as a lesser evil and war as an eschatologically necessary means to the highest good (*iustissimum bellum*, to use the medieval term). Essentially, just war theory is based on the assumption that the nature of acts qualifies the morality of agents, while holy war theory is based on the principle that the nature of agents qualifies the morality of acts: the enemy can only act immorally, so any scruples about them are useless, deceiving and misguided.

However, it would be reductive to attribute the opposition between the two theories solely to the recognition or unrecognition of their equal potential to satisfy the moral criteria required to justify the use of force. As far as *jus in bello* (justice during war) is concerned, just war theory recognises the equal legitimacy of the parties involved regardless of any other considerations, including whether and to what extent each party complies with the requirements prescribed by the criteria pertaining to *jus ad bellum* (justice before war). This is tantamount to saying that, even when confronted with the most ruthless and outlawed of enemies, one side is obliged to respect the rules of war against the other side—except in case of the so-called supreme emergencies (Bellamy 2004; Toner 2005). In doing so, just war theory rejects and even prevents the moral Manichaeism that characterises holy war. This form of extremism leads to a total absence of limits in the conduct of hostilities, which is assumed to be the defining characteristic of this form of war, since it constitutes its end or means. To find a characteristic point of view of the theory of holy war, one need only cite the peculiar form of normative de-responsibility encapsulated in the famous words of Arnaud Amalric (died 1225), the future Archbishop of Narbonne and spiritual leader of the Crusade against the Albigensians. When asked how to distinguish Christians from heretics during warfare, the Cathars in this case, he replied: 'Kill them all: God will recognise his own.'.

It is useful to conclude by making a comparison between the theory of holy war and the alternatives considered so far. While political realism assumes a particularist criterion (self-interest) and applies it universally, recognising the legitimacy of self-interest for every state, the theory of holy war likewise assumes a particularist criterion but applies it in a particularist way. Thus, while political realism recognises each state's right to defend and advocate its religion, the theory of holy war recognises this right only for states that profess a particular religion to the exclusion of all others. The same particularism applies to every other motive and criterion. This shared trait enables us to highlight the differences between political realism and holy war theory, on the one hand, and pacifism and just war theory, on the other. Unlike the former, the latter do not immediately identify with the demands and proclamations of political authorities but instead adopt an attitude of constitutive suspicion towards them. Finally, unlike the other two paradigms, pacifism and just war theory both aim to minimise *overall* violence-related suffering by considering all parties to have equal rights.

References

Ackerman P, DuVall J (2000) A force more powerful: a century of nonviolent conflict. Palgrave, New York
Bainton RH (1960) Christian attitudes toward war and peace: a historical survey and critical re-evaluation. Abingdon Press, Nashville
Bellamy AJ (2004) Supreme emergencies and the protection of non-combatants in war. Int Aff 80:829–850
Bellamy AJ (2006) Just wars: from Cicero to Iraq. Polity Press, Cambridge
Bobbio N (1991) Una guerra giusta? Sul conflitto del Golfo. Marsilio, Venezia
Bobbio N (1997) Il problema della guerra e le vie della pace. il Mulino, Bologna
Brock P (1998) Varieties of pacifism: a survey from antiquity to the outset of the twentieth century. University of Toronto Press, Toronto
Brock P, Young N (1999) Pacifism in the twentieth century. University of Toronto Press, Toronto
Canto-Sperber M (2005) Le Bien, la Guerre et la Terreur: Pour une morale internationale. Plon, Paris
Ceadel M (1987) Thinking about peace and war. Oxford University Press, Oxford
Coates AJ (1997) The ethics of war. Manchester University Press, Manchester
Cortright D (2008) Peace: a history of movements and ideas. Cambridge University Press, Cambridge
Dinstein Y (2005) War, aggression and self-defence. Cambridge University Press, Cambridge
Holmes RL (1973) On Pacifism. Monist 57:489–506
Johnson JT (1975) Ideology, reason, and the limitation of war: religious and secular concepts, 1200–1740. Princeton University Press, Princeton
Johnson JT (1981) Just war tradition and the restraint of war: a moral and historical inquiry. Princeton University Press, Princeton
May L (2015) Contingent pacifism: revisiting just war theory. Cambridge University Press, Cambridge
Narveson J (1965) Pacifism: a philosophical analysis. Ethics 75:259–271
Osiel MJ (1999) Obeying orders: atrocity, military discipline, and the law of war. Transaction, New Brunswick
Regout RHW (1934) La doctrine de la guerre juste de Saint Augustine à nos jours: D'après les théologiens et les canonistes catholiques. Pedone, Paris
Robinson P (ed) (2003) Just war in comparative perspective. Ashgate, Burlington (VT)
Russell FH (1975) The just war in the middle ages. Cambridge University Press, Cambridge
Teichman J (1986) Pacifism and the just war: a study in applied philosophy. Basil Blackwell, New York
Toner C (2005) Just war and the supreme emergency exemption. Philos Q 55:545–561
Walters LR (1973) The just war and the crusade: antitheses or analogies? Monist 57:584–594
Walzer M (1970) Obligations: essays on disobedience, war, and citizenship. Harvard University Press, Cambridge (MA)
Yoder JH (1991) Just war tradition: is it credible? The Christian Century: 295–298
Yoder JH (1996) When war is unjust: being honest in just-war thinking. Orbis Books, Maryknoll (NY)

Democracies at Peace (or at War)? The Rise and Fall of the Democratic Peace Theory

Andrea Carati

1 Introduction

The problem of peace and its preservation has been a subject of interest for generations of scholars. Nevertheless, endeavors to formulate a genuine theory of peace, with the capacity to reveal the mechanisms through which peace can be pursued and sustained, are infrequent. More surprisingly, they have been rare in the field of international relations (IR), which by vocation has the aspiration to explain international dynamics by elaborating explanatory models, investigating the regularities of world politics, and unveiling the ultimate causes of international political phenomena.

Two main reasons help us understand why those theoretical attempts have been so rare. Like most international phenomena involving the entire world order, peace is a research topic that encounters several methodological difficulties. Unlike domestic political phenomena, for which more precise data collection and greater epistemological rigor are possible, the international causes of peace (or, conversely, the reasons why wars break out) do not lend themselves to straightforward scientific investigation. The scale of the phenomenon, the number of actors involved, and the interdependence of several dimensions of international coexistence (economic, political, normative, ethical, cultural, etc.) make it particularly difficult to elaborate a parsimonious, coherent, and comprehensive theory of peace.

In addition, for long periods and especially during the Cold War, IR was dominated by the realist paradigm, in which widespread skepticism prevailed regarding the possibility of achieving a stable, conflict-free international order. From the realist perspective, world politics is fated to suffer from the ills of all time: an anarchic environment (due to the lack of a world government) that condemns states to

A. Carati (✉)
University of Milan, Milan, Italy
e-mail: andrea.carati1@unimi.it

G. Cavaggion (ed.), *The 'Pacifist Principle' in the Italian and Japanese Constitutions in the Wake of the War in Ukraine*,
https://doi.org/10.1007/978-3-032-23108-6_20

inescapable uncertainty and mistrust; the security dilemma, which easily triggers the vicious circle of rearmament through which every state protects itself against external threats but, in doing so, itself becomes a threat for others; the inevitable competition between status quo powers (protecting the international order they dominate) and revisionist powers that, on the basis of the growth of their economic and military capabilities, will sooner or later undermine the existing international order. While realism is not devoid of reflections concerning the preservation of peace—e.g., the *peaceful change* suggested by Carr (2016), Morgenthau's *struggle for peace* (1948), or the balance of power (Kissinger 2017; Waltz 2010; Wight 2002)—it did not elaborate proper theories of peace beyond generic, tentative efforts to avoid wars.

Methodological difficulties and the prominent role of realism, however, have not prevented the emergence of peace theories in the field of IR. Not surprisingly, these were mainly developed by the liberal school. From the institutionalist-liberal strand of IR, in fact, three main peace theories have been proposed in opposition to realism: interdependence theory, institutionalist theory, and democratic peace theory. The latter is the one that has been most successful and appeared the most convincing. Firstly, democratic peace theory incorporates the causal mechanisms proposed by interdependence theory and institutionalism. It does not contradict the other theories but rather appears to propose a more complex and comprehensive type of explanation. Secondly, democratic peace theory has produced a substantial number of empirical studies, many of which are quantitative in nature, that have confirmed its theoretical propositions. Finally, compared to the assorted literature on interdependence and institutionalism, the theory of democratic peace appeared to be much more coherent, based on a more homogeneous scientific literature, whose basic assumptions and propositions are unanimously shared by all its proponents.

The chapter focuses on democratic peace, valuing its merits and shortcomings and concluding that its rise and fall followed the same trajectory of the US-led international liberal order. It is organized as follows: the first section presents the aforementioned theories of peace, the second portrays the origins of the democratic peace theory within IR and illustrates its main arguments and logic, the third section delves into the limits of the theory, and, finally, the concluding part points out how the current demise of the international liberal order seems to confirm the flawed foundations of the democratic peace theory.

2 Liberal Theories of Peace: Interdependence, International Organizations, and Democracy

Liberal theories of IR are diverse; they form a vast literature, including different views and approaches not always consistent with each other (Moravcsik 1992; Van De Haar 2009). Compared with realism, in which different strands of the paradigm stem from the same parsimonious analytical framework, the liberal approach to IR is richer and can be framed as a history of thinkers rather than a development of the same core assumptions like in the realist tradition—i.e., anarchy, security dilemma, centrality of balance of power, pessimistic view on human nature, etc. (Jackson 2005). But for the theories of peace—the democratic peace in particular—liberalism appears much more coherent. In the long history of IR as an academic discipline, three research venues are easily noticeable. They appear, fade, resurface, but are consistently part of the main views of IR. Especially since the 1970s, they have established themselves as well-recognized and compelling theories.

The first is the theory of economic interdependence, which represents a long tradition of international studies whose first classic appeared in 1910, Angell (2010) entitled *The Great Illusion*. Although misunderstood and easily criticized for its unfortunate publication on the eve of the Great War, the book continued to exert a vast influence on generations of IR scholars throughout the twentieth century. Its main argument, the expectation that the industrial revolution, accompanied by an increasing economic interdependence among developed countries, turned war into an unprofitable endeavor, remains inspiring even for contemporary IR scholars (McMillan 1997). Unlike liberal philosophers during the Enlightenment, who anticipated some of his ideas, Angell offered a sophisticated analysis, based on data and rational behavior, it preluded to the positivist approach to the study of economic interdependence in IR. Writing about the unlikelihood of war in Europe just before World War I contributed to the misunderstanding of the book. But Angell's compelling argument was proven by the war rather than disconfirmed—the "illusion" he had in mind was precisely that of European leaders deciding for war in expectation of a short and profitable military effort. Instead, as victims of that illusion, they irrationally precipitated Europe into the spiral of self-destruction. In the end, Angell contended that for rational actors—able to foresee the level of destruction, even for their own countries, in a highly interdependent and industrialized arena—war *should* be unlikely. He was not professing the unlikeliness of war per se as an unfailing result of economic interdependence.

On the eve of World War II, with the failure of the League of Nations and the military competition of the 1930s, realism once again dominated the scene in international studies. The early decades of the Cold War, reflecting the strategic competition between the two superpowers under a condition of mutual nuclear deterrence, confirmed the dominance of realism within the discipline. However, in the late 1970s (not surprisingly following the upheavals produced by the global oil crisis), the theory of economic interdependence made its (re)appearance. With the manifesto book of neo-institutionalism published by Nye and Keohane (1977), *Power and Interdependence*, a new season in international studies opened in which theories of complex interdependence presented themselves as the greatest intellectual challenge to realism in IR. The authors investigated the emerging era of interdependence and how it was changing the very nature of world politics; they concluded that—amid other effects—when complex interdependence prevails, military force loses its usefulness (Nye and Keohane 1977, pp. 25–29). Subsequent theoretical models on interdependence have all invariably been inspired by the contribution of Keohane and Nye on at least one point: the more intertwined national economies are with each other, the less the use of force can be an appropriate way to gain advantage. From this theoretical perspective, peace is necessarily the result not of moral progress or cultural and political changes but of complex economic developments that raise the costs of war to unacceptable levels and drastically lower the benefits to be gained from open conflicts (Barbieri 1996).

The second theory of peace refers to the ability of international multilateral organizations to mitigate the effects of international anarchy and restrain the possibility of states resorting to war. On the one hand, organizations of collective security—i.e., the League of Nations and nowadays the United Nations—add a level of global governance of security by removing it from the free (and dangerous) interaction between self-regarding national securities (Lawson 2023). On the other hand, the proliferation of international organizations, such as the one that began after World War II, creates a dense network of inter- and transnational relations that dilute disputes between states. In this increasingly dense and complex institutional environment, nation-states not only cease to be the most important actors in the international system but also suffer several constraints from outside. Furthermore, the presence of stable international organizations facilitates a permanent channel of communication, the exchange of information, the possibility of mediation, and, in the absence of a legitimate global governing body, the capacity to impose sanctions on states that contravene international norms (Abbott and Snidal 1998; Martin and Simmons 2001). Although they are not perfect or infallible institutional mechanisms, they can certainly more easily avert the use of force than in the case of international systems lacking any multilateral and supranational institutional fabric.

The third strand of peace theories developed by the liberal approach to IR is that of democratic peace, to which the following pages are devoted. In this particular instance, it is not external constraints—such as interdependence or the influence of international institutions—that restrain the actions of states and the use of force; rather, it is the inherent characteristics of the prevailing political regime within the domestic context that serve as the primary restraints. Drawing its origins from the Kantian tradition of the so-called perpetual peace (Kant 2021), contemporary democratic peace theory identifies domestic institutional arrangements as the primary reason for international peace.

Since its emergence in the 1980s, democratic peace theory has been regarded as the most important contribution of the liberal school of IR because, thanks to the countless empirical confirmations produced by rigorous statistical tests, it appeared to be able to defeat all the theoretical propositions of realism (Bridoux 2024). Firstly, democratic peace theory sought to demonstrate, as conclusively as possible, that domestic factors are decisive for world politics. Whereas neo-realism attempted to prove the opposite—namely, that under conditions of international anarchy all states tend to adopt similar behaviors irrespective of their internal structures (Waltz 2010)—democratic peace corroborated that the internal constitutional and institutional arrangements of states profoundly influence relations with one another. Secondly, the democratic peace theory challenged the essence of the realist discourse, which argues that the absence of a world government inevitably produces a kind of Hobbesian state of nature in the international arena. This state of nature is characterized by a persistent state of war (whether threatened or fought) that cannot come to a stable and definitive peace. While it is indeed the case that democracies do not engage in warfare with each other, the absence of a world government does not necessarily produce the same negative effects on interstate relations. Thirdly, democratic peace theory disconfirmed the realist assumption that the nature of international politics is destined always to remain the same (i.e., an eternal struggle between self-interested great powers that, due to anarchy, are never subject to a single global authority capable of imposing shared international norms). Conversely, if the second half of the twentieth century and the first part of the new millennium have been characterized by a gradual spread of democracy, it may also be argued that world politics has undergone a fundamental transformation in its very nature—namely, the capacity to ensure international stability by preventing open conflicts between states. In summary, the simple proposition according to which democracies do not go to war with each other, confirmed by empirical tests, appeared to be the most successful one against the realist paradigm.

3 Why They Do Not Fight: Democracies at Peace

As mentioned briefly in the Introduction, democratic peace has emerged as the most convincing of the three theories of peace just outlined. Apart from the normative aspects (i.e., the commitment to a better, more democratic and just world), it is the scientific nature of the theory that has ensured its success over the past 40 years. Thanks to a rigorous empirical quantitative analysis, the democratic peace "establishes a causal relationship between the type of regime and the prospect for peace in the world" (Bridoux 2024, 314). As Jack Levy (1998) contends, the causal mechanism connecting democracy at the domestic level and peace in the international system comes as close as anything we have to an empirical law in international relations. The scientific status the theory has earned is not comparable to what empirical analysis has produced for the phenomena of economic interdependence and the spread of international organizations. Although authoritative and rigorous analyses also exist in these two areas, these have never gone so far as to confirm the close correlation between democracy and the absence of conflict, as in the case of democratic peace theory.

In addition, the three theories are not mutually exclusive. On the contrary, each seems to support the other. According to Russett and Oneal (2001)'s formula, *Triangulating Peace*, each strand of liberalism (interdependence, institutionalism, and democracy) reinforces each other to increase the chances of peace. Nonetheless, among the three, democracy is the most fundamental political pillar of the triangle for two simple reasons. The first is the fact that free-market democracies have historically proven to be the most prosperous and economically dynamic countries; thus, they are the political regime that can guarantee international interdependence and its continued growth more than any other. The second is that liberal democracies are regimes that, more than any other in history, have been committed to international law and multilateral organizations. So here again, democracies seem to be both preliminary to, and the most consistent with, institutionalism.

However, if the correlation between peace and democracy is indeed a relationship between variables (i.e., a *description* of what occurs in an international order characterized by the presence of a number of democratic states), the theory must propose an *explanation* of the causal mechanism. The vast literature on democratic peace is rather homogeneous in the type of explanation provided (Elman 2001; Gat 2005; Maoz and Russett 1993; Parmar 2013; Russett and Oneal 2001; Rasler and Thompson 2016; Simpson 2019). The explanation is traditionally threefold, based on the effects produced by the internal institutional arrangements of democracies, the normative aspects of liberal-democratic political culture, and the type of interdependence that democracies tend to establish among themselves (Doyle 2005).

First, the so-called *structural causes* of democratic peace focus on the domestic institutional arrangements of a democratic regime. Compared to autocratic regimes, democracies impose a series of institutional, constitutional, and political constraints on democratic leaders, thereby diminishing the likelihood of them inciting their nation to engage in warfare. The system of checks and balances inherent in a democratic constitution imposes institutional mechanisms on political decision-makers that prevent hasty, personalistic, and self-interested choices. Unlike an autocrat or a pure dictator, the democratic leader does not have a free hand in imposing a choice of war. Moreover, democratic leaders are further constrained by the provisional nature of their mandate, the requirement to undergo recurrent electoral consultations within a pluralist party system, and the constant exposure to public opinion. As Maoz and Russett (1993, 626) pointed out,

> International actions in a democratic political system requires the mobilization of both general public opinion and of a variety of institutions that make up the system of government, such as legislature, the political bureaucracies, and key interest groups. This implies that very few goals could be presented to justify fighting wars in democracies. It also implies that the process of mobilization for war in democracies is both difficult and cumbersome. [...] due to the complexity of the democratic process and the requirement of securing a broad base of support for risky policies, democratic leaders are reluctant to wage wars.

Second, the *normative causes* of democratic peace assume that states externalize the norms that are developed within their domestic political processes and institutions. Since democratic regimes are based on political norms that regulate competition and disputes through laws and peaceful means, their foreign policies tend to do the same in the international arena. This is particularly true when two democracies confront one another in a context of conflicting interests: unlike autocracies, they are able to apply nonviolent norms in their interactions. It is therefore more likely for democracies to avoid armed conflicts, preventing escalations to a military level. Their shared norms have better chances than nondemocratic regimes to avert war, thanks to their habits of using legal and peaceful means to manage potentially violent conflicts (Friedman 2008).

Third, peace between democracies is finally the result of the contribution made by economic interdependence between them. Unlike theories of complex interdependence, which do not necessarily discriminate between different types of regimes, the democratic peace theory focuses on the effect that market economies have on international relations (Gelpi and Grieco 2008; Oneal and Ray 1997). Peaceful interactions are likelier among liberal democracies because interdependence arises most naturally between states with open economies. As Russett and Oneal (2001, 125) argue,

> Almost all democracies, though varying to a degree in the role played by the state, have capitalist economic systems that involve extensive competition in free markets among economic agents, including those in other countries. Consequently, democracies tend to trade extensively with one another. Because of the correlation between democracy and open markets we need to reconsider the consequences of democracy through tests in which we control for the influence of interdependence.

The authors eventually demonstrated that, while economic interdependence and international trade reduce conflict in general, open economies are more pacific (Russett and Oneal 2001, 148–155). Since liberal democracies are more oriented toward open markets, while autocracies favor autarchic policies and economic nationalism, they contribute more to the conflict aversion produced by interdependence than nondemocracies.

Ultimately, the democratic peace theory explains the correlation between regime type and the absence of war on the basis of three causal mechanisms: the domestic institutional arrangements that constrain democratic leaders, the set of norms of democratic coexistence that are externalized in international relations between democracies, and the calming effects of economic interdependence, to which open-market democracies contribute most. Although the theory is based on a coherent framework and has considerable empirical support, it has also been criticized in many ways. The next section focuses on these criticisms.

4 Why They Fight: The Flawed Foundations of the Democratic Peace

Proponents of the democratic peace theory have encountered a significant degree of criticism, with objections raised by several scholars, mostly from the realist school of IR (Kinsella 2005). These critiques have focused on both methodological aspects and the theoretical framework itself, including its logical structure and the explanatory power of the theory. While some questioned the measurement and statistical inference, many more tend to accept the democratic peace as an empirical fact, so the aim of their complaints has shifted to the inner logic of the theory—i.e., the three causal mechanisms outlined in the previous section (Rosato 2003).

A first flaw that recurs in critical appraisals is the existence of exceptions to the regularity according to which democracies never (or almost never) go to war with each other (Ray 1993). There are two kinds of exceptions: one concerning interstate wars and the other focusing on the use of force other than war. On the one hand, there are cases in contemporary history where democracies waged war against each other, the most quoted being the following: Germany in World War I (classified as a republic or democracy by most proponents of the democratic peace), which fought against four liberal democracies (Great Britain, France, Italy, and the United States); the Spanish-American War in 1898; the Six-Day War in 1967 with the intervention of Lebanon against another democracy, Israel; and the Kargil war between India and Pakistan in 1999 (Rosato 2003; Russett et al. 1995). On the other hand, some scholars pointed out that while democracies do not wage open wars against each other, on several occasions, they use covert force against elected governments. For instance, during the Cold War, the United States launched several forcible covert actions against other democracies—i.e., Iran (1953), Guatemala (1954), Indonesia (1955), Brazil (1960s), Chile (1973), and Nicaragua (1980s) (Forsythe 1992; Kim 2001). Some others mention the American Civil War, where the warring parties were both democratic regimes, and the only way to reject this case is not to consider internal warfare but focus only on interstate wars (Rauch 2016).

Beyond these exceptions, the most substantial criticism against the theory pertains to the logical coherence of the explanations proposed by democratic peace proponents. Indeed, the (limited) number of exceptions does not appear to provide a compelling argument to disprove the (general) regularity of a political phenomenon. Conversely, causal mechanisms must be convincing, consistent, and coherent with empirical evidence. In the remaining pages, the focus is on three aspects that are deemed to be the most important. These aspects are identified as the greatest shortcomings of the theory and appear to be the most relevant for interpreting the role of democracies in the crisis of the current international order (a subject that will be addressed in the final section).

In the first place, as some realists stressed, the democratic peace is more of a hypothesis than a proper theory (Williams 2011; Mearsheimer 2018, 194–204). Accepting the fact that democracies do not go to war with each other, as an empirical fact based on a robust statistical correlation, the proposed explanations (i.e., structural causes, normative causes, and economic interdependence) do not seem convincing. In other words, they are explanatory hypotheses that have yet to be proven (Rosato 2003). Indeed, as one of the most eminent advocates of the democratic peace, Michael Doyle (2024, 139), conceded, possibly "there are other forces at work in stopping wars between democracies". From this perspective, what needs to be demonstrated is not peace between democracies but rather *whether* democratic institutions at the domestic level, shared norms and economic interdependence are the very causes of peace. Some, in fact, have tried to show that democracies did not fight wars against each other for reasons that have to do with the conditions of the international system. During the Cold War, it was the cohesion of the Western Bloc in an anti-Soviet function that was the real reason that prevented, for example, a North Atlantic Treaty Organization (NATO) country from waging war against an ally (Gowa 2011). In the post-Cold War era, the unipolar moment brought about the bandwagoning effect in favor of the United States (Carter 2022); in this case, it was the asymmetrical hierarchy produced by the unchallenged American hegemony in the democratic front to keep peace among liberal democracies. In summary, although the causal mechanisms identified by democratic peace theory at first appear coherent and defensible, they do not necessarily indicate the root causes of peace between democracies. In other words, the literature on democratic peace is all about the merits of democracies as the most economically efficient, institutionally balanced, and normatively just political regime. But it tends to underestimate, if not disregard altogether, the international constraints and power relations that have allowed the creation of a democratic zone of peace.

In the second place, the structural causes—which in many ways are the most important—are clearly disconfirmed by the statistical records reported in the democratic peace literature itself. The statistical correlation between democracy and peace concerns *only* democracy-democracy dyads in the overall sample of all possible dyads between states in the international system year by year. While democracy-democracy dyads are systematically more peaceful than all other dyads (democracy-autocracy, autocracy-autocracy), democracies historically show a similar propensity for war as nondemocracies (Dixon 1998). This means that democracies are not generally more peaceful; instead, they are war-prone like nondemocracies. This fact disqualifies any explanation assuming that the peaceful effect of democracies in the international arena is due to their domestic institutional arrangements, such as checks and balances, public pressure, and election cycles. In fact, data on the extent to which democracies engage in warfare does not reveal any difference, meaning that democratic political leaders do not face greater constraints than leaders of nondemocratic countries. This aspect undermines the core of the democratic peace. Democratic institutions at the domestic level do not cause international peace. In fact, they tell us nothing about how democracies behave internationally, and their decisions to go to war are not unlike those of nondemocracies.

This is the weakest side of the theory. The point is that there are unspoken assumptions underlying structural explanations that deserve to be verified. While it may seem intuitive to assume that a leader facing elections will tend to avoid making decisions about war before the vote, this assumption is not supported by any empirical research. Indeed, no statistical correlation has been found between decisions about war avoidance and electoral cycles (Gaubatz 1991; Rosato 2003). Similarly, the implicit assumption that leaders exposed to public opinion refrain from making decisions to go to war should be demonstrated and not taken for granted. While democratic publics tend to be more averse to casualties, a conclusive correlation between public pressure and war avoidance has not emerged (Gelpi 2017; Voeten and Brewer 2006). Consequently, the theoretical framework is weakened because causal explanations are founded upon unproven assumptions, such as the supposition that public opinion is systematically war-averse or that the prospect of elections disincentivizes war decisions.

In the third place, democratic peace theory does not seem able to offer a definitive answer to the realist argument that democracies behave in the international arena like any other state. According to the neo-realist perspective, the conditions of international anarchy produce uncertainty and distrust in relations between states that are inescapable; international law and institutions, economic interdependence, or liberal norms can mitigate the effects of anarchy but cannot eradicate them. In the absence of a world government capable of enforcing international law, and thus capable of sanctioning those who defy it (great powers included), democratic states are exposed to the same uncertainties, constraints, and needs as any other state (Waltz 2010). The history of democracies and the way they act in the international system confirms almost all expectations of realism. Like any other political regime, every democratic state—even more so if it is a great or superpower—prioritizes its national security and arms the country to defend itself in the expectation that, ultimately, no international organization will be able to defend it in the event of an attack. Thus, the so-called self-help system (Waltz 2000), according to which every state in conditions of anarchy must provide for its own security either by arming itself or by establishing alliances with stronger countries, applies to democracies as much as to nondemocracies because it is generated by systemic conditions of anarchy from which democracies cannot escape. The same is true for the so-called security dilemma, the mechanism according to which, under anarchy, every state (democracies included) pursues national security by building up its own military capabilities, often with defensive aims. However, doing this generates insecurity in other countries, which in turn have an incentive to build up their own military (Herz 2003; Montgomery 2006).

The history of the Cold War and the likeness of American and Soviet strategies (which were very similar in many ways) seem to confirm the realist view. Western democracies, led by the United States, ended up adopting policies toward the Soviet Bloc that were dictated by international conditions, regardless of domestic political arrangements and democratic norms of coexistence. The Grand Strategy of Containment, mutual nuclear deterrence, and rearmament—policies adopted in a very similar manner by both superpowers—confirm the logic of both the self-help system and the security dilemma. The recent deterioration in relations between NATO countries and the Russian Federation also seems to confirm the same mechanisms: the Kremlin's mistrust of NATO enlargement has stimulated Russian rearmament in an anti-Western function; Russia's rearmament, assertiveness, and aggression against Ukraine have triggered NATO and European rearmament, which in turn will generate suspicion and insecurity for Russia. Again, the peculiarities of democracies do not seem to shelter them from the inner logic of an anarchic international environment.

In essence, democratic peace theory seems to completely ignore these international constraints, in particular the international distribution of power, which, on the one hand, may explain the holding of the democratic zone of peace (but not due to internal arrangements or democratic norms) and, on the other hand, indicate that democracies, under certain international conditions, may in fact adopt foreign policies very similar to nondemocratic regimes.

5 Democracies and the Demise of the Liberal International Order

The criticisms of the democratic peace theory highlighted in the previous section allow us to shed light on the current crisis of the liberal international order from a new perspective. Not only because the most recent competitive dynamics of world politics present themselves as a new test bed for the theory but especially because the history of the rise and decline of democratic peace seems to coincide with the parabola of the US-led liberal order. Indeed, the theory emerged in the late 1980s, at the end of the Cold War, and enjoyed its zenith in the 1990s and early 2000s; it subsequently attracted significant criticism, leading to its marginalization in recent decades.

Not surprisingly, the apogee of the theory and that of the liberal international order both essentially overlap with the so-called unipolar moment (Layne 2006). This phase is characterized by the unchallenged international dominance of the American hegemon and its liberal-democratic allies. In a period of rise and spread of democratic regimes and values on a global scale that was unparalleled in history, the zone of democratic peace expanded and appeared to be unstoppable and unchallenged. In the IR scholarship, it is unsurprising that realism reached its nadir, with liberal theories assuming a dominant position in internationalist studies (Mearsheimer 2025, 7–8). Toward the close of the first decade of the new millennium, the US-led liberal order entered a period of profound crisis (Walt 2018): 9/11 broke the enchantment of an exceptionally secure democratic world, the financial crisis of 2007–2008 shattered the promises of a world dominated by more interconnected and prosperous liberal free-market economies, the military debacles in Iraq and then Afghanistan marked the end of certainties about the infallible military effectiveness of democracies in war, and, finally, the return of competition between great powers (the challenges posed by potential peer competitors like Russia and, prospectively, China) called into question the expectation of the persistence of the unipolar "moment."

The three types of criticism highlighted above seem to be confirmed by the present crisis of the liberal international order. Firstly, the assumption that the explanations for peace among democracies lie in structural causes, norms promoted by democracies, and economic interdependence is further weakened by recent developments in world politics. The invitation of the theory's critics to assess the *other* reasons why democracies have not waged wars against each other so far actually seems more convincing now, especially those that suggest looking at the international distribution of power. Arguably, in light of the international consequences of the American decline, we can now assert that peace between democracies has been possible because it has been intertwined with the distribution of power in their favor. From this perspective, if during the Cold War peace between democracies was due to intra-bloc cohesion and solidarity, peace in the first 15 years after the end of the Cold War depended much more on unchallenged unipolarism than on the goodwill of democratic leaders, the more peaceful culture, and their economic interdependence. From this standpoint, the twofold crisis of unipolarism and the unchallenged power of the United States and its allies is also bound to endanger peace between democracies.

Secondly, the political tensions involving the Euro-Atlantic community in recent years—with an acceleration after the outbreak of war in Ukraine in 2022—again appear to confirm some of the theoretical expectations of realism. In democratic countries, political leaders are not confronted with insurmountable obstacles should they decide to rearm or launch preemptive military strikes (as was the case with the aggression against Iraq in 2003 or the attack on Iran by Israel and the United States in 2025). The tendency to interpret these cases in purely reactive terms, as instances of force employed against nondemocratic states or as a mere response to the aggressive behavior of authoritarian regimes, appears to lack a comprehensive and nuanced understanding of the underlying international dynamics. Conversely, the aggression against Iraq, in addition to Israel's military campaigns in Gaza and the Middle East, appears to demonstrate the ease with which democratic leaders can resort to the use of force (in the case of Iraq, evidently also against those who pose no threat), without necessarily fearing elections, public opinion reactions, or the limitations that legislative power can impose.

Finally, the democracies' reactions to a more competitive world appear to corroborate the hypothesis that the mechanisms of self-help and the security dilemma have been consistent with recent events. Notwithstanding the rejection of the notion that NATO's expansion could provide a justification for the aggression of Ukraine, it is evident that the deterioration of relations between NATO countries and the Russian Federation has been a long process, characterized by a series of misunderstandings and suspicions (D'Anieri 2023; Sarotte 2021). Notwithstanding the defensive intentions of NATO, suspicions have been engendered, which have encouraged Russian rearmament. This, in turn, has increased Western suspicions and so on, evidently triggering the spiral of the security dilemma. Even the tensions between the two sides of the Atlantic—on the one hand, US neo-isolationist aspirations and, on the other hand, Europe's yearnings for strategic autonomy—seem to confirm that common membership in the world of democracies, shared norms, and a very high level of economic interdependence do not always guarantee good diplomatic relations. On the contrary, in an increasingly multipolar world, even Americans and Europeans may develop conflicting interests that do not exclude conflict.

It is premature to argue definitively whether peace between democracies was guaranteed by a historical phase in which, first, the Western Bloc and, then, the unipolar moment favored that outcome or to argue that such a zone of peace was the result of domestic political institutions, a common culture, and a high level of interdependence. Nevertheless, it is evident that peace among democracies is inextricably linked to the fate of the US-led liberal international order. Its resilience may perhaps offer new chances for the confirmation of peace among democracies. An enduring democratic zone of peace is, however, much more unlikely in the event of a final demise of the American hegemonic order.

References

Abbott KW, Snidal D (1998) Why states act through formal international organizations. J Confl Resolut 42(1):3–32

Angell N (2010) The great illusion. Cosimo, Inc., New York

Barbieri K (1996) Economic interdependence: a path to peace or a source of interstate conflict? J Peace Res 33(1):29–49

Bridoux J (2024) Democratic Peace? In: Howard W, Boucher D, Sutch P et al (eds) The Palgrave handbook of international political theory. Springer, New York, pp 309–328

Carr EH (2016) The twenty years' crisis, 1919–1939. Springer, New York

Carter B (2022) Revisiting the bandwagoning hypothesis: a statistical analysis of the alliance dynamics of small states. Int Stud 59(1):7–27

D'Anieri P (2023) Ukraine and Russia: from civilized divorce to uncivil war. Cambridge University Press, Cambridge

Dixon WJ (1998) Dyads, disputes and the democratic peace. In: Wolfson M (ed) The political economy of war and peace. Springer, New York, pp 103–126

Doyle MW (2005) Three pillars of the Liberal peace. Am Polit Sci Rev 99(3):463–466

Doyle M (2024) Why they don't fight: the surprising endurance of the democratic peace. Foreign Aff 103(4):135–141

Elman C (2001) Introduction: history, theory, and the democratic peace. Int Hist Rev 23(4):757–766

Forsythe DP (1992) Democracy, war, and covert action. J Peace Res 29(4):385–395

Friedman G (2008) Identifying the place of democratic norms in democratic peace. Int Stud Rev 10(3):548–570

Gat A (2005) The democratic peace theory reframed: the impact of modernity. World Polit 58(1):73–100

Gaubatz KT (1991) Election cycles and war. J Confl Resolut 35(2):212–244

Gelpi C (2017) Democracies in conflict: the role of public opinion, political parties, and the press in shaping security policy. J Confl Resolut 61(9):1925–1949

Gelpi CF, Grieco JM (2008) Democracy, interdependence, and the sources of the liberal peace. J Peace Res 45(1):17–36

Gowa J (2011) Ballots and bullets: the elusive democratic peace. Princeton University Press, Princeton

Herz JH (2003) The security dilemma in international relations: background and present problems. Int Relat 17(4):411–416

Jackson R (2005) Classical and modern thought on international relations: from anarchy to cosmopolis. Springer, New York

Kant I (2021) Perpetual peace: a philosophical essay. Phoemixx Classics, Poole

Kim J (2001) Covert action and democratic peace: why democracies fight secret wars. Yale University Press, New Haven

Kinsella D (2005) No rest for the democratic peace. Am Polit Sci Rev 99(3):453–457

Kissinger H (2017) A world restored: Metternich, Castlereagh, and the problems of peace, 1812–22. Pickle Partners Publishing, London

Lawson S (2023) International relations. John Wiley & Sons, Hoboken

Layne C (2006) The unipolar illusion revisited: the coming end of the United States' unipolar moment. Int Secur 31(2):7–41

Levy JS (1998) The causes of war and the conditions of peace. Annu Rev Polit Sci 1(1):139–165

Maoz Z, Russett B (1993) Normative and structural causes of democratic peace, 1946–1986. Am Polit Sci Rev 87(3):624–638

Martin LL, Simmons BA (eds) (2001) International institutions: an international organization reader. MIT Press, Cambridge

McMillan SM (1997) Interdependence and conflict. Mershon Int Stud Rev 41(1):33–58

Mearsheimer JJ (2018) The great delusion. Yale University Press, New Haven, Liberal Dreams and International Realities

Mearsheimer JJ (2025) War and international politics. Int Secur 49(4):7–36
Montgomery EB (2006) Breaking out of the security dilemma: realism, reassurance, and the problem of uncertainty. Int Secur 31(2):151–185
Moravcsik A (1992) Liberalism and international relations theory. Cambridge University Press, Cambridge
Morgenthau H (1948) Politics among nations: the struggle for power and peace. McGraw-Hill, New York
Nye J, Keohane RO (1977) Power and interdependence. Brown and Company, New York
Oneal JR, Ray JL (1997) New tests of the democratic peace: controlling for economic interdependence, 1950-85. Polit Res Q 50(4):751–775
Parmar I (2013) The 'knowledge politics' of democratic peace theory. Int Politics 50(2):231–256
Rasler K, Thompson W (2016) Puzzles of the democratic peace: theory, geopolitics and the transformation of world politics. Springer, New York
Rauch C (2016) The power of perception–democratic peace theory and the American civil war. Eur Rev Int Stud 3(1):5–30
Ray JL (1993) Wars between democracies: rare, or nonexistent? Int Interact 18(3):251–276
Rosato S (2003) The flawed logic of democratic peace theory. Am Polit Sci Rev 97(4):585–602
Russett BM, Oneal JR (2001) Triangulating peace: democracy, interdependence, and international organizations. W. W. Norton & Company, New York
Russett B, Layne C, Spiro D et al (1995) The democratic peace. Int Secur 19(4):164–184
Sarotte ME (2021) Not one inch: America, Russia, and the making of post-cold war stalemate. Yale University Press, New Haven
Simpson S (2019) Making liberal use of Kant? Democratic peace theory and perpetual peace. Int Relat 33(1):109–128
Van de Haar E (2009) Liberalism and international relations theory. In: Van de Haar E (ed) Classical liberalism and international relations theory: Hume, smith, Mises, and Hayek. Palgrave Macmillan, New York, pp 125–150
Voeten E, Brewer PR (2006) Public opinion, the war in Iraq, and presidential accountability. J Confl Resolut 50(6):809–830
Walt SM (2018) The hell of good intentions: America's foreign policy elite and the decline of US primacy. Straus and Giroux
Waltz KN (2000) Structural realism after the cold war. Int Secur 25(1):5–41
Waltz KN (2010) Theory of international politics. Waveland Press, Long Grove
Wight M (2002) Power politics. A&C Black, London
Williams MC (2011) The politics of theory: Waltz, realism and democracy. In: Boot K (ed) Realism and world politics. Routledge, Abingdon, pp 63–76

MIX
Papier aus verantwortungsvollen Quellen
Paper from responsible sources
FSC® C105338

If you have any concerns about our products,
you can contact us on
ProductSafety@springernature.com

In case Publisher is established outside the EU,
the EU authorized representative is:
Springer Nature Customer Service Center GmbH
Europaplatz 3, 69115 Heidelberg, Germany

Printed by Libri Plureos GmbH
in Hamburg, Germany